P9-EFI-709

BY JOHN DICKERSON

THE HARDEST JOB IN THE WORLD

On the cover, Lyndon Johnson listens to a tape recording from
his son-in-law updating him on fighting in Vietnam. Here, the
president offers the famously effective "Johnson treatment"
on Republican leader Everett Dirksen.

THE
HARDEST JOB
in the WORLD

The
AMERICAN PRESIDENCY

JOHN
DICKERSON

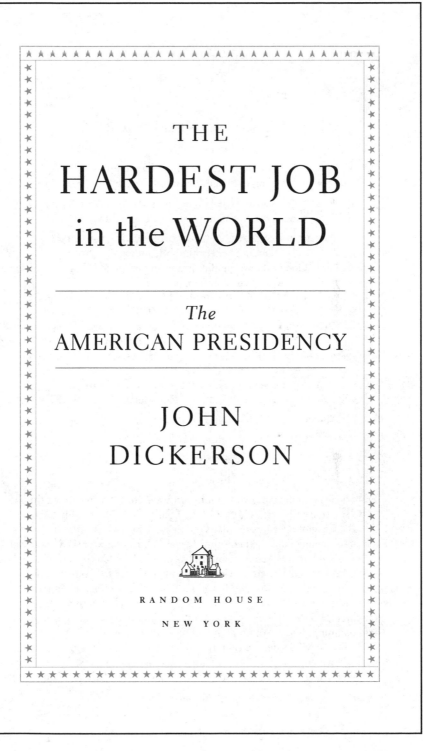

RANDOM HOUSE

NEW YORK

Published in the United States by Random House,
an imprint and division of Penguin Random House LLC, New York.

RANDOM HOUSE and the HOUSE colophon are registered
trademarks of Penguin Random House LLC.

LIBRARY OF CONGRESS CATALOGING-IN-PUBLICATION DATA
Names: Dickerson, John, author.
Title: The hardest job in the world: the American presidency / John Dickerson.
Other titles: American presidency
Identifiers: LCCN 2020001481 (print) | LCCN 2020001482 (ebook) |
ISBN 9781984854513 (hardcover) | ISBN 9781984854520 (ebook)
Subjects: LCSH: Presidents—United States. | Executive power—United States. |
Trump, Donald, 1946– | United States—Politics and government—2017–
Classification: LCC JK516 .D49 2020 (print) | LCC JK516 (ebook) |
DDC 352.230973—dc23
LC record available at https://lccn.loc.gov/2020001481
LC ebook record available at https://lccn.loc.gov/2020001482

Printed in the United States of America on acid-free paper

randomhousebooks.com

2 4 6 8 9 7 5 3 1

First Edition

Front-jacket photograph: Lyndon Johnson listens to a tape recording from
his son-in-law Chuck Robb, a Marine fighting in Vietnam, July 1968
(Jack Kightlinger/Lyndon Baines Johnson Library and Museum)
Back-jacket photographs: (left column) Dwight D. Eisenhower (U.S. National
Archives and Records Administration), Lyndon B. Johnson (Lyndon Baines
Johnson Library and Museum), Harry S. Truman (Harry S. Truman Library &
Museum), Ronald Reagan (Ronald Reagan Library), Barack Obama (official White
House photograph by Chuck Kennedy), Abraham Lincoln (Heritage Auctions),
Franklin D. Roosevelt (U.S. National Archives and Records Administration);
(right column) George Washington (WDC Photos/Alamy), John F. Kennedy
(John F. Kennedy Presidential Library and Museum), Donald Trump (Shealah
Craighead/whitehouse.gov), Jimmy Carter (Library of Congress), Bill Clinton
(Library of Congress), Theodore Roosevelt (Leslie's Weekly/Judge Company)

Book design by Barbara M. Bachman

Contents

"PRAY FOR ME"

On election night 1932, Franklin Delano Roosevelt went to his New York townhouse. The incumbent, Herbert Hoover, had just conceded defeat. His son James helped him to bed and kissed him good night. His father looked up and said, "You know, Jimmy, all my life I've been afraid of one thing—fire. Tonight, I think I'm afraid of something else."

James asked him what he was afraid of.

"I'm just afraid that I may not have the strength to do this job."

As Jimmy left the room, his father said to him, "After you leave me tonight, Jimmy, I'm going to pray. I'm going to pray that God will help me, that He will give me the strength and the guidance to do this job and do it right. I hope you will pray for me too, Jimmy."[1]

On October 23, 1983, the day after President Ronald Reagan approved the U.S. military intervention in Grenada, car bombers attacked the American and French barracks in Beirut, killing 241 Americans and 58 French servicemen, a tragedy Reagan would call the worst of his administration.

Introduction

Anger cannot win.
It cannot even think clearly.[2]

— DWIGHT D. EISENHOWER

O N SEPTEMBER 29, 1956, THE *CEDAR RAPIDS GAZETTE* announced front-page news about the presidency: IKE SETTING UP POLICY OF FIRING BACK.[3] With Election Day just a month away, the incumbent, Dwight Eisenhower, had finally decided to engage his Democratic challenger, Adlai Stevenson. This wasn't big news just in Iowa. In Delphos, Ohio, they woke up to this headline in the *Daily Herald*: FIRE BACK WHEN RIVALS GO TOO FAR — IKE'S NEW POLICY.[4] In Tyrone, Pennsylvania, their *Daily Herald* heralded: IKE DECIDES TO ANSWER DEMO "LIES."[5]

Editors opened the big-type drawer for Eisenhower's decision because the president had previously resisted what he called the "noise and extravagance" of the campaign. Weeks earlier, Eisenhower had waved away an easy chance to attack Stevenson: The Democratic nominee had complained about the state of the economy, and Eisenhower's press secretary had accused Stevenson of cheering for bad news. When reporters asked the president about this, Ike said his rival must have been misquoted.[6] (Ike's press secretary held his next briefing from under the bus where his boss had just thrown him.)

Ike switched his strategy, but the former Supreme Allied Commander hardly stormed the beaches. "Firing back" amounted to instructing the Labor Department to rebut Stevenson's claim about cost of living adjustments.[7]

It's not that Ike was mild-mannered. He wrestled to control his temper all of his life. The White House staff felt the sting of his wrath so often they dubbed him "the terrible-tempered Mr. Bang."[8] He once flung a golf club in anger and almost broke his doctor's leg.[9] When the sport vexed him—which is to say, when he played it—the veins on his temple engorged until one observer said they resembled whipcords.[10] Still, Eisenhower believed he must master his impulses. "Anger cannot win," he wrote in his diary almost a decade before becoming president. "It cannot even think clearly."

Newspaper editors considered it front-page news that President Eisenhower was choosing to confront his opponent. Ike resisted the pull of the campaign trail because he thought getting into the catfight of political competition was beneath the dignity of the office.

Eisenhower believed the presidency was too serious to be concerned with the trivialities of politics. He also believed a president needed self-control to be effective. He didn't attack his opponent, Stevenson, for yet another reason. That reason, according to the *Cedar Rapids Ga-*

zette, was "Mr. Eisenhower's reluctance to engage in name-calling contests that he considers beneath the dignity of the presidency."[11]

Sixty-four years later, under President Donald Trump, the presidency is a name-calling contest in which he appears to be competing with himself. In his first 700 days in office, President Donald Trump insulted 550 people, a brisk rate of one every 1.25 days.[12] "Crooked Hillary," "Leakin' Lyin' James Comey," "Pocahontas" (Elizabeth Warren), and "Little Pencil-neck Adam Schiff" are just some of the names minted by the forty-fifth president. At Trump's rallies, his fans cheer the reveal ceremonies of his latest schoolyard abuses. The catchy ones are printed on campaign T-shirts.

If name calling were still thought to be beneath the presidency, Donald Trump would be seen as governing from the subbasement. Eisenhower's idea of the "dignity of the presidency" is up for grabs. So is the Eisenhower-era idea that the duties and traditions of the presidency should curtail a president's drive for reelection.

Trump's supporters explain that he just has a different style than previous presidents. This undersells him. President Trump is ambitious, and his behavior—the insults, the impulsive competitive maneuvers—are a window into those ambitions, just as Eisenhower's behavior explained his worldview. President Trump is in rebellion against the presidency. Its traditions get in the way of the quick results he wants. He either sidesteps or flattens obstacles or opponents that irritate him or slow him down. In 2019, his desire to circumvent the process when it came to policy toward the country of Ukraine led to his impeachment. Donald Trump is not just a traditional president who happens to have a rough tongue. His rough tongue is a sign of a president who is dismantling the traditional presidency.

Reading these paragraphs, you might feel we are headed toward a predictable story, that this book will chart the stomach-drops of the roller-coaster ride of one president's administration. I would like to interrupt that assumption of a regularly scheduled program to say that this book tells a different, urgent story. The American presidency is in trouble. It is overburdened, misunderstood, an almost impossible job to do. President Trump is a part of that story, but he also obscures it. One of the problems with the presidency is that it has become such a celebrity office that it is defined by the personality of the occupant. But the problems with the job unfolded before Donald Trump was elected, and the challenges of governing today will confront his successors.

To look at the office afresh requires a change of perspective, unhooking from the celebrity headlines in order to understand its evolution and challenges. That is the channel we will switch to now, for a moment, as you imagine hiring someone to be president. Or, better yet, as you imagine what the job might be like if you had to do it yourself.

A PRESIDENT'S TO-DO LIST

WHAT DOES YOUR TO-DO LIST LOOK LIKE? IS IT WRITTEN ON POST-IT Notes? Maybe the app on your phone makes a pleasing noise to prompt you that it's time to go to the meeting, or to get that form notarized. Maybe you've sent yourself an email to remind you to buy those plane tickets before the price goes up. A to-do list can be the source of and answer to the chaos and competing demands of the modern day.

Now imagine a to-do list printed on the kind of paper usually reserved for wedding announcements. Your steward brings it to you each morning with your coffee. It bears the same presidential seal that's on your coffee cup. Most people would recognize it as a schedule, but when you are president of the United States, your schedule is your to-do list. Armies of people fight over its entries, what they will be, how long they will be, or if they should be.

Your time is one of the most precious commodities in the world. How you spend that time, and how it is spent for you, determines the course of your administration and perhaps the country's future. This is why even your free time—those little shards of it you get—are also labeled and scheduled.

The chief of staff knows you are taking the short walk downstairs to your office because he can watch the little red dot that signifies your movements on the White House grounds. You are tracked by your staff because other people are tracking your movements too. They want to kill you. The Secret Service sentinels constantly hovering over your life attest to this, as do the snipers on your roof. Harry Truman could go for a walk through the streets of Washington when the spirit moved him. You can scarcely go to the bathroom without someone's knowing it.

Bill Clinton called the White House the "crown jewel of the federal penitentiary system."

The secretary of state will be calling in a minute. The call is supposed to be about his budget, but he's really using it to argue his case about Iran. He's hoping to get to you before the secretary of defense can make her case about Iran later that day in what she will stage as a casual aside during a photo-op. The most powerful people in government at times behave like high schoolers.

"You know, it's easy for the Monday morning quarterback to say what the coach should have done," said Harry Truman. "But when the decision is up before you—and on my desk I have a motto which says 'The Buck Stops Here'—the decision has to be made."

Before crossing the threshold of your office, you hand your overnight briefing book to your staff secretary. It contains all of the issues that aren't crashing at the moment but that are slowly coming to that. Milk prices are declining, causing lights to go out in barns all across Wisconsin as farmers go out of business. (You barely won Wisconsin in the last election.) Corruption and gang violence in Venezuela are going to spike the number of migrants on the border in the spring.

The top sheet in the briefing binder lists your campaign promises with a red, yellow, or green dot signifying the status of your administration's progress in meeting your priorities. Tabs labeled CHINA and SOTU contain preparation materials for your meeting with the Chinese premier three months from now, and the State of the Union Address a month after that.

The cover of the book is embossed with Q2, which stands for Quadrant Two, a reference to the Eisenhower matrix that drives the daily operations of your White House. The matrix gets its name from Ike because the former president's maxim was that the urgent should not crowd out the important. The matrix helps everyone sort priorities, the most important process in any organization.

IN THE FOUR-QUADRANT SYSTEM, the horizontal axis plots an item's urgency. Is it on fire or merely smoldering? The vertical axis plots an item's importance. Is the smoke coming from a burning family heirloom or last week's funny papers? Defining a problem is the key to solving it. Figure out what quadrant a problem belongs in, and you and your team immediately know the next steps to take. Pick the wrong quadrant, and you waste that precious presidential time, or worse, you miss an opportunity to avert a catastrophe.

	URGENT	NOT URGENT
IMPORTANT	1 ACT	2 PLAN
NOT IMPORTANT	3 DELEGATE	4 DELETE

Quadrant One is America's favorite quadrant. Your allies, opponents, and the media think every problem is urgent and important, and anything you do that isn't tending to what they think belongs in Quadrant One is judged to be a mistake. If you let your Quadrant One be defined this way, the country would have to elect a hundred presidents to shoulder the load.

Every day is a knife fight to move items out of Quadrant One, items that don't really need to be there. Some challenges can't be moved. When Eisenhower learned that the Russians had shot down an American U-2 spy plane, he knew that required his immediate focus. The same was true for Ronald Reagan and the *Challenger* disaster, and for George W. Bush with the attacks of 9/11. Identifying those emergencies is not the real challenge of Quadrant One, however. Actual Quadrant One decisions are the urgent and important ones that no one knows about until months after the crisis has passed: planning to capture or kill Osama bin Laden, removing Iranian nuclear scientists, or finally deciding to replace your national security advisor.

To manage, a president must delegate ruthlessly, ushering or sometimes pushing items from Quadrant One to Quadrant Three, the location for urgent but less important tasks that can be handled by someone else. Day-to-day decisions about how best to combat the spreading Ebola virus in Africa or prepare for hurricane season or reduce opioid addiction will have to be made for you.

Your chief of staff makes a lot of these sorting decisions. This took time to get used to. You like to have control and input, but you had to learn a new, more refined definition of the word "important." Just because an issue is objectively important, or someone claims it is important, doesn't mean it is important enough to warrant spending that precious presidential time on it. Your staff and cabinet secretaries are uncomfortable with being given responsibility. They want you in on the decision because they want cover if things go wrong. And things will go wrong. You'll get blamed for not being in meetings, or reviewing each detail. Taking that flak is part of the job. You'll have to assure those you delegate to you'll take the hits for them.

Guiding you out of the Quadrant One fog is what George H. W. Bush called "the vision thing,"[3] a larger idea that helps you sort. If Quadrant One takes over your life, that leaves no time for Quadrant Two, the non-urgent but important business of your administration that can be solved only through collective action—the issues that humans formed governments to solve. How do we align the incentives in the free market system to prompt people to take risks and protect the people cast aside by its necessary churn? How does the country slow the rate of healthcare spending so that it doesn't bankrupt itself? Eisenhower's farewell address about the danger of the military-industrial complex came from Quadrant Two, as did Reagan's speech to the British Parliament about the duty that democracies have to promote freedom. They were vital issues, but not boiling on the stove in the instant the presidents addressed them. Ignore Quadrant Two long enough, though, and it will grow up to be Quadrant One with no real solutions, because those had to be formed before the problem became acute.

Successful presidents live in Quadrants One and Two, farm out Quadrant Three to their team, and brace themselves against incursions from Quadrant Four. In Quadrant Four, the non-urgent and unimportant topics include the frequency of presidential golf games, commentary about political optics, and well-meaning but wrong analysis of the presidential decision-making process. "The essence of decision making is opaque even to the decision maker," John F. Kennedy said of being president. There is no corollary that says "but it's intimately well known to the cable news pundit."[4]

You walk into the most recognizable office in the world, the Oval Office. George W. Bush said that its oval shape meant the room has no corners to hide in.[15] That is a reminder of your other to-do list, the one buzzing outside your door that will rush in with your first meetings. It is written by the financial markets, or by a white nationalist the FBI believes is plotting in his garage, or the Senate majority leader who can't get enough of himself and wants you to see him today and treat him accordingly. Or you'll have to respond to the latest strategic move by the president of Russia. Every issue involves a decision you will have to make that you know could go wrong, and where you'll be lucky if you have a 60 percent confidence level of success when you make it. "There are no easy matters that will ever come to you as president. If they are easy, they will be settled at a lower level," Dwight Eisenhower told John Kennedy.[16] You'll never have enough information or time to whittle away uncertainty. In some cases, if you fail to act in time, or you delay, the result will be catastrophic.

Today you may have to decide whether to order a drone strike that could cause civilian casualties. Overnight, the second stage of the covert cyberattack you ordered began. It might cause a retaliation, and no one has given a good answer about where or when that might come. It could cripple the entire American banking, electrical, and telecommunications systems. Every meeting about cyberthreats is indeterminate. It's like trying to fight fog with a sword.

During one of your campaign debates, the moderator asked, "What black swan event do you worry about?" Quaint that he thought there was just one in this job. You now know that black swans flock to the White House like swallows to Capistrano. You can try to sort the important from the urgent, but sometimes the real job of being president is simply sorting the urgent.

The sun rises behind the Washington Monument. You laugh and look down at your coffee. You hear the sound track of yourself at a campaign rally when you were running to get this job. You knew the job would be hard when you ran for it, but you and the other candidates had no idea how different the actual job would be from the job you talked about on the campaign trail. You had said in Iowa, Florida, and Ohio: "Each morning when I have my first cup of coffee in the Oval Office and the sun rises behind the Washington Monument, it will be like *your* first cup of coffee, as you look out over the field, or the spreadsheet, or the disordered sheets of a hospital bed. *You* will be on my mind. Your hopes and your dreams will be with me as I think about what I can do as president to help you. We'll always protect your freedom so that you can think about your next great idea, or how to support your spouse or help your son with his homework, or think about nothing at all but the Buckeyes' next victory." (Your speechwriters changed this line to pander to every local audience. You improvised once and got the name of the college football team wrong. The New York tabloids ran front page stories about it for a week.)

It might be the caffeine kicking in, or the memory of the campaign and the thrill of having won the race to get into the Oval Office, but suddenly for a few moments the to-do list shrinks and you feel the thrill of possibility. You think, *I can make lives better now and for a generation. I can touch people and inspire waves of action.* It's corny, but the faces waiting in the hallway for your first meetings represent the vast army of public servants willing to stay up all night, to miss birthdays and anniversaries, because they believed all that stuff you said during the campaign.

Your predecessor testifies that this is a feeling that comes with the office. He left you a letter in your desk drawer, as all presidents leave their successors. The last lines read: "This job will be hard. Harder than anything you've ever done, not just because of the decisions you will face, but because progress will be so slow to achieve what you want. But don't forget, you have the power every day to do good. Sometimes it is just in one life, or on one block, but it can also be in one town, in one state, in one country, and in one world."

The morning knock comes that starts your day. The door pushes open. The first meeting of the day begins. The to-do list awaits for the hardest job in the world.

A President-Obsessed Nation

It is difficult to consider the presidency as an office distinct from its occupant because Donald Trump is its occupant. To a degree greater than any of his predecessors, Trump sees the office as an extension of himself. He does not believe in many of the job's obligations, and his supporters love him for it.

Our view of the office is also warped by the partisanship that Trump has exacerbated. The presidency has become the venue for all high-stakes political combat. Partisans define the standards of the job by the behavior of their preferred president. Or, partisans who oppose a president profess belief in standards that are tailored to make that president seem deficient.

Partisanship also affects how we analyze the presidency. Anyone who identifies a flaw in the office is accused of lowering the bar for the current occupant. If you note that the job is extremely difficult, you might be accused of making excuses, which thankfully is not how we think about brain surgery. Or, if you talk about the specific skills needed to actually do the very difficult job, you are seen as ideologically biased against the occupant who might not have those skills. All of this blocks the ability to examine and evaluate what the job really entails.

It no longer seems possible for a historian or an analyst of one ideology to judge a president of another ideology by a fixed standard, as the liberal Richard Reeves did about the conservative Ronald Reagan when he wrote, "Amazing things, good and bad, happened in the 1980s because President Reagan wanted them to happen. He knew how to be president."[17]

The fact that basic presidential qualities have become a partisan matter shows how far off the rails the office has run. The presidency was originally designed to resist exactly this kind of political infection. Thomas Jefferson and John Adams fought bitterly during the election of 1800, but it was still possible for Jefferson to say that the office would be well served no matter which of them was elected. He might have been hiding his true feelings—he often did when it came to Adams—but that, too, is the essence of the presidency: maintaining public roles that promote the health of the republic.

The White House has hosted forty-three presidents and resisted any one president's effort to put his name on it. The American presidency was created in a moment of desperation and uncertainty about the failing health of the new nation and its experimental democracy. Rival European countries cheered for its failure, awaiting its collapse. They were ultimately disappointed. The shared powers system created by the Constitution, with a chief magistrate chosen by a free people and partially responsible to Congress, has survived for 230 years. It has helped to build the most powerful nation in the world. The traditions and standards of the American presidency have produced heroes and been durable enough to withstand scoundrels, drawing strength and inspiration from the former, shaming and limiting the latter.

The office has a power of its own. Its traditions—embodied in concepts like "the dignity of the presidency" and "acting presidential"—have helped to propel the nation forward and upward. America has been a symbol and beacon for representative democracy to the world, and the standards of its institutions have given hope to people on every continent that self-determination and self-governance are possible.

Donald Trump's tenure has offered the chance to take a sweeping new look at the office. Many of the customs of the presidency were not bolted in place but held there through tradition, restraint, deference, shame, and custom. What held back Eisenhower was an idea in Eisenhower's head, not a wall put there by law. Donald Trump has loosened the bolts on, and dismantled much of, the apparatus, flinging parts onto the White House lawn. To understand what is vital to the office and what is vestigial to the office and to modern governance requires understanding how the presidency has become a job that is out of control.

Many of a president's modern responsibilities were not part of the job's original design. The framers of our Constitution, who launched a successful rebellion against a tyrannical king, envisioned an executive limited in power. The modest design, envisioned as a balance, held for the bulk of America's early history. In 1845, James K. Polk's wife, Sarah, fretted that the diminutive eleventh president might enter a room unnoticed. The original "dark horse candidate" had been Speaker of the House, but even that did not make him a household name. The *New Hampshire Sentinel* wrote of him in jest: "Mr. Polk was the Speaker, we believe, of the House of Representatives."[18] To bolster the president's stature, Mrs. Polk asked the Marine Band to play "Hail to the Chief" when he entered the room so people would swivel their heads in the direction of her husband's arrival.[19]

Today, we notice when the president doesn't show up. We demand presidential comment or action on most events in American public life. We expect the president to hasten to the scene of a natural disaster and comfort the afflicted. We expect the president to administer needle and thread when the national fabric tears, or at the very least to reach for the sewing box of unity. We hope the president will strike deals—or at least strain for bipartisan solutions—by schmoozing with opponents over medium-priced wine in the Blue Room of the White House. We assume the president will promote morality in foreign affairs based on the idea that it makes America safer, and that a country founded on human liberty is obligated to promote it and protect it elsewhere.

When a president has improvised in office, it has often added to the job description. New assumptions of what the job entails are conveyed, like the Oval Office furniture, to the next president. A modern president must now be able to jolt the economy like Franklin D. Roosevelt, tame Congress like Lyndon Johnson, and lift the nation like Ronald Reagan.

In 1956, the historian and political scientist Clinton Rossiter sketched the scope of the office by its chief burdens. Updating his list with subsequent burdens, the president is expected to be: Commander in Chief, Chief Executive, Chief Diplomat, Chief Legislator, Chief of Party, Chief Voice of the People, First Responder, Chief Priest, and World Leader.[20]

"The modern presidency has gotten out of control," says Leon Pa-

President Reagan and his fellow conservative, British prime minister Margaret Thatcher. The duo believed democracies had a duty to promote freedom abroad. In a 1982 speech to Parliament, Reagan predicted that "the march of freedom and democracy" would "leave Marxism-Leninism on the ash heap of history as it has left other tyrannies which stifle the freedom and muzzle the self-expression of the people."

netta, who has served as White House chief of staff, secretary of defense, and director of the CIA. "Presidents are caught in a crisis-by-crisis response operation that undermines the ability of any modern president to get a handle" on the office.[21]

As a president-obsessed nation, we undermine the very idea of our constitutional democracy by focusing so much on one person. No one person can possibly represent the varied and competing interests of 327 million citizens. No one person can perform well the ever-expanding duties of the office while managing an executive branch of 2 million employees (not including the armed forces), people charged with everything from regulating air pollution to X-raying passengers before they board an airplane. Presidential leadership today is not so much the work of an individual, it is the work of an organization, but we nevertheless obsess over the individual.[22]

The presidency has grown not just in size but also in scope and complexity. The role of commander in chief, the weightiest of presidential responsibilities, and the one we will take up first in part I, requires addressing more threats and evolving types of threats. National security risks include stateless terror groups that might weaponize a rented truck, or rogue states that might weaponize an email, in addition to marching armies. Global markets are more interconnected than ever before, which means a president has to be readier than ever to manage a crippling financial emergency before it can destroy the world economy. The threats of pandemics and environmental crises, which know no borders and cannot be stopped by walls, have also grown. Meanwhile, Congress, a president's necessary partner, has increasingly relinquished its role as an institution that tackles the country's big problems.

The country is more complex, too. America is more racially diverse than at any point in history and will continue to be. Just 52 percent of those age six to twenty-one are non-Hispanic whites.[23] A president must know how to read and speak to a wider variety of backgrounds and experiences and a newly forming concept of America.

Jefferson said citizens make presidents the "safe depository of their rights,"[24] but citizens today are fiercely divided. More of us settle into our corners, listening to partisan rants and nursing partisan grudges. Those who might not be so angry about everything are nevertheless confused and frustrated by a fragmented public square in which the media have splintered, allowing pundits with warring opinions and "alternative facts" to respond to the constant stream of social media distractions rather than substantively cover less flashy issues. A president cannot find consensus in this world, which makes it almost impossible to secure public agreement on problems, let alone public support for lasting solutions to them.

The swelling number of presidential duties fills a president's day with whipsawing emotions. In the morning he must console the widow of a soldier who died in combat; that afternoon he will be expected to cheer on and welcome a championship-winning NCAA hockey team to the White House. After that, he will be scared by the briefing about threats to the electrical grid. The grand tour of the office requires stops in places that can seem silly to some. A president must roll eggs on Easter, distribute candy on Halloween, and pardon the Thanksgiving turkey.

The president can never really go on vacation, because even the idea of vacation—a staple of presidents FDR, Truman, Eisenhower, Kennedy, and Reagan—has been bulldozed by partisans who have turned it into a sign of laziness. Everything the president does or doesn't do is processed by a constant, angry babble roaring from cable news to social media and back again.

THE JOB AIN'T AS ADVERTISED

THE PRESIDENCY HAS FACED SIMILAR CHALLENGES BEFORE. WHEN Arthur M. Schlesinger, Jr., published *The Imperial Presidency* in 1973, arguing that the office had gotten out of control, the title term had already been in use for ten years. The former Kennedy staffer warned that the office had become too powerful. Others have warned that the office has shrunk into powerlessness. Over the last four decades two books have been published with the title *Impossible Presidency* (Harold Barger's in 1984 and Jeremi Suri's in 2017).

Both assessments are true. The American presidency is the most powerful and overburdened office on the planet, full of demands, possibility, and frustration. Its occupant is the most famous person in the world, with the power to inspire generations. The president can launch invasions or, by standing aside, let other countries launch theirs. But the president also has very little power to make progress in the domestic sphere on the major challenges of a generation. "In the presidency there is the illusion of being in charge," George W. Bush's former chief of staff Joshua Bolten told me, "but all presidents must accept that in many realms they are not in charge."[25]

Every election campaign offers a chance to look at the office afresh and reset our national expectations, but elections also demonstrate why we need to be better at seizing that opportunity.

Louis Brownlow, who led a commission under FDR in 1937 to reform the presidency, identified the resistance in the populace to critical thinking in politics. "It is harder to think than it is to feel," Brownlow wrote in 1947. "And it is very much harder to think about things that seem to be but unimportant details than it is to feel about the things that seem most important to us."[26]

In campaigns, we reward candidates for behavior antithetical to the qualities, behaviors, and habits needed to perform well as a president.

We encourage impulsive, winner-take-all displays of momentary flash to win a job that requires restraint, deliberation, and cooperation. After competing in an arduous multiyear struggle for their own cause, candidates are expected to switch immediately to an office in which to be successful (and consistent with the founders' intention) they must sublimate their self-interest and ambition for the good of the country.

The office of the presidency we talk about in campaigns is nothing like the actual office of the presidency. In campaigns, it is a magical place where a strong will can solve the thorniest problems. We elect people for that magical job and are predictably disappointed when the wizard's wand wilts against growing entitlement costs or lack of health-care coverage or the warming of the climate.

Presidential campaigns are covered like sporting events, but as the presidential scholar James David Barber put it, "A ball game ends with the final score. The audience does not then put their power in the hands of the winning team."[27] Given the distance between the talents, personal qualities, and skills required to win an election and the talents, personal qualities, and skills required to govern, it's more like the voters are judging a football game and then putting the winning team in charge of synchronized swimming.

The disconnect between campaigning and governing leads to predictable revelations. "I thought it would be easier," President Trump told Reuters one hundred days into his term.[28] A blunt admission—and one much mocked by his critics—but one every president has eventually made after experiencing the shocking disparity between the campaign and the job. "For the last four years I spent so much time getting to know people who could help me get elected President that I didn't have any time to get to know people who could help me, after I was elected, to be a good President," confessed John Kennedy.[29] Lyndon Johnson made the point in his earthy way: "The office is kinda like the little country boy found the hoochie-koochie show at the carnival," he said. "Once he'd paid his dime and got inside the tent, it ain't exactly as it was advertised."

We are also part of the problem in campaigns. We are addicted to distraction. We focus on the glittering controversy of the moment. Instead of measuring candidates for the job, we let the candidates define the job. Campaign discussions center on a candidate's personality and pie-in-the-sky programs while ignoring whether that candidate's qualities and experiences align with the requirements of the job. Or whether they have the ability to accomplish any of the plans being discussed, given the political realities of the day.

The 2020 campaign and those beyond it will continue to test the malleability of presidential standards, which have softened like wax running down the outside of a Chianti bottle. "One reason there are so many candidates for the Democratic nomination for President is that there is no longer much certainty about what qualifies a person for the role," wrote Benjamin Wallace-Wells in *The New Yorker* in 2019,[30] at a time when the number of candidates exceeded the safe occupancy limit for an airport shuttle van.

We are in an age when our presidential candidates go through no apprenticeship process to test whether they have governing qualities. Previous experience in Washington is seen as a liability, but it should be considered an asset. When authenticity and campaign performance become the entire metric for judging whether a candidate should be elevated to such a high-stakes job, we're not simply judging a book by its cover, we're judging a bomb-defusing manual by its cover.

We can't afford to pick our central political player through such a defective system. America faces big challenges: The gap between the wealthy and everyone else is vast and growing. The economic mobility and opportunity that defined the American Dream are weakening. Twenty-seven and a half million Americans lacked health insurance in 2018, according to the U.S. Census.[31] The tensions between rival and warring countries are as complex as they have ever been. The workforce is misaligned with the available jobs. The globe is warming.

America also faces a host of cultural challenges—dislocation, dissociation, the decline of faith in institutions, racial tension. The Constitution doesn't put these tasks on the president's to-do list, but the office that has reached celebrity status influences those parts of the culture. If it shouldn't, we should talk about why not. Fitness for office isn't just a matter of whether a candidate can do the tasks they choose to take on, but also of whether they choose to take on the right tasks.

It is time to reclaim the office of the presidency, separate it from the

"There are no easy matters that will ever come to you as president,"
Dwight Eisenhower told John Kennedy.

presidential election campaign, and define the job's requirements as if we were conducting a job interview, because we are.

WHERE DO THESE EXPECTATIONS that have guided the presidency come from? What is their purpose? What barnacles should we knock off the hull of the job and which neglected elements are vital? Do we even know what the job requires? Are we blind to the skills actually required to be successful as the nation's chief executive because all we want to do is install our preferred party in the driver's seat? What does it mean to have presidential character, and how do you define temperament? Does offering a moral example to the country matter anymore? We interact with presidential history every day as we pass money with the interchangeable faces of its occupants, but what is the value of the legacies of Washington, Lincoln, Jackson, and Grant?

If nothing else, elections are the greatest stretch of time when Americans pay attention to national questions. It's a chance to examine the challenges of the office, to consider whether the presidency has expanded too much, whether the duties have become too demanding, to determine where to trim its responsibilities, and to discuss why Congress has demoted itself to the little brother who can't keep up and how to alter that. Also, have partisans grown so selfish that the idea of creative, collective, workable, and durable solutions are an impossible, even an obsolete goal?

We should probe candidates for information about how they would do the job, not just about what policies they would promote in it. Every time they boast about their plans, we should seek just as much information about how they would go about achieving them, and whether they have the skills necessary to execute them.

The presidency is a job of unrelenting difficult decisions. No one can wait for the president to learn how to make decisions. So we need to ask, what are the hardest decisions a candidate has made and how did they make those decisions? Were any of those decisions any good? What did they learn from their clunkers?

A presidency, like any large organization, requires coordinated action by extremely well chosen teams. How has the candidate selected and led a team? Does that candidate have a theory for building teams and managing them? These are not just questions for challengers but incumbents too.

Which lessons from presidential history do they think are the most instructive and why? Bromides won't do. Unless the candidate knows history, how will he or she have a long view and the context to make decisions?

What is the candidate's leadership style? How do they solve problems? Ask anyone who has ever commanded anything more taxing than a lemonade stand and they will tell you their system for doing it. Tim Cook, the CEO of Apple, told me he thinks of himself as a conductor, guiding a highly talented coordinated operation of colleagues.[32] Secretary of Defense James Mattis explains, "The ideal is a player coach, someone who plays the game well enough that you know what the challenges are but you're coaching others."[33] If voters know how a presidential candidate leads, they will know whether their theory of leadership matches the office and the challenges they'll face.

We should also ask those who want the job or want to stay in it to tell a joke. Former defense secretary Robert Gates said a sense of humor may be one of the most important requirement of the presidency.[34] Humor in the face of unrelenting pressure demonstrates equanimity, a crucial attribute of presidential success. It can also humanize a president, break the ice in tense situations, and win willingness to listen to a president's point of view.

These are questions and topics for governing and leading rather than for campaigning. The questions are vital at this particular moment because what is up for debate in America is not simply the best policies, but the best system of government, and whether the country's institutions and practices are up to the challenges of the day. The debate is about not just the "what" but also the "how."

Until we change our view of the office, presidents will continue to be frustrated by its demands, and Americans will continue to be disappointed in their leader. We will enter this and any presidential campaign season desperate for a good outcome but unprepared to choose someone who can reset the terms of presidential success and protect our country's well-being, or, in a reelection campaign, to demand that the incumbent do so.

Over the past several years, I've interviewed political scientists, historians, dozens of men and women who have worked in the West Wing under presidents of both parties, and some of the men who had the enormous job of sitting behind the Resolute Desk. What they described is an office in dire condition: overburdened, unrelenting in its demands, and unlike anything the founders intended when they met in Philadelphia in that hot summer of 1787 to rescue a fledgling experiment. What you are about to read is an account of the office and how it has evolved over the years to become misshapen, and how our own expectations of it have become warped as well. This book is also an effort to change the way we think about the presidency, particularly when we discuss the competition for the office — during election years and in the off years, when our evaluation of presidential qualities and performance set the conditions for the next contest, including at the congressional, state, and, increasingly, local levels of government.

What might happen if we think differently about the presidency? We will hopefully elect better candidates, or ask better questions of the ones we do elect. We'll stop punishing candidates for having qualities that are actually useful in the job — like experience in Washington, or an ability to reflect, to adapt, and to think about the whole nation. We'll push for policies and staffing choices that would help an overburdened president. Perhaps we might change our expectations so that administrations can stop responding to misplaced outrage in the culture. If presidents are measured against a more targeted critique of the work they do, they might have a better chance at becoming better presidents. Or voters who understand the demands and limitations of the office might look to other avenues—the private sector or Congress—for solutions to problems that have been heaped on the already overburdened president.

On the day of his inauguration in 2009, Barack Obama discussed the office he would occupy with his predecessor. "Ultimately, regardless of the day-to-day news cycles and the noise, the American people need their president to succeed," George W. Bush told him.[35] When Barack Obama met with Donald Trump, he passed on the same message. "Millions have placed their hopes in you," he wrote to the incoming president in the letter he left in the Resolute Desk, "and all of us, regardless of party, should hope for expanded prosperity and security during your tenure."[36] Americans still need their president to succeed. But the presidency as it exists today is set up for failure. It doesn't have to be.

PART ONE

THE OFFICE OF
THE PRESIDENCY

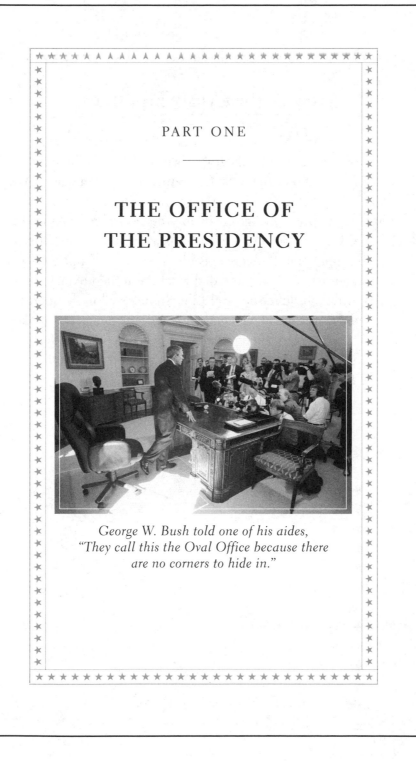

George W. Bush told one of his aides,
"They call this the Oval Office because there
are no corners to hide in."

GABRIEL OVER THE WHITE HOUSE

SEN. LANGHAM: Mr. President, this is dictatorship!

PRESIDENT: Senator Langham . . . words do not frighten me.

LANGHAM: But the United States of America is a democracy. We are not yet ready to give up the government of our fathers.

PRESIDENT: You *have* given it up. You've turned your backs. You've closed your ears to the appeals of the people. You've been traitors to the concepts of democracy . . . upon which this government was founded I believe in democracy . . . as Washington, Jefferson, and Lincoln believed in democracy. And if what I plan to do, in the name of the people . . . makes me a dictator . . . then it is a dictatorship based on Jefferson's definition of democracy. A government of the greatest good, for the greatest number.[1]

—1933 WALTER HUSTON IN
GABRIEL OVER THE WHITE HOUSE

Chapter 1

Executive in Chief

—

It is not because I do less than I might do,
but that I have more than I can do.[2]

—THOMAS JEFFERSON

The president needs help.[3]

—THE BROWNLOW COMMITTEE REPORT, 1937

ON APRIL 7, 1938, PROTESTERS DESCENDED ON WASHINGTON in a state of alarm. The Constitution was in danger. America's chief magistrate, Franklin Delano Roosevelt, was trying to seize power by expanding the size and scope of his office.[4]

Waving placards in front of the White House and marching through the halls of Congress, the protesters represented a host of sturdy citizen organizations: the Committee for the Preservation of America, National Defenders of the Constitution, Women Investors in America, the Paul Revere Riders. Their target was the Reorganization Act, a piece of legislation that would streamline the executive branch and beef up the president's staff.

The excitement in the streets marked a new chapter in a longer, historic clash over the presidency: whether the changes in the presidency, sold as necessary by its occupants, were undermining liberty and the American experiment in self-government.

Mrs. Pauline Revere Auerhamer thought she knew the answer. In 1775, her great-great-grandfather Paul Revere rode his horse through the streets of Lexington, Massachusetts, warning of the British army's advance. In 1938, Mrs. Auerhamer had organized one of the groups marching in what the International News Service called an "almost unprecedented popular protest." The tone of the dispatch then turned sociological: "Thousands of representatives of the 'inarticulate middle class' militantly descended upon the nation's capital."[5]

One protester carried a sign that read WE DON'T WANT A DICTATOR. Another sign demanded NO ONE-MAN LAW! Another pleaded THE COUNTRY NEEDS MEN, encapsulating the American tradition of equating standard-keeping with masculinity (which—in keeping with another stout American tradition—overlooked the fact that much of the energy for the protest came from women). The group did not lack for a theatrical touch. The head of the New York delegation of Revere Riders dressed like the famous silversmith, from the buckles on his shoes to the corners of his tricorn hat.[6]

When President Franklin Roosevelt pushed to reorganize the Office of the Presidency, citizens marched on Washington and pelted their representatives with Western Union telegrams— newspapers noted roughly 330,000—denouncing what they saw as a power grab.

The 1938 protesters might not have wanted a dictator, but five years earlier the country had been in the mood for one. When FDR came to office in 1933, the economic situation was so dire that even sensible people flirted with extreme measures. The presidency had been created to handle emergencies, and America was experiencing one. Why shouldn't the president have the tools to get the job done? A New York

Republican congressman told Roosevelt that Congress should "give you any power that you may need."[7] The columnist Walter Lippmann suggested the same. The *New York Herald Tribune* wrote an editorial entitled "For Dictatorship if Necessary."[8]

In 1933, William Randolph Hearst had tried to show the country just how appealing dictatorship might be. The newspaper tycoon had backed the movie *Gabriel Over the White House*, about a political hack whose bump on the head during an accident and subsequent bedside chat with the angel Gabriel turned him into a benevolent dictator who solved the country's problems with ruthless efficiency.[9] Reform measures included executing his gangster enemies by firing squad in front of the Statue of Liberty, which, as journalist Jonathan Alter points out, was considered by audiences and filmmakers alike as a perfectly fine thing to do.[10] Hearst had hoped the movie might soften up the country for sweeping presidential action. He sent FDR a copy of the script, and Roosevelt returned the pages with a thumbs-up and a series of suggested edits.

With the rise of Hitler and Mussolini, people in polite drawing rooms ended their dalliances with dictatorship, but the taste for quick action would remain. The idea of endowing the presidency with extraordinary powers in times of need stretched back to the founders, who debated giving presidents dictatorial powers at the Constitutional Convention. Even Thomas Jefferson, a skeptic of concentrated power, allowed for strong action by the president in times of crisis. "The laws of necessity, of self-preservation, of saving our country when in danger, are of higher obligation," he wrote. "To lose our country by a scrupulous adherence to written law, would be to lose the law itself, with life, liberty, property & all those who are enjoying them with us; thus absurdly sacrificing the end to the means."[11] This idea has lived on in modern-day clashes over executive power. The Constitution is not a "suicide pact," as Supreme Court Justice Robert Jackson put it in 1947.[12] Or, as Truman put it when he nationalized the steel companies to supply the Korean War, "The president has the power to keep the country from going to hell."[13]

Roosevelt's predecessor, Herbert Hoover, had experienced what happened when a president couldn't take action to fight a crisis. His name became synonymous with every brand of American disaster. Broken cars pulled by mules were known as "Hoover wagons." Shanty-towns were called "Hoovervilles." Soup kitchen meals were "Hoover stew." Newspapers used for warmth were "Hoover blankets," and "Hoover hogs" were the jackrabbits too slow to escape the stewpot.[14]

In a joke at the time, Hoover asked his treasury secretary, Andrew Mellon, "Lend me a nickel, I want to call a friend." Mellon replied, "Here's a dime, call all your friends."[15] The cautionary tale for FDR was how quickly fortunes could turn for a president. Hoover was once a global hero. During World War I, he had managed relief efforts and served as head of the economic restoration of Europe. It was part of his record of accomplishment that helped him get elected in 1928. Then, in a little more than a decade, the man whose ingenuity and skill had fed Europe became a symbol of stasis, hunger, and impotence.[16] When he traveled, rotten eggs pelted his train. When a delegation of Palo Alto Girl Scouts presented Hoover with flowers, he finally let the tears run down his face, and a twelve-year-old asked her mother, "Mommy, what do they do to a president to make a man look like Mr. Hoover does?"[17]

The challenges FDR faced upon taking office were steep. The unemployment rate in 1933, the year after he was first elected, was 25 percent, the highest it has been in modern times.[18] Banks and businesses closed. People were forced from their jobs and homes. Millions starved. Roosevelt responded with "bold, persistent experimentation."[19] "Take a method and try it," he implored in a 1932 commencement address to a younger generation. "If it fails, try another. But above all, try something." President Coolidge, who had preceded Hoover, had usually finished his official day by lunchtime and is said to have believed a national leader should not try to "go ahead of the majestic army of human thought and aspiration, blazing new and strange paths."[20] This sounds like Coolidge, but the quote is actually one written by his secretary who took down his thoughts. FDR opened up new avenues of presidential action each day until after the sun had gone down. He seemed to be living by Ralph Waldo Emerson's maxim "In skating over thin ice, our safety is in our speed."

In his first hundred days alone, FDR pushed through the heavily Democratic Congress the Emergency Banking Act and National Industrial Recovery Act. He launched the Federal Emergency Relief Administration and Agricultural Adjustment Administration.[21] Roosevelt initiated legislation, whereas before, presidents had only implemented policy that had been established by Congress.[22]

The Great Depression and the Second World War presented challenges that only a president could meet. During his time in office, FDR issued 3,522 executive orders, almost surpassing the total that had been issued by the thirty presidents who preceded him.[23] These emergencies increased the presidential role in setting industrial policy and regulating banking, agriculture, monetary policy, housing, taxation, trade, and employment.[24]

As the political scientist Matthew Dickinson notes in his assessment of FDR's request to expand the size of the executive office, Roosevelt not only accumulated power in the office, he created a new habit. In the future, Americans were "more likely to look to [the president] for solutions."[25]

FDR: "I NEED HELP"

THE EXECUTIVE BRANCH HAD BEEN CREATED TO HARNESS THE ENergy of the executive, but it wasn't equipped for Roosevelt's energy. Cabinet secretaries were autonomous and their duties overlapped. Roosevelt had no efficient way to manage the conflicting authorities and egos. He tried and failed five different times to reorganize the relationships among his cabinet departments. Finally, with the capacity of the office stretched to its limit, FDR sounded his own alarm: "The president's task has become impossible for me or any other man."

FDR petitioned Congress for additional staff dedicated to the president. Up to that point, he had been working with aides mostly on loan from various agencies. He also asked for more control over his cabinet departments and for the ability to coordinate them. If Congress agreed, it would be the first major change to the structure of the executive branch since the presidency was created. This is the request that had ignited the sign carriers accusing FDR of a power grab.

Previous presidents had also called for reinforcements. In 1825, when President James Monroe left office after his second term, he sent Congress "a few remarks . . . founded on my own experience in this office." He wrote that "if inferior details are forced upon the attention

of the President he loses time to devote to matters of higher importance."[26] The fifth president suggested that Congress give his successors
some assistance.[27] Congress—certain that power granted to the president would diminish their own—did not whir into action.

In 1905, Teddy Roosevelt sought to improve the administration by
adopting the best practices of the day, particularly the application of
the scientific method.[28] Congress resisted every single recommendation.[29] Lawmakers were so irritated by the encroachments on their
sphere of action that in March 1909, Congress passed the Tawney
Amendment, which prohibited the expenditure of federal funds by any
executive commission looking into improving presidential administration unless Congress authorized such an investigation.

In 1908, the then political scientist Woodrow Wilson observed that
"duties apparently not assigned to [a president] at all, chiefly occupy
his time and energy."[30] Wilson, not yet president, proposed a series of
sweeping reforms of the office. Later, when he took office and had a

*During the Great
Depression, some of
America's wisest
minds flirted with
the idea of giving
President Roosevelt
dictatorial powers,
but six years into
his presidency, the
backlash against
FDR's move to
reorganize his office
was so robust that
he had to issue
a statement: "I have
no inclination to
be a dictator."*

chance to propose these self-help measures, he shrank from taking on the fight with Congress[31]

THE BROWNLOW REPORT

FDR'S REQUEST WAS BUILT ON AN ELEVEN-MONTH STUDY OF THE executive office that he had commissioned. The President's Committee on Administrative Management—known as the Brownlow Committee—was headed by Louis Brownlow, a journalist, city manager, and professor with a perfect memory, a fondness for anecdotes, and an obsession with the presidency. To draw a blueprint for the modern office, Brownlow and two other college professors traveled to Europe to attend meetings of international public administration organizations.[32] The management of governance was a global problem. Industrialization and modern technology had shifted power from elected representatives to appointed government officials who had special expertise and could keep up with the new pace of developments.[33] The report and FDR's staff requests based on it were, as the political scientist Theodore Lowi wrote, "the first of many efforts to adjust an eighteenth century Constitution to the twentieth century."[34] The Brownlow Committee's famous conclusion: "The president needs help."

The authors of the Brownlow Report knew their audience. They emphasized that President Roosevelt was not trying to tread on, or wriggle out from under, Congress's power over executive administration. "The preservation of the full accountability of the Executive to the Congress is an essential part of our republican system," the Brownlow Committee wrote.[35] The authors also made it clear that Roosevelt's new aides, should he get them, would not impinge upon the duties of the elected president or encroach on the prerogatives of elected members of Congress. Should Congress grant the president new staffers, they would be like children in Victorian England—seen and not heard. According to the committee:

> Their effectiveness in assisting the President will, we think, be directly proportional to their ability to discharge their functions with restraint. They would remain in the background, issue no orders, make no decisions, emit no public statements. Men

for these positions should be carefully chosen by the President from within and without the Government. They should be men in whom the President has personal confidence and whose character and attitude is such that they would not attempt to exercise power on their own account. They should be possessed of high competence, great physical vigor, and a passion for anonymity.[36]

THE PURGE

DESPITE THE PROTESTS, THE REQUEST FDR MADE FOR A LARGER staff was actually quite modest. Though the demands of the day were vast, the president recognized that both by tradition and by the Constitution, he couldn't get grabby. Nevertheless, Congress and the public objected. "We are against centralization of too much power in the hands of the Executive," said C. R. Reilly of Chicago, who rode that protest train all the way to Washington. "It is undemocratic."[37] This had been a regular complaint leveled against FDR since the previous spring of 1937, when the president had unveiled his plan to expand the membership of the Supreme Court. All of Roosevelt's experimentation had put opponents on a hair trigger. When Roosevelt's labor secretary, Frances Perkins, testified in Congress on behalf of the Social Security program, a woman leaped up and shouted that the idea had been copied word for word from "page eighteen of the Communist Manifesto, which I have right here in my hand, Mr. Chairman."[38]

Lucille Sharpe, identified by newspapers as a New York housewife, told a reporter covering the protests against the Reorganization Act, "All I want is a chance to see Mr. Roosevelt in person. I think he needs some elementary lessons in American principles of democracy."[39]

Senator Josiah William Bailey of North Carolina, who led the opposition to Roosevelt in the Senate, didn't just oppose the specifics of the request for staff. He didn't like the president's having made the request at all. Reorganizing the office of the presidency was a "legislative power," he said. "Our power." Bailey criticized the president for taking that reorganizing power "from ourselves, to whom it belongs, to one single, sole man, who, until we do transfer it, never had or enjoyed one particle of it."[40]

The original framers of the Constitution anticipated this debate.

They had created the presidency to move quickly in an emergency, but they also knew that presidents were likely to confect emergencies or exploit them and grab more power, replacing the diverse voices of the people with the single voice of the president. Roosevelt denied that he was doing any such thing. He was just trying to keep everything up to date in the capital city. FDR couldn't exert energy in the executive office if he couldn't keep up the pace. "We cannot call ourselves either wise or patriotic if we seek to escape the responsibility of remolding government to make it more serviceable to all the people and more responsive to modern needs," said the president.[41]

Roosevelt devoted a fireside chat to promoting the Reorganization Act.[42] He also put political muscle behind it, targeting members of his own party in primaries who opposed it and were up for reelection in 1938. Despite the magical properties ascribed to FDR's radio addresses, the public did not warm to him on this topic. In an April 1938 Gallup poll, only 18 percent of the country thought the president should have more power.[43] Three hundred thirty thousand Americans sent telegrams to members of Congress denouncing "one-man rule."[44] The legislation became known as the "dictator bill." Several cartoonists portrayed Roosevelt with an outstretched arm in a Nazi salute. Another cartoon, entitled "Oliver Twist," showed a towering FDR with meaty hands encircling a vast soup bowl labeled "power," a bowl almost as big as his smile. In his shadow cowered a little chef dubbed "Congress," holding a ladle and wearing the alarmed expression of one about to meet his doom. The attacks from the citizenry on FDR worked. In the spring of 1938, the House blocked the bill. FULL CREDIT ACCORDED AROUSED NATION read one headline.[45]

This setback did not extinguish Roosevelt's vim. With the election of 1938 ahead, he recast himself. After midnight on April 11, as the ten men in the press pool covering the president on vacation in Warm Springs, Georgia, tossed playing cards back and forth at one another to pass the time, an urgent bulletin interrupted them. It was a statement from the president, in the form of a letter FDR had penned to a concerned constituent.[46] It contained his defense:

> I have no inclination to be a dictator. I have none of the qualifications which would make me a successful dictator. I

have too much historical background and too much knowledge of existing dictatorships to make me desire any form of dictatorship for a democracy like the United States.

The debate during the election of 1938 wasn't just about the size of the office. The Democratic Party was having a fight over other measures Roosevelt wanted to enact with an enlarged presidency. The same Southern Democrats the president targeted over the Reorganization Bill had also helped kill the antilynch law he had supported. But FDR's pressure gambit failed. As Susan Dunn outlines in *Roosevelt's Purge*, which recounts the war the president waged against members of his own party, only one of the Democratic candidates targeted by FDR lost his reelection bid in 1938.[47]

In 1939, Congress finally granted the president some of the help he had asked for, but not at the level he had requested. To dispatch the duties of his office, he would now be allowed six assistants and be given limited authority to reorganize the departments of the executive branch.[48] Congress reserved the right to veto any of the president's plans for further modifications. In other words, they gave the president a little more freedom to run his sector of the federal government, but they also fitted him with an ankle bracelet.

THE IMPERIAL PRESIDENCY

TODAY, THE BATTLE OVER THE REORGANIZATION BILL SEEMS REMOTE. A tale of Congress dominating a president in a clash of wills seems like the kind of distant story of past glory you'd read about in a guidebook of a sleepy country whose tall ships once ruled the seas and dominated the spice routes.

In the decades since Congress granted Roosevelt his elevator full of additional staffers, the executive branch has steadily increased in size and power. The emergencies of the Great Depression and, later, World War II gave FDR more leverage with Congress. The gains he made for the executive branch not only increased its power but provided the opening through which his successors moved to expand the presidency even further. Congress, once a jealous guardian of its role as the primary representative of the people, allowed much of this transformation to happen. The attacks of 9/11 and the military response to them increased the scope and power of the presidency even more.

The president is now the leading actor in the American government. Roosevelt described the branches of government as a three-horse team tilling a field. It could not plow in straight furrows without three-way cooperation. Now the president rides a Clydesdale, dragging along Congress, which many supporters believe exists just to slow the operation. "More and more legislative authority is delegated to the executive branch every year," complained Republican senator Ben Sasse of Ne-

In 1933, FDR and his cabinet of ten could fit behind his desk. Donald Trump's cabinet of twenty-four is larger than a royal wedding party. Eighteen of them are here arranged in March 2017 as six slots remained to be filled.

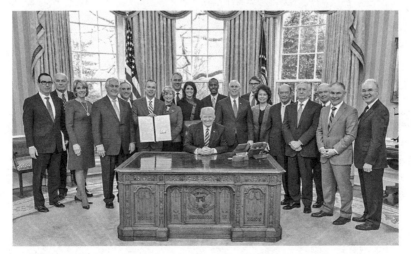

braska in a floor speech in September 2018. "Both parties do it. The legislature is impotent. The legislature is weak."[49] The decline of legislative activity has left America "increasingly governed by negotiations between the imperial presidency and whichever philosopher-king has the swing vote on the [Supreme Court]," wrote the *New York Times* columnist Ross Douthat.[50] No one is happy with the outcome, but no one seems to know how to restore the balance.

Today, about 418 people work inside the 55,000-square-foot White House, in jobs from National Security Advisor to public liaison to special assistant for financial policy.[51] Two thousand more work in the Executive Office of the President. As Congressman Mo Udall once quipped, "The White House now has enough people with fancy titles to populate a Gilbert and Sullivan opera."[52]

When Roosevelt and his first cabinet assembled for a group photo in 1933, all eleven of them could fit behind the desk—a display of wide lapels, pocket watches, and one plain black dress that Labor Secretary Frances Perkins said she wore to keep her colleagues focused.[53]

In 2017, to squeeze the twenty-four members of the Trump administration with cabinet rank behind the desk, the photographer would have had to stack them on risers like a high school glee club. Protesters no longer line up to rail against an office of that size. Instead, the expectation has grown that the president will respond to all public and global questions, which makes sorting priorities the first and most difficult task of the hardest job in the world.

Cyberattack

Last month I convened an emergency meeting of my cabinet and top homeland security, intelligence and defense officials. Across the country trains had derailed, including one carrying industrial chemicals that exploded into a toxic cloud. Water treatment plants in several states had shut down, contaminating drinking water and causing Americans to fall ill.

Our nation, it appeared, was under cyberattack. Unknown hackers, perhaps a world away, had inserted malicious software into the computer networks of private-sector companies that operate most of our transportation, water, and other critical infrastructure systems.

Fortunately, last month's scenario was just a simulation—an exercise to test how well federal, state and local governments and the private sector can work together in a crisis.[1]

—BARACK OBAMA IN *THE WALL STREET JOURNAL*, JULY 19, 2012

The president's morning usually starts with the Presidential Daily Brief, a catalog of the world's most pressing dangers. Presidents should not let the urgent crowd out the important, but "sometimes you don't get to the important," says Obama's former terrorism adviser. "Your day is spent just trying to prioritize the urgent. Which urgent first?"

Chapter 2

Commander in Chief

—

Domestic policy can only defeat us.
Foreign policy can kill us.[2]

—JOHN F. KENNEDY

Many people are always saying the Presidency is too
big a job for any one man. When I hear this assertion,
I always try to point out that a single man must make the
final decisions that affect the whole, but that proper
organization brings to him only the questions and
problems on which his decisions are needed. His own
job is to be mentally prepared to make those decisions
and then to be supported by an organization that
will make sure they are carried out.[3]

—DWIGHT D. EISENHOWER

PRESIDENT EISENHOWER WAS A LIFE HACKER. HE THOUGHT ABOUT not just what he did but how he did it and developed systems to make himself more efficient. He had ideas about different modes of leadership, the power of optimism, and prioritizing vacations to keep himself sharp. When Ike first entered the White House after his inauguration in January 1953, the story goes, an usher handed him a letter and he batted it right back. "Never bring me a sealed envelope!" he said. Nothing, he explained, should come to him without first being screened to see whether it merited his attention.[4]

Ike understood that leaders must prioritize how they apply their attention, because the number of tasks and their weight make presidential time a precious commodity. He also understood the priority cost. If a president dribbles out his focus on the secondary or frivolous, he will have no time for those matters that only he can decide. Eisenhower knew the most basic and important task for a president is simply knowing what his job is.

Presidential time also sends a signal. It tells the rest of the administration what is important. Every staffer wants to please the president, so naturally they gravitate toward areas the president attends to in the hope of perhaps getting noticed. How a president's time is allocated determines the course of an administration and perhaps this or another country's future.

KNOWING WHAT IS TRULY PRESIDENTIAL

IKE ENCAPSULATED HIS APPROACH TO PRIORITIES IN THE MAXIM "WHAT IS important is seldom urgent, and what is urgent is seldom important." The concept has been passed on through the generations. Senator Lamar Alexander remembers working in the Nixon White House as a young staffer under Bryce Harlow, a favorite staff member of Eisenhower.[5] "We had some young guys that were on the White House staff," Alexander remembers. "We'd get impatient and I'd say 'Mr. Harlow, why don't we do this?' and he'd say 'Lamar, our job here is to push the merely important matters out of the White House and reserve for the president what is truly presidential.'"[6]

If a leader is judicious and focused, his team will have a clear understanding of what is important. "Priorities are like arms," the productivity expert Merlin Mann says. "If you have more than two, you are crazy, or you're lying."[7]

A president's top priority is protecting America. "The power of directing and employing the common strength forms a usual and essential part in the definition of the executive authority,"[8] wrote Alexander Hamilton. Or, as President Kennedy said, "Domestic policy can only defeat us. Foreign policy can kill us."[9] Kennedy was even more expansive about this priority in a conversation with Richard Nixon after the Bay of Pigs failure. The president told his vanquished rival from the 1960 race, who shared his view about national priorities, "It really is true that foreign affairs is the only important issue for a president to

*Harry Truman's decision to use two atomic weapons was
the most momentous presidential decision ever made.
His administration would create the CIA, the National
Security Council, and the modern Pentagon, preparing the
way for presidential dominance of national security affairs.*

handle, isn't it? I mean, who gives a shit if the minimum wage is $1.15
or $1.25, in comparison to something like this?"[10]

The national security folder in the president's portfolio has grown
ever larger as the threats to America have grown wider and more complex. World War II caused an enormous expansion of the White House.
In 1947, Truman created the National Security Council to manage
the tasks after a three-year debate with Congress that set the stage for
the modern national security establishment, reorganizing and modern-
izing the U.S. armed forces, foreign policy, and the intelligence community apparatus. What was initially a limited power granted to the
executive grew ever larger. The Cold War required, as Eisenhower put
it, "permanent armaments"[11] to prepare for conflict anywhere the ongoing ideological battle required. Some of those armaments could destroy mankind. Kennedy expanded the National Security Council after
the Bay of Pigs, because he worried that the system for managing threats
was not providing good advice.

If we forget how serious the presidency is, the armor that surrounds the office reminds us. A hulking apparatus protects the presidential body—from the armor-plated eight-ton limousine to the ring of Secret Service agents—and reminds us that the job can become grave in an instant. A military aide travels with the president everywhere, carrying the codes to launch nuclear warheads. Fighter jets fly just off the wings of Air Force One. The president must be protected, because only the president can make the most serious and irrevocable decisions about national safety.

On the morning of his inauguration, Bill Clinton was given his lesson on how to launch nuclear weapons. "There's a difference between knowing about the presidency and actually being President," he wrote about taking on the weight of the job as he moved from the president's guest quarters at Blair House to the president's quarters across the street. "It's hard to describe in words, but I left Blair House with my eagerness tempered by humility."[12]

Even relatively peaceful presidencies are perilous. Jimmy Carter is the only president since Hoover who did not have an active military engagement. Still, he had to manage the Iranian hostage crisis and failed military rescue. There were also the high-stakes presidential moments we didn't hear about at the time. In 1979, Carter was one minute from being awakened with news that twenty-two hundred Soviet missiles had launched and that U.S. planes were in the air ready to retaliate. He would have had only minutes to respond with a counterattack. His National Security Advisor, Zbigniew Brzezinski, had been awakened in the night and informed of the attack. He'd asked for confirmation and received it. Brzezinski had not awakened his wife, reckoning that everyone would be dead in half an hour. Just before calling the president he learned that it was a false alarm. Software simulating a Soviet missile attack "was inexplicably transferred into the regular warning display."[13]

FLATTENED BY HISTORY OR GIVING IT A NUDGE

VOTERS GET ANGRY WHEN A PRESIDENT ISN'T PAYING MAXIMUM attention to the domestic issue they care about, but it could very well be that he is dealing with a secret national security challenge. "When it comes to Donald Trump, the naysayers should be less reflexively accusatory and presumptively negative," says Trump counselor Kellyanne Conway. "Oh, he's just watching TV. No, he's doing things you can't see because his first duty is to protect the American people."[14]

If a president's campaign promises crumble in office, it may be that a president is experiencing complexity they never understood as a candidate. Barack Obama hoped to pull troops out of Afghanistan before leaving office, but he concluded that the United States could not afford to walk away and allow the country to incubate extremists again.[15] When Obama justified the drone program that had killed U.S. citizens aligned with al-Qaeda, the former candidate who came to the office on the strength of his opposition to George Bush's Iraq war sounded a lot like him. "We are at war with an organization that right now would kill as many Americans as they could if we did not stop them first," he said. "So this is a just war—a war waged proportionally, in last resort, and in self-defense."[16] President Trump wanted to remove the thousands of troops Barack Obama had left in Afghanistan, but then during a 2019 Thanksgiving visit to Afghanistan, Trump declared that the United States would leave only when it had achieved "total victory,"[17] an ambitious goal long since shelved as impossible.

How a president sets priorities has periodically been a focus of presidential campaigns. If an administration isn't paying sufficient attention, America is left vulnerable. President Kennedy claimed that his predecessor, Eisenhower, had allowed a missile gap to open with the Soviets. Reagan won, in part, by promising a simple and directed focus. Asked before he was president about how he would deal with Communism and the Soviet Union, he replied: "We win. They lose."[18]

During the 2012 presidential campaign, then candidate Mitt Romney argued that Russia was America's greatest geopolitical foe and that Barack Obama was missing that point. (He was mocked by Obama and pundits, but turned out to be right.) Trump faced a stronger, bipartisan criticism of Russia blindness in response to his accommodationist posture toward Russian leader Vladimir Putin.

Experts from both parties applauded Donald Trump's attention to the national security challenge from China. Though they might disagree with his approach, Trump's focus on China showed he had his priorities in order. By contrast, Trump's focus on debunked theories about alleged Ukrainian interference in the 2016 U.S. election and the activities by Joe Biden's son in that country showed disordered priorities. Neither was anywhere near the top of the administration's list of security priorities or that of any credible expert. Nevertheless, the president engaged his time, his administration's entire policy-making apparatus, and his personal lawyer on these matters. His fixation on the shadow caused end-runs that led to his impeachment.

Richard Nixon's trip to China in 1972 was a triumph of priority setting in national security. Despite the deluge of day-to-day security challenges, including the ongoing war in Vietnam, Nixon stayed focused on the long game of renewing relations with Chinese communists who had been shut out of U.S. foreign policy for twenty-five years since they came to power. The outreach not only opened channels of communication with a potential rival, but created a connection with a country that could be a counterweight to the Soviet Union. It was a vision Nixon had nurtured as vice president under Eisenhower, then as a private citizen, and in careful small public signals when he came into office as president.[19] Developed in secret and carried out against howls from conservatives who saw relations with China as a gross capitulation in the global ideological struggle, the gambit was something only a president could achieve in the American system, fueled by Nixon's vision and view of leadership.[20] The mark of a leader "is whether he can give history a nudge," he told one interviewer.[21] He did so in an extraor-

Richard Nixon's trip to China in 1972 was the culmination of a yearslong strategy. By shaking hands with Chinese premier Chou En-lai, he showed the respect required to thaw a two-decade freeze. "When our hands met, one era ended and another began," wrote Nixon.

dinary act of foresight. "He personally identified one of the great problems of American foreign policy—the isolation and hostility of China—and by over three years of patient effort, brought it to an end," wrote the *New York Times* columnist James Reston.[22] Nixon's old boss Eisenhower would have surely recognized this as the perfect execution of a Quadrant Two—important but not urgent—task.

Don't Duck the Hypothetical!

IF YOU WERE CONSTRUCTING A JOB INTERVIEW BY WHICH TO DETERmine whether candidates could manage the presidency, the role of commander in chief would be the most important part of the conversation. The person across the table from you with their résumé on heavy bond paper and their practiced lines might not fully grasp what they are signing up for. If they get the job, they might have to decide whether to risk thousands of lives, maybe more. If their priorities are wrong, even more lives might be at stake.

Voters can use the Eisenhower decision matrix to see if candidates have their priorities straight. Are they concerned with Quadrant One issues or issues in Quadrant Two, or are they lost somewhere else? Is the press stuck covering non-urgent and non-important events as if they belong in Quadrants One or Two?

Thinking in quadrants can also shape how we look at candidate attributes. Since national security is such a large part of the job, we should spend our time and focus on thinking about whether candidates have the skills to handle those issues. A crisis will come, and when it does, there won't be time to watch a webinar to get up to speed. "If you take the presidency seriously," says Susan Rice, Barack Obama's National Security Advisor, "you're dealing with the toughest issues that any human being on the planet is facing."[23]

The crisis questions we should ask candidates are: What is the most significant challenge the candidate has faced and what did they do about it? How does the person handle pressure? What experience in the past demonstrates that? Can they build a crisis team that will give them good and varied options? When they are alone making the most crucial decisions about life and death, what values will govern their decisions? These topics rarely get a thorough investigation in campaigns.[24]

In the fall of 2019, *The Washington Post* published the Afghanistan Papers, an internal Pentagon review of that war.[25] Members of the military from every level spoke on the record and candidly. They painted a picture of chaos, drift, and ineptitude in an unwinnable war. Yet for eighteen years, successive administrations continued on, offering a protracted campaign of misinformation. Given the history of mistakes in Vietnam, Iraq, and now Afghanistan, any president or candidate who aspires to the job should have to explain what lessons they take from that report and how they plan to avoid repeating the mistakes that are so costly.

When candidates are asked questions related to a national security crisis, they speak in generalities, nervous about demonstrating how they would make hard choices because they don't want to scare or offend voters. Fortunately, we don't pick airline pilots this way, evaluating them for crisis response only after the flock of birds has flown into the engines.

A familiar dodge is for candidates pressed on national security issues to say they won't answer hypothetical questions. This stratagem should lead to a revolt from the citizenry on the grounds that candidates who refuse to entertain a hypothetical question are refusing to demonstrate one of the key skills for the job they want: the ability to think hypothetically and in counterfactuals. In answering a question that requires a little thinking, a candidate shows us that she can contemplate and evaluate a situation. An answer to a hypothetical question demonstrates how a presidential candidate thinks through a specific tough problem, like a runaway pandemic, but it also gives us a view into the general matter of whether a candidate can think about hypothetical outcomes and weigh probabilities, which they will be required to do all the time in the office.

When a candidate chooses *not* to cry "hypothetical," it can be illuminating. During a 2008 campaign debate, Barack Obama was asked a hypothetical question by an audience member: "Should the United States respect Pakistani sovereignty and not pursue al-Qaeda terrorists who maintain bases there, or should we ignore their borders and pursue our enemies, like we did in Cambodia during the Vietnam War?" Senator Obama replied, "If we have Osama bin Laden in our sights and the Pakistani government is unable or unwilling to take him out, then I think that we have to act, and we will take him out."[26] Three years later, the president was presented with the exact situation the questioner had put forward, and President Obama acted as he had said he would during the debate. Imagining what might happen in a presidency is a crucial task for any candidate and for the electorate, because the unimaginable often happens.

"I Can Hear You!"

PRESIDENT BUSH: I want you all to know that America today, America today is on bended knee, in prayer for the people whose lives were lost here, for the workers who work here, for the families who mourn. The nation stands with the good people of New York City and New Jersey and Connecticut as we mourn the loss of thousands of our citizens.

RESCUE WORKER: I can't hear you!

PRESIDENT BUSH: I can hear you! I can hear you! The rest of the world hears you! And the people—and the people who knocked these buildings down will hear all of us soon!

RESCUE WORKERS: [*Chanting*] U.S.A.! U.S.A.! U.S.A.! U.S.A.! U.S.A.! U.S.A.! U.S.A.! U.S.A.![1]

In the 2000 presidential debates between George W. Bush and Al Gore, the word "terrorism" came up only once, and in passing. It would soon dominate Bush's presidency.

Chapter 3

Welcome to the NFL

—

Within the first few months I discovered that being a
President is like riding a tiger. A man has to keep on riding
or be swallowed. The fantastically crowded nine months of
1945 taught me that a President either is constantly on top of
events or, if he hesitates, events will soon be on top of him.
I never felt that I could let up for a single moment.[2]

—HARRY S. TRUMAN

IN THE NATIONAL FOOTBALL LEAGUE, WHEN A ROOKIE GETS KNOCKED
off his feet in his first game by an opposing player who seemed to come
out of nowhere, a veteran or coach will greet his wobbly return to the
sidelines by saying "Welcome to the NFL." This happens in the presidency too: the challenges come with force and sometimes seemingly
from out of nowhere. In 1913, after Woodrow Wilson became president,
he remarked, "It would be an irony of fate, if my administration had to
deal chiefly with foreign affairs, for all of my preparation has been in
domestic matters."[3] His remark was prescient: Wilson soon faced World
War I.

The first thing a new president notices upon moving into the best
address in public housing is that the issues that occupy their time are
not the ones they spent so much time talking about in the campaign.
"The biggest shock they face is that eighty-five to ninety percent of the
job is all about foreign policy, which is about five percent of the campaign," says Elaine Kamarck, author of *Why Presidents Fail*. "All of the
sudden you're having to make decisions and learn about countries and

meet with world leaders and then on top of that there's the secret world of intelligence."[4] Condoleezza Rice worked in the White House during the fall of Communism and during the attacks of 9/11 and its aftermath. "It's the unexpected that will catch them," she says of a new president. "It's this huge machinery. The military is doing things and there are foreign countries and Congress. You don't really have levers on all of it. . . . A president walks into the Oval. There're pictures of Lincoln and Washington. What do I do now?"[5]

George W. Bush faced the most head-snapping switch of the last century between the campaign and the presidency. During the 2000 campaign, terrorism was not an issue. In that election year and the first eight months afterward, no major national survey asked about terrorism when evaluating the candidates.[6] In the three debates between Vice President Al Gore and George W. Bush, the word "terrorism" came up only once, and in passing.

Bush had planned to define his presidency around education policy and domestic affairs. His first foreign policy move was to strengthen ties with Mexico. The Texas governor had campaigned on a promise that he would have a "humble foreign policy," but by the end of his term, his successor, Barack Obama, won office running against Bush's "arrogant foreign policy."

"Almost all of them have foreign policy ideas they come with," says former Secretary of State Rice of presidential candidates. "On day one, 'I will,' and on day one, they don't, because it's so complicated. They're almost all frustrated because the world doesn't accord with the world that they thought they were going to be able to shape. And you really can't see that from the outside. Then you get in there and the stuff starts flowing."

George W. Bush not only had to respond to the threats in the moment, he also presided over the most substantial reorganization of the executive branch since 1947. He expanded his national security staff. He created the largest department in the executive branch, the Department of Homeland Security, and in 2005 another entirely new entity, the Office of the Director of National Intelligence, which itself includes several intelligence agencies founded since Kennedy's presidency.

George W. Bush didn't just expand the presidency's footprint. He expanded the war reach of the office by signing executive orders authorizing warrantless eavesdropping on American citizens and establishing military tribunals for the detention, treatment, and trial of certain noncitizens. When Bush thought legislation infringed on his national security duties, he amended it with signing statements, addenda that expressed his view that while he was signing the law, he would not allow the law to constrain his powers.[7] "War," said James Madison, "is in fact the true nurse of executive aggrandizement."[8]

THE PLATE IS FULL OF HOT POTATOES

PRESIDENTS START THEIR DAY WITH THE PRESIDENT'S DAILY BRIEF, an intelligence assessment of the threats facing America. FDR received an oral briefing. John F. Kennedy requested that his intelligence briefing document be small enough to fit in his pocket. During the Obama years, the PDB was delivered in a stiff leather binder that looked like the guest book at a country club. Inside was a grim iPad containing all of the possible ways the president could fail at his most essential role. Early in his term, Trump reportedly requested an oral digest of the briefings like FDR. The form has not affected the growth in threats. In the post-9/11 presidency, the threats are more numerous and more complex.

"Every morning I would take a blank piece of paper in preparation for the presidential daily brief and I would write down the top things that I thought the president should know," says General James L. Jones, President Obama's first national security advisor. "Generally it was somewhere between ten and fifteen, maybe the average was twelve or thirteen. Occasionally I still do that just for the heck of it. And today, I can go from one to twenty-five without missing a beat."[9] When he left the White House, Jones said, only half in jest, that Obama should have two National Security Councils, one to handle the threats that arise overnight and one to handle the ones that come up during the day. "When I was a twenty-eight-year-old National Security Council staffer," remembers Barack Obama's third national security advisor, Susan Rice, "I had a hip pager that I carried with me wherever I went out of the office. And if the pager went off I had to call into the White House situation room, and the White House situation room would tell me that they're getting reports from embassy X or Y that a plane in Rwanda has been shot down or eighteen American service members were killed in

SECRET

WAR DEPARTMENT
WASHINGTON

April 24, 1945.

Dear Mr. President:

I think it is very important that I should
have a talk with you as soon as possible on a highly
secret matter.

I mentioned it to you shortly after you took
office but have not urged it since on account of the
pressue you have been under. It, however, has such a
bearing on our present foreign relations and has such an
important effect upon all my thinking in this field that
I think you ought to know about it without much further
delay.

Faithfully yours,

Secretary of War.

The President,
The White House.

DECLASSIFIED
E. O. 11652, Sec. 3(E) and 5(D) or (E)
OSD letter, April 12, 1974
By NLT-HC , NARS Date 2-2-76

SECRET

*Harry Truman instituted the practice of giving presidential nominees
CIA briefings because he had learned that America had an atomic
weapon only after he became president. "There were so many things
I did not know when I became President," wrote Truman.*

Somalia. You would get into your car, drive to the White House, try to
get what information you can, and start the process of managing it.
Now, if something like that were to happen before I could get the first
piece of information to be briefed, we'd be bombarded on social media
and in the press with demands for someone to come on television and
explain what's happened when nobody knows what the hell has happened. I mean it's a whole different deal."[10]

Let's do the math and tally the threats the modern president faces:

China is growing economically and militarily and has a plan to replace the Western democratic model with their authoritarian version of one-party capitalism. Russia is concocting virulent and hard-to-detect threats of terrorism and cyberwarfare, hoping to destabilize the Western countries so that they are not in a position to challenge Russia's desire to expand. From North Korea alone, the president faces both Cold War–style nuclear devastation and cyber mayhem.

Democracy, once a force on the move in global affairs in the wake of the end of the Cold War, is under threat as authoritarian leaders seize power, ignoring laws and international agreements. In 2018, Freedom House, which tracks the health of democracies around the world, reported the thirteenth consecutive year of decline in global freedom, spanning a variety of countries in every region, from long-standing democracies like the United States to consolidated authoritarian regimes like China and Russia.[11]

Mature democracies in countries like Italy, Great Britain, and Germany face economic pressure from globalism and migration crises that have made their political systems vulnerable to both voters and leaders who feel threatened and favor quick results. Under this pressure, alliances weaken, as does the binding power of a shared ideological commitment to the values and principles of the liberal order, making it more difficult for the West to push back against China and Russia with one voice. The United States, which, under presidents of both parties, believed in promoting human rights, individual freedom, and democracy, has retreated from this commitment under President Trump's transactional foreign policy. "There have never been more threats than there are today," says Michael Morell, a former deputy director and acting director of the CIA who briefed the previous four presidents.[12] "It's kind of like the plate-spinner in the circus," says Stephen Hadley, National Security Advisor for George W. Bush. "A dozen plates on a narrow spindle, held up only because the spindles keep spinning. And the spin-maker has to go from plate to plate to plate, spin it, spin it, spin it, to keep them from falling."[13]

James Clapper, director of national intelligence under President Obama, adds climate change to the list of big challenges because it will increase competition over access to food and water and other resources, making it harder for governments to control their territories.[14]

It's not just that a president faces new challenges, says General David Petraeus, he also captains a disordered ship. "In Washington, D.C., the center has been hollowed out of Congress because of party primaries, gerrymandering, vast amounts of money (some of it not accountable), the lack of civics education—all different sorts of issues that have led us to a point where the government shuts down and many of the budgets are not approved in time for the start of the fiscal year," he says. "If we're going to do better around the world, we need to do better at home."[15]

The complexity of threats has gone up, and so have the demands of Americans that the president will be intimately involved with the details of each issue. "We elect presidents to be the desk officer, not the chief executive officer as we should," says former deputy director of the Central Intelligence Agency David S. Cohen.[16] This saps the president's ability to do what only he and the executive branch can do. "The American people I think now have an expectation that it's the president's job to make sure no terrorist attacks of any kind ever happen again, and that's a tall if not impossible order," says Susan Rice. "That expectation puts a lot of freight on the president and can overwhelm long-term and strategic thinking on perhaps more pressing problems."[17]

This expectation has been exacerbated by the satellite and Internet Age that brought war into the West Wing—and sometimes into the Oval Office. The president can be hands-on now more than ever. Lyndon Johnson selected bombing targets in Vietnam. President George H. W. Bush and later his son held regular briefings with generals who sat on the edge of the battlefield. Barack Obama watched special forces plow into Bin Laden's compound. Donald Trump watched a similar operation kill the head of ISIS, and the Iranian general Qasem Soleimani. The operation that killed the latter was so detailed, the president was able to reenact it step-by-step for donors weeks later at Mar-a-Lago.[18]

Brett McGurk, who worked for George W. Bush and Barack Obama, watched as both presidents became drawn more and more into the details of national security operations during their presidencies. Neither wanted to be LBJ picking bombing targets, but both realized that unless a president is elbow-deep in the details, the information he possesses can be incomplete. Those giving the president options are often biased because they advocated one approach or another. If given options A and B, a president may not know that option F is available.

"When a president over-delegates to the chain of command . . . the information he's getting can become stove-piped. For Iraq, for example, it's coming up from the team heavily invested in the light-footprint approach, the existing strategy, which was failing," says McGurk of the Iraq war under Bush. "Our team at the NSC did a nightly note for him, which had a different analysis, and I think that was important, ultimately, to shifting course."[19]

Those who worked with Barack Obama say his hands-on approach after he was surprised by the virulence of ISIS was much more effective than his position of delegation beforehand. "Obama and Bush in the last two years in my experience were more of the Eisenhower model, very inquisitive with intense questioning," explains McGurk, who watched both presidents evolve in the job. "They would force you to defend your position on questions large and small. That can be frustrating but given the issues we're talking about, war and peace, life and death, it is essential and leads to better strategy, with lower risk and fewer surprises."

With such an array of threats and potential threats, the challenge for any national security team, explains Trump's former national security advisor, H. R. McMaster, is to get beyond just playing defense. "Most people, I think, are predisposed toward protecting against dangers and don't think opportunistically," he says. "We should be thinking 'What are we not thinking about that we should be?'"[20] He is making the case for Quadrant Two thinking.

"In the Bush administration you had key people there who did not give due attention to the costs and risks of actions," says McMaster. "By the Obama administration you had leaders who did not pay enough attention to the costs and risks of inaction."

In addition to the number of decisions a president has to make, the decisions are qualitatively different for the modern president. At the end of a morning briefing with intelligence officials, a president might be asked whether a specific person should be killed with a drone strike later that day. Conventional warfare followed loose patterns. Cyberwarfare is a new Wild West where electric grids can be shut down, the labels on blood types in military hospitals switched, and airplane navigation systems remotely disabled. "For the first time we have a technology that can be easily weaponized that the government doesn't own," says Condoleezza Rice. "The battle space for cyber is not owned by the government. How does a president see that private public interaction? What does privacy mean?"

After a morning of tough decisions, the modern president can expect to be interrupted later in the day by unanticipated chaos—a shooting, a letter containing an unidentified powder, or an American citizen taken hostage. The president must be interrupted because his counsel must be sought, but also because in the age of terrorism, expectations have grown that a president will be immediately in the Situation Room, or will be up all night monitoring developments, even if there are no presidential decisions to be made. "No one wants to have that moment when you're asked in a hearing why the president wasn't notified," says one former White House staffer.[21]

Monitoring even small threats can take up an entire day. "My definition of a good day was when more than half of the things on my schedule were things I planned versus things that were forced on me," says Jeh Johnson, who served Obama as homeland security secretary.[22] An acute example: In June 2016, Johnson planned to travel to China to discuss the long-term threat from cyberattacks. Hours before takeoff, he was forced to cancel the trip so he could monitor developments after the shooting at the Pulse nightclub in Orlando. (Quadrant One, urgency, had preempted Quadrant Two, importance.)

The presidency has changed so fundamentally since General Eisenhower's day that the task for a president's team is not sorting simply the urgent from the important. "The urgent should not crowd out the important," says Lisa Monaco, Obama's chief counterterrorism adviser. "But sometimes you don't get to the important. Your day is spent just trying to prioritize the urgent. Which urgent first?"[23]

IMAGINATION AND DOUBT

TO DETERMINE WHICH URGENT SHOULD BE MANAGED FIRST, A PRESIDENT needs the best information possible from his intelligence agencies. Since the attacks of 9/11, the job of sifting through information has gotten larger and substantively harder for those intelligence agencies. At the same time, the political environment in which their findings are evaluated has also become more toxic. The president's national security decisions are now caught between imagination and doubt.

No administration wants to get surprised by another 9/11. "My fundamental job was to protect the American people, and I didn't do it," one of George W. Bush's staffers remembers him saying after the attacks of 9/11.[24] After the attacks, the then CIA director, George Tenet, added a threat matrix to the president's morning briefing that delineated all possible threats of terrorist activity. Bush wanted to go through every one.[25] The 9/11 Commission concluded that before the attacks, the intelligence agencies suffered from "a lack of imagination" about the terrorist threat and how creative al-Qaeda might be in staging their attack.[26] If a lack of imagination had allowed the 9/11 attack, the president and his team switched to becoming hyperimaginative, perceiving threats everywhere. Terrorism was so all-consuming that the CIA created a separate report that one intelligence officer referred to as "issues we would have told you about but we haven't had time to."[27]

"After 9/11, we woke up every day behind," says Bush's communications director Dan Bartlett about the news environment. "Every day was catch-up day."[28] Said another national security official from that time, "It was like they all had PTSD from the president on down because they had lived through 9/11 so there was like this mantra of 'Never again on my watch, never again on my watch.'"[29] National security experts were already sweating to imagine the worst, but after 9/11, the incentive increased. Former FBI director Andrew McCabe describes how the age of terror changed vacation days. "Working counterterrorism cases, you begin to dread every holiday. Christmas is the Christmas threat. Thanksgiving is have we checked the traps?[30] Have we heard any chatter from overseas? Who are we looking for this week? You constantly live in fear of the phone ringing in the middle of the night, knowing that that will be the bell that calls you in to work. Some disaster. Some horrible thing that, God help you, you may have been able to prevent and failed to do so. It's a sense of impending doom that you carry throughout your life."[31]

While intelligence officials are watching every shadow, the sour political environment has increased the level of doubt surrounding any warnings they might issue. The country is still suffering from the hang-over of too much imagination, which led to the war in Iraq. The second Bush administration and intelligence agencies from around the world imagined that Saddam Hussein had stockpiles of weapons of mass destruction and launched an invasion to keep him from using them or giving them to al-Qaeda.

Sixteen years after the 2000 election, in which the issue of terrorism wasn't really discussed, Donald Trump declared that George W. Bush's decision to invade Iraq was an impeachable offense. He accused President Bush of lying and labeled the Iraq war the greatest mistake in American foreign policy.[32] He was not penalized for it. In 2019, Lou Dobbs, an adviser and favorite of President Trump, would claim (on the Fourth of July) that American generals had "not won a war since 1991,"[33] as if it was accepted wisdom that America's military was awful. He received no real backlash. According to the Pew Research Center, 58 percent of veterans and 59 percent of adults think the war in Afghanistan was a mistake, and 64 percent of veterans and 62 percent of adults think the war in Iraq was a mistake.[34]

President Donald Trump has consistently raised doubts about the intelligence agencies. "These are the same people who said Saddam Hussein has weapons of mass destruction," said a statement from the president-elect responding to findings that Russia had interfered in the 2016 election.[35] At a summit meeting in Helsinki in 2018, the president gave equal weight to dueling assertions from U.S. intelligence officials and Russian president Vladimir Putin over whether Russia had interfered in the 2016 U.S. presidential election.[36]

After U.S. intelligence officials testifying before Congress contradicted the president's assertions about the health of ISIS, President Trump tweeted that their national security assessments were "wrong!"[37] and that perhaps they "should go back to school."[38] The president has also had public disputes with his intelligence agencies over whether North Korea is a nuclear threat,[39] and whether the Saudi government was involved in *The Washington Post* columnist Jamal Khashoggi's murder.[40]

This battle has a cost. "It makes their jobs harder," says David S. Cohen. "It doesn't bounce off after a while. What it says to the analysts is that their analysis doesn't matter. What you want in an analyst is for them to be meticulous and careful and rigorous, but they're human. If an analyst thinks, 'It doesn't matter what I write here because it's not going to affect anything,' they might ease off a little bit."[41]

How might this tension between imagination and doubt play out for a president alone, late at night, pressed for a decision? The U.S. posture in cyberwarfare is "persistent engagement" and "forward defense," which means taking actions before getting hit.

But what if, as experts have suggested, positioning forward escalates conflict, tipping an adversary and triggering a strike? Will a president get blamed for inviting that strike? What are the costs of being in permanent cyberconflict, and will the American public tolerate those costs? On the other hand, if cyberoperations don't effectively anticipate threats, the president will be blamed for not protecting the country, his primary job.

A president must decide how to strike a balance between having imagination and having too much imagination. "Your imagination can run too wild," says cybersecurity expert Andrew Grotto of Stanford, who worked for presidents Obama and Trump. "The risk is we can end up spreading ourselves so thin with respect to resources and attention . . . that we end up with a pretty watered-down defensive and resilience posture."[42]

To keep from spreading itself too thin, an administration may have to prioritize, putting resources and attention toward protecting electrical, banking, and telecommunications companies and not put as much toward protecting water systems and hospitals. A president must have the guts to make that kind of decision, which has enormous downsides. How confident the president feels about making the call depends on how confident the president feels about the intelligence agencies. "If done right," says Grotto, "making these decisions means conscientiously knowing that you are accepting risk, which is the most vulnerable type of real political exposure."

Welcome to the NFL—but not every challenge a president faces comes from a foreign adversary. The challenges that upset the alarm bell in the night can come from fire, wind, or water, forces that cannot be attacked but that require a president to respond with a mix of command and compassion.

Taft and the Titanic

April 4, 1912

PRESIDENT TAFT STUNNED
Wires White Star Line for News of Major Butt

Special to *The New York Times*

WASHINGTON, April 15—President Taft did not know of the sinking of the *Titanic* or of the danger of his old friend, Major Archibald Butt, when he went to spend the evening at Poll's Theatre, formerly Chase's vaudeville, where "Nobody's Widow" was the play.

The President had read the erroneous accounts of the *Titanic's* accident that appeared in the afternoon papers and thought all on board had been saved and the ship would be taken safely into Halifax. He was nearly frantic when he learned the truth about 11 o'clock, and went at once to the telegraph room at the White House to read the Associated Press bulletins and the bulletins from THE NEW YORK TIMES Washington office. Mr. Taft told the operator to use every effort to get him the news and let him know anything during the night when any was received.

Word was also sent to the telephone operators at the War and Navy Department to forward to the President any information they might get from the wireless stations about the *Titanic*. President Taft for the past three years has regarded Major Butt as his inseparable companion and friend. His fidelity, practical sense, and jovial nature made him exactly the sort of a comrade a man worried with innumerable heavy burdens would desire to have. The President as he appeared at the White House offices tonight was deeply moved. When he knew all that the newspaper dispatches told, he turned like a man that had been stunned with a heavy blow and went slowly back to the Executive Mansion.[1]

Chapter 4

First Responder

—

At an hour and time like this, the federal government
must not be something cold and far away, but a
warm friend and a warm neighbor.[2]

— LYNDON B. JOHNSON

T HE ATTACKS ON PEARL HARBOR ON DECEMBER 7, 1941, AND ON
September 11, 2001, called on the most extreme presidential skills. The
9/11 Commission called these attacks acts of "surpassing dispropor-
tion."[3] Of smaller proportion, but greater frequency, are a set of natural
and man-made disasters that call on the president to perform the role
of responder, consoler, and commander.

Presidential disaster obligations are a relatively new part of the job,
but a politically fraught one. Presidents who have been judged to miss
the mark have been crippled, as George W. Bush was after Hurricane
Katrina. "Presidents don't come in thinking 'Who is my FEMA administrator going to be?'" says Brock Long, Trump's former administrator
of the Federal Emergency Management Administration, which coordinates the federal emergency response. "But it should be thought of as
one of the top five people he picks, because the agency is so volatile. It
will make or break presidencies and determine future elections."[4]

It was not always this way. In the fall of 1955, during the Eisenhower
presidency, a series of storms lashed the United States. At the time, that
hurricane season topped the list of the costliest on record.[5] Given our
modern expectations, you'd think a visit to the newspaper archives
would yield yellowing clippings of the president pointing at maps or

receiving furrowed-brow briefings from meteorologists. But newspaper stories about hurricanes Connie, Diane, and Edith in 1955 barely mention the former Supreme Allied Commander. When Hurricane Audrey killed more than six hundred Louisianans in 1957 (the record in Louisiana until Katrina), Eisenhower did not visit Cameron Parish. His absence was not considered remarkable.[6]

When some of the storms of '55 hit, Ike was on vacation watching the shadows lengthen with his wife, Mamie, at his Gettysburg retreat and fishing with his grandson, David.[7, 8, 9] Pundits did not voice concern. During Hurricane Ione, Eisenhower's vacationing was the subject of a little jocularity from Nixon, his number two. "We get a little more sleep around Washington," the vice president told the hapless reporter who had been assigned the lighter-than-a-feather piece about what it was like when Eisenhower was on holiday. "He has the ungodly habit of getting up early."[10]

This presidential posture of detachment wasn't different for a Republican or a Democrat. Kennedy did not go to the scene of Hurricane Carla, which struck Texas in the fall of 1961.[11] He didn't tour the aftermath of the Atlantic nor'easter that punished mid-Atlantic states six months later.[12] "I have found remarkably few examples of journalists or politicians seeking to exploit evidence that government was in some way complicit in a particular disaster," writes the political and environmental historian Gareth Davies in his study of presidents and disasters.[13]

Neither Kennedy nor Eisenhower was callous. Ike believed, like most did at the time, that local governments, civil defense forces, and the Red Cross were supposed to stack the sandbags and distribute food packets and blankets after a storm hit. The federal government's job was to rebuild structures. Eisenhower believed that if the federal government preempted the local duty to care for neighbors, it would jeopardize the core American value of Americans giving back to their communities. "I regard this as one of the great real disasters that threatens to engulf us, when we are unready as a nation, as a people, to meet personal disaster by our own cheerful giving," Ike said in 1957. "Part of the reason is this misunderstanding that government is taking the place even of rescuing the person, the individual, and the family from his natural disasters."[14]

Democratic president Grover Cleveland held the same view. In 1887, he vetoed a bill that would have provided $10,000 to pay for seeds for farmers in Texas after a drought. Cleveland said:

> I can find no warrant for such an appropriation in the Constitution; and I do not believe that the power and duty of the General Government ought to be extended to the relief of individual suffering which is in no manner properly related to the public service or benefit. . . . The lesson should be constantly enforced that though the people support the Government, the Government should not support the people. The friendliness and charity of our countrymen can always be relied upon to relieve their fellow-citizens in misfortune. . . . Federal aid in such cases encourages the expectation of paternal care on the part of the Government and weakens the sturdiness of our national character, while it prevents the indulgence among our people of that kindly sentiment and conduct which strengthens the bonds of a common brotherhood.[15]

"I AM HERE TO HELP YOU"

THE SHIFT IN THE PRESIDENTIAL FIRST RESPONDER EXPECTATION started during Lyndon Johnson's presidency. LBJ believed in a stronger connection between the people and their president. Whereas Grover Cleveland worried about paternalism, Johnson spoke in terms of government as a family. Implicitly, of course, he was the father. He initiated programs that helped create new federal engagement on the issues of poverty, health, minority rights, environmental protection, and education. "I am interested in the whole man," he said. "I am concerned about what the people, using their government as a tool, can do toward building the whole man, which will mean a better society and a better world."[16]

Johnson wasn't just being empathetic. He used his public role and the comforting hand of government to build political power. It was this merger between the duties of the office and the requirements of politics that gave birth to the presidential first responder obligation.

On September 9, 1965, Hurricane Betsy swamped New Orleans.

The National Weather Service clocked wind gusts approaching 160 mph, making it a Category 4 storm.[17] Seventy-five people died, some from drowning when they were trapped in their attics, where they had fled from the rising water. (It's why locals now keep a hatchet in the attic, to smash through and climb onto the roof.)

Senator Russell Long of Louisiana telephoned President Johnson with an update: "Mr. President, aside from the Great Lakes, the biggest lake in America is Lake Pontchartrain. It is now drained dry. That Hurricane Betsy picked the lake up and put it inside New Orleans and Jefferson Parish and the Third [Congressional] District. . . . Mr. President, we have really had it down there, and we need your help. . . . Mr. President, my people, oh, they're in tough shape."[18]

Senator Long begged for a presidential visit. Johnson said he'd do what he could. If he couldn't make it, he'd send his best man. Long said he didn't want his best man. He wanted Johnson, and knowing Johnson's political needs, he promised a hero's welcome. "You go to Louisiana right now, land at Moisant Airport," said Long, switching into the third person like a Hollywood producer selling a star on a script. " 'The President was very much upset about the horrible destruction and damage done to this city of New Orleans, lovely town. The town that everybody loves'—If you go there right now, Mr. President, they couldn't beat you if Eisenhower ran."

Johnson pondered. He talked to Buford Ellington, his director of the Office of Emergency Planning, who advised him not to go. "Here's my problem," LBJ explained. "Dammit, when I ask a man to do something, I want him to do it, and I've been asking Russell Long all year, and he's had to do a lot of things he didn't want to do at all. And he's emotional . . . and they feel like nobody cares about them and they voted against us and they feel like they're kind of on the outside and I feel like a seventeen-year-old girl. I want to let them know they're loved. I have to pet [my daughter] Lucy sometimes when I don't want to because I don't want her to run away from home."[19]

Johnson decided to show love to the senator he had just compared to a teenage girl and to the people of Louisiana. "I am here because I wanted to see with my own eyes what the unhappy alliance of wind and water have done to this land and its people," said the president upon landing in Louisiana. "I have put aside all the other problems on my desk to come personally to Louisiana . . . when I leave today to go back to Washington, you can be sure that the federal government's total resources will be turned to Louisiana to help this state and its citizens find its way back from this tragedy."[20]

The president's motorcade wound through the wreckage and stopped in front of Washington High School in the 9th Ward. A few flashlights prepared the damp way for Johnson. A shifting mass of bodies and half illuminated faces greeted him. Almost all who had sought shelter there were African American. They were eating cold beans and raw carrots from paper plates on the floor.[21] The official White House log describes the scene as a "mass of human suffering. It was the most pitiful sight of human and material destruction."[22] Johnson spoke to the room: "This is your president. I am here to help you."

The president returned to Washington moved and committed to wrangling the bureaucracy. "In times of distress," he told disaster officials in one coordinating phone call, "it's necessary that all the members of the family get together and lay aside any individual problems they have or any personal grievances and try to take care of the sick mother, and we've got a sick mother on our hands."[23]

Johnson's response is an example of the kind of blunt push a president can provide to spark action. If presidents must know when to delegate in order to cover the sprawling duties, they must also know when to weigh in. "The president is really the only one who can get the bureaucracy to move more quickly," says former Department of Homeland Security Secretary Michael Chertoff.[24] Obama's FEMA director, Craig Fugate, calls it "the ability a president has to cheerfully compel everything from a sub cabinet agency to a governor."[25]

In the days after Hurricane Betsy, in 1965, newspapers portrayed Johnson in action hero terms. *The Washington Post* ran the headline LBJ SEES BETSY TOLL IN HUNDREDS: ASSUMES CHARGE OF DAY AND NIGHT RELIEF OPERATIONS.[26] The *Chicago Tribune* reported that "President Johnson, only hours back from an on-the-spot inspection of Hurricane Betsy's ravages in New Orleans, today ordered extraordinary federal aid to all of Louisiana."[27] In *The New York Times*, JOHNSON DIRECTS RELIEF described how "Johnson had pressed his way through hundreds of

*When Lyndon Johnson visited tornado victims in Indiana, a columnist
initially skeptical about the trip concluded that the president did
have a role to play: "The Presidential visit briefly transforms the
institution into a symbol, a person to be seen and spoken to."*

refugees huddled in the darkened school corridors. . . . It was this
recollection as much as anything, according to the official, that gener-
ated the mood that kept the President at his desk most of this rainy
Sunday."[28]

Soon, the federal government started doing more than just rebuilding structures. It started caring for suffering citizens. Federal disaster
spending under Eisenhower constituted about 6 percent of total disaster spending. By the Nixon era it had grown to nearly 50 percent.[29] On
April 1, 1979, President Carter signed an executive order that created
the Federal Emergency Management Agency (FEMA), which merged
many of the separate disaster-related responsibilities at different agencies to manage emergencies for the federal government. In 2018, FEMA
spent $133 billion on disaster relief.[30] In that same year, 33,041 people
were engaged in the federal disaster workforce.[31] The number of incidents judged to constitute a major disaster increased from about a
dozen per year under Eisenhower to 137 disasters declared by President
Trump in 2017 and 124 in 2018.[32]

The President at His Desk

Television also contributed to setting the stage for the president to play first responder.

Before television entered the home to become the thing we gathered around at the dinner hour, the country might not know about a disaster that hit in some other region of the country. In 1938 the great New England hurricane killed 700 people; 1,754 were injured, and 63,000 lost their homes.[33] It was a greater disaster than the Chicago fire of 1871, the San Francisco earthquake of 1906, or any Mississippi flood, but William Manchester writes in *The Glory and the Dream:* "Long Islanders and New Englanders traveling to other parts of the country that fall were startled by the number of well-informed men and women who knew nothing of the hurricane."[34]

As the television age dawned, severe weather events became national stories. Networks binged on images of Americans waist-deep in water, fishing their heirlooms from ruined living rooms. Edward R. Murrow, the first news correspondent to fly in a plane tracking a hurricane, noted that the movements of even an unexceptional hurricane were "reported as completely as those of the president or a movie star."[35] If CBS's Murrow was going to get bounced around in the sky for viewers' benefit, NBC wasn't going to be outdone. So anxious was NBC News to be first on the scene when disaster struck, it hired private weather companies to help position its television crews ahead of hurricanes.[36] In 1961, working at a Houston TV station, Dan Rather reported live from the heart of Hurricane Carla. It boosted his career. "We were impressed by his physical courage," said Walter Cronkite. "He was ass deep in water moccasins."[37]

Television networks now cover weather events from the moment the barometer fibrillates. The lure of the drama is so inescapable that correspondents are rushed into the middle of the spots from which everyone else is being told to evacuate. They keep a sentinel in empty drugstore parking lots whipped by the wind and pelted by the rain. Implicit in the whole exercise is that viewers might get to see a zooming palm frond or a washing machine on the lam—debris that is of a sufficiently dramatic and dangerous but not life-threatening variety.

This instinct for drama, writes Davies, created a stage that needed a lead actor. The president was the obvious choice. What exactly was the president supposed to do, though? In April 1965, when Johnson visited Indiana to help local politicians coordinate disaster relief, a skeptical columnist writing for the *South Bend Tribune* wondered if the president angling his wingtips through the cinder blocks wasn't interrupting people who were just trying to get their lives back together. He asked "what good a Presidential visit does anybody after a tornado has flattened his home or business, or has killed and maimed his family."[38] The author then revealed that he had had a revelation and praised Johnson for "a demonstration of personal presidential concern." The tour helped personalize "the sprawling bureaucracy that is the Federal Government in the 1960s. The Presidential visit briefly transforms the institution into a symbol, a person to be seen and spoken to," providing evidence to victims that "somebody cares," thereby raising their "distressed spirits." It worked. "I touched the president's hand," exclaimed one girl after Johnson climbed down from the pile of cinder blocks that was once the Baptist church in Goshen, Indiana.[39] The president had delivered temporary excitement to the devastated community.

Until the presidential disaster role was codified in the Disaster Relief Act of 1970, constituents engaged in a "call-and-response" pattern, as historian Andrew Morris has labeled it, pressing the federal government for a special response. After Hurricane Camille hit in 1969, one Gulf Coast resident pleaded with Mississippi's senator James Eastland to "use this moon landing monkey business spending to make our people decent here on earth."[40]

Implicit in this understanding of the presidency is an inescapable cycle. The bigger the government gets, the more a president must show personal concern. In part that's because people want to know what their tax dollars are funding. There's also a political benefit. When Nixon landed in Gulfport, Mississippi, after Camille, he was greeted by 75,000 and a sign, NOT MANY REPUBLICANS HERE BUT LOTS OF NIXON-CRATS.[41] Johnson's role model, FDR, knew how valuable it was to keep tight the connection between empathy and governing. Roosevelt took what he called "look-see" trips to drought-stricken and flood-ravaged areas. He wasn't bringing federal dollars, but he was showing people he cared. He also employed his extraordinary wife, Eleanor, to be his "eyes and ears,"[42] traveling across the country to its poorest and most crippled

Eleanor Roosevelt waits at the start of a two-and-a-half-mile trip into a drift coal mine, part of her forty-thousand-mile tour of hard-hit pockets of America to monitor New Deal programs and identify areas of greatest need. An ambassador from and to her husband's administration, the First Lady served as the eyes and ears for a president dedicated to keeping a close connection with the country.

corners. On a trip to a West Virginia mining community, she donned a helmet and rode down into the mine by the light affixed to it.[43] She greeted a miner who was ashamed to shake her hand, as the miner's daughter recalls. "Mrs. Roosevelt, I can't shake hands with you, my hands are all dirty," said the miner. The First Lady grabbed his hand and said, "You're the kind of man I like to shake hands with. You're a working American. I like to shake hands with people like you."[44]

Roosevelt also shortened the distance between the office and the people through radio, which drew them in using the intimate pull that keeps you listening in your car to a National Public Radio story in your driveway after you've arrived home.

The public soaked up that attention. William E. Leuchtenburg quotes a 1934 dispatch from the journalist and author Martha Gellhorn to the FDR adviser Harry Hopkins:

> Every house I visited—mill worker or unemployed—had a picture of the President. These ranged from newspaper clippings (in destitute homes) to large coloured prints, framed in gilt

cardboard. . . . And the feeling of these people for the President is one of the most remarkable phenomena I have ever met. He is at once God and their intimate friend; he knows them all by name, knows their little town and mill, their little lives and problems. And though everything else fails, he is there, and will not let them down.[45]

Roosevelt's emotional bond with the country during the disaster of the Great Depression and World War II was key to the success of his presidency. When Roosevelt died, mourners wept in the streets. Thousands stood to watch his funeral train take him to Hyde Park from Warm Springs, Georgia. A reporter asked one mourner, "Why are you here? Did you know Franklin Roosevelt?" The mourner replied: "No, I did not know President Roosevelt, but he knew me."[46]

Not long after he was elected, Roosevelt declared that "the Presidency is not merely an administrative office. That is the least of it. It is pre-eminently a place of moral leadership."[47] That kind of leadership doesn't take place simply when a switch is thrown. "To sound a certain trumpet does not mean just trumpeting one's own certitudes," writes historian Garry Wills. "Followers have a say in what they are being led to"[48] To be a moral leader, a president must build his relationship with the public to make an emotional connection. This is done by showing up when they look for solace or guidance, but also by saying the right things. As the nation's moral leader, the president is the one person in the country in a position to provide guidance, meaning, and stability when events make people hungry for consolation. It is a political opportunity and a governing obligation.

On the day of Abraham Lincoln's second inauguration, Pennsylvania Avenue was a bog of mud and standing water from the recent heavy rains. Thousands of spectators let it pool around their boots as they stood on the Capitol grounds. The president stood on a platform in front of the East Portico. Over his head rose the completed Capitol dome—its construction had continued during the war, a sign of continuity amid national distress.

Soldiers were on the lookout for Confederate assassins reportedly in town to kill the president. The war that would go on to kill seven hundred fifty thousand continued. Nevertheless, Lincoln did not treat the South like a conquered nation. He did not revel in the righteousness of the Union cause. Instead, he spoke at that moment of division, revenge, and retribution to an entire nation, and about a time when it would not be consumed with those poisons:

> With malice toward none; with charity for all; with firmness in the right, let us strive on to finish the work we are in; to bind up the nation's wounds; to care for him who shall have born the battle, and for his widow, and his orphan—to do all which may achieve and cherish a just, and lasting peace, among ourselves, and with all nations.

The audience was not sure what to make of the address. The *New York Herald* reported that African Americans "spoke 'bress de Lord,' in a low murmur at the end of almost every sentence. Beyond this there was no cheering of any consequence. Even the soldiers did not hurrah much."[1]

The president returned to the White House, where he sought out Frederick Douglass, who had been a bracing critic of Lincoln's first inaugural address. Lincoln was anxious to know what Douglass thought. "Mr. Lincoln, that was a sacred effort," he said.[2]

Chapter 5

Consoler in Chief

—

The future doesn't belong to the fainthearted; it belongs
to the brave. The *Challenger* crew was pulling us into
the future, and we'll continue to follow them.[3]

—RONALD REAGAN, JANUARY 28, 1986

WHEN A DISASTER HITS, AMERICANS LOOK TO THE PRESIDENT.
The instinct comes from a basic human need that leaders answered long
before America was created. "Since Pericles spoke in ancient Athens,
eulogies have followed a classic form," writes Bill Clinton's speechwriter
Michael Waldman. "Honor the dead. State why it is appropriate that we
do so. Take from their deaths a lesson as to how we should live our lives."[4]

In his Gettysburg Address, Lincoln transformed the tragedy of the
Civil War into meaning for the living: "It is rather for us to be here
dedicated to the great task remaining before us—that from these hon-
ored dead we take increased devotion to that cause for which they gave
the last full measure of devotion—that we here highly resolve that these
dead shall not have died in vain—that this nation, under God, shall
have a new birth of freedom—and that government of the people, by
the people, for the people, shall not perish from the earth." Through
the power of his narrative, Lincoln turned a war that killed six hundred
thousand into a new national commitment to the fundamental promise of the American experiment.

Lincoln spoke in an epochal moment. Those moments don't present themselves often. For the modern president, though, there are frequent calls for public empathy. The public expects the one politician

who represents the whole nation to answer those calls. According to *The Hill* newspaper's 2018 American Barometer survey, 83 percent of Americans now expect a president to play the role of consoler in chief after a tragedy.[5]

In 1986, when the space shuttle *Challenger* exploded 73 seconds after takeoff, President Ronald Reagan delivered a televised address hours later from the Oval Office. The speech became instantly memorable because it transformed tragedy into meaning. "Your loved ones were daring and brave, and they had that special grace, that special spirit that says 'Give me a challenge and I'll meet it with joy,'" Reagan said, knitting the astronauts' sacrifice into the history of explorers who have pushed the boundaries of human understanding. "They had a hunger to explore the universe and discover its truths. They wished to serve, and they did. They served all of us."[6]

Ronald Reagan's response to the space shuttle Challenger *disaster set the standard for how a president should embody the pastoral role in the communications age. "The sense of national catastrophe is inevitably heightened in a television age, when the whole country participates in it,"* wrote Johnny Apple of The New York Times.

Christa McAuliffe, a teacher from New Hampshire, had been on board the mission, which meant schoolchildren were watching the launch. Reagan spoke to them. "I want to say something to the schoolchildren of America who were watching the live coverage of the shuttle's takeoff. I know it is hard to understand, but sometimes painful things like this happen. It's all part of the process of exploration and discovery. It's all part of taking a chance and expanding man's horizons.

The future doesn't belong to the fainthearted; it belongs to the brave. The *Challenger* crew was pulling us into the future, and we'll continue to follow them."

Finally, Reagan planted the flag of freedom: "I've always had great faith in and respect for our space program, and what happened today does nothing to diminish it. We don't hide our space program. We don't keep secrets and cover things up. We do it all up front and in public. That's the way freedom is, and we wouldn't change it for a minute." In the Cold War space competition, it was a thinly veiled reference to the secrecy of the Soviet Union and other totalitarian regimes.

Peggy Noonan, Reagan's speechwriter, captured the alchemy produced by a presidential speech: "We lean forward, hungry to hear. Now it will be said. Now we will hear the thing we long for. A speech is part theater and part political declaration; it is personal communication between a leader and his people. . . . Speeches are important because they are one of the great constants of our political history. They have been not only the way we measure public men, they have been how we tell each other who we are. . . . They count. They more than count, they shape what happens."[7]

Reagan contextualized the heroism of those who had died. He made it a part of the human story and the American story of which the audience was a part too. R. W. "Johnny" Apple of *The New York Times* immediately valorized the moment:

> The need that the President addressed tonight is a need as old as organized societies. In crises past, it has been successfully met by the celebration of heroes and martyrs, by the defiant rhetoric of Charles de Gaulle after the fall of France and Winston Churchill during the Blitz, even by the popularization of gritty, bittersweet songs like "Tipperary" or "Praise the Lord and Pass the Ammunition." Failure to meet the need is inevitably costly. It ruined Herbert Hoover's Presidency after the Great Crash, Lyndon Johnson's Presidency after the Tet offensive, Jimmy Carter's Presidency after the capture of the American embassy in Tehran. The sense of national catastrophe is inevitably heightened in a television age, when the whole country participates in it.[8]

RELEVANT IN AN INSTANT

ON APRIL 18, 1995, BILL CLINTON STOOD IN THE EAST ROOM OF THE White House trying to salvage his presidency with a prime time news conference. He was still recovering from the 1994 elections, in which Republicans won 8 seats in the Senate and a historic 54 seats in the House,[9] taking control of that body for the first time in forty years. The GOP surge was a repudiation of Clinton's first two years in office and his failed healthcare push. Once they came to power, Republicans sprinted to make good on their promises, enshrined in their 1994 campaign document, the Contract with America, passing through the House a balanced budget amendment, welfare reform, and middle-class tax cuts. The political revolution, followed by so much activity, encouraged the view that the House had taken such complete control of the political landscape that they had squeezed the imperial presidency into a Dixie cup.

When a president summons the nation to a televised press conference, he expects to fill the airwaves. In this case, only one of the national television networks answered Clinton's call to carry the press conference live.[10] The president just wasn't the most popular show in town. That show was the one airing on Capitol Hill. The extra lights and cameras were aimed at Speaker of the House Newt Gingrich, who was charging ahead with the conservative Contract with America. Two weeks earlier, Gingrich had addressed the nation at the 100-day mark of his new reign.[11] Looking every inch an American prime minister, he had the furniture to go with it. He stood by a desk that looked as though it would take a half a dozen toughs to move it.

Given that so much public attention was focused on Gingrich— a white-haired baby boomer with expansive appetites who stood at one end of Pennsylvania Avenue—the fellow fitting that description at the other end of the avenue was feeling blue. Judy Keen of *USA Today* didn't make things better. She asked President Clinton at his White House press conference whether he was still relevant.

"The Constitution gives me relevance," Clinton said. "The power of our ideas gives me relevance; the record we have built up over the last two years and the things we're trying to do to implement it give it relevance. The president is relevant here."[12] With each use of the word "relevant," President Clinton seemed to affirm that he was less so.

Less than twenty-four hours later, Bill Clinton would be proved right. On April 19, Timothy McVeigh detonated a car bomb in front of the Alfred P. Murrah Federal Building in Oklahoma City, killing 168 people, among them nineteen children attending day care in the building.[13]

No matter how far a president wanders, or is banished from the noisy end of the room, a crisis can instantaneously put the presidency at the center of American life again. In a flash, the comforts of civilization and progress are removed and a president is tested on all of the qualities of the office—policy, political, and symbolic. The entire country is watching, needing, and grading him.

Over the next week, Clinton instructed the public on the manhunt for McVeigh and the relief and recovery efforts in Oklahoma City. As Reagan had elevated the *Challenger* astronauts' dedication, Clinton praised the federal workers who had been targeted by the antigovernment terrorist, by heralding the nobility of their public service. In the Oval Office, he and the First Lady spoke to schoolchildren, comforting them about the nineteen who had died, just as Reagan had comforted the children who watched the *Challenger* explode.

After the Oklahoma City bombing, Bill and Hillary Clinton spoke with schoolchildren at the White House about the tragedy. "It was the first time Clinton had been a reassuring figure rather than an unsettling one," wrote Clinton's speechwriter Michael Waldman.

Clinton also maximized the political opportunity. His opponents in Washington had profited by and encouraged right-wing opposition to the federal government. Clinton put them on the defensive. "We owe those who have sacrificed the duty to purge ourselves of the dark forces which gave rise to this evil," he said.[14] This hastened Clinton's postelection strategy of positioning himself as less liberal than the person the public had come to fear in his first two years in office. In the aftermath of the bombing, both the Gallup and CBS / *New York Times* polls recorded Clinton's approval rating at 51 percent, up from the low to mid-40s.[15] "It was the first time Clinton had been a reassuring figure rather than an unsettling one," wrote Waldman.[16]

UNDER THE GUN

AFTER THE 1966 SHOOTING AT THE UNIVERSITY OF TEXAS IN WHICH Charles Whitman killed seventeen people and injured thirty, Lyndon Johnson did not assume the consoling role.[17] On July 18, 1984, when James Huberty shot and killed twenty-one people and injured nineteen at a McDonald's in San Ysidro, California, the papers did not report any comment from the administration of President Ronald Reagan. His public papers contain no statements on the subject in the days following.[18]

In the twenty-first century, gun violence has become a frequent event requiring a national response. According to the author and criminologist Grant Duwe, in the sixty-five years before the 1966 Texas tower shooting, there were just twenty-one public mass shootings in which four or more people were killed.[19] In the fifty-four years since then, as of February 2020, the number has increased by more than eight times, to 175 public mass shootings, and the attacks have become increasingly deadly.[20]

According to Tevi Troy, a former deputy secretary of HHS and a presidential historian, Bill Clinton faced eight mass shootings during his two terms, the highest number of any president up to that time. That record was broken during Barack Obama's presidency when there were twenty-four mass shootings,[21] more than in the three preceding administrations combined. Obama addressed sixteen of them personally. In the first three years of Donald Trump's administration, he saw thirty-four mass shootings (defined as a single attack in a public place in which three or more victims were killed) including those at a Las Vegas outdoor concert and at Parkland High School in Florida. He has traveled to eight such shooting-related events.[22]

The most searing moment for Obama came in 2012, when he met with the families of the twenty children and six adults gunned down in Newtown, Connecticut, shortly before Christmas. He held the babies who lost their grandparents, posed with some of the students who survived, and embraced one grieving parent after another. It was a private moment but an obligation he felt came with the office.

Three years later, Obama eulogized parishioners of the Emanuel African Methodist Episcopal Church in Charleston, where a white supremacist had killed nine who had joined for their Bible study.[23] The first African American president spoke just down the road from what had once been the nation's central port of entry for African slaves. Almost half of all of the enslaved Africans who came to the United States first arrived in Charleston.[24] One hundred miles away, the Confederate flag still flew in front of the state Capitol, a remnant of when it had flown atop its dome, raised during the era of Jim Crow when South Carolina politicians denied black citizens their civil rights, as was done throughout the South.

In the traditional form of these speeches, the speaker elevates the victims, and then the audience is connected to that elevation through some common tie. Reagan and Clinton had done this by connecting the departed with the American experience. President Obama picked a larger audience—the human race. He built his speech around God's grace.

When the families of the nine murdered Charleston churchgoers faced the killer at his first hearing, they told him they forgave him. The shooter had sat through a prayer circle before opening fire on his victims. Now their families were putting into practice the faith that their slain relatives had gathered to affirm. The president pointed out that an act that the killer imagined would incite fear and recrimination, violence and suspicion, had created just the opposite effect. Instead of deepening divisions that trace back to the nation's original sin, the massacre gave birth to a stunning act of generosity and forgiveness.

If people who had every reason to be small, vengeful, and unforgiving could, through the power of God's grace, forgive, perhaps their example could offer a lesson to heal a nation still torn over race and hatred. "As a nation, out of this terrible tragedy, God has visited grace upon us, for he has allowed us to see where we've been blind," President Obama said.[25] Intentionally or not, the president's words echoed those of Robert F. Kennedy, who, almost fifty years before, had delivered an extemporaneous eulogy to Dr. Martin Luther King, Jr., at a campaign event to an African American audience as he delivered the news of the assassination. Quoting Aeschylus in a moment of racial horror, Kennedy drew the same link between pain and wisdom: "In our sleep, pain which cannot forget falls drop by drop upon the heart until, in our own despair, against our will, comes wisdom through the awful grace of God."[26]

The goal was not to lecture but to create space for policy evolutions on race and gun violence. Five days after the shooting, South Carolina governor Nikki Haley announced she was removing the Confederate flag from the state Capitol grounds. At the press conference announcing the move, she was joined by RNC Chairman Reince Priebus.[27]

The duty of national consolation is found nowhere in the Constitution, but the presidency is an office dedicated to promoting unity, which faced its greatest test over slavery, the institutional scourge that almost broke the Union. Obama connected the consoler role with the deeper obligation of the job.

Obama closed his remarks by singing "Amazing Grace," written by a white English minister tormented by his past as a slave trader seeking some absolution for his blindness. It is a hymn that has grown to comfort people of all races.

"ON MANY SIDES"

DONALD TRUMP FACED A TEST OF RACIAL HEALING EIGHT MONTHS INTO his presidency in Charlottesville, Virginia. Like Charleston, the city was wrestling with its long histories of enslaved labor and racist policies. Charlottesville is the home of the University of Virginia. It is also the location of Monticello, the home of the school's founder and the third U.S. president, Thomas Jefferson. At Monticello in the summer of 2017, curators applied the last touches to an exhibit commemorating Sally Hemings, a woman enslaved by Jefferson and long bleached from history books, who cared for his children and with whom he fathered several. For years, the university and Monticello had been working to recognize the contribution of the enslaved individuals who arranged the bricks of those buildings that tourists traveled from all over the world to admire, who made possible the very democracy built on ideals of freedom, liberty, and justice propounded by those, like Jefferson, who enslaved them.

While the contributions of the enslaved were being elevated on one side of town, the Charlottesville City Council voted on a petition written and circulated by Zyahna Bryant, a young black woman in high school, to remove a statue of the Confederate general Robert E. Lee, who had fought to maintain slavery.[28] This effort became the pretext for a "Unite the Right" rally on an August weekend, organized by people who protested the removal and the renaming of Lee Park, in which the statue was located.[29] On August 11, white supremacists and neo-Nazis marched through the center of the university jostling tiki torches in a nighttime parade, shouting "Jews will not replace us."[30] The next day, more neo-Nazis, white nationalists, and armed militias pressed their case downtown, carrying Nazi flags and signs that read THE JEWISH MEDIA IS GOING DOWN[31] and DIVERSITY = WHITE GENOCIDE.[32] Clashes ensued in the brutal heat, and one of the skinheads floored his Dodge Challenger into a cluster of counterprotesters, killing thirty-two-year-old Heather Heyer.[33]

It was a ready-made moment for an action-hungry president in which he could fulfill the role of consoler and moral leader. The moral high ground was clear, level, and open. It would be hard to find groups more in conflict with American ideals than white supremacists and neo-Nazis. President Trump, who is constantly alive to personal slights, might also have found it personally offensive that he was being used to support a racist cause. They had invoked his name in their putrid cause. "We are determined to take our country back," said David Duke, a former grand wizard of the Ku Klux Klan, at the kickoff to the rally. "We are going to fulfill the promises of Donald Trump. That's what we believed in, that's why we voted for Donald Trump. Because he said he's going to take our country back. And that's what we gotta do."[34] By custom, duty, and morality, Trump could not be indifferent about the racism in Charlottesville.

The president spoke from his Bedminster, New Jersey, golf course on the day of the clashes. "We condemn in the strongest possible terms this egregious display of hatred, bigotry, and violence on many sides — on many sides," Trump said. "So we want to get the situation straightened out in Charlottesville and we want to study it and we want to see what we're doing wrong as a country, where things like this can happen."[35]

This was not moral clarity, but moral flattening. The point the president chose to stress — repeating it for emphasis — was that the hatred and bigotry were displayed "on many sides." But the only bigots marching for an ideology of hate were the white supremacists. Anger stirred in opposition to them was not a reason for presidential condemnation, but elevation. The president, who has an uncommon ability to single out individuals and groups of people for abuse, did not mention the white supremacists at all in his remarks.

This was part of a pattern first displayed during the campaign. Don-

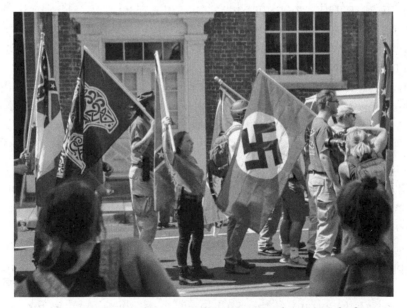

*Among the protesters marching against the removal of
a statue of Robert E. Lee were vocal and visible
white supremacists and Nazi sympathizers.*

ald Trump had been accused by Republican Speaker of the House Paul Ryan of a "textbook definition of a racist comment" when Trump said that Gonzalo P. Curiel, an American judge of Mexican heritage, could not treat him fairly in a case involving Trump University.[36] On another occasion during the 2016 race, the Republican Senate majority leader, Mitch McConnell, chastised Trump for his "seeming ambivalence about David Duke and the KKK."[37]

The response from fellow Republicans in the aftermath of Charlottesville was just as swift. "Mr. President—we must call evil by its name," said Colorado Republican senator Cory Gardner. "These were white supremacists and this was domestic terrorism."[38] Gary Cohn, the president's chief economic adviser, said, "Citizens standing up for equality and freedom can never be equated with white supremacists, neo-Nazis, and the KKK."[39] Secretary of State Rex Tillerson did not defend the president when asked about his remarks on *Fox News Sunday*. "The president speaks for himself," he said.[40]

President Trump has changed the presidency by speaking for himself. A signature aspect of this characteristic is his facility with quick denunciations of melting intensity. In June 2017, the president criticized the mayor of London for being soft on terrorists just hours after his city was attacked.[41] He dinged California forest management officials in the middle of record fires that were scorching acres in November 2018.[42] The president sent twenty-seven tweets about NFL players protesting racial injustice by choosing to kneel during the national anthem, a practice he found repugnant.[43] He tweeted eighty-four times suggesting that President Obama was not born in America.[44] Whether his target is a federal judge, Gold Star parents, or weather-battered officials in Puerto Rico, Donald Trump says what is on his mind immediately and doesn't sweat the nuances.

By contrast, the president's six tweets in the aftermath of the Charlottesville violence never referred to racism or bigotry or white nationalism.[45]

When Trump is passionate about something, it's unmistakable. So why did the president lapse into vagueness when it came to Charlottesville? Theories abound: He didn't want to criticize whites who voted for him out of a sense of racial grievance; he didn't want to disparage Southern whites who share his view that attacks on General Lee are attacks on American heritage; he didn't want to give in to the left on anything, because he believes they are hypocrites for ignoring their own violent fringe.

The White House press office later clarified that the president meant to include the white supremacists.[46] The next day, at a press conference, President Trump did just that, denouncing racists unambiguously in prepared remarks. As the press conference wore on, however, the president strayed from the script and lost his way, or, as his critics would put it, got back on track. He returned to moral equivalence. "You had a group on one side that was bad, and you had a group on the other side that was also very violent," he insisted to reporters, "and nobody wants to say that, but I'll say it right now."[47] At a press conference designed to explain why he hadn't immediately called out the racists, the president was boasting about having immediately called out the people who were attacking the racists.

Speaking of the protesters who wanted to keep the Robert E. Lee statue, the president said that "there were very fine people on both sides." He hastened to add, "I'm not talking about the neo-Nazis and white nationalists, because they should be condemned totally." The president did not say, as has often been claimed, that white supremacists were "very fine people."[48] (How people who march alongside racists and the flutter of Nazi flags can be characterized as "very fine people" is another matter, however.) The president was passionate that these fine people were possibly being maligned. He was also passionate when he interrogated reporters who used the term "alt-right."[49] Why hadn't they used the term "alt-left"?

It was an asymmetric application of outrage and passion, contrary to our expectations of an office whose occupant is meant to use emotion to speak with moral force and to drive the country toward unity and healing. "President Trump took a step backward by again suggesting there is moral equivalency between the white supremacist neo-Nazis and KKK members who attended the Charlottesville rally and people like Ms. Heyer," said Senator Lindsey Graham, a frequent Trump supporter. "I, along with many others, do not endorse this moral equivalency."[50]

The events that took place in Charlottesville cried out for a typical presidential response, answering tragedy by reminding the country of its enduring values. When presidents do this well, they can transform sorrow into inspiration. If they do it exceptionally well, they may one day deserve a monument and the designation of being "presidential."

George Washington wanted a simple inauguration. He set out from Mount Vernon on April 16, 1789, hoping to make the trip to New York in "as quiet and peaceable manner as possible."[1] He wanted no hoopla. "No reception can be so congenial to my feelings as a quiet entry devoid of ceremony," he wrote to the governor of New York, where he would make his final stop.[2]

No one listened.

In Alexandria, Virginia, hundreds of men, women, and children greeted him in the streets. In Baltimore and Delaware, the streets were also lined. Newspapers had printed his travel route. Veterans appeared in their uniforms. Songs were sung to celebrate his life. As he approached Philadelphia, twenty thousand people filled the streets, some yelling "Long live George Washington," which sounded very much like the formula the English used to greet their monarchs.[3] City fathers asked the president-elect to ride a white horse through town. As he crossed a bridge wreathed in laurels and evergreens, a cherubic child was lowered so that he could place a laurel crown on the president-elect's head.[4]

Washington left town to avoid the departure ceremony, but that only made him early for the rose petals in Trenton, New Jersey. A floral arch read "December 26, 1776," the date of his famous victory at that spot. It also read "The Defender of the Mothers will also Defend the Daughters."[5] Thirteen young girls dressed in white walked before him spreading flowers. When he got to New York, they put him on a barge manned by thirteen oarsmen, also dressed in virginal white. A flotilla accompanied him carrying musicians who played and a chorus that sang hymns to him. Cannons fired in celebration.

Chapter 6

Acting Presidential

———

Throughout our history, we have seen the presidency as the repository of all of our highest hopes and ideals and values.[6]

—MIKE PENCE, AS A LOCAL RADIO HOST IN 1992

A PRESIDENT'S POWER TO CONSOLE COMES FROM A CEREMONIAL reverence Americans grant their presidents. To deserve the reverence, a president must act as steward of the dignity and stature of the office. In short, a president must be presidential.

What does it mean to be presidential? Basically, to act in keeping with our highest expectations of the office. "Moral nature is a part of our humanity and people crave the maintenance of principles that have ensured order and prosperity," wrote the conservative political scientist James Q. Wilson about our modern public life.[7] For the ceremonial jobs only a president can perform, we expect behavior consistent with the scope of their duties, just as we'd expect a minister performing a wedding not to hit on the coat check girl at the rehearsal dinner. Whimsical gun instructors and leadfoot babysitters also demonstrate behavior at odds with their duties.

When Donald Trump attacks the suffering after a disaster he is not acting presidential. When he attacks a dead congressman and his widow—also a member of Congress—as he did with Representatives John and Debbie Dingell, he is not acting presidential.[8] When he makes fun of the sixteen-year-old climate activist Greta Thunberg he is not acting presidential.[9]

The president's allies and press secretary say this is part of being a "counterpuncher," an excuse that is beneath the traditional office and has no connection to the values of the office or duties of public life. "The standard in the executive branch was supposed to be different, *higher*, than for the legislative and judicial branches," wrote Bill Bennett in *The Book of Virtues*.[10] He was right. John Adams, who helped create that standard, agrees: "Because power corrupts, society's demands for moral authority and character increase as the importance of the position increases."[11]

The standard of the office is not defined by the occupant any more than the standard for customer service is. At the customer service desk, counterpunching is not an explanation, it is cause for a stern visit from the manager.

President Washington felt the country looking over his shoulder. That's why he was so agitated about the fuss made over his inauguration. The scrutiny is written into the office. "From the very circumstance of his being alone," Hamilton wrote, the president "will be more narrowly watched and more readily suspected."[12] Washington did not want the ceremonial pomp to overshadow his duty to the republic, which was to resist the posture of a monarch.[13] He wanted his ceremonial behavior and public deportment to match his understanding of the job.

Washington's concern carried over even to the way he dressed, because he knew the country was watching. As the historian Joanne Freeman writes, based on "the logic of the time, if national leaders dressed and behaved like aristocrats, the government would take on an aristocratic tone, the American people would adopt it, vote more such people into office, and in no time, the republic would fall."[14]

The idea of acting presidential was around before the presidency even existed. When George Washington arrived in Philadelphia for the Constitutional Convention in May 1787, he was greeted with the same flourishes and fuss that would later accompany his inauguration. Mounted dragoons accompanied his final mile. Young boys and Revolutionary War veterans lined the cobblestone streets and the bells pealed in the tower of Christ Church. Thirteen cannons announced his battered coach, which had traveled 150 miles, jostled by storms and mud. The forced shiatsu from the bad roads was another reminder of the weakness of the government. States, aligned in a loose archipelago of sovereignties, had no central authority able to create an infrastruc-ture of connecting roadways. (The roads were so bad farther south that delegates from the Carolinas and Georgia traveled north by ship.[15])

His head and stomach aching from the ride, the fifty-five-year-old Washington did not pause to rest. Instead, his journals record, he vis-ited Benjamin Franklin moments after putting down his bags.[16] Frank-lin, the president of Pennsylvania, was perhaps the only American more famous than the retired general. Washington's visit showed respect. Their combined stature and reputation lent credence to the entire risky effort.[17] "A union of abilities of so distinguished a body of men, among whom will be a FRANKLIN and a WASHINGTON, cannot but pro-duce the most salutary measures," wrote the *New Hampshire Gazette* of the Convention.[18] "These names affixed to their recommendations . . . will stamp a confidence in them" that the opposition "will not dare to attack, or endeavour to nullify."[19]

Visiting Franklin was the first of Washington's symbolic moves in a public role that he had not formally been assigned, but that he intuited would be crucial to building support for the delegates' radical new di-rection for American government. Washington's role at the Constitu-tional Convention was not to quote Greek philosophers, or to negotiate difficult language in the new governing compact.[20] His "colloquial tal-ents were not above mediocrity," as Thomas Jefferson put it, having "neither copiousness of ideas nor fluency of words."[21] His contribution in Independence Hall would be to light the quiet gray walls and baize-covered desks with the glow of his reputation and character, lending legitimacy and credence to a bold experiment.

Before the delegates started debating the new national government, they had to pick a president of their convention. Washington was the unanimous choice to take the speaker's chair, a finely carved seat with a half sun painted on its crown.[22] Each time Washington walked to the front of the room, his colleagues showed him deference. It was a rule of the order of the proceedings that "every member shall stand in his place, until the president pass him."[23] The ordered behavior was not superficial decorum, but a symbol of all that Washington had accom-plished. All that he stood for in battle, but more important, what he stood for as a national leader who had repeatedly sublimated his per-

"Many of the members cast their eyes toward General Washington and shaped their ideas and powers to be given to the President, by their opinions of Washington's virtue," wrote South Carolina's Pierce Butler of his fellow delegates at the Constitutional Convention.

sonal ambition for the good of the republic. A proceeding that paid daily homage to those ideas, the founders believed, would also infuse a respect for those ideas into their work product.

Washington's aura was ever present in the minds of his countrymen as they did their work. Like a model at the front of a figure-drawing class, Washington was there in that room—the same room where the Declaration of Independence had been signed eleven years earlier—to inspire. John Adams called Washington the finest political actor he had ever seen.[24]

Other great presidents have embraced that title or been given it. Ronald Reagan asked how a president could not be an actor. Franklin Roosevelt said to the famous actor Orson Welles, "Mr. Welles, there are two great actors in the United States, and you're the other one."[25]

The power of Washington's example was so strong that it almost killed the discussion. As delegates addressed the issue of the chief executive of the new government, they weighed whether to create a single president or a committee. Delegate James Madison, who took careful notes during the summer, described the moment when nothing nearly happened:

The Committee of the whole proceeded to Resolution 7, "that a national Executive be instituted, to be chosen by the national Legislature for the term of — — years . . . to possess the executive powers of Congress &c . . ."

Mr. WILSON moved that the Executive consist of a single person.

Mr. C PINCKNEY seconded the motion, so as to read "that a National Ex. to consist of a single person, be instituted."

A considerable pause ensuing and the Chairman asking if he should put the question.[26]

A considerable pause ensuing. The delegates were about to decide the matter of the presidency with no discussion. In the previous days of their deliberations, they had picked over every little question they came upon as they obsessed over how to distribute power so that it would not be abused. In this moment, though, they were ready to decide quickly.

The members of the convention took that "considerable pause" because they all assumed George Washington would take the job they were creating. (As David O. Stewart put it, the framers of the Constitution "wrote General Washington's future job description.")[27] Since that was the case, there was no reason to debate whether the executive should be one man or a committee. Anyone arguing that the executive had to take the form of a committee would be implying that Washington wasn't up to the job, or that he was susceptible to the corruption that a committee was intended to prevent. To argue for a committee would be to argue against Washington's capacity for virtue, the whole reason he'd been put at the head of the class in the first place. Only Benjamin Franklin was brave enough to break the impasse and encourage more debate on the issue.[28]

WHEN THE CONSTITUTION WAS completed and agreed to by the delegates, George Washington signed it first. The presidency created in Article II was tailored for his shoulders, and it was expected that he would break in the garment for future wearers. "In our progress toward political happiness my station is new," he wrote to Catharine Macaulay Graham, "and if I may use the expression, I walk on untrodden ground. There is scarcely any part of my conduct which may not hereafter be drawn into precedent."[29]

From the start, the office of the presidency was imbued with the behavior of its occupant. Jefferson credited Washington's character with nothing less than saving the republic: "The moderation and virtue of a single character probably prevented this revolution from being closed, as most others have been, by a subversion of that liberty it was intended to establish."[30]

Washington felt the weight of the job because he understood that the job would convey expectations on future occupants. "Example, whether it be good or bad, has a powerful influence," wrote Washington as commander of the Continental Army. As president, he knew if he set those expectations high, those expectations, or norms as we call them today, would drive other men's actions. Ambitious men would seek glory by meeting those expectations by acting "presidential."[31]

Washington's desire to be thought well of by public men he admired called him from retirement to join in the creation of the new Constitution. How could a man of honor neglect his country when it was in need? He worried "whether my non-attendance in this Convention will not be considered as a dereliction to republicanism."[32] This is the power of social norms and elite opinion. That same desire later propelled Lincoln. "Every man is said to have his peculiar ambition," said Lincoln. "Whether it be true or not, I can say, for one, that I have no other so great as that of being truly esteemed of my fellow men, by rendering myself worthy of their esteem."[33]

Washington's standard has come to mean not just a specific set of behaviors, but a reminder of the very value of high standards. "Let him remember he sits where Washington sat, and so remembering, let him answer, as Washington would answer," Abraham Lincoln warned President Polk. "As a nation should not, and the Almighty will not, be evaded, so let him attempt no evasion — no equivocation."[34]

How a president acted was an affirmation of the entire enterprise. The political scientist Dennis Thompson expands on this idea with the concept of "constitutional character," namely, "the disposition to act, and motivate others to act, according to the principles that constitute the democratic process."[35] So, for example, the founders believed a president should cool the passions of the people, not inflame them, because the national temperature would have a direct effect on the health of the republic. A president who was acting presidential would constrain his or her behavior accordingly. As Jeffrey Tulis, the author of *The Rhetorical Presidency*, points out, the founders rejected "frequent popular appeals" because a president who governed that way would undermine deliberation and lead to bad public policy.[36]

If a president whipped up the crowd, "the passions . . . not the reason, of the public would sit in judgment," wrote Madison in Federalist No. 49. "But it is the reason, alone, of the public, that ought to control and regulate the government. The passions ought to be controlled and regulated by the government."[37]

President Truman reaffirmed this principle during his tenure: "You can't divide the country up into sections and have one rule for one section and one rule for another, and you can't encourage people's prejudices. You have to appeal to people's best instincts, not their worst ones. You may win an election or so by doing the other, but it does a lot of harm to the country."[38]

President Trump has chosen to govern by a different route, building support among his political base by "weaponizing uncertainty," explains the social researcher Brené Brown, taking people who are uncertain and promising them certainty and giving them someone to blame for whatever they lack.[39] Or, as Trump's former ambassador to the United Nations Nikki Haley put it, referring to the Trump 2016 campaign, "During anxious times, it can be tempting to follow the siren call of the angriest voices."[40] This stratagem is effective, but it also splits the country. Trump's philosophy, said former Tennessee Republican senator Bob Corker, "is based upon division, anger and resentment, and in some cases, even hate. . . . Instead of appealing to our better angels and trying to unite us like most people would try to do, the president tries to divide us."[41]

A president who chooses to fulfill the expectations of the job has an enormous power to inspire. "Great men exist that there may be greater men," Emerson wrote in "Uses of Great Men," a meditation on the power of example and standard-keeping in public men.

FDR's labor secretary, Frances Perkins, said his "capacity to inspire and encourage those around him to do tough, confused and practically impossible jobs was without dispute." After a meeting, she said she "came away from an interview with the president feeling better not because he had solved any problems," but because he had some-how made her feel more cheerful, more determined, and stronger than she had felt when she went into the room.[42]

John Kennedy inspired a generation of Peace Corps volunteers. Ronald Reagan inspired an entire generation of Republican politi-cians. The myth that he never took off his jacket in the Oval Office was repeated often as a symbol of how his deportment matched with the vaulted expectations for the job.

It is this power of example to inspire those who witness it that we hear about regularly at presidential funerals. "Grant that all who attend to these proceedings might be desirous of being our best selves," said House Chaplain Reverend Patrick Conroy when eulogizing George H. W. Bush.[43]

David Cohen, former CIA deputy director and treasury undersecre-tary under Barack Obama, remembers the first time an order came over from the White House and the weight it carried. "I was several layers away from the president at that point, but the idea that we were there at the treasury and what we were going to do in some respects was fulfilling the policy goal of the president—I just remember thinking that is so unbelievably cool." Respect, says Cohen, is an organizing

FDR signs the Social Security Act with members of Congress and Labor Secretary Frances Perkins. FDR's "capacity to inspire and encourage those around him to do tough, confused and practically impossible jobs was without dispute," said Perkins.

principle. "It's the magnet that everybody lines up to."[44] As Eisenhower used to say, "Optimism and pessimism are infectious and they spread more rapidly from the head down than in any direction."[45] Leadership guru John Maxwell turned this idea into one of his twenty-one irrefutable laws of leadership: "Who you attract is not determined by what you want; it's determined by who you are."[46]

For a man to achieve all that is demanded of him, wrote Goethe, he must regard himself as being greater than he is. For a president, the measure of greatness he is aiming for is shaped by public expectations, founded on the idea of being presidential. I asked Lyndon Johnson biographer Doris Kearns Goodwin about Johnson's mottled character and how it fit with the idea of being presidential. Johnson was exceedingly vulgar, a bully, braggart, and manipulator with corrupt business ethics. A man of "monstrous character," as conservative David Frum put it, and yet Johnson was effective and rightfully lauded for improving the lives of millions and millions of Americans.[47] "At some point a great leader transfers that ambition from self to a larger goal," said Goodwin, "to the country and maybe even history."[48] This is how ambition, so frightening to the founders, spurs greatness even in our public figures today. But in the American presidency, the president isn't the only one with ambition. The public has ambitions for the president as well. They can be just as powerful, and just as overpowering.

On August 3, 1981, twelve thousand air traffic controllers walked off their jobs. The men and women, who acted as pilots' eyes at more than four hundred airports, demanded higher pay to compensate for the unique stress of their jobs, in which just one mistake could prove fatal. Air traffic during the heavy summer season stopped.

The new president, Ronald Reagan, recovering from an assassination attempt three months earlier, negotiated with the union that had backed his presidency. After an agreement, the union increased their demands. The president refused.

A stare-down ensued. "Bring the Controllers Down to Earth," wrote *The New York Times*, arguing the controllers had gone too far. Controllers thought no one could replace them. They had unique expertise. The president thought their expertise was so specialized that the union members wouldn't be able to find employment elsewhere. The president spoke to the nation, noting that the federal workers had signed a specific pledge that said they would not strike. "It is for this reason that I must tell those who fail to report for duty this morning they are in violation of the law, and if they do not report for work within forty-eight hours, they have forfeited their jobs and will be terminated."[1]

With no agreement, the president did not blink. New controllers were brought in and there were no incidents. "Ronald Reagan not only transformed his presidency, but also shaped the world of the modern workplace," wrote historian Joseph A. McCartin. "It was still not common for employers to deal with strikes by trying to break them, but once Reagan had successfully broken PATCO and retained his popularity . . . many private-sector employers took a similarly hard line when in the private sector workers went out on strike in the private sector."[2]

Reagan did not fully realize the importance of his decision at the time, but would later say that his action in the strike was "an important juncture for our new administration. I think it convinced people who might have thought otherwise that I meant what I said."[3]

Chapter 7
———

Action Hero President

———

You know, it's easy for the Monday morning quarterback to
say what the coach should have done, after the game is over.
But when the decision is up before you—and on my desk
I have a motto which says "The Buck Stops Here"
—the decision has to be made.[4]

— HARRY S. TRUMAN

Life does not consist in thinking, it consists in acting.[5]

— WOODROW WILSON

IN 1945, A FRIEND OF HARRY TRUMAN'S SAW A SIGN ON THE WARDEN'S
door at the Federal Reformatory in El Reno, Oklahoma.[6] It read: THE
BUCK STOPS HERE. Truman's friend asked if the inmates could make a
copy for his friend in the Oval Office. Truman put the gift on his desk
and referred to it often. "You know, it's easy for the Monday morning
quarterback to say what the coach should have done, after the game is
over," Truman said at the National War College on December 19, 1952.
"But when the decision is up before you—and on my desk I have a
motto which says 'The Buck Stops Here'—the decision has to be made."

The "buck," in this famous phrase that outlines the basic obligations of the presidency, originates from the game of poker. In frontier
days a knife with a buckhorn handle was used to indicate whose turn it
was to deal. A player who didn't want to deal could decline the responsibility by passing the "buck" to the next player.[7]

Truman deployed the expression as a rebuttal to the pundits and smart set who are always so certain about the way things should go. Truman had plenty of critics. He fired General Douglas MacArthur, he nearly seized the train lines, and he did seize the steel mills. When *Washington Post* music critic Paul Hume criticized his daughter's singing, the president wrote to him, "Someday I hope to meet you. When that happens, you'll need a new nose, a lot of beefsteak for black eyes, and perhaps a supporter below!" The intemperate letter caused newspapers to wonder about the balance of the president's mental state. The "Truman talent for trouble," said *Newsweek,* kept the nation nervous. *The Washington Post* predicted his seizure of the mills in April 1952 "would probably go down in history as one of the most high-handed acts ever committed by an American president." Truman, said the *Post,* had grossly usurped the power of Congress, and in a constitutional democracy there was no more serious offense against good government. "Nothing in the Constitution can be reasonably interpreted as giving to the Commander in Chief all the power that may be necessary for building up our defenses or even for carrying on a war." Truman was asked at a press conference if he believed he could seize the steel mills, then under his inherent powers did he believe he could seize the newspapers and radio stations? His equivocal answer satisfied no one.[8]

Often presidential critics are not weighed down with experience about the matter at hand, which seems to add conviction to their opinions. Many of the most vocal in this camp have never been in a situation like the one about which they are presently so certain. Lincoln called them "newspaper generals" during the Civil War.[9] Italians call them *umarell,* which refers to men of retirement age who pass their time watching construction projects and offering unwanted advice. This is also known as being a "sidewalk superintendent." In America, this group is sometimes found on Twitter.

Truman's maxim about buck stopping is a statement of the reality of the presidency. The decisions come to one person, and the choices are often ill-defined. That one person has to assume the overwhelming weight of the consequences and make a decision—often without delay. It is why we value the office and those who take on its burdens willingly. Truman mentioned this idea again in his farewell address in

January 1953: "The President—whoever he is—has to decide. He can't pass the buck to anybody. No one else can do the deciding for him. That's his job."[10]

The phrase encourages humility from the backseat driver. Are you sure you'd do so much better? In 1962, after a visit by a group of judgy historians, John Kennedy said, "No one has a right to grade a President— not even poor James Buchanan—who has not sat in his chair, examined the mail and information that came across his desk, and learned why he made his decisions."[11]

Unfortunately, the audience Truman and Kennedy were speaking to and their present-day colleagues do not share this view. Instead, they have stolen the phrase "buck stops here" for their purposes. The buck-stopping expression has become a cudgel used to blame the president for anything that goes wrong or any problem that is not quickly solved. When the president, or a president's aide, explains that life is a little more complex than the critic thinks, the expression is deployed. The president is accused of making excuses and not understanding a fundamental truth about the presidency: The buck stops at the president's desk.

"Voters would like presidents to be Superman,
but the best they can do is strike that pose."

POLITICAL OPPORTUNITIES

ON APRIL 20, 2010, AN EXPLOSION SHOOK THE DEEPWATER HORI-
zon offshore drilling platform. Eleven people were killed, and a river of
oil was unleashed into the Gulf of Mexico. Two days afterward, the
ocean structure snapped like a breadstick and sank into the water. For
a total of eighty-seven days the oil kept on belching.

It was the first big test of President Obama's ability to respond to an
unfolding catastrophe. The president visited the oil-slicked beaches, updated the public even when there was no progress to report, and counseled patience. He did not stop the oil from flowing, nor did he convey
enough urgency to give people the feeling that his presence would hasten that outcome. For this he received failing grades. The urgent blast of
oil made the president's words seem too synthetic, slipping over the moment. "This is one of the greatest lost political opportunities I've ever
seen," said James Carville, Bill Clinton's political guru.[12]

Cable television networks carved out space in the lower corner of
their screens to show the black oil rushing into the sea. Nick Anderson,
the editorial cartoonist for *The Washington Post*, lampooned the famous Obama poster by Shepard Fairey with the word HOPE by drawing an oil-soaked Obama over the word HELP. The oil was urgent. The
president didn't seem to be.

The restraint and cool-headed reason that had once been seen as
Obama's assets were now seen as fatal flaws. He should be able to get it
fixed! Or at least give the impression through his public appearances
that a solution was coming. The headline on a Peggy Noonan column
in *The Wall Street Journal* rendered the verdict: HE WAS SUPPOSED TO
BE COMPETENT.[13]

In our instantaneous world, a president must be seen to be active
and available for the purposes the public requires. After a disaster, there
is no appetite for a hidden hand presidency. The president is expected
to leave his fingerprints on everything—whether doing so is useful or
not. Sometimes this leads to playacting. The chief of staff to one president said the pressure sometimes caused the administration to stage
events at FEMA headquarters that were merely for the purpose of feeding this expectation that the president must do *something* about whatever looming hurricane was spinning off the coast of Florida.[14]

In the aftermath of the blowout at BP's Deepwater Horizon drilling site, the Obama administration pulled out every public relations stop as the oil continued to billow into the Gulf of Mexico, even taking the rare step of deploying the First Lady to the region, where she urged Americans to support the local economy by vacationing there.

In April 1970, a fire and power failure imperiled the Apollo 13 trip to the moon. There was nothing President Nixon could do in the middle of the night, but his National Security Advisor, Henry Kissinger, says he woke him anyway: "We couldn't tell the public that we had not alerted the president," said Kissinger. "It is important the public has a sense that the president is on top of the situation."[15] During the Cold War, when the space race was on, presidential attention to the heavens was a proxy for American strength in the competition against the Soviet Union. Chief of Staff Haldeman records that the next day there was a "whole review of other alternatives to show [Nixon's] concern and interest."[16]

George W. Bush standing on that pile of rubble in New York City after the attacks of 9/11 set the modern standard for vigorous presidential action. If a president doesn't act—or isn't seen acting—it can damage his presidency. "It used to be that presidents were advised to let the FEMA director and governor handle disaster response," says Andy Card, who managed the Hurricane Andrew response for George H. W. Bush in August 1992 and served as George W. Bush's chief of staff during Hurricane Katrina in 2005. "Now the expectation is that if a president is not talking about it all the time, he is asleep at the switch, or Marie Antoinette."[17]

Card knows how harsh that public judgment can be. In September 2005, when Hurricane Katrina drowned New Orleans, killing at least 1,833 people, Bush flew over the wreckage. Below were miles of snapped trees and houses submerged to the roof. The president and his team were concerned that a presidential visit in the immediate aftermath would disrupt recovery efforts, but the picture of the president looking down from Air Force One was interpreted as a sign of ineptitude. Atop the rubble pile on 9/11, he had taken charge of the moment. From the plane, he looked like a mere spectator.

Would it really have helped the people of Louisiana if the president had landed? His arrival and the preparations for it, including the briefings by officials who had important things to do, might very well have gotten in the way. It didn't matter. The commentary linked the suffering in New Orleans with that image of the president looking down

No one expected Lyndon Johnson to visit the 9th Ward in Louisiana after Hurricane Betsy, because it was not then the custom for presidents to travel to ravaged cities. By the time George W. Bush flew over the 9th Ward after Hurricane Katrina in 2005, the expectation had grown so large that his decision not to land defined the end of his presidency.

from a dry place above it all. Because so many of the dead were African Americans, the rapper Kanye West declared, "George Bush doesn't care about black people."[18]

Bush had been on vacation at his sixteen-hundred-acre ranch while the storm was approaching.[19] "He has to get off his mountain bike and back to work," declared Representative Rahm Emanuel, a member of the Democratic leadership in the House, who would later serve as Barack Obama's first chief of staff.[20] Steve Schmidt, deputy assistant to the president and the vice president's counselor, wrote in an email to a colleague that the image of ineffectiveness would be impossible for Bush to overcome before his term was over in 2008. "This is the end of the presidency."[21]

The Katrina response became a frame for evaluating other presidents. As Obama wrestled with the oil spill, critics labeled it "Obama's Katrina."[22] Stung by that verdict, President Obama interrupted his vacation to tour abandoned beaches dappled with oil tar balls that rolled in with the tide. "There were great inspiring, amazing times in the Obama White House," remembers press aide Ben LaBolt. "But you also remember the times where it just seemed like you couldn't win and there was no way out . . . this is one of those times."[23]

Forty-nine days into the BP oil crisis, solutions with desperate names like "top hat"[24] and "junk shot"[25] had been tried and failed—the latter included pumping golf balls, shredded tires, and knotted rope into the well. It all had the improvised feel of the razzle-dazzle plays cooked up in touch football games. At one point, a suggestion was considered that the military bomb the well head. The spill went into the record books as the largest in American history. NBC's Matt Lauer asked President Obama whether he should spend more time in the Gulf and—using the language of an action hero presidency—"kick some butt."[26] Obama bristled at the suggestion he was being too cerebral and hadn't deployed the weight of his administration behind the response. "I don't sit around talking to experts because this is a college seminar," Obama shot back. "We talk to these folks because they potentially have the best answers, so I know whose ass to kick."

The Obama administration hadn't caused the spill. It was a particularly difficult problem to solve. The Interior Department and Coast Guard oversee deepwater rigs, but capping raging oil gushers was not a governmental skill. Nevertheless, Obama was on the hook for the whole belching mess. "I ultimately take responsibility for solving this crisis," the president said in the midst of the drama. "I am the president, and the buck stops with me."[27]

GREEN LANTERNISM

THE MAXIM "THE BUCK STOPS HERE" IS A SUCCINCT EXPRESSION OF presidential obligations, but as the job and our expectations of it have grown, so has the waistband on the expression. It originally referred to the decisions only a president could make. Now it assigns responsibility to the president for anything that doesn't go well during his presidency.

To a president's supporters, this idea of the presidency seems unfair. Why should the president get the blame for problems that the administration didn't cause and that are too complex to be solved? Real life isn't a Tom Clancy novel. A president can't solve problems with a barrel roll and a well-placed shot from his sidearm.

The political scientist Brendan Nyhan calls this vision of the presidency Green Lanternism, "the belief that the president can achieve any political or policy objective if only he tries hard enough or uses the right tactics."[28] (Nyhan chose the Green Lantern because the DC Comics character's power is determined by his will.)

In a Green Lantern presidency, presidential speeches have nearly magical properties. A president can turn the public to his viewpoint no matter how steep the opposition. If the president doesn't, pundits determine that it's because the speech was not given with enough (a) feeling, (b) authenticity, or (c) attention to the pundit's favorite metric of the moment. In a Green Lantern presidency, negotiations with Congress are supposed to yield deals no matter Congress's partisan makeup.

Green Lanternism makes it hard to identify what might actually be stopping progress, because it's always the president's lack of will that's to blame. It also sets presidential candidates up for failure because they will overpromise in campaigns and underdeliver in office when it turns out force of personality won't do the trick.

Tough luck, says Senator Mitt Romney. The expectations come with the job and force accountability and organizational discipline. "I think the president is responsible for everything that happens in the executive branch—actually, in government," says Romney, who has held a host of executive-level jobs, including governor of Massachusetts, CEO of Bain Capital, and president of the Salt Lake Organizing Committee for the 2002 Winter Olympics. "Corporate executives lose their jobs all the time. That is the nature of the job. What that means is you have to have a talent for saying 'Okay, how do I amass a group of extraordinary people who have amazing capabilities themselves and manage them, oversee what they're doing, guide what they're doing, give them their head, and in many cases recognize they'll make mistakes but not big, serious ones.' It's a whole process. How can I make sure they know what needs to be bumped up to me? I take the blame for anything. I mean for all of it, and I get the credit for everything by the way. So that's how it goes. The deal is you get the credit for everything and the blame for everything."[29]

President Eisenhower was even more committed to the idea of presidential accoountability. The general argued that maintaining the norm that the leader is responsible for all the actions of his subordinates is the true test of virtue. "Character in many ways is everything in leadership," said Eisenhower. "Character is really integrity. When you delegate something to a subordinate, for example, it is absolutely your responsibility, and he must understand this. You as a leader must take complete responsibility for what the subordinate does. I once said, as a sort of wisecrack, that leadership consists of nothing but taking responsibility for everything that goes wrong and giving your subordinates credit for everything that goes well."[30]

Eisenhower recognized an important quality of the presidency and leadership: There is an institutional benefit to practices that cause the leader personal pain in the short term but benefit the organization in the long term. Michael Bloomberg explained this to *Face the Nation*'s Margaret Brennan when talking about why taking the blame for subordinates is so important to building and maintaining a good organization. "When they make decisions that you don't necessarily agree with or that don't turn out to be the right decisions, you have to back them up," said the former New York mayor. "If you don't give people the confidence that you're going to have their backs . . . you're not going to get good people and you're not going to keep them."[31] This is not an invitation to remove accountability, but to embrace a wiser account-

Four days after the nuclear reactor at Three Mile Island suffered a partial meltdown, Jimmy Carter donned plastic booties and visited the facility with his wife, Rosalynn. The president, who had worked with nuclear reactors in the Navy, hoped to calm fears of radiation leakage. "The president of the United States just doesn't walk into a danger area without knowing what is going on," a local resident told The New York Times.

ability whereby a leader protects his subordinates so that they can take risks and show initiative without excessive fear.

Tim Cook at Apple makes a similar case. He explains one of his roles as blocking the "noise from the people who are really doing the work."[32] In this conception of the job, a president takes the heat so that his administration performers can plow ahead with getting their work done.

ACCOUNTABILITY AND DEMOCRACY: THE COMMON VOICE

PRESIDENTIAL ACCOUNTABILITY IS NECESSARY TO MAINTAIN HIGH standards of execution, but it's also necessary to keep democracy healthy. President Obama's former staffers wouldn't wrestle anyone out of taking a more generous view of Obama's response to the BP oil spill. But members of the Obama team also agree that taking heat is a necessary part of the job. America has only one official who represents the entire country, they point out. The office of the presidency provides a location for voters to place their anger and frustration, just as it offers a place where they can turn for hope, inspiration, and comfort. "As long as we as Americans can blame the president, he's accountable to us," says Obama's press secretary Josh Earnest. "Yes, that puts the president in an unfair position, but democracy needs it."[33]

Blunt pressure from the electorate forces a president and his aides who have his interests at heart to push for solutions, or at least progress. This is the upside to tribalism and hero worship, as staffers who swoon over their boss or adhere to the boss because of brute political ties work harder to keep the boss from getting blamed. The fear that the voters might punish the president startles the staff and bureaucracy into movement. It's a voter's job and responsibility to push no matter what, in order to get action.

That's the positive view of this phenomenon. The downside is that if a president does not take this view of their office and its obligations they think they are being unfairly criticized. They take the criticism personally and lash out. Or they talk to the paintings late at night in a paroxysm of self-pity. Or they ignore the criticism as fake news. As a result, they take no steps to address the root cause in the moment and don't order their team to solve the underlying problems.

The other complication of this necessary accountability is that it leads to imprecision in evaluating presidents. Presidents are accountable for everything that happens in an administration but there are some organizational failures that the president has no hand in. When Donald Trump's secretaries of Interior, Environmental Protection Agency, and Health and Human Services were forced to resign for ethical lapses, Donald Trump was not responsible for those. He was accountable—he had hired them—but he was not the proximate cause of the controversies. President Trump, on the other hand, was responsible for circumventing his administration's policy and Congressional legislation on Ukraine. He was also directly responsible for sending his lawyer to investigate Hunter Biden instead of following protocol and having U.S. authorities do it.

This distinction matters because abuse of power—the thing that the founders feared so much—grows from the direct actions of presidents, not the unseen work of a president's agents. President Obama is responsible for his controversial decision to kill U.S. citizens with drone strikes, but he is not directly responsible for the Justice Department program known as Operation Fast and Furious, which permitted guns to be sold to suspected smugglers, some of which ended up at crime scenes in Mexico.[34] There is no evidence he initiated it. The same is true with the IRS targeting conservative groups of which the president was not aware.[35] Understanding this distinction helps us compare presidents across time as well. A president who is a direct participant in a controversy is not the same as one who has a controversy take place on his watch.

What Obama's press secretary Earnest is describing is a view of the presidency and public opinion that emerged in the early twentieth century, backed by reformers like Woodrow Wilson. As a political scientist, Wilson wrote in *Congressional Government* that Congress had grown sclerotic and ineffective, detached from the people. The modern age, he maintained, required presidents to be more responsive to the voters in order to keep democracy working.[36] "The progressives' charge was that the Constitution's ingrained checks on concerted action had come to thwart the organic adaptation of government to the exigencies of national development," writes political scientist Stephen Skowronek.[37] Once again, the debate about the presidency centered on whether the system was too cumbersome to keep pace with modern progress. A closer connection between the people and their president would keep American government grounded in what Wilson called "the common meaning of the common voice."[38]

Obama's chief of staff Denis McDonough embraces this idea of a presidency always in front of the public demonstrating and explaining even when the display is not a stunning success. It's more than just public relations. It is an act of stewardship. "The public parts of the president's job are important because people have to see him working through the things that are on their minds," says McDonough. "He is the public face of their government."[39]

If that's the right view of the office, it highlights just how much risk there is for a president. He has to appear with regularity as the public face when things aren't going well, as Obama did with the BP oil spill. However, that's likely to encourage people to associate their bad mood with the president's face. Moreover, it creates an expectation: A president must show up at the customer service window, dispensing a frown or a thoughtful nod or whatever will respond to the public mind. Since the public is generally angry, this means repeatedly offering them the chance to associate you with their irritation.

A presidency so conceived lengthens the president's to-do list. Answering those calls shreds the attention and crowds out the important, which, if left unattended, will become urgent, and may catch the president and administration unprepared. But if a president isn't always tending the complaint window, he may lose the political standing necessary to gain public approval—or at least a sympathetic hearing—for other actions he might want to take in the future. Also, as anyone who has been on hold with customer service for half an hour knows, the rage can accumulate until it can melt glass. A president who is available to the public can act as a conductor to dissipate some of that heat.

If this vision of the presidency is accurate and a part of a president's duty of state and public stewardship, presidents must take the blame for problems they neither caused nor can solve as fast as the public wants. Lyndon Johnson was right when he said that "being president is like being a jackass in a hailstorm. There's nothing to do but stand there and take it."

"I Hate to Tell You, Puerto Rico": Standards of Presidential Stewardship

DONALD TRUMP REJECTS THE HAILSTORM OBLIGATIONS OF THE presidency. If a tradition asks him to sit there and take it, his response is to punch that tradition in the nose. When personal political survival collides with a stewardship duty, he protects the former at the expense of the latter. Why accept a vision of the job that damages your political standing in a situation where you don't deserve it—a situation you didn't cause and can't change? That just weakens your political standing to address the things you can control.

So what is the standard for presidential stewardship? Are presidents bound to it by anything more than tradition and shame?

In the fall of 2017, Hurricane Maria devastated Puerto Rico. According to the traditional playbook, the president would have been seen in briefings before the storm arrived, and in a windbreaker after it hit. Stories in the papers would have chronicled his impatience with slow recovery efforts, or captured the president's barked commands that everything possible had to be done to speed aid to the crippled island. Without hindering relief efforts, he would have traveled as close as possible to the disaster to lend the symbolic consolation of the office and highlight recovery efforts.

None of this happened. President Trump attended the first situation room meeting six days *after* the storm wiped out vast swaths of the island.[40] In public, President Trump spoke about the island only in passing. No stories in the paper testified to his private passion for helping or for cleaning up the island.

Unlike previous administrations, Trump administration officials don't have to leak stories to the papers about the president's private passions. His Twitter account records his personal feelings in real time. In the week and a half after the storm hit Puerto Rico, the president offered public support and occasional updates about the island, but a full view of his tweets shows that his focus was on healthcare legislation, the Alabama Senate race, and NFL players protesting during the national anthem.

Then, on September 30, ten days after the storm, the president displayed his most concerted energy on the topic. It was prompted not by the plight of U.S. citizens, but by stories about the recovery effort which criticized the slow deployment of Defense Department assets to deal with the devastation of the island. President Trump came alive. In an eleven-hour period, he tweeted eighteen times about Puerto Rico, attacking the news media for their coverage of relief efforts and attacking locals in Puerto Rico.[41]

"I can see why he was frustrated," says Brock Long, Trump's former administrator of FEMA, which coordinates federal emergency response. Long says President Trump "gave me everything I needed and let me do my job."[42] What the president was responding to, says Long, was a disproportionate blame for the federal response when the infrastructure and local conditions in Puerto Rico were highly vulnerable, and local emergency response officials were incompetent or unresponsive. Proof of that unresponsiveness was still coming out two years after the storm hit. The government fired several officials, including the emergency management director, for incompetence when aid supplies intended for hurricane victims were found unused in a warehouse.[43]

Long maintains that what makes the difference in disaster response is not a measure of presidential action, but the quality of local officials and resources. In Texas and California, local officials are experts experienced in working with the federal government. In Puerto Rico, he says, he never met a local emergency coordinator.

Long and other emergency response officials across administrations say blaming a president puts us at the wrong complaint window, which means we are wasting our public useful anger that could be directed at improving disaster response. "Part of the elevation of the presidential role points to how we've turned federalism on its head," says Craig Fugate, who led FEMA under President Obama. "The primary role of responding is the governor's and not the federal government. People expect the president to be in charge, and if something is wrong it's the president's fault, but you elected the governor. Blame them. The primary responsibility is not federal. In many cases it is unfair to say it is all the president's fault when we've seen big failures and structural problems at the local and state level that the federal government can't fix."[44]

Fugate says this applies to the disproportionate blame aimed at George W. Bush after Katrina. "There were a lot of challenges in all forms of government," says Fugate about Hurricane Katrina. "There is no way in hell one person could have screwed up Katrina as much as people think [FEMA director] Mike Brown did."

Also, blaming the president means voters don't step back and look at larger forces at work during a disaster. "We get what we deserve when we build and design our communities in ways that make us vulnerable to events where there is no credible way to respond," says Fugate. If people keep building houses along shorelines, he says, the president and his FEMA director are going to have a harder and harder job. Placing the blame properly does not always mean it is removed from a president. It may just put it in a different place. While local officials are responsible for flood relief, a president is responsible for policies that address climate change, which causes the sea level to rise and increases the potential for flooding. So a president may be to blame not for a Q_1 failure but a Q_2 one instead.

In Puerto Rico, Donald Trump was not the first president to face these kinds of disaster challenges—inadequate or incompetent local help, or conditions on the ground that made the recovery more difficult. What he did that was new, however, was to attack local officials while they were still scrambling to respond to the waves of frantic residents without power, tap water, or cell service.

Donald Trump offered a direct challenge to the idea of the complaint window presidency. As a veteran of the hospitality industry, he does not apply that trade's "the customer is always right" mentality to the presidency. Instead, he was the one banging on the customer service window. Why should he take the responsibility for local failures? Why should he rush to help when they got themselves into this mess?

Enduring the hailstorm is not a president's only obligation in an emergency. A president is expected to dispense constant empathy. It is another way to get the bureaucracy moving, by highlighting the human toll, which calls public servants to even greater efforts. A president who displays empathy also lends symbolic comfort to those directly affected and to the rest of the country, encouraging them to feel empathy for their fellow Americans who they can see on their television screens are suffering.

President Trump directed his passion toward exercising grievance far more than toward displaying empathy for Americans. It wasn't that he said nothing, it's that his passion was so clearly directed at managing political ramifications affecting the president's approval rating or criticisms of his administration. For a president who applies unrelenting pressure to get the job done on an issue like blocking migration at the Southern border, that same level of urgency was not applied to Puerto Rico. No staffer that I talked to could testify that he applied anything close to that level of passion when it came to lessening the human misery in Puerto Rico.

When President Trump visited Puerto Rico, thirteen days after the storm's landfall, he had the chance to rebalance his response. He also had an opportunity to rebut the charge that his public response to disasters in Texas and Florida—states with voters in his political base—had been far warmer. Upon landing, he offered words of support and encouragement and praised the federal response. It was not dazzling, but it was solid presidential stuff.

He did not stop there, though. The president also included detours that reaffirmed the conclusion that his real passion concerned his own administration and not the residents of Puerto Rico. "I hate to tell you,

Puerto Rico, but you've thrown our budget a little out of whack," he said at a news conference with the territory's leaders.[45] He also engaged in a grim and inaccurate squabble about the death count. "Every death is a horror, but if you look at a real catastrophe like Katrina, and you look at the tremendous hundreds and hundreds and hundreds of people that died, and you look at what happened here with really a storm that was totally overpowering. Nobody's ever seen anything like this. And what is your death count as of this moment? . . . Sixteen people, versus in the thousands," he said. "You can be very proud."[46] Afterward, the president tossed paper towels into a crowd of strained faces as if he were trying to win a boardwalk prize. It elevated the impression that the humanitarian toll had not shaken him.

In 2019, two years after Hurricane Maria hit Puerto Rico, the president stayed in this same groove. He greeted the arrival of another storm bearing down on the commonwealth with a tweet that referenced the "incompetent Mayor of San Juan!"[47] The counterpuncher was preemptively swinging even as the island was preparing to get hit again. Never one to forget a grudge, the president was also counterpunching against the hailstorm expectation. If people were going to place blame after yet another storm he wanted that blame to be placed somewhere else.

T.R. and the Gorgon

On February 23, 1902, a group of smartly dressed visitors from New York were admitted to President Teddy Roosevelt's office at the White House. One of the company was the richest man in the world, J. P. Morgan, later the model for the spats-and-monocle-wearing mascot of the game Monopoly. Roosevelt wanted to break up Morgan's Northern Securities Company railroad trust because it had a lock on that mode of transport, which meant it could charge freight companies whatever it wanted. The banker told the president he should have warned him about the suit. "That is just what we did not want to do," answered Roosevelt, in order to "prevent violent fluctuations and disaster in the market."[1]

Morgan, who owned the majority shares in the company, sought a quick fix. "If we have done anything wrong," he told the president, "send your man to my man and they can fix it up." By Roosevelt's "man," Morgan meant the attorney general, Philander Chase Knox. "That can't be done," said the president. Knox was more blunt: "We don't want to fix it up. We want to stop it."[2]

Morgan predicted disaster if a president could just meddle in the nation's financial affairs. "I am neither a bull nor a bear in Morgan stock," responded Roosevelt. "I am President of the United States, and am sworn to execute the law. I would proceed against you or any of your combinations as quick as I would against a [labor] striker—but not because I am opposed to either capital or labor, except as either of them may be violators of the laws of the country."

After the meeting was over and the average net worth of the room had been significantly lowered by the banker's departure, Roosevelt was piping hot. "That is a most illuminating illustration of the Wall Street point of view," he told Knox. "Mr. Morgan could not help regarding me as a big rival operator, who either intended to ruin all his interests or else could be induced to come to an agreement to ruin none."[3]

Morgan was also irked. Later in life, when he heard Roosevelt was going to Africa, the banker reportedly said: "Good. I hope the first lion that finds him does his duty."[4]

Chapter 8

Confidence Man: The Economy

—

Market booms develop acute overoptimism and with it a
corresponding reverse into acute pessimism. They are
equally unjustified, and the sad thing about all that is the
number of unfortunate people that are drawn into the vortex
with the loss of their savings and reserves. But any lack of
confidence in the economic future and the basic strength of
business in the United States is simply foolish. Our national
capacity for hard work and intelligent cooperation is ample
guaranty of the future of the United States.[5]

—HERBERT HOOVER, A MONTH AFTER THE
STOCK MARKET CRASH IN 1929

FORTY-ONE DAYS BEFORE THE 2008 ELECTION, GEORGE W. BUSH
hosted the two men vying for his desk set. The Republican nominee,
John McCain, had asked for the extraordinary meeting to talk about
the imploding economy. The housing market had collapsed, and Congress and the administration were debating emergency legislation that
would amount to the most sweeping economic intervention since the
Great Depression.

McCain's request for the meeting seemed desperate. He trailed
Barack Obama in the polls. He had already taken the dramatic step of
suspending his campaign, arguing that the economic crisis required a
break from politics so that leaders could gather to find a solution, which
came across as an unnecessary and theatrical act.[6] The liberal blogger

Josh Marshall captured the snicker of skepticism that greeted McCain's move, charging that McCain had staged the campaign equivalent of faking an injury when you're down late in the fourth quarter.[7]

Treasury Secretary Henry "Hank" Paulson, who led the administration's push for a $700 billion bailout of the banks, questioned McCain's motives.[8] The GOP nominee needed grassroots conservatives on Election Day, and they opposed the bailout. On the website nowallstreetbailout.com, created to gather opposition to the move, one commenter wrote, "This bailout could end up breaking the spirit that underlies the true American way. The key word is 'RESPONSIBILITY!' WHERE IS IT?!'"[9] Matt Kibbe, the president of FreedomWorks, the conservative pressure group that had set up the website, offered an analogy: "Allowing investment banks to dump $700 billion in 'troubled assets' on the taxpayer is akin to inviting a vampire into the house. If you live, you certainly won't be the same person when you wake up the next morning."[10]

McCain had already swerved once in the campaign, departing from his script by picking grassroots favorite Alaska governor Sarah Palin as his running mate. He had been arguing that foreign policy experience was crucial to serving as president but then picked someone he said was ready to step into the job, should she have to, who had none of the experience he had said was fundamental. Paulson warned McCain that if he torpedoed the rescue legislation, the treasury secretary would publicly accuse the GOP nominee of sabotaging the economy.[11] He said Fed Chairman Ben Bernanke would make the same declaration. As an independent Fed chair, Bernanke would never have done that, and Paulson knew it, but he bluffed out of panic over a looming catastrophe.[12] McCain had called the meeting in order to get the voters to imagine him as a president at the helm. Paulson was threatening to call him Ahab.

House Republicans weren't trying to court a national constituency the way McCain was, so they didn't have to listen to Paulson. Their leader, John Boehner, who also attended the Oval Office meeting with the two candidates, said his conservative members wouldn't vote for Wall Street bailout legislation. His counterpart, Democratic House Speaker Nancy Pelosi, felt betrayed. She explained to the room that her troops had agreed to the politically painful bailout of the Wall Street banks on the promise that both parties would hold hands and jump off the high dive together. Now it looked as though House Republicans were climbing down the ladder, leaving Democrats to face the political plunge all by themselves.

The White House session dissolved in uncertainty and acrimony. Before Pelosi could leave, Treasury Secretary Paulson got down on one knee and pleaded with her not to "blow it up" by withdrawing her party's support from the legislation. "I didn't know you were Catholic," said the Speaker with an uncomfortable laugh (referring to the practice of genuflecting). "It's not me blowing this up, it's the Republicans."

"I know," said Paulson. "I know."[13]

In the end, John McCain, who had called the meeting, didn't say very much during it. What could he say? He had neither the expertise, nor the staff with the expertise, to manage the problem. Like Senator Obama, he had been campaigning, so he hadn't been involved in crafting the legislation in Congress. McCain was trying to look presidential, but the moment revealed something about the difference between the cinematic notion of the presidency as it is imagined in the campaign, and the actual job.

In a moment of crisis, a president doesn't just show up and bend spoons (and minds) with the force of his will. A president tending to an economic crisis requires a team of experts, and engagement.

FORECLOSURE NATION

NOT ALL OF THE DISASTERS THAT PRESIDENTS FACE LEAVE SCATTERED cinder blocks and splintered plywood. In the fall of 2008, the disaster was all the *intact* houses. Scores of empty homes snaked through vast, carefully planned suburban idylls. Streets were lined with For Sale and foreclosure signs in front of homes emptied of owners who had abandoned them or been evicted because they couldn't pay the mortgage.

Just as 9/11 marked an escalation in the complexity and number of security challenges a president must address, the Great Recession of 2007–2009 highlighted how sticky the economy can be in the age of global commerce and lightning-quick transactions. In the fall of 2008, George W. Bush and his team weighed complex and politically volatile decisions under excruciating time pressures. Failure could have meant a collapse of the Western economy.

In economic matters, as with national security, presidents are both stewards and first responders. Stewardship requires promoting policies that prepare for disaster and encourage prosperity and equal opportunity. Quadrant Two responsibilities. In the first responder role, the president must operate in Quadrant One—important and urgent: making quick decisions that have global consequences. The president's two economic jobs are related, of course. The ongoing economic conditions in America, both real and perceived, determine how much political and financial support a president will have when an economic crisis hits and action must be taken.

We don't talk about a president's emergency economic responsibility in campaigns as much as we do the stewardship duties. We vote for someone we trust to do the right thing in a pinch. What does that mean, though, when it comes to the economy? We elect for the best of intentions, but the presidency requires more than that. If an economic crisis hits, we're going to hope that the president has picked the right team, has a system for evaluating information in frantic conditions, and has developed relations with key players, building the kind of trust required when the market arrows are red, angry, and all pointing down.

Men of experience standing in dark suits and ties at the White House lectern are supposed to convey confidence, but in the spring of 2008, President Bush was uncertain about what was going to happen next with the economy. He had to trust his advisers to keep it from crashing.

"We're Not Going to Do a Bailout, Are We?"

The speed and size of the Great Recession of 2008 surprised most experts. "A lot of people talked about slack in the system," says Bill Clinton's treasury secretary Robert Rubin, "but no one talked about the greatest collapse since the Great Depression."[14] In 2008, the financial system seemed stable. There were challenges—increasing income inequality, stagnant wages, slow productivity growth—but the view was that the economy was fundamentally healthy and could handle shocks. Some economists even flirted with the idea that risk, as it was once understood, had been tamed. There were sophisticated equations governing transactions that would temper market swings. Traditional exposures could be mitigated.

The faith in sophistication was the problem. Transactions zipped through the system at an ever-increasing rate, and the computational forces propelling them were opaque. Mortgage-backed securities were top of the class in this category. These financial instruments amounted to a fruit smoothie of a large number of home mortgages, blended on the theory that by mixing enough home loans together, banks could harvest risk-free returns. Sure, some folks might not be able to keep up with their mortgage payments, but that's why banks mixed a lot of mortgages together. Even if a few mortgages failed, the final blended product would still have enough good mortgages on which people were making their interest payments to offer a strong return. One bad berry in a robust housing market wouldn't spoil the smoothie.

That was the theory anyway, but then too much of the fruit went bad.

Housing prices plummeted. Homeowners who couldn't pay their loans couldn't sell their houses for enough to cover their loan obligations.[15] Banks that took over the mortgages couldn't make back the money they had lent by selling the houses put up for collateral. At one point, a quarter of the homes in America with mortgages were valued for less than the mortgage amount their owners owed the banks.[16] By December 2007, as the wave of doom was cresting, there were 97 percent more home foreclosures than there had been by December 2006. A record million homes were vacant.[17, 18]

Owners of those no-risk, sure-thing, good-as-cash, take-it-to-the-bank mortgage-backed securities unloaded them fast. As prices fell, investors who had bought them on credit were asked to cover their shortfall, but they couldn't sell the securities they owned for anything close to what they owed on the loans they took to buy them in the first place. Firms that owned the securities were also in a fix. Over the previous years, those firms had been allowed to expand with scanty cash reserves. They didn't have a cushion and were decimated when the value of the significant amount of mortgage-backed securities in their portfolios collapsed.

Panic in the housing market caused a broader panic in the financial markets through these securities. It wasn't just a few apples that were bad; the apples, the branches, and the orchards were spoiled.

EVERY TELEVISION ON THE PANIC STATION

IN 2008, SIX MONTHS BEFORE SECRETARY PAULSON WOULD GET DOWN on one knee and beg Nancy Pelosi for her support for his proposed bailout, he met with President Bush to go over a speech on the darkening economic picture. The president, who had made increasing home ownership a key objective of his presidency, was no longer in economic stewardship mode. Now he had become a first responder.

In a time of panic, investors lose confidence and sell. Unlike market goods like an orange or a car, where price is determined by quality and availability, financial markets are influenced by people's feelings about stability.

"That's why the word 'credit' comes from the Latin for 'belief,'" write the architects of the Great Recession rescue, Ben Bernanke, Hank Paulson, and Timothy Geithner, in their book about the experience.[19] Geithner was president and CEO of the Federal Reserve Bank of New York at the time and would go on to be Barack Obama's treasury secretary. "Why we say we can 'bank' on things we know to be true, why some financial institutions are called 'trusts.' It's why traditional bank architecture relied so heavily on imposing granite facades and pillars to project an aura of stability and permanence in front of the fragility of finance."[20]

Sometimes, those public feelings about confidence are irrational or "foolish" as Herbert Hoover groused. No president can say this out

After the Panic of 1837, the first major national economic crisis in American history, Americans blamed President Martin Van Buren. In this cartoon, a destitute father hears the pleas of his family. On the wall hang pictures of Van Buren and his predecessor, Andrew Jackson.

loud, however. It doesn't fix the confidence problem, and it invites voters to give the single-finger salute. People sell in a panic. That causes their neighbors to panic. Panic becomes what everyone is wearing this season. Panic gets invited to every dinner party.

The immediate challenge for a president and his staff trying to restore confidence in any financial crisis is how to sound the alarm without alarming people. Robert Rubin experienced this during the Mexican peso crisis of 1995. "I found myself trapped in a kind of Catch-22," writes the former treasury secretary. "On the one hand, I needed to underscore the dangers in order to motivate reluctant legislators—and the public—to support our rescue package. On the other hand, frank talk about what might happen could provoke the very reaction we most wanted to avoid."[21] In 2008, President Bush struggled to strike this balance. When he spoke in public about the economy he referred to "adjustments," "disruptions," and "the situation."[22] It was like talking about "moisture" before a hurricane.

A president can't sound too alarmed, but sounding too sanguine can diminish confidence further. If rosy predictions don't pan out, people might wonder if anyone is in charge. Assuming not, they might hasten their bolt to the exits. Too much happy talk, though, and you land in the history books next to Hoover. In accepting his nomination in 1928, Herbert Hoover proclaimed that Americans were "nearer to the final triumph over poverty than ever before in the history of any land."[23] A year later, more than 60 percent of the country earned less than the amount necessary to support a family.[24]

Presidents who believe in the long-term benefit of minimal government intervention are cured of this view during a panic. It is a presidential truth from the days when transactions took place on a barrelhead. In response to the Panic of 1837, President Martin Van Buren intoned:

> All communities are apt to look to Government for too much. Even in our own country, where its powers and duties are so strictly limited, we are prone to do so, especially at periods of sudden embarrassment and distress. But this ought not to be. The framers of our excellent constitution and the people who approved it with calm and sagacious deliberation, acted at the time on a sounder principle. They wisely judged that the less Government interferes with private pursuits the better for the general prosperity.[25]

This didn't wash. Van Buren was bounced from office in 1840. Heir to Andrew Jackson's populist revolution, Van Buren found himself on the receiving end of public anger. The electorate revolted against his aloof notions of unfettered markets. They wanted government, driven by the president, to bring relief (or at least stop pushing policies they felt were making things worse).

Franklin Roosevelt took office in 1933 and immediately had to wrestle with the confidence octopus. It produced one of the most memorable speeches of all time as he told the country in 1933, in response to the crippling economic conditions, "The only thing we have to fear is fear itself—nameless, unreasoning, unjustified terror which paralyzes needed efforts to convert retreat into advance." He then asked the country in that inaugural address to show that it was not afraid by backing his proposed solutions.

In March 2008, President Bush met with Secretary Paulson to go over the president's next speech on the economy, which was aimed at restoring that sense of confidence. The president hoped to reassure the country with a firm statement on the administration's resolve, but the secretary noticed that the text of the speech included language ruling out any bailouts. "Don't say that," Paulson warned. The president was puzzled. "We're not going to do a bailout, are we?" he asked. Paulson said he wasn't predicting one at the moment, but given the volatility of things, he couldn't rule one out. "Mr. President, the fact is, the whole system is so fragile we don't know what we might have to do if a financial institution is about to go down."[26]

At this point in the movie version of this story, we would have heard the chandelier in the state dining room gently chiming, picking up the first tremors before the tsunami sinks the ship.

Bush listened to Paulson and kept the no-bailout pledge out of the speech. Four days later, the eighty-five-year-old brokerage firm Bear Stearns collapsed. Having lost billions in subprime mortgage investments, it had little cash. Banks would no longer offer Bear Stearns the loans that are a part of the daily flow of commerce.[27] Soon the panic started. If a trusted giant like Bear, which had weathered the Great Depression, could have such hidden rot, it might exist throughout the banking industry.

To stop the panic, the U.S. government stepped in. By September 2008, the government took over the mortgage giants Fannie Mae and Freddie Mac, government-backed institutions created to make it easier for people to buy homes by providing affordable mortgages. The feds hadn't intervened in the financial markets like that since the Depression.[28]

YOU WON'T LIKE TODAY'S SPECIALTY SANDWICH: TARP, THE TROUBLED ASSET RELIEF PLAN

AS THE BUSH ADMINISTRATION TRIED TO SPUR CONGRESS TO SEND money to banks to avoid further panic that would lead to more widespread economic collapse, Democratic majority leader Harry Reid reported that his office fielded five thousand calls opposing the bailout, known as the Troubled Asset Relief Plan (TARP). Only twenty people called in support.[29] Years of income inequality, stagnant wages, and slow productivity had built national resentment against a system in which those at the top got ahead while the other 99 percent trod water or fell behind. "In a natural disaster, relief is a politically attractive bailout," says Paulson. "It hits one group of people. If it's a hurricane, a drought, a wildfire, the national government is supposed to come in. The public believes the funds are going to victims who are harmed through no fault of their own. Everybody wants to see the money go there." But that was not what was happening in the banking crisis. "This was a politically toxic thing no matter how you dressed it up."[30]

Bill Clinton faced similar toxicity in 1995. Just after his State of the Union Address in January, his economic advisers warned that the Mexican economy was imploding from debt. The peso was headed to an all-time low and the country needed to be rescued. If not, migrants would flood into the United States and drug cartels would flourish in the chaos. America's economy would take a hit if its third-largest trading partner imploded. Mexico's failure would spook markets in other developing countries, whose leaders would retreat from their slow adoption of free market systems. Those emerging markets represented 40 percent of the market for U.S. exports.

In the 1980s, emerging market sovereign debt (debt owed by a government) traded in slow private transactions. By the mid-1990s, global transactions moved at fiber-optic speed. Markets that tanked in one place could unsettle countries on the other side of the planet. Problems in countries with currencies most Americans don't recognize can quickly become the reason they don't have a job, whether it's Greek debt weakening U.S. trading partners in Europe, or the collapse of the Mexican peso, or the British departure from the European Union. Nearly 60 percent of the American economy is tied up in foreign trade, which means millions of U.S. jobs and families are linked to the undulations of the global market.[31]

In 1995, Clinton supported his economic team's recommendation to give Mexico a $25 billion bailout. Clinton's political advisers thought that was a bad idea. He had just suffered a stinging defeat in the 1994 election, when Republicans won control of the House for the first time in forty years and took control of the Senate. A bailout might help Mexico, but it would also help protect investors. Why should they be saved from their risky bet on Mexican bonds? "Those who wanted to speed my political recovery after the crushing midterm defeat thought I was nuts, or, as we say in Arkansas, 'three bricks shy of a full load,'" Clinton remembers.[32]

Seventy-nine percent of the country opposed the Mexican bailout, according to a *Los Angeles Times* poll. Congressman Bernie Sanders (I-VT) told Treasury Secretary Rubin in a House hearing that he should "go back to your Wall Street friends, tell them to take the risk and not ask the American taxpayers."[33] From the right, Republican commentator and presidential candidate Pat Buchanan called the Mexican loan "daylight robbery of the nation's wealth. [It is money] the American taxpayers will never see again."

Clinton placed his bet on an uncertain policy. As in all real presidential decisions, there was no one option that guaranteed success. During deliberations, Treasury Secretary Rubin had polled his advisers about the chances that the bailout would work. The answers ranged from one in three to just a little better than 50 percent.[34] The bailout not working would mean that Clinton had ignored the public and wasted money and America would still have suffered the economic turmoil of a collapse of the Mexican economy.

Congress refused to support the move. Clinton responded by creating his own route. He used emergency executive powers to lend Mexico money from the Exchange Stabilization Fund.[35] It was the first time the fund had been used to rescue a foreign currency. It was a stretch of the president's executive powers.

In the end, Mexico borrowed only half of the money it was offered and paid back its loan three years early with $1.4 billion in interest, $600 million more than had the money been invested in U.S. Treasury notes.[36] That wasn't the only way to think about it, argued critics. When investors know they will get bailed out, they make riskier investments. The bailout implanted a mindset out in the world that would only invite more behavior that required bailouts.[37]

Thirteen years after the Mexico bailout, in the mortgage-backed-security crisis, George W. Bush couldn't use the same workaround tools that Clinton had. The problem was too big. He had to work with Congress, but he faced an even tougher political dynamic than Clinton. The divide between the haves and the have-nots in America was even greater than it had been in 1995, putting more populist pressure on the lawmakers inflating the lifeboats for the Wall Street bankers.

In 2008, the interconnectedness of the American economy was greater than it had been during the Clinton administration, also making the need for action all the more urgent. Wall Street pain from the housing-spurred collapse was affecting Main Street businesses. Nearly all lending was frozen as banks responded to the volatility with extreme risk intolerance. Small businesses couldn't get loans for the basic reasons they need them—to meet payroll or expand or continue operations. If the situation continued, TARP advocates argued, companies would close and people would lose their jobs. Home loans were scarce, even for qualified recipients, imperiling all the jobs in housing-related industries. This looming disaster in the rest of the economy became a chief selling point to woo skeptics. The administration hoped to get the banks lending again by buying up the bad securities on their balance sheets. That's what the $700 billion was for.

The demand for speed in an economic emergency increases suspicions that the solution will exacerbate existing inequalities. Democratic leader Harry Reid said the administration was asking the Senate to move too fast in approving the bailout. "It takes two weeks to pass a bill to flush a toilet" in the Senate, Reid said, complaining that the administration was asking Democrats to simply take their word for it. Paulson responded: "If we don't do this, we are flushing the toilet on the American people."[38] GOP House leader John Boehner described the rescue as "a crap sandwich" but said "I'm going to eat it anyway."[39] When he spoke on the floor of the House, where such language isn't allowed, he said: "Nobody wants to vote for this, nobody wants to be anywhere around it. . . . I didn't come here to vote for bills like this. But let me tell you this, I believe Congress has to act."[40]

Despite the push, the antibailout fever in the fall of 2008 was too high. The first vote for TARP failed in the House, with 60 percent of Democrats and just 33 percent of Republicans voting for it.[41] President Bush, who had called all nineteen Republican members of his Texas delegation, had persuaded just four to support the bill. "You were being

Populist rage over a shrinking middle class and unequal distribution of wealth nearly sank the TARP bailout in 2008. Public distrust of Wall Street has not improved, limiting future presidential action in an emergency.

asked to choose between financial meltdown on the one hand and tax-payer bankruptcy and the road to socialism on the other, and you were told to do it in twenty-four hours," said Texas Republican congressman Jeb Hensarling, who voted against the measure.[42]

After the failed vote, the stock market dropped nearly 800 points. By day's end, $1.2 trillion in IRAs, pension funds, and savings was gone—nearly twice the size of the bailout package itself. The VIX index that chronicled market volatility, the so-called "fear index," closed at the highest level in its twenty-eight-year history.[43] The negative market reaction helped convince House members that the dire predictions about economic collapse had been real. The Senate took up the cause, authoring its own bill, which passed, and the newly spooked House members voted for it this time.

PERSONNEL IS POLICY

THE STORY OF THE TARP BAILOUT IS A TALE OF PRESIDENTIAL PERSONNEL. Whether you are a fan or opponent of presidential emergency actions, there is agreement on one thing: In a fast-moving complex economic landscape, personnel is policy. Presidential decisions are highly dependent on the team that joins the president on those couches in the Oval Office. They understand the stakes and frame the options.

Bush trusted his economic advisers. He knew that while his popularity had been damaged by the Iraq war, the economic team had the authority to convince lawmakers to back a policy unpopular with their constituents. "If I hadn't had a year before the crisis struck to build a relationship of trust with George Bush, I don't know what I could have negotiated if I hadn't had that," says former Treasury Secretary Paulson. "And if I hadn't had the opportunity to work with Pelosi and Schumer and Reid and Frank and Dodd, in addition to Republicans and had a president who had encouraged me to do it, I don't think I could have gotten it through."[44]

Picking the right team and retaining them long enough to build rapport are crucial in a presidency when a crisis hits. "What is important during a presidential transition is having a really good process for focusing on and deciding about people," says Secretary Rubin. "You need really good people around you . . . you need people who are conversant with the intersection of politics and policy. If you had a professor who wasn't cognizant of political considerations and he went through some analysis that didn't relate to the world we live in, [it wouldn't work]. It's economics, politics, markets, how business thinks. So you need people who are conversant with the intersection of all those things."[45, 46]

John Taylor, who managed the post-9/11 emergencies of international finance from the Bush Treasury Department as undersecretary of international affairs, notes the importance of clear lines of authority among personnel in such situations: "To deal with emergencies you have to have an incredibly good chain of command," says Taylor. "That's not just the people, it's the whole process. It's the whole chain of command. It's harder in some sense in areas other than the military because [the military is] set up that way. In economics it's zero."[47]

When administrations are granted emergency powers, staffers gain extraordinary discretion to make policy. The relatively loose congressional guidelines on how TARP money would be spent meant that the Bush and Obama administrations could use the money far more freely than is usually the case. This allowed for the emergency rescue of U.S.

car manufacturers. "All we needed was [Treasury Secretary] Tim Geithner to sign this piece of paper," says Steve Rattner, a Wall Street CEO whom Obama brought in to manage the auto industry bailout of 2008–09. "If we'd had to go to Congress, it would have been a hostage situation. One of the car companies would have had to fail for Congress to see how bad it was. Just like Lehman. One of them had to fail for Congress to see how bad it was and then actually do what they needed to do. But we were able to operate as if we were in the private sector. It was amazing."[48]

The car companies survived, but that won't make voters any more anxious to support the next emergency move, nor will the fact that TARP realized a more than $100 billion profit for the government from repayments by bailed-out firms.[49] Critics point out that the success or failure of individual bailouts isn't being measured the right way. These bailouts are proof, say people like Senator Bernie Sanders, that government gets truly energetic on economic matters—and Congress wakes from its slumber—only when wealthy interests and wealthy donors are endangered. Ask for emergency measures to reduce the number of the uninsured or to help with college loan debt or address global climate change, and the money isn't available. That dynamic, argue Sanders and others, is fundamentally unfair, and it will increase populist anger that will be unleashed the next time a president asks for emergency forbearance.

Bailout critics also point to the power of staff. They argue that George W. Bush and Barack Obama were too influenced by establishment figures from Wall Street and Washington. When disaster struck, the two presidents lacked the imagination to reorient the system that was collapsing. Advisers who knew the secret handshakes of the world of finance drove presidential decisions toward outcomes that retained the system with which they were familiar. "President Obama has repeatedly turned to nominees with close Wall Street ties for high level economic positions," Massachusetts Senator Elizabeth Warren wrote in *Huffington Post* in 2014. "It's time for the Obama administration to loosen the hold that Wall Street banks have over economic policy making. Sure, big banks are important, but running this economy for American families is a lot more important."[50]

This is why AFL-CIO president Richard Trumka said in 2014 that the organization would withhold its endorsement of Hillary Clinton if she hired advisers from the Obama and Bill Clinton presidencies. "If you get the same economic team, you are going to get the same results," said Trumka, "and the same results aren't good enough for working people."[51]

A Chicken in Every Pot, but Don't Stir It

As with national security, the most important thing a president can do to manage economic emergencies is to enact policies that reduce the chance that there will be an emergency in the first place.

That's easier to do as commander in chief, where the president has a number of specific tools. A president can push diplomacy, launch wars, negotiate tariffs, and use summitry to influence other world leaders. There are not as many economic analogs. "As a president, foreign policy is yours," says Elaine Kamarck of the Brookings Institution, "but economic policy is barely yours. There is constant pushback."[52] If a president wants to affect the economy, it requires sustained, focused attention and national rallying. It also means fighting with Congress and the army of lobbyists hired to protect the interests of those who benefit from the system you're trying to change.

During the 2020 election campaign, Elizabeth Warren argued that a president has plenty of tools, if she knows how to use them correctly. Through the regulatory agencies, the executive branch can take on monopolistic practices, restructure student loan debt, and reform the banking industry. It's an argument that seeks to use the executive branch for liberal ends the way Donald Trump has for conservative ones.

The conservative economists John Taylor and Michael Boskin know firsthand how hard it is to encourage politicians to address tough economic problems before they become urgent crises. The pair wrote an op-ed in March of 2018 with former secretary of state George Shultz entitled "A Debt Crisis Is on the Horizon," about the necessity of addressing the growing federal budget deficit.[53] With the economy strong, they argued, it was the perfect time to take action. They were rebuffed or ignored. Conservative lawmakers, who talked so passionately about the debt once before, responded with no more than a furrowed brow.

"The structure of what's going on is you have current voters with different interests clashing," says Boskin. "'[The federal government should] spend more' and 'Don't raise my taxes,' to oversimplify the two positions. So what's the default? Stick future voters who don't vote now with the bill. That's the structure of what's going on."[54] Republican reluctance to embrace a traditional GOP economic view of deficit reduction—during good economic times and with a Republican president—is just one example of the way in which promoting a lot of economic policy is hard when there is not a crisis to rally everyone.

If lawmakers tackled the deficit now, it would give them more room to operate when the next crisis hits. If fiscal matters are left unmanaged, deficits will become the ready-made excuse for not taking emergency action on the grounds that emergency action is too expensive. During the 2008 debate over TARP, Congressman John Culberson voted against the bailout because it was "bankrupting our children" by adding to the debt.[55] Other lawmakers—including a number of Democrats—argued that the 2009 stimulus package pushed by President Obama was too puny to help the economy recover in the aftermath of the Great Recession because the Obama administration and conservative Democrats were too concerned about the deficit.

During good economic times, the adventurous spirit deflates. Presidents want to boast about how well things are going. Talking about emergencies yet to happen, or dangers down the road for which we must prepare, darkens the bright picture that's lifting a president's approval ratings. Also, economic Quadrant Two work for the long term inevitably calls for sacrifice. Voters don't like sacrifice, as much as they might tell reporters they are willing to accept their share. Given the brutal priority sorting of the presidency, such gambits toward meeting the challenges of the future either never make it onto the to-do list, or they occupy the immovable basement position. It is extremely hard to build energy and focus for important but non-urgent matters when so many urgent issues fill the president's day.

COMPLACENCY CALLS CATASTROPHE

AS WITH MANY ASPECTS OF MODERN LIFE, THE DISTANCE FROM THE LAST catastrophe creates complacency, and complacency invites the next catastrophe. "The enemy is forgetting," former Federal Reserve Chairman Ben Bernanke told the American Media program *Marketplace* about the lessons of the Great Recession. "As time passes, and the memory of this gets further in the rearview mirror."[56] The Nobel laureate Kenneth Arrow has tried to turn signs of economic certainty into a warning sign. "Vast ills have followed a belief in certainty," he said in his 1992 essay "I Know a Hawk from a Handsaw."[57] "Our knowledge of the way things work, in society or in nature, comes trailing clouds of vagueness."[58] Civil War General William Tecumseh Sherman had his own version of this fear of certainty: "Every attempt to make war easy and safe will result in humiliation and disaster."

Among the most dire economic challenges for a president to tend to in moments of relative calm is income disparity in America. It fueled the populist resistance to the Mexican peso bailout and TARP. The situation continues to get worse.[59] This should be a top priority for all presidents. They are entrusted with fostering equal economic opportunity in a land dedicated to equality. There's also a political reason: Populist rage stoked by unequal outcomes makes the president's job harder.

The great recession of 2008 had a disproportionate impact on middle-income Americans whose financial health is determined by the appreciation of their homes. The wealthy weren't hit as badly because their wealth appreciates from other instruments, like the rise of stock prices. Stocks have grown faster since the last collapse. When people look at the booming stock market recovery but don't feel it in their lives, they conclude that these emergency measures have only widened American disparities.[60]

Polls show that people notice things aren't fair. In April 2019, when *Washington Post* / ABC News pollsters asked Americans whether the economic system in America mainly works to benefit all people or mainly works to benefit those in power, 60 percent said it mainly benefits those in power.[61]

The biggest legislative economic action taken by the Trump administration has only increased the feeling in the United States that the powerful are getting the rewards. According to an April 2019 Gallup poll, only 14 percent of the public believe they received a tax cut (in reality, roughly 8 in 10 did).[62] An internal Republican National Committee poll obtained by Bloomberg News showed that by a 2-to-1 margin—61 percent to 30 percent—respondents said the law benefits "large corporations and rich Americans" over "middle-class families."[63] According to a Pew Research Center poll, 62 percent of Americans say it bothers them "a lot" about the tax cut legislation that "some corporations don't pay their fair share." Even 42 percent of Republicans are bothered "a lot" about this perceived disparity.[64]

Under President Trump, other signs of economic health increased during the first three years. The monthly job growth continued its longest stretch in U.S. history, which had started six years before he became president.[65] The stock market broke record after record. Business confidence hit all-time highs, as did consumer confidence. The recovery after the recession that caused Hank Paulson to plead with Nancy Pelosi at the White House set a record for the longest peacetime expansion. But in a connected global economy, economic emergencies can quickly drive lawmakers back to their knees. Unlike in 2008, though, when Congress and the two parties joined together to respond, the relationship between the two parties has corroded. The state of toxic partisanship is not something that should give anyone confidence that a president will be able to address the next disaster effectively.

REAGAN AND O'NEILL

The seventy-year-old patient lay threaded through the tubes of a George Washington University hospital bed, recovering from a gunshot that had pierced his lung. He had lost half his blood to an internal hemorrhage and was still weak. But he was not so spent that he could not whisper along with his Irish Catholic visitor who had knelt to pray for him. They recited the Twenty-Third Psalm: "The Lord is my shepherd; I shall not want. He maketh me to lie down in green pastures . . ." The bullet had come within an inch of the patient's heart. Death had been close but only the tightest circle of his intimates had known. That circle had to be tight because the exterior circle of interested parties was large—a country of nearly 300 million, who had elected him, the fortieth president of the United States, just four months earlier. Had he died, the man kneeling in prayer would have been second in line after the vice president to replace him. When Speaker of the House Tip O'Neill had finished praying, he hauled himself back up and bent his six-foot-three, 300-pound frame over the bed and kissed President Ronald Reagan on the forehead. "I'd better be going. I don't want to tire you out."[1]

Chapter 9

A Historic Partisan Gap

—

Any discussion of how hard it is to manage the presidency
has to start with the weakness of Congress. You can't have a
president solve problems the legislative branch has not.[2]

—DENIS MCDONOUGH, WHITE HOUSE CHIEF
OF STAFF TO BARACK OBAMA

If Congress is determined not to act, there is
only so much a president can do.[3]

—GEORGE W. BUSH

We're majoring in the minors.[4]

—SENATOR BOB CORKER

I F YOU FIND YOURSELF IN A CONVERSATION ABOUT WHAT'S WRONG
with politics today, you're likely to hear about the relationship between
President Ronald Reagan and House Speaker Tip O'Neill and how
they worked together to save Social Security.

The story goes like this. In the early 1980s, two political giants with
Irish roots and humble beginnings clashed at the end of one era of
American politics and the start of another. Though they hailed from
opposing parties, opposing branches of government, and opposing ide-
ologies, they overcame their differences and reformed one of the most
politically sensitive government programs.

Unlike the glancing sideshow debates of today, the two men fought over central issues: What role should the government play in American life? What does America owe its least fortunate? Is government assistance the best remedy? Does the government threaten or promote individual liberty?

In 1981, when the Republican Ronald Reagan became president, the economy had been sluggish for a decade. America still seemed wobbly in its global standing, still convalescing after the Vietnam War. President Reagan led a conservative revolution to reinvigorate the country by shrinking government, which he believed was undermining American values.

Tip O'Neill stood as the last political giant from the New Deal era. A rumpled bed of a man, he defended policies designed to protect the poor and disadvantaged from the unfettered market. "[You are] the only person in a position to continue representing the ideals of justice and compassion," O'Neill's leadership aide Burt Hoffman wrote to him.[5]

Reagan and O'Neill criticized each other directly and personally. Reagan compared the heavyset O'Neill to the video game character PacMan—"a round thing that gobbles up money."[6] Reagan said he got his exercise by "jogging three times"[7] around the portly Speaker. O'Neill called Reagan "Herbert Hoover with a smile"[8] and "Ebenezer Scrooge."[9] His report card on Reagan in 1983 was withering: "He only works three to three and a half hours a day. He doesn't do his homework. He doesn't read his briefing papers. It's sinful that this man is President of the United States. He lacks the knowledge that he should, in every sphere, whether it's the domestic or whether it's the international sphere."[10]

When O'Neill said Reagan couldn't sympathize with the working man, the president shot back: "I grew up in poverty and got what education I got all by myself, and I think it is sheer demagoguery to pretend that this economic program . . . is not aimed at helping the great cross-section of people in this country that has been burdened for too long by big government and high taxes."[11]

This criticism crossed a line, though as modern readers we would need special glasses to see it. Charging O'Neill with "sheer demagoguery" was considered such an outrageous attack on a coequal branch of

"Politics is politics," said Democratic House Speaker Tip O'Neill. "[President Reagan and I] may disagree during the day, but come six P.M. we become friends." Reagan, seen here with O'Neill at the president's seventieth birthday party, joked that sometimes when they talked and O'Neill got a little too hot, Reagan would set his watch forward to six.

government that it occasioned its own round of concerned news coverage. Reagan ultimately phoned O'Neill to apologize.[12]

Despite the fighting, O'Neill and Reagan socialized. Reagan writes in his diary of a private evening at the White House and a small dinner for six, which included O'Neill and his wife. "It was a nice evening but maybe Tip and I told too many Irish stories."[13] Reagan also records that O'Neill and House Majority Leader Jim Wright surprised him by delivering a birthday cake.[14]

When either of the two men went too far, he apologized to the other. While they went quite far, they maintained norms and limits, because they had to work together in an American system of shared powers. They felt a duty to work together to serve the people who had hired them, and the voters expected them to behave in keeping with their responsibilities.

Perhaps no quote better captures the contours of their relationship than O'Neill's response when asked about the lasting damage of one of his public fights with the president. "Politics is politics," said O'Neill. "We may disagree during the day, but come six P.M. we become friends."[15] (Reagan joked that sometimes when O'Neill got a little too hot during a conversation, Reagan would set his watch to six). This is the spirit that inspired both to work on a legislative solution that extended the solvency of the Social Security system.[16]

This kind of bipartisan animal does not roam anymore, which is why worthy citizens retell the tale, as if they hope by remembering it by the campfire, they can coax it out of the mountains.

Headline writers kindle the same hope. *The New Yorker* asked in 2017, CAN DONALD TRUMP LEARN FROM RONALD REAGAN AND TIP O'NEILL?[17] A 2015 *Hill* newspaper headline reads: HOW TIP O'NEILL AND RONALD REAGAN WOULD MAKE THIS CONGRESS WORK.[18] In 2010: TIP O'NEILL AND REAGAN AND MODEL FOR BREAKING PARTISAN GRIDLOCK.[19] In 2009: BIPARTISAN REAGAN-O'NEILL SOCIAL SECURITY DEAL IN 1983 SHOWED IT CAN BE DONE.[20]

Politicians refer to the deal constantly. "Think of Reagan and Tip O'Neill coming together in the early '80s to raise the age for Social Security," said Majority Leader Mitch McConnell in the fall of 2018 when he blamed "bipartisan reluctance" to reform federal entitlement programs for the increasing federal debt. "It took it out of the political arena and made it possible to be successful."[21]

Isn't it pretty to think so? This is a nice story. It is no longer a realistic one. In 2019, a meeting at the White House broke down when House Speaker Nancy Pelosi challenged President Trump on Russia's involvement in Syria, saying, "All roads with you lead to Putin."[22] President Trump referred to the House Speaker as a "third-rate politician."[23] During a phone interview with *Fox & Friends*, the president was even more personal, referring to Pelosi as "Crazy Nancy . . . crazy as a bedbug,"[24] and responding to a video of the Speaker, "Nancy's teeth were falling out of her mouth, and she didn't have time to think!"[25]

It's not just that things have gotten more coarse. The Reagan and O'Neill working relationship existed within a political structure that no longer exists. The structural incentives are far different now. The chance of such a major deal coming together today without a fundamental shift in our national political life is as likely as Ronald Reagan and Tip O'Neill coming back to life to put it together themselves.

THE SLEEPING PRESIDENTIAL PARTNER

A PRESIDENT CANNOT SUCCEED WITHOUT CONGRESS. THE CONSTITUTION ties the two branches together. At the moment, the relationship is at a low ebb. "Any discussion of how hard it is to manage the presidency has to start with the weakness of Congress," explains Denis McDonough, White House chief of staff to Barack Obama and former congressional aide. "You can't have a president solve problems the legislative branch has not."

Members of Congress represent the diversity and breadth of America. Durable solutions to the toughest problems can come only through a system that passes laws informed by that diversity and in which the process makes everyone feel heard whether they win or lose. A president acting alone can't replicate that diversity of representation. If they act unilaterally, they're likely to galvanize their political rivals. Nor does a president have Congress's tools to address vital issues. Even if the president has massive arm muscles in some areas of government power, the political body cannot ambulate on spindly congressional chicken legs.

When Congress does not address central questions on issues like healthcare, immigration, and economic policy, it lengthens the president's to-do list. The country almost exclusively turns to the president for political solutions and blames him if he doesn't act, so presidents scramble to meet those expectations. Presidents issue executive orders and administrative actions that are either limited—because the president anticipates a court fight over exceeding presidential authority—or they are too broad, and the courts strike them down.

The broken relationship needs repair but lacks an easy fix. The political parties are deeply split. Partisan separations are locked in by election districts drawn to concentrate political power and by the lifestyle choices of people who move to live near others with whom they share cultural and political views. Party control of Congress changes regularly, which discourages compromise and makes fights between parties more frequent and vicious. If these fires of separation start to die down, media and interest groups that profit from conflagration hasten to slosh more gasoline on the floor.

Congress and the president have a difficult time doing the basic three-legged-race work of governing without ending up in a heap. Recent history is punctuated with periodic budget battles that lead to shutdowns or weekslong posturing over the threat of shutdowns.

When presidents do collaborate with Congress on big legislation, the achievements are partisan. Obama signed healthcare reform flanked only by Democrats. Mitch McConnell explains the damage done by taking this approach: "Without some meaningful buy-in, you guarantee a food fight. You guarantee instability and strife. It may very well have been the case that on Obamacare, the will of the country was not to pass the bill at all. That's what I would have concluded if Republicans couldn't get a single Democratic vote for legislation of this magnitude. But Democrats plowed forward anyway. They didn't want to hear it and the results are clear. It's a mess." McConnell had a chance to practice what he preached early in the Trump administration. The tax cut bill was even less popular than Obamacare at the equivalent time, but McConnell helped to pass it with no Democratic support and little effort by the president to get it.[26] Trump celebrated his tax cut bill and was joined by only Republicans in the Rose Garden for the big moment.

The relationship was so poisonous in 2020 that when Trump signed a bipartisan United States–Mexico–Canada Agreement (USMCA), an updated version of the North American Free Trade Agreement, no Democrats were invited.

Early in the twentieth century, Will Rogers joked, "This country has come to feel the same when Congress is in session as when the baby gets hold of a hammer."[27] Now the country is angry not only at what Congress does, but at its repeated demonstration of what it cannot do in hammering out solutions to the difficult issues facing the country. Leaders in Congress wouldn't dare take on an issue as large and politically volatile as Social Security reform the way Reagan and O'Neill did. "We are majoring in the minors," said Republican senator Bob Corker of Tennessee when he looked back on how the Senate spends its time.

BOLL WEEVILS ARE EXTINCT

SAMUEL JOHNSON IS REPORTED TO HAVE SAID THAT SECOND MARRIAGES demonstrate the triumph of hope over experience. A similar hope animates those who tell the Reagan and Tip O'Neill story. They hope, despite recent experience with American politics, that cooperative governing might work again.

For this to happen, though, the political incentives would have to change. When Ronald Reagan took office in 1981, the structure of Congress encouraged cooperation. He won 144 congressional districts represented by Democrats.[28] The Democratic House members representing those districts answered to constituents who liked the new Republican president, which encouraged those Democratic representatives to work with him.

Known as the Boll Weevil Democrats, these members shared Reagan's desire to increase defense spending, shrink the budget, and lower taxes.[29] They took their name from the cotton-destroying beetle that couldn't be eradicated. Their more formal name was the Conservative Democratic Forum: Democrats dedicated to demonstrating that they were not liberals. (The group no longer exists. Turns out the beetle can be eradicated.)

With any piece of House legislation, if Reagan received the support of all 191 Republicans, he needed only a few more than half of the Boll Weevils for the legislation to pass. When Reagan passed tax cuts early in his tenure, 113 Democrats voted with him. When he passed his first budget, 63 Democrats did.

Democratic Speaker Tip O'Neill gave his conservative Democrats room to work with a Republican president because he needed those Democrats to stay in the party. The Democratic Party was undergoing a transition, as FDR's New Deal coalition—Southern Democrats, labor, and urban and blue-collar voters—had started dissolving, with some voters gravitating toward the Republican Party. If some Democrats needed to side with the president in order to stay popular back home, that was fine, just as long as when they got reelected as Democrats they voted for O'Neill as Speaker, which they were likely to do if he gave them room to vote as their district and not their party dictated. And if O'Neill had a good relationship with his conservatives, it also made it easier for him to influence policy in the bills they ultimately supported with President Reagan.

In Congress today, fewer members need voters from outside their party to get elected. In 1984, when Reagan won reelection, 190 districts voted for a presidential candidate of one party and a House member of the other party.[30] In 2016, only 35 districts split their votes that way.[31]

In 2008, Barack Obama won only 34 districts represented by Republicans.[32] Four years later, only seventeen House Republicans represented districts that reelected Obama.[33] In 2016, Donald Trump won only 12 districts represented by Democrats.[34] Remember, Ronald Reagan won 144 Democratic districts in 1980.[35]

Split ticket voting is also disappearing in the Senate. During Nixon's and Reagan's terms, voters in more than half the states who voted for Republican presidential candidates picked Democrats for the Senate. By 2008, 20 percent of the senators from the states Obama won in 2008 were Republicans.[36]

In 2016, for the first time since 1916—which was the second election in which senators were chosen by popular vote—not a single state divided its political preferences.[37] Republicans won 22 Senate seats, all in states carried by President Donald Trump. Democrats won in a dozen states where Hillary Clinton prevailed.[38]

A political marriage of the kind Tip O'Neill and Ronald Reagan formed—as bumpy, acrimonious, and fraught as it was—would not be the same today because so few would attend the wedding.

How Split Ticket Voting Died

To lock in their partisan dominance, parties—particularly Republicans—have drawn congressional districts to maximize the power of their voters. When Barack Obama won reelection in 2012, he carried Pennsylvania by three hundred thousand votes. The state's Democratic congressional candidates collectively outpolled their GOP rivals by nearly one hundred thousand votes. But because Republicans had designed political lines to concentrate Democratic votes in just a few districts, Republicans still won thirteen of Pennsylvania's eighteen House seats.[39] Similarly, throughout the country, even though voters cast 1.4 million more ballots for Democratic House candidates than Republican ones in 2012, Republicans lost only eight seats and maintained control of the House.[40] When districts are drawn this way, members representing them only have to appeal to voters of their party to stay in office.

Demographic patterns have also contributed to voter homogeneity. "When people move, they also make choices about who their neighbors will be and who will share their new lives. Those are now political decisions," wrote Bill Bishop in his groundbreaking 2008 book *The Big Sort*. Voters who share the same cultural habits—churchgoing or hunting, for example—tend to vote for the same kinds of candidates. "The like-minded neighborhood," wrote Bishop, "supported the like-minded church, and both confirmed the image and beliefs of the tribe that lived and worshiped there."[41]

In 1976, fewer than a quarter of Americans lived in extreme landslide enclaves where a presidential candidate won by 20 points or more. By 2004, that share had doubled. Nearly half of all voters lived in landslide counties.[42]

House and Senate elections are now more deeply influenced by national issues, which squeezes out the local factors that encouraged lawmakers to be politically independent. "Fifty years ago, a New Jersey Democrat and a New Mexico Democrat faced different primary electorates," explains Morris Fiorina of Stanford and the Hoover Institution. "Today, both cater to coalitions of public sector workers, racial and ethnic minorities, and liberal cause groups like environmental and pro-choice organizations. Similarly, fifty years ago Ohio and Oregon Republicans depended on different primary electorates. Today both cater to business and professional organizations and conservative cause groups like taxpayers and pro-gun and pro-life groups."[43]

These organizations provide the money to pay for the campaign ads and digital strategies that get more expensive every year. In just the last ten years, the average amount raised to run for a House seat has increased by 50 percent to almost $2.2 million. The average raised for a Senate race has increased by 85 percent to almost $6 million. Winning races cost even more.[44]

Congressional and presidential candidates pulling money from the same pots grow more unified and aligned in their thinking and behavior because they're courting the same tiny audience of power brokers. Increasingly, the national issue voters focus on in both House and Senate races is the presidency. In 2018, the president was not on the ballot, but 60 percent of registered voters—the highest percentage in recent midterm elections—said they used their vote to send a message about

President Trump.[45] In 2010, 52 percent said the same about Barack Obama.[46]

The coagulation of parties has spurred the creation of national bogeymen. Democratic minority leader Nancy Pelosi was portrayed as a dark and shadowy figure in Republican television advertisements across America. According to the media analysis group Kantar/CMAG, Pelosi was featured in 21 percent of all Republican congressional ads in the 2018 general election.[47]

As parties calcify, ideological outliers disappear from within their ranks. According to the political scientist James Lo, conservative Democrats in Congress are now more liberal than the most liberal Republican House members; the most liberal Republican member of Congress is more conservative than the most conservative Democrat. There is no overlap. By contrast, in the 1960s, at times, 50 percent of lawmakers overlapped ideologically.[48]

Americans tell pollsters they want bipartisan cooperation, but those who actually vote don't value that as much. (Or they define bipartisanship as acquiescence by the other party to what their party believes.) In congressional elections, voters mostly pick the party and not the person, which means the member headed to Washington is encouraged to stick with the party and not behave like a person.

JUDGE SENATORS BY THEIR JUDGES

IN THE ERA OF CONGRESSIONAL ELECTIONS DOMINATED BY NATIONAL themes, it's easier for presidents to campaign for members of their party. They don't have to tailor each speech for Joe, Sam, or Carol. They can just make a general pitch.

In 1986, Ronald Reagan embarked on a thirteen-state tour for Republican senators in a last-ditch October effort to lift their chances before Election Day. A key part of his act concerned not senators, but federal judges. "Remember, the Senate has to confirm any judges I appoint," said Reagan. "We've given America tough laws and tough judges. So long as Republicans retain control of the Senate, we can go right on fighting crime." Later, he continued, "I just have to believe it's better to have a Republican running the Senate Judiciary Committee than a liberal Democrat like Teddy Kennedy."[49]

Appointing judges was a topic that appealed to Republican stalwart voters. The conservative concern about judges had its origin in the Supreme Court of liberal chief justice Earl Warren. Since the mid-fifties, Republican diehards had been railing against judicial opinions that they believed coddled criminals and encouraged a general permissiveness in American life. If Democrats took control of the Senate, Reagan warned, they would appoint "sociology majors" to the federal bench.[50]

In his effort to elect more senators, Reagan contributed to a shift in their job requirements. Voters focused on a senator's ability to confirm judges would care less about a candidate's legislative or leadership skills.

Increasingly, it mattered less whether a senator could negotiate for conservative policies in the Senate give-and-take—which requires adaptation, compromise, and emotional intelligence. Instead, it was important to simply hold a seat and vote with the president of your party. When Mitch McConnell raises money from Republican donors who think Maine's Susan Collins is not sufficiently ideological, he reminds them it was her vote that helped put Brett Kavanaugh on the Supreme Court. This is now true of all red-meat national issues like immigration and abortion. Interest groups enforce this. Senators must not waiver. So, for example, in the Democratic Party, it is extremely difficult for a candidate to oppose abortion rights. They will face constant resistance, regardless of what other qualifications they may have.

Congressional reforms have also made it harder for individual members to break out of the partisan pull. Members once had the ability to target spending to their home districts—so-called earmark spending for things like local infrastructure projects. They could build a local reputation on delivering benefits for their constituents that those constituents might value more highly than positions on national interest group issues.

Senator Collins argues that banning earmarks shifted power to the executive branch. "I was amazed when a Republican Congress abolished earmarks during the presidency of a Democrat," she says. "What we did was shift power away from Congress and vest it in the executive branch, which was controlled by the opposing party. And I will never understand why we did that, nor why we thought that federal employees and political appointees know better than we do what our states need."[51]

When appropriators in Congress can't determine where funds go, the president and his cabinet secretaries get to decide how to allocate the money. Earmarks were also the currency that gave lawmakers a reason to vote for bills that contained items the other political party liked, which encouraged bipartisanship: A member would tolerate something she didn't like if she was allowed to benefit from the passage of a line item that benefited her constituents and therefore benefited her politically.

Reagan also had his own reasons to keep voters focused on judges. It was an issue on which a president like Reagan, elected with the support of social conservatives, could show that he was delivering for his team. "It became evident after the first term that there was no way to make legislative gains in many areas of social and civil rights," said Bruce Fein, a Justice Department official. "The president has to do it by changing jurisprudence."[52] Reagan's communications director, Pat Buchanan, argued that the appointment of two justices to the Supreme Court would "do more to advance the social agenda—school prayer, anti-pornography, anti-busing, right-to-life, and quotas in employment— than anything Congress can accomplish in twenty years."[53]

When presidents and their allies make the political case that the president's appointment power is more important than legislation, voters start to look to the issue of appointments when picking presidents and senators, reducing the focus on the ability to make halting, imperfect progress by working with Congress. Donald Trump has employed this trend to its maximum effect. Giving conservatives their dream judicial appointments has contributed to this phenomenon in almost every Republican Senate race: Now, most Republican voters simply want to know whether the Republican running will support the president. A president campaigning for senators in a nationalized election centered around himself has an easy speech to make. He just needs to show up.

THE "BAD PEOPLE" PROBLEM

RONALD REAGAN USED TO SAY LIBERALS WEREN'T BAD PEOPLE, IT'S JUST that their ideas were wrong. That sentiment has been losing ground in recent years. Voters increasingly think the other side is made up of bad people. This undermines compromise, because no one wants their law-maker to compromise with evil.

In a YouGov poll in May 2019, eight in ten who identified with a party did not believe that those across the aisle share the same values. Two-thirds of Republicans regard Democratic policies as bad or dangerous (with 40 percent calling them "dangerous"). Nearly as many Democrats say the same about GOP policies: 63 percent say they are bad or dangerous, with 36 percent using the term "dangerous."[54]

In 2016, according to a Pew Research Center survey, 55 percent of Democrats and 58 percent of Republicans viewed the other party in deeply negative terms. That was a considerable increase from 2000, when only about a quarter of Democrats (23 percent) and Republicans (26 percent) had a very unfavorable view of the other party.[55]

These partisan attitudes bleed into our personal lives as well. In 1958, the Gallup Organization asked a random sample of Americans, "If you had a daughter of marriageable age, would you prefer she marry a Democrat or a Republican, all other things being equal?" Thirty-three percent of Eisenhower-era Democrats wanted their daughters to marry a Democrat, and 25 percent of Republicans wanted their daughters to marry a Republican. By 2016, 60 percent of Democrats and 63 percent of Republicans wanted only intraparty marriage.[56]

Since 1994, the Pew Research Center has been testing views on fundamental political beliefs. They've asked Democrats and Republicans general questions like whether regulations do more harm than good, whether black Americans face systemic racism, whether immigrants are a burden to society, and whether corporations make reasonable profits. In that year of political ferment that changed control of the House for the first time in forty years, members of the two major parties held positions on average only 15 percentage points apart on those issues.[57] Twenty-five years later, 36 points divide the parties. The partisan gap—the largest recorded in that poll—is much larger than the gap between the opinions of men and women, of black and white Americans, and of other socioeconomically differentiated groups.

In this environment, a president can't build a coalition to support healthcare legislation when the two parties fundamentally disagree on whether the government should be involved in healthcare at all. Nor can a president push for a lower corporate tax rate if members of one party think corporations already make unreasonable profits.

The partisan gap in how people view presidents is also as wide as ever. On average, during his two terms, Eisenhower enjoyed the approval of 49 percent of Democrats. Obama had the support of 14 percent of Republicans over the course of his presidency. Just 7 percent of Democrats approved of Trump in October 2019.[58]

If you don't recognize yourself in these starchy positions of both parties, it's likely you are not a political obsessive. You probably don't have a fresh tube of war paint, even if you might say you lean toward one party or another. Less partisan voters like you could force lawmakers to pay less attention to the diehards, but less partisan voters generally aren't as spirited and committed as the most righteous ones. Either the process has pushed voters who hold cross-partisan views aside, or they have retreated in disgust. Or, because they're more flexibly minded, temperate voters are not deeply engaged in the party nominating process. In the 2018 midterm elections, only around 20 percent of us voted in congressional primaries, which means the most active, passionate,

House Speaker Nancy Pelosi confronts President Trump over U.S. policy in Syria during a White House meeting in October 2019. The Trump White House released the photo with the president's caption "Nervous Nancy's unhinged meltdown!" Pelosi made it her cover photo on Facebook and Twitter.

and extreme voters ultimately pick the party candidates.[59] By the time everyone else joins in the process, during the general election, the available candidates have in many cases already been selected by the party's extremes. If you are a nominal member of a party, you might not like your side's offering, but the alternative—pushed to the ideological extreme by primary politics—is likely to be even more at odds with your basic views, so you vote for your team.

No Value in Reaching

For a member of Congress elected by voters who feel such strong antipathy toward the other party, compromise with a member of the opposing party, or with the opposing party's president, equals betrayal. When Republican senator Jeff Flake of Arizona bucked his party by asking for more time to investigate the charges against President Trump's Supreme Court nominee Brett Kavanaugh, the senator confessed he never would have been able to do so if he were up for reelection. "Not a chance," admitted Flake, who was retiring. "There's no value to reaching across the aisle. There's no currency for that anymore. There's no incentive."[60]

Partisan media reinforce this view, particularly on the Republican side. Conservatives fashioned their own networks to bypass the mainstream media and members of the Republican Party they deemed too cozy with American politics as it had been framed after the New Deal. The *National Review* was founded in opposition to Eisenhower's New Republicanism. Talk radio rose with the spirit that invigorated the Gingrich revolution. Fox News followed a similar path, becoming a network whose marquee talents deeply allied with Donald Trump.

Tribal groupings demand loyalty. "During this campaign, voters wanted to know one thing," said Senator Bob Corker about the 2018 elections. "Not policy, not anything else. They wanted to know if you were behind Donald Trump."[61]

The rise in partisan media has also diminished the power of party leaders in Congress. In the past, a member of Congress had to work within the institution to gain clout and fame. When Minnesota senator Hubert Humphrey tried to show off to the press as a freshman, Democratic leaders let him know his future would be brighter if he waited his turn and didn't make them look bad. They controlled the ladder of success, so Humphrey had to listen. Leaders could assert discipline through knuckle-wrapping, which allowed them to pursue long-term goals. Leaders were also insulated from popular pressure, which meant they could make these moves without heartburn.

Now members who can chant the best ideological liturgy hold the attention of voters glued to Twitter or their preferred cable channel, making it hard for leaders to keep order. Any deal making with the other party can be undermined by charismatic members with a direct line to the base crying heresy, regardless of that member's seniority.[62]

Donald Trump is an avid Fox News watcher, which means that an ambitious member of Congress can go on Fox and speak directly to its most important viewer. In the summer of 2019, the president nominated Congressman John Ratcliffe as his next director of national intelligence after admitting he liked Ratcliffe's pro-Trump comments on Fox News, turning the network into a kind of self-reinforcing state mouthpiece.[63] Proof that some boundaries remain, Senate Republicans sent word they would not confirm the unqualified congressman.

Pressure from members who have standing in the green room rather than the congressional cloakroom can overwhelm party leaders. Immediately after the Democrats took back control of the House in 2018, liberal members with a strong social media following like Alexandria Ocasio-Cortez of New York pushed Speaker Nancy Pelosi to act more boldly, calling on her to confront Donald Trump on his immigration policy and start impeachment proceedings. The press turned the early days of the 116th Congress into a conversation about the internal rumble between Pelosi and "the Squad," a small group of liberal freshmen that included Ocasio-Cortez.[64] The real political story at the time was that Democrats had come to power by winning forty-eight races in formerly Republican-held districts. Those winners did not run on a doctrinaire liberal message, but the media appeal of the charismatic liberals in the Squad drove the coverage. "That's like five people," Pelosi said, brushing off questions about liberal pressure she was getting but clearly frustrated that charismatic liberals were disproportionately dictating news coverage.[65]

In 2015, Speaker John Boehner resigned after his clash with Republican absolutists. The final donnybrook was initiated by Texas senator

Ted Cruz's gambit to shut down the government in order to force President Obama to abandon the Affordable Care Act, known as Obamacare. "The Bible says, beware of false prophets," Boehner told me on *Face the Nation.* "And there are people out there spreading noise about how much can get done. I mean, this whole idea that we were going to shut down the government to get rid of Obamacare in 2013, this plan never had a chance, but . . . a lot of my Republican colleagues who knew it was a fool's errand, they were getting all this pressure from home to do this. And so we have got groups here in town, members of the House and Senate here in town who whip people into a frenzy believing they can accomplish things that they know, they know are never going to happen."[66]

In an environment where partisans cause this kind of disruption over purity within their own party, it chills the ardor any member might have to reach out to a president of the other party. "I don't understand how you manage people in Congress in either party into seeing that some level of accommodation is in their interest," says Josh Bolten, former chief of staff to George W. Bush.[67]

Donald Trump's solution has been not to bother much with accommodation, going further in that absolutist direction than any other modern president. It's a brand of highly successful hardball politics that started before Trump and has diverged from presidents of the old style—notably the Republican president George H. W. Bush.

How to Create Contrast

Often we search hard for words to define our opponents. Sometimes we are hesitant to use contrast. Remember that creating a difference helps you. These are powerful words that can create a clear and easily understood contrast. Apply these to the opponent, their record, proposals, and their party:

decay, failure (fail) collapse(ing) deeper, crisis, urgent(cy), destructive, destroy, sick, pathetic, lie, liberal, they/them, unionized bureaucracy, "compassion" is not enough, betray, consequences, limit(s), shallow, traitors, sensationalists, endanger, coercion, hypocrisy, radical, threaten, devour, waste, corruption, incompetent, permissive attitude, destructive, impose, self-serving, greed, ideological, insecure, anti-(issue): flag, family, child, jobs; pessimistic, excuses, intolerant, stagnation, welfare, corrupt, selfish, insensitive, status quo, mandate(s) taxes, spend (ing) shame, disgrace, punish (poor . . .) bizarre, cynicism, cheat, steal, abuse of power, machine, bosses, obsolete, criminal rights, red tape, patronage.[1]

—DOCUMENT DISTRIBUTED TO FRESHMAN REPUBLICAN
MEMBERS OF THE HOUSE IN 1995 BY GOPAC,
THE POLITICAL ACTION COMMITTEE
HEADED BY CONGRESSMAN NEWT GINGRICH

Chapter 10

A New Era of Partisan Warfare

What is good for the president may well be good
for the country, but it is not necessarily good for
congressional Republicans. We need wedge issues
to beat incumbent Democrats.[2]

—CONGRESSMAN VIN WEBER OF MINNESOTA, 1990

IN 1984, WHILE PRESIDENT RONALD REAGAN WAS SPARRING WITH
but also working with Tip O'Neill, Georgia congressman Newt Gingrich was scrambling up the ranks by promoting a tougher form of
politics. Gingrich baited O'Neill into a fight by criticizing Democrats'
national security record. He did so on the floor of the House, late in the
day, when the chamber was empty and none of the named were there
to defend themselves in front of the C-SPAN cameras that captured the
attack. O'Neill thundered the next day that the sneak attack was "the
lowest thing that I have ever seen in my thirty-two years in the House."
His words in the House chamber broke the rules of the body, which
prohibit criticizing a fellow member. Gingrich's allies immediately
asked that they be stricken from the record, which they were, a ceremonial rebuke of O'Neill.[3] It was deft: By using new technology, Gingrich
undermined Democrats and set a trap. When O'Neill fell in, Gingrich
used the ancient norms to punish him.

In the fracas that ensued, O'Neill's number two, Congressman Jim
Wright of Texas, appealed for fellow feeling to members of both parties.
"Nerves are tight like a cotton clothesline after a rain," calmed the rep-
resentative from north Texas. "I rose here to try to assuage that, to try to

put it at rest, to try to make Members feel a little more kindly toward one another."[4]

Five years later, Gingrich would spearhead the move to push out then Speaker Wright. In May 1989, Wright resigned in the wake of sixty-nine ethics charges, including accepting improper gifts and circumventing House rules on outside income through bulk sales of his book, *Reflections of a Public Man*.[5] Gingrich had cast Wright as a malevolent force of the left, skewering him as "the most corrupt Speaker in the twentieth century," a man "so consumed by his own power that he's like Mussolini."[6] Wright's resignation marked another ascension in Gingrich's rise to power, as he educated his colleagues in the win-at-all-costs mindset. One of Gingrich's key tactics was demonizing Democrats. They weren't just wrong, Gingrich deemed them "evil" and "enemies of normal Americans."[7] As Gingrich once correctly said, "The number one fact about the news media is that they love fights. When you give them confrontations, you get attention; when you get attention, you can educate."[8]

Congressman Newt Gingrich led a wildly successful assault on forty years of Democratic rule in the House of Representatives, ushering in an era of brass knuckle politics. Some Republicans of the old order would become casualties.

President George H. W. Bush also reflected on Wright's departure: "In spite of the present situation I believe the Wright tenure was one of effectiveness and dedication to the Congress of the United States."[9] The difference between how Gingrich and President Bush regarded Wright offered a tidy example of the split between the collegiality and restraint of the World War II generation and the cheerful knee-to-the-groin ethos of the young conservatives. That split would have its most cinematic display on a fall afternoon in one of the signature moments marking the new relationship between presidents and partisans in Congress.

September 30, 1990, President Bush stood in the White House Rose Garden before a bank of Brooks Brothers suits containing the leaders of Congress. The government was set to run out of money that day. That's a familiar story to contemporary ears, but the remarks those men made would sound less familiar. The Republican president praised the Democratic leaders, and they praised him right back. Congressional leaders of both parties praised one another. It wasn't just the frivolous Washington meringue of bromides either. They thanked each other for the brutal, slogging efforts that had brought about an agreement. The president and assembled lawmakers announced a Budget Summit Agreement, a mix of spending reductions and tax increases aimed at taming deficits. The agreement capped five months of intense wrangling, which ended in a sprint of negotiations. For eleven days and nights at Andrews Air Force Base, meat-fed men (Monday was prime rib night) debated. The outcome was one the framers would have approved of: Lawmakers of strong opinions representing each branch compromised rather than resorting to open conflict or shutting down the government. The compromise yielded imperfect results but ones preferable to inaction.

That was one way to see it. The alternative view was that leaders of both parties had shed their principles. No one had done so more than Bush himself, having gone back on a "no new taxes" pledge he had made at the GOP convention two years earlier in the 1988 campaign.[10] The latter sentiment played out on one side of CNN's split-screen coverage that overcast day. Juxtaposed with Bush and congressional leaders appeared footage of Representative Newt Gingrich exiting the White House. The second-ranking House Republican refused to add his frame to the bank of suits, or to follow behind his party's president. "It was a betrayal of his pledge and a betrayal of Reaganism," Gingrich said.[11] He headed back to the Hill, where the new breed of Republicans waited to swarm him as a rebel hero.

Bush's decision sowed the seeds of his defeat in the 1992 election. "It did destroy me," Bush later revealed to his biographer, Jon Meacham, in *Destiny and Power*.[12] After this, it was taken as truth that no Republican politician could survive disappointing the party's conservative core. "Why am I running?" Pat Buchanan asked the day he announced his primary challenge to George H. W. Bush in the 1992 election. "Because we Republicans can no longer say it is all the liberals' fault. It was not some liberal Democrat who declared, 'Read my lips, no new taxes,' then broke his word to cut a seedy backroom budget deal with the big spenders on Capitol Hill."[13] Bush saw the fundamental nature of governing differently from Gingrich. "I was elected to govern and to make things happen and my . . . view is, you can't do it through confrontation," he said.[14]

This is not the cover of the 1990 Brooks Brothers fall catalog, but President Bush and congressional leaders of both parties announcing their hard-fought budget agreement. Bush's reversal of his "no new taxes" pledge would cost him the presidency.

The split screen that day encapsulated the dilemma for modern presidents: Work with the other side and accept the title of traitor, or refuse to work with them and get nothing done. Days after the Rose

Garden ceremony, the deal announced there collapsed. Liberal Democrats voted against their leaders because they wanted more government spending. Conservative Republicans voted against their leaders because they opposed tax increases and wanted more spending cuts. Republicans running for reelection in the 1990 midterm elections needed their base to turn out at the polls, and the base is not inspired by capitulation. "What is good for the president may well be good for the country, but it is not necessarily good for congressional Republicans," Representative Vin Weber of Minnesota, a Gingrich ally, told *The Washington Post* at the time. "We need wedge issues to beat incumbent Democrats."

Eight years later, Newt Gingrich fell victim to the forces he had unleashed. Heading into the 1998 election, the Speaker predicted big Republican gains in House elections. When the opposite happened and Republicans lost several seats, a number of different factions that had already been grumbling about Gingrich called for his removal. The cabal consisted in part of conservatives who accused the Speaker of betraying their principles.[15] Facing purity attacks of the kind that he had taught his protégés to wield, the Speaker resigned, charging that "cannibals" within the House GOP conference wanted to destroy the party from within.

CONTROL SWAPPING

THE REAGAN AND O'NEILL AGREEMENT ON SOCIAL SECURITY IN 1983 coincides with the end of one party's dominance in Congress and the rise of permanent combat over institutional control that Newt Gingrich exemplifies. For decades after 1932, Democrats were essentially the majority party in Congress. Between 1980 and 2018, however, the Senate majority has changed hands six times. The House majority shifted four times during the same period. Political scientist Frances Lee has argued the constant back-and-forth has fundamentally changed the incentives for members because every election offers a chance for a change in party control.

"Intense party competition for institutional control focuses members of Congress on the quest for partisan political advantage," writes Lee. "Members and leaders of both parties invest more effort in enterprises to promote their own party's image and undercut that of the op-position."[16]

This makes Congress less effective and nastier. The minority party has no incentive to work with the majority for fear of relegating them-selves to permanent minority status by adding to the lustre of the party in the majority. You can't froth up your voters to cast the bums out if the bums have been achieving things you've voted for. The majority and minority do not work on the most important issues, but on issues that highlight differences with the other party and keep their coalitions intact. When you highlight those differences, the authors of fundrais-ing letters, rattling the cup for more money for your next race, have ready material and can claim the other side threatens the health of the republic. In 2014, when Republicans controlled the House, they did not confront the difficult question of immigration reform, instead push-ing the issue aside for fear that internal party division would make them vulnerable in the election and risk losing or weakening control of the chamber.

In the earlier era, before party control switching in Congress was the norm, Democrats extended deference to the leaders of the opposite party. In December 1988, after George H. W. Bush had won, Demo-cratic House Ways and Means chairman Dan Rostenkowski, perhaps the most powerful committee chairman in Congress, promised that he would "avoid embarrassing the new President on taxes for one year."[17] The chairman could afford that deference. Democrats held a 10-seat advantage in the Senate and an 81-seat margin in the House. Bush knew this too, of course, which meant he had to work with—and give in to—Rostenkowski in order to make the progress he wanted.

Twenty years later, the battle for majority status helped kill the hon-eymoon. "If you act like you're the minority, you're going to stay in the minority," House Republican Whip Kevin McCarthy told his GOP troops in 2009 after Obama was elected. "We've gotta challenge them on every single bill."[18] In the Senate at about the same time, Mitch McConnell said his main priority as the leader of the minority was to make Barack Obama a one-term president.[19]

Party switching also makes it hard to get work done. Legislating re-quires institutional knowledge and a system for managing a complex process. Committee chairmen with experience can develop that process. New presidents often rely on those grooves to make progress toward their goals. That's harder to do if the president is new and the majority staff has just retaken control.

When elections aren't making things topsy-turvy, well-intentioned reforms in Congress dilute this expertise. In 1994, when Republicans took control of Congress, they voted to limit committee chairmen to six-year terms. This limit was intended to discourage fiefdoms, freshen thinking with new blood, and give the Speaker the power and control necessary in an era of nationalized politics when parties want to cohere around one unified message and not be defined by powerful committee chairmen. However, it also meant all of those committee chairmanships would be turning over in 2000, when George W. Bush was elected. The new president was getting his sea legs just as the leaders in the House were settling in. "I understand the instinct," says Karl Rove, who served as deputy chief of staff under Bush. "When you're a Republican and you have term limits it means you don't have somebody who has been there and a staff that has been there and a structure that you can deal with. When you have to deal with the congressional leadership it's sort of nice if there's some stability, but if there's instability, you come in and the chairman of the Armed Services Committee is only in his second year."[20]

The instability of Congress is now the new normal in American politics. A hero president might break through the current system and make it work better, but it's not clear that the current system is susceptible to heroism or in a mood to elevate that kind of hero. Plus, the search for a presidential savior is itself a sign of how far off track things have gotten. The framers hoped to create a system which would force balance in all the ways the current system has come to work against that balance.

"No Intrusion from the President"

"The most eminent senators . . . would have received as a personal affront a private message from the White House expressing a desire that they should adopt any course in the discharge of their legislative duties that they did not approve. If they visited the White House, it was to give, not to receive, advice. Any little company or coterie who had undertaken to arrange public policies with the president and to report to their associates what the president thought would have rapidly come to grief. . . . Each of these stars kept his own orbit and shone in his sphere, within which he tolerated no intrusion from the president or from anybody else."[1]

— Massachusetts Senator George F. Hoar, 1903

Chapter 11

On the Separation of Powers

—

The great security against a gradual concentration of the
several powers in the same department consists in giving to
those who administer each department the necessary
constitutional means and personal motives to
resist encroachments of the others.[2]

— JAMES MADISON, FEDERALIST NO. 51

A frame, a scheme, a system, a combination of powers for a
certain end, viz the good of the whole community.[3]

— JOHN ADAMS

THERE IS NO REFEREE IN A PICKUP BASKETBALL GAME. PLAYERS
abide by a common understanding of the rules of the game, which
keeps it from turning into rugby. Every player presses their advantage,
but when there is an obvious foul, the injured party speaks up, the person who committed the foul fesses up, and an accommodation is made.
Play ball. The interruption is so short that the players' sweat barely has
time to cool. The commitment to individual success and team success
does not override the broader spirit that is necessary for the game to be
played.

This is also how the founders conceived of the rules separating the
political branches. Each would push their advantage but would recognize when they went too far and abide by the shared ethos of the system.

Over time, however, the balance has been disrupted in the same

*Professor Woodrow Wilson stumped for the League of Nations but was
ultimately thwarted by the Senate, a body he referred to as "a little group
of willful men, representing no opinion but their own," which has "rendered
the great Government of the United States helpless and contemptible."*

way that balance can collapse in a pickup basketball game. An afternoon at the local playground goes sour when a single player gets too
aggressive, hacks away at opponents, or cries foul when another player
merely looks at them sideways. Such spoilsports usually come from
outside the neighborhood, or they're somebody's friend. They ruin the
game. They're not invited back.

An equivalent behavior threatens the presidency. The founders expected that presidents would act with energy, but that they would also
show deference. There would be clashes, but a virtuous president
would abide by the spirit of the balance. In this conception of the office, the president would be an advocate for his branch, but also a steward of the larger separation of powers system. When another player
cried foul, the president would not press his interest to the maximum
extent. This would keep the pickup game going.

This spirit animated the delegates to the Constitutional Convention
during their discussion of the presidential veto power as a way to check
Congress from going too far. While weighing whether to allow Con-

gress to override a presidential veto, some delegates argued there would be no reason to give Congress that power because it would never come to that. If a president saw that Congress really favored a course of action, he would stand aside and not oppose its will.

The framers chose to allow Congress to override the president, but for much of the early republic, presidents deferred to that branch's powers. When William Henry Harrison ran for president in 1840 he did not talk about policy, because, he said, to do so would encroach on Congress's prerogative.[4] Congress made the laws and the president simply executed them.

In 1907, Woodrow Wilson, in his study of how the Senate interacted with the presidency—a post he would take six years later—wrote about the "unmistakable condescension with which the older members of the Senate regard the President of the United States." Senior senators treat the president "at most as an ephemeral phenomenon," because they have served longer than presidents and their "experience of affairs is much mellower than the President's can be; [they look] at policies with steadier vision than the President's; the continuity of the government lies in the keeping of the Senate more than in the keeping of the executive, even in respect to matters which are of the especial prerogative of the presidential office. A member of long standing in the Senate feels that he is the professional, the President an amateur."[5]

In 1969, when Vice President Spiro Agnew asked Idaho Republican senator Len Jordan if the administration had his vote, the senator replied curtly, "You can't tell me how to vote! You can't twist my arm!" Afterward Jordan announced the "Jordan Rule." If the vice president or anyone else from the administration tried to trample on the separation of powers by lobbying him on anything, he would vote the other way. Agnew later apologized.[6]

Today this spirit is largely gone. A president drives his party in Congress and is considered derelict if he doesn't take advantage of every opening—real or imagined. Presidents now determine whether the country goes to war, though the Constitution vests that power in Congress. Presidents set the tone on foreign affairs, either by dominating Congress or by going around Congress and paying no price for it.[7] Presidents choose not to interpret laws, as Barack Obama did with the Defense of Marriage Act, or to interpret them in ways at odds with congressional intent, as the Obama administration was accused of with the Affordable Care Act.

Passage of bipartisan bills like measures to confront opioid addiction or reduce mass incarceration pass either because the need is so overwhelming and immediate, as was the case with deaths from opioid overdoses, or because coalitions form in both parties outside Washington, pressuring lawmakers for different reasons from each ideological side. In many areas, the president is encouraged to push because Congress either doesn't act or has shown it will give in when a president pushes. "Congress chose to abdicate by choosing not to govern," says NYU public service professor Paul Light. "It has totally acquiesced to the White House."[8]

Members of Congress agree that they've lost sway, and they're sad about it. "We should have three coequal branches," Senator Ron Johnson told *Meet the Press* moderator Chuck Todd in February 2019. "Right now, the presidency is probably the most powerful, and then the Court. And Congress is really diminished. And we should start taking back that congressional authority. It'd return that balance. But that's the way it is. And again, particularly when Congress has given the president authority, it's really when that president's authority is even stronger than just what's written in the Constitution."[9]

This sounds good in theory, but senators mostly press to take back authority only when it is in the hands of a president of the other party. President Trump knew he would face no real opposition from his Republican allies in Congress when he denied Congress's will and diverted money to build a border wall or blocked congressionally mandated money for Ukraine.[10]

The Government Accountability Office found that Trump had delayed that money illegally, but his allies in Congress were not concerned that he had usurped their authority. When Trump was impeached by the House for doing so, they compounded this acquiescence by supporting and in some cases applauding his lawyers' claim that Congress had no right to check any presidential abuse of power.[11]

Republican majority leader Mitch McConnell said several times that Senate Republicans were waiting to hear from President Trump before moving forward on legislation; he feared no outcry for letting the executive branch have total say.[12] It made good political sense. Your political fortunes in Senate races are determined by national feelings about the president, so you don't want to do anything the president might dislike or that makes the president look bad politically.

Donald Trump has remade the Senate Republicans just as he has the Republican Party. Ambitious senators of the new generation, such as Tom Cotton, Ted Cruz, Lindsey Graham, and Marco Rubio, don't just support the president's programs, they risk their credibility to defend him. Nikki Haley, who once censured Trump for his rhetoric during his 2016 campaign, has adopted his jagged-edged style. After Trump ordered an air strike to kill an Iranian general in early 2020, the former UN ambassador claimed that the "only" people "mourning the loss" of the general were "Democrat leadership and our Democrat presidential candidates."[13]

When newly elected Senator Mitt Romney of Utah criticized Trump's character in a *Washington Post* opinion piece in 2019,[14] the blast from fellow Republicans was steady. In an editorial titled "Romney's Harsh Trump Critique Shows Why He Lost to Obama in 2012," *Investor's Business Daily* wrote, "What's at issue is a newly elected Republican senator has used a plainly anti-Trump newspaper to trash a sitting U.S. president. You might think Romney would wait until he himself had done something in the Senate."[15]

When Mitt Romney became the first senator to ever vote to impeach a president of his party, he did so citing his commitment to his oath of office and oath to God. The president vilified him and the White House targeted him for retribution.[16]

In 1938, the idea of senators swaying in such synchronicity moved former president Herbert Hoover to a Nazi analogy. "Mr. Hitler also has a parliament," said Hoover. "You may not know it. It was also once upon a time an independent arm of the German government. But Mr. Hitler has rearranged its function. I quote him: 'Individual members may advise but never decide; that is the exclusive prerogative of the responsible president for the time being.'"[17]

Lockstep unity between a president and members of Congress in the same party would lead to "the malignant growth of personal power," warned Hoover. "Liberty never dies from direct attack. No man ever arises and says 'Down with Liberty.' Liberty has died in 14 countries in a single score of years from weakening its safeguards, from demoralization of the moral stamina of the people. . . . If we examine the fate of wrecked republics throughout the world we find their first symptoms in the weakening of the legislative arm. Subservience in legislative halls is the spot where liberty and political morals commit suicide."[18]

In his speech decrying the consolidation of the Democratic Party, Hoover read headlines from Democratic papers saying that even they didn't support the idea. "*The New York Times* exclaims: 'How great an intellectual servitude the President now requires from his followers.'" Quoting from a Lynchburg, Virginia, paper, Hoover read: "Are the people of the forty-eight states to select their representatives in Congress or is the President of the United States to perform that duty for them and thereby become a national dictator?"[19] Were Hoover alive today, he would have an easier time finding a partisan paper criticizing senators for being out of lockstep with the president than one worrying about whether the party regularly marched too precisely in step with him.

FDR, *depicted here as a hulking Oliver Twist, overwhelms his masters in Congress with demands for more power. The president was arguing he could not do his job without more authority. "The president's task has become impossible for me or any other man," said Roosevelt.*

STEP BACK TO THE FRAMERS

IT IS NOT FROM THE BENEVOLENCE OF THE BUTCHER, THE BREWER, or the baker that we expect our dinner, Adam Smith explained. William Galston of the Brookings Institution connects this famous formulation to the framers, who shaped the American system of government around an identical view of political self-interest.[20] They believed it was not the virtue of presidents and members of Congress that brings liberty and security. By building a governmental system that acknowledged, anticipated, and accommodated self-interest and ambition, the framers thought they could design a thriving government that could work in the real world, despite the low instincts of the human characters who cycled in and out of it.

The framers of the Constitution who created the separation and sharing of powers system would be terrified by its current flabby condition. To understand why requires a brief visit to the sweaty hall in Philadelphia where the delegates to the Constitutional Convention did their work in the summer of 1787. For four hot summer months they held a roiling debate about the nature of ambition and power and how each might warp Congress and the new office of the presidency they were creating.

The remedy on the drawing board was to consolidate national power, which included a robust executive office. Though just ten years earlier they had revolted against a tyrannical king, they were forced to look for more executive power because the presidency that existed under the Articles—known as President of the United States in Congress Assembled—was a watery and largely ceremonial post. It couldn't spur action, particularly when it came to defending the nation.

The president created under the Articles of Confederation was also unable to check Congress when it acted as a tool of popular passion. As much as the founders feared the tyranny of a king, they also worried about the mob. "The evils we experience flow from the excess of democracy," said delegate Elbridge Gerry of Massachusetts. "The people do not want virtue, but are the dupes of pretended patriots. They are daily misled into the most baneful measures and opinions by the false reports circulated by designing men, and which no one on the spot can refute."[21] The new office, this presidency they were creating, would have the power to act, but not so much power that it turned its occupant into a tyrant. "You must first enable the government to control the governed," James Madison wrote in Federalist No. 51, "and in the next place oblige it to control itself."[22]

The fifty-five men who met in Philadelphia were both eggheads and men of practical experience, not a bad model for our presidents today. They had read Aristotle, Plato, Cicero, Montesquieu, and Locke. They had studied human nature and read history to understand where the theory clashed with reality. They had also served in colonial assemblies, local conventions, and the Continental Congress, and as governors and members of the legislature. They included plantation owners, farmers, and merchants.

To design a system that could achieve these dual goals of action and restraint, the delegates to the Constitutional Convention examined the basics of human nature. Was ambition a good thing or a bad thing? How much power can a leader have before becoming a tyrant? How much natural virtue is required for the office? How should presidents be evaluated to know whether they can do their job? What are the qualities that make for success in the job? Who represents the people, and where should fealty to the people's voice begin and end? When and how should citizens and lawmakers stop abusive presidents? All of these questions, founded on the challenges of human nature, are still with us today.

The presidency the founders contemplated was a risk. The delegates were willingly inviting into government two forces they knew could destroy it: power and ambition. A president would need power to be effective, but power was a rapacious force. The framers referred to power as "a cancer," an "ocean" that had an "endlessly propulsive tendency to expand itself beyond legitimate boundaries," as Bernard Bailyn describes it in *The Ideological Origins of the American Revolution*.[23]

Men were no match for power's sway.[24] Patrick Henry warned, "If your American chief be a man of ambition, and abilities, how easy it is for him to render himself absolute."[25] Samuel Adams also argued that power could not be contained by any man. "Such is the depravity of mankind that ambition and lust of power above the law are predominant passions in the breasts of most men," he said. "[Power] converts a good man in private life to a tyrant in office."[26]

The founders were realistic about human weakness, but they believed that because they were so aware of its shortcomings, they could design a new government that not only accounted for man's weakness but used it to keep balance. "They did not believe in man," the historian Richard Hofstadter wrote of the framers, "but they did believe in the power of a good political constitution to control him."[27, 28]

Their government would take advantage of the ambitions and desire for power the way a pocket watch takes advantage of tension between the parts. Each branch of government in the separation of powers system would be aligned so that while the executive, judicial, and legislative branches might grind against each other, the collective interlocking nature of the system would allow that those branches' pushing against each other would keep the system running. "The great security against a gradual concentration of the several powers in the same department," wrote James Madison, "consists in giving to those who administer each department the necessary constitutional means and personal motives to resist encroachments of the others."

No one piece would spin faster than another, but all would spin together. "The doctrine of the separation of powers was adopted by the Convention of 1787, not to promote efficiency," wrote Supreme Court Justice Louis Brandeis in 1926, "but to preclude the exercise of arbitrary power. The purpose was not to avoid friction, but, by means of the inevitable friction incident to the distribution of the governmental powers among three departments, to save the people from autocracy."[29] If future generations could maintain the system, that would protect the values encased in it.

Designing a system that could achieve this balance took months of wrangling. The delegates "were perplexed with no part of this plan so much as with the mode of choosing the President," wrote Pennsylvania delegate James Wilson.[30] The very idea of handing power to a president was an invitation to abuse. "The first man put at the helm would be a good one," said Franklin, referring to his friend George Washington, but "Nobody knows what sort may come afterwards. The executive will always be increasing here, as elsewhere, till it ends in a monarchy."[31]

Madison, who must have gone through a barrel of ink as the official note taker, got a little tired of the delegates' endless obsession with how to circumscribe the president. He wrote to Jefferson, "as it respects the

Executive, [discussion] was peculiarly embarrassing. On the question whether it should consist of a single person, or a plurality of co-ordinate members, on the mode of appointment, on the duration in office, on the degree of power, on the re-eligibility, tedious and reiterated discussions took place."[32, 33] (Madison here identified the eighteenth-century equivalent of a phenomenon that still makes congressional deliberations drag on today: Everything has been said, but not everyone has said it.)

The debates trended to the tedious because the delegates were obsessed with balancing the distribution of power. Each time a grain of power was given to one branch, or removed from another, forces arrayed to argue for rebalancing the system to make sure the grains of power reached equipoise. Founders who argued one side of an issue jumped to the other side of the same issue depending on what the overall power picture looked like.[34, 35]

The debates always kept in mind the human impulses of the people who would serve as presidents in the future. The structure of government might change, but like gravity, human impulses would always be the same. Pennsylvania delegate Gouverneur Morris, who spoke more than anyone else at the Convention, argued, for example, that the nature of ambition meant the chief executive should not be limited to one term.[36] Anyone fit for the job would be ambitious, he explained. Close the door to a second term and that would stifle that ambition, which might encourage presidents to stay in office by force. Limitations, Morris said, "may give a dangerous turn to one of the strongest passions in the human breast. The love of fame is the great spring to noble and illustrious actions. Shut the civil road to glory and he may be compelled to seek it by the sword."[37]

The framers' obsession with balance offers some indication of how they might act if they saw the state of their carefully arranged system today—if they saw leaders in the legislative branch taking direction from the president about which laws to pass, or what legislation to even debate. Today, Supreme Court justices are presented as a method of wooing voters in elections for the president of the executive branch. Presidential action on foreign agreements, wars, and expenditures are only lightly massaged by a drowsy legislative branch originally entrusted with these responsibilities. The government lurches like a harried beast driven one way by executive overreach and then occasionally driven back the other way by the Solomonic decision of the single Supreme Court justice who occupies the ideological middle of the judicial branch.

Given their view of human nature, the founders would have greeted these kinds of imbalances with the pale face of horror. To allow the safeguard of equipoise to slip, they believed, would invite all the baleful effects of power, ambition, and mob rule to romp, just as surely as leaving the rabbit pen open would invite nearby wolves to dinner. They would have quoted Montesquieu: "When the legislative and executive powers are united in the same person or in the same body of magistrates, there can be no liberty."

The balance of powers system exists to do more than simply check the inevitable abuses of power. When Congress has a say, it brings in representation of a more diverse range of viewpoints. When it comes to war, for example, a president may want to act. Her job is to move, and everyone is looking at her. But members of Congress represent the districts and states where constituents have been fighting those wars for two decades. It is the "most exact transcript of the whole society," as delegate James Wilson put it.[38] They have a better understanding than the president about how those people doing the war-fighting feel. A system in balance allows both to be heard in making high-stakes decisions.

While there is debate over how literally to take each utterance from the men who crafted the founding instructions, it is clear from the spirit of their debates that they were obsessed with balance. A government in which power was wrongly distributed could create a president who was at once too powerful and yet not powerful enough to bring the system back into balance. It would also make bad laws. Nowadays, instead of looking to bolster Congress's powers and expect less from the president, we remain in thrall to the presidential habit. We still look to a president who, through force of will, can recalibrate the system and snap Congress into action. For this we should blame Lyndon Johnson.

"IF WE FAIL ON THIS, THEN WE'LL FAIL ON EVERYTHING."

LYNDON B. JOHNSON: We're going to have to get a discharge petition. I can't say that myself, but it's already filed and we're going to either rise or fall. . . . And I think if there's ever a time when you really talk to every human you could, even the boys in Houston and any other doubtful areas, you ought to do it. I don't think it ought to come from me. If we could possibly get that bill out of the rules committee—they won't even give them a hearing . . . that means we've got to get about 219. We'll start at about 150 Democrats. That means we've got to get sixty, seventy Republicans.

DAVID MCDONALD: Well, fine.

JOHNSON: They'll be saying they don't want to violate procedure—

MCDONALD: Yes, I can imagine that.

JOHNSON: —our answer will have to be, "Well, a man won't give you a hearing at all." That's the way they treat [Lee Harvey] Oswald in Dallas. They just shoot him down without a hearing. A man's entitled to a hearing. And if they won't give you a hearing, let's get the hearing on the floor. But I sure wish you'd give that your personal attention and see that every man that you've got is up there next week talking to them. And I don't want it coming from me.

MCDONALD: I will do it.

JOHNSON: But if we could get that, that would almost ensure passage in the Senate, because they could see it—we had the power to discharge them and therefore we'd have the power to apply cloture.

. . .

MCDONALD: Okay, Mr. President. I'll have all of my legislative people report to Nordy [Hoffman] immediately.

JOHNSON: You tell Nordy [Hoffman] I appreciate very much his working with us—never needed him as much as now—but don't be quoting the fact that I'm calling you, because—that'll just create problems.

McDONALD: Mr. President. I'll go to working—we've already telegraphed all of our local unions.

JOHNSON: I know that.

McDONALD: We'll have all of our people . . . report to Washington right away.

JOHNSON: That's right. I just—I'd keep that out of the paper. I'd do it quietly . . . I'd just say, "We've been talking for a hundred years. And they won't give us a hearing on this thing, so we've got to do something about it."

McDONALD: Alrightly, I'll do that.

JOHNSON: Until we get 219, we'll be a failure. And if we fail on this, then we'll fail on everything.[1]

—NOVEMBER 29, 1963, PRESIDENT JOHNSON ENLISTS
DAVID McDONALD, PRESIDENT OF THE
UNITED STEELWORKERS OF AMERICA, IN AN EFFORT
TO START STALLED CIVIL RIGHTS LEGISLATION.

Chapter 12

Just Be Like LBJ!

———

Don't let those [liberal] bomb throwers, now, talk you out of
seeing Dirksen. You get in there to see Dirksen. You drink
with Dirksen! You talk with Dirksen! You listen to Dirksen![2]

— LBJ TO HUBERT HUMPHREY

Why don't *you* get a drink with Mitch McConnell?[3]

— BARACK OBAMA

*Lyndon Johnson allied with Dr. Martin Luther King, Jr., to push Congress
to do what it was unprepared to do. "I want to tell you how grateful I am,
and how worthy I'm going to try to be of all your hopes," he told the civil
rights leader in a phone call on November 25, 1963. Cautious aides
counseled patience, but he dismissed their concerns, asking:
"Well, what the hell is the presidency for?"*

VERY PRESIDENT JOLTS ALONG THE DISAPPOINTING ROAD ON which hope is replaced by experience, but Woodrow Wilson had a particularly jarring ride. As a political science professor, he had proclaimed that a president "is at liberty, both in law and conscience, to be as big a man as he can."[4] Once in office, he learned how limiting the job could be. In 1917, railing against an unproductive Senate after his plans had been stymied by the body's tradition of unlimited debate through filibuster, Wilson pointed the finger at "a little group of willful men, representing no opinion but their own . . . [who] have rendered the great government of the United States helpless and contemptible."[5]

Today, the filibuster vexes presidents even more than it did President Wilson. Anything the majority wants to pass through the Senate requires 60 votes to close off the unlimited debate the minority can engage in through a filibuster. That means a president needs sixty senators to vote with him to pass anything difficult. Donald Trump regularly pressures Mitch McConnell to get rid of the filibuster so that legislation can pass with a simple majority. McConnell has resisted, arguing that someday Republicans will be in the minority again and they will want the filibuster to help block the majority from doing as they please.

Despite the blockages, presidential candidates find willing applause from audiences eager to hear promises that when they take office, bipartisan cooperation will return. In 2008, Barack Obama told Steve Kroft on 60 Minutes, "One of the things I'm good at is getting people in a room with a bunch of different ideas, who sometimes violently disagree with each other, and finding common ground and a sense of common direction."[6]

By the end of the Obama administration, the level of disagreement between parties was even greater than before, but that didn't stop Hillary Clinton in 2016 from campaigning on a groovy version of successful compromise. She committed that as president she would "bring people from right, left, red, blue, [and] get them into a nice, warm, purple space where everybody is talking and where we're actually trying to solve problems."[7] Donald Trump promised he'd work similar bipartisan magic: "With Congress, you have to get everybody in a room and you have to get them to agree. I'm really a great negotiator. I know how to negotiate. I like making deals, preferably big deals."[8]

The power of the charismatic actor who claims to be able to get everyone in the room to reach an agreement carried over to the 2020 campaign. Vice President Joe Biden pointed to his thirty-six years as a senator from Delaware. "I'm the only one who has passed major pieces of legislation across the board," boasted Biden, before listing those pieces of legislation: "The Violence Against Women Act, the assault weapons ban and the Chemical Weapons Treaty. By bringing Democrats and Republicans together."[9] (All of those bills passed fifteen years ago, proof, some would say, that the model of congressional compromise is an antique one.)

Why does the idea of the magical negotiator-president persist? One reason is President Lyndon Johnson. He secured the right to vote for Southern blacks and created Medicare and Medicaid. He did all of it with a cinematic flourish. Photographs and telephone recordings testify to a colorful and sweeping display of his special talent for negotiating. Johnson is also the only president who had been a Senate majority leader, in which role he had honed special skills.

Johnson's success has encouraged the idea that personal application of attention can solve problems. His example fuels the legislative action hero image of the presidency, which for a period during 2013 caused news coverage to fixate on why President Obama would not "schmooze" with Republican lawmakers. "The president has got to start inviting people over for dinner," Michael Bloomberg, former New York City mayor, advised during Obama's tenure. "He's got to play golf with them. He has to pick up the phone and call and say, 'I know we disagree on this, but I just want to say—I heard it was your wife's birthday' or 'your kid just got into college.' He has to go build friendships."[10]

Pundits regularly advised Obama to sit down and have a drink with Senate minority leader Mitch McConnell, in the same way Truman sipped bourbon with congressional leaders. "Really? Why don't *you* get a drink with Mitch McConnell?" Obama joked in response. By the end of his first term, the president and his aides had given up entirely on the idea of making deals with Republicans, because they concluded that if they made a deal on immigration, for example, the Republican base would punish, or threaten to punish, the cooperating members of their party, and the deal would collapse. Privately, little irked Obama more than the claim that he should do more to work with an opposition that he believed had no interest in working with him.

The opposition has a different view. McConnell describes negotiating with Obama like a visit to the principal. Obama would offer lectures about how wrong McConnell and his fellow Republicans were. Joe Biden, on the other hand, was someone McConnell could work with, said the Republican leader, and with whom he negotiated budget and tax agreements. What was the difference? Biden spent his time more effectively. "Joe . . . made no effort to convince me that I was wrong," wrote McConnell, "or that I held an incorrect view of the world. He took my politics as a given, and I did the same, which was what allowed us to successfully negotiate."[11]

Democratic senators in the Obama years are also critical. "Obama had no real personal chemistry with members that weren't in the circle," said one. "He had his pets but he did not cultivate relationships" outside that. He never called to say, "Okay, what are the two things you need us to do that could be really helpful?" When you went to the Oval, it was very formal. . . . He's funny, and I think he's smart but he's basically an introvert."[12]

The difference between Obama and Biden is an echo in miniature of Kennedy and Johnson. Kennedy tried to work Congress but he just wasn't as good at it. "I never realized how powerful the Senate was," Kennedy complained, "until I left it and came up to this end of Pennsylvania Avenue."[13] It wasn't that Kennedy didn't spend the time trying, he just didn't have the instincts. Similarly, Obama had not "climbed the greasy poll of politics," as Democratic leader Chuck Schumer put it when describing Obama's unfamiliarity with the source code of most members of Congress.

Still, a look at the relationship between Senate leaders and the presidents during the Johnson era and today explains why replicating Johnson's effectiveness requires more than just presidential schmoozing skill and willpower. In 1954, as Senate minority leader, LBJ, a Democrat, helped Republican president Eisenhower defeat conservative Republican John Bricker's amendment to limit presidential power in foreign affairs.[14] As president, Johnson worked with the leader of the opposition party in a similar way. Republican minority leader Everett Dirksen helped Johnson pass civil rights legislation over the opposition of conservative Democrats and Republicans.

"You and I are going to get Ev," Johnson told Senator Hubert Humphrey, later his vice president, about working with Dirksen to break the Southern filibuster of the Civil Rights Act. "It's going to take time. We're going to get him. You make up your mind now that you've got to spend time with Ev Dirksen. You've got to let him have a piece of the action. He's got to look good all the time. Don't let those [liberal] bomb throwers, now, talk you out of seeing Dirksen. You get in there to see Dirksen. You drink with Dirksen! You talk with Dirksen! You listen to Dirksen!"[5]

In June 1968, months before the election, Chief Justice Earl Warren announced his retirement from the Supreme Court. Johnson nominated his friend and fellow Texan, Homer Thornberry, an Appeals Court judge, to the Court and proposed elevating Associate Justice Abe Fortas, also a friend of his, to the position of Chief Justice. Republican Minority Leader Dirksen agreed to help him do it.

Forty-eight years later, Barack Obama faced a similar situation. On his way out of office, he was presented with a Supreme Court vacancy in an election year. The difference this time was the political climate of partisanship, with the Republican Party in the majority and its leader wielding more power. Within a few hours of the announcement of Associate Justice Antonin Scalia's death, Senate majority leader Mitch McConnell announced he would not let the Senate take up any nomination Obama might make. "The American people should have a voice in the selection of their next Supreme Court Justice. Therefore, this vacancy should not be filled until we have a new president," declared McConnell.[16]

McConnell was repeating the identical argument that had been used when Johnson was president and had a vacancy to fill. In 1968, conservative Republican senator Robert Griffin of Michigan had tried the same gambit. "In this century there have been no 'lame duck' nominations to the Supreme Court," said Griffin, "made by a president in the final year of his last term in office."[17] The Republican leader, Everett Dirksen, dismissed Griffin's made-up rule about lame duck presidents as "frivolous, diaphanous and gossamer." When the leader was asked about whether Griffin would continue to push the case, Dirksen erupted. "No one challenges my leadership, nothing happens around here without me."[18]

Denied the chance to make up a new rule, Griffin and a group of Republican senators threatened to filibuster President Johnson's picks, and GOP nominee Richard Nixon spoke out from the campaign trail, claiming that while he wasn't going to weigh in on who Johnson had selected, he did not support blocking the president's choice by filibuster.

Fortunately for the Republicans, Fortas had to withdraw his nomination after a conflict of interest surfaced. Thornberry, who was tied to Fortas's ascension, never made it onto the Court, and Nixon got to make the call after he won in 1968, appointing Warren Burger to replace Earl Warren.

Fortunately for Donald Trump and the Republican Party, Mitch McConnell did not share Dirksen's interest in working with the president. Instead, he pressed his partisan advantage. Obama's nominee, Merrick Garland, was blocked, and Donald Trump was elected, in part (or in whole) because conservatives knew they could lock in a conservative seat on the Supreme Court by making him president.

It was a triumph for Republicans, but it came at a cost, Democrats say. "The question turns on whether or not you think you want to be able to have this exercise in self-government go on forever," says Senator Michael Bennet when reflecting on how McConnell blocked the Senate consideration of Merrick Garland for the Supreme Court.[19] Bennet argues that the norms that McConnell and Trump ignore are the undefined guardrails that allow the American system to operate. "If you don't care about that, if this is the end of the Roman Republic, it doesn't matter. You might as well grab everything that you can possibly grab. I have a more optimistic view of where we are and a more confident view in our democracy."

Bennet and others argue that if there is any chance for the O'Neill and Reagan kind of relationship to work in today's partisan politics, leaders have to stop short of pressing their maximum partisan advantage. Reagan and O'Neill restrained themselves from crossing certain boundaries in the interest of the longer-term goal of maintaining the working relationship between the institutions they led. When they did cross a line, they called each other to apologize; they joked to reestablish their baseline after brutal fights.

"Why don't you get a drink with Mitch McConnell?"
joked Barack Obama about the Republican leader, who redefined the
relationship between the branches by declaring that his goal was to
make Obama a one-term president.

Pressing things to the limit, as is fashionable today, just increases the acrimony and invites the other side to respond in kind, initiating a brutal tit for tat. Bennet also criticizes former Democratic Senate majority leader Harry Reid, who changed the Senate rules to make it easier for Barack Obama to confirm judges,[20] a rule Mitch McConnell has used to great effect.

Given how much the relationship between the president and Congress has changed since Johnson held office, perhaps the message of his presidency is not that his tactics can be repeated but that a modern president should try to replicate the creativity, dash, and focus Johnson applied to the task.

Johnson used John F. Kennedy's death to turn his predecessor's program into "a martyr's cause," as Johnson put it.[21] It would be ridiculous to suggest that a modern president could replicate those circumstances, or to wish for conditions that would allow him to, but Johnson's immediate recognition of the opportunity, and his immediate work to take advantage of it, represent an instinct for risk taking that a modern president might do well to emulate. LBJ's biographer Robert Caro details in *The Passage of Power*, Johnson was so constantly attuned to his per-

sonal power and prestige that even when he was weighed down by duties in the immediate aftermath of the assassination, he was calculating
how to build authority.[22] It's the kind of risk Donald Trump could have
embraced, for example, with a grand immigration deal or sweeping
infrastructure program, or a risk that Barack Obama could have taken
to win a deal on a bipartisan budget agreement.

Steven Gillon in *The Pact: Bill Clinton, Newt Gingrich, and the
Rivalry that Defined a Generation* chronicles a set of secret negotiations between Bill Clinton and Newt Gingrich in 1998 when the two
leaders, like Reagan and O'Neill, met to discuss how they might hammer out a grand agreement on Social Security and Medicare entitle-
ments. Both men kept the discussions within a tiny group of close aides.
Despite their animosity and past acrimony, they both wanted to do
something big. The project fell apart in early 1998 when Clinton's affair with Monica Lewinsky was revealed, leading to a protracted partisan battle.

It's difficult to make progress in politics today, but Johnson didn't
exactly have a layup in defeating the segregationist South in the House
and Senate, including overcoming the resistance of his patron and
sometime ally Richard Russell of Georgia. He might have lost Southern support for the Democratic Party forever, as he predicted and as
came to pass, but he was courageous enough to take the chance.

As Todd Purdum sketches in *An Idea Whose Time Has Come*, Johnson knew what members of Congress needed, so he purchased votes by
working the other parts of the system. To shut off debate on civil rights
legislation, he flattered one senator by consulting him on Latin American affairs, won the vote of another by supporting a water project, and
banked a few more by arranging emergency aid and lending Air Force
Two over to both Alaska senators after that state's massive earthquake.[23]
"Time and again you hear him listening for the words," describes Robert
Caro, talking about what it is like to listen to Johnson talk to a member
of Congress. "What does this guy really want? I mean, it's almost palpable. You can hear what he's doing. And, of course, when Johnson finds
out what a guy really wants, he will work to give it to him."[24]

Johnson knew how to use flattery and self-abnegation in pursuit of
his goals. "I've got a surprise for you, Harry," Johnson wooed in a phone
call to Virginia senator Harry Byrd, whose vote he needed to pass a

budget, adding, "I've got the damn thing down under one hundred billion . . . way under," since Byrd was pushing for reduced federal spending. "It's only 97.9 billion. Now you can tell your friends that you forced the president of the United States to reduce the budget before you let him have his tax cut."[25] As the political commentator David Frum wrote, "If the price of being the winner was to look like the loser, Johnson would pay."[26]

IS THERE A BIPARTISAN DUTY?

THE CALL FOR PRESIDENTS TO SIT DOWN WITH THE LEADERS OF THE opposing party is a vestige of a time when presidents and lawmakers were less connected to their party, and parties were more ideologically, demographically, and geographically heterogeneous than they are today. Presidents could appeal to ad hoc coalitions in Congress, which formed around beliefs on specific issues. I've interviewed senior staffers in the Trump and Obama administrations, and these ideas about bipartisanship are either scoffed at or politely entertained—mostly for the reasons I've already outlined in the previous chapters. It is unimaginable that Republicans would drop resistance to a Democratic priority like Medicare for All in exchange for unrelated pork or goodies from the executive branch beneficial to their states. When Barack Obama tried this by offering a permanent exemption from the state share of Medicaid expansion to Senator Ben Nelson of Nebraska to win his vote for the Affordable Care Act, it was labeled the "Cornhusker Kickback," and had to be scrapped after a public outcry.[27] The level of secrecy in the negotiating process in the 1960s and tolerance for transactional politics would also be impossible in our modern media and social media age.

But if it's not possible to be LBJ, is the yearning for presidents to wear the LBJ cape a sign of a constant need in the electorate? Bipartisanship is hard, but is it still important in the American system to get caught trying? If the very idea of durable bipartisan solutions is under threat from virulent partisanship, isn't that an urgent national problem a president should tackle? Despite the challenge, no president would stop working to reduce unemployment just because it's hard for a president to control the economy.

Any president who made real bipartisan moves—large enough to compel action from the other side—might be taking a big political risk. Voters of both parties might very well not reward a president who puts together a bipartisan deal or even tries to. Bill Clinton helped pass the North American Free Trade Agreement to open commerce with Canada and Mexico on a bipartisan basis, and it was not a political boon. (Liberals didn't like it and Republicans didn't give him credit for it.) Trying might also expend a lot of time and undermine the final product. Barack Obama's effort to work with Republicans on the Affordable Care Act bore no fruit. He was told by Republicans not to make public statements on immigration reform or gun control for fear of spooking Republicans who might sign on if the legislation was closely associated with the president.

Still, the president is the leader of one of the Constitution's three branches: Isn't there a duty to contribute to the repair of the broken machine? "The political system acts against success for a president," says Mitch Daniels, who served as the director of the Office of Management and Budget under George W. Bush. "The new tribalism is right up there with the national debt as the biggest threat to our nation."[28] Former secretary of defense James Mattis agrees: The greatest threat America faces, he told me, is "the lack of political unity."[29]

Bipartisanship represents a great American tradition. "If you are cast away on a desert island with only a screwdriver, a hatchet, and a chisel to make a boat with, why, go make the best one you can," advised Teddy Roosevelt. "It would be better if you had a saw, but you haven't. So with men."[30] Or, as Ronald Reagan put it: "I'd learned while negotiating union contracts [as president of the Screen Actors Guild] that you seldom got everything you asked for. And I agreed with FDR, who said in 1933: 'I have no expectations of making a hit every time I come to bat. What I seek is the highest possible batting average.' If you got seventy-five or eighty percent of what you were asking for, I say, you take it and fight for the rest later, and that's what I told these radical conservatives who never got used to it."[31]

A president who can help America inch closer to a more durable and less vicious operating environment will be remembered for more than the sum of their tweets. Their actions will move the government back to operating collectively to address collective challenges. It will lighten a president's load by sharing the burden with Congress. A presidency that works in partnership with a Congress embracing its role as the strong first branch of government might not only make better laws, but will keep the country from turning to more violent options, as Ronald Reagan pointed out at a tribute to Tip O'Neill in 1986: "The fact of our friendship is testimony to the political system that we're part of and the country we live in, a country which permits two not-so-shy and not-so-retiring Irishmen to have it out on the issues rather than on each other or their countrymen."[32] Ronald Reagan knew that conflict did not always mean irrevocable gridlock. Even former enemies could be encouraged to work toward a common goal. He applied this broad vision to picking his White House staff too.

In the summer of 1855, Cyrus Hall McCormick, the inventor of the reaper, brought suit against a competitor, John Henry Manny. Manny's legal team included a roster of famous patent lawyers, including the brilliant Pittsburgh lawyer Edwin McMasters Stanton. Since the trial was to be held in Cincinnati, the team needed a local lawyer. Their first choice from nearby Illinois wasn't available, and they didn't think much of the second, the earthy Abraham Lincoln. "Why did you bring that damned long armed Ape here," Stanton asked his partner. "He does not know any thing and can do you no good." For the next several weeks the legal team ignored Lincoln, which is a hard thing to do with a man of his height. They stayed at the same hotel but "never conferred with him, ever had him at our table or sat with him, or asked him to our room, or walking to or from the court with him, or, in fact, had any intercourse with him," remembers one of Stanton's partners. Lincoln wrote a brief, but the fancy lawyers from the East Coast didn't read it. It was humiliating, and Lincoln complained of being "roughly handled by that man Stanton." He was so glum that he vowed to the wife of a local lawyer that he would never return to Cincinnati. "I have nothing against the city, but things have so happened here as to make it undesirable for me ever to return here."[1]

Despite the wounding, six years later Lincoln appointed Stanton to be his secretary of war, the most powerful post in his cabinet, because Lincoln thought Stanton's bluntness and single-minded intensity were precisely the qualities needed in the war effort.[2]

After Lincoln died, his son Robert recalled how Stanton called on the family "for more than ten days . . . every morning in my room, and spent the first few minutes of his visits weeping without saying a word."[3]

Chapter 13

The End Depends on the Beginning

The press wants to write the 100-day story. They asked:
"What'd you do in the first 100 days?" And I said, "I built my
team." And they responded, "Yes, but what legislation did
you pass? What did you accomplish?" And I said, "I built
my team." They never got the concept.[4]

— MICHAEL BLOOMBERG ON HIS TERM AS MAYOR

The best executive is the one who has sense enough to pick
good men to do what he wants done, and self-restraint
enough to keep from meddling with them while they do it.[5]

— ATTRIBUTED TO THEODORE ROOSEVELT

*"These were the very strongest men. I had no right to deprive
the country of their services," said Lincoln of his cabinet,
packed with political rivals and divergent opinions.*

THE PRESIDENCY HAS BECOME MORE DIFFICULT, AND YET THE applicants keep lining up for the task. Is it still possible to do the job well? Over the years, as I have tried to answer the questions raised in this book, I have asked the same question: If you were hiring the president, what questions would you ask the job applicant? What qualities would you look for?

If answers were based on what gets the most press coverage in presidential debates, you might imagine the responses to have been: "Zingers! I want to make sure the next president has zingers at the ready." Or you might think that the presidency is a job where emergencies and vital challenges can be solved by highlighting small differences with political allies.

Running for president requires begging for dollars much of the time. According to Federal Election Commission data compiled by *The Washington Post*, together Donald Trump and Hillary Clinton raised close to $2.4 billion—the most on record—for the 2016 presidential election.[6] If you reverse-engineered the presidency from the time, attention, and passion candidates display in their campaigns, you'd expect the presidency to be a job devoted to endless Oval Office telethons.

The answer I actually received was about team building: picking and managing personnel. This topic is not likely to rouse the stadium crowd if a candidate talks about it during a campaign. No one squanders a foam finger wag for a candidate who explains their theory of building talent. Nevertheless, I heard this answer so often and from so many different kinds of people, I started to think my sources were on an email chain I didn't know about. Team building is vital to the presidency, but we don't talk about it much.

The consensus view from senators, presidents, CEOs, billionaires, nonprofit leaders, and generals is that first choices determine future outcomes. Furthermore, the team-building job doesn't stop after creating the first roster. Leaders must maintain the team and retune it as circumstances change. They've even got to devote some of their attention to future hires, lining up candidates who are on deck to fill key spots even when the current performer is doing well. Or they've got to hire someone very good who can manage all of these team-building tasks for them.

In the business world, team building is an obsession. It is the subject of many CEO aphorisms and of many books given to fresh business school graduates. "The most important decisions that businesspeople make are not *what* decisions," says Jim Collins, author of *Good to Great*, "but *who* decisions."[7] "I'd rather interview fifty people and not hire anyone than hire the wrong person," says Jeff Bezos, the founder of Amazon.[8] "The secret of my success is that we've gone to exceptional lengths to hire the best people in the world," said Apple's Steve Jobs.[9] The management guru Peter Drucker argues that leaders who focus on team building have a deeper understanding of organizations. "The leaders who work most effectively, it seems to me, never say 'I,'" Drucker wrote. "And that's not because they have trained themselves not to say 'I.' They don't think 'I.' They think 'we'; they think 'team.' They understand their job to be to make the team function. They accept responsibility and don't sidestep it, but 'we' gets the credit. . . . This is what creates trust, what enables you to get the task done."[10]

"We tend to think that the leader is going to solve the problem," says retired four-star army general Stanley McChrystal, who made a study of leadership after his military career. "It's not the leader solving the problem. It is the team solving the problem, the interaction between leaders and followers. And so we're much healthier if we pull back from the idea that the leader is all powerful."[11]

"More than anything else [I'd ask] is what their track record would be for hiring people," said Admiral Mike Mullen, former chairman of the Joint Chiefs of Staff, when I asked him what he would look for.[12] David Rubenstein, the CEO of the Carlyle Group, turned the job interview notion into a debate question. "Nobody ever asks presidents about their management style," he said. Rubenstein worked for Jimmy Carter as a young man and turned his expertise on the presidency into the book *The American Story*. "In all the debates they say, 'What's your position on Medicare?' Okay, but what's your position on how you would run the government? Who's going to be your top person?"[13]

In 2012, Newt Gingrich actually did run for president on this idea and several others that reflected his attention to what the job would actually require. In his Contract with America (the presidential candidate version), he promised a training program for executive branch employees, because he recognized that while teams are crucial to a successful presidency, there's no process for building good ones. "You can't just appoint smart people," he said of the presidency. "You have to have a team and operate as a team, and any corporation would have a training program to acculturate people."[14]

When I interviewed Senator Mitt Romney, he was so enthusiastic about the topic of building a presidential team that I could feel the residual propulsive force left over from his 2012 presidential campaign. In his career, Romney repeatedly built teams in the private sector, as cofounder and CEO of Bain Capital, later CEO of Bain & Company, then as president and CEO of the 2002 Winter Olympics and governor of Massachusetts. "Once you know where you are and what your focus should be, you say, 'Okay, what is the team I need to accomplish those things?'" says the freshman senator. "At the Olympics I came into an existing organization, but it was clear to me that I needed a Chief Operating Officer because I couldn't do it all. I looked and said, 'I can do half the job. I can't do the whole job.' So I need a Chief Operating Officer. Number two, I need a better Chief Financial Officer. Number three, I need a much more effective person building the benches. Those were gaps. So then I went out to recruit. . . . Every executive has a different approach. I try and hire people who are really smart, smarter than me. Number two, I look for people who have an unusual area of skill or talent. I don't worry about their flat sides. I don't try and correct their weaknesses. If someone's got a weakness, I'll hire someone else to fill that gap."[15]

The skill for building teams can't be conjured after the votes are tallied in early November. "Management is like skiing," says Michael Bloomberg. "You don't read a book on skiing and then go out and ski double black diamonds. Management is something you learn over a period of time, and you have to manage larger and larger groups of people and make more and more difficult decisions and live with those decisions as you go."[16]

Attention to a functioning team sometimes means being hands-on, and sometimes it means allowing uncomfortably free rein to subordinates. Knowing which circumstance requires which approach is the art of leadership. Knowing how to pick a president who understands all of those things is the voters' job, but at the moment we don't even ask the first question, or know how to assess for this quality.

Ronald Reagan followed a model of hiring similar to the one Romney described. On the morning after he won the 1980 election in a landslide, he called James Baker's hotel room and asked him to serve as his chief of staff.[17] Baker had been on the other side of Reagan twice, working for his 1980 rival George H. W. Bush and counting noses for Ford during the pitched nomination battle against Reagan in 1976. Conservative pooh-bahs who backed Reagan, and saw his presidency as a chance to change the ideological trajectory of America, were deeply

Though Jim Baker had worked to defeat Ronald Reagan in the 1976 and 1980 presidential campaigns, the incoming president hired him as his first chief of staff, knowing he would need an experienced Washington hand to make progress on his administration's agenda.

suspicious of Baker. "President Reagan understood what many of his followers did not," wrote Baker. "It's more important for the chief of staff to be competent and loyal than to be a so-called true believer. . . . He also understood that one of the most important tasks of a White House chief of staff is to look at policy questions through a political prism."[18]

Reagan headed to Washington in 1980 with a mandate to shrink the government and spark a conservative revolution. This could have given him a Jacobin temperament, but his early hiring of staff reflected a key understanding that he knew what he didn't know. He was looking to fill in his weak spots. The former two-term California governor knew he would be judged by what he achieved through the Washington process. As a Washington neophyte, he needed an expert to manage that process. "He did not know one missile system from another and could not explain the simplest procedures of the federal government," Reagan's biographer Lou Cannon wrote of the president. "But he understood intuitively that the political process of his presidency would be closely linked to his acceptance in Washington. In this he was the opposite of Jimmy Carter, who knew far more and understood far less."[19]

During the 2016 campaign, I asked President Obama about the qualities voters should look for in a president. "The first thing I think the American people should be looking for is somebody that can build a team and create a culture that knows how to organize and move the ball down the field," he said, sitting in the old family dining room of the White House.[20]

Obama argued that teams were so important because a president's time is so limited. If a successful president wants to make his priority sorting as brisk and effective as possible, he needs a good team to which he can delegate. That team needs to understand its own priorities and manage them so that the president is not overburdened with issues that could have been addressed by subordinates who showed good planning and leadership. "No matter how good you are as president, you are overseeing two million people and a trillion-dollar-plus budget, and the largest organization on earth," said Obama. "You can't do it all by yourself. And so you are reliant on really talented, hardworking, skilled people, and making sure they're all moving in the same direction, and doing it without drama, and not worrying as much about who is getting credit, and creating all those good habits inside of an organization that I think are critical."[21]

YOUR FOUNDATION KEEPS THE HOUSE STANDING

THE MINDSET THAT A SUCCESSFUL PRESIDENTIAL CANDIDATE BRINGS to building a team sets the trajectory for the entire administration. When a president picks a congressional liaison, for example, you can tell whether the presidency will be committed to finding bipartisan solutions or to endless rounds of partisan swordplay. If the liaison, whose job is to help midwife legislation and tend relationships, is a congressional staffer with a good reputation with both parties and who understands how the system works, then it is an indication the president has put a premium on bipartisan, durable solutions. If the president picks a liaison who likes to flash his serpent teeth, then the president is planning to dominate the other party, or to clash a lot in the attempt.

How a leader designs a team also tells you whether they understand presidential priority setting. Senator Lamar Alexander started his first term as Tennessee governor in 1979 and modeled his office on the presidential structure outlined by Lyndon Johnson's aide George Reedy. "One, see an urgent need; two, develop a strategy to meet the need. And three, persuade at least half the people you're right," Alexander remembers. "I adopted that as a young governor. I delegated to others the operation of the government. I had a chief operating officer of the government and cabinet members, and I didn't fool with it. I spent my time being governor."[22]

As they build a team, savvy presidents recognize that governing and campaigning are two different things, and they require teams with very different skills. This is easier said than done. Even the presidents who know it have a devil of a time implementing it. Campaign staffers have devoted their lives, marriages, and health to a president's election. It's hard to abandon such loyal soldiers. They were the ones who helped build the team that won.

"I know thee not, old man" may have worked for Shakespeare's Prince Hal when he became king and had to set aside his old pal Falstaff, but a president who leaves his campaign team in the wings for opening night of the Big Show equips an army of angry Falstaffs ready to grumble to the press about how their old friend is disloyal and has lost his way. As the presidency wears on, this chorus will always be there ready to handle press phone calls.

"The real problem with the staff was that most of them came out of the campaign or Arkansas," remembered Bill Clinton, "and had no experience in working in the White House or dealing with Washington's political culture. My young staffers were talented, honest, and dedicated, and I felt I owed many of them the chance to serve the country by working in the White House. In time, they would get their sea legs and do very well. But in the critical early months, both the staff and I would do a lot of on-the-job learning, and some of the lessons would prove to be quite costly."[23]

If a president decides to welcome into the administration the campaign team, they'll rejoice over memories of foxhole triumphs, but soon will struggle to do the kind of work that is unlike the work they just accomplished, and therefore, work for which they may have little to no experience.

"Dance with the one that brung you" makes sense only if you are going to continue to dance. Governing is not the same as dancing. Or if it is dancing, it is a quadrille and not the jitterbug everyone has been doing in the presidential campaign. "The tendency to hire who you know and who you worked with before is actually not a good thing," says Max Stier, president and CEO of the Partnership for Public Service, which works to bring private sector leadership excellence to government. "The question is, do you invest in the up-front work that has to be done to create a high-functioning team? Do you understand the importance and value of working together as a team, and do you have people who are skilled in doing that?"[24]

TEAM OF RIVALS

A PRESIDENT'S FIRST CHOICES ALSO INDICATE WHETHER THEY PLAN to lead as a conductor managing a team whose individual members have autonomy and expertise, or whether they'll be hovering over every detail like the instructor in shop class on the first day with the coping saw. Will they hire people who are leaders in their own right to handle those Quadrant Two tasks—important but not urgent—and Quadrant Three tasks—urgent but not important—or will they operate from fear and insecurity and keep decision making close at hand?

Abraham Lincoln is associated with the best strong leader anecdote. Surveying his cabinet and finding all opposed to him, he raised his hand and said, "Seven noes and one aye, the ayes have it." The tale is apocryphal but typical of the decisiveness we look for in leaders. The true story of Lincoln's relationship to his cabinet is more nourishing for future leaders and is far more bold than that anecdote. Doris Kearns Goodwin's book *Team of Rivals* tells the extraordinary story of how the sixteenth president built a team of sharp, divergent personalities and made that team work, despite the risk of hiring people who had spent the previous years trying to defeat him.[25]

Lincoln formed a mixed cabinet—former Whigs and Democrats, conciliators and the inflexible. Each of his rivals in his cabinet was "sure to feel that the wrong man had been nominated," as Lincoln's secretary, John Nicolay, put it.[26] Lincoln told a Senate ally of his picks, "their long experience in public affairs, and their eminent fitness" gave them "higher claims than his own for the place he was to occupy."[27]

"We needed the strongest men," Lincoln said, responding to Joseph Medill of the *Chicago Tribune*, who asked Lincoln why he had chosen a cabinet comprised of enemies and opponents. "These were the very strongest men. I had no right to deprive the country of their services."[28] Lincoln knew that unless he united the factions in support of the Union, he could not keep the Union together. Nicolay later wrote Lincoln's "first decision was one of great courage and self-reliance."

What made Lincoln's cabinet choices all the more amazing—and all the more of a risk for him—is that the president was relatively inexperienced as a team builder. "The construction of a Cabinet," one editorial advised, sounding almost exactly like Michael Bloomberg, "[is] like the courting of a shrewd girl, it belongs to a branch of the fine arts with which the new Executive is not acquainted. There are certain little tricks which go far beyond the arts familiar to the stump, and the cross-road tavern, whose comprehension requires a delicacy of thought and subtlety of perception, secured only by experience."[29]

That Lincoln was able to summon this kind of wisdom with very little experience invites humility about judging presidential candidates based on their experience. They may understand what the job requires and just not show it, or have a chance to show it in a campaign. On the other hand, there was only one Lincoln, and the transition into office for a new president makes it nearly impossible for that person to start in a way that takes maximum advantage of the skills they bring with them.

TRUMAN LEARNS ABOUT THE MANHATTAN PROJECT

That first meeting of the cabinet was short, and when it adjourned, the members rose silently and made their way from the room—except for Secretary [of War] Stimson.

He asked to speak to me about a most urgent matter. Stimson told me that he wanted me to know about an immense project that was under way—a project looking to the development of a new explosive of almost unbelievable destructive power. That was all he felt free to say at the time, and his statement left me puzzled. It was the first bit of information that had come to me about the atomic bomb, but he gave me no details. . . . The next day Jimmy Byrnes, who until shortly before had been Director of War Mobilization for President Roosevelt, came to see me, and even he told me a few details, though with great solemnity he said that we were perfecting an explosive great enough to destroy the whole world.[1]

— THE MEMOIRS OF HARRY S. TRUMAN, APRIL 12, 1945

Chapter 14

Lost in Transition

It would be goddam easy to run this office,
if you didn't have to deal with people.[2]

— RICHARD NIXON

I loved my previous life. I had so many things going.
This is more work than in my previous life.
I thought it would be easier.[3]

— DONALD TRUMP

A PRESIDENT AND WHITE HOUSE STAFF HAVE ABOUT SEVENTY-five days between the blast of the confetti cannons on Election Day and taking the helm of the $5 trillion presidential enterprise.[4] In the business world, a takeover—which is the closest thing to what a presidential exchange is—would take months of planning. In 2012, Mitt Romney's team realized that no team could be assembled in such a short amount of time. Top talent like to keep their private sector jobs and have to be coaxed into service. Plus, after selections are made, candidates for top posts have to have their backgrounds scrubbed for conflicts. To get a jump on the task, Romney's advisers started preparing his team long before he knew whether he would get the job. If they could build an operating rhythm quickly, they'd be ready once the new enterprise kicked off.

The product of that six months of work was printed in "The Romney Readiness Project."[5] The 140 pages are filled with organizational charts and prioritization matrices. White House staffers in both parties describe chaos in the early days of an administration when a new staff of ambitious Type A people are thrown together without a clear organizational chart, like cats in a tumble dryer. So one of the operation's most useful functions was matching jobs with responsibilities.

Six hundred people had a hand in planning for a Romney transition. They ran through exercises planning for how a Romney administration would move ideas and legislation through the federal system. When people talk about the benefits of having a businessman in the White House, the careful attention the Romney team put into personnel and organization is no doubt what they are talking about.

Move-in day 1969. The Nixons meet the Johnsons on the day the new president was sworn in. Nixon had just seventy-six days to get ready for the most important job on the planet. The next day he told staff he intended to "get up early and work late so this house will always be a happy house."

BAD KARMA

THE ROMNEY TEAM NEVER GOT TO TEST WHETHER THEIR PREPLANning would work. The next GOP nominee from the business world was much more successful and would test a different proposition: What happens when you follow the opposite of the Romney approach?

After the 2012 race, Congress passed the Presidential Transitions Improvement Act of 2015 to push candidates to start work on their transition in May of an election year. The new federal requirement removed the political liability for candidates who thought too early about the job they were running for. Candidates used to have to worry about being accused of "measuring the drapes" in the Oval Office.[6] The term refers to the tradition of redecorating the White House with each new administration. It is supposed to suggest that a candidate is haughty, or imprudent, or disrespecting voters. Obviously, though, a candidate who plans in advance respects the voters and wants to do a good job for them.

In 1992, George H. W. Bush produced a spectacular three-car-pileup metaphor as he leveled a version of the "drapes" charge at Bill Clinton: "I half expected, when I went over to the Oval Office, to find him over there measuring the drapes. Well, let me say, as the first shot out of the barrel, I have a message for him. Put those drapes on hold; it is going to be curtain time for that ticket. And I mean it."[7]

The new law didn't remove fear of that charge from Donald Trump, who internalized it. He appointed then New Jersey governor Chris Christie to fill the congressionally mandated post of running the transition but then told him he did not want to hear about Christie's work. He said it was bad luck. "When he hired me he said to me I'm picking you because I want nothing to do with this," says Christie. "It's bad karma. . . . If the transition ever came up [in conversation] he'd flip out."[8]

Students of presidential transitions and Obama staffers who worked with the Christie-led team said the former New Jersey governor did a sturdy job of preparing the Trump administration for the enormity of governing.[9] That effort produced more than two dozen binders of information to jump-start the Trump presidency, including lists of possible appointees whose backgrounds had already been scrubbed by the team of former U.S. attorneys Christie had hired. A Harvard professor who taught classes on the presidency interviewed members of the Trump organization and wrote memos about how Trump's style could be integrated into presidential traditions.[10] A daily plan for the initial days of the administration was created, along with a phone call list of foreign leaders to reach out to based on U.S. foreign policy interests.

The vision of the authors of the 2015 Improvements Act came to life in those binders. Up to a point. Shortly after Trump won, Christie and his work were ejected. "I gave them to them Monday," Christie said of the binders of transition material. "They threw them out Friday."[11] Trump's chief strategist at the time, Steve Bannon, and Trump's son-in-law, Jared Kushner, thought Christie was trying to use the transition to put his own imprint—and not Donald Trump's—on the presidency. Christie says he had kept the campaign in the loop about his process, but jealousies, suspicions, and power struggles combined to feed those binders into the shredder.

This is not a new story in transitions. Though the Trump team has brought to the presidency idiosyncrasies like no other in modern times, the Trump experience does flow along familiar historical lines. It is often the case that those who have been closest to the president, in a campaign or in his family, clash with the members of the staff concerned with governing.

As a candidate in 1976, Jimmy Carter designed a separate governing team—separate from his campaign team—before he even won the Democratic Party's nomination. After he won the election, an epic skirmish broke out between Carter's campaign team and governing team. "Our biggest problem during the transition was a problem of internal conflict," remembers Jack Watson, who led Carter's governing-focused transition team. "We had, surrounding us on all sides, a very large, far-flung campaign operation . . . much more oriented to politics, campaigning, and to winning the election. . . . That very large group of folks wanted, of course, to come into the transition and ultimately into the government after the election had been won. The problems between [campaign manager] Hamilton Jordan and me, about which so much was made, stemmed not from personal matters, but from inevitable and very powerful external forces as in a Greek tragedy."[12] It was, Watson told Chris Whipple for his book on White House chiefs of staff, *The Gatekeepers*, "a very bloody beginning. . . . It was two months into the transition before I felt safe starting my own car."[13]

This tension between the staffers tasked with preparing for the office and those who helped the candidate win the office explains why Clark Clifford told John Kennedy in 1960 that he would advise him on building a good White House staff but would not serve on that staff. It clarified his role as a disinterested outsider.[14] Kennedy later quipped that Clifford had asked him for nothing except the right to advertise his law firm on the back of the one-dollar bill.[15]

With Donald Trump the resistance to structure was even greater. "Donald was an unconventional candidate," Jared Kushner told Christie, according to the governor. "He is going to be an unconventional president."[16] It is traditional for the winning team to come into their new job with a head of steam and skepticism about the folkways within their new headquarters. The Trump team, like previous insurgency candidacies, won by spotlighting how poorly things were going in Washington. They had the fresh biofeedback of their extraordinary victory. With that mindset, it's tempting for the new victors to condemn worthy traditions as needless bureaucracy. The presidential scholar Richard Neustadt identified this feeling in 1960 and the pitfalls that come with it:

> Everywhere there is a sense of page turning, a new chapter in the country's history, a new chance too. And with it, irresistibly, there comes the sense, "they" couldn't, wouldn't, didn't, but "we" will. We just have done the hardest thing there is to do in politics. Governing has got to be a pleasure by comparison: We won, so we can![17]

While in most organizations, the new boss seeks out the "institutional memory," a new presidential team ejects it immediately. Craig Fugate, Barack Obama's FEMA director, witnessed this phenomenon across several administrations during his time in public service. "They're used to barking out orders and having them followed," says Fugate of administrations that form just after successful campaigns. "And now they move into the bureaucracy—which I don't use as a derogatory term—and those career folks help you achieve your agenda. Every administration needs to have someone in there to shape that. Those that ignore that at their own peril impale themselves."[18]

The botched Trump start led to cascading staffing catastrophes and a historic number of departures. Donald Trump repeatedly promised he would hire "the best people."[19] He did not. That is not my opinion; it is President Trump's, which he expresses frequently. Trump has said his first secretary of state, Rex Tillerson, was "dumb as a rock" and "lazy as hell." His attorney general, Jeff Sessions, was "scared stiff and Missing in Action," "didn't have a clue," and "should be ashamed of himself." Trump described one of his assistants, Omarosa Manigault Newman, as "wacky," "deranged," "vicious, but not smart," a "crazed, crying lowlife," and finally a "dog." After lasting only eleven days as communications director, Anthony Scaramucci "was quickly terminated 'from' a position that he was totally incapable of handling" and was called "very much out of control." An anonymous adviser to the president was called "a drunk/drugged-up loser." Chief strategist Steve Bannon was "sloppy," a "leaker," and "dumped like a dog by almost everyone." His longtime lawyer Michael Cohen was "TERRIBLE," "hostile," "a convicted liar & fraudster," and a "failed lawyer." The president was "Never a big fan!" of his White House counsel Don McGahn and "not even a little bit happy" with Jerome Powell, his selection to head the Federal Reserve, whom he called an "enemy." His third national security advisor, John Bolton, was mocked as a "tough guy [who] got us into Iraq." When the president was irritated with his former chief of staff, John Kelly, the president's press secretary, Stephanie Grisham, declared that Kelly "was totally unequipped to handle the genius of our great president."

Trump insisted that Michael Flynn become his National Security Advisor despite warnings from Christie, President Obama, and a host of military officials that Flynn lacked the judgment and temperament for the job. Flynn would resign twenty-four days into the new administration for, among other things, lying about his contact with the Russians, for which he would later be indicted.

Candidates at the Department of Labor (Andrew Puzder), Veterans Affairs (Ronny Jackson), and the Federal Reserve (Herman Cain and Stephen Moore) were hastily put forward and collapsed before the Senate voted for lack of qualifications or conflicts or a combination of other problems. This also happened in the highly sensitive posts of secretary of defense (Patrick M. Shanahan). Other cabinet candidates who had been hastily vetted, like the secretaries of the Departments of Health and Human Services (Tom Price) and the Department of the Interior (Ryan Zinke) and Environmental Protection Agency administrator Scott Pruitt, imploded in the job.

According to a Brookings Institution study, in the first three years of the Trump administration, it lost 82 percent of its "A-team" White House staffers, a category that refers to the top noncabinet officials. That set a record. Thirty-eight percent of those key spots experienced "serial turnover." A president who promised to hire "the best" presided over a firing and shuffling process unprecedented in the White House.[20]

The shortages have undermined the president's agenda. Adam White of the Hoover Institution argues that the disordered personnel process has made it harder to follow through on the president's push to deregulate. Were there more Trump allies in executive agencies, there would be better follow-through in shepherding the laborious process of undoing regulations, a Trump priority.[21]

The staffing issues have also harmed the president's priorities at the Pentagon. In the spring of 2019, according to *Politico*, a quarter of the Pentagon's most senior civilian posts remained filled by temporary personnel unconfirmed by the Senate.[22] The collection of placeholders couldn't make decisions as crisply. The staffing issues also handicapped the department in disputes with other agencies, which slowed or thwarted their objectives. When agencies are understaffed, decision making shifts to the White House, complicating an already complex system and adding to a lengthy presidential to-do list.

After Secretary of Defense Mattis resigned in December 2018, it was seven months before a full-time successor was confirmed to head the agency the president says he cares about the most. "When you're the Secretary of Defense, you're handling life or death issues for other countries. They have to be sure they are talking with someone in charge," said Republican senator James Inhofe, chair of the Armed Services Committee. "You're not in charge if you're acting, in my opinion."[23] The ranking Democrat on the Armed Services Committee, Senator Jack Reed, explained why acting officials are less effective. "Anyone who's in an acting capacity, people are wondering, 'Will he be the nominee?' And then, 'Should we follow through with this initiative—if it's the personal initiative of this individual—and how much energy should we put into it?' That's natural in any organization: 'You're acting? That's nice, somebody's coming after you.'"[24]

Admiral Mike Mullen explains why the lack of permanent department leadership matters. Without a confirmed secretary of defense, the military lacks a forceful, independent voice in national security discussions. An acting secretary can't push back as hard against bad ideas or lean forward in advocating for the soldiers, sailors, airmen, and marines.[25] Ultimately, this also means the president who has a bunch of "actings" doesn't get the best advice for doing his primary job, keeping America safe.

OUT OF SYNC WITH BUSINESS

PRESIDENT TRUMP'S WHITE HOUSE PERSONNEL RECORD IS NOT JUST out of sync with traditional presidential structures, it is at odds with the best practices in the business world. Top-selling business books revolve around a core set of concepts—the necessity of organization, the benefit of building cooperative teams and elevating employees. The titles of recent bestsellers tell the tale: *The Advantage: Why Organizational Health Trumps Everything Else in Business* and *Team of Teams: New Rules of Engagement for a Complex World* and *Bringing Out the Best in People: How to Enjoy Helping Others Excel.* The chapter headings in leadership books are remarkably similar: tell the truth, elevate subordinates, trust your team. These books sell well at graduation time because they include checklists for any aspiring leader to emulate. The Trump White House seemed designed to flout almost all of these rules.

Of all the campaign promises Donald Trump has kept, the one he has kept with the most fervor has been his promise to be an unconventional president. Unconventional is good, particularly in getting a sclerotic system to start moving. Unconventional is the engine of U.S. innovation and spark behind the biggest cliché of the modern business age: disruption. But there is a difference between unconventional and untethered. Unconventional is driving from the passenger's side to get a better view of the road when the windshield is iced over. Untethered is throwing the steering wheel out the window—or, in this case, all of those transition binders.

HARPER'S

Every president needs about twelve months to get his executive team organized, to feel his way into the vast and dangerous machinery of the bureaucracy, and to lay out guidelines of policy for both of them. The policies drafted during the campaign, and earlier, always have to be revised. For nothing looks quite as simple from the Executive Office as it did from the outside. Mr. Eisenhower, for example, stepped into the White House full of confidence that he could, in short order, balance the budget and slice Big Government down to size; he was astounded to discover he could do neither.

This shakedown period is difficult enough under tranquil circumstances. For Mr. Kennedy it was further troubled by a sudden series of emergencies: Cuba, Berlin, and Southeast Asia. While he was still trying to move in the furniture, in effect, he found the roof falling in and the doors blowing off.[1]

—JOHN FISCHER, HARPER'S MAGAZINE, FEBRUARY 14, 1962

Chapter 15

Hard at the Start

For the last four years I spent so much time getting to know
people who could help me get elected President that I didn't
have any time to get to know people who could help me,
after I was elected, to be a good President.[2]

—JOHN F. KENNEDY

Can a hard-driving, fast-moving bunch of egotists be so
metamorphosed between November 5 and January 20?[3]

—BRADLEY PATTERSON, WHITE HOUSE STAFFER
FOR DWIGHT EISENHOWER, RICHARD NIXON,
AND GERALD FORD

I F TRANSITIONS MOVE TOO FAST, PRESIDENTS LEARN RIGHT AWAY
that the office of the presidency moves too slowly. "When the president
makes a decision, it's like a penny dropping down in the top of a machine," explains Fran Townsend, who worked in the justice department
during the Clinton administration and as George W. Bush's homeland
security and counterterrorism adviser. "A president wants the penny to
come out at a certain place, but what actually has to happen with the
human beings to make sure the penny comes out where he wants it to
come out is a little bit of a mystery. And you've got bureaucrats who if
not properly motivated and organized can undermine you just by not
moving it. They just hold on to the penny in the box. And you can't
find it."[4]

A White House quaintly understaffed in 1938 is now overstuffed.
Even in the smoothest-running administrations, the overabundance

creates traffic jams at the Oval Office door. In the White House, power is proximity. Staffers want power, so they're always trying to get near the president. This leads to a lot of loitering outside office doors, overstaying your welcome after a meeting in the Oval Office, and bothering the president with unworkable or half-baked ideas. "The guys around the president want to show their stuff. They want him to look at my program, look at my issue," says Joseph Califano, Jr., who served as the chief domestic policy adviser under Lyndon Johnson and as Jimmy Carter's secretary of health, education, and welfare. "So many issues get to the president's throat that shouldn't really get there"—issues "better left down in the bureaucracy to resolve."[5] The framers worried that power would corrupt the president; it has that same effect on those who work for him, which makes it hard to maintain a disciplined organization. "Power is so tempting when it's sitting right there," explains Senator Lamar Alexander, who worked for Nixon and George H. W. Bush. "You want to get your sticky fingers all over the decision. So you have White House aides running around who have no business making decisions."[6]

The authors of the Brownlow Report of 1937, who studied FDR's White House, promised Congress that White House aides would be anonymous. Seventy years later, many who work in unelected White House positions wield more power and influence than elected members of Congress. Some, like Oliver North, Jim Baker, and Karl Rove, have become household names or are recognizable at the supermarket. Donald Trump's aide Stephen Miller—whose Rasputin-like influence is a regular topic of Washington whispers and grumbles—felt the juice of his new post after being there only a few hours. "The whole world will soon see as we begin to take further actions, that the powers of the president to protect our country are very substantial and will not be questioned," Miller told me during an interview in 2017 on *Face the Nation*.[7]

All those bodies in the White House mean a lot of egos poised to clash. Whether staffers are motivated by a sense of duty, arrogance, or ideology, many try to engrave their initials on the administration. When they don't get their way in internal deliberations, they vent, maneuver, conspire, and peddle notions to the media. As a journalist, I don't want to sound ungrateful, but from a White House management standpoint, the leaking creates hours of work mopping up messes. Staffers—and sometimes the president—swerve to correct a story leaked to the press, and in future deliberations they are suspicious of one another. The leaking can also give the public an incomplete picture. People who leak because they were shut out of a decision often don't know what they are talking about.

Retribution becomes a fixation. Jimmy Carter's chief of staff promised to fire anyone speaking critically of the administration. Various Trump officials have promised this as well. In neither instance did it stop the leaking.

Creating a healthy White House environment in which everyone feels they are on a team helps cut down on the leaking. "If they feel like they are a part of a team and you are working with them and listening to them, [even if] they don't always prevail, [they feel] that you are at least giving them the benefit of being a part of the team, [and] that sense of team is important," says Leon Panetta, Clinton's former chief of staff. "You have to be honest with them and they with you, and if you don't have that trust but it's built on suspicion and power egos or who puts a knife in somebody's back, if that's the interplay, then it's not going to work."[8]

"In any White House there are three types of people: those there to serve the president," says Trump's former national security advisor H. R. McMaster; "those there for their own agenda, to advance their own careers; and those there to save the country from the president. These exist in all presidencies."[9] Aides who have worked in multiple administrations say that the Trump administration had a greater share of the last two, including a new twist: A staffer penned an anonymous opinion piece in *The New York Times* announcing a secret plot to save the country from the president. "I work for the president but like-minded colleagues and I have vowed to thwart parts of his agenda and his worst inclinations," wrote the author.[10] According to some stories, intelligence officials kept some information from the president—particularly about Russia—to prevent him from getting upset and blocking actions necessary to meet the threat. These tales delight Trump critics but represent a perversion of democracy. Unelected individuals who deny the president information deprive the American people's representative of having information necessary to do the job.

You Can't Repair the Plane and Fly It Too

IT IS TEMPTING TO SAY A BUSINESSMAN OR MILITARY LEADER COULD break open the mysterious box of an administration bureaucracy and straighten things out with a bracing application of common sense. But this is a fantasy, and maybe a dangerous one. Being a CEO and being a president are two very different tasks, and any CEO who wants the job of being president who doesn't recognize the difference immediately should probably be disqualified.

"You can't hire or fire whoever you want," explains Stanford's Amy Zegart, ticking off the ways in which the presidency is distinct from the corner suite. Zegart spent three years working on organizational change as a management consultant at McKinsey & Company before teaching political economy. "You have no clear metrics of success in a White House. It's not revenues and profits. How do you measure success? Success is only whether they're going to get reelected. You have to work with people who hate you and who profit by not working with you. Your incentives across your organization are completely not aligned. In fact, some organizations or part of your organization will benefit the more you fail. . . . It's a completely different skills set. You have to actually be able to get people to do what you want them to do when they have incentives not to." Truman certainly felt this way. The thirty-third president said, "I learned that a great leader is a man who has the ability to get other people to do what they don't want to do and like it."[11]

The framework for legislation in Washington is also the opposite of the framework that leads to success in the business world. In Washington, lawmakers are praised for the plan more than for the follow-through. "The incentives for political appointees is to get their signature legislation or executive order signed by the president," says Jeffrey Zients, who served as the acting director at the Office of Management and Budget and the head of Obama's National Economic Council.[12]

For corporations, the strategic plan activates the process that leads to the product, which can be measured. In government, legislation — the equivalent to the strategic plan — *is the objective*. Everyone crowds behind the president for the photo signing, and the lucky ones go home with one of the pens he used to sign the legislation. "The president's signing is the equivalent of the Board's approval of a company's strategic plan," says Zients, who also worked in the private sector as chairman and CEO of a variety of companies. "It is the first ten percent of the process. Ninety percent is implementation and execution. Unfortunately, there's no equivalent of a signing ceremony for execution. All the people who crowded around the desk for the signing ceremony are long gone when it comes time for the hard work of implementation."

WE JOIN THIS PROGRAM ALREADY IN PROGRESS

A PRESIDENT WITH A YEN TO REFORM THE INEFFICIENT SYSTEM FINDS it almost impossible, because the plane in need of repair is the one the president is flying. When Kennedy came into office, the Bay of Pigs operation was nearly under way. On inauguration day, George W. Bush briefed Barack Obama on an active computer hacking of Iranian missile systems known as Operation Olympic Games.[13] Legacy items from the previous administration face every top official throughout the organization before they have a chance to hang a picture of their mother on the wall.

If Donald Trump loses his reelection bid, the incoming FEMA director will manage legacy items from 2017's Hurricane Maria, just as Trump's FEMA director dealt with the aftermath of 2012's Hurricane Sandy and 2005's Hurricane Katrina. The new secretary of energy will have to decide how to store tons of nuclear waste created under Donald Trump.[14]

Once a president and the president's team get in sync with ongoing operations, they have to put aside their reformer's impulse and tackle the in-box, which immediately starts filling up with snakes.

If, for some reason, history stopped and a new White House team took the field in unnaturally placid early weeks, they might find the time to spread the schematic across the floor in order to figure out how to streamline things. Without a guide, would they know what they were looking at? Duties overlap, lines of authority are fuzzy, and departments that should work together are in constant conflict. Some of the organizational chart is written into legislation, which means an administration can't change it to be more responsive even if they wanted to. "Nobody knows what their job actually is," says Mona Sutphen, who served on the National Security Council in the Clinton White House and as deputy chief of staff for policy under President Obama, "unless you have been in government and are at the same agency you were in before. [But] most people don't go back into their old job. You get a bunch of really Type A super-successful people in a room and give them lots of power and no job description and that's what the West Wing looks like. People are jostling around going 'I don't even really know—is this my territory? How do we have a meeting?'"[15]

Kellyanne Conway describes a version of this in the early days of the Trump administration. "Things were happening that didn't seem normal but could have been perfectly normal in a White House since few of us had ever worked in one," she says. "It turns out some White House officials were playing games and curating their own images. They are nearly all gone."

The Presidential Records Act of 1978 requires a White House to send all of its material to the National Archive after a president departs. This makes for a stark first day for the new administration, as a former national security official described it: "You go to the luncheon in the

Kennedy and Eisenhower confer after the Bay of Pigs invasion three months into the new president's tenure. "Victory has a hundred fathers and defeat is an orphan," said Kennedy after the failed raid. "I am the responsible officer of the government, and that is quite obvious."

Capitol and Statuary Hall and you stand there while they play 'Hail to the Chief' for the first time for your guy. It's just really this high. And then you arrive at the National Security Council, and there's nothing. The desks are cleaned. They filed away everything."[16]

Once a president's team learns to identify the component parts of the presidential operation, they then have to find someone who knows which pieces of the organization to salvage and which ones to put on eBay. There aren't that many experts you can call to know what happens if you chuck the wrong item, because that expertise requires an understanding of both the organization and the goals and skills of the new team.

Some presidents deputize "czars" or special assistants to unstick the process, which offers the self-soothing feel of a solution (I'll put my best person on it!), but that often compounds the complexity. "We have a terrible process for selecting presidents, but then there are also mistakes that presidents make over and over and over again. Even if you select a good one, they make the same mistakes," says Zegart.[17]

Those who support shrinking the government applaud Donald Trump's personnel approach of atrophy and neglect. By one estimate, Trump's staff is as small as the White House staff has been in twenty years, in line with Calvin Coolidge's preference for the federal workforce. When asked how many people work in the White House, the thirtieth president reportedly answered, "About half."

Richard Nixon was even more peppery. "We've checked and found that ninety-six percent of the bureaucracy are against us," he groused, early in his tenure, about the permanent administrative staff of the executive branch. "They're bastards who are here to screw us."[18] This is why Nixon, like Trump, mostly disowned the bureaucracy. When questioned about problems at the Bureau of Indian Affairs, the president agreed. "It's a horrible mess," he said. "Someone ought to do something about it."[19]

Trump's strategist Steve Bannon promised the president would bring about the "deconstruction of the administrative state."[20] But downsizing in the federal government follows the same rules that downsizing does in the private sector. Streamlining doesn't bring efficiency unless it follows some considered plan. An administration that throws an ax at the bureaucracy instead of precision cutting with a scalpel ignores the expertise at the ready. "Trying to run a government without its support is like trying to run a train without an engine," wrote Stephen Hess in *Organizing the Presidency,* a study of several theories of presidential management.[21] If an administration ignores government workers, as Michael Lewis demonstrates in his book *The Fifth Risk,* they leave vast key parts of the government unattended, like the portion of the Department of Energy in charge of hunting down weapons-grade plutonium and uranium or that part of the administration working to harden the vulnerable electric grid to cyberattack.[22]

Reduced staffing and inattention are not leading to better outcomes. An investigation by *Politico* in 2020 found that a host of Agriculture Department decisions affecting farmers, food stamp recipients, and meatpacking workers were based on sloppy data and carelessness.[23] The problem for the modern president is that government agencies are not modern. Arcane rules about buying and selling products and hiring and firing people hamper the executive's ability to manage agencies. Regulations and unions further complicate the goal of running the organization based on efficiency and productivity. The penny does not bounce smoothly and elegantly as it moves through the machine. It goes silent, emerges dusty from unexpected parts, and sometimes comes out as a nickel.

FUNCTIONAL FIXEDNESS

EXPERIENCE OF THE WRONG KIND CAN BE AN IMPEDIMENT IN THE new environment. "The natural instinct of a newly elected president is to approach the job like they operated in their previous roles," explains Mike Leavitt, who served as administrator of the Environmental Protection Agency and as secretary of health and human services, both under George W. Bush. He was also CEO of the Leavitt Group, today known as Leavitt Partners, the nation's second-largest privately held insurance brokerage. "If you are a business executive with a consistent pattern of success, and supreme confidence in your own judgment, you are naturally going to assume your success formula is good enough for your new job. So if it was your practice to swoop into the details, it would be natural to do the equivalent as president. Every president has to learn this, I suspect. They know how to get elected, but they have to learn how to govern."[24]

The highly accomplished incoming presidents and their staff need to understand that they are in an environment unlike one they've ever been in before. "When I was at the inauguration in the first term in '93 I was walking with a friend from the administration who said 'We've done very well in the world we're in, and we should do things that way here,'" remembers former treasury secretary Robert Rubin. "I said, 'I don't think so. I think we're in a complex new world, and yes, there's experience we have that could be very valuable, but the key is to recognize how different this world is and see how to function effectively in that world.'"[25]

In private enterprise, companies seek to break this "functional fixedness" (seeing solutions only by the patterns of your previous expertise). In presidencies, there is no systematic process for jolting presidents out of their patterns other than trial and error. Having just won an election, a president may have a strong instinct to stick to the patterns that worked in the past. Voters and pundits encourage this fixed view. When experimentation with a new mode of working goes wrong, a president or White House is judged to be in disarray. In Silicon Valley the expression "fail fast" exemplifies the culture of experimentation and learning through iteration. It means take risks, recognize your mistakes quickly, adapt, and move on. In politics, iteration is called "flip-flopping."[26] "If we took trial and error seriously, 'flip-flopper' would be a badge of flexibility; worn with pride," writes Tim Harford in *Adapt: Why Success Always Starts with Failure*.[27] Donald Trump has a high tolerance for iteration. He could establish a new tolerance for it in the office. However, since he never admits to changing positions or failing, he actually reinforces the old way of thinking: that iteration is something to be ashamed of.

The Partnership for Public Service has tried to help private sector employees make the leap into public life. It hopes to attract more qualified people into government positions by making the transition easier. A graphic on the cover of the PPS training pamphlet shows which skills overlap between the public and private sectors. Both reward "achieving results" and "leading change"—but challenges distinct to governing include "stewardship of public trust" and "commitment to public good."[28] PPS doesn't have a presidential training course, but as voters seem determined to elevate candidates with little or no experience in public service, perhaps they should start one.

For a president who seeks to govern all Americans, these new skills are particularly important. Success in a presidency is not about simply winning for your political party or yourself but is measured by a president's stewardship, trustworthiness, and commitment to the public good. The PPS program explains why: "As Americans we have only one institution with the resources and public mandate to address our nation's most vexing problems: the federal government."[29]

CONFIRMATION BIAS

FINALLY, A PRESIDENT TRYING TO MAKE A CLEAN START FACES THE maddening delays associated with getting political appointees confirmed. Even if a president could field a complete team, in the pinched period alotted for transitions they get stuck in the locker room waiting to get the Senate's seal of approval. Roughly four thousand political positions require background checks and Senate confirmation. Once the team does get going, it takes a while to grasp the idiosyncratic job duties. Meanwhile, as partisanship escalates, the flame on the burnout rate burns hotter.

The reputational cost of working for an administration in a time of high partisanship affects the labor pool. Experts who aren't political and shy away from the partisan combat increasingly become reluctant to take jobs. Instead, partisan warriors will be attracted (or they'll be the only ones left in the employment line). Administrations will start to fill up with a greater share of staffers armed with hard partisan skills, rather than with policy knowledge and expertise in executing government.

A new president with an organizing bent also has to weigh whether making progress getting the organization in order is a sunk cost no one will recognize. There's no political reward for time spent on the internal process, building teams and systems. If a president bounded into the press briefing room to announce a sparkling initiative on cross-departmental integration, he or she would most likely be met with an arcade of raised eyebrows. "I've never seen an elected official get elected for land use planning and mitigation codes. We don't elect people for that," says former FEMA administrator Brock Long.[30]

To make organizational headway, a White House must resist the strong political pull of fixating on tasks that pay off today but disappear tomorrow rather than investing in organizational practices that might reap greater benefits down the road. This is an unrealistic demand. The presidency operates under hyperunrealistic time lines, none more idiotic than the notion that something dramatic must get accomplished in the first one hundred days. This is a media construct left over from FDR's first term. He had a genuine emergency and conditions such as no other president has faced. Nevertheless, administrations are measured by this flawed metric. "The press wants to write the 100-day story. They asked: 'What'd you do in the first 100 days?'" explained Michael Bloomberg. "And I said, 'I built my team.' And they responded, 'Yes, but what legislation did you pass? What did you accomplish?' And I said, 'I built my team.' They never got the concept." In the real world, CEOs are advised to take their time. "You may feel the need to validate yourself by proving your creative genius," writes Michael Watkins in *The First 90 Days*, the seminal work on starting in a new organization. "Instead, feel confident that you're there, and at least initially, listen carefully rather than talk. Find ways to highlight the strengths of others. As for your own genius, there will be plenty of time for that."[31]

TRY, TRY AGAIN

OVER THE LAST 120 YEARS, ALMOST EVERY PRESIDENT HAS TRIED TO reform the way his administration does business. They created task forces to expand accountability, increase efficiency, and streamline presidential authority.[32] Teddy Roosevelt, a progressive reformer who had served as civil service commissioner, was the first. In 1905, his Committee on Departments and Methods sought to "place the conduct of the Government on the most economical and effective basis in the light of the best modern business practice."[33] In its investigations, the commission found confusion and overruns that would sound familiar today: 28 different kinds of ink, 278 kinds of pens, 11 different kinds of typewriter ribbons, and 132 grades of pencils.

Then came the Taft Commission on Economy and Efficiency in

1910. Herbert Hoover had a special affection for the topic. As commerce secretary under Harding in the 1920s, Hoover became so effective and powerful that he elevated the sleepy new department and became known around the White House and Washington salons informally as "Secretary of Commerce and Under-Secretary of all other departments."[34] After his presidency, Hoover led not one, but two commissions on executive branch operations.

Many presidents have tried to inject the whiz-bang innovations of private enterprise into the poky policies of the federal government. Bill Clinton created the National Performance Review, which the political scientist James Q. Wilson described as "marrying the youthful spirit of Silicon Valley to the old traditions of official Washington."[35] Its purpose was to "reinvent government" by making it more transparent and responsive. George W. Bush instituted a government rating system to evaluate operations—his administration gave every department a red, yellow, or green "traffic light" score.[36] Obama tried to streamline regulations and launched a number of experiments to make government more effective through the use of social science.[37] Donald Trump attempted to make it easier for agencies to fire federal workers, though a court ruled he overstepped his authority by trampling workplace protections Congress had put in place for federal workers.[38]

Along the way, some reforms have taken hold to keep duties from overlapping, and to improve hiring and purchasing methods, but most reform efforts have petered out. The frustrated energy of failed efforts is palpable and can be found in a paragraph in the report of the subsequent reform effort that looks back on all the failed gambits that have crashed before: "All of these bodies made serious studies," reads the Hoover Report of 1955, "and most of them made important reports to the Congress or the President. Yet for the most part they were ineffectual. They did not get public support. Little or nothing was done about their recommendations, and the reforms they proposed died a-borning."[39]

Presidents have to operate while straining against Lilliputian ropes, from the rules and folkways of the bureaucracy to the congressional demands enshrined in legislation. When an administration tries to improve, Congress ignores them. "We spent a lot of time talking about putting the 'management' back in the Office of Management and Budget," says Mitch Daniels, who served as its director under George W.

Bush. "It was the right thing to do to evaluate every program and rate it whether it was working or not, but Congress in the end ignored it. It didn't matter if it was working or not. They were funding it whether it was working or not."[40]

If you want a taste of the sorrow that overcame many of the energetic reformers who tried to streamline the executive branch, do a little reading in the rules governing when and how an administration can reorganize itself. The Constitution vests in Congress the power to reorganize the executive branch. So a president has to ask Congress for permission to make improvements in the operation of his own administration. There are laws and regulations governing how to make such requests. Reading those laws and regulations can make you want to nap. Multiply the complexity associated with attempting to make things more efficient across all the places one would want to apply those efficiencies, and you have some sense of the thicket presidents and their administrations face in trying to improve their working environment.

As Teddy Roosevelt pushed to improve how the federal government operated, he told a story of its inefficiencies as a way to highlight the need for making things a little more shipshape: An officer in charge of an Indian agency made a request in autumn for a stove costing seven dollars to keep the infirmary warm during the winter. "Thereupon the customary papers went through the customary routine," Roosevelt wrote in his autobiography. "The transaction moved like a glacier with dignity to its appointed end, and the stove reached the infirmary in good order in time for the Indian agent to acknowledge its arrival in these words: 'The stove is here. So is spring.'"[41]

"I'm National Security Advisor for President Reagan. One morning I go into the Oval Office, and I'm alone with the president. He's sitting in his chair right in front of the fireplace. You know the scene. I'm sitting on the couch off to his left. And I'm telling him about this terrible problem I'm working on. You know the State Department and the Defense Department are mad. Commerce is involved. Treasury is involved. 'Mr. President, it's just a mess. I'm trying to solve it today.' He's paying no attention to me whatsoever. He's looking over my shoulder right into the Rose Garden. So I talk louder and talk faster. Nothing. And so I don't know what's wrong, what's going on. And so finally when I'm about out of anything to say or do, he perks up, and he says, 'Colin, Colin, look, look! The squirrels just came and got the nuts they put in the Rose Garden this morning.' And I said, 'Yes, Mr. President, I've got to go now.' And so I left his office and went back to my office, the corner office of the West Wing, and just sat there thinking, 'What the devil was that all about?' And then it struck me. It should have been baldly obvious. What he was saying was, 'Colin, I love you, and I will sit here for as long as you want me to, listening to you tell me about your problem. You let me know when I have a problem. And until then, I'm going to watch the squirrels in the Rose Garden go for the nuts.'"[1]

—GENERAL COLIN POWELL

Chapter 16

How a President Decides

The public have no idea of the constant accumulation of
business requiring the President's attention. No President
who performs his duty faithfully and conscientiously can
have any leisure. If he entrusts the details and smaller
matters to subordinates, constant errors will occur. I prefer to
supervise the whole operations of the Government myself
rather than entrust the public business to subordinates,
and this makes my duties very great.[2]

—JAMES K. POLK IN 1848

In the discharge of the duties of the office there is one rule
of action more important than all others. It consists in never
doing anything that someone else can do for you. Like many
other good rules, it is proven by its exceptions. But it
indicates a course that should be very strictly followed in
order to prevent being so entirely devoted to trifling details
that there will be little opportunity to give the necessary
consideration to policies of larger importance.[3]

THE AUTOBIOGRAPHY OF CALVIN COOLIDGE, 1929

T HE DIFFERENCE BETWEEN A MOVIE ABOUT BASEBALL AND A LIVE
baseball game is that in a movie the boring parts are edited out. Hero
sluggers are always getting hits. Many of them are home runs. No film
could sustain showing the boring truth that even Ty Cobb, the greatest
hitter ever, got a hit fewer than four out of ten times at the plate.[4] No
director would find much drama in the long pauses during play. Base-

*Outside the Oval Office on November 16, 1983, Ronald Reagan
feeds some squirrels (not pictured) in the White House Rose Garden,
a lesson in delegation and focus.*

ball is, after all, the only spectator sport that encourages fan calisthenics to make it through the game.[5]

This is true with the presidency as well. In dramas like *The West Wing* and *House of Cards*, Rushmore-ready presidents fold their towering frames into the Oval Office and deliver a series of politically dexterous and rhetorically pleasing solutions. This has conditioned many of our expectations about what a president could do if we just held the right kind of casting call.[6]

In the actual presidency, decisions are slower, more complicated and opaque. Calvin Coolidge wasn't sure the nature of the office could be captured at all. The job "does not yield to definition," he said, before lapsing into lyricism. "Like the glory of the morning sunrise, it can only be experienced — it cannot be told."[7]

John Kennedy described the presidency as a riddle: a job about making decisions, where the decisions are sometimes unclear even to the person making them. "The secret of the presidential enterprise is to be found in an examination of the way presidential choices are made," he wrote, but "the essence of ultimate decision remains impenetrable to the observer—often, indeed, to the decider himself."[8]

The keys to effective presidential decision making are put in place long before the acute moments that make it into our affirming dramas. Proper staff selection, planning, and delegation are important, but they are dry topics that can't be much improved by a swelling soundtrack or smoldering leading man. Some of the best presidential decision making takes place when a president chooses not to act, which is very hard to film. Finally, there is one other way that drama and reality diverge: You pretty much know how a movie is going to end. In reality, heroic presidents can do everything right and the ending still may be a disaster.

KNOW WHEN TO CUT IT

THE FIRST THING A PRESIDENT LEARNS ABOUT MAKING DECISIONS IS that they are never clear-cut. "Nothing comes to my desk that is perfectly solvable," President Obama explained to the author Michael Lewis. "Otherwise, someone else would have solved it. So you wind up dealing with probabilities. Any given decision you make you'll wind up with a thirty to forty percent chance that it isn't going to work. You have to own that and feel comfortable with the way you made the decision. You can't be paralyzed by the fact that it might not work out."[9] Thomas Jefferson explained this to his secretary of the treasury: "What is good in this case cannot be effected. We have, therefore, only to find out what will be least bad."[10]

Obama's national security advisor, Susan Rice, points to the discussion over intervention in the Syrian civil war as typical of a presidential-level decision with tough outcomes. Syria's President Assad had killed almost two hundred thousand people and displaced three million.[11, 12] "Do you intervene militarily and try to take out Assad?" she says, reeling off the set of questions. "You can't really accomplish that from the air, so that's a ground invasion again in the Middle East. But then if you don't, you've seen what happens. [Assad continues to slaughter his people.] Do you focus on those threats that are directly threatening the United States and our allies like ISIS? Yes, that's what we did, but then you leave other stuff unattended. I could go on and on, but the point is, that's an example, one of many, of a case where the sins of omission and commission kind of merge into all not good options. You're literally choosing from the least bad options and trying to minimize the downside to U.S. interests, recognizing there will be a downside under any course of action."[13]

The human response to uncertainty is to research a problem more. Presidents often don't have the time. Many presidential problems also don't get easier with further investigation; some grow hairier the more you hit the books. Bill Clinton learned this early in his administration. He encouraged a free-flowing atmosphere in which he could sample ideas, bat them around in ad hoc meetings, and test drive his thinking. "The meetingest person I've ever met" is how his treasury secretary, Lloyd Bentsen, referred to the late-night dorm room atmosphere.[14] "There was a tendency for people just to wander and walk into meetings," Chief of Staff Leon Panetta explains. "So we clearly limited that." Panetta told the program *Frontline* that he set new rules: "I will approve who goes on Air Force One with the president. I will determine who sits in those meetings in the Oval Office, so that we don't have people coming out of the wall sitting there. . . . There were so many things happening that it was pretty clear that the president really needed to have clear focus."[15]

President Clinton ultimately recognized that his decision-making process was too flabby for the job. "I always think that everything can be worked out, you know," Clinton told the talk show host Arsenio Hall. "Sometimes you can't work everything out. You've just got to cut it. And you've got to know when to cut it and when to work things out. That's something I've done a lot of work on, trying to make sure I overcome that weakness."[16]

A president who waits too long to decide either misses the moment to act or clogs up the conveyor belt carrying other decisions that need to be made. "You can never reduce all of the questions down to a certainty," Henry Kissinger has said about being president. "Sometimes you just have to leap."[17]

Presidents must get comfortable with a process they don't control. Staffers do the preliminary work and present options. Many decisions must be made very quickly with no time even to reframe the question. "What Presidents do every day is make decisions that are mostly thrust upon them," wrote the presidential scholar Richard Neustadt. "The deadlines are all too often outside their control, on options mostly framed by others."[18]

The President's Son of a Bitch

To make crisp decisions, the president needs a crisp team directed by a strong and independent chief of staff. "Every president reveals himself by the presidential portraits he hangs in the Roosevelt Room, and by the person he picks as his chief of staff," historian Richard Norton Smith told Chris Whipple.[19] What is revealed in a president's choice of chief of staff and the marching instructions he gives that person is how the president thinks about priorities, receptiveness to bad news, and delegating decision making.

The chief of staff enforces the president's quadrant system, whether the president employs the Eisenhower schematic or not. The president sets priorities and decides how much to delegate, but it's the chief of staff who takes those orders and keeps everyone on task. Meanwhile, the world conspires against order. Sometimes it's the president flinging wrenches into the works. The chief of staff has to read that evolving picture and either redirect the president or redirect the operation.

Since the president's time is the most valuable commodity in the world, the chief of staff must be miserly with the clock. This does not make him popular (there hasn't been a woman in the role yet). In Whipple's book about the post and its history, the term "son of a bitch" appears fifteen times. They must act like an SOB and are often called one by those who are denied access to the president.

People who can get fussy when the chief of staff exercises dominion over the hours and minutes include cabinet secretaries and family members. "I strongly believe there must be cabinet access to the president," huffed Jimmy Carter's transportation secretary, Brock Adams, who resigned when he was denied it. "I could not function under those circumstances. I suppose others can."[20]

Donald Trump's United Nations ambassador, Nikki Haley, complained about being shut out by Chief of Staff John Kelly. "I requested a meeting with the president. Chief of Staff Kelly stalled on it and would never call me back. Finally, I called the president and told him

I had been requesting a meeting for days and wasn't getting a response. Within an hour I had the meeting. Kelly didn't appreciate it and let me know."[21]

What a chief of staff must think about is the opportunity cost of presidential time. When a president spends time on one thing, he is not spending it on another. A chief of staff is responsible for knowing the entire range of presidential obligations and playing gatekeeper with that in mind. Interest groups, cabinet secretaries, and ideologues want the president devoting maximum attention to their cause. It may be a perfectly worthy issue, but it must be worthy relative to the other issues the president faces and toward which he and his team have calculated he can maximize his utility.

A smooth decision-making system allows a president to move from only reacting to threats to being able to advocate for their priorities. George W. Bush's PEPFAR program, the President's Emergency Plan for AIDS Relief, targeted relief toward millions of mothers and saved hundreds of thousands of babies from contracting AIDS on the African continent. The signature achievement was possible because enough time and attention was cleared to think boldly and not simply to react to events incrementally. When Bush pushed staffers to do more than their original blueprint imagined, the system could accommodate the larger vision. There was also a system in place that could respond with a plan when Bush returned from summer vacation and handed his homeland security adviser Fran Townsend John Berry's book *The Great Influenza*, on the 1918 flu, and asked her to create a response should they face that kind of outbreak.

Don't Snicker at "Executive Time"

On President Trump's daily schedule, several hours are devoted to "Executive Time." This became a subject of ridicule in 2019, when the president's schedule was leaked, presumably by someone who worked for the president but didn't think the president worked. It was true that the president's free time coincided with spells of rage-tweeting in response to Fox News programs airing at that time.[22] But whatever the specifics of Donald Trump's day, they should not obscure the general proposition that clearing time for the presidential brain is crucial. Top executives know that free time is important to think about strategy and vision. A Harvard Business School study called "The Leader's Calendar" found that top CEOs carve out about a quarter of their day for such creative thinking.[23]

We should not obsess about a president's schedule but instead focus on what a president actually does with his time, says Dan Pink, author of *When: The Scientific Secrets of Perfect Timing.* "One type of thinking is systematic, analytic, linear, and rigorous," explains Pink. "The other is more freewheeling, creative, iterative, and big-picture. We obviously want presidents to do both. We want them to pay attention to the data and the intelligence briefings and to think logically. But at other times we also want them to be more imaginative."[24] It's that second category that is most under threat from the busy presidential day, but where important Quadrant Two thinking can take place.

No Improvisation, Please

Nixon installed and empowered his chief of staff, H. R. Haldeman, to build a White House management system that became the template for many of his successors. Nixon hoped Haldeman's experience as an advertising executive would introduce "more advanced management procedures and . . . a tighter staff arrangement," as the *Los Angeles Times* reported on the eve of Nixon's presidency.[25] "Haldeman is the Lord High Executioner," the president told his staff. "Don't come whining to me when he tells you to do something. He will do it because I asked him to and you're to carry it out!"[26]

Haldeman's key principle was that improvisation was deadly. To minimize it, he designed a rigorous system. "Nothing goes to the president that is not completely staffed out first, for accuracy and form, for lateral coordination, checked for related material, reviewed by competent staff concerned with that area—and all that is essential for Presidential attention."[27]

Presidential decisions are complex and interconnected. A person operating outside the system created to accommodate that complexity might naively take a shortcut thinking it will speed up a result. Instead

Shown here aboard Air Force One (Spirit of 1976), *Richard Nixon's chief SOB, H. R. "Bob" Haldeman, tried to bring order to the White House in his role as chief of staff. Permit no "end-runs," he decreed, even by the president. Nixon's end-run on Watergate would cost Haldeman his liberty (he went to jail) and Nixon his office.*

of hastening the process, though, the shortcut may cause collateral damage because its author didn't have a view of the whole operation's activities.

"At any given moment there are dozens of interagency councils happening inside the White House, all hoping to get 'decision time' in the Oval to resolve their matter," says former secretary Mike Leavitt. "It's like an air traffic control tower managing a hundred airplanes [that all] think they have an emergency and need to land, now. To work well, the presidency has to have order and structure. To someone supremely confident in their ability to instinctively know the answer to every question, this could seem overly bureaucratic. However, when the process is not allowed to operate, the consequence is a lot of crashes and unexpected outcomes."[28]

Haldeman was a brute about anyone who might think about doing what he called an "end run" around the system. "Do not permit anybody to end-run you or any of the rest of us," he told his staff. "Don't become the source of end-running yourself, or we'll miss you at the White House."[29]

The chief of staff must control access not only to the president's time but also to his brain share. Information that reaches the president must be in the best form possible. You know about this in your own life. You don't want fourteen weather reports, for two weeks, if you're only deciding whether to take an umbrella. You need one weather report, the moment before you walk out the door. And you want that weather report to be of the greatest possible accuracy. On the other hand, if you've scheduled a church picnic, it does you no good to learn rain was scheduled when you're spreading out the blanket if that information has been in the forecast for a week. A chief of staff strives to make sure bad news makes it up the chain of command in time. Information must be fully baked and pass the clean toothpick test before it gets to the president. Otherwise, he will go off half-baked, initiating a cascading series of reactions.

The reason a president has to show faith in the system is that it encourages other people to operate within the system too. That discourages inefficient end-runs and also allows information to flow. Max Stier describes the presidency as an office encased in a set of force fields created to prevent bad information from getting from the bottom to the top, where leaders can actually act on it. Unless a president allows the system to work and fights his own impulses, the force fields will keep the president isolated. "Someone is going to do something dumb someplace, somewhere," says Stier. "The question is, does that information actually get to the people it needs to so that they can actually do something about it."[30]

The White House employee most prone to end-runs that a chief of staff has to worry about is the president. He's not like any other staffer, of course, which is why the president thinks end-runs are just fine. Action hero presidents take action! But a president can't know everything that is going on, and shouldn't. This means a president should not be tempted to give in to his worst instincts. Haldeman instructed the staff to incorporate the president's bad instincts in their planning. "If you go to him and say, 'I need an hour,' he will say, 'Sure, come in tomorrow at five,' and seventeen people will be there tomorrow at five."[31]

Mitt Romney tells the story of how this affected his father, who served as secretary of housing and urban development under Nixon. "My dad got very upset about the president's policy on a housing matter and met with the president and said, 'Here's what I want to do. This is very important.' Nixon said 'I agree, George. That's good.' Then my dad got back to his office, and the phone rang. It was Haldeman saying, 'That's not going to happen. That's not what we're doing.' The president doesn't like conflict. He doesn't want to sit there and disagree with you. He and I have talked since you've met, and that's not what we're going to do. So, George, this is the new marching order.' And of course, it infuriated my Dad. But that's how Nixon made it work given his personality."[32]

You'd think maybe the Nixon White House wouldn't be a model for operations, given how things turned out. But things turned out as they did not because of the weakness of the Haldeman system, but because Nixon and his team deviated from it. As Dick Cheney, who served as Ford's chief of staff, said, "There was nothing immoral or unlawful about the system."[33]

Haldeman's schematic for the chief of staff became such a model for the job that Clinton aide George Stephanopoulos handed Leon Panetta a copy of *The Haldeman Diaries* with the page turned down to the passage where Nixon empowered Haldeman in front of the staff. "You need the power not to be overridden," Stephanopoulos told Panetta, "not to have to deal with three different White Houses. You need to be a dictator."[34]

SAYING NO TO THE PRESIDENT

IT MIGHT NOT SEEM THAT HARD TO LET SOMEONE BE YOUR SOB, BUT what if that also means allowing your chief of staff to be an SOB to you?

I have interviewed chiefs of staff going back to the Reagan presidency, and each one has said the job sometimes requires being tough with the boss. "That's the most important quality that I think an assistant or chief of staff certainly can present to the president," says Jim Baker. "You've got to be able to say 'This doesn't make sense. Don't do it.'"[35] Robert Gates, who served as defense secretary for Bush and Obama and was CIA director under George H. W. Bush, told me "the subordinate

When Leon Panetta came into the White House as chief of staff, he dispelled the late-night dorm room atmosphere and helped the president learn when to "cut it," that is, when to stop seeking more information and make a decision.

needs to be willing to tell the truth to power, [and] the boss needs to be big enough to recognize that person is actually trying to help them."[36]

A president who allows a system where he can be told no must have a balanced temperament, because presidents are oriented toward action. They "find identity in the action," as Theodore White put it. Being told *no* robs them of their identity.

In an interview early in his tenure, I asked President Trump who on his staff told him no in his administration and who he relied on to help him identify his blind spots. "I guess it's one of those things in life you have to be able to figure out," he said. "Maybe I've been figuring that out anyway long before I got here."[37]

George W. Bush's chief of staff Josh Bolten explains that this ability to tell a president no highlights an important distinction in what makes a good or a bad chief of staff. Those who can tell a president no are working for the presidency and not just the president. If the duty is to the presidency, then the chief of staff serves the institution and its goals as set by the president's process, but also has an eye on the institutional role in American government. If the chief of staff believes the job is to serve the president, then the administration goes off course and the office becomes disconnected from its larger obligations in the American system, turning into a vanity project. Instead of following the plan informed by the president's vision, the ship of state veers off after the momentary impulses of the president's emotions.

CONDUCTOR

To make presidential-level decisions, a president needs space. This is created by delegating ruthlessly, pushing decisions to cabinet secretaries and staff. Warren Buffett describes the skill of delegating as cultivating an air of indifference.[38] Apple CEO Tim Cook describes his job as being like a conductor, in that a central part of his role is not performing but creating the perfect conditions for other great performers.

Ronald Reagan, as a former Hollywood actor, understood this idea of leadership. In his world, the star had one job and did it best when the rest of the crew did all of their individual jobs. "I've got a role to play," Reagan explained to his political guru Stu Spencer. "I've got a script to learn—and you're a producer, you're a director, and you're a cameraman: Now you do your job and I'm gonna do mine."[39]

In horse racing, this view of leadership is called "giving the horse its head," meaning don't hold the reins too tightly, let the horse think for itself. Mitt Romney and Michael Bloomberg both used the expression when talking about running a team. In their conception of the term, it means allowing your subordinates enough independence that they can do their best work. "Get people regardless of their political persuasion who have expertise in each of these areas that you're not an expert on, defense and business, and economics, and international relations, and give them authority to go along with responsibility and then let them do it even when there are things that you don't agree with," says Bloomberg.[40]

Shortly after Donald Trump won, I asked former secretary of state George Shultz what advice he would give the new president. "There has become a tendency to put decision making and even operational things in the White House," said Shultz, who served in the Eisenhower,

Nixon, and Reagan administrations. "The White House staff has grown a lot, the National Security Staff has grown a lot, with the result that that's a dominant place. . . . I would hope, once [President Trump] gets things settled down, the president might say something like this: 'I consider my cabinet and sub-cabinet people to be my staff. Those are the people I'm going to work with to develop policy. And they're the ones who are going to execute it under my supervision. But they're gonna execute it.' When you do that, you get good people. You get all people who have been confirmed by the Senate, people who can be called to testify at any time so they're responsible, accountable people. And you get better people and you get better execution. And it's much less expensive. You don't need these big White House staffs."[41]

CLEANING OUT THE CABINET

THAT ADVICE SOUNDS GOOD, BUT IT MAY BE NEARLY IMPOSSIBLE FOR a president to follow. Political considerations are just too great. Those pressures push against excessive delegation.

President Carter tried exactly what George Shultz suggested, instituting a "cabinet government" in which he gave power and autonomy to his cabinet secretaries. The idea—like many of Carter's disruptive gambits—crashed. Given free rein, cabinet secretaries started to build their fiefdoms, muscling in on the territory of the others. It was chaos.

Carter handed energy policy to his energy secretary, James Schlesinger, who created a product that irritated the other parts of government who were cut out of the process. A single cabinet department isn't designed to manage and coordinate with other agencies who feel they have a stake in the outcome. Left unattended, vanities, envies, devices, and jealousies flourish.

The best evaluation of the problem with the Carter presidency came from former Carter speechwriter James Fallows.

"Carter seemed to think that organizations would run in practice as they did on paper," Fallows wrote in *The Atlantic* in May 1979 after he had left the administration.

> People would perform their assigned functions and seek no orders; orders, once given, would be carried out; when people

were asked to direct specific bureaus or departments their loyal-
ties would still lie with the larger interests of the Administration.
Recent history was taken by Carter to prove his point: one of
Nixon's worst sins was his abuse of cabinet departments—he
stacked them with political flunkies and destroyed the secretaries' control over their own shops. With Watergate over and Nixon
deposed, cabinet government became a good-government rallying cry. . . .

If a president wants to allow cabinet secretaries full day-to-
day control, he must make special, almost daily efforts to find
out how that control is being used. Otherwise, when a president
declares hands off the departments, a depressingly predictable
sequence will begin. The White House staff will defer to the
departments—until the first big calamity happens. A secretary
might play to the department's constituents rather than the president's. . . . A big scandal might arise. . . . A secretary might appear to be building his own empire. Deception, inefficiency, a
dozen other ills infecting the various government departments,
whatever the origin, will make a president angry. He will feel
frustrated. . . . He will feel especially frustrated if, like Carter, he
has put extra stress on governmental performance and results. If
he cares about his policies and his political future, he will feel
compelled to act. He will send in his own people, good loyal
people, to get the job done right.[42]

To get the job done right, Carter not only sent in his people, he also
sent out his people. In the space of one day in July 1979, the president
fired five cabinet members. Gone were his secretaries of health, education, and welfare, the treasury, transportation, and energy, along with
his attorney general.

This upheaval caused a rolling tremor of snickers and chuckles
across Washington. The normally sedate *Washington Post* columnist
David Broder had a rollicking time at his typewriter, comparing the
Carter purge to a piece of space debris: "Skylab missed Washington
D.C. last week. But yesterday, the Carter Cabinet fell out of orbit 18
months ahead of schedule, breaking up into red-hot chunks of flaming
political ego and scattering debris across the bureaucratic landscape."[43]

Robert Strauss, a veteran of Democratic politics, was asked about whether he'd keep his job. "I expect to serve as trade representative for a rather extended period of time—perhaps until next week."[44] The comedian Mark Russell quipped that Rosalynn Carter was writing an article for *Ladies' Home Journal* titled "How We Turned Our Cabinet Room into a Spare Den."[45]

Did giving his cabinet secretaries their head, as Romney, Schultz, and Bloomberg suggest, not work for Jimmy Carter alone, or will it never work in a world where a president must have enough control to manage the hyperpolitics of our age? The American system elevates a president, but voters, pundits, and fellow politicians expect the president to be at the center of things.[46]

To make good decisions, a president needs to maintain two delicate balances. The chief of staff must be a whiz at building and keeping a system that presents decisions at just the right moment, and delegation must be robust but not so extensive that it exposes the president to political harm. It's hard to imagine that there is a human on the planet who could pull off both of those difficult balancing challenges perfectly.

If the delicate balances required to maintain a funtioning presidency are so difficult, what happens in an emergency? It is vital for a presidency to have a working decision-making system in an emergency because once it arrives, a system can't be built on the fly. "Even if you have a 1920s vision of what the American government should be, you have to believe that in moments of crisis and flux, the role of the president becomes incredibly important," says Harvard's Gautam Mukunda. "Having an effective government is like an airbag. When things go really, really wrong you want it to be there."[47] That's a moment when a presidency is like what we see in the movies, and when the cinematic moment comes, the president alone has to act.

Truman Seizes Steel Mills

On Tuesday, April 8, 1952, the furnaces in American steel factories slowed. The next day, 650,000 members of the millworkers' union were set to go on strike to protest the lack of a wage increase.

While furnaces cooled, President Truman grew hotter. With the country at war in Korea it could not afford the delay in its means of production. That night he spoke to the country.

"The plain fact of the matter is that the steel companies are recklessly forcing a shutdown of the steel mills. . . . As President of the United States it is my plain duty to keep this from happening. And that is the reason for the measures I have taken tonight. At midnight the Government will take over the steel plants. Both management and labor will then be working for the Government. And they will have a clear duty to heat up their furnaces again and go on making steel."[1]

A scathing *Washington Post* editorial two days later prophesied, "President Truman's seizure of the steel mills will probably go down in history as one of the most high-handed acts ever committed by an American President."[2]

The steel mills took to the courts to win back their property, leading to an exchange that captured just how far the president thought his power extended. United States District Court Judge David A. Pine asked Attorney General Holmes Baldridge, "You contend the executive has unlimited power in an emergency." Baldridge replied, "He has the power to take such action as is necessary to meet the emergency." Judge Pine: "If the emergency is great, it is unlimited, is it?" Baldridge: "I suppose, if you carry it to its logical conclusion, that's true." Judge Pine: "And that the executive determines the emergencies, and the courts cannot even review whether it is an emergency." Baldridge: "That is correct."[3]

Chapter 17

Impulse Presidency

—

As a very active President with lots of things happening,
it is not possible for my surrogates to stand at podium
with perfect accuracy![4]

—DONALD TRUMP TWEET, MAY 12, 2017

T HE STRUCTURE OF A WHITE HOUSE MIGHT SEEM ABSTRACT, BUT
John Kelly thinks it can determine presidential survival. Trump's second chief of staff saw the president's impeachment as the inevitable
result of a disordered White House. "I said, 'whatever you do, don't hire
a 'yes man,'" Kelly remembered telling Trump when he left the post in
December 2018, "someone who won't tell you the truth—don't do that.
Because if you do, I believe you will be impeached."[5]

Kelly was articulating the SOB model of his job, whereby a president must sometimes be saved from himself by a loyal staffer. Clark
Clifford rescued President Truman from a fit of pique by toning down
a rhetorical flourish in which the president called for hanging labor
leaders in order to resolve a railroad strike.[6] During Nixon's tenure,
these interventions happened so often, Henry Kissinger explained Watergate by saying: "Some damn fool went into the Oval Office and did
what Nixon told him to do."[7]

When asked about Kelly's tenure, a former colleague said, "You'll
never know the disasters he prevented."[8] In an interview with the *Los
Angeles Times*, Kelly hinted at this himself, saying his tenure should be
judged by all the calamities he prevented the president from launching.[9]

Former House Speaker Paul Ryan spoke in the same fashion about the president. In an exit interview with Mark Leibovich of *The New York Times* before retiring from public office, he summed up his time during the Trump period by saying, "I can look myself in the mirror and say 'I avoided this tragedy, I avoided that tragedy, I avoided that tragedy.'"[10]

Trump's former United Nations ambassador Nikki Haley held a different view of how presidential staff should behave. A former executive herself, as governor of South Carolina, she chided Kelly for what she characterized as an effort to undermine President Trump. "It should've been, 'Go tell the president what your differences are,'" Haley told CBS's Norah O'Donnell on the eve of impeachment, "'and quit if you don't like what he's doing.' . . . To undermine a president is really a very dangerous thing. And it goes against the Constitution, and it goes against what the American people want. And it was offensive."[11] Like so much, this view of leadership can be influenced by where people stand politically. Conservatives cheered insubordination when it was General Douglas MacArthur doing it. He became a hero by disobeying Democratic president Harry Truman. When Truman fired him, the belch of messages at the Western Union Offices testified to the national disapproval. Members of Congress read the choice ones into the Congressional Record. "Impeach the imbecile"; "We wish to protest the latest outrage on the part of the pig in the White House"; "Impeach the Judas in the White House who sold us down the river to the left wingers and the UN"; "Impeach the little-ward politician stupidity from Kansas City"; and "Impeach the red herring from the presidential chair." Senator William Jenner said, "This country today is in the hands of a secret coterie which is directed by agents of the Soviet Union." Senator Joe McCarthy told a Milwaukee meeting that the president was "a son of a bitch" surrounded by henchmen drunk on "bourbon and benedictine," and Congressman Joe Martin, the Republican leader in the House, told reporters that "the question of impeachments was discussed" among Republicans in their conference after MacArthur's firing was announced.[12]

The antipodal views of a staffer's duty illustrate the added complexity of working for a highly improvisational president. It is difficult

Former ambassador to the United Nations Nikki Haley chided Trump officials for trying to thwart their boss even when he made illegal requests. Haley's rule: Implement the president's goals or resign.

to agree even on a standard of staff behavior. The difference between Kelly and Haley is about more than the etiquette of managing up, though. They are clashing over a traditional tension in the presidency between leadership and management. A leader must push and be innovative. They must break some eggs to make the omelet, if you'll pardon the old cliché. A manager, on the other hand, must make sure the place runs efficiently so that there's a pan to make the omelet in and gas in the stove to cook it and the kitchen is orderly, so that no one winds up with egg on their face. A president leads, staff manages, and both must come to an accommodation that allows the place to operate.

Most presidents are elected to change the accepted way of doing things, which ensures tension in the kitchen. Since Jimmy Carter's election in 1976, voters have shown an overwhelming desire to elect outsiders. Even Senator Barack Obama was barely a Washington figure. His 2000 campaign ran on an explicit non-Washington message. This inclination helps explain why the American National Election Study found that 13 percent of Trump voters in 2016 backed Obama in 2012.[13] A *Washington Post* analysis after the 2016 election found that of the nearly seven hundred counties that twice voted for Obama, one-third had gone to Trump.[14] Voters are going to keep cycling through outsiders until they find one they like.

The modern president arrives with a mandate to renovate, but faces opposition from the zoning commission—the media, government workers, and Washington wise owls who fashion conventional wisdom. It's a group the energetic newcomers often give an unflattering nickname. Barack Obama's Deputy National Security Advisor Ben Rhodes called it "the blob," an inchoate entity made up of the foreign policy thinkers who criticized Obama's desire to change U.S. commitments in the Middle East.[15] (Most of them supported the Iraq war, which Obama had opposed.) There is a domestic equivalent, too—practitioners who have always done things a certain way. Donald Trump calls this force by various names like "the swamp" or the "deep state."

The blob smiles because they have seen this before in government and private enterprise where certainty is not leavened by ignorance. Not every new idea is a good one, they remind. Some traditions offer the stability that create the conditions for entrepreneurial thinking. "The one thing that members of that elite group have in common is experience," former defense secretary Robert Gates told me when I asked about the blob, of which he was a member. "Some of us have given bad advice in the past. Some of us have given pretty good advice. But to lump everybody together and say—and really the [presidential] candidates kind of do that—and to say 'I don't need those people, I don't want those people,' is to dismiss an awful lot of experience and a very great diversity of views on the challenges we face and how to deal with them."[16] A president must find a balance between these views, pressing against established thinking without discarding its necessary wisdom.

Donald Trump did not carry a concern about this balance to Washington with him. He brought a wrecking ball. This put him in a different category altogether than previous presidents who wrestled with the tension between innovation and tradition. In the extremity of his approach, though, President Trump offers a lens through which to look at the larger presidential challenge of being an agent of change in the modern presidency. To be successful, a president must do more than just disrupt the regular order of things. That may be what their voters are satisfied with, but greatness lies in replacing it with a better alternative.

THE TRUMP WAY

H. R. HALDEMAN WARNED AGAINST "END RUNS," EVEN FROM THE president. Donald Trump has been an end-run president. He outsourced his Ukraine policy to his private lawyer, Rudy Giuliani.[17] He tasked the White House lawyer with firing special counsel Robert Mueller.[18] When his Homeland Security director, chief of staff, and secretary of state told him that various demands he had made would break the law, he sought ways to go around staffers who were so sensitive about law breaking. "When the president would say, 'Here's what I want to do and here's how I want to do it,' I'd have to say to him, 'Mr. President, I understand what you want to do, but you can't do it that way. It violates the law. It violates a treaty,'" former secretary of state Rex Tillerson told Bob Schieffer.[19] "You know, he got really frustrated."

President Trump has operated as he did in the private sector, say his closest aides, impatient with what he sees as the time-wasting impediments to progress erected by the bureaucracy. One Trump ally sought a metaphor from the New York real estate business to explain the president's worldview. In real estate, mountains of red tape can be avoided if you find the right person, a "fixer," who can work the system and bypass the nine-to-five drones running it. "There are really only five people who need to make decisions," says one former Trump staffer of running a White House, "everyone else is just kind of getting in the way."[20]

Another Trump veteran describes what it is like to encounter the bureaucracy: "The problem presidents have when they come into office is they all have their own feelings about engagement with the world, but they walk into this fifty-thousand-person department that wrote the policy on Ukraine, Afghanistan, and the world. They own the policy; it's their life's work. You look at the National Security Council and it's made up of many of the same people who own and believe in our existing foreign policies. So you have these discussions with a president who doesn't want to be screwing around in Afghanistan and NSC people who wrote our policy on Afghanistan. They're fighting changes because they can't believe these new people have ideas. It's not that they inhabit the swamp. They built it. It is abnormal to question them."[21]

The job for any adviser, then, explains H. R. McMaster, is to find a way to match the system to its new leader. "We can design the perfect process and products and bring them to the president and say, 'Hey, conform please to this,'" says McMaster of working with President Trump. "I jokingly said, 'How do you think that's going to work?' What we have to do is run a process and develop products and create venues that are consistent with the way the president receives information and makes decisions. If I tried to hide that and say, 'Hey, here's the one shiny option we all agree on, he's going to say 'forget it.'"

Afghanistan offers a stark example of how abysmal conventional wisdom can be. The Afghanistan Papers, published by *The Washington Post* in late 2019, revealed the candid assessments of top military officials as a part of a federal project examining the root failures of the longest armed conflict in U.S. history. The interviews and findings, which were not supposed to be made public, showed that top officials did not tell the truth about the eighteen-year war, making, as the *Post* put it, "rosy pronouncements they knew to be false and hiding unmistakable evidence the war had become unwinnable."[22]

The Afghanistan Papers are much like the Pentagon Papers, the secret report on the disastrous decision making and deception behind the Vietnam War. The author David Halberstam used the term "the best and the brightest" to refer to the policy experts who had all the credentials and right opinions but were wrong about that war.[23] Kennedy's secretary of state, Dean Rusk, exemplified the cocooned thinking that preferred the well-known path. "His mind, for all its strength and clarity, was irrevocably conventional. He mistrusted what he called 'the flashy or sensational' and rejoiced in the role of 'tedium' in diplomacy," historian Arthur M. Schlesinger Jr., wrote about Rusk in *Life* magazine in 1965. "He seemed actually to prefer stale to fresh ways of saying things. One felt that he regarded novelty as an effort to shock or make mischief."[24]

IDENTIFYING A PROBLEM IS NOT THE SAME AS SOLVING IT

ONE OF THE GREAT MAXIMS ABOUT INNOVATION IS ATTRIBUTED TO Henry Ford: "If I had asked people what they wanted, they would have said faster horses." It is a truly innovative expression, for it is likely made-up and not something Ford said, but it neatly captures his spirit. Ford matched that passion for the new and innovative, with an appreciation for considered thinking and precision. To build his product, he adapted the moving assembly line. That's what turned a good idea into one that he could execute with such success. Creativity in the idea-forming phase was necessary but would have been deadly when it came to designing a system of interchangeable parts for assembly of that idea.

The regularity of production Ford revolutionized is what would be derisively called the bureaucracy in government—standardization, a regular order of doing things, lines of authority and review. In a presidency, innovation and a disruptive approach are not at odds with an orderly White House of the kind Haldeman created. "Structure and process make it possible to make decisions with the widest amount of information and the most complete set of options and examine issues quickly, thoroughly, and intimately," says Karl Rove. "The absence of process is disorganization and makes it dependent less on a careful examination of the facts and more on who got into the office last." In a White House, Rove explains "information jumps up and grabs you, but [where there is a system] it'll be informed by people thinking and discussing and writing about these things for months."[25]

Donald Trump brought an instinct for doing things in a new way, but it is the missing second part of this formula for success that has wracked his White House. "I wouldn't go to war with you people," President Trump told his military leaders during a discussion of Afghanistan, according to Philip Rucker and Carol Leonnig in their book, *A Very Stable Genius*. "You're a bunch of dopes and babies."[26]

The word "chaos" comes up so frequently in interviews about Trump's process, you'd think it was his Secret Service code name. Lines of authority were crossed, staffers were pitted against one another, and competing fiefdoms were allowed to flower and climb up the facade. When I hosted *Face the Nation* I would get regular Sunday phone calls from representatives of each faction calling to point fingers at the other in order to shape the program's discussions.

The president's impulsivity and the culture it fostered have undermined his goals. Off-the-record conversations with those who have worked with the president describe a path as predictable as the movement of the sun. Plans were made, hours of work completed, the playing cards placed in their fragile tower. Then the president thundered in with demands to do the illegal, impractical, or unwise and the cards scattered as though someone had turned on the leaf blower. Instead of Ford's steady assembly line, the process was more like the rush at the mall on Black Friday.

This was the Trump way. "He's the kind of guy who likes throwing hand grenades in the room," said his friend Richard LeFrak. "It's kind of his personality that—you know, he likes to see how people react to some statement or act that he does."[27] Having destabilized the room, as the author of the chaos, Trump could manage it while everyone else was getting their bearings and waiting for their ears to stop ringing.

This approach creates some fellow-feeling among former senior White House staffers in the Bush administration who sympathize with what it must be like to work for a random-task-switching president. "I don't know what it would be like to wake up every day and have no idea what the president was going to say," said one.[28] A former Trump administration official refers to people who were "used up" by working under the strain of Donald Trump.[29] Conversations with Trump administration cabinet secretaries and senior Trump officials had the aspect of a man chasing the bull in the china closet, trying to catch the vases and plates before they hit the ground.

There were advantages to Trump's chaotic approach. The president gave his national security officials flexibility and a free hand to carry out the campaign against ISIS in the early period of his presidency. Vast sections of the administration are also free from the president's micromanaging. His son-in-law, Jared Kushner, won praise from Democrats in deftly handling criminal justice reform. Ivanka Trump has effectively spearheaded worker retraining and family leave policies, and counselor Kellyanne Conway aided the push to pass legislation to attack opioid addiction. In areas outside his observations, if Trump could boast about a development in his administration, that made him happy; he was not concerned with the details of how it had been accomplished.

A senior staffer who had also served under President Obama marveled at how quickly work could get done in the Trump administration, which lacked the traditional process of review. "The executive order was a stark contrast with Obama," says the official of a policy authored early in the term. "It would have taken us eighteen months to do that. Was that a feature or a bug? It depends. If you're working on motherhood-and-apple-pie stuff and you know what you're talking about, you can do it. When you look at the travel ban executive order, it did not benefit from the same lack of process. They undermined themselves."[30]

The travel ban was the first example of many executive actions in which the president's intervention and brash approach worked against his goals, exacting costs in the process. The travel ban order blocked entry into the United States for people from seven terrorist-related countries. When the order was issued, neither border and customs officials nor the secretary of defense had been brought into the decision-making process. This omission created days of chaos in the green card system as officials straightened out whether the rule affected green card holders or not. "There aren't a lot of answers as of today," said Senator Marco Rubio after the order was issued. "In fact, my staff was told the State Department as of today was ordered not to talk to Congress about the issue."[31]

Iraq, one of the countries on the list, was actively assisting the United States in military operations against terrorists. The hastily authored order not only offended the U.S. ally but blocked Iraqi officials from coming into this country to coordinate with military officials.

It is easier to ask forgiveness than permission, perhaps, but that's not a wise way to make government policy. Time, energy, and manpower are wasted in the effort to undo the mess created by the lack of planning. The wording of the travel ban itself was so rushed that it required three revisions before it passed through the court system.

"If you don't have a process," says Josh Bolten, "it doesn't matter how smart the people are. If you don't have a process to bring some focal point, then you'll miss something important." Either a president won't know what they don't know, or they'll miss the bad information that a good system will allow to make it to the right decision makers. "The travel ban is a classic case," says Bolten. "Had there been a process in place, the president never would have been given an option that was clearly a surprise to people who needed to know about it."[32]

As a sign of the self-healing instincts that kick in during an administration, when I asked Trump staffers to recount when it had first hit them that they were responsible for the enormous duties of the presidency, several mentioned the chaotic days of the travel ban. They told stories of the media frenzy and the confusion in agencies as if everything they were describing had been initiated from outside the administration rather than from the chief executive.

SYRIA SWERVES

PRESIDENT TRUMP REPEATEDLY SURPRISED HIS ADVISERS ON MILItary policy in Syria, a key part of his objective of defeating the terrorist group ISIS. In December 2018, the president announced on Twitter that the United States was withdrawing from Syria.[33] Nobody in the administration—not his National Security Advisor, not the head of the CIA, not the chairman of the Joint Chiefs—knew about his decision. Less than two weeks before, Secretary of Defense James Mattis and Brett McGurk, the president's special envoy for the coalition fighting ISIS, were in Canada trying to persuade the seventy-nine-member global coalition to stay in the fight. McGurk had also explained during a State Department briefing a week before Trump's announcement why it was U.S. policy that forces should stay: "It would be reckless if we were just to say, well, the physical caliphate is defeated, so we can just leave now."[34] Then, that's exactly what the president did say.

The president had said, in announcing his withdrawal, that ISIS had been defeated, but his advisers had repeatedly told him that while ISIS had lost its geographical foothold, thousands of ISIS fighters remained in the area, ready to move in if U.S. forces backed off. If the president wanted to make good on his boast of defeating ISIS, they told him, the United States had to stay in the fight.[35]

President Trump was so abrupt and dismissive of his military team, including Secretary of Defense Mattis, that Mattis resigned. After fighting so long and hard to defeat the terrorist group, he said, he wasn't going to preside over its return.[36] McGurk, who had been contemplating delaying his planned departure from the administration to finish the fight, retired immediately as well.

The announcement set off a four-day scramble to get the president to either reverse or delay the decision, which he ultimately did. Said an ambassador to a key U.S. ally: "We have no understanding what will happen on any given day and whether what happens on one day will last to the next."[37]

Several months later there was another policy jolt. In October 2019, President Trump spoke with Turkey's leader, Recep Tayyip Erdogan, who threatened to launch a military operation against U.S.-backed Kurdish rebels in northeast Syria.[38] Erdogan had made this threat many times before and Trump had pushed back, boasting about how he was not going to abandon the U.S. allies, the Kurds, who had been crucial in the fight against ISIS. A year earlier, Trump explained in a press conference, "They fought with us. They died with us. They died. . . . Tens of thousands of Kurds died fighting ISIS. They died for us and with us. . . . We don't forget—I don't forget."[39]

A year later, the president reversed this position. He gave his endorsement for a Turkish military operation that would sweep away the American-backed Kurdish forces near the border in Syria.[40] After the White House announced the surprise policy change, Turkey moved in and shelled the former U.S. allies, took over former U.S. positions, or allowed its allies to. Hundreds of Islamic State prisoners either escaped or were freed from detention in northern Syria as the Kurds turned their attention to fighting for their own survival. Senator Lindsey Graham, a staunch Trump ally, called it "irresponsible" and a "stain on America's honor. . . . We have sent the most dangerous signal possible—America is an unreliable ally."[41]

The Pentagon inspector general later reported that the president's move had undermined his goal of defeating ISIS. "ISIS exploited the Turkish incursion and subsequent drawdown of U.S. troops to reconstitute capabilities and resources within Syria and strengthen its ability to plan attacks abroad," the inspector general wrote.[42] The Pentagon spent months managing the wild swerve, and six months after the fire drill, the same number of U.S. troops were in Syria as had been there when the president announced the withdrawal. "Trump doesn't pay attention, there's no process, and then he's suddenly surprised by one event or another. That just compounds risk in a wartime situation because new facts arise all the time—mostly manageable if there's a process, totally unmanageable if the commander in chief has no idea what's going on or feel for things," says McGurk. "So on Syria, it's a call from Erdogan, who has tried this gambit before: 'I'm going to invade Syria, so get your people out of there. I'll take care of ISIS. You have nothing to worry about.' The right answer is 'No, you're not, don't come near my people, let's work this out.' But Trump, who doesn't want to be there anyway, hasn't internalized the situation at all, and never prepares for calls with counterparts, says, 'Sounds great, it's all yours. I'm out of there.'" As if to prove how vital U.S. action in the region was to defeating ISIS, it was during this confused period that U.S. forces killed the ISIS leader Abu Bakr al-Baghdadi.

The president's impulsive decisions—calling for a meeting with the Taliban at Camp David (which he then called off), ordering an Iranian air strike that he called off only after pilots were in their planes ready to fly, ending U.S.–South Korean joint operations—also caught his military officials off guard. So has his rough treatment of allies like the European Union, which he labeled America's foe, and his gentle treatment of adversaries like Russia.[43] Pentagon planners had to expand their planning, incorporating the president's impulsiveness into their blueprints for the future. They drew up contingencies for an immediate withdrawal from Afghanistan in case Trump called for a pullout as he had in Syria. It was possible, since Trump has long pushed for just that. On the other hand, in a Thanksgiving 2019 visit to Afghanistan, he promised "total victory," an extraordinarily large pledge which military officials were not expecting.[44]

Presidents get to make these kinds of decisions, but the manner in which they make them matters, as surely as a cabdriver's rightful use of a steering wheel matters if they are to avoid taking everyone up over the curb. Innovation without execution is hallucination, they say in Silicon Valley, modifying the Japanese proverb "Vision without action is a daydream."

DISRUPTION PRICE TAG

THE IMPROVISATIONAL PRESIDENCY ALSO HAS A DOLLAR COST. PRESIdent Trump has challenged independent agencies, breaking with decades of practice intended to promote economic stability. When the president's trade actions against China, Europe, Canada, and Mexico weakened the economy, he berated the Federal Reserve for not lowering interest rates. He suggested that Fed chairman Jerome Powell was as great an enemy of the United States as the Chinese.[45] He called Powell and the other Fed board members "boneheads."[46]

This isn't just rhetoric. It's bad for business when the president gives the Fed the business. A paper published by the National Bureau of Economic Research found "The average effect of these tweets on the expected fed funds rate is statistically significant and negative . . . market participants believe the Fed will succumb to the political pressure from the President."[47]

In 2019 the president shut down the federal government when he couldn't reach a deal with Democrats on funding his border wall. "If we don't get what we want, one way or the other," he promised congressional leaders, "whether it's through you or through the military or whatever you want to call it, I will shut down the government."[48] This cost $3 billion, according to a partial accounting by the Congressional Budget Office.[49] Other costs not counted in the tally included disruption to private enterprise which relies on government business and permits. Roughly one million government contractors also received no back pay after the shutdown was over.[50]

The president's unilateral action has led to the repeated spectacle of the president contradicting or exposing his top staff as dishonest. When Trump fired James Comey, Vice President Pence offered a dramatic and earnest explanation for the decision, suggesting the president's move was based solely on the recommendation from Deputy Attorney General Rod Rosenstein: "A man of extraordinary independence and integrity and a reputation in both political parties of great character," explained Pence about Rosenstein, came to work, sat down, and made the recommendation for the FBI to be able to do its job that it would need new leadership."[51] The next day, the president explained that he decided to fire Comey before Rosenstein's letter because of the Russia investigation, not for the reasons Pence had cited.

When his National Security Advisor H. R. McMaster said Trump had not revealed sensitive information to the Russians, the president undermined him moments later, announcing in a tweet that he had a right as the president to reveal the information.[52] True, a president can declassify anything, but it put his aides in the position of looking as if they were trying to mislead the public about what had happened. Garden variety spin, which all administrations engage in, takes on a more sinister shape when it is directly contradicted by the boss.

After a few of these incidents, the president explained in a tweet that his staff couldn't speak for him because they don't always know what he's doing: "As a very active President with lots of things happening, it is not possible for my surrogates to stand at podium with perfect accuracy!"

It can also be more difficult to stand in a courtroom. In July 2019, a government lawyer tried to explain to a judge why his position about the census was different from the one the president had just tweeted. "The tweet this morning was the first I had heard of the president's position on this issue, just like the plaintiffs and Your Honor," Josh Gardner, a lawyer for the Justice Department's civil division, who served under multiple administrations, told the judge. "I do not have a deeper understanding of what that means at this juncture other than what the President has tweeted. But, obviously, as you can imagine, I am doing my absolute best to figure out what's going on."[53]

THE SAVING GRACE OF INSUBORDINATION

DESPITE AMBASSADOR HALEY'S POSITION ON STAFF FREELANCING, it is likely that Donald Trump was saved on at least one occasion, if not more, by the insubordination of his staff members. According to sworn testimony by his former White House lawyer, Don McGahn, President Trump told him to shut down Robert Mueller's investigation into whether the Trump campaign worked with Russia to influence the 2016 election and whether the president obstructed the investigation into that matter. McGahn ignored him, concluding, rightly, that firing Mueller would have given evidence and ammunition to obstruction of justice charges.

According to Ruth Marcus in *Supreme Ambition*, during the fight over Supreme Court Justice Brett Kavanaugh's nomination battle, McGahn refused to take a phone call from the president when he thought Trump wanted to pull the nomination because of the political heat. Kavanaugh was later confirmed by the Senate.

National Security Advisor John Bolton tried to block the president from making aid to Ukraine contingent upon that country's investigating Joe Biden's son [54] Bolton failed, and the president was impeached for conditioning U.S. assistance on the announcement of an investigation into the Bidens.

"Beware the Spokes of the Wheel"

When Jimmy Carter and his team arrived at the White House, they found a bicycle wheel left by Gerald Ford's chief of staff, Dick Cheney. It was a regifting. When Ford lost the 1976 election, Cheney's colleagues gave him the wheel mounted on a board as a going-away present. All the spokes except one had been busted, bent, and twisted. The gift was an ode to Cheney's view of the management structure of the presidency. If everyone had access to the president through their own channels—the spokes on the wheel—the system broke down. No decisions got made until the president signed off. That created bottlenecks and burned out the president.

"Power in Washington is measured by how much access a person

Beware the spokes of the wheel! During the transition, President Gerald Ford's outgoing chief of staff, Dick Cheney (center), and head of his transition team, John Marsh (left), warned Jimmy Carter's transition chief, Jack Watson (right), against allowing the new president to make himself available to everyone. Carter's team didn't listen.

has to the president," wrote Gerald Ford in his autobiography. "Almost everyone wanted more access than I had to give. I wanted to have an 'open door,' but it was very difficult. . . . I was to discover soon enough that it simply didn't work."[55]

Cheney's modification was to break all the other spokes and have the organization run through him. "Somebody's got to be in charge. Somebody's got to be the go-to guy who can go into the Oval Office and deliver a very tough message to the president," Cheney explained. "You can't do that if you got eight or nine guys sitting around saying, 'Well, you go tell him.'"[56]

The inscription on the plaque read, "The spokes on the wheel are a rare form of management artistry . . . modified by Dick Cheney." Cheney decided to pass on this wisdom and left the wheel on his desk for Carter's top aide, Hamilton Jordan, along with a note: "Ham, beware the spokes of the wheel."[57]

The advice did not convey. Jordan and Carter didn't listen. Like Donald Trump almost forty years later, Carter and Company had come to town to disrupt the order of things.[58]

Nixon had a regimented system. Carter would have a looser system. The former submarine officer and Georgia governor decided he would be his own chief of staff. He'd be more available to his staff and cabinet. He'd listen to a wide range of views and be more transparent.

Carter was soon overburdened. The reviews in the newspapers were withering. "The president decides even the petty questions himself," one Democratic Senate staff member was quoted in the *Boston Sunday Globe* in 1978.[59] "He attends to minute details to an obsessive degree." *Saturday Night Live* lampooned Carter's penchant for managing everything with a skit in which he talked down a caller who had taken too much acid.[60]

The central story that typified this tendency was Carter's management of the White House tennis court schedule. The story conjures images of the president at a folding table checking in staffers on a clipboard. It wasn't exactly that bad. Carter had told his staff that the court was for his family and to run any request for the court by him. Stuart Eizenstat, a former Carter adviser, explains why it was necessary: Carter slipped off to play one day and returned shortly thereafter.

The court was occupied. "Some OMB guys" are playing, the president said glumly.[61]

Democratic wise men staged an intervention with Carter. The "spokes of the wheel" approach had to be scrapped.[62] Carter agreed, at least to his diary, in which he wrote, "It's become obvious to me that we've had too much of my own involvement in different matters simultaneously. I need to concentrate on energy and fight for passage of an acceptable plan."[63] His new chief of staff, Hamilton Jordan, told *The New York Times*, "I think he's going to be different in his approach, with less inclination to jump into details, and more listening, thinking and reflecting."[64]

President Trump's former White House counsel Don McGahn describes the structure of Trump's world as "hub and spokes," but the president has added special features to his rims. According to Jonathan Swan of *Axios*, McGahn said "no member of staff is empowered because Trump is the hub and he makes the decisions; all the senior aides are spokes." Trump often assigns "the same task to multiple people," and "there is no chief of staff in the usual sense."[65] Trump has called Jimmy Carter "a terrible president," but his management style became a hypercharged version of it.[66] "He has turned a presidency-centered government into an Oval Office–centered government," says Stier.[67]

Unlike Carter, Donald Trump largely stuck with his management approach even after a series of crackups. "The idea that someone or some plan is going to manage Donald Trump is not true," says a former senior White House staffer. "No one is going to tell him what to do. The idea that one of these guys [from past administrations] would know what to do with Donald Trump? They'd have a stroke. The best you can do is have a policy of containment."[68] Donald Trump has transformed the office of the presidency into an office of one, whipsawed by the dictates of the chief executive even if those dictates are at odds with his own policies or verifiable fact.

What is most extraordinary about President Trump's commitment to chaos is that he has been able to sustain it. Usually chaos exacts a psychological toll in high-pressure jobs, and there is no greater psychological wringer than the presidency.

ALL EYES ARE ON YOU, MR. PRESIDENT.

All eyes are on you, Mr. President.
In the audience, the eyes of "The Press," "Congress,"
"The People," "Economy," "The Trusts," and
"Teddy Roosevelt," among others, look on.

THE PRESIDENT WILL SEE YOU NOW

At 12:45 P.M. on March 15, 1913, 125 newsmen appeared in the new president's office. They had been called there by his private secretary to meet him for the first time.[1] They stood in a semicircle, four deep, in sack coats and vests, waiting for the new tenant to start pushing around some words. "I did not realize there were so many of you," said President Wilson, piercing the awkward pause. "Your numbers force me to make a speech to you en masse instead of chatting with each of you."[2]

The speech "en masse" would later receive the formal name "press conference," a Wilson innovation. Presidents have come to be wary of them, but in their early days, press conferences were a balm to the troubled chief executive. WILSON WINS NEWSPAPERMEN read the *New York Times* headline of the encounter. The accompanying article is a warm bath from top to tail. The newspapermen liked Wilson, and Wilson seemed very much indeed to like them, too! "As he went on talking, the big hit he was making with the crowd became evident," gushed the *Times* reporter. "There was something so unaffected and honest about his way of talking under this unexpected call on him that it won everybody."[3]

The *Washington Post* reporter wasn't going to be outdone in this apple polishing contest. "Wilson, in friendly chat, says he likes reporters," read the *Post* story, which then went soft in the knees, describing Wilson "standing there, where he could take in all with a sweep of his kindly eyes and with a genial smile."

Chapter 18

The Expectation

—

Mommy, what do they do to a president to make
a man look like Mr. Hoover does?[4]

— GIRL SCOUT FROM PALO ALTO

Short day in office — left for 1st weekend in Camp David.
It was great to be in a house with the knowledge you could
just open a door and take a walk outdoors if you wanted.[5]

— RONALD REAGAN

When I took office, only high-energy physicists had
ever heard of what is called the Worldwide Web. . . .
Now even my cat has its own page.[6]

— BILL CLINTON

AT THE CONCLUSION OF MOST RECENT PRESIDENCIES, THE official White House photographer compiles a book of their favorite pictures of the president. The turn of the pages offers a tour through the psychological landscape of the modern presidency. The president appears at the bedside of wounded soldiers he sent into battle or greets caskets arriving at Dover Air Force Base wrapped in the American flag. The president bears witness to grief in gymnasiums, town squares, churches, and schools in the aftermath of tornadoes, floods, and shootings. The presidential body leans, paces, and slumps through an endless string of meetings. In the pictures with world leaders, the president's posture is a little more straight.

In almost all of the images, the president is the focal point of all the eyes. Everyone wants something: comfort, an answer, a salute, a signature, news, approval, encouragement, inspiration, the truth, a thumbs-up or a thumbs-down. A president travels with The Expectation just as much as he does the presidential seal.

The pictures in the book are arranged by theme, but The Expectation follows no orderly pattern. A president must switch from serious to congenial to contemplative and back again, a kind of performance that would be trying for even a professional actor. In the morning, the trade staff may need a decision on the next round of negotiations with China. Then it's time to welcome the college football champions, followed by a phone call with the British prime minister.

The unrelenting pace and variety can distort reality. Denis McDonough, who served President Obama as chief of staff, says time occasionally became unhooked from its normal signifiers. "It required a rare ability to know what day it was," he said. "Every night felt like Tuesday night."[7]

This is an awful lot for one consciousness to handle. One of the most iconic presidential photos is titled "The Loneliest Job." It captures John F. Kennedy standing alone staring out the south window of the Oval Office.[8] It depicts an essential truth: This job rests on one human body and one mind. Bill Clinton thought the photo captured the presidency so perfectly that he hung it in his private office.

The presidential brain must handle a wider variety of acute experiences than perhaps any other brain on the planet. Meanwhile, the president lives in a most peculiar unreality. A president travels not only with a doctor but with bags of his blood type and a room for surgery on Air Force One. If the Secret Service thinks the marble on the bathroom floor in a foreign country might cause the president to take a digger, they will lay down protective strips to give him traction when he gets out of the tub. Grover Cleveland used to answer his own front door; now presidents' lives are baby-proofed.

Shortly after the attacks of 9/11, George W. Bush asked for ice cream, and when he noticed it wasn't his favorite from Blue Bell, he was told that the Secret Service was worried that those who would try to do him harm would know of his fondness for Blue Bell and poison the White House supply.

The president cannot get away from the president. In the White House working offices, the president's picture is on almost every work-place wall—it is where the White House photographers put their daily work. The other walls contain paintings of the men who achieved greatness in the job, as well as those who muddled through. It's like taking a test with your competitors' scores posted around you.

The strain of the job reportedly caused Nixon to talk to the paintings. Harry Truman thought they might talk back. He wrote in his diary that the disconnect between what the people want and what a president can deliver was so strong it caused the ghosts of his predecessors to roam the halls: "The tortured souls who were and are misrepresented in history are the ones who come back."[9] That's a crowded group.

Harry Truman called the White House the "great white jail."[10] Obama called it "the bubble,"[11] and told an aide that he had a recurring dream. In it he was enjoying a peaceful walk. He was alone and undisturbed. Then he was noticed. That turned the dream into a nightmare, and he awoke. "You have no freedom, you can't walk out of the White House," says Obama's National Security Adviser Susan Rice. "To get fresh air you're either on the south lawn, which gets very confined, or you're playing golf in a bubble. You literally can't get out. If you want to watch a movie, you have to watch it in the White House theater. If you want to see your friends, you basically have to invite them over. If you go to their house, it's a whole production. They've got to sweep the house. It's ridiculous. You really feel that the walls are closing in on you. Obama fantasized about being able to put on a baseball cap and sunglasses and walk through Central Park and just look like some normal black guy. And even if he tried to do that now, everybody would recognize him. You never escape that. Once you've given up your independence you never get it back, and one shouldn't underestimate what that does to people."[12]

Ronald Reagan's diary captures his delight upon grabbing a sliver of freedom when he first spent a night at Camp David. "It was great to be in a house with the knowledge you could just open a door and take a walk outdoors if you wanted."

The presidency contains an irritating disparity. The president of the United States is simultaneously the strongest and the weakest of all national leaders. A president can unleash armies and turn the emotions of stadiums full of people but is powerless in battles against the media, the bureaucracy, and Congress when it wants to stand up and assert itself. If there is another election coming, a president feels the voters tapping their toes on the sidelines every time he makes a decision.

A president has valets, butlers, aides, and bodyguards watching for the sign of some need they can fulfill, but the things a president truly wants—quick action in Congress, the agreement of a foreign leader, walking to get an ice cream cone on a summer night—are maddeningly out of your reach. You can shake your scepter and sometimes it's just a rattle.

This is frustrating to a president, because anyone who gets the job likes to take action. "The one thing that energizes any president is the ability to get things done," says Leon Panetta.[13] Ike Hoover, a longtime White House usher, described that at the end of a busy day, Teddy Roosevelt, still bursting with energy, would slip out the back of the mansion and run around the base of the Washington Monument until he had blown off his excess steam.[14]

Grover Cleveland testified to his restlessness when he left office. "After the long exercise of power, the ordinary affairs of life seem petty and commonplace," he wrote. "I thought I was glad when Mr. McKinley came to Washington to be inaugurated. . . . But I miss the strain, the spur to constant thinking, the consciousness of power, the knowledge that I was acting for seventy million people daily."[15]

That strain of meaningful action is the glorious upside of the job. "They're president because they like to be in charge," says Josh Bolten, George W. Bush's chief of staff. "It's like a football running back waiting for the blocking to develop. Their instinct is to just sprint."[16] When the historian Richard Reeves challenges the myth of Ronald Reagan's passivity, it is this instinct that he uses as proof. "I found in the course of my research [that he] was a gambler, a bold, determined guy. On Halloween night in 1975, he told his wife he was running for President again, no matter what: 'I'm entering the race. Otherwise I'd feel like the guy who always sat on the bench and never goes into the game.'"[17]

You can't sprint through a ribbon cutting, though. Perhaps some of the most frustrating parts of the job are the purely symbolic aspects. "You can't be fired for waking the president, you can only be fired for not waking him," a White House staffer told the former *New York Times* columnist Les Gelb when talking about how to handle responses to emergencies while in the White House.[18] This mind-set leads to a lot

President George W. Bush tried to write a discreet note about the "call of nature" during a United Nations Security Council meeting in 2005. When you are president, the whole world hears that call, too.

of presidential activity that amounts to protecting appearances in the chance that something might go wrong. This wears on the most powerful person in the world who is being used as the prop.

A chief of staff to a recent president complained that briefings at FEMA before and after a disaster often felt like theater to protect the president from looking aloof, as George W. Bush did during Hurricane Katrina.[19] For the president whose to-do list awaits, sitting through a briefing with no great purpose is as exciting as a teeth cleaning.

"The White House is first and foremost a place of public leadership and that brings to bear on the president intense moral, sentimental, and quasi-religious pressures which can, if he lets them, distort his own thinking and feeling," wrote James David Barber in *The Presidential Character*. "If there is such a thing as extraordinary sanity, it is needed nowhere so much as in the White House."[20] George Reedy, Lyndon Johnson's press secretary, described "an environment in which no man can live for any considerable length of time and retain his psychological balance."[21] When I asked one senior Trump official what he considered the most important test of whether a presidential candidate was up for the job, he replied: "A psychological exam."[22]

MEDIA QUICKENING

PRESIDENTS HAVE FELT PRESSURE SINCE THE OFFICE ROLLED OFF THE production line. "I greatly apprehend that my countrymen will expect too much from me," George Washington wrote, worrying that the extravagant "undue praises which they are heaping upon me at this moment" would quickly turn to equally extravagant "censures."[23] Thomas Jefferson complained that the presidency "brings nothing but unceasing drudgery and daily loss of friends."[24] On New Year's Day in 1926, Calvin Coolidge wrote to his father: "I suppose I am the most powerful man in the world, but great power does not mean much except great limitations. I cannot have any freedom even to go and come. I am only in the clutch of forces that are greater than I am."[25]

What has changed considerably for the modern president, though, is the amount of public and media scrutiny. The proliferation of media, most notably twenty-four-hour cable television, has turned the presidency into an around-the-clock reality show. The president is the biggest celebrity in the world. Eyes are constantly watching, ready to imbue his every grimace with meaning.

The scrutiny started slowly. The first press conference in Woodrow Wilson's office would be followed by years of accommodating coverage from the White House press corps. FDR held congenial off-the-record gatherings with reporters, where he shaped their stories. Newspapers didn't publish pictures of the president in his wheelchair and no one wrote about his affairs. John F. Kennedy carried on a reckless string of predatory affairs as president. Aides knew about them, as did the members of the Georgetown party set, which included prominent journalists. Stories of those affairs never surfaced. Even Nixon, who ordered the IRS to investigate prominent members of the press, could call reporters late at night, sodden with drink, and those reporters did not report on his slurred ramblings.[26]

James Deakin, in his account of presidential press relations, pinpoints Eisenhower's heart attack as the moment the relationship started to change. Eisenhower's doctor first reported that Ike had merely had a bout of indigestion. (Too many onions on the hamburger, they said.)

The Eisenhower team's deception was well within the existing norms of the office for hushing up personal health issues. In 1893, Grover Cleveland, informed that he had cancer of the mouth, sneaked away to a friend's yacht and had part of his jaw removed. He conspired with his doctors to conceal the procedure for twenty-four years. Woodrow Wilson covered up his stroke and lived out the last seventeen months of his presidency as more or less an invalid. His wife, Edith, helped run things.[27]

The Cold War changed the sense of urgency. With nuclear war a possibility, the president had to be fit and ready to respond. This is what made the Kennedy cover-up of his health issues so much more deceitful during his 1960 campaign. Kennedy lied and staged a wide and prolonged cover-up of the fact that he suffered from Addison's disease—a possibly fatal malfunctioning of the adrenal gland. He and his doctors covered it up because public disclosure of the illness would have ruined his chances.[28]

Press scrutiny increased most acutely after a string of lies and deceptions surrounding the U.S. war in Vietnam and the Watergate break-in.

After two presidents, one from each party, fed the country a series of corrosive lies, the press became more aggressive. Public trust in the office and government plummeted.

In 1964, the share of the country saying they could trust the federal government to do the right thing nearly always or most of the time reached an all-time high of 77 percent in a Pew Research study.[29] Within a decade—a period that included the Vietnam War, civil unrest, and the Watergate scandal—trust had fallen by more than half, to 36 percent. By the end of the 1970s, only about a quarter of Americans felt that they could trust the government at least most of the time. Today the number is 18 percent.

With trust so low, coverage of the presidency and presidential character grew hotter. A new generation of reporters sought to emulate Watergate heroes Bob Woodward and Carl Bernstein. Wilson greeted reporters in his office who remarked on the kindness of his eyes, but by 2017, an Oval Office interview could become pointed enough that President Trump abruptly ended it and walked away. Americans have always been fascinated by every corner of a sitting president's life. In 1925, *The New York Times* wrote five hundred words on Coolidge's indigestion (it was the cantaloupe!),[30] but the incursions were infrequent. There were some barriers. The scrutiny has gotten to the point where if a president jots a note about needing a bathroom break, it becomes worldwide news, as it did when George W. Bush needed a moment during a United Nations meeting in 2005.[31] Every moment is on display either in the moment or in the eventual tell-all book some staffer will write.

As news competition has increased, the White House press experience has become frenzied. Andy Card witnessed the change as a staffer for George H. W. Bush and then as chief of staff for his son. Under the father, says Card, the news day ended in the late afternoon when the White House declared a "lid," meaning there would be no more news for the day. "After four thirty there was a lid and everybody breathed a sigh of relief because we were done for the day," Card remembers.[32] If the White House declared a lid, it meant that only the most urgent breaking news would warrant a response. That meant more time to work on the actual business of the White House, rather than responding to agenda items dictated by rumors from the Hill, angry statements from the opposition, or other surprises that stew in the Washington atmosphere.

As news outlets proliferated and technology provided twenty-four-hour coverage, White House staffers had to field more queries. At the same time standards of the journalism declined. Instead of asking the White House only about stories that had a possible basis in fact, some reporters started pushing lower-grade stuff. White House staff couldn't ignore their requests because news outlets were dropping their standards and going with stories that lacked the same kind of verification as before. "With cable and the competition between outlets, if you could get a single source instead of two, or get someone to comment on a rumor, that meant a story," continues Card. "Then that meant the White House had to comment on it. That encouraged reporters to just troll for rumors, which empowered the ego of the White House staff to start leaking rumors. The change in the news cycle has had the greatest impact on discipline, or been the greatest invitation to a lack of discipline, in the presidency."

Kellyanne Conway describes what first contact with the press was like for the Trump administration. "There was no honeymoon period whatsoever. As we were preparing to take the reins, I remarked, 'The White House and the press will share joint custody of the nation for the next four or eight years; we should find a way to responsibly co-parent.' And it was just divorce and deadbeat Dad immediately."[33]

Simply tending to this loopy cycle of rumor and reaction can consume a White House operation. The top staff must chase down and disarm rumors before they take on a life of their own. Social media has quickened and supercharged this cycle. Tweets, in particular, strip quotes and moments of their context. They don't include comments from relevant parties. The site encourages people not to read beyond the headlines, which are often inaccurate or incomplete.

In July 2017, a video rocketed through social media of President Trump shaking hands with people invited to attend a healthcare speech at the White House.[34] A little boy sat in a wheelchair and the president passed him by. Hundreds of people sent around the video as proof of President Trump's shriveled spirit. J. K. Rowling, the author of the Harry Potter novels, gave the video a particular boost on Twitter, writing that Trump appeared "frightened he might catch his condition."[35] How could a person not even stop to notice a child in a wheelchair? This was unfair. In reality, the first thing the president had done upon entering the room was stop, bend over, and talk to the child.

The president is under constant scrutiny, and those who think the worst of him have a platform to broadcast their unfettered scorn. Even though he is a victim of this environment, Donald Trump was also one of its most prolific and successful instigators of this kind of presidential smear, as he carried out a five-year crusade to prove Barack Obama was an illegitimate president based on the lie that Obama was born in Kenya.

To fight back, President Trump has become an expert—perhaps *the* expert—on the platform at using its direct line into his supporters. "One thing that Donald Trump has done that I think is permanently transformative of the presidency is the daily, transparent, unedited way that he communicates directly with the public, everybody at the same time," says counselor Kellyanne Conway. "So the stay-at-home mom, the plumber on the job, and the billionaire CEO who has fifteen people watching his social media feeds, all get the same info at the same time. They all receive a personal presidential communication at the same time. He cut out the middle man though, so I know the middle man doesn't like it."[36] A CBS News/YouGov poll has found that just 11 percent of strong Trump supporters trust the mainstream media—while 91 percent turn to the president for "accurate information."[37]

The president can bat down rumors immediately with his Twitter account, which allows him to bypass the media filter. That's an advantage technology brings, but the ease of tweeting has also created presidential missives that have sent the White House bucket brigade scrambling to define what he means or create post hoc rationalizations for his claims.

CAN A PRESIDENT HANDLE THE STRAIN?

CAN ONE PERSON HANDLE THE EMOTIONAL AND PSYCHOLOGICAL STRAIN of the presidency? Professional psychologists and armchair ones have diagnosed Donald Trump as unfit. In *The Dangerous Case of Donald Trump*, twenty-seven psychiatrists and mental health experts concluded that the president's mental state presented a danger to the nation and the well-being of its citizens. They argued that his intense focus on himself, his constant state of grievance, and his lack of restraint were classic markers of narcissistic personality disorder.[38]

At a White House ceremony, President Trump stopped to visit with Montgomery Weer, a three-year-old boy with spina bifida. Critics on a hair trigger jumped on a video clip from later in the event that falsely made it appear the president had ignored the boy.

In *The Atlantic,* the conservative lawyer George Conway, the husband of Trump's top counselor Kellyanne Conway, argued that "Donald Trump's narcissism makes it impossible for him to carry out the duties of the presidency in the way the Constitution requires."[39]

Wherever one falls on the question of Donald Trump's mental fitness for office, the question of the mental and physical strain of the job existed before the forty-fifth president started posting on his Twitter account pictures of himself oiled up in boxing trunks like the movie character Rocky.[40]

In 1955, former president Herbert Hoover completed his second review of executive-branch efficiency and suggested the addition of an administrative vice president to help the overloaded president. (The existing vice president was apparently too busy.) Hoover knew about the burden firsthand. One afternoon shortly before he left office in

1933, he told his secretary, "All the money in the world could not induce me to live over the last nine months."[41] Henry Stimson, the secretary of state, said a tête-à-tête with Hoover during his lowest ebb after the 1929 economic crash was "like sitting in a bath of ink."[42]

Hoover's report was issued a few months before President Eisenhower had his first heart attack in 1955. It was the fourth heart attack or stroke to hit a sitting president since the severe stroke that left Wilson incapacitated until his administration ended in 1921.[43] (Coolidge died from a heart attack just four years after leaving office.) This caused the columnist Walter Lippmann to wonder whether the stresses of the job were too much for one man to bear. Addressing the "intolerable strain" on the president, Lippmann wrote, "The load has become so enormously greater . . . because of the wars of this century, because of the huge growth of the American population, of the American economy, and of American responsibilities."[44]

The decision to wage war weighs heaviest on a president. In one decision, Harry Truman ordered two nuclear strikes that killed about eighty thousand people instantly. Close to a hundred thousand more died from the long-term effects. The decision changed the course of the twentieth century, though Truman said it was the decision to go to war in Korea[45] that had been the hardest of his presidency. A letter sent to him by the father of a soldier who died in that war, returning his son's Purple Heart, suggests just how difficult it was:

Mr. Truman,

As you have been directly responsible for the loss of our son's life in Korea, you might as well keep this emblem on display in your trophy room, as a memory of one of your historic deeds.

Our major regret at this time is that your daughter was not there to receive the same treatment as our son received in Korea.

Truman kept the letter in his desk drawer long after his term ended, a testament to the weight that remained on him even after he left the Oval Office.

Since the attacks of 9/11, being president means being a war president. George W. Bush's communications director Dan Bartlett says that when the president was deciding whether to send more troops into Iraq in 2007, at a time when the public and members of his own administration wanted the United States to withdraw, he began wearing a mouth guard at night because he was grinding his teeth so much in his sleep.[46] President Trump explained, "The hardest thing I have to do, by far . . . is sign letters to parents of soldiers that have been killed."[47]

When I asked Trump counselor Kellyanne Conway to name a moment that conveyed the weight of the job, she described Trump's first trip to witness a dignified transfer of remains of the first known casualty from an operation Trump ordered. "The gravity of that hits you because it's no longer this out-of-body experience that you're witnessing from afar," she said of the visit to Dover Air Force Base in February 2017. "You're a participant. You're no longer a spectator. You're a participant."[48]

A president can't be stymied into inaction, though. If a president thinks too much about the widows he's making or the children who will never know their mother because of his orders, he might not be able to take action that would forestall greater carnage. This is why General James Mattis never had casualty reports delivered to him while combat was under way. "I don't take casualties well," says Mattis, who led the Marines in the U.S. invasion of Iraq in the Second Gulf War. "It cuts to the core of me. So I would tell my subordinates, 'Do not report casualties to me, medevac them as quickly as you can, keep moving, keep fighting, and if you've taken so many casualties and you can't keep fighting, let me know, but we'll grieve afterwards. I want you to stay focused on the enemy and keeping the men alive who are still in the fight.'"[49]

A PRESIDENT WEARS MASKS

MODERN PRESIDENTS HAVE BEEN RELATIVELY HEALTHY, BUT THE LOAD of the job has grown even heavier. As the job of responder and consoler has become a part of the presidential portfolio, the president has also had to learn to take on the human weight that comes with those duties. "He told me of a man who rushed up to him and cried 'I've lost my baby,'" wrote Lady Bird Johnson of her husband's tour of Louisiana in the wake of Hurricane Betsy in 1965. "Lyndon's face contorted just as the man's had, as though he were about to cry. He said it was horrible."[50]

The hardest day of Barack Obama's presidency came in December 2012 in Newtown, Connecticut, where he met and comforted the families of the twenty-six victims massacred at Sandy Hook Elementary School. When a mother broke down, the president handed her a tissue. With the younger siblings of those who had died, he lifted them into the air, tried to coax a smile, and handed them White House M&M's.[51]

The emotional distance of the job cycles between M&M's and a tissue. Presidents aren't trained as pastors, but they have been thrust into that role. A presidential brain has to be emotionally alive enough to a situation to reflexively hand a tissue to a mother, but also closed off enough to not become consumed with the sorrow your decisions will create.

There is no staff for this. A president can't delegate these duties, and it's not even clear what life experiences train a person for that range of emotional chutes and ladders. After the president consoles the nation, who consoles the president?

The term "temperament" is the closest thing that captures a president's ability to manage the emotional aspects of the job. The notion encompasses the grace under pressure required to make the hardest decisions and the emotional intelligence to read other human beings. Temperament also contains the stability to move easily in and out of the darker parts of the job. A president must be comfortable with deceit in negotiations and know how to keep parts of his brain hidden even from those closest to him.

Senator Huey Long complained about Franklin Roosevelt's skill at hiding himself: "When I talk to him, he says, 'Fine! Fine! Fine!' But [Senator] Joe Robinson goes to see him the next day and he says, 'Fine! Fine! Fine!' Maybe he says 'Fine!' to everybody."[52] This is why FDR's opponent Herbert Hoover called him a "chameleon on plaid."[53] New York governor Al Smith was once asked whether he had gotten a commitment from Roosevelt, and he responded, "Did you ever nail a custard pie to a wall?"

New York Times journalist Elmer Davis said Roosevelt thought "the shortest distance between two points is not a straight line but a corkscrew."[54] FDR cultivated this quality. "You know," he told his friend Henry Morgenthau, Jr., in 1942, "I am a juggler, and I never let my right hand know what my left hand does. . . . I may be totally inconsistent, and furthermore I am willing to mislead and tell untruths if it will help win the war."[55] Roosevelt won the war and helped lift a frightened nation, but, as the Roosevelt biographer Geoffrey C. Ward writes, that sense of mission also caused him to "mislead and tell untruths" not just for the good of the nation but in the "interest purely of his own advancement."[56]

David Herbert Donald, the famous Lincoln biographer, uses Keats's phrase "negative capability" to describe the sixteenth president's mental suppleness. Keats described the skill as "when a man is capable of being in uncertainties, mysteries, doubts, without any irritable reaching after fact and reason."[57] The mythical view of the president is of a bold planner who wills the country to his view of things. The great presidents, though—Lincoln and FDR—had the capacity to allow situations to develop, and they were not overcome when situations did not develop as quickly as they would have liked. Donald Trump, famously impatient about issues like immigration, shows this kind of ease with uncertainty when progress with North Korea or trade talks with China dribble on. This quality helps a president understand when action is most effective. They're not just stabbing frantically at any chance they get. It also keeps them from expending mental energy on situations they can't yet change, and allows them to be comfortable with situations whose outcome was uncertain. "Only a leader with an experimental temper could have made the New Deal possible," wrote Richard Hofstadter of FDR.[58]

Roosevelt's flexibility was considered a great and necessary presidential skill, but his deceptions and emotional distance also had a darker side. FDR's untroubled conscience allowed him to carry on affairs in his private life. In his public office, despite his claims about its moral nature, he did not stir to respond to the Holocaust though he knew Jews were being rounded up and sent to their death, and he ordered Japanese Americans into detainment camps.

A man who wears masks and exchanges them so freely must strain to keep them from slipping. It's not a weightless process. If it were, that might be even more dangerous.

This is the heart of the critique of Donald Trump's presidency—that he is unburdened by conscience, that he tells repeated falsehoods with ease. He has affection for dictators in Russia, Turkey, and Saudi Arabia not for geostrategic reasons, but because he admires power with no moral brake on its execution.

Alexander Hamilton listed the president's duties as "decision, activity, secrecy and dispatch."[59] That is a description for a lonely office with weighty decisions, or, as Lyndon Johnson wrote, "If I was seldom lonely, I was often alone. No one can experience with the President of the United States the glory and agony of his office."[60]

Much of the weight of national security environment bears down in secret, taking up space in the president's brain in a way the public never knows. In 2006, British intelligence officials told their U.S. counterparts that an al-Qaeda offshoot was planning to mix chemicals brought on planes in carry-on bags to stage a coordinated attack on a dozen U.S. planes leaving from Europe.[61] Officials didn't want to foil the plot immediately, because more surveillance might lead them to the ringleaders. The danger was that the plot might be farther along than they knew. Every day George W. Bush asked his homeland security adviser Fran Townsend if the planes leaving for the United States would be safe. For several days, those in the tiny circle that knew about the plot had to sweat the several hours during which planes took off from Europe to the United States, hoping that whatever meeting they were in might not be interrupted by bad news.

The night before the raid that killed Osama bin Laden, President Obama addressed the White House Correspondents' Association dinner. He told jokes, as is the custom, and appeared to have a great time, a man breezily at ease in a world of glamorous sophistication. But he was on the cusp of possibly the defining moment of his presidency.

In the previous weeks, Obama had chaired national security meetings about the raid. The events that took place immediately before and after those secret Bin Laden meetings give a sense of the different roles a president must play even while burdened by his toughest call: an education policy speech; meetings with leaders from Denmark, Brazil, and Panama; meetings to avert a government shutdown; a fundraising dinner; a budget speech; a prayer breakfast; immigration reform meetings; the announcement of a new national security team; planning for his

A president must wear masks. On April 29, 2011, President Obama authorized the highly risky secret raid on Osama bin Laden's compound. The next day, as tradition dictated, Obama passed the waiting hours by telling jokes at the White House Correspondents' Association dinner. On May 2, he watched the raid in real time.

reelection campaign; and a military intervention in Libya. On April 27, 2011, the day before Obama chaired his last National Security Council meeting on the Bin Laden raid, his White House released his long-form birth certificate to answer persistent questions about his birthplace raised by the man who would be his successor.

In the joke-writing process for the White House Correspondents' Association dinner, the president removed a quip about Bin Laden.[62] His aides were given no hint as to why. On the most secret matters of state, the president carries information that is locked away from those who might be most helpful in shouldering the burden. Barack Obama also never told his wife about the planning for the raid.

Under that kind of pressure, a president is also denied the normal tools of relaxation. He can't take a stroll through Georgetown. He can't drink too much or blow off a Sunday in sweatpants watching football in a friend's basement. Lincoln went to the theater one hundred times during the Civil War. If a president goes on vacation at the wrong time or in the wrong way, he catches hell. "Presidents don't get vacations — they just get a change of scenery," said Nancy Reagan in 1985 in defense of her husband's frequent trips to his ranch in California.[63]

Golf must now be played be in moderation. If a president once enjoyed journaling, the White House counsel will explain that journals can be subpoenaed, so that needs to stop. If a president is ever caught whining on a bad day, it will define the presidency more than a hundred good days.

Nevertheless, presidents have to find some way to cope with the job. To do so, they construct their own coping mechanisms. Mostly that means constructing a mental sanctuary from the torrent of constant criticism.

Robert Dallek describes how FDR took solace from Lincoln's equanimity and decided not to respond to his critics, because it would consume his ability to attend to all other work. FDR identified with Lincoln's reflections on his efforts to "do the best I know how, the very best I can; and I mean to keep on doing it to the end. If the end brings me out all right, what is said against me will not amount to anything. If the end brings me out all wrong, then angels swearing I was right would make no difference."[64] Lincoln had "kept his peace — that was and is the great lesson," Roosevelt told Margaret (Daisy) Suckley, his distant cousin. "You won't always be right," he remarked to his adviser Rexford G. Tugwell, "but you mustn't suffer from being wrong. That's what kills people like us."[65]

Eisenhower believed in "the virtues of a complete and absolute rest," writing in a letter to his brother while Ike served as president of

"Presidents don't get vacations—they just get a change of scenery,"
said Nancy Reagan in 1985 in defense of her husband's
frequent trips to his ranch in California.

Columbia University that "My experience this spring convinced me that there most certainly is such a thing as overwork—for the rest of my life I am going to work at avoiding that particular disease."[66] Mostly, the thirty-fourth president avoided overwork with rounds of golf. During his presidency he played nearly eight hundred rounds of golf,[67] a record for the office not likely to be matched.

Lincoln, Truman, and Obama all addressed the frustrations of the job by writing long venting letters that they then crumpled up and threw away. Eisenhower engaged in an abbreviated form of that practice to master his temper. "I make it a practice to avoid hating anyone," he wrote in his memoirs. "If someone's been guilty of despicable actions, especially towards me, I try to forget him."[68] To help him do this, Eisenhower would write the person's name on a piece of paper "and drop it into the lowest drawer of my desk, and say to myself: 'That finishes the incident, and so far as I'm concerned, that fellow.'"[69]

That might have worked for Eisenhower, but he didn't have to work in a building where a television on every desk broadcast a news channel with people claiming to have perfect knowledge of what he did or why he didn't do what he did. Barack Obama once walked by a television on which a pundit was claiming to explain his moves and said to no one in particular, "Oh, so that's why I did it?" He couldn't hide the irritation, which is why Obama usually had the television tuned to ESPN. "One of the things you realize fairly quickly in this job is that there is a character people see out there called Barack Obama. That's not you," President Obama told Michael Lewis. "Whether it is good or bad, it is not you."[70]

That sounds like a sensible view, but in a job that requires wearing so many different masks and playing so many different roles—sometimes just in an afternoon—and in which there are so many other people creating alternative versions of you, the hardest task for a president may be knowing who "you" is. It may be one of the aspects of the job that could be managed, if that were all you had to contend with, but when added to all the other things a president and administration must get right, it may make the job essentially impossible.

Chapter 19

The Impossible Presidency

—

Presidential contestants make extensive preparations
to enter a no-win situation.[1]

—THEODORE LOWI

Ulysses S. Grant, the victorious Union general,
stoops beneath the burdens of the presidency, a job that may
have been designed to be too much for any one person.

WHEN LOOKING AT THE COMPLEXITY OF THE PRESIDENCY AND
how hard it is to manage its duties, the job can seem beyond any one
person. Just a partial list of all that must go right in a presidency starts

to stretch the limits of human endeavor: A president needs to pick the right team in a hurry, including a chief of staff who gets the balance of information flow, delegation, and gatekeeping just right. The cabinet needs to be filled with leaders who have autonomy, but not so much ego that they create political disasters. A president must have exquisite fingertip feel for prioritization, communication, and political nuance.

Bread that good cannot be made of wheat.[2]

What if the job actually is impossible? What if efforts to tune it, by worrying about the skills of a chief of staff or a president's delegating or management acumen, are too puny to fix what ails the office? Those tweaks, made in good faith perhaps, obscure the big fact about the job, which is that it needs enormous, generational changes.

This is Jeremi Suri's claim in his book *The Impossible Presidency*, in which he argues that the office is more broken than we know. "Even the most capable modern presidents are doomed to fail," he writes. "Limiting the failure and achieving some good along the way—that is the best we can expect." The office was never designed to take on what it has now been asked to tackle, and tinkering isn't enough. "The inherited presidency is no longer the correct presidency for the twenty-first century."[3]

Yes, the presidency has always been hard. Suri's *The Impossible Presidency* of 2017 has the same title as Harold M. Barger's *The Impossible Presidency* of 1984. Barger writes, "The expectations for success and the public's expectations for results are based on a model of executive leadership more appropriate to a prime minister–cabinet system of government than to our own system."[4]

It's tempting to collapse into "It has always been thus," but that's a dodge. Americans have reformed their institutions when they needed it. The Constitutional Convention of 1787 was itself an effort to remedy the weakness of the first try. No one says "It has always been thus" when faced with America's other chronic challenges over equality and protection of liberty. When the complexities of the past have challenged American government, it has responded with repair and reform.

America's expectations of the presidency are out of alignment. We must think more boldly about the presidency, including the bold proposition (for a book about the presidency) that we should stop thinking about the presidency as much as we do. We ask the president to do too much, so what should we remove from the office? What can Congress do to come off the sidelines? What can we ask of local government? Should we stop running every public issue through the presidency, and should we stop expecting everything of an office never intended to be the vessel for all our hopes?

A presidential campaign is the perfect time to discuss the presidency because the public is focused on the office. The wisest voices write books and articles that are the result of deep-considered thought about the American system to coincide with the moment of national interest. The problem, however, is that elections are a forum for all of the things that are undermining representative government and our ability to answer those larger questions: the cultural obsession with the self, the fixation on performance, and the interest in immediate action at the expense of long-term planning. Talking about the problems of the presidency during a campaign is like talking about the danger of sugar while your child is snapping on the Halloween Spider-Man mask.

It doesn't have to be this way. Of all the many reforms that might bring the office back in line with its original design and American values, the first step to thinking about the presidency differently is changing the way we think about the office during our presidential campaigns.

PART TWO

PRESIDENTIAL CAMPAIGNS

*Senator Hubert Humphrey said, while competing in
the primaries against Kennedy, "I felt like an
independent merchant competing against a chain
store." Nixon called Kennedy's campaign a
"slick high-octane publicity machine."*

THE BEST MAN

PRESIDENT HOCKSTADER: "Power is not a toy we give to good children. It is a weapon. And the strong man takes it and uses it. If you don't go down there and beat Joe Cantwell to the floor with this very dirty stick, then you've got no business in the big league. Because if you don't fight, the job is not for you. And it never will be."[1]

—GORE VIDAL, *THE BEST MAN*,
A PLAY ABOUT RUNNING FOR PRESIDENT

Chapter 20

Candidate of the People

—

Elections, my dear sir, Elections to offices which are
great objects of Ambition, I look at with terror.[2]

—JOHN ADAMS, IN A LETTER TO THOMAS JEFFERSON
AFTER READING A COPY OF THE NEW CONSTITUTION

I enjoy these runs away from home to meet nonpartisan
bodies of men, because I regard a campaign as a great
interruption to the rational consideration of public
questions. I think that we have a very bad American habit
of changing our point of view for a few months during the
time when we are determining the character and personnel
of our government. Therefore, I think it is useful as well as
refreshing to look at things, sometimes at arm's length,
to withdraw from the mêlée, and to see things as you
would try to see them at other seasons.[3]

—WOODROW WILSON, 1916

IN 1959, SENATOR JOHN KENNEDY PUBLISHED A PIECE OF PUNDITRY
in *TV Guide* announcing a revolution in American government. In a
piece entitled "A Force That Has Changed the Political Scene," the
senator argued that nothing in modern politics "compares with the
revolutionary impact of television." The television revolution meant
that politics would henceforth focus on how voters felt about the candidates, not on the candidate's positions on the issues. "Honesty, vigor,

compassion, intelligence—the presence or lack of these and other qualities make up what is called the candidate's 'image,'" wrote Kennedy. That image on the box in the den would rule future contests, ushering in a "new breed of candidates" with a "particular reliance on TV appeal."[4]

Kennedy did concede that television would make political contests vulnerable to "manipulation, exploitation, and gimmicks . . . and public relations experts," and that television costs would make candidates even more beholden to "big financial contributors." Nevertheless, Kennedy kept things sunny, arguing that television would counteract those forces by revealing elemental truths about the candidate. It would offer voters a distillation, like a bouillon cube of candidate character, leaving impressions that "are likely to be uncannily correct." Once those impressions had been made, party leaders would be "less willing to run rough-shod over the voters' wishes and hand pick an unknown, unappealing, or unpopular candidate in the traditional 'smoke-filled room' when millions of voters are watching, comparing, and remembering."[5]

Two months later, Kennedy announced his candidacy for the presidency. His use of television, and its use of him, would hustle in the revolutionary change he predicted. It would also hasten the change to an era of presidential politics focused on the momentary appeal of theatrical candidates performing for voters who had ever more control of the selection process.

In the article, the upstart senator stretched to make the wish the father of the thought—or rather, the punditry the father of the candidacy. Kennedy hoped to maneuver around those party bosses he'd written about, because they were not likely to pick him as their candidate. To do this, he had to build a permission structure within the party to make it okay to support him. By elevating the value of the medium in which he excelled, he hoped to boost the impressions of his campaign. Television didn't elevate the superficial, he argued, but the opposite. It allowed voters to delve into the essential character of the politician. Therefore, if they liked the fresh-faced Massachusetts fellow on TV, it meant they'd come to an "uncannily correct" view about him. And who didn't want to be uncannily correct?

Having learned that essential truth through television, voters shouldn't let party bosses press someone else into their lap, particularly someone our pundit senator had predefined as "unknown, unappealing, or unpopular." Having shined up the qualities of any candidate who came across well on television, Kennedy made it a fatal presidential flaw to be unknown, cold, or dull on the screen. Fifty-six years later, Donald Trump channeled the same spirit when he boasted about his ratings and taunted his competitors who made viewers change the channel. If you could generate excitement, you were ready for the presidency.

Kennedy had to build a side road to the presidency because the main road was closed. In 1960, the *New York Times* columnist James Reston surveyed the "old pros" and found they favored Senate majority leader Lyndon Johnson for the nomination. Other columnists dialed up state Democratic Party chairmen and Democratic members of Congress to compile a list of likely nominees. Jack Kennedy wasn't on that list. House Democrats liked Senator Stuart Symington (D-MO). Senate Democrats favored Majority Leader Lyndon Johnson (D-TX). At Georgetown cocktail parties, men in narrow ties and black-framed glasses spoke knowingly about the Democratic convention and predicted that Adlai Stevenson, Stuart Symington, and Lyndon Johnson would emerge ahead of Kennedy, and that out of the deadlock, the nomination would go to Johnson.

Kennedy could not rebut those claims in Georgetown salons because while he lived just down the street, the people he needed to convince were not in Georgetown. Kennedy's counterargument lived out in the rest of the country, where he hoped to win primary contests and show the party bosses that while he might not have seniority and as much experience as the favorites, he had the support of the people. Those bosses wouldn't dare tell the people they couldn't have Jack if Jack had been the one they voted for. Also, primary victories would prove Kennedy a winner, which might mean he actually had the right stuff to win in the general election.

Kennedy's case rested on an idea of the presidency in the Wilsonian mold—an office in constant communication with voters. A candidate couldn't truly understand the country and know what policies were best for the people in it if he hadn't been out there and among them.

"Primary contests not only educate the public—they educate the candidate as well," Kennedy said.[6]

> For if a candidate wishes to understand the needs and aspirations of the people he seeks to serve—he must go among them. He must view the cities and towns and factories and farms firsthand—not merely read secondhand reports from local supporters or look at the nation through the wrong end of a television camera. He should see the poverty of West Virginia, the depressed dairy farms of Wisconsin, the unemployment in Maryland—if he is to deal with these problems effectively in January. He must campaign in all sections of the country—the East, the West, and the Far West—if he is to understand the problems of all sections—and not merely his own. He must listen as well as talk, see as well as be seen, learn as well as teach. And the primary is the greatest instrument there is for that kind of education. For after the nomination it is often too late—for the candidate and for the country.

Kennedy didn't invent this workaround. In 1912, Teddy Roosevelt tried to use primaries to beat his old protégé William Howard Taft. The Republican party bosses backed Taft, so Roosevelt took his message to the people. He roared and waved his arms from the stage, insisting that the survival of the republic depended on listening to the voice of the people, as conveyed in the primaries. "The right of the people to rule," he told a Carnegie Hall audience, is "the great fundamental issue now before the Republican Party and before our people."[7]

Necessity had caused a drastic change in Roosevelt's view of campaigning. Twelve years earlier, as McKinley's vice presidential candidate, he had pouted when campaign strategists tried to roll him out on the stump: "I must make the most emphatic protest against the plan for me to speak all day long in the open air from the tail end of the car. I do not think such a course is wise or dignified."[8] When you're trying to elbow your way back into power, though, your ideas of dignity can evolve. (*We warned you about this*, the founders would say.) Still, in 1912 it didn't work. The states Roosevelt won in the primaries assigned him their delegates, but he fell 70 delegates short of beating Taft.

Months after Republican bosses thwarted TR's "Let the People Rule" campaign, he faced a campaign moment that did prove Kennedy's case that how a candidate behaves in the crucible of the campaign tells you something about their fitness for the job. Before speaking at the Milwaukee Auditorium on October 14, 1912, Roosevelt campaigning on the Bull Moose ticket was shot by a deranged saloonkeeper who imagined TR had killed President McKinley. Bleeding from the bullet lodged against his fourth rib, the former president took the stage. "Friends, I shall ask you to be as quiet as possible," he said. "I don't know whether you fully understand that I have just been shot."[9] It was a mic-dropping moment, but Roosevelt held on to the mic because he had more to say. He spoke for the next ninety minutes, reading through his fifty-page speech that had saved his life by slowing the path of the bullet. (Despite the extraordinary display of fortitude, Roosevelt lost the 1912 election.)

In 1952, Tennessee senator Estes Kefauver tried to sneak past the Democratic Party establishment by running in state primaries. He won

Teddy Roosevelt sniffed at the idea of campaigning when he was a vice president, but when fighting to return to the White House as president, he said primary elections were crucial: "The right of the people to rule is the great fundamental issue now before the Republican Party and before our people."

twelve of fifteen elections, but since delegates were chosen by bosses at state party conventions, the presidential nomination went to former Illinois governor Adlai Stevenson, who hadn't competed in a single primary.

The bosses thought Stevenson the better general election candidate, but they also thought Kefauver was a pill. Kefauver's crusading investigations into big city crime had made him a national television figure. Thirty million people watched his hearings into organized crime. He was a political star. (This was perhaps the last clash between a television candidate and party bosses in which the party bosses won.) But those investigations also revealed connections between the mafia and Democratic political organizations. Kefauver's investigation into a Chicago police scandal, for example, helped torpedo the 1950 reelection of the Senate Democratic majority leader, Scott Lucas.[10] Helping knock off your party's leader in the Senate will hurt you with your bosses.

In 1952, Eisenhower had used television "spots" in his campaigns. The ads, created by the inventor of the M&M's "melts in your mouth, not in your hand" campaign, showed Ike answering questions from "ordinary citizens."[11] The D-Day commander already had the towering credentials for the job. The ads were intended to show that the general was just a regular fellow.

Eight years later, Kennedy didn't have Eisenhower's stature, so he used television to build the appearance of qualifications in real time. If he showed people pictures of himself doing presidential things, they would be able to see him as president. Advertisements in West Virginia showed him shaking hands with miners before they dropped down 500 feet to start their eight-hour shift.[12] He used television to introduce himself, on his terms. Footage from a town hall with voters was used to educate viewers about his religious faith. He appeared on *The Tonight Show*, the first presidential candidate to be a guest on a late night talk show. "They had never before seen such a young, attractive senator," remembered host Jack Paar, who received a congratulatory phone call from Kennedy's father after the appearance.[13] This started the process of luring voters into casting their vote for candidates based on what they saw in the moment. Candidates would soon be in charge of writing the standards by which they would be judged for election.

Kennedy promised he would deliver on these connections he was making. Because he had been with the voters, he would pay special attention to their needs when he got to Washington. A Kennedy newspaper ad showed votes for his Democratic primary opponent, Hubert Humphrey, landing in a garbage can. Votes for Kennedy, by contrast, dropped from the ballot box through the roof of the White House. West Virginia Democrats voting on who could deliver the goods for them picked Kennedy. When he became president, his first executive order increased the amount of food distributed to needy Americans in economically distressed areas, a direct result of his time spent in West Virginia. The votes did indeed go right into the White House, as Kennedy had promised.

Kennedy's success in the primaries helped sway the power brokers at the convention in Los Angeles that year. If the primary voters of West Virginia were okay with his Catholic faith and youth, the country would be too. Still, the debate inside the party continued right up until the last minute. Kennedy might be able to woo voters in the downtown square, but would he have the skills needed to actually do the job as it came rushing at him?

President Truman had called the primaries "eyewash."[4] Others complained the selection process had degraded into a popularity contest. "Senator, are you certain that you are quite ready for the country,

Senator John Kennedy meets with West Virginia coal miners on his way to winning the state in 1960. He built in authority for the presidency by demonstrating capability.

or the country is ready for you in the role of president in January 1961?" Truman asked on the eve of the Democratic National Convention. "I have no doubt about the political heights to which you are destined to rise. But I'm deeply concerned and troubled about the situation we are up against in the world now and in the immediate future. That is why I hope that someone with the greatest possible maturity and experience would be available at this time. May I urge you to be patient."[5]

Truman knew what the job demanded. By citing maturity and experience he offered a counterargument to the case Kennedy had made in *TV Guide*. The job required something more than what could be divined through the camera lens. It required something more than a candidate could pick up on the road shaking hands in front of department stores and giving speeches to the auxiliary club. Truman offered this view even though he was a beneficiary of a powerful road show himself. His 31,700-mile whistlestop train trips in the 1948 general election as an incumbent had helped him defeat Tom Dewey, by putting Truman in touch with the people in just the way Kennedy was advocating.[6] Still, Truman argued, the job required something deeper.

Kennedy persisted and won the Democratic nomination. The tide was turning. Party insiders would thin to a shadow over the coming years and exert less and less influence. Candidates would woo the party's most ardent voters (the ones who participate in primaries) directly, and they would increasingly use television to do it.

The new power of the performance crystallized in the mythology surrounding Kennedy's successful debates in the general election campaign against Vice President Richard Nixon. Conventional wisdom held that Kennedy won the presidency because he looked better on the revolutionary living room medium. Whether that was true or not, future candidates took that lesson from the contest and copied it. "Kennedy's victory created a bipartisan political belief that constructing a celebrity image and building a well-oiled media exploitation machine could be more than a controversial sideshow or distraction to American politics," argues the historian Kathryn Cramer Brownell. "It could become a source of political authority and serve as a path to the American presidency."[7]

The legendary CBS producer Don Hewitt, who put together the famous Kennedy/Nixon debates, predicted every candidate would conclude "That's the only way to campaign." One of the great storytellers in television, Hewitt nevertheless worried that the show of politics would come to eclipse everything else. "Great night for John Kennedy," he said. "And the worst night that ever happened in American politics."[18]

What worried Uncle Don? The answer ran on the cover of *TV Guide* in 1964 as the magazine cheered the coming political conventions. "This is our Super Bowl," one television executive said. Sports dramas like the Super Bowl need heroes. If television executives wanted a Super Bowl–like event, then they'd have to treat its main actor as a star. To crank up the drama, they turned up the promises for excitement. A *TV Guide* headline heralded THE NEWS, THE COLOR, THE DRAMA, THE EXCITEMENT. News comprised only one-quarter of the nouns in that headline. The other three-fourths were show business words. The networks, having promised a show with drama, had to haul out the spotlights. The parties and candidates, eager to stir voters in order to spur them to the polls, were only too happy to assist with the production. As with any good show, the actors, producers, and audience all engaged in and applauded the creative license required to keep everyone entertained. After a few seasons, the presidential show grew less and less connected to the reality it originally sought to portray.

Dear Mr. President,

Congratulations on a remarkable run. Millions have placed their hopes in you, and all of us, regardless of party, should hope for expanded prosperity and security during your tenure.

This is a unique office, without a clear blueprint for success, so I don't know that any advice from me will be particularly helpful. Still, let me offer a few reflections from the past 8 years.

First, we've both been blessed, in different ways, with great good fortune. Not everyone is so lucky. It's up to us to do everything we can [to] build more ladders of success for every child and family that's willing to work hard.

Second, American leadership in this world really is indispensable. It's up to us, through action and example, to sustain the international order that's expanded steadily since the end of the Cold War, and upon which our own wealth and safety depend.

Third, we are just temporary occupants of this office. That makes us guardians of those democratic institutions and traditions—like rule of law, separation of powers, equal protection and civil liberties—that our forebears fought and bled for. Regardless of the push and pull of daily politics, it's up to us to leave those instruments of our democracy at least as strong as we found them.

And finally, take time, in the rush of events and responsibilities, for friends and family. They'll get you through the inevitable rough patches.

Michelle and I wish you and Melania the very best as you embark on this great adventure, and know that we stand ready to help in any ways which we can.

Good luck and Godspeed,
BO[1]

—Letter from Barack Obama to Donald J. Trump

Chapter 21

No Hiring Manual
for the Presidency

—

It will be allowed that, in an operation so all-important as
that of an election of a President, every process should be
regulated with the utmost exactness and precision; and, yet,
there is scarcely an officer, great or small, important or
unimportant, in the State government, or in the United
States Governments, who is elected or appointed by a rule
so undefined, so vague, so subject to abuse, as that by which
we elect the Chief Magistrate of the Union.[2]

— SENATOR MAHLON DICKERSON, AMENDMENT
TO THE CONSTITUTION, 1818

JOHN KENNEDY COULD CREATE HIS OWN CRITERIA FOR HIS ELECTION
and then use them to get the job because there are few fixed hiring
guidelines for the presidency. When he made his pitch for the importance of the primary election system, he quoted Lord Bryce, a British
academic and politician who wrote a three-volume history of American
politics published in 1888. (In 1960, voters were okay with erudite quo-
tations; it's hard to imagine a candidate landing with the home crowd
these days by quoting the musings of a British academic.)

Bryce had observed that primaries determined the shape of the presidency more than the general election did. Kennedy used this point to
bolster his claim that primaries had something fundamental to say
about the presidency and direction of America. What Kennedy did not
say is that Bryce also had other views about the presidency that rather
undermined the spunky candidate's argument. They are expressed

most succinctly in his chapter entitled "Why Great Men Are Not Chosen Presidents."[3]

Bryce argued that the process for electing presidents focused too much on political victory and not enough on what it took to do the job. As a result, mediocre men of average intelligence blundered into a post for which they were unprepared. Bryce enlivened his analysis with wry anecdotes: "An eminent American is reported to have said to friends who wished to put him forward, 'Gentlemen, let there be no mistake. I should make a good president, but a very bad candidate.'"[4]

The selection criteria for picking and evaluating good presidents have been up for grabs from nearly the beginning. The founders discussed the method for picking presidents at the Constitutional Convention, but they could do no better than to settle on the clumsy workaround of the Electoral College, cobbled together in a rush to overcome an impasse in discussions and to accommodate southern slave states.[5] As William Grayson, who participated in the Virginia ratifying convention, put it, the Electoral College was "rather founded on accident, than any principle of government."[6]

Hamilton didn't see it that way, of course. Desperate to sell the underlying product, he argued in the Federalist Papers that the Electoral College guaranteed that America would have only virtuous presidents:

> The process of election affords a moral certainty, that the office of President will never fall to the lot of any man who is not in an eminent degree endowed with the requisite qualifications. Talents for low intrigue, and the little arts of popularity, may alone suffice to elevate a man to the first honors in a single State; but it will require other talents, and a different kind of merit, to establish him in the esteem and confidence of the whole Union, or of so considerable a portion of it as would be necessary to make him a successful candidate for the distinguished office of President of the United States. It will not be too strong to say, that there will be a constant probability of seeing the station filled by characters pre-eminent for ability and virtue. And this will be thought no inconsiderable recommendation of the Constitution, by those who are able to estimate the share which the

executive in every government must necessarily have in its good or ill administration.[7]

Hamilton wasn't just arguing that the Electoral College was sufficient, he was arguing that the system of allowing elites to pick presidents *ensured* premium leaders. It was such a good feature, he argued, that the Electoral College alone recommended supporting the entire constitutional system.

The idea of a selection process that would elevate a virtuous president helped the framers elide problems during drafting. As the historian Joseph Ellis points out, the Constitution "devoted more space to the rules for electing or removing the president than to delineating the powers of the office itself."[8] That ambiguity, Ellis argues, allowed consensus. If there had been too much specificity about presidential powers, those on the lookout for incipient monarchy would have pounced, wide-eyed about the number of items on that list. For those who wanted an active president, on the other hand, a specific list of powers would look too small for an office designed to combat the passions of the people and encourage the kind of energy for which the founders were creating the office in the first place.

In retrospect, Hamilton sounds naive and foolish, a little too desperate to sell his product. His vision of the Electoral College, like much of the presidency itself, depended on future generations' keeping the faith and tending the norms of the founding generation. They didn't tend them for long. As early as the election of 1800, electors gave up on the idea of being philosophers picking the best of their lot. They picked based on faction and made their choices based on political advantage, not reason. As the political scientist James W. Ceaser points out, the presidential selection process immediately became the "product not of a conscious design of certain statesmen to fashion constitutional doctrine, but rather a search by pragmatic politicians for the most effective way to win power."[9] The founders obsessed over the corrupting nature of power when they created a system of shared powers, but they left the selection of those who would wield that power open to abuses.

The looseness and malleability of the presidential selection process has caused perpetual frustration. In 1818, Senator Mahlon Dickerson (no relation) asked whether there was any office "elected or appointed by a rule so undefined, so vague, so subject to abuse, as that by which we elect the Chief Magistrate of the Union." To tighten standards, Congressman George McDuffie a few years later pushed for a uniform system of appointing electors, pointing out, "An attentive consideration of the nature and functions of a written constitution will lead us to the extraordinary but manifest conclusion that . . . we have no constitutional provision at all" to regulate the election of a president. This left the country vulnerable to "the violent tyranny of successive and temporary factions, and also [to] the more systemic encroachments of ambition."[10]

It's hard for politicians to stick to reason and virtue when power is the prize. So, over time, everything the founders worried about rushed into the American electoral system—political parties, presidents who campaigned for the job, popular elections. The fountainhead of the presidency would not be the virtuous Electoral College that Hamilton imagined but the shove and grab for power. Presidential politics would become vulnerable to the infections of passion, ambition, and the whims of the mob that had so concerned the framers when they created the office in 1787. A contest with no brakes on the quest for power encouraged candidates to do whatever it took to get that power. That a candidate would do whatever it took to get power is now proof that a candidate is fit for the job—a perfect reversal of the founders' intent.

AN OFFICE OF VIRTUE: STANDING FOR THE OFFICE

AT THE START OF THE AMERICAN EXPERIMENT, CANDIDATES RAN FOR office in sync with the founders' wishes, which is to say that they didn't run for office at all. To stump for the job would show excessive ambition, that volatile quality which the country's architects spent so much time in Philadelphia that summer trying to squeeze out of the governmental system. "They wanted an ideal man, hovering above the people," writes Gil Troy in *See How They Ran*, a history of presidential campaigning. "To demonstrate virtue, a presidential candidate had to remain silent and passive, trusting his peers to choose wisely."[11]

In standing for office and not campaigning, a candidate showed he could restrain his ambition. He had the muscles to resist self-interest and the lure of corrupting power. The nation could only hand power to someone who had the internal structure to avoid its lure. "Never trust political power to anyone who seeks political power" was the rule, says Jennifer Mercieca, historian of American political rhetoric.[12] Once in office, presidents had to continue to refrain from political behavior. In 1904, Teddy Roosevelt complained to his son, "I could cut [Alton Parker, the Democratic nominee] into ribbons if I could get at him in the open. . . . But of course a President can't go on the stump . . . and so I have to sit still and abide by the result."[13] (The man who charged up San Juan Hill identified so closely with the prevailing traditions of restraint that he sat on his hands when it came to politics.)

Challengers to incumbent presidents were constrained too. As the political scientist Jeffrey Tulis notes, "Presidents generally did not give partisan or policy-oriented speeches, so presidential candidates were expected to refrain from such undignified behavior also."[14] The president was to be "vigorous," but within his limited sphere. He'd know where the lines of that sphere were drawn and why they should not be crossed. Only a sufficient emergency would prompt him to do so.

Without a constant need to court voters, the founders reasoned, presidents could calmly pursue the best interests of the country. They would not be swayed by public passions, of which the founders were distrustful. Jefferson spoke about trusting the people, but that didn't mean handing over power to them. For Jefferson and his colleagues, public opinion was the starting point of governing, but not its end. Reason and deliberation were necessary to refine public opinion. Politicians were not supposed to be mere instruments of the mob. The "republican principle . . . does not require an unqualified complaisance to every sudden breeze of passion, or to every transient impulse," wrote Hamilton. When "the interests of the people are at variance with their inclinations," it is the representatives' duty "to give them time and opportunity for more cool and sedate reflection."[15]

The president would be the one representative of all the people, but he was expected to have enough virtue to thwart the people when their passions bubbled over. Pennsylvania delegate James Wilson, one of the most influential voices for a strong chief executive, argued the "republican temperament" of American politicians would keep presidents from abusing the office. "One such attribute [of the presidency]—and a crucial one," explains the political scientist James W. Ceaser, "was the ability of the president to withstand popular pressure when it conflicted with the public good."[16] How would the president know how to divine the public good? How would the president have the fiber to do the right thing, instead of responding as if filled with nougat and doing the popular thing? Personal virtue was the answer.

George Mason of Virginia was a little more frank. He said letting the voters decide on candidates for president would be like referring the choice of colors to a blind man.[17] Hamilton argued that the genius of the people was not that they had varied ways of voicing loud, ill-informed opinions in public, but rather, that they knew how ill-informed they were. That they knew they had a tendency to "err." Therefore, they wisely chose and deferred to "guardians . . . to withstand the temporary delusion[s]."[18]

The American presidency in this conception required balance. The people must be listened to, but elites must sift their views. The people were the font of wisdom, but too much from that font could drown the country. That notion did not last.

PEOPLE POWER ON THE RISE

SOON ENOUGH, THOUGH, THE PEOPLE WHO HAD BEEN ASKED TO DEFER GOT antsy. They wanted a say in picking the person to whom they were granting power to affect their lives. Those who wanted to act in their name were happy to engage on the stump. Those who wanted power saw appealing to the people as a new route to acquiring it.

The change was gradual. In 1824, Andrew Jackson of Tennessee spoke for the Western spirit of the emerging nation. Unhappy with the decisions of the distant counsels in Washington, his supporters pushed for more representation. "This is a great national crisis," wrote the *Louisville Public Advertiser*, "involving the question, whether the PEOPLE are sovereign in elections, or whether their servants shall rule them!"[19] This spirit helped kill "King Caucus," the prevailing system in which Democratic-Republican members of Congress picked their party nominee. Since only one party existed at the time, the caucus essentially picked the president.

Jackson didn't campaign. He outwardly eschewed the practice, but he didn't stop his supporters from campaigning for him among delegates in key states. It became a clash between insiders and outsiders, between standards and interests. Henry Clay, Jackson's nemesis, disliked "appealing to the feelings and passions of our countrymen rather than to their reasons and judgments."[20]

When Jackson lost in 1824, his supporters cried that the election had been stolen. In 1828, Jackson's supporters promised he would "sweep the Augean stables" of Washington,[21] just as Donald Trump promised to "drain the swamp."[22] (Hercules had been tasked to clean out in a single day the stables of King Augeas, who owned more cattle and horses than anyone in Greece.)

When Jackson, "the people's president," won, his unwashed supporters arrived in Washington and wrinkled the noses of the political class, just as would later happen when Donald Trump raised his right hand in 2017. Daniel Webster of Massachusetts reported of Jackson's inaugural day, "I never saw anything like it before. Persons have come 500 miles to see General Jackson and they really seem to think that the country is rescued from some dreadful danger."[23]

In 1840, William Henry Harrison broke with tradition by actually appearing at a few Whig rallies as a presidential candidate, though that's about all he did. (Those in attendance may not have remembered though, because the Party had lubricated the audience by distributing hard cider.) Harrison was incidental to the process. The political parties ran politics. They mobilized turnout rates of 80 percent or more of the electorate at the time (which was more limited than it is today).[24] They did this by doling out jobs, providing favors, or acting as a social club. As Michael E. McGerr writes in *The Decline of Popular Politics*, the time of highest voter participation in the mid-nineteenth century was a time of extreme partisanship. Political combat was "aggressive, demonstrative, contentious and often vicious . . . few men chose to reject partisanship and stand as independents. Those who did were excoriated, their manhood questioned."[25]

As parties came to power, tending the norms against campaigning wasn't just about promoting virtue in a future president. The wire pullers, as political strategists were called at the time, didn't want to be interfered with by the candidate at the end of the wire. Parties were so powerful during the nineteenth century that when the Whig Party nominated General Winfield Scott in 1852, party bosses worried that the orotund and self-important general, who liked to refer to himself in the third person, would get into office and believe he had achieved the victory on his own. "I know you made him and we've got him and it's better Scott than anybody else," one New Yorker confided to William H. Seward in August, "but I am a little afraid that . . . if elected he may be apt to say 'my own right arm hath gotten me the victory.'"[26]

A candidate who thought they had gotten themselves elected wouldn't bend a knee to the party hacks when in office. The norm against campaigning continued through the nineteenth century, though various candidates employed stratagems to wriggle around it. In 1860, Stephen Douglas pretended to be going to visit his mother when in fact he was campaigning.[27] By 1880, a hundred years after the nation's founding, James Garfield thought it a "foolish custom which seals a presidential candidate's lips,"[28] but he was advised by President Hayes and other Republicans to "sit cross legged and look wise until after the election." Nevertheless, he felt the pull of the electorate, so he split the difference. He adhered to the tradition that candidates should await the country's call, but he left the gate open—literally. He ran a "front-porch" campaign, greeting throngs of visitors at his Mentor, Ohio, home.[29]

In 1952, "Citizens for Eisenhower" lofted the general to victories in party primaries, which helped force Republican Party officials to drop insider favorite Senator Robert Taft. Increasingly, both parties bound their national convention delegates to the outcome of the primaries, inserting a structural barrier to block meddling by party elites who might have made a different choice than the rank and file who expressed their preferences in the primaries. Under these rules, if the people spoke, the party insiders could not unwind their decision in a back room. In 1976, Ronald Reagan took advantage of primaries that locked in delegates as he rallied the conservative grassroots voters against the incumbent, Republican Gerald Ford, almost defeating him.

In 1972, on the Democratic side, previously marginalized groups like women and minorities pushed for more say in the fights for the nomination. The reforms of that year, which included delegate quotas for representation by previously sidelined groups, opened the nomination to the voice of the people even further. With the party elites weakened, the grassroots nominated the liberal George McGovern. "If people could be made to feel there was still hope through working in the system, they might draw encouragement and inspiration," wrote Gary Hart, McGovern's campaign manager.[30] Kennedy had argued that exposure to the people through the primary process filled him with a special understanding about the country. By opening up the process, Hart argued, the people would not only have more influence over their nominee but would feel better about their party and, if their party won, their country.

Even after formal backroom deliberations were largely gone from party nominations, a popular political science theory held that nominations were driven by a process by which "the party decides." Party strategists, pollsters, and donors selected the preferred candidate through an informal consensus. This helped Hillary Clinton, whose allies in the Democratic National Committee favored her over rival Bernie Sanders, but the fact that she barely beat a man who didn't identify as a Democrat suggested how weak the parties had become. On the Republican side, Donald Trump rewrote the textbooks. The party didn't want him, but the people did. "Donald Trump won not because of the party but in spite of it," says Carlos Díaz-Rosillo, a former Harvard professor and member of the Trump administration.[31]

WHAT YOU MISS WHEN YOU
CLOSE THE BACK ROOM

AS VOTERS REPLACED THE PARTIES AS THE MAIN FORCE IN SELECTING candidates, the criteria for evaluating presidents became even more fluid.

Voters don't like the sausage-making aspect of politics. Politicians make promises and then break them because they get infected by the political process. Lobbyists, or the Washington culture of favor trading, distracts them from doing what the people want. So voters tend to penalize candidates from the political world.

During the 2016 campaign, while Chris Christie's wife, Mary Pat, knocked on doors for him in New Hampshire, a woman invited her inside. She really liked the governor. She stacked compliments on his wife's lap like blankets. So, Mrs. Christie asked, was the woman going to vote for her husband? No, she said. As much as she might like Christie, she was voting for Trump. "Dear," she said, "we don't need another politician."[32] Whether a candidate promises to sweep the stables, as Jackson did, or drain the swamp, the passion for disruption in the name of connecting the people to their government is rich and long-standing.

The problem with downgrading the sausage-making skills is that government is still a sausage-making enterprise in which ugly compromises are made for partial progress in the name of the greater good. This is not a theory. It is the instruction left by the framers in the Constitution: Make sausage. The Constitution was designed to restrain ambition and excess through a system of shared powers which would force bargaining and compromise.

Thomas Jefferson described the process of give and take when determining the location of the capital in Washington, D.C. "I thought it impossible that reasonable men, consulting together coolly, could fail by some mutual sacrifices of opinion to form a compromise which was to save the Union." What the third president goes on to describe is a determination by all parties to look to the higher good — "the preservation of the Union and of concord among the States was more important," even though backing down off their previous positions meant "the pill would be particularly bitter" and cause "a revulsion of stomach almost convulsive."[33]

Now, candidates aren't allowed to boast about talent as a horse trader during primaries, because ideological voters expect maximalist positions from which they won't wobble. They don't want to hear about a skill for compromise with the other side.

John Kennedy announced his candidacy from the Senate. No senator would do that today because the institutions of Congress have become associated with capitulation. In the Democratic race in 2020, Joe Biden tried to boast that his Senate career demonstrated he could make progress by working with the other side. His opponents pointed out that men he made deals with in the seventies were segregationists. Senators who run for president now run away from their day job, often promising, as John McCain and Ted Cruz did, that while they've been in Washington they've been a subversive.

As voters gained more control over the nominating process, the standard for the office became whatever voters settled on the standard being at the time of the election. "When we elect someone who hasn't spent time in politics it's not just that we are electing someone with no experience in the job," says Harvard's Gautam Mukunda, whose book *Indispensable* studies the essential characteristics of great presidents and leaders. "We are electing someone where we have no information to judge whether they are able to do the job."[34]

With standards up for grabs, candidates define the job not by the duties it requires, but by the attributes they happen to have. (This works in much the same way I might persuade you that true happiness in life can be achieved only by buying this book.)[35] The criteria for election became not what the job required but what the candidate could sell. The country just had to hope that what the candidate was selling to get the job was remotely connected to the job they were going to do.

In 2007, Arkansas governor Mike Huckabee told Tim Russert that he sought to be a president who led "a revival of our national soul."[36] It was a wise tactical move for a man who had been a former Baptist preacher, but as Gene Healy writes, in *The Cult of the Presidency*: "What sort of office did Huckabee imagine he was running for? Is reviving the national soul in the job description? And if reviving the national soul is part of the president's job, what isn't?"

"I'M THE ONLY ONE"

VOTER DISAPPOINTMENT WITH POLITICAL PROMISES AND POLITICIANS is familiar, because no one on the hustings or the used car lot makes a sale by promoting middling outcomes. *What's it going to take to put you in a new car today (because you'll be disappointed soon enough and we might as well get the process started)?* The gap between promise and practice gave H. L. Mencken a lifetime of material. Politicians, he wrote in 1936, have "no special talent for the business of government; they have only a talent for getting and holding office. Their principal device to that end is to search out groups who pant and pine for something they can't get and to promise to give it to them. Nine times out of ten that promise is worth nothing. The tenth time is made good by looting A to satisfy B."[37]

Herbert Hoover would never have subscribed to such a cynical view, but he did confide that the system of campaign promising in 1928 had overshot the mark. "My friends have made the American people

A Chicken *for* Every Pot

Wag — 30 Oct. 1928

THE Republican Party isn't a *"Poor Man's Party:"* Republican prosperity has erased that degrading phrase from our political vocabulary. The Republican Party is *equality's* party — *opportunity's* party — *democracy's* party, the party of *national* development, not *sectional* interests — the *impartial* servant of every State and condition in the Union.

Under higher tariff and lower taxation, America has stabilized output, employment and dividend rates.

Republican efficiency has filled the workingman's dinner pail — and his gasoline tank *besides* — made telephone, radio and sanitary plumbing *standard* household equipment. And placed the whole nation in the *silk stocking class.*

During eight years of Republican management, we have built more and better homes, erected more skyscrapers, passed more benefactory laws, and more laws to regulate and purify immigration, inaugurated more conservation measures, more measures to standardize and increase production, expand export markets, and reduce industrial and human junk piles, than in any previous quarter century.

Republican prosperity is written in *fuller* wage envelops, written in factory chimney smoke, written on the walls of new construction, written in savings bank books, written in mercantile balances, and written in the peak value of stocks and bonds.

Republican prosperity has *reduced* hours and *increased* earning capacity, silenced *discontent,* put the proverbial "chicken in every pot." And a car in every backyard, to boot.

It has *raised* living standards and *lowered* living costs.

It has restored financial confidence and enthusiasm, changed *credit* from a *rich* man's privilege to a *common* utility, *generalized* the use of time-saving devices and released women from the thrall of *domestic drudgery.*

It has provided every county in the country with its concrete road and knitted the highways of the nation into a *unified* traffic system.

Thanks to Republican administration, farmer, dairyman and merchant can make deliveries in *less* time and at *less* expense, can borrow *cheap* money to refund exorbitant mortgages, and stock their pastures, ranges and shelves.

Democratic management *impoverished* and *demoralized* the *railroads,* led packing plants and tire factories into *receivership,* squandered billions on *impractical* programs.

Democratic maladministration issued *further* billions on mere "scraps of paper," then encouraged foreign debtors to believe that their loans would never be called, and bequeathed to the Republican Party the job of *mopping up the mess.*

Republican administration has *restored* to the railroads solvency, efficiency and par securities.

It has brought rubber trades through panic and chaos, brought down the prices of crude rubber by smashing *monopolistic rings,* put the tanner's books in the *black and* secured from the European powers formal acknowledgment of their obligations.

The Republican Party rests its case on a record of stewardship and performance.

Its Presidential and Congressional candidates stand for election on a platform of sound practice, Federal vigilance, high tariff, Constitutional integrity, the conservation of natural resources, *honest* and *constructive* measures for agricultural relief, sincere enforcement of the laws, and the right of *all* citizens, regardless of *faith* or *origin,* to share the benefits of opportunity and justice.

Wages, dividends, progress and prosperity say,

"Vote *for* Hoover"

Paid for by a member of the Republican Business Men, Inc.

Those wishing to see similar advertisements in other New York papers may send cheques to the Republicans Business Men, Inc., 4 West 40th Street

GENERAL COMMITTEE
George Henry Payne, Chairman

L. F. Loree, M. Vanclain, Wm. H. Hamilton, Julius Rosenwald, Albert I. Grey, Edson S. Lott, F. H. McKnight, Wm. Cooper Procter, R. B. Strassburger
George Whitney, Henry Rogers Winthrop, Frank C. Munson, J. Horace Harding, Gen. W. W. Atterbury, Wm. Ziegler, Jr., Kermit Roosevelt, Edmond K. Wise, Albert Tersch

Hoover's boosters ran this ad promising voters the moon.
Democrats lampooned him with it later, when the soup lines and
high unemployment of the Great Depression made his
fantastical 1928 campaign promises seem like a cruel joke.

think me a sort of superman, able to cope successfully with the most difficult and complicated problems," he told a friend. "They expect the impossible from me and should there arise in the land conditions with which the political machinery is unable to cope, I will be the one to suffer."[38] And how.

Hoover could blame his friends because in 1928 he was not as involved in making the direct pitch as candidates are today. With the dawn of the television age, the candidate became not only the chief actor in the drama, but the chief salesman. Other attributes were less important than your skills as a pitchman.

When the parties atrophied, the connection between the needy candidate and the needy public grew tighter. "The political parties no longer have either intelligible boundaries or enforceable norms, and, as a result, renegade political behavior pays," writes author Jonathan Rauch.[39] As a result, in 2016, Donald Trump and Bernie Sanders were only nominal members of the parties whose nominations they sought. Sanders was a lifelong independent and Donald Trump was a donor and member of both parties. In 2020 the Democratic Party would see a battle between Mike Bloomberg and Bernie Sanders, neither of whom had been longtime members of the Party. Ted Cruz came to power as a candidate by tearing down his party establishment, including the Senate majority leader Mitch McConnell who he targeted as a liar.[40]

The nominating process was "transformed from a mixed system, in which control over the nomination was shared by the people and the party organizations, to what can be termed a plebiscitary system in which the key actors are the people and the individual aspirants," writes political scientist James W. Ceaser. This ushered in "a new method of generating support in presidential campaigns: 'popular leadership,' or the attempt by individual aspirants to carve out a personal mass constituency by their own programmatic and personality appeals and by the use of large personal campaign organizations of their own creation."[41]

The pressure to sell encourages candidates to make vast promises. Even self-styled serious candidates cannot resist the pull to light the roman candles to keep the crowd in a roar. Howard Dean explained what this was like when looking back on his 2004 presidential campaign. "I'd get out there and I would talk about policy and there was no adrenaline rush," he told the documentary producers at FiveThirtyEight .com. "People kind of went 'uh-huh, uh-huh,' and I really wanted that huge charge of being able to crank them all up and to believe in themselves again and get enthusiastic, and I would succumb to that."[42] It was this pull that led Dean to produce the "scream" of elation as he tried to whip his crowd into excitement after his disappointing third-place showing in the 2004 Iowa caucuses.

"I really wanted that huge charge of being able to crank them all up and to believe in themselves again and get enthusiastic," Howard Dean told FiveThirtyEight.com, "and I would succumb to that."

Once candidates get to the general election, they shift from boasting about how ideologically pure they are to boasting about how much they are going to get done. "Longer and longer campaigns have contributed to a prolonged bidding war of candidates making more and more promises as to what government will do if they are elected," says Roger Porter, who served in the Reagan and Ford administrations and now teaches at the Harvard Kennedy School.[43]

The American presidential election has become what William Henry Harrison, the ninth president, had feared. Examining "the history of all Republics," Harrison discovered that "as they receded from the purity of Representative Government, the condition of obtaining office was the making of promises." Ambition often made "men of the fairest characters" act like "auctioneers selling . . . linen," advocating for anything for "a temporary gain."[44]

In the 2004 campaign, John Kerry's running mate, John Edwards, sounded like a revivalist preacher at a rally in Newton, Iowa, as he touted the promise of stem cell research to cure paralysis: "If we do the work that we can do in this country, the work that we will do when John Kerry is president, people like Christopher Reeve are going to walk, get up out of that wheelchair and walk again."[45] Barack Obama unleashed this grandiose version of his presidency as a candidate in 2008, when he clinched the nomination: "Generations from now, we will be able to look back and tell our children that this was the moment when we began to provide care for the sick and good jobs to the jobless; this was the moment when the rise of the oceans began to slow and our planet began to heal."[46] The crowds roared and helped deliver Obama to the White House.

In 2016, Donald Trump built the tower of promises higher. "Nobody knows the system better than me," he told the GOP convention, "which is why I alone can fix it."[47] Throughout the campaign he continued to make the same pitch. "Politicians have used you and stolen your votes. They have given you nothing," Trump said on the day he cleared the number of delegates required for the nomination. "I will give you everything. I will give you what you've been looking for for fifty years. I'm the only one."[48] At regular intervals, candidate Trump tied the highest possible achievements of American government to himself: "The only one to fix the infrastructure of our country is me."[49] "I am going to save Social Security without any cuts. I know where to get the money from. Nobody else does."[50] "Nobody but Donald Trump will save Israel."[51] An office that once required no displays of ambition was won by repeated displays of self-aggrandizement.

In 1950 the American Political Science Association published a report on the health of political parties as concern grew that presidents were dominating the political system. Their conclusion about trends halfway through the last century sound almost as prescient as Kennedy's about television: "When the President's program actually is the sole program . . . either his party becomes a flock of sheep or the party falls apart. In effect this concept of the presidency disposes of the party system by making the President reach directly for the support of a majority of the voters. It favors a president who exploits skillfully the arts of demagoguery, who uses the whole country as his political back yard, and who does not mind turning into the embodiment of personal government."[52]

An Off-the-Cuff Opinion

Truman's new technique in addressing the people was illustrated by his extemporaneous speech for the National Conference on Family Life. He spoke with complete lack of formality and undoubtedly succeeded in communicating his ideas to the audience in a personal manner. That sort of address certainly holds his listeners more effectively than the reading of a set speech which has been prepared and combed over carefully by presidential advisers. It is said that the President intends to employ this new technique when he makes his tour of the West. . . . Mr. Truman cannot get away from the fact that his words become those of the President of the United States. When the President speaks, something more than an off the cuff opinion or remark is expected, unless he is talking informally and off the record for a small group. Much as we applaud the President's courage and flexibility in experimenting with a new technique, therefore, we cannot suppress the hope that when he speaks for the whole nation for the whole world to hear, that the advantages of weighing his words will not be overlooked.[1]

—*Washington Post* editorial, 1948

Chapter 22

What Got You Here
Won't Get You There

—

Whoever steps into this office, whether it's Obama or
McCain, they're going to learn there's a big difference
between campaigning and governing.[2]

—GEORGE W. BUSH

Coolidge became a man who believed that a national leader
should not try to "go ahead of the majestic army of human
thought and aspiration, blazing new and strange paths."[3]

—BENJAMIN GINSBERG, *PRESIDENTIAL GOVERNMENT*

MARSHALL GOLDSMITH COACHES HIGH-PERFORMING CEOs.
His bestselling book *What Got You Here Won't Get You There* warns
that success can limit the successful. As ambitious people zip up the
rungs of the ladder, they rely on past skills, but to truly thrive, the exceptional executive is aware they have to lose some successful old skills
and learn, adapt, and change.

Goldsmith says it's hard for successful people to recognize this pit-
fall because success blinds them. "Successful people are delusional
and the more successful we *become*, the more delusional we *get*."[4]

Former defense secretary James Mattis offers a similar sermon:
"Success is one of the biggest penalty boxes you can get into if you live
in it because you can start thinking you know all that you need to do,
you've done all the learning that you need to do, and so it's probably
the most injurious thing out there in terms of stunting one's personal
development and continued lifelong learning."[5]

After winning the election, incoming presidents should book some hours with Goldsmith. As extraordinary as it is to triumph in a campaign, governing is a different job. What got you to the White House won't necessarily get you to Mount Rushmore. Our modern campaigns promote the opposite impression, but the faster a president recognizes the difference, the better off he or she will be.

A new president turns the first page of the transition briefing book, propelled by a strong ego boost. They have just convinced millions of Americans that they are worthy of the most powerful job in the world. They've done so after a grueling two-year battle with no days off. Soon enough for a president, though, they bonk their nose against the sliding glass door of reality.

Understanding that campaigning is not governing is one of the first big tests a new president faces. If a president gets this wrong, he builds the wrong kind of team and launches an administration under the wrong heading. Each subsequent day the vessel plows on in the wrong direction, changing course becomes harder.

The best leaders understand that different situations call for different talents. Harry Truman once snickered that Eisenhower would face a big surprise because the presidency would not snap with the command-and-control efficiency of the military. "He'll sit here, and he'll say, 'Do this! Do that!' And nothing will happen. Poor Ike—it won't be a bit like the Army. He'll find it very frustrating," Truman said.[6]

The Missouri pepperpot misunderstood Ike. The former general and Columbia University president knew different tasks required different leadership approaches and that a key skill of a leader was identifying what the moment required.[7] He'd studied leadership throughout his career. His private correspondence and diary entries are dotted with asides about what he had accumulated in his rise.

In a 1943 letter to General George Marshall, Eisenhower, then serving as assistant chief of staff in charge of the Operations Division, describes why Patton, who was so good at one kind of leadership, would not be good at another kind:

> Patton's strength is that he thinks only in terms of attack . . . the man has a native shrewdness. . . . Personally, I doubt that I

would ever consider Patton for an army group commander or for any higher position [but] under a man who is sound and solid, and who has enough sense to use Patton's good qualities without becoming blinded by his love of showmanship and histrionics, he should do as fine a job as he did in Sicily.[8, 9]

The analysis applies almost perfectly to the difference between campaigning, which is all about attack, and the obligations of governing, which is more akin to rebuilding after a war.

In a campaign, candidates have to do one thing: convince voters to pick between two alternatives. All the smaller choices lead to the larger one. If you don't like my opponent's views on the Supreme Court, vote for me. If you don't like the way my opponent talks, vote for me. All action focuses on a single deadline day in early November. The binary choice works as a shield, too. If, as a candidate, you face a problem, you can deflect attention from it by highlighting your opponent's problems.

Campaigns center on constant confrontation. Durable and successful governing, on the other hand, requires building coalitions through conciliation and cooperation. Campaigns offer no partial victories. In governing, durable solutions with lasting impact are partial solutions. Everyone gets something. A president or voters who demand total victories are campaigning, not governing. Victories through unilateral action are brittle. Often they can be undone by the next president. These victories are also likely to be puny. The great national challenges a president should address, like healthcare, economic prosperity, climate change, and immigration, can be effectively tackled only through collective action. As Bill Clinton has said, the subtext of the Constitution is "Let's make a deal."[10]

In an election, voters are prepared for change. It is embedded in the process. With governing, presidents face the resistance to change that Machiavelli identified five hundred years ago: "There is nothing more difficult and dangerous, or more doubtful of success, than an attempt to introduce a new order of things. . . . Hence it is that, whenever the opponents of the new order of things have the opportunity to attack it, they will do it with the zeal of partisans, whilst the others defend it but feebly, so that it is dangerous to rely upon the latter."

The comedian Stephen Colbert says the fun of campaigns for political humorists like him is that the audience meets you halfway. The audience knows the players and what the stakes are when you hit the stage. You don't need to set up the joke or explain the premise. You just get to dunk the ball again and again. This is true for candidates too; the audience is ready to buy what they are selling.

During a campaign, we know why they are at the microphone. The stakes are high, so we're apt to listen. When a president steps up to speak, however, people have to be given a reason to tune in. There is no deadline like Election Day to focus the public mind. A president making a case for a policy is arguing in a more complex environment. There isn't just one choice—Candidate A or B—but competing and complex policies and policy options to grab public attention. Health-care reform, for example, is hard to boil down to a single yes or no decision. The issue spiders off in all directions. Interested parties engage in heated debates using non-user-friendly terms like "community rating," which lose people if you use them as a president. Opponents pelt the process with disinformation about "death panels" that pull the conversation into an area of emotion and theater and away from focused attention on trade-offs that are the natural result of governing.

Presidents turning the wheel from campaigning to governing must also worry about the supporters who all clambered onto the bus. They were promised a package tour of quick solutions that would be painful only for the undeserving or for members of the other party. If the champion that they pounded yard signs for starts talking about complexity and delay, supporters will feel betrayed.

I CAMPAIGN, THEREFORE I AM

DESPITE THE GULF BETWEEN CAMPAIGNING AND GOVERNING, CANDIDATES and their supporters promote the idea that they are the same thing: that campaign success will lead to success in office.

In 1992, after Bill Clinton beat George H. W. Bush, Vice President Dan Quayle said, "If he governs as well as he campaigned, the country will be all right."[11] Republicans had argued during the campaign that Clinton's character faults disqualified him from office. Quayle, acting generously in defeat, suggested Clinton's campaign skills were the more important indicator about the future of the republic.

When Steve Kroft of 60 Minutes asked Barack Obama about his lack of executive experience in 2008, the one-term senator pointed to his successful campaign as proof he could manage the presidency. "I know how to make things run and get things done," he said. "Otherwise I wouldn't be here sitting having this interview with you."[12] Bill Clinton echoed this sentiment as he campaigned for Obama. "If you have any doubt about Senator Obama's ability to be the chief executive," Clinton said at one of Obama's vast rallies in October 2008, "just look at all of you. . . . He has executed this campaign."[13]

Donald Trump weaponized this idea. When challenged on various policies, or whether those policies are working, he drops his campaign victory as a conversation ender. "I can't be doing so badly," he told Time magazine, "because I'm president, and you're not."[14] To Lesley Stahl of 60 Minutes he tied off a back-and-forth by saying, "Lesley, it's okay. In the meantime, I'm president, and you're not."[15]

The presidency has become so much like the campaign, argues the political scientist Jeffrey Tulis, that the country is now effectively governed by a second Constitution, one that clashes with the first one. In Constitution One, Tulis explains in his seminal work The Rhetorical Presidency, "candidates exemplified a public teaching that political campaigns were beneath the dignity of men suited for governance, that honor attended more important activities than campaigns." The second Constitution puts a premium on active and continuous presidential courtship of popular opinion—hot action over cool deliberation. "In a striking reversal," writes Tulis, "campaigns are becoming the model for governing."[16]

If the presidency is just a Broadway upgrade of the off-Broadway campaign, then "How could a president not be an actor?"[17] as Ronald Reagan asked. Or, in keeping with the escalation of the entertainment product, how could he not be a reality TV star?

THE TALKING CURE

MODERN PRESIDENTS WIN ON THE STRENGTH OF THEIR RHETORIC and showmanship. Naturally, they reach for those same tools to meet the early challenges of the office. "It's a malady and it's a dangerous one," says the Texas A&M political scientist George C. Edwards III.

"They have been talking for two years, and that's nearly all they've been doing. When they win, they conclude that they can convince people of anything. The feedback is pretty strong."[18]

Candidates spend most of their campaign with the communications team, or talking about communications. They bring that apparatus with them to the White House, which means the pattern of crisis management has already been set in deep grooves.

Every White House seems to have the same meeting early in its tenure. The president, still high on the feedback loop of the campaign rallies, says that the problems they're having can be solved through better communication. "What I've got to do is to spend more time communicating with the American people about what we've done and where we're going," Bill Clinton said in a 1994 interview, at a low point in his first term.[19]

In 2010, President Obama explained that "as president, the symbols and gestures—what people are seeing coming out of this office—are at least as important as the policies we put forward."[20] Two years later, asked to identify his biggest mistake, he pointed to communication. "When I think about what we've done well and what we haven't done well, the mistake of my first term—couple of years—was thinking that this job was just about getting the policy right. And that's important. But the nature of this office is also to tell a story to the American people that gives them a sense of unity and purpose and optimism, especially during tough times."[21]

When supporters deflate about their president, they also diagnose communications failures. "Mr. President, you're not leading this nation," Jimmy Carter told the nation about himself in a 1979 national address known as the "crisis of confidence" speech.[22] He was repeating the criticism that he had heard from a Southern governor he'd talked to: "You're just managing the government. You don't see the people enough anymore. . . . Don't talk to us about politics or the mechanics of government but about an understanding of our common good. Mr. President, we are in trouble. Talk to us about blood and sweat and tears."

Carter started the famous speech promising to be the president "who feels your pain." This is an example of what Jeffrey Tulis was talking about—a president who is in constant symbiosis with the public.

Jimmy Carter speaks to the nation about shared sacrifice and a flabby national spirit. Dubbed the "malaise" speech for its tone (though Carter himself did not use that word), it temporarily improved Carter's political standing. His fortunes fell a few days later when he fired a chunk of his staff.

This phrase has since come to be associated with Bill Clinton. That's fitting, because Bill Clinton was the Southern governor whose criticism Carter quoted in the speech. Both men would learn that no matter how many speeches you gave that showed you understood the country's pain, communication alone could not protect you from more powerful forces.

Franklin Roosevelt was one of the best at using communications and empathy to rally the country. But Roosevelt's skills could not protect him from the "Roosevelt Recession" of 1937–38, which contributed to enormous losses for his fellow Democrats in the midterm presidential elections. Nor could he convince the country that the Supreme Court should be expanded or that Democrats should be punished for blocking his reorganization plan.

In 2011, the Emory psychologist Drew Westen published a three-thousand-word *New York Times* op-ed asking "What Happened to Obama?" It argued the president had failed to tell a compelling tale about the Great Recession in a way that would shame the opposition, inspire supporters, and promote effective solutions. "There was no story," Westen said of Obama's inauguration speech, "and there has been none since."[23]

The piece received a wave of amens, attesting to the number of Obama supporters who had been muttering the same thing in private for months. Liberals felt that Barack Obama, who had won so handily, and made them feel so good, should unpack his campaign skills and apply them to governing. "This was without a doubt the most insightful and compelling dissection of where this president is and why," wrote one reader in response to the Westen piece. "He seems to so many people, including past supporters like me, to have become this inert and feckless non-presence. 'Leader of the free world' indeed."

Columnists joined the chorus. In *The Washington Post*, Richard Cohen charged that Obama's speech and behavior were cool to the economic suffering in the country. When he did speak, Cohen wrote, Obama lacked "the rhetorical qualities of the old-time black politicians." He could not, Cohen, said, "recall a soaring passage from a speech."[24]

On the other side of the scrimmage line, political scientists, and the columnists who study their work, sharpened their cleats. They claimed that Westen, and everyone reading his piece out loud to their spouses at the breakfast table, fundamentally misunderstood how presidential rhetoric works. "It's hard to exaggerate just how wrong Westen's argument is, starting with his assumption that policies flow 'naturally' from this 'simple narrative,'" wrote the Middlebury political scientist Matthew Dickinson. "In this regard, Westen falls prey to a basic misconception: that a President can control the narrative by which the public defines his presidency."[25] John Sides, a political scientist at Vanderbilt University, made the same observation: "There is precious little evidence that presidents accomplish much by rhetoric—least of all large shifts in public opinion. In fact, when presidents start giving barnburning speeches and drawing lines in the sand, guess what often happens? It makes it harder for presidents to get things done."[26]

TALKING UP THE ECONOMY

IF THE ECONOMY IS BAD, IT'S PARTICULARLY HARD FOR A PRESIDENT TO talk his way out of a fix. When President Obama's supporters were imagining that stronger rhetoric would dominate his opponents, the unemployment rate was at 9.3 percent.[27] Getting a hearing in that kind of environment is extremely difficult. Studies show that the media cover bad economic news more than good or neutral news. (You probably didn't need to read a study to know this.) During George Herbert Walker Bush's presidency, for example, the evening news broadcasts devoted almost thirty minutes to the economy each week—times were bad—as opposed to the Clinton years, when times were good. During that period, the issue received an average of sixteen minutes of coverage per week.[28]

The political scientists Matthew Eshbaugh-Soha and Jeffrey S. Peake looked at the type of media coverage accorded to the presidency and put the fix plainly for presidents trying to shake off the weight of a bad economic storyline: "Presidents do not typically influence the attention devoted to economic issues by either the news media or Congress, but are instead primarily responsive to media attention. . . . George H. W. Bush fell victim to this relationship in 1992. . . . His experience is not rare, but a function of the presidency's limited influence on the economic policy agenda, particularly when the economy is weak."[29]

WE SHALL NOT BE MOVED

WAIT—HOW CAN PRESIDENTIAL SPEECHMAKING BE SO INEFFECTIVE when the books of great speeches have so many presidential entries?

The answer is that the power of speechmaking depends on the circumstances and the topic. Presidential speeches can define a moment, give language to inchoate thoughts, and gather together a stunned country. They can also be brilliant in a losing cause, which wins them a place in the hearts of wordsmiths but not in the breasts of the citizenry. But speeches are not magical in all instances. The belief that they are—encouraged by rhetoric-heavy campaigns and our theater reviews in the media—has warped our understanding of what a president should and can do to be successful.

History is full of examples of presidents failing despite deploying every rhetorical tool hanging on the White House Peg-Board. Woodrow Wilson's vision of the power and necessity of presidential oratory is credited (or blamed) for sparking the modern reliance on presidential oratory. After World War I, Wilson nearly killed himself trying to persuade Americans to support the League of Nations. He traveled ten thousand miles by train to twenty-nine cities and spoke nearly forty times, pleading with Americans to join European countries in building a system that would keep mankind from filling up muddy fields with the bodies of another generation of young men. "He envisioned the president serving as the spokesman for public opinion in great national debates," writes J. Michael Hogan in *Woodrow Wilson's Western Tour*. "Rather than promote some narrow partisan agenda, Wilson's rhetorical president assumed the obligation to educate, interpret, and give expression to public opinion. He did not manipulate or even persuade public opinion, but rather served as a 'spokesman for the real sentiment and purpose of the country.'"[30]

Republicans saw Wilson not as a neutral arbiter, but rather as a president trying to rally the country against their party, and using the casualties of the Great War to do so. They were right. "Some men in public life who are now opposing the settlement for which these men died could visit such a spot as that," the president said about the American graves in Europe. "I wish that they could feel the moral obligation that rests upon us not to go back on those boys, but to see the thing through."[31] Wilson's faith in his own righteousness and power of persuasion encouraged his belief that he could pressure Republicans rather than compromise with them, which infuriated those Republicans and doomed his efforts.

Presidents who try to replicate their campaign success on the stump also face an opposition with far better weapons than their campaign opponent had. The president's opposition has powers granted them by the Constitution. Republican Henry Cabot Lodge fought Wilson on the League with a passion. "I never expected to hate anyone in politics with the hatred I feel toward Wilson," he told his friend Teddy Roosevelt.[32] Lodge was not only the majority leader, he was chairman of the Senate Foreign Relations Committee. He scheduled a month of hearings on the League, hoping that the more the public learned about it, the more they would discover they didn't like it. To slow things down further, he called for a reading of the entire two-hundred-page treaty, which took him a fortnight. He read it himself. (A luxury a politician could afford when he didn't have to spend so much time raising money.) After the reading was done, Lodge called the first of sixty witnesses.

Wilson failed to persuade Congress and the country, but he defined the moral benefits of presidential action even in defeat. "I would rather lose in a cause that will some day win," he said, "than win in a cause that will some day lose."

President Trump has offered the opposite maxim. When asked if he had spoken too harshly during the campaign, he said, "No, I won."[33] When asked if he went too far in making fun of Christine Blasey Ford, who alleged that the president's U.S. Supreme Court nominee Brett Kavanaugh sexually assaulted her, he reportedly said, "It doesn't matter, we won."[34] Winning is the only thing.

John F. Kennedy's words are among the most repeated in the presidential canon, but his eloquence didn't help him rally the public behind his Medicare program. On May 20, 1962, Kennedy addressed the country from Madison Square Garden about the issue of reform. "In this free society of ours the consent and support of the citizens of this country is essential if this or any other piece is going to be passed," he said to an estimated television audience of 20 million. The next night a family physician, Dr. Edward Annis, gave a televised rebuttal. More than 30 million people tuned in to that, according to one report. The president did not sway his audience, and the measure died in Congress.

George Edwards looked at key moments when presidents drew themselves to their full rhetorical height in order to persuade the public—Oval Office speeches, State of the Union Addresses, prime time press conferences—and found a weak power of persuasion. "There is not a single systematic study that demonstrates that presidents can reliably move others to support them," says Edwards. "Equally important, we now have a substantial literature showing that presidents typically fail at persuasion."[35]

Ronald Reagan, despite his reputation as "the great communicator," could not convince even a plurality of Americans that the United States should provide military aid to the Contra rebels fighting Nicaragua's Sandinista government, despite three Oval Office addresses on the issue between March 1986 and February 1988.[36] "During the eight years of my presidency, I repeatedly expressed my frustration (and sometimes my downright exasperation) over my difficulties in convincing the American people and Congress of the seriousness of the threat in Central America," wrote Reagan. "Time and again, I would speak on television, to a joint session of Congress, or to other audiences about the problems in Central America, and I would hope that the outcome would be an outpouring of support from Americans who would apply the same kind of heat on Congress that helped pass the economic recovery package."[37]

After winning reelection in a landslide victory in 1984, Reagan made another run at pitching support for the Contras. In April 1985, his pollster Richard Wirthlin wrote him a memo outlining the limits of his persuasive power. It's a memo all presidents should keep handy. Reagan had been successful, wrote Wirthlin, "when the issue considered *already* has strong grassroots support." He had been able to pressure Congress "if that issue has, from the outset, broad support." In other instances Reagan had been successful because he "amplified the public's political voice," meaning he galvanized popular sentiment that had been dormant.[38]

Wirthlin explained that if the people were not with him, the president could not change minds. (Reagan's position of providing aid to those fighting the regime in Nicaragua was favored by 28 percent of all Americans; 70 percent opposed it.) In fact, Wirthlin explained, the more the president spoke about the issue—even from a position of principle—the more his prospects would decline. His stumping for the idea turned it into a partisan issue his opponents would want to scuttle just to deal him a defeat. Supporters couldn't counterbalance that, because there weren't that many people who were stirred by the underlying policy. "By raising the political stakes and the public saliency of this particular issue," wrote Wirthlin, "you would not only put into jeopardy the favorable job approval you now enjoy, but, more importantly, you will generate more public and congressional opposition than support."[39]

Analysts at the Pew Research Center looked at their polls and also found presidents aren't very persuasive. When George H. W. Bush appeared in prime time to defend and promote passage of his famous 1990 deficit reduction deal, it did not build support.[40] Bill Clinton traveled to nearly two hundred cities and towns during the first two years of his presidency. He sold his healthcare bill, his budget stimulus, himself, and his party. Ultimately, his healthcare bill did not pass, his poll numbers fell, and Republicans took control of the House of Representatives for the first time in more than forty years. Chuck Meyer of WWWE Radio in Cleveland, Ohio, summed up the dire picture by saying, "You're getting blamed for just about everything going on in the country today, including the heartbreak of psoriasis."[41]

In 2005, after George W. Bush won a second term, he sought to turn his victory into momentum for a plan to allow Americans to own private Social Security accounts. He campaigned on the idea and he was making good on the promise. "I earned capital in the campaign, political capital, and now I intend to spend it," said Bush, articulating the traditional view of how rhetoric and presidential persuasion are supposed to work.[42] He planned to travel to sixty cities in sixty days to sell the package. The barnstorm strategy employed every campaign gimmick: the manicured crowds, the carefully choreographed presidential movements, and the full weight of presidential rhetoric. The president also addressed the country in prime time.

The audience did not rise to applaud the show. They rose to leave. Poll numbers for the privatization plan, and the president's approval rating, dropped. To bolster his case, Bush included ideas for implementing the program proposed by a Democratic economist. He hoped to buy Democratic votes, or at least look as if he was extending a hand to the opposition by including ideas they once supported. The move brought neither votes nor public support.

Members of the president's party reacted to the political reality by stepping back. "If you lead, we'll be behind you," one House leader said, "but we'll be way behind you."[43] In the end, Bush, who had worked so hard to sell his plan, recognized the limits of presidential persuasion. The sixty-city tour never made it past twenty-five.[44] "The failure of Social Security reform shows the limits of the president's power," Bush wrote about the defeat. "If Congress is determined not to act, there is only so much a president can do."[45]

In 2007, Bush made a national appeal for a "path to citizenship" for undocumented immigrants. It did not move support for the issue, even in his own party. Nine years later, his party would nominate Donald Trump on a platform explicitly antithetical to what Bush had proposed.

President Obama entered office with a Reaganesque reputation for the power of his speechmaking, and he immediately put his silver tongue behind selling healthcare reform. He had run on the issue, and prospects looked good at the start. In April 2009, 59 percent of respondents in a Kaiser healthcare poll believed healthcare reform was more important than ever. Only 37 percent said the weak economy made reform too difficult.[46] Obama went to work on the legislation, and as he did so, Wirthlin's Law—that advocacy for a cause can rally your opposition more than your team—kicked in. Partisan Republicans associated the reforms with a president they didn't like, and the numbers turned against Obama. Like Bush on Social Security, Obama tried to woo Republicans by including some of their ideas in his plan. He pointed out that the individual mandate that was causing opposition— compelling people to buy insurance as a way to spread risk—was originally a Republican idea.[47] The opposition did not bend.

In February 2009, when Obama started pitching, his approval rating on the question of healthcare stood at 57 percent favorable to 41 percent unfavorable. By the time he signed the law in March 2010 with no Republican support, those numbers had flipped.

When President Obama pushed for immigration reform in his second term, Republicans who shared his objectives asked him not to speak in support of the plan, to keep from riling up their party base against it. When gun reform measures couldn't pass the Senate, Republican senator Pat Toomey of Pennsylvania said Obama's support had weighed down the legislation. "There were some on my side who did not want to be seen helping the president do something he wanted to get done, just because the president wanted to do it," he said.[48]

Donald Trump looked as if he might reverse this pattern of presidential persuasion. His Twitter account is a presidential innovation on par with FDR's fireside chats; perhaps he had a new kind of magic. Even though it has tremendous power in his party, driving opponents from the field and muting others, the president's Twitter feed has not been a persuasive tool for the larger country. His signature legislative achievement, the tax cut, passed in 2017 with only 29 percent of the country supporting it. A year later, according to the Gallup poll, only 41 percent approved of it, and the vast majority of the country believed it benefited the already very wealthy—a direct contradiction of the case the president had been making on its behalf.[49]

During President Trump's monthslong battle over healthcare, his proposal to replace Obamacare had only 31 percent approval in the month that it passed the House.[50] Though the president has been promoting a border wall since the first days of his candidacy in 2015, four years later, 60 percent of Americans opposed the idea.[51]

When a president speaks, lobbyists and special interests hand out luxury earmuffs. Any issue important enough to require sustained presidential action that hasn't already slipped into law will have lobbyists and special interests protecting the status quo. There are more lobbyists than ever before in Washington, and their ties to lawmakers are more robust. Many of them are former lawmakers who have special insight and ability to influence the process for private clients. Of the 106 members who exited their congressional offices in January 2019, 41 percent now work for a lobbying firm.[52] Of the former members of the previous Congress, the number was 60 percent.[53] Presidential rhetoric has to be so strong that the public pressure it creates is specific, and sustained enough to make lawmakers worry about their political future more than they worry about that future when they disappoint the lobbyists who are a crucial source of campaign cash that will help them get re-elected.

IF PRESIDENTS WEREN'T FIXATED on applying their rhetoric to the problems they face, the press would blame them for not trying hard enough. The media are addicted to presidential communication. Broadcast and cable networks need pictures and sound. Presidential speeches fill the bill.

This is why the State of the Union speech is covered with such a sense of moment, despite its limited utility in the progress of American life. The pageantry is covered as if it were leading to something. It rarely is.[54] Nevertheless, analysts give the words of the speech the steady kneading of a dozen loaves of sourdough. The speech takes place in an exciting present where history and context that might undermine the pageantry are furloughed off to the side of the stage so as not to distract the audience from the spectacle of the moment.

In 2014, Barack Obama declared in his State of the Union Address that he would use his pen and his phone to bypass a reluctant Congress. The press covered the declaration as if sweeping possibilities were galloping just beyond the horizon and would be in town by noon. In reality, the president could not do much through executive orders, as Obama had told audiences years earlier when he still had faith in the legislative process to try and compel it into action.

In 2019, Donald Trump's team declared his State of the Union Address would be about political unity. There were many reports uncritically announcing this gambit despite the fact that the president had shown no interest in unity during the previous twenty-five months of his presidency. After the speech concluded unblemished by offers of cooperation or olive branches to the other side—which are the component parts of creating unity—the idea of unity nevertheless did not die. It flopped around on the deck as analysts filled airtime during the State of the Union analysis period noting that the White House had said it would be a speech of unity.

Having invested these high-profile speeches with all of this attention, we expect the polls to change. We judge the president to have failed if they don't. Your correspondent was guilty of this view. In 2010 I wrote about President Obama's failure as a pitchman, and the political scientist Brendan Nyhan introduced me to the research that has formed the basis of this chapter.

"I CANNOT GO ANY FASTER"

THE TWO GREATEST PRESIDENTS, ABRAHAM LINCOLN AND FRANKLIN Roosevelt, understood the limits of their persuasive powers. "With public sentiment," Lincoln said, "nothing can fail; without it, nothing can succeed."[55] When Roosevelt met with the progressive reformer Upton Sinclair, he responded to the author's entreaties, "I cannot go any faster than the people will let me."

In an oft-quoted but likely apocryphal conversation between FDR and A. Philip Randolph, the civil rights leader and labor activist, the president told Randolph, "I agree with you—now convince me to do it." Even if the exchange didn't happen, the reality of public pressure—or the threat of it—did move FDR. In 1941, Randolph's call for a march on Washington pushed FDR to sign an executive order banning discrimination in government and defense industry employment.[56]

Wise presidents discover they are not directors but facilitators of events. "When broader forces align—public opinion, the right number of legislators—presidential action is a useful addition of momentum to that change," says the political scientist John Sides. "It's not going to create that change by itself, but it can direct it."[57]

It is in this realm where campaign skills benefit a president. A candidate's skill for reading the country helps a president know when the public is ready to move. The challenge for presidents is that the office thwarts the president's ability to get out and read the nation. To break through the bubble, Lincoln walked the streets taking "public opinion baths."[58] "Men moving only in an official circle," said Lincoln, "are apt to become merely official—not to say arbitrary—in their ideas." Wood-

The civil rights leader A. Philip Randolph pushed FDR to end discrimination in government employment. An oft-quoted but likely apocryphal conversation between the two addresses the need for public pressure to create the conditions for presidential action. After a conversation, the president is said to have told Randolph, "I agree with you—now convince me to do it."

row Wilson asked reporters not to report on Washington but to report back to him about the country, and Barack Obama asked his staff to curate letters from Americans to give him a read of the country.[59] Donald Trump stays connected with his base through close attention to Fox News, which is in constant touch with that portion of the country.

Despite the limited power of rhetoric in the presidency, the myth persists during presidential campaigns that presidents are mountain-movers. "You see, Mr. President—real leaders don't follow polls," New Jersey governor Chris Christie thundered at Barack Obama at the 2012 Republican convention.[60] "Real leaders change polls." How? Conviction and principles, Christie said. This is how presidents wrap everything up neatly by the end of an hourlong television show like *The West Wing*. Presidential rhetoric mows down opposition and crystallizes realities, making change happen before the last set of commercials.

This formula makes for very soothing entertainment, but maintaining a grand vision of the power of presidential rhetoric leads to disappointment. When presidents can't change conditions with speeches, they get antsy. If we lowered the expectations for rhetoric in office and stopped paying so much attention to it in campaigns, we might spend a minute or two evaluating whether candidates have the attributes that will be required to actually make progress instead of just talking about it.

Once the president is in the job, we might look at actions taken that are unrelated to rhetoric, which can be more productive. "Modern presidents have lost the balance required for good leadership," writes Elaine Kamarck in *Why Presidents Fail*; "they spend so much time talking that they mistake talking for doing."[61] The time devoted to communications could be spent building alliances with Congress and with foreign and national leaders.

The challenge for the modern presidency is restoring the equilibrium when the incentives to focus on communication are so strong. The place to shift our thinking is during the presidential campaign. Newt Gingrich, who identified this imbalance as a presidential candidate in 2012, promised that if he were elected, he wouldn't talk much. If he talked all the time, he said, it would take away from the focus and attention he needed to apply to the tasks of the day. It would also, he said, diminish the power of his words as a president. Senator Michael

Bennet of Colorado offered a version of this pledge in the 2020 campaign: "If you elect me president, I promise you won't have to think about me for two weeks at a time. I'll do my job watching out for North Korea and ending this trade war. So you can go raise your kids and live your lives."[62]

Increased skepticism about the power of rhetoric might also lead the president and administration aides to better self-diagnosis. What they've identified as a communications problem may be a policy or political one. Put another way, instead of redoing the commercial, the administration might recognize that the consumers don't like the product.

As we run campaigns ever more devoted to the show, and presidents focus more and more on making the sale, those who succeed are likely to be better at the show and less interested in the painstaking process of governing or building relationships. This leaves the presidency exposed when reality can't be solved by the magic of the show—whether in the form of Oval Office addresses or a never-ending Twitter stream. Having overemphasized communication at the expense of execution, presidents will find they'll need their speechwriting teams soon enough though, to try to explain their way out of the fix they find themselves in. But, you can't talk your way out of a crisis any more than you can talk your way out of gravity. There is one other option a president could try when moved to speak: Sometimes in the presidency, the right thing to say is nothing at all—showing restraint, perhaps the greatest test of governing in the age of impulsivity.

BUSH '88

Almost from the moment candidate George Bush became President-elect George Bush, he underwent a remarkable transformation. There were no more references to liberals from Massachusetts who opposed recitation of the Pledge of Allegiance in classrooms. There were no more references to Willie Horton and murderers being turned loose to rape and pillage. Nor did he have anything to say about card-carrying members of the ACLU.

The reason was all too obvious: President-elect Bush recognized as his first priority the need to cleanse the air of division and partisanship that had poisoned the political atmosphere throughout the presidential campaign of 1988. Only then could the act of governing responsibly in a system of divided partisan responsibility and power go forward.[1]

—JACK W. GERMOND AND JULES WITCOVER,
WHOSE BROAD STRIPES AND BRIGHT STARS:
THE TRIVIAL PURSUIT OF THE PRESIDENCY, 1988

Chapter 23

Restraint

—

Next to knowing when to seize an opportunity, the most important thing in life is to know when to forgo an advantage.[2]

— BRITISH PRIME MINISTER BENJAMIN DISRAELI

"Anyone who felt good about American politics
after the 1988 presidential campaign probably also
enjoys train wrecks, or maybe a day at the beach
watching an oil slick wash ashore."[3]

— NEWSWEEK, 1990

O N NOVEMBER 9, 1989, WEST BERLINERS ATTACKED THE WALL that had divided them from the East. Known as *mauerspechte*, or "wall woodpeckers," they used hammers, picks, and pieces of the wall that had already broken off. On the other side of the barrier rumbled bull-dozers and cranes from East Berlin. More than 2 million people participated in what one journalist described as "the greatest street party in the history of the world." Soon the wall was down and Berlin was united for the first time since 1945. "Only today," one Berliner spray-painted on a piece of the wall, "is the war really over."[4]

The spasm of freedom should have been a banner moment for President George H. W. Bush. The symbol of the unsettled post–World War II order and the source of constant clashes between Communism and capitalism was crumbling into spiky chunks. But as the wall came down, the White House briefing room remained president-free. The speechwriters were not clattering at their keyboards about the unstoppable power of liberty. The champagne stayed corked in its bottles.

White House reporters crowded into the Oval Office. Lesley Stahl of CBS News took up a position close to the seated president. Stahl, the president recalled, was "poised over me." This gave Bush the posture and aspect of a man waiting for a teeth cleaning, even though Stahl was not that physically close. "This is a sort of great victory for our side in the big East-West battle," said Stahl, heading for the bicuspids, "but you don't seem elated, and I'm wondering if you're thinking of the problems." Bush responded: "I'm just not an emotional kind of guy." Later, Bush dictated what he was really thinking into his microcassette recorder: "The press gets all over me," Bush told his diary a few days later. " 'Why aren't you more excited?' 'Why aren't you leading?' 'Why aren't you doing more?' "[5]

Doing, doing, doing. We expect doing from our presidents. As candidates they promise us nothing but successful doing. The cable channels need pictures of doing. No one clicks on a YouTube link to a clip of a president not rushing to the Situation Room. Why wasn't George Bush doing the easiest form of doing in the job devoted to doing?

Bush wasn't emoting because he was exercising restraint, one of the most important and least appreciated presidential qualities.

THE DISCONNECT BETWEEN THE attributes we reward in campaigns and the ones actually required in a president is widest when it comes to the quality of restraint.

The presidency is an office of balance. It requires dash and quick action. As Eisenhower said, "Occasions arise when one has to remember that under particular conditions, boldness is ten times as important as numbers."[6] "A president either is constantly on top of events," said Truman, "or, if he hesitates, events will soon be on top of him."[7] On the other hand, a president must also be patient. "We shall sooner have the fowl by hatching the egg than by smashing it," reminded Lincoln.[8]

Campaigns reward the dash and punish the patience. In an always-running show to win public approval, action gets noticed. Distinction and confrontation get noticed most of all, which encourages hot takes from the media about you—as a candidate you want those because they fire voters more than winding essays about your nuance. Because candidates are defined in the starkest terms, so that a single deficiency can be framed as a fundamental flaw. Those who pause to think are characterized as too cerebral. Stumble in an answer and you are either too old or too dumb for the job. Push for incremental solutions on healthcare and you don't care about the uninsured. Push for tough enforcement of immigration laws and you are heartless. Warn about the danger of coal to a warming planet and you want to close down cities. The stark evaluation scheme makes it easy to dismiss a candidate who shows restraint as too timid for a job of action.[9]

Enlisting in the Reserve

In the age of instantaneous assessment, restraint is lampooned as a lack of leadership. A president who does not act in front of everyone is "leading from behind." Or worse, a president is "prudent," the anvil that the comedian Dana Carvey draped on George Herbert Walker Bush.

Plus, restraint is booooring. Donald Trump explained this during a rally. When Peggy Noonan suggested he should be more presidential,[10] the president acted out what that would look like. He stood artificially straight, moved in staccato like a robot, and dished out inoffensive pap in monotone, thanking the troops and asking God to bless America. "I could be presidential," he joked before launching into his Disney Hall of Presidents routine. "You'd be so bored. . . . This got us elected. If I came like a stiff, you guys wouldn't be here tonight."[11]

When Eisenhower didn't meet expectations of actions, critics joked that his chief of staff, Sherman Adams, was in charge. If Adams dies, went the joke, Eisenhower will become president. As historians and political observers gained access to Ike's personal correspondence and memoranda, they found his fingerprints all over administration actions. He wrote key lines that were inserted in speeches that members of his cabinet gave at opportune moments. He phoned television network executives to blunt Senator Joseph McCarthy's demagogic rot from harming the Republican Party. He directed covert operations and secret diplomacy.[12]

In an almost perfect inversion of the Trump approach, Eisenhower refrained from showy displays, because he believed they detracted from his ultimate goals. "A covert preoccupation with getting political results while appearing publicly nonpolitical was central to Eisenhower's leadership style," writes Fred Greenstein, whose book *The Hidden Hand Presidency* reoriented how people thought about the thirty-fourth president.[13]

In 1812, Thomas Jefferson offered perhaps the best early articulation of the quality of presidential restraint. In 1807, a British warship sank the USS *Chesapeake*. The nation and Congress demanded a gunpowder response. As Michael Beschloss details in *Presidents of War*, the pundits were rattling their quill pens. "O! for a Washington or Adams to Wield the sword of state!" wrote the Federalist *Courier* of Charleston, South Carolina.[14] "Never since the battle of Lexington have I seen this country in such a state of exasperation as at present, and even that did not produce such unanimity," Jefferson wrote to a friend.[15]

Jefferson weighed action and restraint in response. He understood the country's mood and made preparations for war (without asking congressional approval). On the other hand, he had philosophical objections to action. He believed that war encouraged the federal government to centralize power under the pretext of emergency, and that once enlarged, federal power would not shrink back, endangering liberty.[16] Jefferson also had practical reservations. He knew the nation could not prepare fast enough to fight.

The third president chose restraint, enacting an economic embargo instead. It damaged the nation's economy, but he believed it was a better option than bloodshed. Looking back on the experience in a letter in 1812—a year in which James Madison did not resist similar provocations and blundered into war—Jefferson wrote of the presidential power of restraint: "The affair of the *Chesapeake* put war into my hand. I had only to open it and let havoc loose. But if ever I was gratified with the possession of power, and of the confidence of those who had entrusted me with it, it was on that occasion when I was enabled to use both for the prevention of war, towards which the torrent of passion here was directed almost irresistibly, and when not another person in the United States less supported by authority and favor, could have resisted it."[17]

INFORMED RESTRAINT

AFTER THE BERLIN WALL FELL, GEORGE H. W. BUSH'S POLITICAL opponents criticized him for not gloating. "I urge President Bush to express the sense of elation that all Americans feel as the East German people erase barriers that have imprisoned them for decades," said Democratic Senate majority leader George Mitchell.[18] The House majority leader made the same point. "Even as the walls of the modern Jericho come tumbling down, we have a president who at least for now is inadequate to the moment," said Dick Gephardt. "At the very time freedom and democracy are receiving standing ovations in Europe, our president is sitting politely in the audience with little to say and even less to contribute."[19]

Bush got it from the home team too. "I was one of those who thought he should go to Berlin, he should be at the wall; for Kennedy, for Reagan, for all of those who had wanted the wall to come down, he should go there," said Condoleezza Rice, Bush's adviser on Soviet policy and later secretary of state in his son's administration.[20]

If it was a moment calling for an end zone dance, Bush, who had helped bring it about, would have had the right to spike the ball. "Never before in human history had a great power broken apart with more than twenty thousand nuclear weapons in its midst," writes the diplomatic historian Jeffrey A. Engel. "There were no helpful precedents" for Bush to follow, he adds, "and no guarantees it would all end well."[21]

What Bush knew is that actions have consequences. By showing restraint, he mitigated the set of challenges he would face in the future. Bush wanted unification to be Germany's triumph so that it would also be its future obligation. That would hopefully diminish how much the United States would have to manage in the future.

Giving others ownership through your restraint is another lesson Marshall Goldsmith teaches his executives. A leader who hears an idea from an energetic subordinate will feel inclined to add his two cents, but that has a cost most managers don't recognize. "I am young, smart, enthusiastic. I report to you. I come to you with an idea," says Goldsmith, laying out the scenario. "You think it's a great idea. Rather than saying it's a great idea our tendency is to say 'That's a nice idea. Why don't you add this to it?' The quality of the idea may now go up five percent from your contribution, but my commitment to its execution may now go down fifty percent. It's no longer my idea."[22]

The difference between restraint and dithering or cowardice is that restraint is informed. Bush wasn't just winging it in the moment. He had taken a read of Soviet leader Mikhail Gorbachev through a constant regimen of diplomatic outreach and relationship building. When the wall fell, Bush sent a message to Gorbachev letting him know that "the U.S. has no intention of seeking unilateral advantage from the current process of change."[23] At the Malta Summit in December 1989, almost a month after the wall fell, Bush made sure Gorbachev took note of what the United States was doing by not acting. "I hope you noticed that the United States has not engaged in condescending statements aimed at damaging the Soviet Union," he told him. He also specifically mentioned the accusations at home that his approach was overly cautious. "I am a cautious man, but I am not a coward; and my

President Bush's careful tending of relationships with global leaders
and his long view of international relations guided his initial reaction to
the fall of the Berlin Wall. On December 3, 1989, President George H. W.
Bush and Soviet leader Mikhail Gorbachev declared an end to
the Cold War at the Malta Summit.

administration will seek to avoid doing anything that would damage your position in the world."[24]

If the United States had rubbed Soviet noses in the defeat, Gorbachev might have been pressured to crack down hard on Germany and other countries struggling for their independence. "We were all haunted by the crushing of the uprisings in Hungary in 1956 and in Prague in 1968," Bush told his diary at the time.[25]

"What he understood that very few of his critics understood was that Gorbachev's position in Moscow was relatively perilous," remembers former defense secretary Robert Gates, who was Bush's Deputy National Security Advisor at the time. "The concern that he had was that if he celebrated too much it could serve as a provocation to the conservatives in the Soviet Union who were still powerful in the KGB, the army, and the party. In fact the same people who launched a coup against Gorbachev two years later. And I think in retrospect he felt and we all felt that had he pushed too hard, had he celebrated too hard that November, it might have in fact precipitated the coup against Gorbachev a couple of years earlier and he may not have survived it."[26]

According to Bush's biographer, Jon Meacham, Bush told his diary at the time, "If we mishandle this and get way out [in front] looking like [the rebellions are] an American project—you would invite crackdown, and invite negative reaction that could result in bloodshed. The longer I'm in this job, the more I think prudence is a value and experience matters."[27]

Restraint in the moment is a cousin of the larger discipline required in the job, which is understanding that not everything is transactional and momentary. The presidential scholar Richard Neustadt frames patience as a way of banking influence for later, a matter of "trying to judge influence prospectively, as it might be available for still-to-be specified use, rather than reviewing current conditions for particular use at the moment."[28]

Bush tended relationships with international leaders in ways the hungry cameras never captured, or cared about, but that would pay off later. He believed in toiling in Eisenhower's Quadrant Two, where leaders tend to the important but (not yet) urgent. It served him when he worked leader after leader at the end of the Cold War to manage the transition for formerly Soviet-dominated countries into the democratic order.

In August 1990, Bush didn't respond militarily to Iraq's invasion of Kuwait until he had patiently built a coalition of partners. After removing Saddam from Kuwait, he did not order the United States to go into Baghdad as a conquering army, an act of restraint that looks all the wiser in the light of his son's Iraq invasion.

Stanley McChrystal, who commanded special forces in Iraq and Afghanistan, came to the view that the United States should have followed a policy of restraint after the attacks of 9/11 instead of what he calls the "spasmodic response." "In the case of Afghanistan, immediately after 9/11, in terms of military action we should have done nothing initially," he told the National Defense University. "I now believe we should have taken the first year after 9/11 and sent 10,000 young Americans—military, civilians, diplomats—to language school; Pashto, Dari, Arabic. We should have started to build up the capacity we didn't have. I would have spent that year with diplomats, traveling the world as the aggrieved party. We had just been struck by al-Qaeda. I would have made our case around the world that this is a global problem and that the whole world has to deal with it. I would have spent the full year in preparation."[29]

George H. W. Bush's career in public service, and the skills it gave him, were not ready-made for campaign videos, but they gave him instincts—about his opponents, about the sequencing of events—that helped in the actual job. During the 1988 campaign, Bush was accused of lacking "the vision thing"—a phrase he coined because pundits and allies were always trying to get him to put on the Ronald Reagan costume and give a big, sweeping speech.[30] Bush did have a vision, though, about how a president carries out the job so that he is ready for a crisis.

"What It Takes"

Elevating restraint in the campaign conversation is not an argument for polishing only that attribute or for judging a president on that skill alone. No one would argue for a president of restraint only. The patience of a statue won't make you worthy of a statue. President James Buchanan, whom a journalist described as "the personification of evasion, the embodiment of an inducement to dodge,"[31] did little to fight the forces that ultimately led to the Civil War. That restraint dooms him to the basement position in presidential rankings. George H. W. Bush's inadequate response to the AIDS crisis was worsened by restraint. His restraint in not telling the country what he actually knew as vice president about the Reagan administration's swapping arms for hostages was not prudence but dishonesty.[32]

Nevertheless, Bush's restraint in office is worth studying as an example of that undervalued attribute. It also rewards examination because his display of it contrasted with his 1988 campaign, in which he won because he was not restrained. If the changes in campaigning that make it more cutthroat and shallow are to be kept from infecting the presidency, which has been allowed to become more and more like campaigns, it will require a president who, like Bush, recognizes the obligations of the office are different from those of the campaign.

In the 1988 campaign, by design and circumstance, George Bush pushed the limits of what was acceptable. In order to win, he played dirty and pledged to do things that were ideologically and temperamentally at odds with his values and experience. The campaign centered largely on social and cultural issues, like the Pledge of Allegiance, prison furloughs, and capital punishment, that he knew had almost nothing to do with governing.

Bush's campaign was considered to have set a new low-water mark for restraint-free campaigning. (Until the 2016 campaign reset the clock). The journalists Jack Germond and Jules Witcover made the subtitle of their book *The Trivial Pursuit of the Presidency* because they judged the 1988 race to be "perhaps the most mean-spirited and negative campaign in modern-day American political history."[33] Elizabeth Drew of *The New Yorker* wrote that the contest "did something new to our Presidential elections. A degradation occurred which we may have to live with a long time. The Bush campaign broke the mold of modern Presidential politics. Negative campaigning of a new order of magnitude has now come to Presidential politics. And it worked."[34]

In 1988, and when Bush was eulogized in 2019, his campaign choices were characterized as proof he had "what it takes." That's the name of the famous campaign book about the 1988 race by Richard Ben Cramer, devoted to the idea that success went to the candidate who was willing to do all that was necessary to win the job. Implicit in the idea was the notion that if you did what it takes in the campaign you would be worthy of the job. Jack Germond and Jules Witcover entitled their chapter characterizing Bush's limit pushing "Anything Goes."

Thinking back on his 1988 run, Bush wrote, "If you want to be President—and I do—there are certain things that I have to do."[35] He told his biographer, Jon Meacham, "Politics isn't a pure undertaking— not if you're going to win, it's not. That's the way politics is, unfortunately."[36] Bush believed the maxim that the first job of leadership is obtaining power. This view of how to achieve the presidency clashes with the ideals of the framers of the Constitution. No-holds-barred campaigning for personal ambition is precisely what they were worried about. A brute who showed no virtue in attaining power would torch the presidency when grafting that ethos onto the office.

On the other hand, George H. W. Bush was the epitome of what the framers wanted in a president. The historian Richard McCormick defines that standard this way: "The ideal candidate in a republic was a man who, through his dedicated and disinterested public service, acquired a reputation for probity and integrity and accepted the call of his fellow citizen to successively higher offices."[37] Bush fit that description. He had patiently served throughout his career, in China, at the CIA, and as the head of the Republican Party.

Although Bush fit the framers' mold, when he ran for office in 1980 and 1988, the voters had long since taken evaluating candidates into their own hands. Bush was considered too weak for the position that prioritized ambitious action as the key criterion for a successful candidate. In 1980, the first time Bush ran for his party's nomination for president, he had been upstaged by Ronald Reagan at a Nashua debate. Bush had arranged a one-on-one face-off with Reagan, whom he had just bested in the Iowa caucuses. He thought it would be the fatal blow. At the last minute, the former California governor suggested that the other candidates—Robert Dole, John Anderson, Philip Crane, and Howard Baker—be allowed onstage. They showed up and, finding no chairs or microphones to accommodate them, petitioned for remedy. In the confusion, Bush insisted that the rules and agreement said it was to be a two-man debate only. It looked like a lawyerly dodge.

After more confusion, Reagan, who had paid to put on the debate, seized the microphone and scolded the moderator: "I am paying for

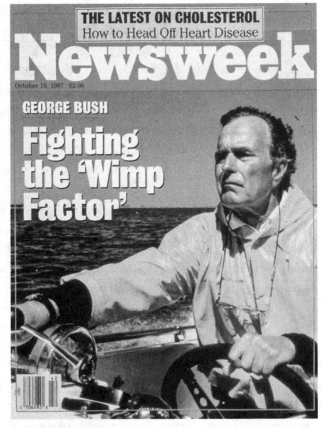

George H. W. Bush was accused of not having "the vision thing." During the 1988 campaign, Newsweek magazine asked whether he had what it takes to win and handle the presidency.

THE LATEST ON CHOLESTEROL
How to Head Off Heart Disease

Newsweek

October 19, 1987 · $2.00

GEORGE BUSH

Fighting the 'Wimp Factor'

this microphone, Mr. Green!"[38] The crowd in the high school gymnasium loved it; the press gobbled up the moment and it slipped into presidential campaign lore as the moment Reagan turned things around in New Hampshire and won the nomination. Though it wasn't that simple or pat, never mind, it affirmed the conventional wisdom: Voters wanted John Wayne Reagan and not WASPy Bush in the presidency.[39]

In 1988, after eight years as vice president, Bush faced the same issue: Did he have the mettle for the presidency? Conservatives suspected he wasn't one of them, and when they criticized him, they used the language of weakness. "The unpleasant sound Bush is emitting as he traipses from one conservative gathering to another is a thin tiny 'arf,'" wrote George F. Will. "The sound of a lap dog."[40]

Never mind that Bush had been a bomber pilot in World War II who survived parachuting from his plane. Never mind that he had been the nation's top spymaster. *Newsweek* echoed Will's sentiment by putting Bush on the cover and declaring that he was battling the "Wimp Factor."

To erase that image in the 1988 race, Bush embarked on a display of impetuosity. In theatrical outbursts choreographed by the media guru and image crafter Roger Ailes, Bush fought with reporters at a *Des Moines Register* forum, and then famously in a set-to on CBS News with Dan Rather. Before the Rather rumble, Ailes wound up Bush like a top. "You've either got to go in there and go toe to toe with this guy," said Ailes to Bush, "or you're going back to Kennebunkport."[41]

Bush's campaign strategist, Lee Atwater, matched the theatrics with a systematic and withering assault on the Democratic nominee, Michael Dukakis, challenging not just his policies, but whether the son of Greek immigrants was a worthy American. The most memorable fight was about patriotism. Dukakis had accepted a Massachusetts Supreme Court judgment that mandatory Pledge of Allegiance recitations in public schools were unconstitutional; he had vetoed legislation that would have mandated it. "What is it about the Pledge of Allegiance that upsets him so much?"[42] Bush asked at one of his rallies. Bush visited Findlay, Ohio, known as Flag City, and used a rally at a flag factory in New Jersey to keep these themes alive.

During the 1988 Democratic primaries, then Senator Al Gore had brought up the Massachusetts furlough program that allowed convicted criminals time off during the weekend. One of the convicts who had taken advantage of the program, Willie Horton, had committed murder and rape while out of prison. The victims had been white; Horton was black. An ally of the Bush team turned the story into an ad and the campaign ran with it, with Atwater boasting that he was going to make Willie Horton such a close association with Dukakis that people would think he was running on the same ticket.[43]

The strategy was so poisonous that Atwater apologized for it on his deathbed. "Fighting Dukakis, I said that I would 'strip the bark off the little bastard' and 'make Willie Horton his running mate,'" Atwater repented. "I am sorry for both statements: the first for its naked cruelty, the second because it makes me sound racist, which I am not."[44]

It was not a campaign founded on elevating George Bush's governing qualifications, but built instead on tearing down his opponent, a strategy with which Atwater was familiar. "Republicans in the South could not win elections by talking about issues," he said. "You had to make the case that the other guy, the other candidate, is a bad guy."[45]

When the political need arose, Bush was also willing to trade away that experience and governing seriousness. He picked the forty-one-year-old junior senator from Indiana, Dan Quayle, as his running mate to shore up his support among conservative voters. The senator opposed abortion, held hawkish foreign policy views, and opposed new civil rights measures, but he lacked the experience of other, more experienced politicians Bush could have picked, such as Senate Minority Leader Bob Dole of Kansas or Representative Jack Kemp of New York. Should Bush's vice president have to serve as president, as nine vice presidents had before, two of whom were called into service in the previous twenty-five years, he would lack the kinds of qualifications Bush believed were fundamental to the office.

Michael Dukakis, by contrast, showed restraint during the campaign, choosing to focus on issues and to let the attacks go unanswered until it was too late. "We didn't do what, I'm sorry to say, you have to do in these campaigns, and that's one of the great lessons of '88, sadly," said Dukakis, "and that is you've got to anticipate an attack campaign and you've got to have a carefully thought-out strategy for dealing with it in advance of when it happens . . . preferably one that frankly turns it into a character issue on the guy that's doing the attacking."[46] When Dukakis was asked whether he would support the death penalty if his wife were raped and murdered, his restrained response was seen as politically deadly.[47] Dukakis, who had once been ahead by 17 points in the polls, lost by seven percentage points and 315 electoral votes.

Bush did what it took, including making over-the-top promises about taxes. Looking back on the legacy of making his famous "Read my lips: no new taxes" boast at the Republican convention, Bush acknowledged the moment of maximum macho hemmed him in as a president. He told his biographer, Jon Meacham, "The problem with the tax pledge was the rhetoric was so hot . . . 'I'm the man' and that kind of stuff. I felt uncomfortable with some of that. But it was persuasive—the convention loved it."[48]

The theatricality of the campaign came back to bite Bush when the reality of the job turned out differently than the unreality of the campaign trail and he couldn't keep his tax boast. "It was a mistake," Bush said of the pledge, "but I meant it at the time, and I meant it all through my presidency. But when you're faced with the reality, the practical reality, of shutting down the government or dealing with a hostile Congress, you get something done."[49]

"THERE ARE CERTAIN THINGS THAT I HAVE TO DO"

ALMOST THIRTY YEARS AFTER GEORGE BUSH DID WHAT IT TOOK TO beat Michael Dukakis, his son Jeb stood on the debate stage in South Carolina trying to lift himself off the mat. Just feet from him stood the phenomenon Donald Trump, who had overtaken the Republican Party and was headed to the 2016 nomination.

Just as George H. W. Bush had torn apart Dukakis, Trump shredded the second Bush son and the Bush family. Trump faulted the forty-third president, Jeb's elder brother, for the terrorist attacks of September 11, 2001, that brought down the World Trade Center. "That's not keeping us safe," Trump said.[50] He went on to say that George W. Bush lied about weapons of mass destruction in Iraq and that the invasion was the greatest mistake in American history, for which Bush should have been impeached. Jeb Bush was trying to remind the voters of all that his family had done for the country. Each time he did, Donald Trump ordered in another wrecking ball.

George H. W. Bush exemplified the clear distinctions between the ethos of campaigning and the ethos of governing. He demonstrated that it is possible to show no restraint in campaigning and yet set a modern example for it in the job. That was then. The Bush family's next generation would experience the sting of a candidate who demonstrated what it takes by crushing the entire Bush family.

Donald Trump's antics should have hurt him in South Carolina. The state had a higher proportion of evangelical voters among the GOP primary electorate than did other states. Trump's divorces, admitted adultery, and nearly imperceptible religious faith, matched with prideful worldly obsessions, seemed like a nearly purposeful effort to offend those voters. Attacking the Bush family in the state should also have set him back. George W. Bush had won the South Carolina primary in 2000 and was still popular there. Nevertheless, Trump won the primary by 10 points. He beat all of his competitors among the 72 percent who identified themselves as born again or evangelical.[51]

Trump's crass and offensive behavior and the disrespect he had shown previous presidents and the office of the presidency were not only not impediments, they were a boon in an era of impulse campaigning. "When you vote for Trump, it's almost giving the middle finger to the establishment or the status quo," Sean Higgins, a college professor and Trump supporter, told CNN.[52]

Donald Trump *Had. What. It. Takes.* The lengths to which he was willing to go to win were seen as proof that he was the man for the job. That his opponents cried foul and wanted to stick to the issues was only proof that they weren't in the same league as the slugger from Queens. If Trump had followed the George H. W. Bush model, restraint would have kicked in during the presidency, but unlike Forty-One, who recognized that the obligations of winning were different from the obligations of the job, Trump has carried over the unrestrained rhetoric and behavior of the campaign into the presidency. He has elevated victory above all. It was revealed, after Barbara Bush died, that she hadn't liked Trump, on account of his treatment of her sons and husband. On Twitter, the president took a swipe at her.[53] It was indecorous for a sitting president to take a poke at the recently deceased former First Lady. Not so, said Trump's longtime friend and political adviser Roger Stone, reminding everyone of the primacy of winning: "Well, she's dead and he's president. Who won that one?"[54]

As campaigns promote impulsivity and governing continues to become more like campaigning, there is little structural incentive for restraint. While restraint remains crucial in the job, it's now up to the president to find that quality within. How can the electorate figure out whether a candidate will be able to do so in office? George H. W. Bush dedicated his life to public service. That calling demands sublimation of personal impulses for the larger cause, requires putting personal ambition, avarice, and passion to work in the service of the nation and its ideals. If a candidate doesn't have that background, it is very hard to discover in a campaign whether they have the restraint required to govern. The way campaigns are run today, the situation may be even more dire. Modern campaigns are so broken, they work to pound the restraint out of candidates and the electorate.

Radiola Ad

No "influence" needed this year for a gallery seat at the big political conventions! Get it all with a Radiola Super-Heterodyne.

When the delegates march in—their banners streaming; when the bands play and the galleries cheer—be there with the "Super-Het." Hear the pros and cons as they fight their way to a "platform" for you. Hear the speeches for the "favorite sons." The sudden stillness when the voice of a great speaker rings out. The stamp and whistle and shrill of competitive cheering. Hear the actual nomination of a president.

It used to be all of the delegates' wives and the "big" folks of politics. Now it's for everybody. Listen in. Get it all! With the newest Radiola.[1]

—1924 Radiola ad

Chapter 24

The Church of
Perpetual Disappointment

A whole year we shall hear nothing else but abuse
and scandal, enough to ruin and corrupt the minds
and morals of the best people in the world.[2]

— ABIGAIL ADAMS, 1800

In regard to the method pursued by political parties,
with reference to electing their respective candidates,
there seems to be just one opinion: That "it is
disgraceful to the country."[3]

— *NEW YORK MIRROR*, 1852

The organized bigotry, the like of which I have never seen. I
feel as if some poison gas had spread over us, and that our
democracy will suffer from this for many years to come.

— LILLIAN WALD, NEW YORK AUTHORITY ON SOCIAL
WORK, ABOUT THE 1928 CAMPAIGN[4]

In selecting those who might occupy the most important office in this country—the Presidency—we put our potential
leaders through a process that is both strange and brutal.
The people who might make crucial decisions about war
and peace, about our taxes, who will have enormous effect
on the quality of our lives, our social order, the civility of our
public discourse, undergo an experience from which few
human beings could emerge whole. Some do not.[5]

— ELIZABETH DREW, *THE NEW YORKER*, 1975

J UST FORTY MINUTES INTO THE FIRST DEBATE OF THE 2012 CAMPAIGN between Barack Obama and Mitt Romney, Ben Smith of *Buzzfeed* wrote a story headlined HOW MITT ROMNEY WON THE FIRST DEBATE.[6] Smith was only saying out loud what the political press sitting in the filing room near the stage was thinking. President Obama had stumbled out of the gate. Reporters joked about it on Twitter.[7] They passed around gags from the professionals. "I can't believe I'm saying this, but Obama looks like he *does* need a teleprompter," wrote the comedian Bill Maher on Twitter.[7] Television executives reading Twitter encouraged their analysts to adopt the same damning view. The reinforcement cycle spun into full whirl.

Twitter set a record of 10.3 million tweets during the debate. In previous election cycles blogs had opened the political conversation to voters, amateurs, passionate observers, and cranks. Now the bar got noisier. An even larger group joined in an even faster conversation. "These tweets tend to frame how people are reading this and how they are evaluating what they are seeing," David Axelrod, a top adviser to President Obama, told CNN's Peter Hamby.[8]

Snap judgments frame the first pieces of analysis on television and determine which 20-second clips are replayed in the post-debate conversation. You're familiar with this scenario: When a show host immediately after the debate says "Let's listen to this exchange, and then I want to get your reaction," the footage chosen is almost always the snap judgment consensus moment from early in the debate. Those clips selected based on early impressions then echo through social media until being reincarnated as memes.

How the media describe debates drives public opinion far more than the impressions people form during the debates.[9] If the media make snap judgments after only a third of the contest, that becomes the public consensus.

The writer Andrew Sullivan worried after the first Obama-Romney debate that voter impressions from the first thirty minutes would metastasize. "How do you erase that imprinted first image from public consciousness: a president incapable of making a single argument or even a halfway decent closing statement?"[10]

In a Pew poll out shortly after the event, Romney had a 49–45 lead over President Obama, a 12 point swing from Obama's 51–43 lead before the debate.[11] Beforehand, Obama dominated on every policy issue and personal characteristic; after the debate, Romney led in almost all of them.

Candidates surrender to the tempo of this market. They choreograph mini speeches they can give in the early moments of debates. (You are familiar with these; they have the determined theatricality of local dinner theater.) Though debates are supposed to be an issue-oriented oasis from campaign ephemera that helps people figure out whether the candidates can do the job, the reality is that if a candidate is not punchy and entertaining, minds take a stroll. "I started zoning out after about 30 minutes," wrote the Princeton professor and liberal blogger Sam Wang of that Obama-Romney contest.[12]

After Obama's dismal first debate in 2012, the president's team told him to pick up the pace and pep. Ron Klain, his debate adviser, boiled the instructions down to the phrase "fast and hammy."[13] When Obama lapsed into professor mode in practice sessions, down came the ruler on his knuckles: *Fast and hammy!* The most powerful and complex office on the planet hinged on a command a waitress might shout through the short order window.

In 2016, Donald Trump bored no one. For his campaign, the pop of the show was an end in itself. "He turned traditional debates into 'must-see TV,'" applauded his son Eric.[14] The Trump-Clinton debates were the most watched ever, and they were the most sordid. Before the second debate, a video leaked of Trump bragging about trying to seduce a married woman, boasting about committing repeated sexual assaults and gearing up for another one. "I just start kissing them," he was heard saying. "It's like a magnet. Just kiss. I don't even wait. And when you're a star, they let you do it. You can do anything."[15]

To distract from the charge, Trump invited three women who accused Bill Clinton of sexual assault to sit in the debate audience.[16] The circus surrounding the second debate got everyone's attention, but in the same way inflight turbulence does, and bringing with it the same queasy feeling of doom.

THE USUAL COMPLAINT

AMERICANS HAVE BEEN MOANING ABOUT ELECTIONS SINCE THE beginning. During the election of 1800, partisanship had grown so virulent, party regulars lunged at one another's throats. Editors of rival newspapers threw haymakers in the streets. (Some of them landed.) "This election of a chief magistrate for the whole Union will never be settled to the satisfaction of the people," said John Quincy Adams, a few years later.[17]

Thomas Jefferson's attack dog James Callender wrote a 183-page pamphlet in which he called President Adams a "repulsive pedant," a "gross hypocrite," and a "hideous hermaphroditical character which has neither the force and firmness of a man, nor the gentleness and sensibility of a woman."[18] He was such a pest that President Adams plunked him in jail for it. Others kept up the pace. Democratic-Republicans claimed that Adams sent his running mate, Charles Pinckney, to England to procure a couple of mistresses for each of them. (When Adams heard about this, he exclaimed, "If this be true, General Pinckney has kept them all for himself and cheated me out of my two!") Federalists warned that Adams's rival, Jefferson, would confiscate Bibles. They asked, "Are you prepared to see your dwellings in flames . . . female chastity violated, [your] children writhing on the pike?"[19]

This history is often used by the sophisticated fellow (and it's usually a fellow) to wave away modern disappointment with elections by alleging that democracy has always been messy. I tried this theory out on Stanford's David Kennedy, the renowned American history scholar. "I'm deeply skeptical of that false intellectual comfort," he said of the idea that conditions will inevitably improve, as they have from those more vulgar times. "It's intellectual laziness to assume that there is a mystical corrective. I think that this moment could be some kind of god-awful inflection point."[20]

The standards for selecting a president should match the power and prestige of the presidency itself, but no one would accuse our infrequently rational modern campaigns of matching our highest aspirations. Today, we face more than the usual complaint. Our generation has done more than merely contribute to the disappointing trends of the past. The age of massive digital connectivity has encouraged campaigns that are hyperfocused on the immediate, in which self-expression is valued above nearly all other qualities. The brisk and shallow process pushes all participants—candidates and voters—to relinquish restraint and patience, two of the most crucial attributes required for the job, and it invites America's foes to manipulate the outcome. The way we pick presidents in the digital age undermines the presidency.

ATTENTION K-MART VOTERS

TODAY'S HYPERDEMOCRACY HAD NOBLE BEGINNINGS. JEFFERSON believed a well-informed electorate was necessary for the country's survival. James Madison expressed a similar view: "A people who mean to be their own governors, must arm themselves with the power knowledge gives."[21] The two were talking about more than just public familiarity with candidates' position papers. To be vigilant citizens, Jefferson argued, voters had to study history in order to understand the corrupting influence of human weakness—like excessive ambition—that existed across time, so that they could be on the lookout for the warnings of their age:

> The most effectual means of preventing [the perversion of power into tyranny are] to illuminate, as far as practicable, the minds of the people at large, and more especially to give them knowledge of those facts which history exhibits, that possessed thereby of the experience of other ages and countries, they may be enabled to know ambition under all its shapes, and prompt to exert their natural powers to defeat its purposes.[22]

A regimen with that goal cannot be fulfilled by scanning Twitter or sampling cable debates featuring pundits tweezing the latest momentary thing. If someone were to bring up the naturally corrupting influence of ambition in most venues where politics is discussed today, they would receive puzzled stares.

In the 1908 election, the five-hundred-page voter's guide titled *Great Issues and National Leaders: Live Questions of the Day Discussed* outlined the regimen required of individuals to be informed participants:

It is every voter's duty to study the issues and the men now before the country. Every Democrat should be as familiar with the Republican issues and leaders as with his own. Every Republican should be familiar with the Democratic claims and their champions. Every Socialist, Populist, Prohibitionist, Independent, and members of all political parties, should be familiar with the claims and the principles of the other parties. It is a privilege that every man should avail himself of as well as a duty that he owes to his country to study all the platforms and all the issues, otherwise he cannot be informed and do his duty as a patriot at the polls.[23]

This patriotic routine was linked to selling books. No better way to push goods than to make them a part of your sacred duty to your country. The pamphlet provided to the door-to-door salesmen offering *Great Issues* instructed them to pitch homeowners that it was "a book which will be an ornament for the home table." They were to show prospective purchasers, while holding a sample of the handsome cloth-covered volume, which of their neighbors had also made commitments to buy. "You will see from these names what kind of people are attracted by it," reads the sample sales patter, "and I am sure you will want your name down with the rest." Taking the election seriously meant you were keeping up with the Joneses.

No one makes that kind of pitch anymore. The sales patter of American politics today does not use the campaign to sell goods; the techniques for selling goods have become the way candidates sell themselves. Now political strategists study what bourbon you drink, what department store you frequent, and a whole host of other lifestyle choices to divine your political leanings. Our modern disappointment with presidential campaigns has formed in the gap between our marble-statue view of the office and the low-rent sales routines increasingly employed to win it.

In 1896, the political strategist Mark Hanna sculpted William McKinley's campaign so thoroughly that Teddy Roosevelt compared the process to hawking "patent medicine."[24] In 1920, Warren Harding hired Chicago advertising wizards to improve his campaign. As David Greenberg details in *Republic of Spin*, they brightened up the merchandise with photography, illustrations, radio, and billboards to present Harding as a handsome and authentic leader. It didn't do much good. H. L. Mencken compared Harding's rhetoric to "a string of wet sponges. . . . tattered washing on the line . . . stale bean soup."[25, 26]

When Eisenhower ran television ads in 1952, his opponent Adlai Stevenson sniffed, "I think the American people will be shocked by such contempt for their intelligence. This isn't Ivory Soap versus Palmolive."[27] Stevenson aide George Ball predicted that "presidential campaigns will eventually have professional actors as candidates." (That, of course, would never happen.)

In 1960, John Kennedy capitalized on what Nixon called a "slick high-octane publicity machine." Echoing Teddy Roosevelt, Nixon dubbed the Kennedy extravaganza a "modern medicine show." (The "Kennedy, Kennedy, Kennedy" jingle was in fact based on a cereal commercial.)[28]

John Kennedy broke the late night talk show barrier during the 1960 campaign, but his appearance on *The Tonight Show* was flat. It's not that Jack Paar didn't try to spark something. The host prodded Kennedy for an amusing campaign anecdote, and Kennedy said, "I was made an honorary Indian."[29] For Kennedy, who was a genuine wit, it was a subpar performance.

In the 1968 campaign, Richard Nixon told the young media guru Roger Ailes that he didn't like television "gimmicks." Ailes responded, "Television is not a gimmick." The future Fox News founder then went about proving it, selling Nixon in extended infomercials as a more likable fellow, deftly answering scripted questions from sympathetic audiences.[30]

Bill Clinton appeared on talk shows hosted by Larry King and Phil Donahue. George Bush resisted at first, arguing that those shows were beneath the dignity of the office. King hosted a wide variety of other guests, including slapdash celebrities and gadflies. Donahue devoted his shows to topics like polygamy. Ultimately, Bush succumbed and sat for an interview with Larry King.

By taking advantage of modern sales and communications techniques, candidates sought voters where they lived. Once there, successful candidates tailored their behavior to fit the medium. This won them the coveted pundits' claim that they were showing "authenticity," a laurel bestowed on candidates who usually achieve this impression through acts of artifice. It is true in politics what George Burns said about show business: "The most important thing is sincerity. If you can fake that, you've got it made."[31]

In 1992, Bill Clinton rigged himself in black sunglasses and played "Heartbreak Hotel" on the saxophone on the Arsenio Hall show. Unlike Kennedy, Clinton grooved to Hall's talk show, and young voters grooved right back. "I like the sax because it has sex appeal," Alison Huff, twenty-five, an assistant to the curator of American music for the Smithsonian Institution, told *The Washington Post*. "And I'm for candidates with sex appeal."[32]

CHEAPENING THE BRAND

THOSE INCLINED TO TUT-TUT DID IN FACT TUT. "A LOT OF THE MAINSTREAM media, the established Sunday show crowd, they were aghast and appalled," remembers Clinton campaign adviser Paul Begala. "I'd say the more upset they were, the more we were sure we were right."[33] *The Washington Post*'s David Maraniss characterized the criticism this way: "Clinton [had become] a metaphor for all politicians these days, diminished by cultural forces that have rendered them little more than sidemen in the band."[34] Clinton media adviser Mandy Grunwald said the old guard's criticism was founded on ignorance. "It was the end of one way of communicating with voters and the beginning of another. They just didn't know that yet."[35] Begala and Grunwald themselves represented how much had changed in presidential campaigns in the modern age. They managed the television campaign and image buffing that Kennedy had predicted would become commonplace in 1959 in *TV Guide*.

Since Kennedy's 1960 victory, campaigns have started earlier and become more frantic. Candidates hammer through a series of staccato acts to keep pace: short television appearances followed by hurried voter contact, followed by fundraising required to pay for the advertisements required in the television age.

Bill Clinton's sunglasses moment raised the same question that met other campaign innovations: Will embracing a popular medium, and the sales techniques used to create appetites in people that they didn't

Bill Clinton was a policy wonk who nonetheless appealed to more than just the cerebral. "I like the sax because it has sex appeal," said one voter. "And I'm for candidates with sex appeal."

know they had, trivialize the process of selecting someone for such a serious job? Will the process encourage voters to pull the lever for superficial reasons? Will we look for the skills that move the goods off the shelves, instead of the skills needed for governing? And will the process train presidents to respond to vexing problems with those superficial sales instincts in office, instead of responding with wisdom and seeking durable solutions to the most pressing problems?

If patent medicine promises are being sold and bought, it is a process that trains the electorate to stop thinking, the way one must stop thinking in order to believe that a furniture polish scent reminds you of a mountain stream.

More Information than Ever Before

The route to the Oval Office grew noisy and coarse with the tacky consumer strategies used to hook the public on ever larger soft drinks and the vehicles with multiplying cupholders to house them. But not every innovation of popular culture made the presidential selection process worse.

In 1858, people worried that the telegraph was "too fast for the truth,"[36] but as the second industrial revolution ribboned the country with train tracks and cities bulked with sprawling factories, the telegraph helped unite a people that, as the historian Walter A. McDougall put it, had "one foot in manure and the other in the telegraph office."[37]

A 1924 ad for the RCA Radiola Super-Heterodyne radio explained how filling living rooms with brown boxes would help expand politics to "everybody" rather than just "the delegates' wives and the 'big' folks of politics." Radio linked rich and poor, rural and urban. The winner of that 1924 campaign, Calvin Coolidge, said technology had elevated the campaign dialogue. Radio allowed him to communicate without resorting to snazzy stunts on the stump. "I am very fortunate that I came in with the radio," Coolidge said. "I can't make an engaging, rousing or oratorical speech . . . but I have a good radio voice, and now I can get my message across to [the public] without acquainting them with my lack of oratorical ability."[38]

As campaigns adopted the tricks of the times, it altered the substance of politics. When Franklin Roosevelt mastered radio, candidate acceptance speeches shortened by 60 percent and became less nutritious. After FDR, only half of the words concentrated on issues, compared to the 84 percent devoted to issues in the previous thirty years of Democratic acceptance speeches.[39]

The railroad and highway systems meant more people could inform their vote by looking at the candidates in the flesh. Candidates and presidents looked right back. "I went by train. I wanted to talk to them face-to-face," Truman said of his famous 1948 train trips. "I knew that they knew that when you get on television, you're wearing a lot of powder and paint that somebody else has put on your face, and you haven't even combed your own hair."[40]

In 1992, when Bill Clinton revealed his preference for boxers over briefs on MTV, standard-keepers identified his appearance as a swerve to perdition, but national familiarity with his undergarments did not dilute the high-fiber content of his campaign, which contributed to Clinton's label as a "policy wonk."[41] Clinton seemed to prove that moments of lightness did not necessarily come at the expense of policy discussions.

In that same election, Ross Perot popularized the campaign innovation of the infomercial. The technique had originally been designed to entice late night viewers to splurge on hair restoration products and food vacuum sealing solutions. Perot used it to educate the country about the dangers of the growing deficit.

Sixteen and a half million people watched the millionaire executive pad through a stack of rudimentary charts and graphs.[42] His presentation received higher ratings than most regularly scheduled entertainment shows on all three networks. It also beat the National League playoff game that followed it.[43]

Today, voters can access candidate positions and detailed discussions of the issues on their phones while waiting to pay for groceries. (Writers thinking about the same issues can write sentences from that same spot—which is where the one you just read was typed.) Voters can devote weekend mornings to thorough online research on the key issues facing the nation.

On the Democratic side in the 2020 primaries, this attention to detail and policy drew voters to Bernie Sanders and Elizabeth Warren, who deluged the electorate with plans and proposals. This spurred a policy footrace among all the candidates in which each tried to outdo the other with their specificity, an explicit counterpoint to the attitude of Donald Trump, who said in 2015, "I don't think people care" about fourteen-point plans.[44]

The information revolution has also increased transparency about the relationship between lawmakers and the $3.4 billion influence business of lobbying.[45] First, it allows us to know who they are. You can look up who is a registered lobbyist. You can also identify the 281 lobbyists ProPublica identified who have worked in the Donald Trump administration[46] and remind yourself that he promised to hire no lobbyists because they tend to promote the worldview of their former employers, which can conflict with the public good. Anyone concerned about draining the swamp in Washington can easily keep track of this, because broken campaign pledges and falsehoods are checked far more thoroughly and more quickly than ever before.

HACKING OUR REASON

THE INFORMATION REVOLUTION COULD SPUR BETTER PRESIDENTIAL campaigns, but as you've already said to yourself—or demonstrated by looking at your phone while reading this book—there are powerful forces in this technology that will swamp its benefits. Just because we have technology that can make us more informed, doesn't mean we are more informed. As Henry David Thoreau wrote in 1854, "We are in great haste to construct a magnetic telegraph from Maine to Texas, but Maine and Texas, it may be, have nothing important to communicate."[47]

One must check the optimism about technology or risk winding up like the *New York Times* editorial that cheerfully applauded the state of campaigning in 1928, before the brutal anti-Catholic contest of that year: "There are many things to deplore; some things to make us ashamed; others to stir our zeal for reform; but, on the whole, there is

Sarah Polk, wife of the eleventh president, James K. Polk, worried that her husband would not be recognized when he walked into a room, so she had the band play "Hail to the Chief" to herald his arrival. Now, in a presidency-obsessed nation, the president is the most recognizable American anywhere, with or without musical accompaniment.

reason enough for all Americans to look forward with happy confidence to another twelve months of keeping step with what Rufus Choate called the glorious music of the American union."[48]

It is difficult to hear that glorious music of the Union through the distraction of email, Twitter, cable news, and Instagram. Social media thrives on snatching attention, which means that the very medium through which we debate politics is structured to undermine those debates by making us less attentive. Who can remember, much of the time, what they were looking for when they first started that Google search? Studies show that we check our phones about every twelve minutes.[49, 50] Which doesn't leave much time for focused thought.

It's easy to veer away from, or never get to, the useful information we might seek to inform our political decisions. "An endless bombardment of news and gossip and images has rendered us manic information addicts," wrote Andrew Sullivan, who ultimately evacuated himself from the life of digital addiction.[51] This distraction detracts from our democratic instinct—or, better, duty—to inform ourselves, but the new media are even more dangerous than that. As the conduit through which we consume political information, the new media condition our political consumption, encouraging us to be less discerning and more volatile.

LITTLE JOLTS OF PLEASURE

A SALESMAN TRYING TO SELL *GREAT ISSUES* DOOR TO DOOR IN TOday's political living room must compete with partisan talk show hosts, shortened attention spans, and brains wired at the chemical level to be lured by the extreme, the flashy, and the immediate. Campaigns now take advantage of best practices from the consumer world, where experiences and purchases are tailored to fit our impulses with as little friction as possible. "Our job is to give the user a steady stream, almost a synthetic or personalized channel," YouTube's chief product officer, Neal Mohan, boasted in 2018 at the annual consumer tech conference in Las Vegas.[52] Or, as Mark Zuckerberg put it, "A squirrel dying in front of your house may be more relevant to your interests right now than people dying in Africa."[53]

In the Year of Our Lord 2019, Bethany Gaskin became a YouTube celebrity by engaging in mukbang, the gratuitous consumption of food. Hundreds of thousands of people tune in each week to watch her binge-eat shellfish.[54] Amusement and distraction are a click away, and we expect everything else to be, too—including our political opinions and information. "Virtually every consumer proposition today, from fast food and entertainment to social interactions, is deliberately crafted so that rewards are immediate while costs are deferred, and deferred so seamlessly that they almost disappear," writes Paul Roberts in *The Impulse Society*. "Speed of gratification is now the standard against which all consumer experiences are judged."[55]

We want our movies instantly. We order our groceries at lunchtime and expect them to arrive in time for dinner. We punch up cars to deliver us to our whims. The largest companies in America, from Amazon to Uber to Facebook, want to fill the air with buzzing drones dropping from the skies whatever you want and more of it. Manna is now always on the delivery menu. The incoming CEO of Alibaba, potentially the world's largest online commerce company, calls on-demand delivery the future of retailing.[56] "Consumers expect to summon retail experiences as they would a genie from a lamp," claps trendwatching.com.[57] We want what we want when we want it. This is true of political opinions too.

In the digital age, these techniques of delivering immediate gratification and stoking our appetites for it reach deep into the brain stem, the same neighborhood where we house the faculties of reason and critical thinking we'd like to think we apply to public issues. Dopamine is the binding agent that locks us to the consumption—it's the little jolt of pleasure that humans associate with beneficial actions. The reward comes after each affirmation either in the form of a "like" on Facebook, a little heart on Instagram, or delivery of information that confirms our worldview when we turn to Twitter. Studies show we will chase the reward of that neurotransmitter dopamine with the passion of a gambling addict or smoker.

When there is no immediate reward, we keep hunting. Disappointment makes us more fervent. This is why people open the Instagram app, find the results unsatisfying, close it, and then, without thinking, swipe their thumb and open it again. Like poison ivy, dopamine creates a fever. Each time we scratch, the desire to scratch grows.

The cycle saps our ability to concentrate, which invites us to speed up the search-for-reward cycle. Deliver us please from that itchy feeling of being insufficiently entertained. "The attention industry needs people who are in a distracted state," says Tim Wu, a Columbia Law School professor and the author of *Attention Merchants*. "[People] who are perpetually distractible, and thus open to advertising. And so it has a strong influence on the content of the media, which becomes increasingly attention-seeking and clickbaity, for want of a better term, and ultimately affects us because the kind of media that you're exposed to starts to influence your own brain and your own personality."[58]

The original objective for Facebook, says Sean Parker, the company's first president, was "How do we consume as much of your time and conscious attention as possible?" Parker says it's "exactly the kind of thing that a hacker like myself would come up with, because you're exploiting a vulnerability in human psychology."[59]

HAIL TO THE SELFIE

THE FAST REWARD WE WANT IS AVAILABLE TO US IN THE ANTICS OF presidential candidates groomed since Kennedy on providing an appealing and immediate message for the audience.

In 2019, Congressman Beto O'Rourke launched his presidential campaign on a feeling. A cover story in *Vanity Fair* that accompanied the former three-term congressman's entrance into the contest described a "near-mystical experience" at a campaign rally during O'Rourke's failed Senate run in 2018.[60] It was the moment when his wife "first witnessed the power of O'Rourke's gift" that represented the rationale for his presidential candidacy. The candidate felt this gift too. "I don't know if it's a speech or not, but it felt amazing," O'Rourke said. "Because every word was pulled out of me. Like, by some greater force, which was just the people there. Everything that I said, I was, like, watching myself, being like, How am I saying this stuff? Where is this coming from?"

This mystical feeling of connection convinced the candidate he should make a go for the most powerful job in the world. "I just knew it. I just felt it," O'Rourke said about his failed run for the Senate. In what the magazine writer, without disparagement, describes as "a politics not readily accessible by reason," O'Rourke was propelled by this feeling into a presidential campaign. "It's probably not the most professional thing you've ever heard about this, but I just feel it."

In case anyone missed the ambition of the launch, O'Rourke was photographed on the cover of the magazine wearing a blue shirt, blue jeans, and brown belt with his hands in his back pockets, a real-life duplicate of the well-known painting of Ronald Reagan in which the former two-term governor and two-term president was dressed the same way and stood in the identical posture. As the piece concludes, the candidate describes being inspired by the power of his own performance. "The more he talks, the more he likes the sound of what he's saying," read the closing lines. "I want to be in it," he says, now leaning forward. "Man, I'm just born to be in it."

The image and article made a false equivalency between Reagan, a three-term governor and two-time presidential candidate who had considerable leadership skills built over time, with a three-time congressman hooked on a feeling. O'Rourke's candidacy did not last long, but it was a candidacy based upon the spirit of his age, a candidacy elevated by self-realization and self-expression, quickened by social media. Before announcing, O'Rourke published diaries of his travels across the country and posted video of his teeth cleaning on Instagram. Far from being laughed off the stage, O'Rourke was encouraged to be on it by pundits who predicted he could go all the way and who prophesied that if he didn't, he would at least be a top finisher.

This political shift to the immediate and personal has been under way for decades. The generation raised during the Great Depression valued shared sacrifice, modesty, and self-discipline. These private behaviors created social cohesion in American institutions and the white male candidates who ran for president reflected those norms on the stump.

The baby boomers started to crack that standard. Individual fulfillment moved into the forefront in the culture, as libertarians from the right wanted to do their own thing and liberals kicked off the constraints that valued conformity over individual freedom and equality.

A split in the generation can be seen in the public careers of John McCain and Donald Trump. McCain committed to serve his country at a young age as a Navy pilot. He was shot down during the Vietnam

War and held prisoner for five years. In his public life and presidential campaign he ran on the idea that he could encourage a new generation to follow "a cause greater than their self-interest."[61]

Donald Trump represented the other half of that generation. Born into privilege like McCain, his life of self-fulfillment and self-aggrandizement made him one of the best-known celebrities on the planet. For many Americans, he is the embodiment of the American Dream. ("I'm really rich, okay?" Trump said at his campaign announcement.)[62] In keeping with this stance, Trump told Howard Stern in 1997 that avoiding sexually transmitted diseases from the many women he slept with was his "personal Vietnam."[63] He joked with the shock radio host, "I feel like a great and very brave soldier."

Social media, which dominates our public and private lives, has quickened this trend toward the centrality of the self. Our public heroes are those who give us a steady stream of costume changes to keep us coming back for the dopamine hit. The planet now contains beings known as "influencers," individuals who through their acts of self-expression on social media have become famous consumers, sought out by advertisers to hypnotize the public.

When Michael Jordan was at the top of his game, Gatorade turned the expression "Be like Mike" into a successful ad. Jordan was one of the greatest basketball players ever. Now people want to be like Mike, but Mike is a guy standing next to expensive cars flexing in a funny hat.

Social media flattens context and encourages us to respond to the world directly in front of us. This hypercharges what the CBS producer Don Hewitt worried about after the Kennedy-Nixon debates turned the campaign into a television contest. Our quickened media encourage our inclination to think that the candidate who performs well is fit for the office. Today we ask: Did a candidate have a good launch? Were they commanding onstage? Did they pause too long before giving a debate answer? What does it say that they cook dinner the way that they do in their online video?

The performance overshadows the search for the prosaic presidential qualities—reason, experience, temperament, restraint, and having faced tough challenges—or these qualities are intuited from a momentary performance in the shortened window of a feed scroll.

Donald Trump benefited from this in two ways. As a "reality television" star, he gained notoriety as a businessman from playing a cartoon-ish sort of businessman on *The Apprentice*—which is to healthy business practices what *The Bachelor* is to stable relationships. As a candidate, Trump embraced the modern appetite, both at rallies and in constant television appearances, rewarding audiences and television networks with a string of fresh, instantaneous hits of dopamine.

In 1948, *The Washington Post* criticized President Truman for going "off the cuff" during campaign stops.[64] In the world of immediacy, this has flipped. To some, the candidate who prepares is somehow unquali-fied. President Ronald Reagan helped to perfect the use of the tele-prompter, but now it is seen as a sign of duplicity. "I've always said, if you run for president, you shouldn't be allowed to use teleprompters," Trump said in a typical remark as a candidate. "We should have non-teleprompter speeches only when you're running for president," he said. "You find out about people. The other way you don't find out about anybody."[65]

PARTISANSHIP AND DOPAMINE

IMMEDIACY OBSCURES CONTEXT, BUT SOME VOTERS AREN'T INTERESTED in context in the first place. Close to 90 percent of voters affiliated with a political party vote for that party's candidate in a presidential elec-tion.[66] For these voters, campaigns are not a chance to make a carefully reasoned choice between competing parties and ideas. They are a venue for team enthusiasm and a place to affirm group identity.

Social media offers the team a place to gather, just as the all-day Whig rallies in the 1840 campaign offered a place for the hard-cider-drinking citizens to swarm and sway in support of William Henry Har-rison. What's new is that we can march in the parade all day long at our computers. We consume information from sources we self-tailor, con-ditioned by a market that encourages frictionless interaction.

Sixty-eight percent of us get our news from social media.[67] This turns our individual experience into a group one. "When we encoun-ter opposing views in the age and context of social media, it's not like reading them in a newspaper while sitting alone," writes Zeynep Tufekci of the University of North Carolina, who studies the social impact of technology. "It's like hearing them from the opposing team while sitting with our fellow fans in a football stadium. Online, we're connected with our communities, and we seek approval from our like-minded peers. We bond with our team by yelling at the fans of the other one. In sociology terms, we strengthen our feeling of 'in-group' belonging by increasing our distance from and tension with the 'out-group'—us versus them."[68]

The political scientists Rose McDermott at Brown University and Peter Hatemi at Penn State have identified how populist leaders use extremity to build cohesion.[69] "Populist movements," they write, "rely on inflammatory rhetoric to create a tribal 'us versus them' condition—this type of environment instigates neural mechanisms from the evolutionary desire to be part of the group." Social media exacerbates this effect by offering "more immediate, emotional, and personal forms of political communication" through which the gatherings can take place. The tactics are ancient, but the delivery mechanism makes them more powerful.

Frictionless doesn't mean without confrontation. If we are righteous in our cause, we're happy to fight with the ignorant. That's not uncomfortable. That's an act of self-affirmation. When it's done on social media for all to see, it's a war dance of belonging.

Partisans gravitate toward affirmation rather than toward information that might create doubt or contradiction. Those who form a heterodox thought hasten to conform. Studies show that after a big political event like a debate, partisans who form their own opinions independent of the tribe will change them and steer their views to line up with the consensus after being exposed to it.[70]

When we aren't self-tailoring our experiences, or moving in line with the herd, political strategists keep us in line through narrow casting. They use sophisticated targeting techniques to identify the issues about which we are most passionate or with which we identify most closely. If the issue you care about the most is abortion, gun rights, or the contribution of fossil fuels to climate change, you will be fed a diet of awful and alarming articles on that topic. This is red meat served for one, just the way you like it. If the issue we are most passionate about is kept in the forefront, we are less likely to swerve off and examine other opinions. Or we'll make our candidate choice based on that issue even if it is not the objectively most important issue a candidate can address in office.

Campaigns and social media companies benefit from the same tactic: keeping voters at the boil. When users are motivated, they are clicking, which increases profits. For a candidate, all that clicking keeps voters immersed in the cause and keeps them connected to the campaign so they can receive future information.

PARTISANSHIP AND REASON:
WHATABOUTISM AND NEGATIVE PARTISANSHIP

AT THE UNENDING TRIBAL POT LUCK, BOOSTERS BARELY HAVE TO WAVE an idea under the warming lights before it's cooked enough for a hungry audience. Whataboutism is the favorite dish.

Here's how it works: When you or someone in your party is accused of falling short of a standard, mention a time that some member of the other party fell short of a standard. It doesn't have to be the same standard or the same magnitude. It's just important that someone in the other party did something wrong, since the goal is deflecting and confusing the issue.

So, for example, if a person says the president from Party A has lied, one of his supporters will note that the president from Party B has lied too. The lies do not need to be of the same type or magnitude. In fact, better that they not be, because you want to send your critic into a sputtering whirl. Suddenly, the person who leveled the original charge is explaining why the situations are wildly different, or defending the president of Party B. Each defense or explanation becomes implicit exculpation of the president from Party A who was the original target of the criticism because, well, who can know anything in this crazy world.

Whataboutism does not work with the police, judges, or our mothers. If you work in customer service, do not try this. If you work for an airline, when a customer comes to you complaining that the airline has lost his family's luggage, it will not lead to job retention if you say, as a representative of the airline, that the other airlines lose luggage too. If you're in a partisan fight with short attention spans, however, whataboutism is effective in at least confusing things.

Whataboutism is the state flower of negative partisanship, one of the strongest forces keeping political tribes together and reducing reflection on the immutable standards that are supposed to govern presidential and personal behavior. In the age of hyperpartisanship, the sins of the opposing party motivate voting more than do the positive aspects of a voter's own party. As anyone who has ever received mail from a campaign knows, the mail pieces are usually about the dire threat posed by the blind ideologues on the other side or the opposition candidate. No one asks for money saying the other guy has a point.

In 2016, the Pew Research Foundation found that among Republicans, 68 percent said a major reason they identify with the GOP is that "the Democratic Party's policies are harmful to the country." Among Democrats, 62 percent said a major reason is that Republican policies harm the country.[71]

The Emory University political scientists Alan Abramowitz and Steven Webster found that in the 2016 presidential election, the key factor in predicting whether a member of a party would vote for that party's candidate was how voters felt about the opposing party's presidential candidate. It was twice as important in predicting loyalty as one's feelings about the candidate from one's own party.[72]

Among those highly engaged in politics—those who say they vote regularly and either volunteer for or donate to campaigns—fully 70 percent of Democrats and 62 percent of Republicans say they are afraid of the other party.[73] When we think the other side is awful, we are fine with treating them that way. So a liberal gadfly gets acclaim for posting a video of Mitch McConnell stumbling on a stage (McConnell has difficulty walking due to childhood polio).[74] Or President Trump wins cheers for promoting a wholly made-up claim that Bill Clinton was responsible for convicted sex offender Jeffrey Epstein's death.[75]

When the other side's failings are posted in neon, there is little a home team president or candidate can do that won't be excused by the ready-to-rally anxious to block the other party from power. There is only winning and losing. "I'm not sure he's a conservative," said Newt Gingrich about Donald Trump, "but he's the most effective anti-liberal in my lifetime."[76]

Preemptive whataboutism is even more powerful than garden variety whataboutism. Instead of measuring a president against a standard, or against the qualifications of another candidate, a partisan compares their candidate to the worst caricature of an imagined candidate of the opposition. "The President may be nuts in his behavior," wrote the conservative pundit Erick Erickson, "but I'll take his crazy over the insanity the Democrats would unleash on the United States."[77]

At a biological level, partisans view an attack on an issue or a favorite candidate as a personal attack, creating an almost physical discomfort when new information contradicts their worldview. "The brain's primary responsibility is to take care of the body, to protect the body," Jonas Kaplan, a psychologist at the University of Southern California, told *Vox*. "The psychological self is the brain's extension of that. When our self feels attacked, our [brain is] going to bring to bear the same defenses that it has for protecting the body."[78] In one study, supporters and opponents of same-sex marriage were offered money to read findings that contradicted or supported their worldview. They were willing to take less money to avoid reading ideas that challenged their positions.[79]

If the stakes are high and personal, we'll applaud anyone who rallies to our side, and we won't be fastidious about the tactics they use. When the blood is up we're not bothered if our gladiator doesn't hue to the facts or rules. As Tufekci says, "Belonging is stronger than facts." Or, as the political scientist Brendan Nyhan says, "partisanship is a hell of a drug."[80]

Debates over facts or expectations with Donald Trump turn into commitment ceremonies, as highly adhesive voters reaffirm their passion and rally behind him. This phenomenon is what makes contemporary political debate such a chore. Writing in the *National Review*, Jim Geraghty explains how the power of identity has overcome our reason and ruined our debates: "Some of us want to argue that certain policies are good and certain policies are bad. But a vocal chunk of Americans don't really care about what the policies are; they would much rather argue that their side is right. They don't care if these are the same policies or comparable to those they denounced earlier. The system is clogged with bad-faith arguments, hypocrisy, and flip-flopping."[81] The discerning Jeffersonian voter doesn't have a chance, so how healthy is a selection process that depends on that voter's discernment?

In *Attention Merchants,* Tim Wu explains how our modern distractions differ from the amusements of the past. "There were technological limits on what we could do to keep ourselves amused. Sustained periods of boredom were unavoidable. Today, boredom is an option. To the extent that boredom is a lack of stimulation, we have cured it, and this isn't necessarily a good thing. If you can endure boredom, you can devote yourself to deep and serious projects. If you can't endure boredom, how do you write a book or enter into reflection?"[82] Wu's questions present challenges for electing presidents as well. If you can't endure boredom, how can you devote yourself to the project of elections in the Jeffersonian model where you evaluate ideas based on reason, which requires patient, focused thought? If only boredom were the only problem. The righteous voter willing to fight the lure of the Turkish delight of Dopamine has another gauntlet to run that is exhausting, simply trying to get accurate, useful information.

"HE'S AN ARAB"

"I can't trust Obama. I have read about him, and he's not—um—he's an Arab," a woman said to McCain at a town hall meeting in Lakeville, Minnesota, in October 2008.

McCain grabbed the microphone from her, cutting her off. "No, ma'am," he said. "He's a decent family man [and] citizen that I just happen to have disagreements with on fundamental issues, and that's what the campaign's all about. He's not [an Arab]."[1]

Chapter 25

Amping Up the Awful

—

When one side only of a story is heard and often repeated,
the human mind becomes impressed with it insensibly.[2]

— GEORGE WASHINGTON

I F A VOTER ESCAPES THE FORCES PUSHING THEM INTO UNTHINKINGLY
pulling the lever based on emotion or belonging, they might search for
nonpartisan information to help them make their choice. Alas, they'll
discover the river of quality information is clogged with old shoes, re-
frigerators, and rotary phones tossed there by partisans, donors, interest
groups, or mischief makers who exaggerate numbers, snip quotes to
remove context, and edit videos to convey a false impression.

The first discovery to be made by this simple information hunter is
that everyone is behaving like brutes. The structure of online communication encourages coarseness because the extreme gets more attention.[3] It also might get more votes. Social scientists at Berkeley's Haas
School of Business found that most people, whether they identified as
moderate liberals or conservatives, viewed politically incorrect statements as more authentic, a quality voters like. The study further showed
that candidates who use politically incorrect language are seen as less
malleable, a second attribute voters like because voters think candidates who behave like that will be impervious to Washington's compromises.[4]

In a political contest, the structure that encourages extremes elevates conspiracy theories, racist appeals, and lies. Extreme views wriggle their way in front of the merely curious in a format where the old

signifiers between quality and crank are gone. You might not have liked the newspaper that landed on your front porch, but journalists would get fired for knowingly printing lies. Now, you get an article from your brother-in-law you trust but who is gullible. Because you agree with him, you agree with the content and pass it on. The malevolent can win the race for eyeballs.

CHAOS ACTORS

ALSO POLLUTING THE RIVER OF INFORMATION ARE ONLINE POLITICAL actors who are simply interested in muddying the water. In 2019, at the annual meeting of the American Political Science Association, the winning paper in the political psychology division identified how stoking chaos has become a form of expressing discontent.

In their paper entitled "A 'Need for Chaos' and the Sharing of Hostile Political Rumors in Advanced Democracies," Michael Bang Petersen, Mathias Osmundsen, and Kevin Arceneaux report on their research that identified participants in the social media conversation who seek to stoke conflict for its own sake. These people are not promoting a particular ideology. They want to weaken political elites and politicians of whatever party. They do not "share rumors because they believe them to be true," write the authors. "For the core group, hostile political rumors are simply a tool to create havoc."[5]

Examples of this behavior include the allegations that Hillary Clinton's campaign ran a secret pedophile ring, that Barack Obama was born in Kenya, and that the Sandy Hook Elementary School shooting that left twenty children and six adults dead was a "complete fake" staged by the government to promote gun control.

The poison spreads through social media channels. "A few chaotic thoughts that lead to a few clicks to retweet or share is enough. When the echoes of similar processes across multiple individuals reinforce each other, it can add up to cascades of hostile political rumors," conspiracy theories, and fake news.[6]

This chaos attack on authority, expertise, and institutions has some hold in 40 percent of the American population, according to the authors. They claim that this free-floating antagonism has attached to Donald Trump, who is also a fan of chaos. Jeb Bush said during the

Republican primaries in 2016 that Donald Trump was "a chaos candidate, and he'd be a chaos president." He meant it to be a criticism, but it wound up being a commercial. Some of Trump's voters liked that he was a chaos agent.

IN THIS ENVIRONMENT OF emotionally charged partisanship whipped up by the political class and the sensation-seeking media business model, reason and critical thinking have a steep hill up which to drag their slide rule and pocket protector. It's even harder if reason isn't what we thought it was. Hugo Mercier and Dan Sperber argue in *The Enigma of Reason* that reasoning exists not to help us gain greater knowledge, but to make us better at producing justifications and arguments to convince others of conclusions we've come to by emotion or impulse. In that case, the evolutionary use of reason is to embrace Whataboutism, illogic, and the other tantalizing types of online argumentation.[7]

THE ILLUSORY TRUTH EFFECT

TO CLEAN THE RIVER, MANY HAVE ADVOCATED THE USE OF FACT-CHECKING in order to identify the garbage so that no one gets confused. This is a noble goal, but it may make the situation worse. Exposing the lie may promote it, building more adherents than detractors, or causing more chaos than order.

The seed of this notion is contained in a possibly apocryphal story about Lyndon Johnson. During one of his early campaigns, he claimed his opponent had amorous relations with pigs. When told that he couldn't say that because it wasn't true, Johnson said he simply wanted his opponent to have to deny it.

During the 2016 campaign when Donald Trump lied repeatedly, commentators wondered why he kept telling lies after he had been fact-checked. He was constantly "doubling down," to use an unfortunate cliché from the gambling world that describes increasing a bet despite risk. The phrase has termited its way into the lexicon to explain why lawmakers repeat falsehoods despite proof that what they're saying isn't so. Politicians like President Trump don't mind being fact-checked—

indeed, they welcome it, because the additional coverage from the controversy publicizes the original lie. The president is happy to say that the economy has never been better or that his tax cut was the largest in history because a fact check about how those two are wrong adds to the amount of time people are exposed to hearing about how good the economy and tax cut are. The benefit of Donald Trump's campaign claim that Mexico was going to pay for his border wall (which is being paid for by diverting Pentagon funding) was that every time he was pressed on it or fact-checked on it, he was getting coverage of just how committed he was to stopping border crossing. True believers hear the fact-checking and become more devoted to the liar.

Studies show that even a single exposure to false information increases subsequent perceptions of its accuracy, something psychologists call the "illusory truth effect." In a study of dubious political claims, Yale psychologists found that "only a small degree of potential plausibility is sufficient for repetition to increase perceived accuracy of even the most implausible claims."[8] George Washington didn't need to do any studies to know this. "When one side only of a story is heard and often repeated, the human mind becomes impressed with it insensibly," he wrote to the Virginia politician Edmund Pendleton about negative impressions of Native Americans, which Washington believed had grown because they "have no Press thro' which their grievances are related."[9]

One root of this phenomenon may be that old devil, pride. We retain our beliefs even in the face of learning we're dead wrong because we don't want to admit that we were wrong. Studies have shown that even when people are told, on good evidence, that the information they believe to be true was completely fabricated, they cling to their original understanding.

Social media makes this worse. Recent research in the *Journal of Experimental Psychology* shows that "social media platforms help to incubate belief in blatantly false news stories, and that tagging such stories as disputed is not an effective solution to this problem."[10] In other words, once a lie is repeated, continuing to repeat it is more effective with susceptible audiences than the power of a fact check to convince those audiences otherwise. A lie gets halfway around the world, goes the old expression, before the truth has a chance to get its boots on. In the social media world, a lie has an Instagram page and your uncle is forwarding you pictures of its weekend parties before the truth can bestir itself.

This is why Donald Trump repeated nineteen times in six weeks that China, not the United States, is paying for the tariffs Trump imposed on imported Chinese goods. The president's own economic advisers, along with a breathtaking number of professional economists, say this is deeply incorrect. President Trump doesn't mind. His supporters have stronger ties to his successes than to abstract ideas about truth telling. As Donald Trump once boasted, "I could stand in the middle of 5th Avenue and shoot somebody and I wouldn't lose voters."[11]

THE RUSSIANS ARE PAYING ATTENTION

IN THE 2016 CAMPAIGN, THE RUSSIAN GOVERNMENT TOOK ADVANTAGE of the obvious vulnerabilities of the American political conversation. According to a bipartisan Senate Intelligence committee report, the Russian Internet Research Agency's disruptive efforts reached 126 million people on Facebook, posted 10.4 million tweets on Twitter, uploaded more than a thousand videos to YouTube, and reached more than 20 million users on Instagram.[12]

The techniques they used took advantage of our psychological wiring and the patterns of permanent outrage and group sorting that pass for political debate. The report reads like one of a political psychologist's studies of our worst modern tendencies. "[The Russians] created strong ties by posting a majority of content designed to generate in-group approval and camaraderie," explains one of the investigations commissioned by the committee, "then posted occasional content that was either designed to sow division from out-groups, explicitly partisan and election-related, or focused on a theme that Russia cared about (Syria)." The goal was to stoke social, cultural, and political unrest by feeding disinformation to narrow categories of users—from black or gay users to fans of Fox News.

According to a research project by the University of Oxford provided to the Senate Select Committee on Intelligence, the Russian effort "demonstrates a sustained effort to manipulate the US public and undermine democracy. . . . to target US voters and polarize US social media users. The Russian effort targeted many kinds of communities within the US, but particularly the most extreme conservatives and those with particular sensitivities to race and immigration."[13]

The committee concludes that the Russian efforts were almost entirely devoted to helping Donald Trump. The only pro-Hillary group, "Muslims for Hillary," was designed not to help her in that community, but to associate the Democratic nominee with a group her Republican rival demonized and wanted to ban from the United States. Whether or not these methods determined the election outcome, the American electorate's psychological vulnerability was glaring enough that it could be targeted.

It was as though in a community susceptible to alcoholism, the Russians placed liquor bottles on every doorstep, and the press, the public, and Donald Trump encouraged everyone to open the door.

PART THREE

THE WAY WE
LIVE NOW

*Donald Trump and Vice President Mike Pence
on election night, November 9, 2016.*

Chapter 26

Winning Above All

———

I won.

—DONALD TRUMP

SIXTY YEARS AFTER IKE MADE FRONT PAGE NEWS BY BARELY
responding to his opponent, Republican senator Marco Rubio of Florida tried to stand athwart the 2016 presidential campaign and yell
"Stop!" What Ike had called the "noise and extravagance of the campaign" had grown into a roar. The Florida senator and former GOP
presidential candidate had been consumed by it, questioning during
one debate whether Donald Trump was well endowed. One month
before Election Day, however, Rubio stood on higher ground. He
asked his party to refrain from using information the Russians obtained
through espionage as a campaign weapon. There were limits to how far
a party should go in pursuit of victory because in winning, the party
would irrevocably destroy the prize. Senator Rubio was arguing for
standards in a process that was rapidly shredding them.

Rubio was referring to well-known public information about the
Russians. On October 7, 2016, the intelligence community had issued
a rare declaration. The director of national intelligence announced
that the Russian government had hacked Democratic nominee Hillary
Clinton's campaign manager's email account and passed the contents
on to WikiLeaks in an operation "intended to interfere with the U.S.
election process."[1]

The emails dominated the headlines and cable news crawls. Rubio,
a member of the Senate Intelligence Committee, refused to talk about

them. "Our intelligence officials who are not partisan people have told us this is the work of a foreign intelligence agency and we cannot be a country where foreign intelligence agencies can interfere or influence our political process," he declared. "What I'd say to Republicans who may be disappointed in my position is today it's them, tomorrow it could be us."[2]

The leaked correspondence was politically tempting. It suggested Clinton was a hypocrite. Included in the trove were rough drafts of Hillary Clinton's paid speeches to the investment bank Goldman Sachs.[3] Criticism of her high-fee appearances had nagged her throughout the campaign. As a declared candidate, she sounded tough on the Wall Street banks, which had contributed to the Great Recession. In the rough draft of the private six-figure speeches, however, she rapped no knuckles. LEAKED SPEECH EXCERPTS SHOW A HILLARY CLINTON AT EASE WITH WALL STREET read one *New York Times* headline.

The emails were mostly embarrassing. In them, aides and allies spoke bluntly and not always favorably about their boss. The political class tucked in their napkins and dined on every morsel because it was good gossip. Rubio refused to partake and suffered the fate of all kill-joys. He sat alone with only his principles to warm him. No one in the Republican Party joined the senator's call not to give aid and assistance to the Russians.

Donald Trump did not listen to Rubio any more than he had during the primary contest against him. The GOP nominee zoomed off in the opposite direction. He criticized journalists for not making *enough* of the Russian WikiLeaks material that intelligence officials said was intended to undermine democracy. "WikiLeaks has provided things that are unbelievable," Trump informed his supporters at a Colorado rally. "The media, you have to remember, is an extension of the Hillary Clinton campaign. It's an extension. And without that, she would be nowhere."[4] (We would later learn from the Trump Justice Department that WikiLeaks consulted with the Trump campaign.)[5]

Donald Trump knew what the Russians were up to. He had inside dope. The U.S. intelligence agencies had briefed him, in keeping with a tradition started in 1952 when President Truman asked the CIA to brief Eisenhower and Adlai Stevenson during their campaign contest. Truman explained at the time, "There were so many things I did not know when I became President."[6] There was one gargantuan thing: Upon taking office after FDR died, Truman learned the military was working on a weapon capable of destroying the world.

The tradition of candidate briefings recognizes a distinction between the world of campaigning, where each contestant makes self-interested moves to win the office, and the world of governing, where the victor represents the entire country.

During the election of 1916, which took place during World War I, Woodrow Wilson considered a plan that recognized this important continuity. If his opponent, Charles Evans Hughes, won, Wilson would allow him to take the job immediately. According to Wilson biographer A. Scott Berg, the president's plan was to ask his secretary of state and vice president to resign, appointing Hughes to secretary of state, then Wilson would resign, allowing Hughes to take office immediately instead of having to wait until the following March. "It would be my duty to step aside so that there would be no doubt in any quarter how that policy was to be directed. . . . I would have no right to risk the peace of the nation by remaining in office after I had lost my authority."[7]

Presidential campaigns have interacted with foreign countries before. During the 1968 presidential campaign, GOP nominee Richard Nixon sent a back-channel message to South Vietnamese leaders attending peace talks in Paris. Using an intermediary known as the "Dragon Lady," Nixon promised a better deal under his administration than whatever the South Vietnamese might get from Lyndon Johnson.[8] Nixon was trying to freeze progress, because if there had been a breakthrough on the eve of the election, voters might have credited President Johnson with ending the fighting, and by association, Nixon's opponent, Vice President Humphrey, would have benefited.

Lyndon Johnson learned what Nixon was up to through intelligence intercepts and held a meeting with his advisers to discuss what to do about it. "Well, Mr. President, I have a very definite view on this, for what it's worth," his secretary of state, Dean Rusk, told him. "I do not believe that any president can make any use of interceptions or telephone taps in any way that would involve politics. The moment we cross over that divide, we're in a different kind of society."[9] Johnson never used them.

Ronald Reagan's 1980 presidential campaign was accused of coordinating with the Iranians holding American hostages to delay the release of those hostages until the election was over. Subsequent congressional investigations concluded the allegations could not be proved.

In 1968 Nixon kept his gambit secret. Trump, on the other hand, spoke clearly and into the microphone. "Russia, if you're listening, I hope you're able to find the thirty thousand emails that are missing," he said at a press conference in July 2016.[10]

TRUMP IN OFFICE AND ESPIONAGE

TWO YEARS LATER, PRESIDENT TRUMP FACED THE SAME QUESTION HE had as a candidate: how to balance political expediency and national duty. ABC's George Stephanopoulos asked him what he would do if his reelection campaign received stolen material from a foreign country. "I think you might want to listen," said President Trump. "I don't— there's nothing wrong with listening. If somebody called from a country, Norway, we have information on your opponent. Oh. I think I'd want to hear it."[11] Stephanopoulos hadn't mentioned Norway; that was Trump's own innovation, in order to strip the question of the menace of China or Russia, the two countries most likely to meddle. Nevertheless, Trump's national security obligations were clear. As commander in chief, he was obliged to thwart espionage, not encourage it. Taking such material would also be illegal. No candidate can take anything of value from a foreign entity. But Donald Trump, whose presidency has been a constant test of the obligations of office, was not going to let the obligations of the office get in the way of keeping him in office.

The obligations of the presidency are not just some tradition like wearing white only before Labor Day. President Trump's Justice Department explained this rule in a legal argument early in his tenure. The Trump administration argued in court that there was a distinction between campaigning and governing, particularly when it comes to national security. As Benjamin Wittes and Susan Hennessey point out in *Unmaking the Presidency*, the DOJ explained that candidate Donald Trump's promise to ban Muslims from the United States was not relevant in assessing his intent as President Trump. The legal argument was presented in court during a debate over Trump's executive order to ban travelers from mostly Muslim countries. "Taking the oath marks a profound transition from private life to the nation's highest public office," the department wrote, "and manifests the singular responsibility and independent authority to protect the welfare of the Nation that the Constitution necessarily reposes in the Office of the President." One cannot evaluate an "action by the President of the United States because of his statements as a private citizen—before he swore an oath to support and defend the Constitution, formed his Administration, assumed the responsibilities of governance, and consulted with Executive officials."[12]

The national security obligations President Trump recognized in law he did not recognize in his answer to Stephanopoulos. A month later, the president put his theory from that interview into practice in real life. He encouraged the Ukrainian president to investigate Vice President Joe Biden and his son.[13] The president claimed that Biden, while in office, had leaned on the previous Ukrainian government to fire a prosecutor who was looking into his son's business dealings in the country. There was no evidence that that had happened, and the narrative was wrong in key places.[14] Nevertheless, on a phone call with the new Ukrainian president, Trump raised issues related to his election and political standing eight times.

Trump had leverage when he put the arm on his counterpart. He had delayed congressionally mandated U.S. foreign aid to Ukraine, which Congress had appropriated to help the former Soviet bloc nation defend itself against Russian interference.

The call came at a particularly notable time in the Trump administration.[15] The president invited a foreign government to offer him help in the U.S. election one day after Robert Mueller's testimony in the Senate about his report that said the president had not coordinated with a foreign government in the last election. On the call, Trump mentioned that he had tasked his personal attorney, Rudy Giuliani, with investigating the meritless story that Ukraine had possession of a Democratic Party computer server that had contained those emails Rubio was concerned about. That theory—that it was Ukraine and not Russia that had interfered in the 2016 U.S. presidential election—had been debunked by Trump's national security officials, Republican-led Senate committees, and intelligence agencies, but it, too, was part of the president's political obsession. If he could prove that the unicorn story of the server was true, then it would cast doubt on the consensus view of U.S. intelligence agencies and other countries that the Russians had interfered in the 2016 election to help him. The president was looking to both validate his 2016 victory and help his next run.

The extraordinary moves had no parallel in previous administrations. The layer separating the president's duty of his office from his desire to stay in it was already nearly translucent, but in his relations with Ukraine, President Trump found a way to use the mandolin to shave one more layer from it.

In 1992, George H. W. Bush had made a different choice. During the campaign against Bill Clinton, a group of House Republicans suggested that the Bush White House reach out to the Russians to get information on Clinton's time protesting the Vietnam War while overseas. White House chief of staff Jim Baker shot them down. "They wanted us to contact the Russians or the British to seek information on Bill Clinton's trip to Moscow," Baker wrote in a memo later that day. "I said we absolutely could not do that."[16] Bush and Baker, who had done what it took in 1988 against Michael Dukakis, recognized that the obligations of the office required something different.

The line between a president's duty to his nation and his duty to his reelection is clear, but what about other types of underhanded presidential campaign behavior? The presidency does not attract saints.

In 1940, FDR, a philanderer, personally taught his aides how to spread rumors about his Republican challenger Wendell Willkie's extramarital affairs. "Spread it," he told his aide Lowell Mellett, after instructing him as to how rumors could be introduced into the press without fingerprints, "spread it as a word of mouth thing, or by some people way, way down the line. We can't have any of our principal speakers refer to it, but people down the line can get it out. . . . They can use raw material as a matter of fact."[17]

President Trump has adopted the social media techniques of the Russian disruption campaigns, which seek to sow chaos and create disorder. In May 2019, when a doctored video appeared to show Nancy Pelosi slurring her words, the president's personal attorney, Rudy Giuliani, forwarded it on Twitter, asking, "What's wrong with Nancy Pelosi?" (The tweet was since deleted.) The president then forwarded another selectively edited video of Pelosi from the same footage to his more than 60 million Twitter followers with the line: "Pelosi Stammers Through News Conference."[18]

The president also forwarded a deceptively labeled video of Democratic congresswoman Ilhan Omar, a Somali American who came to America as a child. The video showed her dancing and claimed it was on the solemn anniversary of 9/11. It wasn't. Nevertheless, the president wrote: "The new face of the Democratic Party." Twitter took down the original post the president had forwarded because it was fake. The president did not remove his retweet.[19]

After the disinformation campaigns used in the 2016 campaign, the FBI and Department of Homeland Security actively sought to eliminate false and incendiary videos that might disrupt American politics. The president's tweets represented the kind of disinformation they were targeting. "We are trying to rid the Internet of the kinds of things he is spreading," said one senior Trump administration official.[20]

The separation between campaigning and governing is now prosciutto thin. For the president's supporters, this is reason to praise Donald Trump. In 2016, he depantsed a field of experienced politicians and fooled the political class; why shouldn't he replicate that same spirit in office? He is a winner. Elite criticism—that Trump is not "presidential," or vaporous exhalations about flouting "norms"—is for losers.

The president promotes this winning-is-everything attitude. He expressed himself in a video shortly after details of the Ukraine pressure campaign were revealed. Senator Mitt Romney criticized Trump for using his office to target his likely opponent. The president responded by releasing a video showing Romney's election night loss in 2012 followed by election night coverage of 2016 when Trump won. "Mitt Romney never knew how to win," wrote Trump in a subsequent tweet.[21] That was the only rebuttal he needed.

If winning is all that matters in the presidency, what becomes of presidential standards that were cultivated and passed on to protect the office and American system? What are those standards and when should they apply? Even asking this question distorts the traditional understanding of standards. Standards are supposed to be bolted to the floor, informed by immutable American values. Their immutability locks in a concern for the long term and not simply the immediate moment. It's the kind of thing Senator Rubio was talking about. Immutability gives standards fortitude against the pressures of culture that would push the country into the haze of the momentary and away from its founding principles. Donald Trump's presidency raised these questions. For some of his supporters it was familiar territory. They had raised these questions regularly during the presidency of Bill Clinton. If there are no standards, then the whatever-it-takes mentality that has ruled in campaigns becomes the standard for the presidency, turbocharging the office and throwing the system of shared powers out of balance.

HONEST OLD ABE

ABRAHAM LINCOLN

Engraved & Published by Ed. Mendel 162 Lake St. Chicago

LINCOLN
&
HAMLIN

Chapter 27

Resolve to Be Honest

I cannot tell a lie.

— GEORGE WASHINGTON (APOCRYPHAL)

Resolve to be honest at all events; and if, in your own
judgment, you cannot be an honest lawyer,
resolve to be honest without being a lawyer.
Choose some other occupation.[1]

— ABRAHAM LINCOLN

I N 1992, BILL CLINTON'S RISE IN THE PRESIDENTIAL CAMPAIGN prompted the guardians of culture to stack sandbags against the tides that would sweep in a baby boomer of uncertain rectitude. His opponent, incumbent president George H. W. Bush, charged that he lacked the character to be president. Bush said Clinton was "slippery when wet," explaining during one of the debates, "I believe that character is a part of being president. I think you have to look at it. I think that has to be a part of—of a candidate for president, or being president."[2]

When Clinton won, his critics identified a challenge to America that went beyond the presidency. The American president occupied a special cultural position as the best-known person in the country and the most closely followed. Clinton had cheated on his wife and sought to avoid service in Vietnam. That set a horrible example, said conservative critics. His shifting answers about both during the campaign increased their fears that he would trim and prevaricate in office.

FDR said the presidency was primarily a moral office. What would happen if it became inhabited by a person of such liquid standards? "Throughout our history, we have seen the presidency as the repository of all of our highest hopes and ideals and values," wrote Vice President Mike Pence, who was a local radio host at the time. "To demand less is to do an injustice to the blood that bought our freedoms."[3]

As a bulwark against this cultural change on the eve of a new century, those concerned with standards formed a citizen's patrol against corrosion. Good people had to stand up against relativism. If they didn't, the moral rot would spread to the next generation. "For children to take morality seriously they must be in the presence of adults who take morality seriously," wrote Bill Bennett in *The Book of Virtues*.[4] "And with their own eyes they must see adults take morality seriously." The book, published in 1993, the year after Clinton's election, occupied the *New York Times* bestseller list for eighty-eight weeks. It was described as an "antidote" to the cultural decline Bennett and other conservatives saw abetted by the Clinton ascendancy. As Rush Limbaugh put it on the book blurb: "*The Book of Virtues* is built on an old philosophical principle nearly forgotten in the public discussion (and in certain presidential campaigns) but it is an idea I have long championed: Character matters."

I Cannot Tell a Lie

STANDARD-KEEPING AND PRIVATE INTEGRITY CONTINUED TO BE A Republican principal throughout the Clinton years, which came to a close with a test for those who would protect standards. Bill Clinton had lied to a grand jury and he had repeatedly lied to the American public. He was impeached, but the country didn't seem to care. Was telling the truth of so little weight in the American system?

In the 2000 campaign, George W. Bush concluded every speech with an implicit reference to the collapse of standards in the White House. He promised if elected he would "restore honor and integrity" to the Oval Office. When asked to name his favorite philosopher during a Republican primary debate, Bush named Christ, a perfectly reasonable answer for any Christian. For Bush's supporters, the answer was proof he had moral instincts in his bones, the kinds of standards the nation should expect in that office. The pundit class snickered.

By their debate answers ye shall know them. Donald Trump showed voters something different in his presidential debates. At the third debate in the 2016 presidential race, Donald Trump revealed one of his signature attributes. "You had talked a little bit about Marco Rubio," began the questioner, Becky Quick of CNBC, in a question to Trump. "I think you called him Mark Zuckerberg's personal senator." Before Quick could finish her question, Trump cut her off. "I never said that," he interjected. He denied having expressed the sentiment in any form and took umbrage. "I was not at all critical of him," Trump said, categorically. He then blamed Jeb Bush for the quote. He accused the moderators of "really doing some bad fact-checking." Quick promptly apologized to Trump.[5]

You know how this story ends even if you don't know the facts of it. After some rudimentary checking, everyone realized what those of you holding this book have already anticipated. Donald Trump was lying. Not only had he called Rubio Mark Zuckerberg's personal senator, as Quick had suggested, Trump had done so in his own immigration policy document, *the signature policy of his campaign.* "Mark Zuckerberg's personal Senator, Marco Rubio, has a bill to triple H-1Bs that would decimate women and minorities," read Trump's website. Jeb Bush, whom Trump had accused, had said no such thing.

By the quaint standards of the late fall of 2015, Trump's assertive denial was considered a gaffe. Candidates weren't supposed to tell lies or to be so unfamiliar with the positions they'd founded their campaigns on that they denied what was clearly true. It wasn't just the Trump skeptics who viewed this as a gaffe. The website *Breitbart*, whose executive chairman, Steve Bannon, directed Trump campaign strategy as its chief executive, wrote, "Donald Trump was doing well at the GOP Debate on Wednesday evening until a blunder in which he claimed not to have called Marco Rubio 'Mark Zuckerberg's personal senator.'"[6]

By January 2020, about 1,095 days into his administration, the number of false or misleading claims made by President Trump reached 16,241, according to *The Washington Post*'s fact-checker database.[7] The variety was sweeping. He told outright lies, repeated lies even after having been fact-checked repeatedly, and made up stories when the truth would do. He lied about little things and he lied about the most important issues a president must handle. He took credit for things he had nothing to do with and denied involvement in matters he orchestrated. To list the individual examples would fill the next twenty pages. Even the president's supporters admit this. In an article praising Trump for keeping his promises on the travel ban and tax reform, conservative *Washington Post* columnist Marc Thiessen writes, "Don't get me wrong, Trump lies all the time."[8]

Other presidents have lied, but President Trump does so with such frequency and sweep that to put his behavior in the same category as theirs undersells the level of his accomplishment. A person who occasionally drinks and drives is not in the same category as a person who irrigates from the keg he has installed in the passenger's seat for his long-haul trips.

The October 28, 2015, debate "blunder," as *Breitbart* called it, was no blunder at all. Donald Trump offered the audience a peek into his communications innovation. By offering a steady flow of disinformation, he controlled the news cycle and rallied his supporters. At times the president's constant and remorseless pace rendered only one conclusion possible: that he sought to overwhelm the system with so many falsehoods as to challenge the very idea of knowable information. He also hoped to just tucker people out.

In July 2019, only 34 percent of voters polled by Gallup found President Trump honest and trustworthy. That was 12 points lower than Bill Clinton at the same period of his presidency and nearly half of the rating voters accorded George Bush and Barack Obama at that point in their presidencies.[9] In early November 2019, in an NBC News / *Wall Street Journal* poll, 27 percent of respondents said Trump is "honest and trustworthy." Also, 27 percent said he has "high personal and ethical standards."[10]

HONESTY AND THE PRESIDENCY

IN THE AMERICAN PRESIDENCY, HONESTY ISN'T A MERE NICETY, IT IS one of the two pillars of the office. Donald Trump isn't just shilly-shallying around playing low-grade politics. His presidency is testing a basic concept of the office and possibly writing a new definition of it.

When Parson Weems wrote the first biography of George Washington, just after the great general's death, he sought to describe a leader of such radiant quality and virtue he would lift every citizen of the young nation and set a marker for all presidents thereafter. Weems rolled the entire virtue message into one story about honesty—a kind of virtue turducken:

"When George," said she, "was about six years old, he was made the wealthy master of a hatchet! of which, like most little boys, he was immoderately fond, and was constantly going about chopping everything that came in his way. One day, in the garden, where he often amused himself hacking his mother's pea-sticks, he unluckily tried the edge of his hatchet on the body of a beautiful young English cherry-tree, which he barked so terribly that I don't believe the tree ever got the better of it. The next morning the old gentleman finding out what had befallen his tree, which, by the by, was a great favorite, came into the house, and with much warmth asked for the mischievous author, declaring at the same time that he would not have taken five guineas for his tree. Nobody could tell him anything about it.

Presently George and his hatchet made their appearance. "George," said his father, "do you know who killed that beautiful little cherry-tree yonder in the garden?" This was a tough question, and George staggered under it for a moment; but quickly recovered himself; and looking at his father, with the sweet face of youth brightened with the inexpressible charm of all-triumphant truth, he bravely cried out, "I can't tell a lie, Pa, you know I can't tell a lie; I did cut it with my hatchet." "Run to my arms, you dearest boy," cried his father in transports, "run to my arms; glad am I, George, that you ever killed my tree, for you have paid me for it a thousand-fold. Such an act of heroism in my son, is worth more than a thousand trees, though blossomed with silver and their fruits of fairest gold."[11, 12]

The story about lying is itself not true—it didn't happen—but as the American philosopher William Ernest Hocking said, "there are myths which displace truth and there are myths which give wings to truth." The popularity of the tale tells us something about what we Americans want to believe about our presidents. Standards exist to call us to our highest and best. Even when we fall short, standards encourage us to lift our game.

Weems's hope has carried into this century. In 2010, Mississippi governor Haley Barbour referred to the cherry tree story at a breakfast of reporters. He said voters didn't know much about Barack Obama's origin story, the way voters know about George Washington. "We don't know if he chopped down a cherry tree," the governor said.[13] Washington wasn't the source of the cherry tree story—he was too honest for that—but it fitted with his conception of himself. His greatest achievement upon retirement, he wrote, would be to maintain the "most enviable of all titles, the character of an honest man."[14]

The cherry tree story blossomed into the next generation of great American presidents. The first book Abraham Lincoln reportedly read cover to cover was the Washington biography, with its moral code and lessons about honesty.[15] It wound its way into Lincoln's own myth. When Lincoln borrowed a copy of the Washington biography and water ruined it, he worked for three weeks to earn the wages to pay for it. Lincoln's childhood exploits would twine with the Weems model as

In 1945, Franklin Roosevelt had these sentences from a letter John Adams wrote to his wife, Abigail, engraved on the State Dining Room mantel: "I pray Heaven to bestow the best of blessings on this house and all that shall hereafter inhabit it. May none but Honest and Wise Men ever rule under This Roof."

an Aesop's fable for a growing nation. When Lincoln served as a young store clerk in New Salem, Illinois, so the hagiography goes, the future president could not stand it if he shortchanged a customer and would walk whatever distance was required to deliver the correct change.

Mary Todd Lincoln once wrote to a friend, "Mr. Lincoln . . . is almost monomaniac on the subject of honesty."[16] (It was Mrs. Lincoln's difficulty with honesty—disguising her clothing and furniture purchases as White House gardening fees, for instance—that so racked her husband with anguish. He was also worried that Congress would find out.) "Resolve to be honest at all events," Lincoln told young lawyers, "and if in your judgment you cannot be an honest lawyer, resolve to be honest without being a lawyer. Choose some other occupation, rather than one in the choosing of which you do, in advance, consent to be a knave."

The truth-telling standard is even part of the official graffiti of the presidency. In 1945 FDR asked that excerpts from a letter written by John Adams to his wife be chiseled into the State Dining Room's white marble fireplace, including the sentence "May none but Honest and Wise Men ever rule under This Roof."[17]

The voters give the president power to act in their name. That contract requires the president to be honest about how he uses that power. Furthermore, a president, as the most powerful public information officer, owes a duty to be truthful with the public so they can make wise decisions and feel confident about their world.

Honesty is also at the center of a president's persuasive power. He cannot move the public or lawmakers to support military action or emergency economic moves if they don't trust him. A president's staff takes no risks if they think they're being asked to do something under false pretenses. They'll only fight so hard if they fear the president to whom they are loyal is not telling the truth. If a president lies consistently, they'll stop looking to the president for leadership. Or they'll take notes and refer to them when the president sells them out and they get their revenge by writing a tell-all.

Other staffers will do the opposite and rally around a lying president, which can be catastrophic. Administrations aren't built to fight lies. They're built to protect the president and the president's policies. Fealty, loyalty, cowardice, and partisanship overcome conscience, prompting staffers to circle the wagons around a lying president. The lies compound themselves until everyone is culpable or compromised.

This happened during the Vietnam War, when the music of patriotism and service and duty was used to mask a series of deceptions. As Trump's former National Security Advisor H. R. McMaster wrote in his book *Dereliction of Duty*, "arrogance, weakness, lying in the pursuit of self-interest, and, above all, the abdication of responsibility to the American people" paved the way to an ever deeper U.S. involvement in a war that "led Americans to question the integrity of their government as never before."[18] In the aftermath of that compounding set of lies, tens of thousands were dead and Americans never fully regained their trust in the presidency or institutions of national government.

After Vietnam and Watergate forced Richard Nixon from office, Jimmy Carter promised in his presidential campaign, "I will never lie to you." Could he really keep that promise? I asked him this question when I visited him on the Habitat for Humanity construction site where he was working, at age ninety-three, to put up a new house for a family in need. I suggested that shading the truth must be necessary now and again in order to get things done in the presidency. "I disagree with that," he said. I asked him if he kept his "never lie" promise. "I think I went through my campaign and my presidency without ever lying or making a deliberately false statement," he replied. "And I think that would be a very worthwhile thing to reinsert into politics." He added, "I think I did, and everybody that worked for me, as far as I know, kept that promise too."[19]

This standard cannot be met. It may not even be wise for it to be met. Presidents must shade the truth now and again, if only to do the very thing for which the people gave them power. "Think of it, George Washington could not lie," wrote Mark Twain. "Grown person, you know—could not lie. Comes right out and says it. Seems to me I'd 'a known enough to keep still about an infirmity like that."

Washington liked honesty, but not when it was dangerous. When he hired spies and used his personal funds to pay for clandestine operations during the Revolutionary War, he never told the Continental Congress. Though he was not president yet, in 1777 he started to define the criteria for justifiable presidential lying: "There are some secrets, on the keeping of which so, depends, oftentimes, the salvation of an

Army: secrets which cannot, at least ought not to, be entrusted to paper; nay, which none but the Commander-in-Chief at the time, should be acquainted with."[20] Great presidents like FDR and Lincoln succeeded, in part, because they hid their true intentions until the right time.

Eisenhower said a leader must always show optimism, even if on the inside he longed to be in the fetal position. To paraphrase the writer Michael Kinsley, the perfect president shows the public an optimistic face that sees the silver lining of the cloud, but is privately worried about the cloud and working hard to dispel it.

The public can have too rigid a view about presidential prevarication. That doesn't allow the president the room to maneuver. If the standards are too strict, they won't be enforced. So how do we evaluate lies so that we don't become mindless hanging judges? Recognizing nuance in this volatile area of the presidency is just one way to more finely hone our understanding of the job.

First, put the lie in context. Is the lie about a personal matter or a professional one? Is it vital to the republic that the truth be known? Might a president have a defensible basis for not telling the truth in the furtherance of a larger goal? Lying about covert operations in order to protect an ongoing mission is one thing. Lying about the Chinese paying tariffs to disguise the pain resulting from your economic policies is another. When Barack Obama said you could keep your health insurance to minimize people's fears about the Affordable Care Act, he was deceiving people in a similar way.[21] But neither of these is as deceptive as repeatedly making up events that did not happen or saying that you did not participate in events that you participated in as Donald Trump has.[22] This leads to the next criteria. Is the lie an outlier—the rare glass of spilt milk—or a regular serving from the presidential udder? By the logic of The Book of Virtues, the lies also have a corrosive effect. When they are tolerated or encouraged, they deprive children of being in the presence of adults who take morality seriously.

Lies aren't just about morality. They also send a signal about presidential priority setting. Is whatever the president lied about important enough to burn that valuable political and social currency of trust? Even if the lie itself doesn't require a strong response, it can signal a disorder in the president's internal balance and a confusion about priorities, a crucial element of the job. The founders imagined that presidents would be ambitious and would need to be checked, but they also expected that they have character and virtue. "I go on this great republican principle, that the people will have virtue and intelligence to select men of virtue and wisdom," wrote James Madison. "Is there no virtue among us? If there be not we are in a wretched situation. No theoretical checks—no form of government can render us secure."[23]

The Commander in Chief of the Continental Army Takes His Leave, 1783

On December 22, 1783, just three months after the Revolutionary War ended, George Washington, the commander in chief of the Continental Army, attended a ball in his honor. The night was fit for a king. Thirteen toasts were raised to "His Excellency." Thirteen cannons were discharged. The guest of honor dined with two hundred or so of America's perfumed and powdered worthies. After dinner, women stood in line to take a turn with the guest of honor. He "danced in every set, so that the ladies might have the pleasure of dancing with him," wrote James Tilton of Delaware, "or as it has since been handsomely expressed, get a touch of him."[1]

The next day, Washington appeared before the Confederation Congress to give up his position as commander of the Continental Army, and the dance steps were just as formal. The protocol was even written down: "When the General rises to make his address, and also when he retires, he is to bow to Congress, which they are to return by uncovering without bowing."[2]

The protocol for the moment Washington resigned his military commission was important enough that a three-man committee—which included Thomas Jefferson—was created to plan the ceremony of resignation. Despite the military commander's popularity, the ceremony was designed to show that Congress was preeminent. Washington bowed to the people's representatives in Congress. In response, its members did not bow, but merely removed their hats as a sign of respect.

When Washington willingly gave up his power, putting
his country before his own interests, King George III
reportedly told the American-born artist Benjamin West,
"If he does that, he will be the greatest man in the world."

"Having now finished the work assigned me," Washington said, his voice cracking at times and the paper from which he read shaking in his hands, "I retire from the great theater of action . . . and take my leave of all the enjoyments of public life." Several participants reported tears in the eyes of the people in the audience.

Horses stamped at the door, awaiting their rider. Washington stood to receive his answer (item number 5 on the protocol list) and was instructed to "take his leave" (item number 7 on that list). Then private citizen Washington mounted his horse. At his departure, the crowd cheered.[3]

Chapter 28

Character Counts

—

Liberty cannot be preserved without a general knowledge
among the people, who have a right, from the frame of
their nature, to knowledge, as their great Creator, who does
nothing in vain, has given them understandings, and a desire
to know; but besides this, they have a right, an indisputable
unalienable, indefeasible, divine right to that most dreaded
and envied kind of knowledge, I mean, of the characters
and conduct of their rulers.

—JOHN ADAMS, 1765

A VAST OIL PAINTING HANGS IN THE CAPITOL ROTUNDA, DEPICTING the moment George Washington willingly handed back power. That moment joins other signature founding American moments like the embarkation of the Pilgrims and the signing of the Declaration of Independence. For a country whose system of government sought a novel way to manage the rapacious desire for power in its leaders, it was an example of personal conduct that would protect the republic from the destruction that had befallen other governments. "Tis a Conduct so novel," said John Trumbull, the American painter who commemorated Washington's scene, "so inconceivable to People, who, far from giving up powers they possess, are willing to convulse the Empire to acquire more."[4]

By giving up power, Washington demonstrated his mastery of the personal impulses that had cracked kingdoms and felled republics. When King George III heard the general had put his country's interest above his own, he reportedly told the American-born artist Benjamin West: "If [Washington] does that, he will be the greatest man in the world."[5]

Washington had shown character, the second fundamental presidential attribute.

The idea of character is so central to the office that a PBS series on the presidency is titled *Character Above All*. The concept gets a fresh boost with the challenges of each generation, but the basic idea is that character is the instinct to do the right thing rather than the expedient, comfortable, or impulsive thing. "Virtue may be defined as the love of the laws and of our country," said Jefferson paraphrasing Montesquieu. "As such love requires a constant preference of public to private interest, it is the source of all private virtue. . . . Now a government is like everything else: to preserve it we must love it. . . . Everything, therefore, depends on establishing this love in a republic."[6]

The American presidency was created during the summer of 1787, but the first blocks of its foundation were placed four years earlier in George Washington's "preference of public to private interest." Nine months before his resignation, Washington had faced an even more powerful test of his character.

After defeating the British, Washington continued to train the Army. Pay for the men was spotty. The weak national government under the Articles of Confederation couldn't come up with the cash. The national government had to cajole the funds from each individual state, and the states were not paying their fair share—even for worthy causes like back pay for the soldiers who had fought and given those states their liberty.

To get their paychecks, officers under Washington's command conspired to threaten Congress. When Washington learned of their plot, he surprised his men at one of their secret counsels held in Newburgh, New York. "Gentlemen," he said, "by an anonymous summons, an attempt has been made to convene you together—how inconsistent with the rules of propriety! how unmilitary! and how subversive of all order and discipline."[7]

Washington sympathized with their grievance, but he violently disagreed with their methods—dishonorable conduct that amounted, in his view, to bullying and threatening a military coup. He heaped shame on them. Their plan soiled what they had fought for, and stained *his* integrity—since he had put his reputation behind the cause of forming a republic and gambled his virtue in support of it. "As you respect the rights of humanity, & as you regard the Military & national character of America, to express your utmost horror & detestation of the Man who wishes, under any specious pretences, to overturn the liberties of our Country, & who wickedly attempts to open the flood gates of Civil discord, & deluge our rising Empire in Blood."[8]

Midway through his remarks, Washington paused to put on his reading glasses. "Gentlemen, you must pardon me, I have grown grey in your service and now find myself going blind."[9] Soldiers in the audience reportedly wept.

The general could have joined his men in threatening Congress. He had the manpower and stature to have taken control as head of the new government.[10] He would have had a noble rationalization. What better cause than paying the soldiers, whose wives had been reduced to begging and whose children were starving?[11] The historian Richard Beeman identifies the choice Washington faced: Should he "remain loyal to his long-suffering troops or to honor the rule of law"?[12] Washington chose the rule of law. The ends did not justify the means. "The reasons for his behavior were so deeply buried in his character," writes the historian Joseph J. Ellis in *His Excellency*, "that they functioned like a biological condition requiring no further explanation."[13]

The framers of the Constitution, in search of a way to empower a president without inviting tyranny, found a solution in Washington's character. His restraint in favor of republican government bolstered the country's view of itself and its mission. He reaffirmed—and the protocol of his departure codified in official ceremony—that in America, no matter how powerful or famous one person might be, the republic and its values mattered more.[14]

CHARACTER'S COMPONENT PARTS

IN 1995, JAMES Q. WILSON UPDATED THE DEFINITION OF CHARACTER for modern times, breaking it into two component parts. "To have a good character means at least two things: empathy and self-control," he wrote in his book *On Character*, devoted to the topic. "Empathy refers to a willingness to take importantly into account the rights, needs, and feelings of others. Self-control refers to a willingness to take importantly into account the more distant consequences of present actions; to be in short somewhat future oriented rather than wholly present oriented."[15]

This definition of character locates the attribute in the office, taking the concept out of the realm of personal behavior (the realm, for instance, of affairs, or alleged affairs), where it is often discussed when referring to presidents, but where it ultimately is not that important to the job.

EMPATHY

EMPATHY IS A CRUCIAL ASPECT OF PRESIDENTIAL CHARACTER BECAUSE it is the bridging mechanism between what's required in modern campaigns, which force candidates to focus their attention on their political base, and the presidency, a job that requires representing the entire nation. The willingness to take into account the rights, needs, and feelings of others is necessary in order to represent everyone and not just the tribe whose chariot you rode in on.

Donald Trump has no time for empathy. That's not an opinion. It was his campaign position. When Jeb Bush suggested that undocumented immigrants fled to America out of love for their family, Donald Trump mocked him repeatedly. He also mimicked the idiosyncratic movements of a disabled reporter for his rally crowds in order to ridicule him. (The reporter's sin was accurately characterizing a newspaper article in which Trump was quoted.) Trump belittled the mother whose son, an Army captain, had been killed in combat. He said of Senator John McCain of Arizona, once a prisoner of war in Vietnam, "I like people that weren't captured." Bob Woodward reported that Trump's first chief of staff, Reince Priebus, said, "The President has zero psychological ability to [experience] empathy or pity in any way."[16]

Empathy is not merely a laudable human trait. It is politically useful. When a tragedy hits, the human impulse is to feel for those who suffer. When a president's empathy matches the public's human impulse, he improves his stature by being in sync with public feelings. In September 2019, at the swearing-in ceremony for Chairman of the Joint Chiefs of Staff Mark Milley, President Trump rushed to hug injured

Army captain Luis Avila after he sang "God Bless America."[17] Avila had been paralyzed by an improvised explosive device blast while deployed to Afghanistan. The singing was a part of his recovery therapy. Only the hardest heart would have let antipathy for the president get in the way of acknowledging the human moment.

Usually President Trump splices in a self-serving response when an empathetic one is expected. When fifty people died in the massacre at an Orlando nightclub, Trump responded by writing, "Appreciate the congrats for being right on radical Islamic terrorism, I don't want congrats, I want toughness & vigilance. We must be smart!"[18] The normal (and political) human reaction would be to feel shock and horror at the deaths, not to see them as validation of a policy position.

President Trump's bond with his supporters represents a certain kind of empathy. He understands their motives, can read their moods, and knows how to use both to his advantage. He doesn't face the challenges they do in their lives, or go to their churches, or even, in many cases, share their ideological views, but he understands them in a way they don't feel Barack Obama ever did. "What I read during 2016 about Trump from Trump supporters sounded like what fans said about Rush Limbaugh in the late '80s and early '90s," says historian Brian Rosenwald, author of *Talk Radio's America*. "You had a segment of society who felt like the rules had changed on them, and values they considered dear—and the key to American greatness—were under siege. They felt condescended to and voiceless. And while Reagan and Bush 2 were conservatives, and the latter was an evangelical, they looked up and saw that, if anything, they were further behind in the culture wars than they were in 1980s. And they wanted someone, who like their favorite broadcasters, didn't care about norms set by people whom they saw as hypocrites and fundamentally opposed to their values."[19] That understanding is the key to Trump's success, because many in his base have felt not just misunderstood, but inadequately represented by leaders who think they are not worth understanding. Part of Trump's power comes from being so quick to respond to these voters, to show respect for them, to affirm that they are not beneath notice.[20] This is a high-quality political skill, but it is a form of sympathy, not governing empathy of the kind Wilson writes about.

"Fellow-feeling, sympathy in the broadest sense," wrote Teddy Roosevelt, "is the most important factor in producing a healthy political and social life." The "broadest sense," as T.R. put it, means empathy that goes beyond the rally's edge.[21] That's what presidents are called to show. The professor of bioethics Peter Singer defines true empathy as an "expanding circle of moral concern," beginning with our own families and tribes and expanding outward to eventually include all of humanity.[22] Shared grievance and tribal ego can enable any of us to light up a certain group, but a president's job is to bind a nation and work for everyone in it.

Empathy between the president and the country presents itself in many different ways. When First Lady Betty Ford announced she had breast cancer, it brought the topic out of the shadows. Waves of women called their doctors. "Lying in the hospital, thinking of all those women going for cancer checkups because of me, I'd come to recognize more clearly the power of the woman in the White House," she wrote. "Not my power, but the power of the position, a power which could be used to help."

Empathy beyond the clubhouse requires making a pitch to transcendent ideas—common kinship or the American character. When candidates competed for a broader, less polarized electorate, a candidate couldn't get elected without knowing how to play broadly popular music. Pointing to the team jersey was not sufficient. Candidates thought about broader reasons the country was connected, so they could woo as many Americans as possible. This mode of campaigning prepared them for moments of national empathy in the job that required them to comfort a nation after a crisis.

It is a tough job, taking on the feelings, aspirations, and needs of people who didn't vote for you, but when leaders don't send a signal to all segments of the population, it creates the building blocks for upheaval. "Demand for recognition of one's identity is a master concept that unifies much of what is going on in world politics today," writes the Stanford political scientist Francis Fukuyama. Political leaders mobilize "followers around the perception that the group's dignity had been affronted, disparaged, or otherwise disregarded. This resentment engenders demands for public recognition of the dignity of the group in question. A humiliated group seeking restitution of its dignity carries far more emotional weight than people simply pursuing their economic advantage."[23]

When Hillary Clinton referred to Trump supporters as "deplorables," it burned long after she was no longer a candidate. When Barack Obama tried to explain how the forces of modern life caused certain voters to "cling to their guns and religion," it also left an indelible mark that lasted long after he was out of office.

Leaders who appear to have little use for the humanity of a group create the glue that keeps their opponents aligned against them. Donald Trump was elevated by this feeling, and as political scientists Lynn Vavreck, John Sides, and Michael Tesler show in *Identity Crisis*, he kept the campaign centered on it. As a president, he knows how to exploit this with the group that supports him, but that comes at the expense of kindling it in others.

SELF-CONTROL

THE SECOND ELEMENT OF JAMES Q. WILSON'S DEFINITION OF CHARacter is self-control: the ability to recognize the larger long-term obligations of the presidency and stick to them even when impulse and pique urge you in the opposite direction.

Self-control is the key attribute of President Eisenhower's Quadrant Two. It directs a president's time and attention to important issues that might not be the subject of today's news crawl on cable television but will be on there in the future. It sustains a president through the spadework of delivering for a member of Congress on some issue they care about in order to build obligations for a future request. It is the patience at the heart of politics that allows the negative capability ascribed to the best presidents who know how to let moments develop instead of stabbing for immediate results.

In our private lives, it is the spirit behind the savings account. It keeps you from yelling at your neighbor when he temporarily blocks your driveway, because you know you'll need his forbearance (or his snowblower) later. In governing and negotiations, self-control is the distance each side gives the other to keep from ruining negotiations. It recognizes that continuing to talk is better than going to war.

Maintaining self-control is a constant challenge for presidents. They tend to feel that because they're the most powerful person in the world, they should be able to get things to move quickly. When they can't, they want to lash out.

On May 24, 1946, Harry Truman handed his press secretary, Charlie Ross, twelve pages of ruled tablet paper, of the kind that children of a certain generation used to practice their letters. It was the script for a coast-to-coast radio broadcast about Truman's dispute with American labor leaders. The steel and railroad bosses had threatened to strike if the government didn't lift postwar wage controls. Truman asked Ross to type up the speech. "I'm going to take the hide right off those sons of bitches," he said.[24]

The curled pages Ross held in his hand were the product of a splenetic outburst in which President Truman charged the labor bosses with greed stretching back to the recently concluded world war. Truman charged that their worker strikes were "worse than bullets in the back of our soldiers." The speech amounted to a national locker room oration. "Let's give the country back to the people," he planned to say. "Let's put transportation and production back to work, hang a few traitors, and make our own country safe for democracy. Come on, boys, let's do the job!"

The former haberdasher was calling for a necktie party. Ross showed the "hang a few traitors" language to Truman adviser Clark Clifford. "It was surely one of the most intemperate documents ever written by a president," Clifford recalled. "The president's handwritten message struck me as perilously out of control."[25]

Truman's team rewrote the speech. Truman had fired off these "longhand spasms" before, and it met the same end. "He expected his trusted inner staff to prevent him from going public with his fury," wrote Clifford of the episode. (The tablet pages now rest in the Truman presidential library as a symbol of the time the president nearly forgot himself in public.)[26]

Presidential character is an individual and group effort. If the chief executive can't stay on the rails, aides nudge him back so that he doesn't act so foolishly that voters, congressional rivals, and world leaders stop taking him seriously. A president can sap the confidence and authority needed for future national conversations or push negotiating partners into corners those adversaries can't get out of without losing too much face.

Understanding the power of speech and self-control over what you say is as important for CEOs as it is for presidents. When Marshall Goldsmith worked with the pharmaceutical CEO Jean-Pierre Garnier, he asked him what he had learned about leadership as the head of GlaxoSmithKline. "My suggestions become orders," Garnier told him. "If they're smart, they're orders. If they're stupid, they're orders. If I don't want them to be orders, they're orders anyway." He continued, "Before I speak, I breathe and ask myself, is this worth it?"[27]

With Donald Trump there is no distance between the president's pique and his public expression of it. Donald Trump's Twitter account pings with the frequency of radar offering a real-time picture of the location of his id. The press briefing has given way to chopper talk, as the president shouts answers to reporters over the deafening whir of his helicopter on the South Lawn of the White House.

The institutional filter between the president and the public is gone. This gives a president the ability to quickly change the narrative, but it also diminishes the brand. President Trump is the wallpaper of American life. The special power of presidential communication is diminished. It also runs the risk of becoming annoying. As FDR wrote, "I know . . . that the public psychology and, for that matter, individual psychology cannot, because of human weakness, be attuned for long periods of time to a constant repetition of the highest note in the scale."[28]

During the 2016 campaign, the media lapped up the Trump show. Cable channels carried Trump speeches live. Sometimes cable news channels showed an empty podium awaiting his arrival into the throbbing auditorium. "The aim of life is not autonomy in the sense of a life regulated by exacting standards," writes George F. Will of the age of Trump, "but rather 'authenticity' in following strong feelings."[29] Authenticity in the instant has eclipsed self-control and everything else as a key presidential attribute. Wilson's criteria for character are not just gone, in Donald Trump's case they have been replaced with an affection for the exact opposite value. "I like Trump on Twitter," said a participant at a *Face the Nation* focus group, "because you know everything he posts is coming directly from Trump. It's what he thinks himself, no one else."[30] Immediacy and authenticity are more valuable than substance.

This instinct has carried over to his party. When Trump was accused of self-dealing by scheduling the G7 at his Doral, Miami, golf club, Senator Kevin Cramer of North Dakota applauded him. "It may seem careless politically, but on the other hand there's tremendous integrity in his boldness and his transparency."[31] How much has that standard changed? Ronald Reagan, by contrast, removed George Allen as head of the president's physical fitness program because the private interests of the former Redskins coach created an ethical conflict.[32]

With no guidelines in modern campaigns, voters refashion their standard for presidential behavior based on what they see immediately before them. "Having that celebrity personality and projecting an image in the media is more important than traditional qualifications," Bob Tyson, a retired database consultant and Trump supporter, told *The Washington Post*'s Dan Balz. "It's made me think differently about what it takes to be elected president. The traditional path of being a state governor or U.S. senator doesn't seem to count as much. It's being able to manage your image in the media and galvanizing your base."[33]

During the campaign, Donald Trump pumped constant high-octane authenticity. He was self-indulgent and brash in the incendiary way that wins big ratings on reality shows. "I know more about ISIS than the generals do! Believe me," he told an Iowa crowd. "I always wanted to get the Purple Heart," he said at a Virginia rally when a supporter gave him one. "This was much easier." When the frantic pace of the campaign seemed to slow, he punctured another norm to a roar of approval.

Pundits wondered whether he was "presidential," which only thrilled his allies more. It was like criticizing a contestant on *Survivor* for bad spelling. "My use of social media is not Presidential," Trump tweeted. "It's MODERN DAY PRESIDENTIAL. Make America Great Again!" Jerry Falwell, Jr., enthused in a tweet: "Complaining about the temperament of the @POTUS or saying his behavior is not presidential is no longer relevant. @realDonaldTrump has single-handedly changed the definition of what behavior is 'presidential' from phony, failed & rehearsed to authentic, successful & down to earth."[34]

A campaign that so thoroughly rewarded showing no self-control invites a presidency without it. "When somebody says something about me, I am able to go bing, bing, bing and I take care of it,"[35] Trump said about using his Twitter account to attack actors and television personalities from Alec Baldwin to Debra Messing to Stephen Colbert. When Fox News anchor Ed Henry suggested the president had done something wrong by pressuring the president of Ukraine to do him a political favor, the American president shared more than twenty tweets disparaging Henry in a period of twenty-one minutes.[36]

The presidency was once primarily an interior job. Presidents had any number of experiences the public never witnessed or even knew had occurred. It has now become external and iterative, and with Donald Trump, raw and public. We used to have to wait for diaries to understand how a president felt. Donald Trump tweets his diary in real time. Quiet, unseen acts have been replaced by constant output designed to generate ratings and excitement and distraction. It's a marvel that the presidential Thanksgiving turkey pardoning ritual hasn't been turned into more of a cliff-hanger, though with presidential standards of basic attributes like honesty and character being rewritten, that possibility is still open.

Chapter 29

It's My Party

—

I could stand in the middle of Fifth Avenue and shoot
somebody and I wouldn't lose voters.[1]

— DONALD TRUMP

DONALD TRUMP HAS REWRITTEN THE FUNDAMENTAL RULES
of the presidency through modification of its basic tenets of character
and honesty. His party, whose members believed in the necessity of
maintaining the sturdiness of those tenets, has not penalized him but
has rallied to his cause. Whether this represents a permanent change in
the presidency depends on whether Democrats who identify each of
Trump's transgressions will use his techniques when they regain presidential power.

To understand why President Trump's approval rating remains
stratospheric among his party, we must return to the Cedar Rapids
newspaper from September 29, 1956, cited at the start of this book.
Printed above the breathless news on that day about Ike's new campaign strategy was even bigger news: DEMOCRAT TO THE HIGH COURT.
Just a month before Election Day, Eisenhower, the Republican president seeking reelection nominated a Democrat, William Brennan, to
the Supreme Court.

Eisenhower named a Democrat in order to help him with the 1956
electorate, in which Democrats crossed over to vote for members of the
other party. Eisenhower won twenty-two states that had at least one
Democratic senator. By 2016, the structural political encouragement

for bipartisanship was gone, and an open seat on the Supreme Court revealed a clear ordering of priorities within the Republican Party. For Republican voters, having a say in the cultural and identity issues influenced by the court was the most important issue. To secure influence on the court, they'd back a candidate who flouted the moral and policy standards they had once believed were inviolate.

In March 2016, Barack Obama nominated Merrick Garland to the Supreme Court in that election year just as Eisenhower had. Garland was no Republican, but he had received 32 Republican votes when he last faced Senate confirmation to the D.C. appellate court in 1997.[2, 3] Seven of the Republicans who had voted for him still served in the Senate. Nevertheless, the GOP Senate majority leader, Mitch McConnell, blocked the nomination from consideration in the Senate. Leader McConnell knew his party would benefit with their voters by blocking the Supreme Court pick more than they would be penalized by Democrats, or nonaffiliated voters who might think his denying the president's nominee consideration was dirty pool. Donald Trump cheered him on. He did not follow the Eisenhower tradition or Nixon's position in 1968, when in the summer of that election year, as the GOP nominee, Nixon said the Senate should not block a Democratic president's Supreme Court nominee from consideration.

Conservatives focus on the Court so much, in part, because of President Eisenhower. Ike was broadly popular in the nation, but conservatives hated his court picks. They saw unelected men making generations-long decisions that trampled freedom, created new rights for criminals, and undermined the other branches of government. William Brennan would go on to form a liberal bloc on the court, along with Eisenhower's other pick, Earl Warren. (Eisenhower would say later in his career that he regretted picking both men because they were so liberal.)

Republican diehards had other complaints in 1956 with Ike. They believed Ike had been too soft on the New Deal. He had accommodated the government blob, allowing a big, intrusive bureaucracy to trample the core American values of self-reliance and freedom. Barry Goldwater, the party's nominee in 1964, scorned the two-term general's "modern Republicanism" as a "dime store New Deal."

The conservative movement that couldn't scratch Ike back then,

*"Nobody's done more to change the court system in the history
of our country than Donald Trump," said Senate Majority Leader
Mitch McConnell at a Make America Great Again rally.
"And Mr. President, we're gonna keep on doing it.
My motto is, 'Leave no vacancy behind.'"*

now dominates his party. The bloc cares so much about the makeup of
the court that they don't leave it to the president. For the last thirty-
eight years, the Federalist Society has groomed lawmakers and candidates to ensure that conservative justices are placed in the lower courts
and elevated to the top spots. In 2016, the Federalist Society achieved
its greatest victory when the Supreme Court seat opened up after the
conservative justice Antonin Scalia died.

When Scalia's death was announced, a moment of instantaneous
sync took place between Donald Trump and the GOP establishment.
They had not been cozy before. At one point during the campaign,
Trump said he wasn't even a member of the Republican Party. Mitch
McConnell agreed, privately predicting that Trump would lose the primaries because "the Republican Party is not going to nominate someone who isn't a conservative."[4]

When it came to the issue of judges, though, Trump performed all
the compulsory routines of his party with perfection and wowed the
Federalist Society judges with innovation in the freestyle competition.
Trump released a list of preapproved conservative judges he promised

he would elevate to the high court. The list had been formed with the advice of his future White House counsel Don McGahn, a Federalist Society stalwart.

Trump's list of names not only helped convince voters he would elevate a conservative into that slot, but that he would elevate the right kind of conservative. Mitch McConnell and a host of others believe that naming a specific list of conservatives won Trump the election. No matter what people thought of Trump, they knew if they put him in office, they would be able to influence the direction of the courts.

As president, Donald Trump kept his promise. He named two conservatives to the Supreme Court—Neil Gorsuch and Brett Kavanaugh—locking in a conservative majority. In his first year, he appointed more judges to the appeals court than any previous president, flipping the ideological balance of three of the thirteen circuit courts from liberal to conservative.[5] By November 2019, Trump celebrated getting more than 150 federal judicial nominees confirmed by the Senate.[6, 7] Since these judges have lifetime appointments, these changes will transform America for the next generation.

Ken Starr, the special counsel who investigated President Bill Clinton and wrote the famous report detailing Clinton's sexual relationship with Monica Lewinsky, explained how Trump's judicial picks work on Republican voters. "People sign up with a political party and now the loyalty to President Trump—not because of his personality," he said. "I think people have to look past his personality . . . because of what his agenda has been. Remember the Supreme Court appointments; that covers—as we say—a multitude of sins."[8]

"It's transformational," says Leonard Leo, executive vice president of the Federalist Society, of Trump's court picks. "There are probably more consequential five-to-four decisions sitting there right now in the Supreme Court of the United States than there have been through most of modern history."[9] Leo also notes the historic number of conservative lower court judges that have been appointed during Trump's tenure, creating a farm team of conservative jurists who can be elevated to the Supreme Court one day and whose conservative decisions not only affect the kinds of cases the high court will rule on but often set the legal parameters for how the Supreme Court will view those cases.

"What puts him in best of class here is his determination, his entrepreneurial spirit, his willingness to take risks on this issue," says Leo of Trump. "If you look at what presidential candidates like Mitt Romney and the Bushes and so forth said about judges, it was all well and good but there was no real risk in saying I'm going to appoint justices in the mold of Scalia and Thomas. Trump went well beyond that and both in terms of who he was talking about but also how he talked about the issues."

DEREGULATION ENERGY

TRUMP HAS APPLIED THE SAME PATTERN TO REDUCING REGULATIONS, another area of key concern to Republican voters. He has even followed the same management approach he did on judges, outsourcing the strategy and implementation to staff that could work on those areas relatively unfazed by the excitement he was creating in the day-to-day West Wing operations.

George W. Bush's political guru and White House strategist Karl Rove started the process of identifying regulations before Trump was ever elected. He worked with Steven Law, a Republican strategist and former aide to Mitch McConnell, backed by the cofounder and first CEO of Home Depot, Bernie Marcus, one of Donald Trump's largest donors. Rove and Law gathered a team of conservative lawyers, some who had worked in federal agencies under George W. Bush. They drew up a plan of attack to unwind regulations in agencies through every tool available.[10]

The Congressional Review Act was a key device. This law allows regulations to be removed by Congress sixty days after they've been written. In its history, it had eliminated only one rule—a regulation on ergonomics Bill Clinton enacted during his final year in office. In less than four months during the Trump administration, Congress and the president wiped away fourteen rules covering everything from limits on the dumping of waste from surface mining operations to expanding states' power to offer retirement accounts to private sector workers.

A host of executive orders in the early days of the Trump administration pushed agency heads to use their discretion to target everything from Obama's clean power plant rule to rules that regulate for-profit colleges. "Hamilton talks about energy in the executive. This administration really used executive orders as the transmission belt for that energy," says Adam White, a regulatory expert at the conservative Hoover Institution. "It used executive orders, political appointees, and real investment of political capital."[11]

President Trump has not built a record of achievement in the traditional sense—marshaling public will and Congress to meet the biggest challenges of the day that can only be attacked through collective action. His record of legislative achievement is weak, particularly given that he controlled both houses of Congress in his first two years. What Trump has done is deliver for his base. In addition to the issues of regulation and judges, he has cut personal and corporate taxes. Together, these three issues represent the top domestic Republican priorities. He has also increased Defense spending and given military leaders a freer hand on the battlefield to make decisions, other long-standing Republican priorities.

Donald Trump is operating in the presidency as it is. In a time of high partisanship, he is using the levers he can to achieve results for the people who elected him. "You've got to find areas where you can flex your muscles," says Leo. "In a place where there's congressional malaise or inaction, [regulations and judicial appointments] are two areas where you can do that."

Tim Cook talks about blocking noise for his employees as a mode of leadership; Trump has done that for these priorities. He has taken the political heat for the entrepreneurial activity of members of his administration—whether it is military operations that cause more casualties, separating migrant children from their parents and putting them in caged cells, or new rules that limit food stamp distribution or encourage more coal production. Trump has been willing to take on the moral sanction for these policies with a thickness of skin few other presidents would show on behalf of their team's priorities.

This has made the forty-fifth president very popular among the GOP stalwarts. During periods when Trump's average approval rating in the country was the lowest among all recent presidents, his popularity within his own party was as high as his more popular predecessors' had been with their parties. He has also been the most popular politician in conservative media.

These achievements make it difficult for Trump's critics within his party. Senators Jeff Flake, Bob Corker, and Mitt Romney all criticized Trump in strong rhetorical blasts, but that did not stop them from voting with him regularly. This ratifies the low opinion Trump supporters have of career politicians. They are all talk. Whatever complaints GOP critics might make, at the end of the day, they like winning too.

RESHAPING THE REPUBLICAN PARTY

THE SUCCESS THAT TRUMP HAS ACHIEVED THROUGH HIS LACK OF INTEREST in feigning interest in bipartisanship or unity has significantly reoriented his party. To accommodate their new leader, Republican politicians have dropped previous positions on significant issues like trade, the federal budget deficit, comprehensive immigration, and military intervention. On cultural issues, the GOP base has become more tolerant of transgressions they once identified as threats to the family and fabric of American life—including the moral relativism that excuses transgressions in the light of political achievement.

It is not new that a party in power would excuse itself from breaking the specific rules it said were cast in iron. The feminist icon Gloria Steinem found ways to defend Bill Clinton amid the tumbling revelations that he had made several unwanted sexual advances. What is new with the support for Donald Trump, though, is the number and scope of the reversals in GOP ranks.

"I was a Republican in the Senate for twelve years and we cared about fiscal issues, world leadership, and free trade," former Tennessee senator Bob Corker said in October 2019. "I look at the Republican Party now and we are isolationist, protectionist, and care nothing about keeping these institutions that have kept the world safe in many ways."[12]

The Republican Party's reversal on immigration policy offers the starkest shift. After the 2012 election, the Republican Party commissioned an "autopsy" to explain why it had lost the popular vote in five of the last six elections. Most of the report was vague, but that vagueness was pierced by one clear policy recommendation: "We must embrace and champion comprehensive immigration reform," wrote the autopsy's authors. "If we do not, our Party's appeal will continue to shrink to its core constituencies only."[13] The Fox commentator Sean Hannity had a public revelation and supported comprehensive immi-

gration reform. "You create a pathway for those people that are here—
you don't say you've got to go home," he said. "And that is a position
that I've evolved on. Because, you know what, it's got to be resolved.
The majority of people here, if some people have criminal records you
can send them home, but if people are here, law-abiding, participating
for years, their kids are born here, you know, it's first secure the border,
pathway to citizenship, done."[14]

Then Donald Trump arrived, winning the nomination and presidency with positions that were on the metaphysically opposite side of
the party position and the position of GOP elites like Hannity. Trump's
position caused a complete reversal. It now dominates the GOP.
Reince Priebus, the previous chairman of the party, who commissioned
the autopsy containing pro-immigration stances, became the first chief
of staff of the Trump presidency. His successor as head of the Republican Party, Ronna McDaniel, defended a Trump television commercial
about a caravan of migrants that even Fox News would not run because
it was considered too racist.[15]

Republicans have also stowed their free trade principles. The last
significant bipartisan pieces of legislation to warrant a bipartisan signing ceremony during the Obama administration gave the president
authority to make trade deals more easily. Even in a time of high partisanship, Republicans turned out for a Democratic president's signing
ceremony because the issue of free trade was noncontroversial. Republicans now support the policies of a president who calls himself "Tariff
Man."

Trump's commitment to restricting trade has been so thorough—in
the name of rebalancing U.S. trade disadvantages with countries like
China—he was willing to tolerate a slowdown in the economy. In October 2019, Trump's trade policies led to the lowest level of manufacturing since the great recession in 2008. The conservative Tax Foundation
found the Trump administration had so far imposed nearly $80 billion
worth of new taxes on Americans by levying tariffs on thousands of
products, which is equivalent to one of the largest tax increases in decades.[16]

The reversal on trade has led to a reversal on the GOP's view toward
government assistance. Conservatives have opposed bailouts of various
kinds, most notably the Troubled Asset Relief Program after the

mortgage-backed securities collapse, as well as assistance to the auto industry. By the fall of 2019, that historic opposition had been reversed The GOP-backed bailouts to farmers harmed by Trump's trade wars were twice the size of the auto bailout.[17]

The Republican Party's starkest rhetorical deficit relates to the fiscal deficit. For my entire career covering American politics, there was one topic certain to come up at the GOP's Lincoln Day dinners or rallies: the coming collapse if the United States didn't address its debt and deficits. Candidates running for dogcatcher campaigned on fiscal responsibility.[18] The Republican Party used to be described as a three-legged stool, and one of those legs was represented by "fiscal conservatives." (Evangelical voters and voters who cared about national security made up the other two legs.) The Tea Party movement arose in 2009 out of a professed aversion to deficit spending.

Now the issue of debts and deficits has virtually disappeared from the Republican conversation. As President Trump's director of the Office of Management and Budget, Mick Mulvaney, admitted, "My party is very interested in deficits when there is a Democrat in the White House. The worst thing in the whole world was deficits when Barack Obama was the president. Then Donald Trump became president, and we're a lot less interested as a party."[19]

Donald Trump's policies, including his signature domestic achievement, the tax cut, have ballooned the deficit beyond even the most pessimistic estimates. Long-term entitlement costs continue to rise with no plan for reform in place or advocated by the president or leaders in Congress. At President Trump's 2020 State of the Union, Republicans responded with a standing ovation when the president announced a new benefit of paid family leave, the kind of federal guarantee party leaders once used to rail against.

Overseas, Trump has replaced the idea of American Exceptionalism with America First. The two sound the same, but the latter lacks the moral component, which was once a part of Republican politics. As a self-declared "nationalist," Trump is skeptical of the conventions of interconnectedness—support for allies, promotion of institutions of liberal democracies—that he believes restrict America from pursuing its interests. He has repeatedly asserted, for example, that the United States is in no position to make moral claims in Russia, Turkey, Saudi

Arabia, or the Philippines because our own nation is "no saint." In this conception, America pursues an America First policy not because it is uniquely morally right—or because it has been the guarantor and promoter of the liberal order for decades—but because it, like all nations, should pursue the maximalist advantage for its own ends.

NEW GOP VALUES

PRESIDENT TRUMP HAS CHANGED REPUBLICAN VIEWS ABOUT VALUES too. In a 2011 poll conducted by the Public Religion Research Institute (PRRI) and the Religion News Service, 60 percent of white evangelicals believed a public official who "commits an immoral act in their personal life" cannot "behave ethically and fulfill their duties in their public and professional life."[20] Five years later, an October 2016 poll by PRRI and the Brookings Institution—after the release of the infamous *Access Hollywood* tape—found that only 20 percent of evangelicals, responding to the same question, thought private immorality meant someone could not behave ethically in public.

In 1976, Jimmy Carter had been wounded politically by his revelation in a *Playboy* interview that he had "lusted in my heart" by thinking about other women. In forty years, the moral relativism that conservatives worried was allowing standards to slip had taken hold.

Broader ideas of morality have also taken a hit. Between 1994 and 1999, 86 percent of Republicans thought it was important for the president to provide moral leadership.[21] In 2018, 63 percent of Republicans agreed with that statement, a 23-point decrease.

Honesty isn't what it used to be either. In 2007, an Associated Press / Yahoo! poll found 71 percent of Republicans saying it was "extremely important" for presidential candidates to be honest, similar to 70 percent of Democrats and 66 percent of independents.[22] A 2018 *Washington Post* poll showed identical shares of Democrats and independents prioritizing honesty in presidential candidates, but the share of Republicans who said honesty was extremely important had fallen to 49 percent,[23] 22 points lower than in the AP / Yahoo! poll from the pre-Trump era.

The change in standards is not happening quietly. There are ugly public bursts. To square Trump's private behavior with the office, some

Few thought it could happen, but Donald Trump beat the more experienced politicians of his party and reoriented it toward his vision. Once a candidate who flirted with leaving the party, President Trump came to define it.

of his evangelical supporters simply made things up. The Reverend Robert Jeffress defended Trump's private behavior by saying evangelicals had also supported the "known womanizer" Ronald Reagan. Tearing down the patron saint of the Republican Party to make excuses for Donald Trump was startling enough, but it wasn't even true. Reagan was not a known womanizer, and when Republicans supported him for the presidency, he had been married to Nancy Reagan for nearly thirty years.

In April 2018, the Trump administration took a "zero tolerance" stance against anyone who attempted to enter the country illegally, which led to the separation of children from their guardians at the U.S.-Mexico border. The number of detained migrant children reached its highest—12,800—in June 2018, according to data obtained by *The New York Times*.[24] A year later, reports surfaced that hundreds of migrant children were being detained at a Texas border facility in "perilous conditions." Russell Moore, president of the Southern Baptist Convention's Ethics and Religious Liberty Commission, tweeted, "The reports of the conditions for migrant children at the border should shock all of our consciences. Those created in the image of God should be treated with dignity and compassion, especially those seeking refuge from violence back home. We can do better than this."[25]

The plaintive cry received a klaxon blast in return from Jerry Falwell, Jr., the president of Liberty University. Falwell's endorsement had helped Trump build support in the evangelical community during a crucial turn in the primaries. He asked: "Who are you @drmoore? Have you ever made a payroll? Have you ever built an organization of any type from scratch? What gives you authority to speak on any issue? I'm being serious. You're nothing but an employee—a bureaucrat."[26]

One did not need a seminary degree to recognize that this was a secular, not religious, denunciation. Moore is an ordained Southern Baptist minister who has been the head of a church. Falwell was trying to cancel Moore's right to speak from a religious perspective because he lacked secular qualifications. "It has caused us to call evil good and good evil," wrote the evangelical author Nancy French of the affection for Donald Trump. "Very quietly, the 'lesser of two evils' edict morphed from 'opposing Hillary Clinton at all costs' into even attacking good people who question the president."[27]

Trump's Standards Have Changed

President Trump has changed his standards too. As a private citizen, Donald Trump served as a sentinel of presidential propriety, weighing in on everything from presidential golf to the president's style of negotiating. The man who announced his candidacy with an escalator ride even had a stance on stair etiquette. "The way President Obama runs down the stairs of Air Force 1, hopping & bobbing all the way, is so inelegant and unpresidential," he wrote in April 2014. "Do not fall!"[28]

The president's censures as a civilian have become uncanny predictors of his future behavior as president. Just about everything he once identified as unpresidential he has now done: attacking Syria without congressional approval; golfing excessively, including during an emergency; campaigning while in office; criticizing Bob Woodward; bantering with a rapper during a national emergency; and replacing his chief of staff three times in the first two years.[29] "Repubs must not allow Pres Obama to subvert the Constitution of the US for his own benefit and because he is unable to negotiate w/ Congress," he wrote on November 14, 2014.[30] Five years later, on February 14, 2019, President Trump announced executive action to fund his border wall, circumventing the will of Congress after negotiations crumbled. Even *Air Force One* etiquette occasioned a parallel, when President Trump mounted the stairs and discarded an open umbrella at the top, leaving it to loll in the wind until someone fetched it.

The list of contradictory Trump tweets scrolls out for several feet. There are so many that a hashtag #theresalwaysatweet has evolved to highlight a tweet from Donald Trump's past that directly sanctions his present behavior.

Political parties rarely turn the wheel as hard and fast as the Republican Party has under Donald Trump. However, the Trump revolution may not be a revolution at all. When LBJ signed the Civil Rights Act in 1965, he prophesied that he had just lost the Democratic Party in the South for a generation because so many conservative Democrats didn't support the rights he was protecting for black Americans. He was right, and it created a shift in American politics. Donald Trump took the helm of his party and there were few real defections. He has been supported at nearly every turn by an overwhelming majority of lawmakers, including some he has publicly and personally humiliated.[31] So he may not have changed his party as much as he brought it in line with its core supporters by stripping away the elite level.

Not everyone has fallen in line. The shift in positions has given rise to a species known as the Never Trumper, a small band of former Republicans opposing the president by making the case for presidential standards. They clash with former allies who have chosen to ride the Trump train and who see criticism about their choice as moral smugness and elitism. They argue that the Never Trumpers cling to outdated manners inadequate to the demands of the age.

Chapter 30

The Uncertain Never Trumper

—

If we don't go off script, our country is in big trouble.[1]

—DONALD TRUMP

MEMBERS OF MAGA NATION CHEER PRESIDENT TRUMP by the glow of burning norms. His departures from traditional presidential standards illustrate Donald Trump's essential insight: The old codes of the job hurt the country and hurt those voters who support him. Norms are the white-glove traditions of special interests and political elites. Victor Davis Hanson in his book *The Case for Trump* summed it up by quoting Kissinger: "I think Trump may be one of those figures in history who appear from time to time to mark the end of an era and to force it to give up its old pretense."[2]

Trump operates in the world as it is, not a phony world bobbing on the foam of Washington politesse. Unburdened by political correctness and the old rules, the president doesn't let table manners get in the way of taking care of business. Breaking the rules is proof he's doing as he promised. It's not cacophony you hear; it's industrious hammering on the institution. As Trump told the Conservative Political Action Conference during a two-hour stream-of-consciousness oration, "if we don't go off script, our country is in big trouble."

Why should President Trump push for quick results in Puerto Rico when the island's poor planning and weak infrastructure have made success impossible? Why should he waste time trying to court Democrats who will never work with him anyway? If North Korea can be brought to negotiate over its nuclear weapons, why shame its leader for his regime's raft of murders, including that of a young American college student? It is true, as the president says, that America spies on its allies and has supported coups and assassinations.

Trump supporters don't quote George Washington, they quote Machiavelli: "The fact is that a man who wants to act virtuously in every way necessarily comes to grief among the many who are not virtuous. Therefore, if a prince wants to maintain his rule he must learn how not to be virtuous, and to make use of this or not according to need."

Conservatives who raise questions about standards are mocked. Anyone who raises a hand and points out that the president lied or is acting boorishly, crudely, or in an unchristian way is lampooned. Trump critics "suffer from a terrible case of moral superiority and put their own vanity and taste above the interest of the country," said Bill Bennett, the author of *The Book of Virtues*, in defense of Trump.[3]

The change in tone is stark. It would be the equivalent of a Democratic president in 2021 after the rise of the Me Too movement teaching his party to snicker at anyone who complained about a few fanny pats at work.

"Yes, the president is speaking mistruths," explained Trump's evanescent communications director Anthony Scaramucci on Bloomberg TV. "Yes, the president is lying. But he's doing it intentionally to incite certain people which would include left-leaning journalists and most of the left-leaning politicians. So what ends up happening is they come out like a hall monitor in the elementary school or your high school and they say, 'Oh, wow, the president is lying.' And his base is basically laughing at them. If someone is taking your lunch money in the cafeteria, if you call the hall monitor it's not going to help you."[4]

The GOP used to be the hall monitors. It was the conservative refrigerator on which the Emerson quotation was taped for the kids to look at in the morning before school: "There never was a strong people that did not rank subordination and discipline among the signal virtues. Subjection to moods is the mark of a deteriorating morality. There is no baser servitude than that of the man whose caprices are his masters, and a nation composed of such men could not long preserve its liberties."[5]

The classicist and war historian Victor Davis Hanson compares Trump to a long line of flawed heroes whose deficiencies are an impediment to the job as conventionally conceived, but who are nevertheless necessary to meet the unconventional moment. He cites Homer's Achilles, Sophocles' Ajax, and the western film heroes Shane, the Magnificent Seven, and Marshal Will Kane. Pious townspeople call in the gunslinger because they can't do the job themselves. They know he is not a good person, but they need his skills.

Hanson doesn't defend Trump's character. He calls him "vulgar, uncouth and divisive" but then reminds readers of the personal flaws of Democratic presidents John Kennedy, Lyndon Johnson, and Bill Clinton.[6] Hanson argues that the times call for sublimating character to effectiveness. Only someone unburdened by the niceties—or "presidential" qualities, as Hanson puts it—can get the job done.

The real moral question, Hanson writes, is not whether the gunslinger Trump could or should become civilized (or "presidential"). Instead, "the key is whether he could be of service at the opportune time and right place for his country, crude as he is. After all, despite their decency, in extremis did the frontier farmers have an orthodox solution without Shane? Mexican peasants did not enjoy a realistic alternative to the Magnificent Seven, and the town elders of Hadleyville had no viable plan without Marshal Will Kane in the streets."[7]

What justifies hiring the gunslinger, in Hanson's view? The threat from China, mostly. Trump has used his brash and unpredictable ways to rebalance the adversarial relationship. Even Democrats like the goal, even if they don't think much of the way President Trump is carrying out his trade war. Trump has also maneuvered North Korea into at least having conversations with the United States. Trump's economic policies have contributed to strong growth and low unemployment across all groups and some wage gains in areas that were stagnant.

These might be preferred outcomes but are they really outcomes for which there was no "orthodox solution"? Mitt Romney would have confronted China with just as much focus. The Trump process with North Korea looks no more profitable than the Clinton team's approach, which was labeled "appeasement."[8] The gunslinger is supposed to save the whole town, not just those who have hired him.

The useful gunslinger analogy also works against Trump. His considerable partisan victories work for those who hired him, but not the whole town. It also elides consequences. We never get to see how the town got on after the gunslinger headed over the hills.

In elections dominated by negative partisanship, Hanson's hired-gunslinger framing builds in a ready-made excuse for anything the president may do. Voters spurred by negative partisanship think the other party is destroying the country. Therefore, the other party is always the danger that justifies doing whatever it takes. That was the argument at the heart of the essay written before the 2016 election by Trump's national security spokesperson, Michael Anton, who dubbed it the "Flight 93" election, referring to the plane whose passengers rushed the cockpit to crash it in a Pennsylvania field on 9/11 in order to save the targets on the ground from the terrorist hijackers.[9] Anton argued that the consequences of a Hillary Clinton victory would be so dire that it was worth electing Donald Trump.

Creating an excuse structure for basic partisanship invites the opposite party to do it as a response, which already crept into the 2020 Democratic primary as candidates promised executive orders and administrative actions to undo Trump's actions. On the left, the existential threats from climate change, mass gun violence, and the human rights abuses of children held in cages at the border are sufficient emergencies to flatten anyone making structural objections to how a Democratic president might use the office. If Democrats use Trump techniques for their ends, it would invite a similar response to continue the cycle. This escalation was all foretold by the authors of the Constitution.

NEVER TRUMPERS

A SMALL GROUP OF CONSERVATIVES HAS RESISTED THE TRUMP presidency. Known as "Never Trumpers," these pundits, former GOP officials, and campaign operatives ask how a movement that once cared so much about standards could shed those standards, and even the idea of objective measurement, so quickly. This is about more than Donald Trump. The transactional justifications made for his presidency could just as easily be made for a Democratic candidate. At issue in the era of Trump is whether the core elements of the presidency are not as fixed as was once believed. If that's so, what really constrains the office? The presidency is overburdened and needs an update. Is abandoning moral standards and the values that have governed America the solution?

The matter of presidential standards is a concern that was raised at the creation of the office. At the Constitutional Convention, South Carolina delegate Pierce Butler was skeptical that a presidency founded on the virtue of its occupant could be maintained. He worried that presidents motivated by personal gain rather than virtue would take advantage of the loose construction of the office. "Many of the members [at the convention] cast their eyes toward General Washington and shaped their ideas and powers to be given to the President, by their opinions of Washington's virtue," he said. "So that the man, who by his patriotism and virtue contributed largely to the emancipation of his country may be the innocent means of its being, when he is laid low, oppressed."[10]

Butler worried that the presidency contained a Washington weakness. Affection for Washington, and for the office made in his image, allowed delegates to project appealing qualities upon the office that it did not inherently have, or lulled them into letting down their guard in protecting the future against encroachment by designing presidents. Washington injected virtue into the marrow of the office, but would that make the nation vulnerable in the future to a poisonous president who would inject something darker?

Never Trumpers are unconvinced by justifications that the country needs Donald Trump to save America from the forces of evil. The expedient have always used ends-justify-the-means arguments. The power-seeking have always been ready authors of emergency narratives that justify their actions. The framers of the Constitution set up the system of shared powers to block just such use of emergencies as a pretext for excessive behavior. Trump's partisan successes in nominating conservative judges and deleting regulations from the Federal Register are not worth the long-term cost of splintering the party, hollowing out its moral core, and dividing the country, say the Never Trumpers. In short, they argue, winning at all costs has costs and the ends for which their former allies are sacrificing themselves will increasingly become the president's personal preferences, making them harder to defend.

They point out that the Republican Party was once defined by opposition to the relativism now used to defend Donald Trump. William

Buckley, founder of the *National Review*, described the conservative magazine's mission: "It stands athwart history, yelling Stop, at a time when no one is inclined to do so, or to have much patience with those who so urge it."[11] The modern Republican Party grew from the idea that stable, traditional notions about individual freedom and proper conduct were the shield against corrosive fads of the moment. Tom DeLay, the Republican House majority whip, argued that the Clinton impeachment proceedings were "a debate about relativism versus absolute truth."[12]

Now, Jonah Goldberg of the *National Review* asks: If conservatives are going with the flow by supporting Donald Trump, on what basis will they yell "Stop" in the future?

> "What can the next Democratic president do that you won't look like a hypocrite for criticizing?" No doubt there are some plausible policy answers to this. After all, Trump hasn't pushed socialized medicine—at least not as president. But in terms of almost every other metric of the president's role and responsibilities, Trump's most unequivocal defenders are leaving themselves stranded on a very small parcel of ground to stand upon once the Trump presidency is over. And their new attitude toward the issue of character barely leaves enough ground to stand on one foot.[13]

MORALITY AND ECONOMICS

DEFENDERS OF TRUMP POINT TO THE CONTINUING STRENGTH OF the economy under his presidency as a justification for his methods, but their former fellow-travelers point out they once had a different view. "The American republic has stood in support of, and been governed by a clear proposition: there are things that matter more than gold," wrote Bill Bennett in *The Death of Outrage*, a volume dedicated to sounding the call against the moral slippage in the age of Clinton. "Do Americans still acknowledge, implicitly, or explicitly, that core ethical values like honesty, respect, distinguishing right and wrong— good character—are important and often decisive?"[14]

Americans do appear to still believe in these values, even if some of the public advocates of morality have stopped asking the question. In March 2019, a Quinnipiac University poll asked about the president's character in exactly the way Bill Bennett's *The Book of Virtues* would have—with an eye toward the next generation. The poll asked "Is Donald Trump a good role model for children?" Only 21 percent of the respondents said yes. Despite Trump's rock-solid support in the Republican Party, only 50 percent of Republicans said yes.[15]

A 2020 *Washington Post* investigation found that the role model is being followed. After reviewing 28,000 news stories, they found that Trump's words had been used by students to put down their peers and teachers at least three hundred times since the start of 2016. Three-quarters of those attacks were directed at people who were Hispanic, black, or Muslim.[16]

Conservatives, including Vice President Mike Pence, once believed the private behavior of a president rendered an irrevocable judgment on their fitness for office. Evangelical leaders in particular cared about this connection. "If he will lie to or mislead his wife and daughter," wrote Franklin Graham before becoming a Trump supporter, "those with whom he is most intimate, what will prevent him from doing the same to the American public?"[17] Now, as Peter Wehner, a former aide to Bennett, writes, these same people support "a foul-mouthed, non-church-attending former casino owner and reality television star who once endorsed partial-birth abortion and was convincingly accused of paying hush money to cover up an affair with a porn star, which took place after his third wife gave birth to their son."[18] Trump also made payments to a former *Playboy* model. He has also been accused of sexual misconduct by more than two dozen women, some of whom have alleged rape.[19] Vice President Pence has defended President Trump at every turn, including when it was revealed in court documents and with audio recordings that Trump had lied about his knowledge about the payments he made to the adult film actress Stormy Daniels.[20] This is a long way from the Mike Pence who argued that members of a president's party had a duty to abandon a president who lies, even if the lies were about private matters, as they were in Bill Clinton's case. "If our leaders flinch at this responsibility," wrote Pence in the late 1990s, "they would do well to heed the Proverb 'If a ruler listens to lies, all his officials become wicked.'"[21]

It may be a proper and more evolved stance to separate private virtue from public virtue. Perhaps George Washington was wrong when he said "the foundation of our national policy will be laid in the pure and immutable principles of private morality."[22] Many of the Watergate participants were privately virtuous. So perhaps there is a new standard: Private behavior is not really that important.

Though the character question is not being raised by its traditional champions, some in positions of leadership are speaking up. Stanley McChrystal, the former U.S. commander in Afghanistan, called on every American to "stand in front of that mirror and say, 'What are we about? Am I really willing to throw away or ignore some of the things that people do that are—are pretty unacceptable normally just because they accomplish certain other things that we might like?' If we want to be governed by someone we wouldn't do a business deal with because their—their background is so shady, if we're willing to do that, then that's in conflict with who I think we are. And so I think it's necessary at those times to take a stand."[23]

The commander of special forces who came after McChrystal also raised questions. Retired Navy admiral William McRaven, who served George W. Bush and Barack Obama, told CBS's Major Garrett, "Every public servant who fails to do things that are moral, legal, and ethical, ought to be held accountable. . . . The danger is, we lead the country down a path that no longer is this kind of beacon that the world is looking for."[24] Shortly thereafter, Trump restored the rank of disgraced Special Warfare Operator Edward Gallagher, who was convicted of posing for photos with a deceased ISIS fighter in 2017. The standards that McRaven was talking about were not just changing in the abstract.

The path is set, and Donald Trump isn't changing his path, but it did not necessarily have to be the path the Trump presidency has taken. Donald Trump has a set of skills that could have made his a transformational presidency of a different kind.

Chapter 31

Donald Trump's America

—

"You're going to be so sick and tired of winning."

—DONALD TRUMP

Donald Trump has been a successful partisan president. His effect on the federal judiciary will live long after the last outraged reaction to his presidency has faded. His achievements in cutting taxes and regulations might be undone by future presidents, but appointments to the judiciary are for life.

Trump's political legacy is less certain. Will he transform the presidency and politics in his image, as he has transformed the Republican Party? The two are related, but the former is disconnected from the latter.

From the start of his presidency, Donald Trump chose to govern for his base. His first target was the Affordable Care Act, the signature achievement of his predecessor. His biggest domestic achievement, the tax reform bill, contained a host of provisions to weaken states that typically elect Democrats. "It's death to Democrats," explained his economic adviser Stephen Moore.[1]

These moves have made Trump's base more solid than ever. But not all Republicans that voted for him in 2016 fall in that category. Suburban Republicans—particularly women—who took a chance on

Trump in 2016 moved away from him over time. So to win re-election, Trump must go for the throat, pushing his strategy against Democrats even further than he already has, in an effort to split the Democratic Party apart by encouraging infighting that makes Democrats less likely to vote, or baiting them into fights that make the Democratic Party unattractive.

Liberals pushed Barack Obama to be equally aggressive with Republicans at the start of his second term. Given Obama's considerable ambition and his conclusion that Republicans were not going to work with him, they wanted him to pick fights over immigration reform, gun control, fiscal policy, and climate change. They hoped the GOP would have broken apart in the fracas as the most ideological voices asserted themselves.

Obama tried some of this, but with nothing like the gusto with which Donald Trump has wielded the ice pick. Throughout his presidency, Trump has sought to bait liberals into clarifying fights over national identity. He singled out NFL players protesting racial injustice. He suggested that four young congresswomen of color should "go back" to the "totally broken and crime-infested places from which they came."[2] (Three of them were born in the United States.) He has worked a variety of angles on issues related to immigration, warning of an "invasion" at the southern border. When Democrats have protested the treatment of children at the border, he has accused them of favoring unlimited immigration of criminals. "A Blue Wave means Crime and Open Borders. A Red Wave means Safety and Strength!" he posted on Twitter in 2018.[3] The president has also tried to define Democrats as economic socialists, gun grabbers, and advocates of special rights at the cost of traditional values and religious liberty.

His campaign manager, Brad Parscale, boasts that these fights over immigration will be the single reason voters reelect Trump. "If you look at the people who are kind of these swing voters, these people who possibly don't like him for personality or different reasons, the number one reason they will vote for him is because of his stance on border security."[4]

Steve Bannon, Trump's former strategist, explained early in Trump's tenure, "The longer [Democrats] talk about identity politics, I got 'em. I want them to talk about racism every day. If the left is focused on race and identity, and we go with economic nationalism, we can crush the Democrats."[5] Trump is hoping not just to crush Democrats by making them sound like special pleaders for a rainbow of groups, but to eat into traditional Democratic strength with minority groups. Just after he won the 2016 election, I asked President Trump how he was going to reach out to minority voters who had not supported him. His answer was that the economy would be so good that they would rally behind him.

The strategy has had mixed results. In the 2018 elections, President Trump attempted to paint the entire Democratic Party as supporting the international gang MS-13. Despite the effort, Democrats won 41 House seats, many of them in swing districts, where Trump's strategy would have had the best chance of working, since those districts are not liberal hotbeds. It was the largest gain of House seats for Democrats since the post-Watergate 1974 elections, when they picked up 49 seats.

In the 2020 election, Democratic presidential positions shifted leftward, as Trump had hoped. To counter Trump's harsh stance on immigration, Democratic candidates have loosened theirs. Almost all the Democratic presidential candidates supported providing healthcare to illegal immigrants, a position 59 percent of the country opposes.[6] A decade ago, a Democratic-led Congress barred undocumented immigrants from buying health insurance in the exchanges set up under the Affordable Care Act.[7] In the 2008 presidential race, the idea of even giving undocumented workers driver's licenses was considered going too far.[8]

The public may not favor the position Democrats take on immigration, but they don't like Donald Trump's positions either. Support for the border wall has decreased since Trump has been advocating for it. In August 2019, 72 percent of voters backed "a path to legal status for undocumented immigrants," according to the Pew Research Center.[9]

But the point is not really about policy alternatives. Trump is trying to define Democrats as culturally outside the mainstream. Former speaker Newt Gingrich, citing a playbook that predates Trump, predicted these positions would create a gap with the electorate and drive voters to Trump: "The crazier the Democrats get on tax-paid healthcare for illegal immigrants, abortion through the ninth month (and infanticide after), taking away every American's health insurance, massive tax increases, talking about reparations as though it was a reasonable idea, etcetera etcetera, the greater the gap is going to get."[10]

President Trump's strongest argument for reelection is the strength of the U.S. economy. Democrats who predicted dire consequences after his election have been proved wrong. "We are very probably looking at a global recession, with no end in sight," said Paul Krugman after Trump's election.[11] Three years into his term, the stock market was up and unemployment was down. Wage growth, which had been sluggish, was also slowly picking up. The economic disparities Donald Trump promised to eradicate still persist—benefits from his tax cut overwhelmingly favored the already wealthy, which is why 60 percent of the country believes the economic system still favors the rich. In October 2018, almost a year after Trump's sweeping tax overhaul was signed into law, 46 percent of Americans disapproved and 39 percent approved of the bill, making it less popular than the Affordable Care Act, at an equivalent time after its passage.[12] Nevertheless, end-of-the-year Gallup polls from 2017 to 2019 consistently show almost 40 percent of the country thought economic conditions were "good."[13]

For Trump to create a new political coalition he would need to do more than bait liberals; he would need more conservative Democrats to break ranks. These would be members of the party whose public disagreement with the party over its direction might validate Trump's claims about Democrats. In 1984, Ronald Reagan won over Democrat Jeane Kirkpatrick, a former adviser to Vice President Hubert Humphrey. She spoke at that year's Republican convention. Democratic senator Zell Miller of Georgia spoke at the 2004 GOP convention in support of George W. Bush.

Such defections are rare nowadays. New Jersey congressman Jeff Van Drew defected late in 2019, but a recording of a phone call by the former Democrat telling a constituent he would never support or vote for Donald Trump just weeks before his party switch made his pledges of fealty to Trump somewhat muddled.[14]

No Democrat of stature has defected to support Donald Trump. The larger political universe has gone the other way. The growing segments of the population—minorities, younger voters—are violently opposed to Trump. They also have negative views of the Republican Party.

WHAT IF?

DONALD TRUMP COULD HAVE PURSUED A DIFFERENT PRESIDENCY. He could have applied his love of disruption with a more mainstream mind-set. He could have served as the president of my in-laws. You don't know my in-laws (unless you do, in which case please tell them hello), but they are patriotic, dedicated members of their community. They have some practical notions and behave mostly the way the characters do in those books about virtue. They are the voice of the roughly 75 percent of people who say they want the parties to work together, according to a September 2019 *The Hill* / HarrisX Daily Poll.[15] They hold the views of the reasonable people interviewed by local television stations who tell reporters they hate negative ads and want candidates to stick to the issues. They are irritated by the three things that lock up Washington: lobbyists, partisanship, and cowardice.

Donald Trump entered the Oval Office with attributes that could have been applied to all three. He ran for office promising not to hire any lobbyists and seemed to attract a following around the idea of "draining the swamp." Trump also came to Washington without strong ideological beliefs. He shifted in and out of political parties for most of his life—five party shifts since 1987. He has been all over the map on hot-button issues. He has supported abortion, legalizing drugs, and a 15 percent tax on the wealthy. He has supported government-run healthcare. He also came to the presidency with an affection for the horse-trading required to make deals. In fact, he said his deal-making skills would change Washington. "I don't like executive orders," he told me during the campaign. "That is not what the country was based on. You go, you can't make a deal with anybody, so you sign an executive order. You really need leadership. You have to get people into a room and get something that is good for everybody, whether it is compromise or whatever, but you have to get them into a room and you have to lead."[16]

He could have applied all of these traits toward building bipartisan coalitions to address key issues of the day like America's incomplete healthcare system, failing infrastructure, high prescription drug prices, comprehensive immigration, and tax breaks for the middle class.

This may sound like a fantasy. Embracing this scenario requires a suspension of disbelief about what is possible in Washington, but remember who we are talking about here. Donald Trump has done some unbelievable things during his presidency. If he had been cowed by conventional wisdom about what was possible and allowable, he would have sat on his hands while watching the Hallmark Channel and never entered the race.

For the purposes of this exercise, take the gumption and risk taking President Trump has applied to the office while in it and use them to prop open your window of disbelief for the next paragraph or two.

If Trump had focused on infrastructure legislation first, members of both parties would have backed him. If Trump had started with that and held a big Rose Garden ceremony, he could have built goodwill, softened up the Democrats he needed for future legislation, and given pundits and the public the storyline they were nearly waiting on the doorstep of the White House to receive. This was the approach George W. Bush took when he focused first on reforming education. After an election in which he had prevailed despite losing the popular vote, Bush sought to build bipartisan authority by notching an early win with the help of Democrats.

Writers—particularly Shakespeare—love a turnaround story. The script was already written for the brash presidential candidate who transformed himself once in office. It's a patriotic story: that's how powerful the American presidency is, that it can transform a man like Donald Trump.

Another big prize, comprehensive immigration reform, might have had a chance, because it had already received 68 votes in the Senate in 2013. On tax cuts, Trump would have had a chance to build a bipartisan coalition too. Moderate Democrats negotiated with White House economic adviser Gary Cohn for a series of additions to the tax cut bill that would have helped the middle class more and corporations less. That those negotiations in the early days of the Trump administration took place at all suggests that there was some possibility for a bipartisan deal on that issue too.

There are considerable obstacles to this fantasy. Making these deals would have angered the Trump base who would have cried capitulation. "You're not going to pass an infrastructure bill right away that most of the Republican lawmakers campaigned against," says a former senior Trump official.[17]

In response to these gambits, the president's favorite TV network, Fox News, would have melted down. To contain the carnage in his caucus, Mitch McConnell would have used maneuvers to block the deal-making. Liberals would have said their leaders were sellouts for even thinking about working with Donald Trump. Remember all those voters who wore pink hats and marched in opposition against Trump the day after his inauguration? They would have marched right to Senate Minority Leader Chuck Schumer's front lawn and taken up residence there.

Let's stick to the fantasy for a minute longer, though. This chaos strategy would have thrilled its author. The president loves to be at the center of chaos. He could have made surprise visits to the Hill, trailing clouds of cameras. He would have cornered Senators and asked them to speak to the cameras to explain why they weren't voting his way, especially after he'd raised all that money for their campaigns (he'd be able to say this to members of both parties, because he's raised money for members of both parties in his career). Maybe the president would remind McConnell that his wife works in his cabinet. It would be hardball, but it would keep the attention on the president. He likes that.

Maybe this gambit would have worked and maybe it wouldn't. The whopping chaotic mess would have gotten ratings, which the president likes, and it would have won pundit approval, something the Queens native is not impervious to. They'd have cheered his efforts to give voters exactly what they want: collective action to solve big problems.

Okay, now you can let the window fall. There are a number of additional reasons that this scenario is implausible that limit its utility as a thought exercise. President Trump was elected with the help of a base he cannot abandon. Support from that base gives him leverage over Republican lawmakers. Those politicians don't dare buck him for fear of being faced with a primary opponent supported by Trump diehards. His base also gives him emotional uplift. "His rallies are like oxygen to him," says senior adviser Kellyanne Conway.[18]

The president's instincts are also not really geared toward deal-making bonhomie. He and his supporters like "owning the Libs," doing things to upset liberals for their own sake. His first significant act fell into this category. "If you want to generate goodwill you don't poison the well immediately with a travel ban," says Matt Glassman, a Senior

Fellow at the Government Affairs Institute at Georgetown University. "His first move went right to the heart of what made his candidacy so divisive. He's never taken his foot off the gas pedal since."[19] Even when there is bipartisan cooperation the president has told the opposite story. The president told his audiences the opioid bill passed with "very little Democrat support."[20] The vote was 98 to 1, with only Republican Senator Mike Lee of Utah opposing it. The House passed it 393 to 8. Even a rare bipartisan achievement was not framed that way.

The president is a pugilist who likes the roar of the crowd. He prefers crossing lines to coloring inside them. You don't get the really enjoyable decibels from the people who have waited in line by being "presidential," as the president has pointed out. Occasionally he mimics what it would look like to be "presidential," to the amusement of his rally crowds. "I always tell you, it's so easy to be presidential," Trump said. "But instead of having ten thousand people outside trying to get into this packed arena, we'd have about two hundred people standing there. It's so easy to be presidential."[21]

To make a pitch across parties to build bipartisan coalitions also requires transcendent appeals to fellow-feeling and a shared spirit that works with a wide audience. Deal-making in this fantasy mold requires character, as James Q. Wilson describes it. When you negotiate and debate, you do it in such a way that you recognize that the other side has a right to speak. While making a point, you address yourself to the argument and not the personality. Views are attacked, but not the other person's self-esteem. "Character is not the enemy of self-expression and personal freedom, it is their necessary precondition,"[22] Wilson wrote, because without these there cannot be an exchange of ideas or orderly familial and communal lives.

These are not Donald Trump's skills, nor are they the skills rewarded in the immediate culture of Twitter, social media, and reality television that he used to get elected. Those venues light up when the president makes personal attacks. He's not going to shut off that oxygen. "His Twitter feed is sometimes an electronic version of his rallies," says Conway. "And he communicates with the public both ways."

Also, while Trump may not have held firm positions along the traditional Washington spectrum, he has been consistent on issues that make working with Democrats impossible. Since his campaign announcement speech, he has referred to people of color in dehumanizing ways. "When Mexico sends its people, they are not sending their best. They are sending people that have lots of problems, and they are bringing those problems to us. They are bringing drugs and they are bringing crime, and they're rapists," he said when announcing his candidacy, adding parenthetically, "And some, I assume, are good people."[23] With the treatment of kids in cages, despite public outcry, he has shown no interest in moving from this policy. Indeed, he has pushed his aides more forcefully on this than any other issue.

This strategy destroys bipartisanship. In order to create fervor among the in-group, it requires lampooning the out-group, which makes future appeals to that out-group impossible. "To propel themselves forward, such figures latched onto the resentments of ordinary people who felt that their nation or religion or way of life was being disrespected," writes political scientist Francis Fukuyama.[24] Success requires portraying the out-group as the wolf always at the door ready to lunge in. That makes it really hard to then turn around and make legislation with the enemy.

Trump might also not have found many Democrats to work with. As the political scientist Frances Lee has argued, the power structure in Congress pushes parties to maximize their differences in order to keep or attain control. For the minority party, cooperation blurs those differences. Why should Trump try to bring Democrats on board when they have no incentive to do so, and why should Democrats work with him and his Republican colleagues when it would only diminish their chances of retaking the majority?

There were other, perhaps more deeply felt reasons Democrats wouldn't have worked with him. The election had been bitter. For five years, Donald Trump had been the country's chief "birther," alleging that Barack Obama was not a legitimate president because he was born in Kenya, which is no more true than that I was born there. African American voters who have witnessed generations of authenticity claims used to deny them their place in America might not have been quick to reconcile with a presidential candidate who spread that kind of poison. Women in the Democratic Party would also not have been likely to forgive his treatment of women, either in reality or on reality TV or in an audio recording.

The immediate fight to fill the Supreme Court early in Trump's tenure would have reminded Democrats that Obama had been denied consideration of his nominee to the seat. The fight over Trump's nominee would have exacerbated every hot-button debate in politics. Interest groups would have made sure those debates raged and would've punished any Democrat who worked with Trump.

Trump was also elected to repeal and replace Obamacare, the signature legislation of his predecessor. Delaying that effort would have caused chaos in his ranks, and finding compromise on that particular issue with Democrats would have been extremely difficult. Bipartisan progress on immigration would also have been nearly impossible. Any deal the president might have struck with Democrats would have outraged the base that elected him. This happened every time Trump even played footsie with the idea of a deal.

When Trump met with a few moderate Democrats in February 2017, they raised the issue of comprehensive immigration reform. The president sounded as though he might go for it after West Virginia Democrat Joe Manchin and Tennessee Republican Lamar Alexander separately made the pitch that Trump could have a "Nixon goes to China" moment. They raised the 2013 "Gang of Eight" bill that had won 68 votes. Then John Cornyn, a Republican senator from Texas, reminded the president he had labeled the components of the deal as amnesty.[25] Trump could have switched positions—he's done that often enough—but his base is adamant on this point.

In late 2017, when a deal seemed imminent on protecting the status of the children of undocumented workers, Trump received a blast from base-connected talk show hosts and backed out of the deal. "President Trump, you'll remember, ran for office promising to fix immigration, make good deals and, in general, do a better job than the corrupt, incompetent lawmakers, he said, were wrecking the country. And he was right, they were wrecking the country," said Fox News' Tucker Carlson. "And yet, today, in a remarkable twist, the president held a televised meeting with the very swamp creatures he once denounced. He told them he trusted them to craft immigration policy without his input."[26]

Progress on other possible bipartisan solutions would have also taken a level of negotiation the president does not seem to want to engage in. He has called various senators and applied flattery and mild rhetorical pressure over the course of his tenure, but he has never deployed any of the real techniques that seasoned deal makers in Washington have used to get the job done.[27] He has certainly taken no bipartisan risks.

For better or worse, Donald Trump has governed exactly as he campaigned. He has been a chaos president. There is no plan for him to change. Not changing is his reelection strategy. When President Trump is replaced—whether it is after eight years or sooner—he will have created an appetite for a presidency that follows a traditional path. A president who replaces him will have done so with the explicit or implicit promise to return to the patterns and expectations of the office before it contained its forty-fifth occupant. Whether that is a good or a bad thing depends on which traditions stay and which ones are replaced by a more streamlined office. It also depends on how the next occupant governs. Donald Trump has created an opportunity for a future Democratic president who will claim powers and offer the excuse that extreme measures are required to reverse what transpired during the Trump years. Resisting temptation is just one of the many challenges that still face the American presidency.

"I Sacrifice to the Public Good"

As the delegates to the Constitutional Convention completed their work on September 17, 1787, Benjamin Franklin prepared to speak, but at eighty-one, found that he could not. Instead, he asked Pennsylvania delegate James Wilson to read his remarks to the room:

"I confess that there are several parts of this constitution which I do not at present approve, but I am not sure I shall never approve them: For having lived long, I have experienced many instances of being obliged by better information, or fuller consideration, to change opinions even on important subjects, which I once thought right, but found to be otherwise. It is therefore that the older I grow, the more apt I am to doubt my own judgment, and to pay more respect to the judgment of others. Most men, indeed as well as most sects in Religion, think themselves in possession of all truth, and that wherever others differ from them it is so far error. . . .

"I agree to this Constitution with all its faults, if they are such. . . . For when you assemble a number of men to have the advantage of their joint wisdom, you inevitably assemble with those men, all their prejudices, their passions, their errors of opinion, their local interests, and their selfish views. From such an assembly can a perfect production be expected? It therefore astonishes me, Sir, to find this system approaching so near to perfection as it does; and I think it will astonish our enemies, who are waiting with confidence to hear that our councils are confounded like those of the Builders of Babel; and that our States are on the point of separation, only to meet hereafter for the purpose of cutting one another's throats. Thus I consent, Sir, to this Constitution because I expect no better, and because I am not sure, that it is not the best. The opinions I have had of its errors, I sacrifice to the public good."[1]

Conclusion

I know of no soil better adapted to the growth
of reform than American soil.[2]

— FREDERICK DOUGLASS, SPEECH ON THE
DRED SCOTT DECISION, NEW YORK CITY, MAY 1857

"Having an effective government is like an airbag. When
things go really, really wrong you want it to be there."[3]

— GAUTAM MUKUNDA

THE MANAGEMENT GURU PETER DRUCKER IS THE ALEXIS
de Tocqueville of business writing. It's hard to get through a book
about American government without finding an observation from the
nineteenth-century French diplomat, and it is also hard to turn many
pages of a business volume without finding one of Drucker's durable
insights. When talking about how difficult it is for managers to hire
good people, Drucker cited the eighteenth-century statesman the Duke
of Marlborough. "The basic trouble in coalition warfare," said Marlborough, "is that one has to entrust victory, if not one's life, to a fellow
commander whom one knows by reputation rather than by performance."[4]

Managers have Marlborough's problem, Drucker argued. They
have to pick people without knowing how they will perform. CEOs say
this is their biggest worry. The nonprofit research organization The
Conference Board interviews business leaders, and almost every year
they report that their biggest concern is attracting and retaining top tal-

ent.[5] Most companies don't know how to test whether the skills a candidate says they have will fit with the ones they'll need when their nameplate goes on the door.

This is a relatively new challenge. Before the 1970s, employees commonly worked for one company their entire career. Bosses filled roughly 90 percent of their vacancies through promotions and lateral assignments.[6] Nowadays, career mobility is the norm, and bosses tap a smaller in-house candidate pool.

Companies responded to this market change by searching for lost certainty. A multi-billion-dollar industry sprouted to help managers divine whether those smiling faces on the other side of the conference room table had the skills those companies really needed. Management and human resources consultants push psychological screening techniques and computer models to intuit skills in various areas. Business authors promise they'll help companies find "'A' players" and "hire for attitude."

In the federal government, the Office of Personnel Management has also tried to follow a reliable system when hiring the people who keep our food safe, watch the locks on the nuclear weapons, and provide healthcare and retirement security to hundreds of millions of people. OPM suggests that managers use a psychological test known as the "Realistic Job Preview," which can "provide a prospective employee a realistic view of what the job entails." Another technique seeks to measure "job fit." OPM also advises that managers administer emotional intelligence tests and "integrity and honesty tests . . . because integrity is strongly related to conscientiousness, itself a strong predictor of overall job performance."[7]

Imagine if we used any of those methods to evaluate presidential candidates. While the rest of the world has sought rigor in making selections, the presidential hiring process has gone in the other direction, becoming more reliant than ever on a grab bag of evaluation criteria that shifts with the impulsive nature of the times.

I have interviewed thousands of voters over the years as they assess candidates for office. Those voters are a source of hope and vision and durable faith in our country, but their approach cannot be called systematic. They say they don't like negative ads, but they repeat the claims made in them. They are critical of the news, but their opinions

are shaped by what they hear on cable TV. They claim they are independent, but they have voted for one party all of their lives. They say
they don't care about the candidate horse race, but it consumes their
conversations.

The media have often failed the voters. We focus too much on the
polls, treat the campaign as theater, simplify complex problems into
binary choices, and stoke conflict, while abdicating our responsibility
to help people get through the conflict. We don't stretch often enough
to explain whether, and why, the flashpoint moment we're focusing on
is actually important, or test our assumptions about what we've chosen
to elevate. I myself have contributed to all of this drift, even when I
thought I was being rigorous.[8]

Political combat encourages quick disqualifications of those who
would seek to lead us, but every leader is flawed. "We want to believe
the mythology, that the leader is 10 feet tall, never scared, never wrong,
has the answer to all of our questions. That's never correct," says Stanley McChrystal. "We're very disappointed when we see how they are in
private because it just doesn't match part of the mythology that we
have, but the reality is that every person is a human being."[9] The question in campaigns then is to identify what we think are the disqualifying
characteristics, not simply if a candidate happens to have any flaws.

The presidential hiring process is administered by voters who trust
a wide variety of folk wisdom. People watch a debate or catch a scrap of
news coverage and form a "gut" feeling. The signal from the biome is
often related to a face they already recognize. Or, voters play mix and
match. We know an anecdote about a favorite president and see something of that same quality in a member of the current field. Some
single-issue voters care only about the candidate who makes maximum
promises about their favorite cause.

The voices of people from the real world are vital to our democracy.
If nothing else, they are a counterweight to the cocooned thinking of
the talking-head set. But if the real world is a source of stable thinking,
then we should acknowledge that no one in the real world with responsibility for anything important would choose and evaluate leaders
through the slapdash method the public uses to measure presidents.

We allow any old selection criteria in politics because, unlike in
business or sports, if you don't participate in selecting a person from

your pool of applicants in politics, a selection will be made for you, and that selection may well be made from the pool of applicants in the opposite political party. If you prefer apples to oranges, you'll accept a bruised apple and eat around the brown spot rather than pick up a Sunkist.

When party pooh-bahs picked presidential candidates, they promoted a whole basket of bad fruit—Warren G. Harding, James Buchanan, Andrew Johnson. All hang from the bottom of presidential lists. That doesn't mean, however, that the ad hoc system that has replaced the back room of cigar ash is better, or that it can't be improved.

Few successful institutions remain the same today as they were eighty, forty, or even twenty years ago. Leaders in business, education, and entertainment constantly try to improve how they do what they do. One recent adaptation in the corporate world, for example, is the rise of CEO coaches. Bill Campbell, Marshall Goldsmith, and Teri-E Belf have tutored some of the highest-performing humans on the planet—from Eric Schmidt to Jeff Bezos and Mark Zuckerberg—to keep them nimble. Coaching is not a momentary fad, argue the authors of *Trillion Dollar Coach*. It is a requirement. "Any company that wants to succeed in a time where technology has suffused every industry and most aspects of consumer life, where speed and innovation are paramount, must have team coaching as part of its culture."[10] Coaching is an adaptation that seeks to improve adaptation.

If we are to repair the presidency, then politicians, the public, and the press need to change how we think about the institution. "The presidency needs to be cutting edge because it is the tip of the spear for dealing with our biggest problems," says Max Stier of the Partnership for Public Service.[11] This chapter offers some suggestions that might change our perspective. The suggestions are modest because humility is one of the main suggestions. Our view of the presidency is distorted by our inflated expectations about what a president can do and warped by a candidate's immodesty about what they will do. To promise grand solutions would only compound this error.

We should also be realistic about the challenges facing the American system that contains the presidency. The balance of powers system is out of whack. Partisanship is not channeled productively and creates gridlock in our institutions and public debate. The political class, traditional media, and social media have all responded to this moment of conflict by magnifying and increasing the emotional appeals and coarseness of our public discourse.

A comprehensive discussion of reforms that would address these problems—and others beyond the scope of our work here, such as the role of money in politics and improving ballot access or reforming the Electoral College—would fill several books. I do hope that at the very least, though, we can develop habits for sorting public events— particularly the presidential campaign—in ways that are more realistic and useful. Understanding the presidency in this moment can give voters a sense of control when witnessing the events of the day and making the choices they do.

THE CAMPAIGN ≠ THE PRESIDENCY

WE MUST NO LONGER CONFUSE GOOD CAMPAIGNING SKILLS WITH GOOD governing skills. The jobs are different. As Reagan's chief of staff Kenneth Duberstein explained, campaigns encourage "destroying your adversary." Governing requires the art of "making love to your adversary."[12] Campaigns demand overpromising—we can have guns *and* butter. Governing requires ruthless prioritization based on the idea that everyone can't have everything at the same time, including the president's attention. Campaigns float on waves of rhetoric; in office, talking gets you only so far. Candidates can't change their positions on issues—or they'll be accused of flip-flopping—yet governing requires adapting. Candidates and partisans make issues seem simple, but solutions to any tough problems are intricate.

When we misunderstand what the office requires, we misapply our outrage. We rail at the mechanic fixing our car's exhaust problem because we expect him to be hunched over the tailpipe. We're ignorant that the problem comes from the engine, and that we should actually be applauding him for what he's doing at that end of the vehicle.

We also accept solutions that are momentarily pleasing but have long-term costs. We applaud presidents who issue executive orders that work for our team but ignore how they ultimately weaken Congress. Executive orders can also build up the appetite for a savior from the other team who will sashay in and graft on their own executive orders.

"That's basically the only way to govern now," the Democratic strategist Andrew Feldman told *Politico* in 2019 about executive actions. "It's kind of a way of life."[3] Governance by executive order is frantic and fragile and makes it harder to address America's biggest problems.

REPLACE ABSOLUTES

CAMPAIGNS PUSH US TO DEFINE PRESIDENTIAL QUALITIES IN ABSOLUTES. Voters in diners across the country put down their forks and tell reporters they want truth-telling, authentic candidates, for example. But presidents must wear masks.

Presidents must flatter and elevate politicians to get their vote, even if they don't respect them. They must sometimes fib to their supporters to get them to back the steps the president has to take to accommodate the other side (a motivation that might incite supporters to label them a sellout if they knew the truth of the matter).

Defining attributes by absolutes stops us from thinking more intelligently about the office and what it really requires. It also makes us the willing dupes of candidates and their handlers. They define attributes starkly so that an opponent who shows any variability can be immediately disqualified from the job.

Instead, we should think about presidential skills like honesty, political awareness, and decisiveness on a continuum. Within each, there is a range. We don't want presidents who are completely political, driven only by the pursuit of power, with no underlying values at all. We also don't want to embrace the other extreme, electing a candidate who is too fastidious to succeed in politics.

If we are going to reject a candidate we might do so because they are "too political" for the job or too political for the moment, but not because they merely show political instincts. We should find them dangerous not because they sometimes wait to decide, but because they dither when the moment calls for a decision to be made.

Here are some of the key presidential attributes and the ways we might think about them:

ADAPTABILITY: To stay sane, a president must ignore advice. So much of it is uninformed. So much of it is self-serving. So much of it is unworkable. So much of it is mean. But a successful president must mix the fortitude and stability needed to stick to the plan with a nimbleness that leaves them open to surprise and opportunity. If they change course, they risk being called a flip-flopper—soft as an éclair, as Teddy Roosevelt put it—but that's better than blundering as a result of being cut off from reality.

AMBITION: A president must want to be great and want to achieve great things. The country needs that personal fuel. But acclaim must be linked to service on behalf of American values and goals. Otherwise, the country would be poisoned by what the founders believed to be the most corrosive of the human attributes.

CONSTITUTIONAL CHARACTER: A president must know that they are a steward of the American system. They are not simply the quarterback of the executive branch. In a perfect balance-of-powers system, each branch seeks its advantage and the joint tension makes the machine work, but if a president knows the system is out of whack, they must help to restore that balance to protect the overall experiment.

COURAGE: A president must be bold. Without courage, a president may not be able to take advantage of their other attributes. But a president must know the difference between a risk and a gamble. A risk can be repaired if things go wrong. A gamble cannot.

Teddy Roosevelt had "what it takes." At a stop in Wisconsin during the 1912 presidential campaign, he was shot by a saloon-keeper who had had a premonition in a dream. The bullet passed through his notes and eyeglass case and lodged in his chest. He gave the speech anyway. "It takes more than that to kill a bull moose," Roosevelt assured the audience.

WE ARE AGAINST HIS POLITICS. BUT WE LIKE HIS GRIT

CURIOSITY: "A president can't know everything," says former Russian Ambassador Michael McFaul. "They have to ask questions and know how to prod information out of experts."[14]

DECISIVENESS: A president must make a decision with clarity, knowing that the outcome could be murky. A great president knows how to build a system that delivers the right information at the right time, including unpleasant information, and then knows when to stop asking for more information and make the call.

EMPATHY: Identified by political scientist James Q. Wilson as the first component of character, empathy refers to an understanding of the issues that affect all Americans, because a president represents the entire country. The danger of having too much empathy is that it can spur a president to lead by emotion. Military action might appeal to a president who has an emotional connection with a suffering population across the globe, but restraint might be the better call. Or, a president might not take military action because of empathy for those who might lose their lives, a decision that might risk greater loss of life.

HISTORICAL PERSPECTIVE: A president must understand what has shaped America. Familiarity with past events will help them anticipate how actions are likely to play out and get ahead of potential repercussions and consequences. But a president must not let the calamities of history freeze the instinct to act or let themselves be obsessed with fighting the last battle.

HONESTY: A president must be truthful with regard to fundamental values but understand that some situations require withholding the truth, or some parts of it, to achieve goals that would become impossible if every fact is known.

LEADERSHIP: A president is not a ruler who barks out commands. A president is not a weathervane, either, listening only to the public outcry. Instead, a president must know when the people are ready to be led in a new direction. A president who has a close relationship with the people can create the conditions for leadership, but action hero presidents who wildly shift public opinion exist only in the movies.

MANAGEMENT: A president must understand the scope of his or her administration and the necessity of building a strong team which they neither micromanage nor delegate to in a way that removes them from the decisions only a president can make.

POLITICAL FEEL: A president must know how to flatter, give credit, and construct events that make people feel grateful. All of this helps get others to do what you want them to. A president must know how to leverage the frantic desire to be near power, and not mind that it's so embarrassing to watch people scramble to be near it. Politics is the water in which a president swims, but a president must frequently return to the surface, bobbing above politics, or risk drowning. Too much focus on politics warps policy in the direction of parochial claims and away from the greater good.

PRIORITIZATION: A president must pick among the country's urgent needs and pursue the goals that can be achieved through the applications of time and attention. A president must also know that some actions might exact too high a price and imperil the ability to act on other matters.

RESTRAINT: The second component of character, restraint, keeps a president from acting when no action at all is the best course.

RHETORICAL FLAIR: A president needs the ability to move audiences from sorrow to action. He must be able to effectively explain events so that even when the way forward is unclear, a president's aura of command gives people a sense of control.

TEMPERAMENT: A president must have a finely calibrated emotional rheostat. When stakes are high, and staffers are taking their emotional cues from you, a well-regulated mind allows focus and reserve. Presidents must know how to control their emotions. In a job with irritating uncertainty, a president must be able to weather the itchy delays and unresolved questions, devoting their mental and emotional energy to those things they can control. They must also recognize when an emotional spark is required; in the face of a moral outrage, icewater responses won't do.

THEATER: Like George Washington seated at the head of the Constitutional Convention, a president provides a model of behavior that inspires and leads, but a president who is too addicted to the show and the adulation and roar of the crowd bends his actions so as to inspire public adulation and thus serves himself instead of the country.

VISION: Great presidents have a vision of how to use the power of their office to improve the world, a vision that shapes their days and directs their administration when they aren't even in the room to give orders. "The achievement of the great Presidents springs precisely from the fact that they had a deeper sense of reality than most of their contemporaries and penetrated to problems their fellow countrymen preferred to ignore," wrote the historian Arthur M. Schlesinger, Jr., in 1973.[15] Vision allows for that penetration. If their eyes are constantly off in the clouds, though, a president's vision will fail from lack of hard-eyed execution.

Also, a president must be able to make fifteen-minute brownies in five. No president can achieve all of these balances, obviously, but a good president will have more strengths than not, know how to hire to cover the patchy parts, and make adjustments within each attribute based on the circumstance.

The presidency requires "different talents exercised at different tempos," as the presidential historian Thomas Bailey put it. "Washington had to build the Union. Lincoln had to put it back together. One is a constructive job and the other is restorative."[16]

Our job as voters, newly informed about the gradations of presidential skills, is to evaluate presidents on whether they have applied their skills as the moment requires. When the decision-making skill is required, rhetoric is a mistake. Protecting your political flank at the expense of the good of the nation is a blunder.

SHIFTING OUR PERSPECTIVE ON presidential attributes can carry a risk of technocratic deafness. A lot of commentary about our political system strangles itself in the real world because it is unrealistic or contains no allowance for human behavior. With that in mind, we need to remember that political change comes, in part, from holding presidents to impossible standards. Set the bar high, and even if a president falls short, they will have achieved something. Set the bar low, and the results will be correspondingly mediocre. The activists who forced FDR and LBJ to act on civil rights didn't make small requests.

In evaluating presidents, Frederick Douglass offered a critique that is perhaps a useful model. "Viewed from the genuine abolition ground, Mr. Lincoln seemed tardy, cold, dull, and indifferent," he wrote about the sixteenth president, "but measuring him by the sentiment of his country, a sentiment he was bound as a statesman to consult, he was

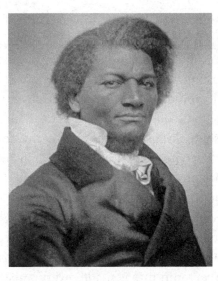

Frederick Douglass criticized Abraham Lincoln regularly, but he also offered a nuanced example of how to evaluate a president in context. "Viewed from the genuine abolition ground, Mr. Lincoln seemed tardy, cold, dull, and indifferent," he wrote about the sixteenth president, "but measuring him by the sentiment of his country, a sentiment he was bound as a statesman to consult, he was swift, zealous, radical, and determined."

swift, zealous, radical, and determined." This vision of the presidency recognized both the necessarily high standard of the office and the human limitations of circumstance.

The Platonic ideal of a president would have strong ratings across all attributes, with the ability to make adjustments within each attribute based on the circumstance.

HIRE FOR BLACK SWANS

A PRESIDENT WILL BE SURPRISED AND TESTED. EARLY IN THEIR TERM there's a good chance they will have to react to a national security threat. Before the attacks of 9/11, George W. Bush had to manage the Chinese capture of an American EP-3 spy plane. Barack Obama learned upon taking office that a covert cyberwar was under way with Iran.[17]

Candidates should be asked what surprise events they might anticipate. Their answers will let us know whether they have scope and vision for the unpredictability of the job they're vying for. We should ask whether they have been in a tough spot before that will give them some reference for enduring the difficulty that will hit them hard and fast. How did they handle that tough situation? What lessons have they taken away from the emergency responses, both diplomatic and military, of previous U.S. presidents?

When pressed on their foreign policy credentials, Democratic candidates in 2020 pointed to their opposition of the Iraq war as proof of their sound judgment. That's a start, but it's only a sliver of the answer. Judgment is good, but execution, follow-through, and determination are what translate good judgment into reality. Those are the qualities that are built by experience. If a candidate lacks that experience, we should interrogate them about the trade-offs of foreign policy. Included in our interrogations should be some discussion of the domestic costs of military action. Debate moderators press candidates about how they are going to pay for their domestic programs, but they rarely raise the issue when it involves spending on military adventures. This allows the belief to flower that national security is somehow too important to be limited by prosaic matters of accounting. But President Eisenhower, whose military record perhaps gave him the standing to make that case, drew the connection directly: "Every gun that is made, every warship launched, every rocket fired signifies, in the final sense, a theft from those who hunger and are not fed, those who are cold and are not clothed."[18]

National security challenges should occupy more of our time because they come in an area of the presidency where the chief executive has the most unchecked power and where the stakes are the highest. What is a candidate's theory about the appropriate use of presidential power? When they are in office facing the pressures of national worry and incentives to act, how will they approach their power and the question of expanding that power to meet the needs of the moment?

As a candidate, Donald Trump said he would reinstate torture in order to combat ISIS. When I asked him about this statement, he said it was weak for the United States to follow rules when ISIS didn't follow any.[19] It was a window into the "whatever it takes" mind-set President Trump would bring to the office. In January 2020, he warned Iran that he would target cultural sites—a war crime that would make U.S. cultural sites more vulnerable—if Iran chose to retaliate for the United States' killing of Iranian general Qasem Soleimani. What we learned in the campaign told us something about how he would govern.

Most candidates will not have Donald Trump's candor about the lines they will cross. They will disappoint us when we ask these questions. Thoughtfulness on complicated issues is not usually rewarded by enough voters on Election Day. However, the administrations that fought wars in Vietnam, Afghanistan, and Iraq have all misled the public at a tremendous cost. Even if the candidates aren't brave enough to answer these questions we should push to debate these issues among ourselves in these terms.

PRIORITIES AND OPPORTUNITY COSTS

CAMPAIGN PROMISES ARE LIKE VACATION PHOTOGRAPHS. THE NUMber of pictures you take of a spot usually indicates how much you loved it more than does the quality of any one photograph. A presidential candidate who talks all the time about immigration, as Donald Trump did, is going to push on that issue when they get in office. That's important to know, but we shouldn't ignore the quality of the picture. How far are candidates willing to go to achieve their goals? How ingenious will they be? How much political capital will they torch to get the job done? Answers to these questions, or at least the back-and-forth over them, will give us some indication about whether a candidate can pull off what they say they want to do, and whether they understand the costs.

When a candidate promises to create a revolution in the country that will change Washington, it rouses the audience, but it raises questions about how effective the revolution will be. Every revolution powerful enough to create change excites a counterrevolution devoted to stopping it. How will the candidate overcome that resistance? When a candidate promises to do something thoroughly objectionable to the other side, like Donald Trump's Muslim ban, we should reevaluate any promise the candidate makes about legislation, because the toxicity created by the promise will foreclose opportunities of working with the opposition.

Beyond the nuts and bolts, presidential priorities need to be understood in terms of opportunity cost. When an administration pushes for something big, that will consume a lot of its time and attention. If a candidate promises to revamp the entire entitlement system, significantly reduce the number of uninsured, and rebuild America's middle class, they will have to pick one, and that will significantly affect their ability to achieve the others.

Understanding priorities and opportunity costs also helps us to evaluate incumbent presidents. A president's supporters are fond of talking about "promises kept." Keeping promises is laudable, but it's not the end of the evaluation process. Was keeping that promise worth all the time and attention needed to do so? Was the impact of the result worth the effort? Was the result worth not spending the same time and attention on other, potentially more important issues? What political damage was caused, or opportunities uncovered, in the process of achieving that result? Would other approaches have yielded a better, longer-lasting result?

Donald Trump has kept his promise to be tough on China. What are the mitigating costs from the effect those tariffs have had on farmers and manufacturing? What are the costs of not pursuing the regional trade deals that might have pressured China more? What are the costs to taxpayers who must fund the bailouts required by the tariff war? What is the cost to the global economy of the uncertainty created by it? The policy might be worth all the collateral issues, but they should at least be tallied.

Can They Build a Team?

A PRESIDENT'S PROMISES WILL NOT AMOUNT TO MUCH IF THEY CAN'T build a team to execute those promises. "Presidents alone rarely accomplish great things," said the national security expert Philip Zelikow about his former boss George H. W. Bush. "He understood that. Presidents accomplish great things because they create teams that can do great things with their leadership."[20]

The best way to test whether a candidate can inhabit the CEO-like role of a presidency is to check their previous experience. If they don't have any experience managing a complex team, we need to determine what their theory of management is, and how they would delegate effectively. Lincoln hadn't run a team, but he knew how to build one.

Does a candidate understand how much of their job they will actually do themselves and how much of it they will delegate? Do they understand how important hiring is? If they haven't even thought about these matters, voters are hiring someone who can make promises but will be a sweaty, panicking mess when they get into office. Without a team or an operating tempo they'll be even worse in an emergency.

When Herman Cain ran for the Republican nomination in 2012, he refused to open the doors on his kitchen cabinet. "They're all gonna ask me, well, who are your economic advisers? And they hate it when I say, I'm not gonna tell you. 'Well, don't you think the American people want to know who's advising you on these new radical ideas?' I'm not gonna tell you. They're my advisers, they're not yours. They just wanna know who my smart people are so they can attack them. That's why they wanna know. And then when I come up with my foreign policy philosophy, they said, well, who are you consulting with on foreign policy? I'm not gonna tell you. They wanna know everything so they can have more ways to try to attack you."[21]

It was a theatrical bit of political spin that might have gotten Cain through the interview, but it should have made voters shudder. Focusing on presidential teams isn't important simply because voters need to know whether the candidate understands how to operate in the structural environment of the job; voters should care about the makeup of presidential teams because those advisers will have a great deal of power if the candidate gets elected. Those who make up presidential teams will heavily influence the departments they run and the kinds of options they present to the president.

Don't Diminish Washington Experience

We should stop treating experience in Washington as a liability. This is not a new tension in American politics. Herbert Hoover noted, "When we are sick, we want an uncommon doctor; when we have a construction job to do, we want an uncommon engineer; and when we are at war, we want an uncommon general. It is only when we get into politics that we are satisfied with the common man."

Today, candidates who have no familiarity with Washington enjoy a distinct advantage; those who have a Washington connection are seen as denizens of "the swamp." This bias ensures that the president lacks all of the skills and relationships honed by years of service that might give them a fighting chance of breaking through the partisan gridlock to create durable solutions. This encourages presidencies led by executive order rather than governing through the legislative process.

Experience in Washington can blind a president by limiting vision to only a Washington view, but it can also offer insight. A president with experience could know how to circumvent the red tape and generally see through the traditional Washington tricks that allow lobbyists, the bureaucracy, and congressional staff to form an iron triangle that thwarts progress. In an emergency, they would know where to push.

Now, of course, simply serving in Washington isn't proof that a lawmaker has any of the relevant experience. Given how easy it is to run against the establishment as a lawmaker in Washington, there are many who seek to rise through the ranks unblemished by the skills, relationships, and leadership qualities necessary to be effective outside the cable network green room.

DON'T HIRE "BUSINESSMEN," HIRE BUSINESS ATTRIBUTES

VOTERS ROMANTICIZE THE CAN-DO SPIRIT OF THE CORPORATE CEO. "What earns him my support is his business acumen," said Liberty University president Jerry Falwell, Jr., when asked what in Trump's Christianity he found attractive. "Our country was so deep in debt and so mismanaged by career politicians that we needed someone who was not a career politician, but someone who'd been successful in business to run the country like a business."[22]

Being a "businessman" can mean anything the person wielding the term would like it to mean. In this case, it meant that Donald Trump would be attentive to the debt and deficit, but little in his record suggested that Donald Trump was a good fiscal steward. There was plenty of proof that he was not. He had repeatedly filed for bankruptcy and stiffed contractors.[23] More directly to the point, he promised not to touch the biggest drivers of budget costs and promised to increase defense spending, the very biggest piece of the pie.[24] Candidate Trump effectively promised to swell the budget, and he has.[25]

The presidency is nothing like a business. Those who promote this idea expect finger-snapping prowess to bring a broken system into shape. But presidents don't have the unilateral power CEOs do. Nor does a president have the forcing mechanism of quarterly reports and stock prices that bring focus and measurement to the enterprise.

A more sensible way to draw from the business world's experience with managing large and complex institutions would be to emulate the way companies select their executives. Gautam Mukunda, a Harvard political scientist who has studied the relationship between how corporations pick leaders and the presidential selection process, points out that businesses rely on a filtering system that seeks leadership candidates who have the basic attributes needed for the job. "We shouldn't believe that a good CEO [necessarily] makes a good president," Mukunda says, "but we should notice that CEOs are selected through a process that is far more careful and deliberate and rationally destined to pick candidates who fit the job."[26] Americans who allege a fondness for the effectiveness of the business world could apply some business-world wisdom to their own decision making by picking leaders the way companies do: by favoring, not punishing, candidates with pertinent experience, or those who have at least thought about how to do the job they're being hired for.

IMPROVING THE PRESIDENCY

Limit the Goals

FORMER INDIANA GOVERNOR MITCH DANIELS, WHO WORKED FOR Ronald Reagan and George W. Bush, argues that presidential overload can be solved only by radically pruning the office. This might require a break between the functional role of the job (defending the nation and building consensus for important legislation, areas where the presidential brain and only the presidential brain can be applied) and the ceremonial parts of the job (visiting disaster sites and welcoming NCAA champions). The latter category might be impossible to avoid altogether, but much of it could be outsourced to the vice president. In his 2017 book *The Impossible Presidency*, the University of Texas historian Jeremi Suri goes further, suggesting we add a European-style prime minister who could take work off the president's desk. A future president might also redefine the role of the First Spouse, tasking her—or him—with a set of duties as Franklin Roosevelt did with Eleanor Roosevelt. "The next successful president is likely to be somebody who concentrates relentlessly on a few well-chosen goals," Daniels says. "Someone who makes it plain that 'there is only so much of me and there are only so many days. We have big problems. It's not that I don't care. I care deeply, but you're not going to see me doing these things. You hired me to do a different job.'"[27]

This idea has an equivalent in the business world. Jim Collins, the author of popular business books including *Good to Great*, writes that creating a "stop doing" list changed his life and put him on his current successful path. He discovered what made the difference between mediocre and successful companies: "Many of the big decisions were not what to do, but what to stop doing."[28]

What should the president stop doing, and how would a president pull this off? This may be another way in which President Trump may have given the country an opportunity to address a problem it has long ignored. Some of Trump's norm-flouting has gotten him in trouble. On other occasions, he's done the previously unimaginable, and the world has kept on spinning. Perhaps this might embolden the next president to give an uncommon inaugural address:

> My fellow Americans, for generations presidents have stood where I stand now and built a tower of disappointment. They have stacked promise upon promise. We will not judge their heart. This great country calls us all to be generous. But it is not generous to the institutions created by our founders to stretch these institutions beyond their limits. Therefore, I will devote my presidency to two essential goals: ensuring your safety and your prosperity. I will take no part in ceremony enjoyed by my predecessors if it does not align with these goals. Instead, America will have the pleasure of coming to know my vice president, cabinet officials, and husband. Congress, too, will enjoy the opportunity to show its generous temperament by returning to American government as an active and equal participant.

Cynics, pundits, and the Extremely Online would roll their eyes. The opposing party would accuse the president of shirking her duties. But the American people might appreciate the candor, the humility, and the signal of focus on the work that really matters. They might also appreciate a president who is not jumping into and out of every issue and making the presidency a reality show. "A rational, experienced president is going to be very, very boring," says Leon Panetta.[29]

Onboard the President

WHATEVER SET OF DUTIES A PRESIDENT DECIDES TO TACKLE, THEY NEED time to get up to speed. Every presidential campaign should go through a process like the one Mitt Romney's undertook in 2012. "It's not fair to the American public," says the Partnership for Public Service's Max Stier, "for a candidate to say, 'You know what, I'm going to go through that "Now what?" moment when I get into office, and you're all just going to suffer along with me on that.' "[30]

Voters and the media could do their part by shelving the idea that it is a display of hubris for a candidate to think about the nuts and bolts of the presidency before the first Tuesday in November. Or at least not snicker, as elites did when Michael Bloomberg suggested he would redesign the West Wing to an open office plan the way he did his offices in public and private life.

We should do the opposite: Evaluate candidates based on their commitment to the transition, using it as a sign of seriousness. How they think about the transition offers a view into how they would approach the job: Can they focus on an important long-term task while engaged in the day-to-day urgency of the campaign? Can they put the right people in place?

Retire the 100-Day Measurement

EVERY PRESIDENT SINCE FDR HAS HAD TO ACCOUNT FOR HIMSELF after the first one hundred days. Only a president facing an extraordinary emergency should have to meet that artificial deadline for significant action. Instead, we should encourage a new norm: If a president wants to move fast, then they have to start slow. Team building and learning the new landscape of a job take time and require exercising new skills. The press and the president's opponents should allow a new administration more time to settle in. Otherwise, current trends are going to lead to calls for resignation that start almost as soon as the rookie president lowers their hand from the Bible.

This will be hard. Presidents are flushed with power when they come to office. On Christmas morning, no one wants to wait for Mom and Dad to get up before opening presents. Most new presidents campaigned on the idea that they would not fall prey to the incumbent's sluggishness and lack of will. However, unrealistic expectations and an unrealistic schedule encourage rushed stabs at action that are more for show than for durable progress.

Give the President His Staff

IT TAKES TOO LONG FOR THE PRESIDENT TO GET HIS TEAM ON THE FIELD. FDR's cabinet was confirmed in fifty-five minutes. Now it takes months. Administrations have to vet candidates down to their socks for fear that some political liability will arise. Then they have to manage the sticky Senate confirmation process. Congress has an important role keeping the executive branch in check, but the process should move faster. Either start the background check process during the campaign, find a way to speed up the congressional approval process, or let presidents have their staff right away and make it easier for Congress to bounce wayward members.

Perhaps some jobs can be taken out of the political process by making them like the Federal Reserve chairman or FBI director, posts that extend across administrations. Brock Long, Donald Trump's former FEMA director, suggests that the disaster management position is too important to be politically appointed. As it stands, new presidents have to appoint someone to a post that can be politically vital with very little idea of what the job really entails. When an emergency hits, the political needs overload the ability to manage emergencies. This can cost lives. "Presidents don't understand the mission until they're in it. It is out of sight and out of mind until the moment everything is broken. Because it's an appointed office, it means it's a make or break agency for legacy. I would never recommend anyone become FEMA administrator under the current conditions."[31]

Elevate the Bureaucracy

THE ADMINISTRATIVE PROCESS IN THE EXECUTIVE BRANCH IS A KEY part of the presidency that goes neglected, argues Elaine Kamarck of the Brookings Institution. It's easy to see why the subject gets little attention in campaigns. There are no moving pictures or exciting drama.

Presidents behave as if the huge federal bureaucracy they lead is something that happened to them, rather than a vital asset to their job and something they must manage and direct. The executive branch, according to the Constitution, sees that the laws are faithfully executed. The agencies are where that executing happens.

If you're an ideologue, you should care about the bureaucracy because that's how many of the things you want to do will get done with a weak Congress. Conservatives, who dislike the entrenched waste of the bureaucracy, should welcome better management. Liberals, who believe in a larger role for the federal government, should welcome the goal of making it better at delivering services. As Michael Lewis detailed in *The Fifth Risk*, federal agencies oversee vast and vitally important parts of American life. They make sure our water is clean, nuclear weapons are secure, unsafe planes are grounded, and drugs heal instead of harm.

The political scientist John J. Dilulio, Jr., who worked in the George W. Bush administration, argues that despite what conservatives have long argued, the federal civil service is not bloated but overloaded.[32] To make do, the government relies on contractors, which adds a duty to the full-time government employees who oversee the vast number of contracts and grants that attenuate accountability. "Leveraged government," he argues, has replaced big government. It's a sloppy workaround. A professional, transparent workforce would make government more efficient and accountable.

Restore the American Tradition of Reform

ONE OF THE BEST WAYS TO REPAIR THE PRESIDENCY IS TO STOP FOCUSING on it. We take all of our problems to the presidential complaint window, but on certain matters, we're going to the wrong office entirely. We should be looking to other institutions — Congress, state and local government — and looking at the electoral process that picks those lawmakers. Those are the institutions where we can effectively address many of our national challenges. Some of them need repair to be in a position to fulfill their duties.

The first step in reform may be believing that our systems can be reformed at all. A January 2020 Gallup poll shows that only 23 percent of the public has faith in Congress. Who wants to throw their back into improving an institution we dislike? On the other hand, the low opinion of the institutions that were once a modern marvel of the world is a sign of how much they need to be repaired. Reform is in the American tradition. After all, the Constitutional Convention was assembled to repair the Articles of Confederation just ten years after they were written. Congress must reassert itself again, taking the lead in writing legislation to meet great national needs and at least weighing in on enormous questions like war and peace. This would relieve pressure on the executive and return to the model the founders designed.

To come back online, Congress must change how it operates, and the electoral process must change so that the structure of elections doesn't continue to make partisanship worse and impossible to get away from. If elections are not structurally slanted toward picking inflexible partisans, they might pick candidates encouraged to make progress through compromise. Since gerrymandered districts lock in partisanship, some states are entrusting nonpartisan panels with drawing district lines instead of giving that job to politically motivated legislators. Ranked-choice voting in states like New York and California uses a format in which voters pick multiple candidates. This seeks to encourage centrist candidates and possibly diminishes outcomes in which a less popular ideological candidate wins because candidates with similar views split the vote.

The Senate filibuster, which allows any senator to engage in unlimited debate until sixty votes are found to stop it, should be reformed, suggest analysts like Ezra Klein, in order to allow legislation to flow and to put senators on the record on key issues so voters know where they stand. Senators of both parties say they would like to vote more and be judged on the votes they take, rather than let their leaders limit what comes to the floor because votes on the record might hurt vulnerable senators and imperil a party's majority status.

The Brookings Institution scholar Jonathan Rauch argues for a political realist approach to politics. This assumes conflict is a constant part of the system and calls us all to take a more transactional approach to the way Congress works. This would allow removal of many of the good-government changes instituted in Congress that, while well intentioned, have had the perverse effect of draining the institution of its lawmaking power. Eliminating earmarks, for example, has put more power in the executive branch's hands and removed the grease that used to bring about legislative compromise. Rotating committee chairs faster was meant to freshen thinking and give congressional party leaders more power, but it has sapped expertise.

The unintended consequences of past reforms should give us humility about advocating for new ones. Advocates of term limits for members of Congress say they would reduce the influence of lobbyists and wealthy interests who have control over lawmakers because they provide the financing for their campaigns. Perhaps, but lobbyists will be happy to be rid of lawmakers with expertise so they can hoodwink the newcomers. Reducing experience also empowers administrative employees who don't change with administrations.

Just because there are challenges with implementing term limits doesn't mean the idea is not worth exploring, however, or that the goals that that remedy seeks to repair are suspect. This is true of reform more generally: The worst fear about a given idea is not necessarily the most likely outcome of that idea. Put another way: Don't let opponents of an idea dismiss it by conjuring the most objectionable implementation of that idea.

Act like Ben Franklin

IT IS POSSIBLE TO REVERE THE FOUNDERS TOO MUCH. THEY HAD MANY flaws. They wrote a document that sought to ensure liberty while it institutionalized slavery. Excessive reverence for the founders also makes our debates lazy. We hold an opinion, search for the founder's quote that affirms it, and wait for the applause from people who agree with us on Twitter. But a quote from the founders is not the last word. They couldn't even agree with one another. Alexander Hamilton and James Madison fought over George Washington's authority to declare the United States neutral in a war between Britain and France. They helped write and sell the Constitution, but they disagreed about what it meant not long after it had been ratified.

Instead, we should interrogate the thinking behind the founders' work to see if it applies today. Their view of power, for example, was based on a notion about ambition and its rapacious unstoppable char-

Ben Franklin was not a paragon of virtue, but we could all take a lesson from his equanimity. In agreeing to the final copy of the Constitution, he said, "The opinions I have had of its errors, I sacrifice to the public good."

acter. They feared ambition not because it made leaders a bore at the dinner table, but because their understanding of history made them believe that unbridled ambition inevitably corroded republican government. Do we see leaders with bulldozing ambition today? Does ambition still maintain that same baleful quality? If so, should we react with the alarm the founders felt when they identified ambition as the greatest threat to the republic?

The founders represented a class of thinkers and a concentrated body of thought focused on how government should work to improve human liberty while guarding against the negative effects of human weakness. Their work, with its flaws, was still durable enough so that Frederick Douglass could use the structure they framed as a tool to repair their work. "Interpreted as it ought to be interpreted, the Constitution is a glorious liberty document," he wrote. Slavery could be supported, he argued, only "by disregarding the plain, common-sense reading of the Constitution itself."

While keeping a wary eye on founder worship, we can still admire some of their habits. We should all look to Benjamin Franklin's final remarks at the close of the Constitutional Convention, and seek to emulate his cognitive equanimity and spirit of putting the general good ahead of personal desires. Hamilton was a hothead in debate, but we also see that he was conscious of excessive righteousness, observing that "so powerful are the causes which serve to give a false bias to the judgment, that we, upon many occasions, see wise and good men on the wrong as well as on the right side of questions of the first magnitude to society. This circumstance, if duly attended to, would furnish a lesson of moderation to those who are ever so much persuaded of their being in the right in any controversy."

Delegate Gouverneur Morris of Pennsylvania was chosen to draft the final wording of the Constitution because he had shown a self-effacing instinct like Franklin's.[33] According to Madison, he showed "a candid surrender of his opinions when the lights of discussion satisfied him that they had been too hastily formed, and a readiness to aid in making the best of measures in which he had been overruled." Nevertheless, Morris was no marshmallow. His outrage at his colleagues who would pretend to write a document focusing on liberty while institutionalizing slavery is a jewel, and a prime example of what we mean when we say someone was on the right side of history.[34]

When we talk about the presidency, we should stretch for this balance between immutable beliefs and open-mindedness. How? The first step is not to cede ground to the partisans. We are trapped in a time of high partisanship, when so many forces, either through design or error, seek to either separate us or define us by our most agitated members. As we walk to the voting booth or into the public square, politicians, pundits, the press, and social media drive us deep into the woods and rob us of our phones and shoes before abandoning us there. Good luck making it back.

We need to know better than to get into the car.

Americans are better than our political class. The group More in Common, which seeks to repair America's political divide, commissioned extensive polling to examine the actual contours of America's landscape. It found that much of our polarization is driven by roughly one-third of the population, ideologues on both wings who are highly engaged with social media and their causes. These activists have noble impulses when they are viewed in the abstract—personal responsibility, equality—but it's their tactics that divide us. They use a noble starter to bake toxic bread.

A survey by The New York Times found that only 16 percent of people placed their political party affiliation among the top three terms they used to describe themselves.[35] For nearly five years, beginning in

2012, the writers Deborah and James Fallows flew across the country in a single-engine Cirrus SR-22 to learn what makes communities thrive. One of their central findings: Those who prospered had not been infected by national politics, either the obsession with Washington or the tactics of motive questioning and bad-faith argumentation that reign there. "Across the country, in towns outside the media spotlight, a new America is being built—one that is innovative, compromise-minded, optimistic, and working toward practical solutions to the problems of this age," they write. This is more proof that we should stop being so obsessed with the presidency. Governors, mayors, and local governments are doing amazing things to help people, and many of them are doing these things in better faith than our politicians at the national level.

If polarization is not the natural condition of most of the country, then defining our national life by the views of those who are political obsessives is a misrepresentation of American national life and also affects that life, creating a profound weariness that cripples the will to participate in public affairs. Those of us in the press have an obligation to be clear that America is not defined by its most partisan citizens.

More in Common hopes to recapture the public square from souring forces by reminding Americans that we are larger and more unified than what is reflected back at us through the political process. It also seeks to create a new obligation for lawmakers, that they should speak to the whole nation, not just to the partisans that keep them in power and comfort. They hope to make building unity a political obligation.

The political scientists Samara Klar, Yanna Krupnikov, and John Barry Ryan have found that Americans are not as polarized as our political combat suggests, but that it is our corrosive language and behavior around the subject of politics that people don't like. They conducted a series of experiments and surveys with more than six thousand people during the 2016 and 2018 national election seasons.[36] They asked people whether they would be "happy" or "unhappy" if they had a child who married someone from the opposing party, Republican or Democratic. For the two-thirds of Americans who do not strongly identify with a party, fewer than 20 percent said they would be unhappy with an in-law from the opposing party—as long as that in-law rarely discussed politics. If their child's partner was talkative, the number doubled to 40 percent. Clearly, how, and how much, we talk about politics makes us more divided.

The Stanford political scientists James Fishkin and Larry Diamond have tried to put this insight into practice through methods designed to build a deliberative democracy. In October 2019, they brought a scientific sample of 523 registered voters together for a weekend in Dallas. The voters took part in diverse small-group discussions facilitated by moderators and sessions featuring experts and presidential candidates from both parties who answered questions from participants. The voters spoke face-to-face across their divisions with neutral facilitators. The most polarizing proposals, whether from the left or the right, generally lost support, and a number of more centrist proposals moved to the foreground.

After the weekend, the percentage of participants saying the system of American democracy was "working well" doubled from 30 to 60 percent. The researchers found that participants are more empathetic and reasonable when they're not just relying on sound bites and tribal chants.

If we are not a country of partisans, we can take actions to stop living in their world. Joseph Califano, Lyndon Johnson's former domestic policy aide, suggests that one possible way to interrupt the present system is for centrists to storm the primaries. Only a small percentage of party members currently take part in the presidential nominating process. The majority of that group is ideologically extreme and more interested in litmus tests. If people with fewer fixed opinions participated more consistently, they might select candidates who demonstrate the preparedness and open-mindedness to govern.

In our everyday political lives and conversations we can recognize the tricks of partisan whataboutism. In a debate, we shouldn't let politicians duck a question by pointing to some flaw in a candidate of the opposing party. They should answer for their own behavior, explain their own positions, and trust voters to be smart enough to judge the other party on the same set of fixed standards.

We shouldn't let partisans pick the topics of national debates. They'll often focus on a side issue that roils emotions in order to set us against one party or another. So enraged, we'll vote on that one issue and not bother thinking through the many larger issues worthy of our attention.

We should also be more discerning about news and information so that the partisans and the Russians aren't influencing our thinking. The managing editor of Snopes, the website that helps you debunk the urban myths your uncle forwards to you, has a rule: If a story arouses an emotional response in you, double-check it. Or, as reporters say: "If your mother tells you she loves you, check it out."

We should recognize, and resist, the simple narratives pushed by partisans and lawmakers. To be sure, there are true American values that don't change, but problems are usually more complex than presented. As voters, we should ask for more from our lawmakers than red meat. And we should call them out when their answers contain no nourishment at all. There is a difference between an answer and a response. Candidates and lawmakers often give the latter as if they've given the former. It is an odd quirk of the modern campaign that we judge candidates on whether they have "what it takes," but protect them from the mildly abrasive duty of answering potentially risky questions.

White House of the Rising Sun

The presidency was a risky bet when it was created. Four years after ending a revolution against a monarchy, the founders established a post that carried elements of what they once despised.

After months of debate at the Constitutional Convention, Benjamin Franklin approved of the final product and rendered his verdict on its promise. "I have often looked at that sun behind the president without being able to tell whether it was rising or setting," he said of the chair Washington occupied during deliberations. "But now I . . . know that it is a rising . . . sun."

George Washington offered no monumental words of hope and change at the conclusion of the delegates' work, but he did commemorate the moment. Before making his way back to Mount Vernon, the future president visited a local bookshop. At a price of 22 shillings sixpence in Pennsylvania currency, he purchased a four-volume copy of

Don Quixote, a book about pursuing worthy dreams even if it is not certain they are going to come true.

There was no guarantee that Washington's dream and the dream of his colleagues would come true. They were rewriting the country's founding principles just ten years after the Articles of Confederation had been adopted, and they knew they might be rewriting their new Constitution in another ten years. By 1802, Alexander Hamilton lamented that the Constitution was a "frail and worthless fabric." The fabric has held, though. The document has endured, as has the founders' carefully balanced system of separate powers. The words and the patterns of behavior that drove the founders have been conveyed from age to age, guiding the character of the chief executive and the nation.

The success and prosperity of the United States of America, though, are still not guaranteed. They are dreams that are tested with each new presidency and that will be tested for as long as the office shall last. In our present moment of partisanship, distraction, and expectation, the office is stretched and misshapen. After 230 years, the challenge remains to keep the sun rising.

Acknowledgments

FIRST, ANNE. SHE HAS BEEN A CRITICAL EAR, A FIRM EDITOR, AND a generous soul from the moment this project started, which, depending on how you count, was either eight years ago or thirty years ago. It is not easy to live with someone who talks about presidential attributes on every dog walk or in the middle of a chore he then doesn't complete. Nevertheless, Anne Dickerson has shouldered that burden and an infinite number of other ones. I'd also like to thank Brice and Nan for their love, the inspiration of their example, and humoring me when I listed all the things I was going to do when I finished the book. It's nice to let a man have his dreams. I love you all very much.

My editor, Kate Medina at Random House, has been a dream. That might read as an obligatory sentence. As such, it's just the kind of bauble Kate would strike out. She is on the lookout for every word that isn't sincere and sharp. But those words are deeply heartfelt. She is precise and wise—in person and in the margins of the pages she sometimes delivered by hand on a Saturday night. And she is an enthusiast, which is my favorite kind of person. Noa Shapiro shepherded endless details and treated me with the patience I might not always have deserved. I am grateful to Carol Poticny for her tireless work tracking down all of my picture requests. Thank you to Benjamin Dreyer, Rebecca Berlant, Kelly Chian, and Sandra Sjursen in production for countless acts of reclamation and binding the wounds after my assaults on language, punctuation,(!) and grammar.

I'd also like to thank Gina Centrello, Robin Desser, Andy Ward, Tom Perry for making this book possible, and Lucas Heinrich, Barbara Bachman, Joseph Perez, Paolo Pepe for making it look so good. All those hours struggling alone would mean nothing without a team to give these thoughts a platform. Thank you to Susan Corcoran, Maria

Braeckel, London King, Ellen Folan, Michelle Jasmine, Steve Boriack, Ayelet Gruenspecht, Leigh Marchant, Barbara Fillon

Elizabeth Hinson has been with me on this project every step of the way, though on the other side of the country—running down facts, obscure newspaper articles, questioning slapdash sentences, and fielding urgent requests for material she had already found. Scores of Google Documents were created and five books could be written from the exchanges in its comments section. She saved me from a thousand blunders, which means those that remain are mine alone. Apologies to Liv and Will and Mary Anne for taking so much of Elizabeth's time. Thank you also to Michelle Ciarrocca, who fact-checked the original *Atlantic* article that gave rise to this book and then signed on for the book-length effort.

My mother used to say that to understand politics, "you have to have history in your bones." I have been the beneficiary of many skeletons. First among them is Brian Rosenwald, Scholar-In-Residence at the University of Pennsylvania, who has worked with me for the last four years on the *Whistlestop* podcast gathering mountains of research upon which we built those episodes, which then provided ballast when I needed it during the book-writing process. He helped banish a lot of my glib certainties and arrived with generous regularity in my in-box with a new prompt or idea about something I should consider. I am also thankful to Dr. Carah Ong Whaley, associate director of the James Madison Center for Civic Engagement at James Madison University whose comments on the manuscript were invaluable.

I am grateful, more broadly, for all the historians and political scientists who work so patiently and thoroughly to create the work that has done so much to shape my thinking. I have benefited not just from the product of their work but from their example. I am also grateful to all of the reporters who I've traveled with and competed with covering this beat.

The impetus for this book came from a conversation with *Atlantic* editor Jeffrey Goldberg years ago after we'd finished taping *Face the Nation*. I am grateful to him for that conversation, which led to an *Atlantic* cover a year and a half later. It was expertly edited by John Swansburg. He not only sharpens the work and finds the most precise version of what you are trying to say, he makes you a better thinker. I am also thankful also to Yoni Applebaum and Don Peck and Scott Stossel. Thank you also to David Bradley for devoting so much to *The Atlantic*.

Before *The Atlantic*, the themes of this book were spooled out in a five-part *Slate* series which wouldn't have existed if its then-editor, David Plotz, hadn't forced all of us to leave our day-to-day reporting and take on a huge project that Will Dobson and Michael Newman helped bring to life.

I am also immensely grateful to my colleagues at CBS. Susan Zirinski gave me the summer to work on this and Bill Owens and Tanya Simon at 60 *Minutes* welcomed me while I was wrestling the pages into their final order. At *Face the Nation*, Executive Producer Mary Hager took a risk on guests and questions framed around the ideas in this book and she and Chris Isham and Steve Capus and David Rhodes all enthusiastically backed them when they turned into debate questions during the 2016 campaign. Thanks also to producer Joey Annunziato who worked with me on these ideas at *CBS This Morning*.

I have been the beneficiary of two excellent assistants in Claire Fahy and Cara Korte. I am very grateful for their constancy, friendship, generosity, and brains.

At the Partnership for Public Service, Max Stier has been a constant source of advice and friendship. I have been a beneficiary of the Miller Center's scholarship and am grateful particularly for its director, Bill Antholis. I am grateful also to the Hoover Institution for inviting me to be a media fellow while I was working on the book and for the generous guidance of its constellation of fellows. I benefited from the keen eye, encouragement, and suggestions of Elliana Bisgaard-Church, Eliza McGraw, David Onek, Amelia Wooldridge, who read the book at various stages.

I am sustained by friendships that bring so much light into my life and that make this kind of book possible. Thank you to Stephen and Evie, Pac and Katherine, David and Liz, Brandon and Alex, Jim and Megan, David and Kara, Penelope and Alex, and Amelia and Adrian. For the last fifteen years, I have spent every week with David Plotz and Emily Bazelon recording the Political Gabfest where I test drove a lot of these ideas. I am grateful for their patience, wisdom, skepticism, and their love, and to all our listeners who have sustained the experiment. Thank you to Jocelyn Frank who brings it to life each week.

To my siblings and the entire Dickerson, McKeehan, and Sharp clans, thank you for your love and support and tolerance even when mine was absent.

Bibliography

BOOKS CONSULTED

Adams, Charles Francis, ed. *Memoirs of John Quincy Adams: Comprising Portions of His Diary from 1795 to 1848*. Philadelphia: J. B. Lippincott & Co., 1876.

Adams, John. "John Adams, Clarendon, no. 3." In *Papers of John Adams*, edited by Robert J. Taylor et al. Cambridge, MA: Belknap Press of Harvard University Press, 1977. http://press-pubs.uchicago.edu/founders/documents/v1ch17s12.html.

Adams, Sherman. *Firsthand Report: The Story of the Eisenhower Administration*. New York: Harper & Brothers, 1961.

Administrative Management in the Government of the United States. Washington, DC: U.S. Government Printing Office, 1937.

Alexander, Robert M. *Representation and the Electoral College*. New York: Oxford University Press, 2019.

Algeo, Matthew. *The President Is a Sick Man*. Chicago Review Press, 2011.

Allbeury, Ted. *Show Me a Hero*. Mineola, NY: Courier Dover Publications, 1992.

Allison, Graham, and Philip Zelikow. *Essence of Decision: Explaining the Cuban Missile Crisis*. New York: Addison-Wesley Longman, 1999.

Allison, Robert J., and Bernard Bailyn, eds. *The Essential Debate on the Constitution*. New York: Literary Classics of the United States, 2018.

Alter, Jonathan. *The Defining Moment: FDR's Hundred Days and the Triumph of Hope*. New York: Simon & Schuster, 2006.

Ambrose, Stephen E. *Eisenhower: Soldier and President*. New York: Simon & Schuster, 1990.

———. *The Supreme Commander: The War Years of General Dwight D. Eisenhower*. New York: Anchor Books, 2012.

Angerholzer III, Maxmillian, James Kitfield, Norman Ornstein, and Stephen Skowronek, eds. *Triumphs and Tragedies of the Modern Presidency*. Santa Barbara, CA: Praeger, 2016.

Annals of the Congress of the United States: Fifteenth Congress—First Session. Washington, DC: Gales and Seaton, 1854.

Annual Historical Association for the Year 1902. Washington, DC: Government Printing Office, 1903.

Arnold, Peri E. *Making the Managerial Presidency*. Lawrence: University Press of Kansas, 1998.

Arrow, Kenneth J. "I Know a Hawk from a Handsaw." In *Eminent Economists: Their Life and Philosophies*, edited by Michael Szenberg, 42–50. New York: Cambridge University Press, 1993.

Auden, Wystan Hugh, and Louis Kronenberger. *The Viking Book of Aphorisms*. New York: Dorset Press, 1981.

Bailey, Thomas A. *Presidential Greatness: The Image and the Man from George Washington to the Present*. New York: Appleton-Century-Crofts, 1966.

Bailyn, Bernard. *The Ideological Origins of the American Revolution*. Cambridge, MA: Belknap Press of Harvard University Press, 1967.

Baker III, James A. *Work Hard, Study . . . And Keep Out of Politics!* New York: G. P. Putnam's Sons, 2006.

Baker, Peter. *Days of Fire: Bush and Cheney in the White House*. New York: Anchor Books, 2013. Kindle.

Balogh, Brian, and Bruce J. Schulman, eds. *Recapturing the Oval Office: New Historical Approaches to the American Presidency*. Ithaca, NY: Cornell University Press, 2015.

Barber, James David. *The Presidential Character: Predicting Performance in the White House*. Englewood Cliffs, NJ: Prentice-Hall, 1992.

———, ed. *Choosing the President*. Englewood Cliffs, NJ: Prentice-Hall, 1974.

Barger, Harold M. *The Impossible Presidency: Illusions and Realities of Executive Power*. Glenview, IL: Scott, Foresman, 1984.

Barnett, Randy E. *Restoring the Lost Constitution: The Presumption of Liberty*. Princeton, NJ: Princeton University Press, 2004.

Barnett, Randy E., and Josh Blackman. *An Introduction to Constitutional Law*. New York: Wolters Kluwer, 2020.

Beeman, Richard. *Plain, Honest Men: The Making of the American Constitution*. New York: Random House, 2009.

Beerbohm, Max. "The Happy Hypocrite." In *The Yellow Book*, vol. 11, London: Ballantyne Press, 1896.

Bennett, Anthony J. *The American President's Cabinet: From Kennedy to Bush*. London: Macmillan Publishers, 1996.

Bennett, William J. *The Book of Virtues: A Treasury of Great Moral Stories*. New York: Simon & Schuster, 1993.

———. *The Death of Outrage: Bill Clinton and the Assault on American Ideals*. New York: Simon & Schuster, 1998.

———. *The Moral Compass*. New York: Simon & Schuster, 1995.

Bennis, Warren, and Burt Nanus. *Leaders: Strategies for Taking Charge*. New York: HarperCollins, 2007.

Berg, A. Scott. *Wilson*. New York: Simon & Schuster, 2013.

Bergner, Jeff. *The Vanishing Congress: Reflections on Politics in Washington*. Norfolk, VA: Rambling Ridge Press, 2018.

Bernanke, Ben S., Henry M. Paulson, Jr., and Timothy F. Geithner. *Firefighting: The Financial Crisis and Its Lessons*. New York: Penguin Books, 2019. Kindle.

Beschloss, Michael. *Presidents of War*. New York: Crown, 2018.

Bishop, Bill. *The Big Sort*. Boston: Houghton Mifflin Harcourt, 2008.

Blight, David W. *Frederick Douglass: Prophets of Freedom*. New York: Simon & Schuster, 2018.

Bloom, Harold. *Genius: A Mosaic of One Hundred Exemplary Creative Minds*. Burbank, CA: Warner, 2002.

Bohn, Michael K. *Presidents in Crisis*. New York: Arcade Publishing, 2015.

Boller, Paul F., Jr., *Presidential Campaigns*. New York: Oxford University Press, 1984.

Boorstin, Daniel J. *The Image: A Guide to Pseudo-Events in America*. New York: Vintage Books, 1992.

Borneman, Walter R. *Polk: The Man Who Transformed the Presidency and America*. New York: Random House, 2009.

Bowen, Catherine Drinker. *Miracle at Philadelphia*. New York: Little, Brown and Company, 1986.

Brauer, Carl M. *Presidential Transitions: Eisenhower Through Reagan*. New York: Oxford University Press, 1986.

Brettschneider, Corey. *The Oath and the Office*. New York: W. W. Norton, 2018.

Brinkley, Douglas, ed. *The Reagan Diaries*. New York: HarperCollins, 2007.

Britten, Loretta, and Sarah Brash, eds. *Hard Times: The 30s (Our American Century)*. Richmond, VA: TIME-LIFE, 1998.

Brownlow, Louis. *The President and the Presidency*. Chicago. Public Administration Service, 1953.

Bryce, James. *The American Commonwealth, Vol. 1*. London: MacMillan and Co., 1891.

Bush, George. *All the Best, George Bush: My Life in Letters and Other Writings*. New York: Simon & Schuster, 2014.

———. *Public Papers of the Presidents of the United States: George Bush, 1992–1993*. New York: Best Books, 1993.

Bush, George W. *Decision Points*. New York: Crown, 2010. Kindle.

Campbell, Kurt M., and James B. Steinberg. *Difficult Transitions: Foreign Policy Troubles at the Outset of Presidential Power*. Washington, DC: Brookings Institution Press, 2008.

Cannon, Lou. *President Reagan: The Role of a Lifetime*. New York: PublicAffairs, 2000.

Caro, Robert A. *The Passage of Power: The Years of Lyndon Johnson*. New York: Knopf Doubleday Publishing Group, 2012.

Carroll, Andrew, ed. *Letters of a Nation: A Collection of Extraordinary American Letters*.

Carter, Jimmy. *White House Diary: Jimmy Carter*. New York: Farrar, Straus and Giroux, 2010.

Ceaser, James W. *Presidential Selection: Theory and Development*. Princeton, NJ: Princeton University Press, 1979.

Chace, James. *1912: Wilson, Roosevelt, Taft and Debs—The Election That Changed the Country*. New York: Simon & Schuster, 2004.

Chadwick, Bruce. *The General and Mrs. Washington: The Untold Story of a Marriage and a Revolution*. Naperville, IL: Sourcebooks, Inc., 2007.

Chafetz, Josh. *Congress's Constitution*. New Haven, CT: Yale University Press, 2017.

Chapman, Robert J. *The Rules of Project Risk Management: Implementation Guidelines for Major Projects*. New York: Routledge, Taylor & Francis Group, 2016.

Chernow, Ron. *The House of Morgan: An American Banking Dynasty and the Rise of Modern Finance*. New York: Grove Press, 2010.

———. *Washington: A Life*. New York: Penguin Press, 2010.

Chollet, Derek, and James Goldgeier. *America Between the Wars: From 11/9 to 9/11: The Misunderstood Years Between the Fall of the Berlin Wall and the Start of the War on Terror*. New York: PublicAffairs Books, 2008.

Clements, Kendrick A. *The Presidency of Woodrow Wilson*. Lawrence: University Press of Kansas, 1992.

Clifford, Clark M. *Counsel to the President*. New York: Knopf Doubleday, 1992.

Clinton, Bill. *My Life*. New York: Alfred A. Knopf, 2004. Kindle.

Collier, Christopher, and James Lincoln Collier. *Decision in Philadelphia: The Constitutional Convention of 1787*. New York: Ballantine Books, 2007.

Collins, Jim. *Good to Great: Why Some Companies Make the Leap . . . And Others Don't*. New York: Harper Business, 2011.

Congressional District Atlas. 95th Congress 1977. HathiTrust. https://hdl.handle.net/2027/puri .32754073474441.

Congressional Record: Proceedings and Debates of the United States Congress. vol. 83, part 9. Washington, DC: U.S. Government Printing Office, 1938.

Congressional Record: Proceedings and Debates of the United States Congress. vol. 107, part 15. Washington, DC: U.S. Government Printing Office, 1961.

Congressional Record: Proceedings and Debates of the United States Congress. vol. 113, part 6. Washington, DC: U.S. Government Printing Office, 1967.

Cook, Blanche Wiesen. *Eleanor Roosevelt*. Vol. 3, *The War Years and After*. New York: Penguin Random House, 2016.

Coolidge, Calvin. *The Autobiography of Calvin Coolidge*. Walking Through The Word Publishers, 2014. Kindle.

Craig, Richard. *Polls, Expectations, and Elections: TV News Making in U.S. Presidential Campaigns.* Lanham, MD: Lexington Books, 2014.

Cramer, Richard Ben. *What It Takes.* New York: Random House, 1992.

Cronin, Thomas E. *The State of the Presidency.* Boston: Little, Brown, 1980.

——. *The Swelling of the Presidency and Its Impact on Congress.* Washington, DC: U.S. Government Printing Office, 1973.

Cronin, Thomas E., and Michael A. Genovese. *The Paradoxes of the American Presidency.* New York: Oxford University Press, 2010.

Cummings, K. Ward. *Partner to Power.* Amherst, NY: Prometheus Books, 2018.

Cummins, Joseph. *Anything for a Vote: Dirty Tricks, Cheap Shots, and October Surprises in U.S. Presidential Campaigns.* Philadelphia: Quirk Books, 2007.

Dallek, Robert. *Camelot's Court: Inside the Kennedy White House.* Sydney: HarperCollins, 2013.

——. *Franklin D. Roosevelt: A Political Life.* New York: Penguin, 2018.

Davidson, Donald J., ed. *The Wisdom of Theodore Roosevelt.* New York: Citadel Press Books, 2003.

Davis, Kenneth C. *Don't Know Much About the American Presidents.* New York: Hyperion, 2012.

The Debates and Proceedings in the Congress of the United States. Fifteenth Congress—First Session. Washington, DC: Gales and Seaton, 1854.

Dickinson, Matthew J. *Bitter Harvest: FDR, Presidential Power and the Growth of the Presidential Branch.* Cambridge: Cambridge University Press, 1996.

DiIulio, John J., Jr. *Bring Back the Bureaucrats.* West Conshohocken, PA: Templeton Press, 2014.

Doherty, Brendan J. *The Rise of the President's Permanent Campaign.* Lawrence: University Press of Kansas, 2012.

Donald, David Herbert. *Lincoln.* New York: Simon & Schuster, 1995. Kindle.

Donaldson, Gary A. *Truman Defeats Dewey.* Lexington: University Press of Kentucky, 1999.

Douglass, Frederick. *The Speeches of Frederick Douglass: A Critical Edition.* New Haven, CT: Yale University Press, 2018.

Draper, Robert. *Do Not Ask What Good We Do: Inside the U.S. House of Representatives.* New York: Simon & Schuster, 2012.

Drucker, Peter. *Managing the Non-Profit Organization: Principles and Practices.* New York: HarperCollins, 2010.

DuBois, Joshua. *The President's Devotional: The Daily Readings That Inspired President Obama.* New York: HarperCollins, 2013.

Dunn, Susan. *Roosevelt's Purge: How FDR Fought to Change the Democratic Party.* Cambridge, MA: Belknap Press of Harvard University Press, 2010. Kindle.

Duwe, Grant. *Mass Murder in the United States: A History.* Jefferson, NC: McFarland & Company, 2014.

Edwards III, George C. *Overreach: Leadership in the Obama Presidency.* Princeton, NJ: Princeton University Press, 2012.

Eisenhower, Dwight D. *Mandate for Change: 1953–1956.* New York: Doubleday, 1963.

Eizenstat, Stuart E. *President Carter: The White House Years.* New York: St. Martin's Press, 2018. Kindle.

Elliot, Jonathan, ed. *The Debates in the Several States on the Adoption of the Federal Constitution, as Recommended by the General Convention at Philadelphia in 1787.* Vol. 5. 2nd ed. Buffalo, NY: William S. Hein & Co., 1996.

Ellis, Joseph J. *His Excellency: George Washington.* New York: Vintage Books, 2004.

——. *The Quartet: Orchestrating the Second American Revolution, 1783–1789.* New York: Vintage Books, 2016.

Ellis, Richard J. *The Development of the American Presidency.* New York: Taylor & Francis, 2012.

———. *Speaking to the People*. Amherst: University of Massachusetts Press, 1998.

Engel, Jeffrey A. *When the World Seemed New: George H. W. Bush and the End of the Cold War*. Boston: Houghton Mifflin Harcourt, 2017.

Engel, Jeffrey A., Jon Meacham, Timothy Naftali, and Peter Baker. *Impeachment*. New York: Modern Library, 2018.

Farrell, John A. *Richard Nixon: The Life*. New York: Doubleday, 2017.

———. *Tip O'Neill and the Democratic Century: A Biography*. New York: Little, Brown, 2001. Kindle.

Felzenberg, Alvin S. *The Leaders We Deserved*. New York: Basic Books, 2008.

Fink, Gary M., and Hugh Davis Graham, eds. *The Carter Presidency: Policy Choices in the Post–New Deal Era*. Lawrence: University Press of Kansas, 1998.

Freedman, Lawrence. *Strategy: A History*. New York: Oxford University Press, 2013.

Freidel, Frank. *Franklin D. Roosevelt: Launching the New Deal*. Boston: Little, Brown, 1973.

Fukuyama, Francis. *Identity: The Demand for Dignity and the Politics of Resentment*. New York: Farrar, Straus and Giroux, 2018.

Germond, Jack W., and Jules Witcover. *Whose Broad Stripes and Bright Stars: The Trivial Pursuit of the Presidency*. New York: Warner Books, 1989.

Gibbs, Nancy, and Michael Duffy. *The Preacher and the Presidents*. New York: Center Street, 2007.

———. *The President's Club*. New York: Simon & Schuster, 2012.

Gillon, Steven M. *The Pact: Bill Clinton, Newt Gingrich, and the Rivalry That Defined a Generation*. New York: Oxford University Press, 2008.

Gingrich, Newt. *Understanding Trump*. New York: Center Street, 2017.

Ginsberg, Benjamin. *Presidential Government*. New Haven, CT: Yale University Press, 2016.

Gitenstein, Mark. *Matters of Principle: An Insider's Account of America's Rejection of Robert Bork's Nomination to the Supreme Court*. New York: Simon & Schuster, 1992.

Goldsmith, Marshall. *What Got You Here Won't Get You There*. London: Profile Books, 2013.

Goodwin, Doris Kearns. *The Bully Pulpit: Theodore Roosevelt, William Howard Taft, and the Golden Age of Journalism*. New York: Simon & Schuster, 2013.

———. *Leadership in Turbulent Times: Lessons from the Presidents*. New York: Simon & Schuster, 2018.

———. *Team of Rivals: The Political Genius of Abraham Lincoln*. New York: Simon & Schuster, 2005.

Gordon-Reed, Annette, and Peter S. Onuf. *"Most Blessed of the Patriarchs": Thomas Jefferson and the Empire of the Imagination*. New York: Liveright, 2016.

Gould, Lewis L. *The Modern American Presidency*. Wichita, KS: University Press of Kansas, 2003.

Greenberg, David. *Republic of Spin: An Inside History of the American Presidency*. New York: W. W. Norton, 2016.

Greene, Robert. *The 48 Laws of Power*. New York: Penguin Books, 2000.

Greenstein, Fred I. *The Hidden-Hand Presidency: Eisenhower as Leader*. Baltimore: Johns Hopkins University Press, 1994.

———, ed. *Leadership in the Modern Presidency*. Cambridge, MA: Harvard University Press, 1988.

———. *The Presidential Difference: Leadership Style from FDR to Barack Obama*. Princeton, NJ: Princeton University Press, 2009.

Gross, Daniel. *Forbes Business Stories of All Time*. New York: John Wiley & Sons, Inc., 1996.

Halberstam, David. *The Best and the Brightest*. New York: Fawcett Books, 1992.

Haldeman, H.R. *The Haldeman Diaries: Inside the Nixon White House*. New York: G. P. Putnam's Sons, 1994. Kindle.

Haley, Nikki. *With All Due Respect: Defending America with Grit and Grace*. New York: St. Martin's Publishing Group, 2019.

Hanson, Victor Davis. *The Case for Trump.* New York: Basic Books, 2019.

Harford, Tim. *Adapt: Why Success Always Starts with Failure.* New York: Farrar, Strauss and Giroux, 2011.

Hargrove, Erwin C. *Jimmy Carter as President.* Baton Rouge: Louisiana State University Press, 1988.

Hart, Gary. *Right from the Start: A Chronicle of the McGovern Campaign.* Princeton, NJ: Quadrangle, 1973.

Hart, John. *The Modern Presidency: From Roosevelt to Reagan.* New York: Harper & Row, 1987.

Hart, Roderick P. *The Sound of Leadership.* Chicago: University of Chicago Press, 1987.

Harvard Business Review. *The Peter Drucker Reader.* Boston: Harvard Business Review Press, 2017.

Healy, Gene. *The Cult of the Presidency.* Washington, DC: Cato Institute, 2008.

Helferich, Gerard. *An Unlikely Trust: Theodore Roosevelt, J. P. Morgan, and the Improbable Partnership That Remade American Business.* Guilford, CT: Lyons Press / Globe Pequot, 2018. Kindle.

Henderson, Phillip G. *Managing the Presidency.* Boulder, CO: Westview Press, 1988.

———, ed. *The Presidency Then and Now.* Lanham, MD: Rowman & Littlefield, 2000.

Hershey, Marjorie R. *Guide to U.S. Political Parties.* Washington, DC: CQ Press, 2014.

Hess, Stephen. *Organizing the Presidency.* Washington, DC: Brookings Institution Press, 2002.

———. *What Do We Do Now?* Washington, DC: Brookings Institution Press, 2008.

Hill, Doug, and Jeff Weingrad. *Saturday Night: A Backstage History of "Saturday Night Live."* San Francisco: Untreed Reads, 1986.

Hilpert, John M. *American Cyclone: Theodore Roosevelt and His 1900 Whistle-Stop Campaign.* Jackson: University Press of Mississippi, 2015.

Hirschfield, Robert S., ed. *The Power of the Presidency.* New York: Aldine de Gruyter, 1982.

Hoar, George F. *Autobiography of Seventy Years.* Vol. 2. New York: Charles Scribner's Sons, 1903.

Hobbs, Joseph P. *Dear General: Eisenhower's Wartime Letters to Marshall.* Baltimore: Johns Hopkins University Press, 1999.

Hodgson, Godfrey. *All Things to All Men: The False Promise of the Modern American Presidency.* New York: Simon & Schuster, 1980.

Hofstadter, Richard. *The American Political Tradition and the Men Who Made It.* New York: Vintage Books, 1989.

Hogan, Michael J. *Woodrow Wilson's Western Tour: Rhetoric, Public Opinion, and the League of Nations.* College Station: Texas A&M University Press, 2006.

Howell, William G. *Power Without Persuasion: The Politics of Direct Presidential Action.* Princeton, NJ: Princeton University Press, 2003.

Hughes, Emmet John. *The Ordeal of Power.* New York: Dell, 1963.

Humphrey, Carol Sue. *The Press of the Young Republic, 1783–1833.* Westport, CT: Greenwood Press, 1996.

Hunt, Gaillard, ed. *The Writings of James Madison.* Vol. 11, 1819–1836. New York: G. P. Putnam's Sons, 1910.

Johnson, Lady Bird. *A White House Diary.* Austin: University of Texas Press, 1970.

Johnson, Richard Tanner. *Managing the White House: An Intimate Study of the Presidency.* New York: Harper & Row, Publishers, 1974.

Jones, Charles O. *The American Presidency.* Oxford University Press, 2007.

Jordan, Amos A., William J. Taylor, Jr., and Lawrence Korb. *American National Security.* Baltimore: Johns Hopkins University Press, 1993.

Kaiser, Robert G. *Act of Congress.* New York: Alfred A. Knopf, 2013.

Kamarck, Elaine C. *Why Presidents Fail and How They Can Succeed Again.* Washington, DC: Brookings Institution Press, 2016. Kindle.

Kean, Thomas, ed. "Foresight—and Hindsight." *The Final 9/11 Commission Report*, 339–60. https://govinfo.library.unt.edu/911/report/911Report_Ch11.pdf.

Kelly, C. Brian, and Ingrid Smyer. *Best Little Stories from the White House*. Naperville, IL: Cumberland House, 2012.

Keltner, Dacher. *The Power Paradox: How We Gain and Lose Influence*. New York: Penguin Press, 2016.

Klein, Ezra. *Why We're Polarized*. New York: Avid Reader Press, 2020.

Kling, Arnold. *The Three Languages of Politics*. Washington, DC: Cato Institute, 2017.

Konig, David Thomas, and Michael P. Zuckert, eds. *Jefferson's Legal Commonplace Book*. Princeton, NJ: Princeton University Press, 2019.

Lamb, Brian, Susan Swain, and C-SPAN. *The Presidents: Noted Historians Rank America's Best—and Worst—Chief Executives*. New York: PublicAffairs, 2019.

Landy, Marc, and Sidney M. Milkis. *Presidential Greatness*. Lawrence: University Press of Kansas, 2000.

Lanthem, Edward Connery. *Your Son, Calvin Coolidge: A Selection of Letters from Calvin Coolidge to His Father*. Montpelier: Vermont Historical Society, 1968.

Larson, Edward J. *George Washington, Nationalist*. Charlottesville, University of Virginia Press, 2016.

———. *A Magnificent Catastrophe: The Tumultuous Election of 1800, America's First Presidential Campaign*. New York: Free Press, 2007.

———. *The Return of George Washington*. New York: William Morrow, 2014.

Larson, Edward J., and Michael P. Winship. *The Constitutional Convention: A Narrative History from the Notes of James Madison*. New York: Modern Library, 2005.

Lasby, Clarence G. *Eisenhower's Heart Attack*. Lawrence: University Press of Kansas, 1997.

Lasswell, Harold D. *Politics: Who Gets What, When, How*. Cleveland: Meridian Books, 1966.

Lee, Bandy X., ed. *The Dangerous Case of Donald Trump*. New York: St. Martin's Press, 2017.

Lee, Frances E. *Beyond Ideology: Politics, Principles, and Partisanship in the U.S. Senate*. Chicago: University of Chicago Press, 2009.

———. *Insecure Majorities: Congress and the Perpetual Campaign*. Chicago: University of Chicago Press, 2016.

Lengel, Edward G. *General George Washington: A Military Life*. New York: Random House, 2007.

Leuchtenburg, William Edward. *The American President: From Teddy Roosevelt to Bill Clinton*. New York: Oxford University Press, 2015.

———. *In the FDR Years: On Roosevelt and His Legacy*. New York: Columbia University Press, 1995.

Levin, Mark R. *Liberty and Tyranny*. New York: Threshold Editions, 2009.

Levin, Yuval. *A Time to Build*. New York: Basic Books, 2020.

Lewis, Michael. *The Fifth Risk*. New York: W. W. Norton, 2018.

Light, Paul C. *The Tides of Reform: Making Government Work, 1945–1995*. New Haven, CT: Yale University Press, 1997.

Looking Toward the Constitutional Bicentennial: A Proposed Amendment to Permit Members of Congress to Serve in Key Executive Branch Offices. Washington, DC: U.S. Government Printing Office, 1980.

Lowi, Theodore J. *The Personal President: Power Invested, Promise Unfulfilled*. Ithaca, NY: Cornell University Press, 1985.

MacMillan, Margaret. *Nixon and Mao: The Week That Changed the World*. New York: Random House, 2008.

MacNeil, Neil, and Harold William Metz. *The Hoover Report, 1953–1955: What It Means to You as a Citizen and Taxpayer*. New York: MacMillan, 1956.

Maltese, John Anthony. *The Selling of Supreme Court Nominees*. Baltimore: Johns Hopkins University Press, 1998.

Manchester, William. *The Glory and the Dream: A Narrative History of America 1932–1972.* Vols. 1 and 2. Boston: Little, Brown, 1974.

Marcus, Ruth. *Supreme Ambition: Brett Kavanaugh and the Conservative Takeover.* New York: Simon & Schuster, 2019.

Martin, George W. *Madam Secretary Frances Perkins.* Lexington, MA: Plunkett Lake Press, 2019.

Matthews, Chris. *Tip and the Gipper: When Politics Worked.* New York: Simon & Schuster, 2013.

McCartin, Joseph A. *Collision Course: Ronald Reagan, the Air Traffic Controllers, and the Strike That Changed America.* New York: Oxford University Press, 2011.

McChrystal, Stanley, Jeff Eggers, and Jason Mangone. *Leaders: Myth and Reality.* New York: Portfolio/Penguin, 2018.

McConnell, Mitch. *The Long Game.* New York: Penguin Publishing Group, 2019.

McCormick, Richard P. *The Presidential Game: The Origins of American Presidential Politics.* New York: Oxford University Press, 1982.

McCullough, David. *Kissinger: A Biography.* New York: Simon & Schuster, 2005.

——. *Truman.* New York: Simon & Schuster, 2003. Kindle.

McDonald, Forrest. *The American Presidency: An Intellectual History.* Lawrence: University Press of Kansas, 1994.

——. *Novus Ordo Seclorum: The Intellectual Origins of the Constitution.* Lawrence: University Press of Kansas, 1985.

McGerr, Michael E. *The Decline of Popular Politics.* New York: Oxford University Press, 1986.

McMaster, H. R. *Dereliction of Duty.* New York: HarperCollins, 2011.

Meacham, Jon. *Destiny and Power: The American Odyssey of George Herbert Walker Bush.* New York: Random House, 2015.

——. *The Soul of America.* New York: Random House, 2018.

——. *Thomas Jefferson: The Art of Power.* New York: Random House, 2012. Kindle.

Mercier, Hugo, and Dan Sperber. *The Enigma of Reason.* Cambridge, MA: Harvard University Press, 2017.

Milkis, Sidney. *The President and the Parties.* New York: Oxford University Press, 1993.

Miller, Merle. *Plain Speaking: An Oral Biography of Harry S. Truman.* New York: Berkley Books, 1981.

Miscellaneous Documents of the House of Representatives, Second Session of the Forty-Fourth Congress, vols. 292 and 294. Washington, DC: Government Printing Office, 1877.

Morris, Andrew. *Race, Rights, and Disaster Relief: Hurricane Camille, Mississippi, and the Transformation of American Disaster Policy.* Philadelphia: University of Pennsylvania Press, forthcoming.

Muirhead, Russell, and Nancy L. Rosenblum. *A Lot of People Are Saying: The New Conspiracism and the Assault on Democracy.* Princeton, NJ: Princeton University Press, 2019.

Murphy, Mark. *Hiring for Attitude.* New York: McGraw Hill, 2017.

Nelson, Michael, ed. *The Evolving Presidency: Landmark Documents, 1787–2015.* Los Angeles: CQ Press, 2016.

Neustadt, Richard. *Presidential Power and the Modern Presidents.* New York: Free Press, 1990.

Newbold, Stephanie P. *All But Forgotten: Thomas Jefferson and the Development of Public Administration.* Albany: State University of New York Press, 2010.

Nichols, David K. *The Myth of the Modern Presidency.* University Park: Pennsylvania State University Press, 1994.

Noonan, Peggy. *What I Saw at the Revolution: A Political Life in the Reagan Era.* New York: Random House, 2002.

Nye, Joseph S., Jr., Philip D. Zelikow, and David C. King, eds. *Why People Don't Trust Government.* Cambridge, MA: Harvard University Press, 1997.

Pariser, Eli. *The Filter Bubble: What the Internet Is Hiding from You.* London: Penguin Books, 2011.

Patterson, Bradley H. *To Serve the President.* Washington, D.C.: Brookings Institution Press, 2008.

Paulson, Henry M. *On the Brink: Inside the Race to Stop the Collapse of the Global Financial System.* New York: Business Plus, 2010. Kindle.

Perlstein, Rick. *Nixonland: The Rise of a President and the Fracturing of America.* New York: Scribner, 2008.

Phillips, Donald T. *Lincoln on Leadership.* New York: Business Plus, 1992.

Pink, Daniel H. *When: The Scientific Secrets of Perfect Timing.* New York: Riverhead Books, 2018.

Pinkett, Harold T. *The Keep Commission, 1905–1909: A Rooseveltian Effort for Administrative Reform.* Menasha, WI: George Banta, 1965.

Plutarch. *Roman Lives: A Selection of Eight Roman Lives.* Translated by Robin Waterfield. New York: Oxford University Press, 1999.

Purdum, Todd S. *An Idea Whose Time Has Come: Two Presidents, Two Parties, and the Battle for the Civil Rights Act of 1964.* New York: Henry, Holt and Company, 2014.

Puryear, Edgar F. *Nineteen Stars: A Study in Military Character and Leadership.* Novato, CA: Presidio Press, 1981.

Quint, Howard H., and Robert H. Ferrell. *The Talkative President: The Off-the-Record Press Conferences of Calvin Coolidge.* Amherst: University of Massachusetts Press, 1964.

Rakove, Jack. *Revolutionaries: A New History of the Invention of America.* Boston: Houghton Mifflin Harcourt, 2010.

Randall, Henry S. *The Life of Thomas Jefferson.* Vol. 1. Philadelphia: J. B. Lippincott & Co., 1871.

Raphael, Ray. *Mr. President.* New York: Vintage Books, 2013.

Rappleye, Charles. *Herbert Hoover in the White House: The Ordeal of the Presidency.* New York: Simon & Schuster, 2016.

Ratcliffe, Donald John. *The One-Party Presidential Contest: Adams, Jackson, and 1824's Five-Horse Race.* Lawrence: University Press of Kansas, 2015. Kindle.

Reagan, Ronald. *An American Life: The Autobiography.* New York: Simon & Schuster, 1990.

———. *Book 1: January 1 to June 28, 1985.* Washington, DC: United States Government Printing Office, 1988.

Reedy, George E. *The Twilight of the Presidency.* New York: New American Library, 1970.

Reeves, Richard. *President Reagan: The Triumph of Imagination.* New York: Simon & Schuster, 2005. Kindle.

The Reports of the Committees: The Senate of the United States. First Session of the Thirty-Fourth Congress. Washington, DC: A. O. P. Nicholson, Senate Printer, 1855–56.

Richardson, James D., comp. *Compilation of the Messages and Papers of the Presidents.* Frankfurt, Germany: Outlook Verlag, 2018.

Roberts, Paul. *The Impulse Society: America in the Age of Instant Gratification.* London: Bloomsbury, 2014.

Roosevelt, Franklin D. *Public Papers of the Presidents of the United States: Franklin D. Roosevelt.* Vol. 9, 1940. Washington, DC: U.S. Best Books, 1941.

Roosevelt, James. *My Parents: A Differing View.* Chicago: Playboy Press, 1977.

Roosevelt, Theodore. *An Autobiography.* New York: Charles Scribner's Sons, 1921.

Rossiter, Clinton. *1787: The Grand Convention.* New York, W. W. Norton, 1966.

———. *The American Presidency.* New York: Time Inc. Book Division, 1963.

Roth, Timothy P. *Morality, Political Economy and American Constitutionalism.* Cheltenham, UK: Edward Elgar Publishing, 2007.

Rubin, Robert E., and Jacob Weisberg. *In an Uncertain World: Tough Choices from Wall Street to Washington.* New York: Random House, 2003.

Ryfe, David Michael. *Presidents in Culture*. New York: Peter Lang, 2005.

Safire, William. *Before the Fall: An Inside View of the Pre-Watergate White House*. New Brunswick, NJ: Transaction Publishers, 2005.

Sanger, David E. *Confront and Conceal: Obama's Secret Wars and Surprising Use of American Power*. New York: Penguin Random House, 2012.

Schlesinger, Arthur M., Jr. *The Imperial Presidency*. New York: Houghton Mifflin Harcourt, 2004.

Schmidt, Eric, Jonathan Rosenberg, and Alan Eagle. *Trillion Dollar Coach*. New York: Harper Business, 2019.

Shogan, Robert. *None of the Above: Why Presidents Fail—and What Can Be Done About It*. New York: Nal Books, 1982.

Simonton, Dean Keith. *Why Presidents Succeed: A Political Psychology of Leadership*. New Haven, CT: Yale University Press, 1987.

Singer, Peter. *The Expanding Circle: Ethics and Sociobiology*. Princeton, NJ: Princeton University Press, 2011.

Skowronek, Stephen. *The Politics Presidents Make: Leadership from John Adams to Bill Clinton*. Cambridge, MA: Belknap Press of Harvard University Press, 1997.

——. *Presidential Leadership in Political Time*. Wichita, KS: University Press of Kansas, 2011.

Slayton, Robert A. *Empire Statesman: The Rise and Redemption of Al Smith*. New York: Free Press, 2001.

Smith, Richard Norton. *An Uncommon Man: The Triumph of Herbert Hoover*. Worland, WY: High Plains Publishing Company, Inc., 1984.

Sorensen, Theodore C. *Decision-Making in the White House: The Olive Branch or the Arrows*. New York: Columbia University Press, 2005.

——. *Kennedy*. New York: Harper & Row, 1965.

Stauffer, John, and Henry Louis Gates, Jr., eds. *The Portable Frederick Douglass*. New York: Penguin Books, 2016.

Stedman, Edmund Clarence, ed. *A Library of American Literature*. Vol. 3, *Literature of the Revolutionary Period*. New York: Charles L. Webster & Company, 1888.

Stephanopoulos, George. *All Too Human*. New York: Little, Brown, 1999.

Sterling, Bryan B. *The Best of Will Rogers*. New York: M. Evans, 1979.

Stewart, David O. *The Summer of 1787: The Men Who Invented the Constitution*. New York: Simon & Schuster, 2007.

Suri, Jeremi. *The Impossible Presidency: The Rise and Fall of America's Highest Office*. New York: Basic Books, 2017.

Suskind, Ron. *Confidence Men: Wall Street, Washington, and the Education of a President*. New York: Harper, 2012.

Taranto, James, and Leonard Leo, eds. *Presidential Leadership: Rating the Best and the Worst in the White House*. New York: Free Press, 2005.

Taubman, William. *Gorbachev: His Life and Times*. New York: W. W. Norton & Company, 2017.

Thomas, Evan. *Ike's Bluff: President Eisenhower's Secret Battle to Save the World*. New York: Little, Brown and Company, 2012.

Thoreau, Henry David. *Walden*. Mount Vernon, NY: Peter Pauper Press, 1966.

Troy, Gil. *See How They Ran: The Changing Role of the Presidential Candidate*. Cambridge, MA: Harvard University Press, 1996. Kindle.

Truman, Harry S. *Memoirs by Harry S. Truman, 1945: Year of Decisions*. New York: Smithmark, 1995.

——. *Public Papers of the Presidents of the United States: Harry S. Truman*. Vol. 8A, 1951. Washington, DC: U.S. Government Printing Office, 1966.

Tulis, Jeffrey K. *The Rhetorical Presidency.* Princeton, NJ: Princeton University Press, 1987. Kindle.

Valley, David B. *A History and Analysis of Democratic Presidential Nomination Acceptance Speeches to 1968.* Lanham, MD: University Press of America, 1988.

Vidal, Gore. *The Best Man.* Dramatists Play Service, 2001.

The Voter's Non-Partisan Handbook and Campaign Guide: Great Issues and National Leaders of 1908. Philadelphia: W. E. Scull, 1908.

Waldman, Michael. *POTUS Speaks: Finding the Words That Defined the Clinton Presidency.* New York: Simon & Schuster, 2000.

Walker, Mike. *Rather Dumb: A Top Tabloid Reporter Tells CBS News How to Do News.* Nashville, TN: Nelson Current, 2005.

Ward, Geoffrey C. *A First-Class Temperament: The Emergence of Franklin Roosevelt.* New York: Vintage Books, 1989.

Washington, George. *The Writings of George Washington: 1785–1790.* New York: G. P. Putnam's Sons, 1891.

Watkins, Michael D. *The First 90 Days: Critical Success Strategies for New Leaders at All Levels.* Boston: Harvard Business Review Press, 2013.

Wehner, Peter. *The Death of Politics: How to Heal Our Frayed Republic After Trump.* New York: HarperCollins, 2019.

Whipple, Chris. *The Gatekeepers: How the White House Chiefs of Staff Define Every Presidency.* New York: Crown, 2017. Kindle.

White, Jr., Ronald C. *Lincoln's Greatest Speech: The Second Inaugural.* New York: Simon & Schuster, 2002.

Wildavsky, Aaron, ed. *The Presidency.* Boston: Little, Brown and Company, 1969.

Will, George F. *The Conservative Sensibility.* New York: Hachette Books, 2019.

Wills, Garry. *Certain Trumpets.* New York: Simon & Schuster, 2013.

———. *Cincinnatus: George Washington and the Enlightenment.* Garden City, NY: Doubleday, 1984.

Wilson, James Q. *Bureaucracy: What Government Agencies Do and Why They Do It.* New York: Basic Books, 1989.

———. *The Moral Sense.* New York: Free Press Paperbacks, 1993.

———. *On Character: Essays.* Washington, DC: American Enterprise Institute, 1995.

Wilson, Woodrow. *Congressional Government: A Study in American Politics.* Boston: Houghton, Mifflin and Company, 1885.

———. *A Crossroads of Freedom: The 1912 Speeches of Woodrow Wilson.* New Haven, CT: Yale University Press, 1956.

———. *The Papers of Woodrow Wilson.* Edited by Arthur S. Link. 69 vols. Princeton, NJ: Princeton University Press, 1966-1994.

Witcover, Jules. *No Way to Pick a President.* New York: Farrar, Straus and Giroux, 1999.

Wittes, Benjamin, and Susan Hennessey. *Unmaking the Presidency: Donald Trump's War on the World's Most Powerful Office.* New York: Farrar, Straus and Giroux, 2020.

Woll, Peter. *American Government: Readings and Cases.* Boston: Longman, 2012.

Wood, Dan B. *The Politics of Economic Leadership: The Causes and Consequences of Presidential Rhetoric.* Princeton, NJ: Princeton University Press, 2007.

Wood, Gordon S. *The Creation of the American Republic 1776–1787.* Chapel Hill: University of North Carolina Press, 1998.

———, ed. *The American Revolution: Writings from the Pamphlet Debate.* New York: Literary Classics of the United States, 2015.

Woodward, Bob. *Fear: Trump in the White House.* New York: Simon & Schuster, 2018.

Young, Jeremy C. *The Age of Charisma: Leaders, Followers, and Emotions in American Society, 1870–1940.* Cambridge: Cambridge University Press, 2017.

The Youngstown Sheet and Tube Company, et al., Republic Steel Corporation, Armco Steel Corporation, et al., Bethlehem Steel Company, et al., Jones & Laughlin Steel Corporation, United States Steel Company, and E.J. Lavino & Company v. Sawyer. 744, 579-768 (1951).

NEWSPAPERS AND PERIODICALS CONSULTED

"The 3 A.M. Phone Call." The George Washington University National Security Archive Electronic Briefing Book no. 371, March 1, 2012. https://nsarchive2.gwu.edu/nukevault/ebb371/.

"192. Telephone Conversation Among President Johnson, Secretary of Defense Clifford, Secretary of State Rusk, and the President's Special Assistant (Rostow)." Department of State: Foreign Relations of the United States, 1964–1968, Vol. 7, Vietnam, September 1968 – January 1969. https://history.state.gov/historicaldocuments/frus1964-68v07/d192.

"1928." New York Times, January 1, 1928.

"1952 Eisenhower vs. Stevenson." The Living Room Candidate: Presidential Campaign Commercials 1952–2016. http://www.livingroomcandidate.org/commercials/1952.

"1980 Presidential Election, Results by Congressional District." Dave Leip's Atlas of U.S. Presidential Elections. https://upload.wikimedia.org/wikipedia/commons/2/29/1980_Presidential_Election%2C_Results_by_Congressional_District.png.

"The 1992 Campaign; Transcript of 2d TV Debate Between Bush, Clinton and Perot." New York Times, October 16, 1992. https://www.nytimes.com/1992/10/16/us/the-1992-campaign-transcript-of-2d-tv-debate-between-bush-clinton-and-perot.html.

"2008 Electoral College by Congressional District." FrontloadingHQ, March 10, 2009. http://frontloading.blogspot.com/2009/03/2008-electoral-college-by-congressional.html.

"2017 Hurricanes and Wildfires: Initial Observations on the Federal Response and Key Recovery Challenges." United States Government Accountability Office: Report to Congressional Addresses. September 2018. https://www.gao.gov/assets/700/694231.pdf.

Abbot, Blake. "'A Widespread Loss of Confidence.' TARP, Presidential Rhetoric, and the Crisis of Neoliberalism." Communication Quarterly, 66:5, 463–480. doi.org10.1080/01463373.2018.1446034.

Abramowitz, Alan I., and Steven W. Webster. "Negative Partisanship: Why Americans Dislike Parties but Behave Like Rabid Partisans." Advances in Political Psychology 39, (2018). doi: 10.1111/pops.12479. http://www.stevenwwebster.com/negative-partisanship-rabid.pdf.

Adams, John. "Quotes on Power." John Adams Heritage Historical Society. http://www.john-adams-heritage.com/quotes/.

Adler, Lynn. "Foreclosures jump 57 percent in last 12 months." Reuters, April 15, 2008. https://www.reuters.com/article/us-usa-mortgages-foreclosures/foreclosures-jump-57-percent-in-last-12-months-idUSN1435957820080415.

Adler, Stephen J., Jeff Mason, and Steve Holland. "Exclusive: Trump Says He Thought Being President Would Be Easier than His Old Life." Reuters, April 27, 2017. https://www.reuters.com/article/us-usa-trump-100days/exclusive-trump-says-he-thought-being-president-would-be-easier-than-his-old-life-idUSKBN17U0CA.

Ajemian, Robert. "Where Is the Real George Bush?" Time, January 26, 1987. http://content.time.com/time/subscriber/article/0,33009,963342-1,00.html.

"Alexander to Obama: No 'enemies list.'" Politico, October 21, 2009. https://www.politico.com/story/2009/10/alexander-to-obama-no-enemies-list-028549.

Alfred, Randy. "Aug. 9, 1854: Thoreau Warns, 'The Railroad Rides on Us.'" Wired, August 9, 2010. https://www.wired.com/2010/08/0809thoreau-walden-published/.

"Alibaba CEO: On-Demand Delivery Is Infrastructure for Future of Retail." CNBC News, November 12, 2018. https://www.cnbc.com/video/2018/11/12/alibaba-ceo-on-demand-delivery-is-infrastructure-for-future-of-retail.html.

Allen, Mike. "Sean Parker Unloads on Facebook: 'God Only Knows What It's Doing to Our

Children's Brains.'" Axios, November 9, 2017. https://www.axios.com/sean-parker-unloads
-on-facebook-god-only-knows-what-its-doing-to-our-childrens-brains-1513306792-f855e7b4
-4e99-4d60-8d51-277555926 /1.html.

Amadeo, Kimberly. "Unemployment Rate by Year Since 1929 Compared to Inflation and
GDP." The Balance, February 7, 2020. https://www.thebalance.com/unemployment-rate
-by-year-3305506.

——. "US Federal Budget Breakdown." The Balance, December 31, 2019. https://www
.thebalance.com/u-s-federal-budget-breakdown-3305789.

"American Experience: George H. W. Bush." PBS, Part 1, 2008. http://www.shoppbs.pbs.org
/wgbh/amex/bush41/program/pt.html#part1.

Andrews, Travis M. "From Kennedy to Trump, the much-deplored history of presidential
candidates on late-night TV." Washington Post, September 22, 2016. https://www
.washingtonpost.com/news/morning-mix/wp/2016/09/22/from-jfk-to-nixon-to-trump
-presidential-candidates-and-their-goofiness-on-late-night-tv/?noredirect=on.

Andrzejewski, Adam. "Trump's Leaner White House 2019 Payroll Has Already Saved Taxpayers $20 Million," Forbes, June 28, 2019. https://www.forbes.com/sites/adamandrzejewski
/2019/06/28/trumps-leaner-white-house-2019-payroll-has-already-saved-taxpayers-20
-million/#1f7233b9386d.

Apple, Jr., R. W. "The Shuttle Explosion; President as Healer." New York Times, January 29, 1986.
https://www.nytimes.com/1986/01/29/us/the-shuttle-explosion-president-as-healer.html.

"April 2009 Health Tracking Poll." Henry J. Kaiser Family Foundation, April 1, 2019. https://
www.kff.org/health-reform/poll-finding/april-2009-health-tracking-poll/.

Arnold, Peri E. "The Brownlow Committee, Regulation, and the Presidency: Seventy Years
Later." Public Administration Review 67, no. 6 (2007): 1030–40. www.jstor.org/stable
/4624663.

"Assessment & Selection: Realistic Job Previews." Office of Personnel Management. https://
www.opm.gov/policy-data-oversight/assessment-and-selection/other-assessment-methods
/realistic-job-previews/.

Associated Press. "Katrina disaster prompts Bush to cut his vacation." NBC News, August 31, 2005.
http://www.nbcnews.com/id/9134533/ns/us_news-katrina_the_long_road_back/t/katrina
-disaster-prompts-bush-cut-vacation/#.XlhXRWhKhPY.

Associated Press. "President Trump picks Ratcliffe to be top intelligence official again." Fox10
News, February 28, 2020. https://www.fox10phoenix.com/news/president-trump-picks-ratcliffe
-to-be-top-intelligence-official-again.

Associated Press. "Rapper Blasts Bush Over Katrina." CBS News, September 3, 2005. https://
www.cbsnews.com/news/rapper-blasts-bush-over-katrina/.

Associated Press. "Rep. DeLay's Remarks on Impeachment." Washington Post, December 19,
1998. https://www.washingtonpost.com/wp-srv/politics/special/clinton/stories/delaytext121998
.htm.

Avirgan, Jody, and Clare Malone. "Why the Dean Screams Sounded So Different on TV."
FiveThirtyEight, February 4, 2016. https://fivethirtyeight.com/features/why-the-dean
-scream-sounded-so-different-on-tv/.

Badger, Emily, and Quoctrung Bui. "Americans Say Their Politics Don't Define Them. But
It's Complicated." New York Times, October 12, 2018. https://www.nytimes.com/interactive
/2018/10/12/upshot/us-politics-identity.html.

Balz, Dan. "Nos. 44 and 45 Broke the Mold. What Does That Mean for the Future of the
Presidency?" Washington Post, May 18, 2019. https://www.washingtonpost.com/politics
/nos-44-and-45-broke-the-mold-what-does-that-mean-for-the-future-of-the-presidency/2019
/05/18/97d64320-77e9-11e9-bd25-c989555e7766_story.html.

——. "The Whip Who Would Be Speaker." Washington Post, October 20, 1994. https://www
.washingtonpost.com/archive/politics/1994/10/20/the-whip-who-would-be-speaker
/9e5dfbdd-808a-4ca6-aff1-70d6980c2ff6/.

Baker, Peter. "'We Absolutely Could Not Do That': When Seeking Foreign Help Was Out of the Question." *New York Times*, October 6, 2019. https://www.nytimes.com/2019/10/06/us/politics/trump-foreign-influence.html.

"Barack Obama defends 'just war' using drones." BBC, May 24, 2013. https://www.bbc.com/news/world-us-canada-22638533.

"Barack Obama's Remarks in St. Paul." *New York Times*, June 3, 2008. https://www.nytimes.com/2008/06/03/us/politics/03text-obama.html.

Barmore, Jasmin. "Bethany Gaskin Is the Queen of Eating Shellfish Online." *New York Times*, June 11, 2019. https://www.nytimes.com/2019/06/11/style/youtube-mukbang-bloveslife-bethany-gaskin.html.

Barrett, Ted, Phil Mattingly, Ali Zaslav, et al. "McConnell denies he told Trump his call with the Ukrainian President was perfect." CNN.com, October 22, 2019. https://www.cnn.com/2019/10/22/politics/mcconnell-denies-trump-call-ukraine-perfect/index.html.

Bauer, Shane. "Part One of Two: Behind the Lines." *Mother Jones*, May/June 2019. https://www.motherjones.com/politics/2019/06/behind-the-lines-syria-part-one/.

Beamon, Todd. "Steve Bannon, Unrepentant, Dismisses Far Right as 'Clowns.'" Newsmax, August 16, 2017. https://www.newsmax.com/Politics/bannon-dismisses-far-right-clowns/2017/08/16/id/808082/.

Bedard, Paul. "Tip O'Neill and Reagan and Model for Breaking Partisan Gridlock." *U.S. News & World Report*, February 17, 2010. https://www.usnews.com/news/blogs/washington-whispers/2010/02/17/tip-oneill-and-reagan-and-model-for-breaking-partisan-gridlock.

Beggin, Riley. "Trump again boosts a baseless conspiracy theory, this one about Jeffrey Epstein." Vox.com, August 11, 2019. https://www.vox.com/policy-and-politics/2019/8/11/20800787/jeffrey-epstein-donald-trump-conspiracy-theory-clinton-body-count-retweet-killed-death-by-suicide.

"Benjamin Franklin's final speech in the Constitutional Convention, 17 September 1787." *The Papers of Thomas Jefferson*, The Trustees of Princeton University, 2018. http://jefferson3volumes.princeton.edu/?q=content/benjamin-franklins-final-speech-constitutional-convention-17-september-1787.

Berkowitz, Bonnie, Chris Alcantara, and Denise Lu. "The Terrible Numbers That Grow with Each Mass Shooting." *Washington Post*, February 26, 2019. https://www.washingtonpost.com/graphics/2018/national/mass-shootings-in-america/.

"Berlin Wall." History.com, November 9, 2019. https://www.history.com/topics/cold-war/berlin-wall.

Berman, Russell. "Hillary Clinton, Uniter?" *The Atlantic*, February 27, 2015. https://www.theatlantic.com/politics/archive/2015/02/hillary-clintons-warm-purple-space/386288/.

"Beyond Distrust: How Americans View Their Government." Pew Research Center, November 23, 2015. https://www.people-press.org/2015/11/23/beyond-distrust-how-americans-view-their-government/.

Bianchi, Francesco, Howard Kung, and Thilo Kind. "Threats to Central Bank Independence: High-Frequency Identification with Twitter." National Bureau of Economic Research, Working Paper No. 26308 (September 2019). https://www.nber.org/papers/w26308.

Blake, Aaron. "Trump's extraordinary Oval Office squabble with Chuck Schumer and Nancy Pelosi, annotated." *Washington Post*, December 11, 2018. https://www.washingtonpost.com/politics/2018/12/11/trumps-extraordinary-oval-office-squabble-with-chuck-schumer-nancy-pelosi-annotated/.

Bloomberg, Michael. Interview by Margaret Brennan. "Transcript: Cotton, Feinstein, Bloomberg." *Face the Nation*, CBS News, April 22, 2018. https://www.cbsnews.com/news/full-transcript-face-the-nation-on-april-22-2018/.

Boerma, Lindsey. "Cain: No need to name my economic, foreign policy advisers." CBS News, October 14, 2011. https://www.cbsnews.com/news/cain-no-need-to-name-my-economic-foreign-policy-advisers/.

——. "Obama reflects on his biggest mistake as president." CBS News, July 12, 2012. https://www.cbsnews.com/news/obama-reflects-on-his-biggest-mistake-as-president/.

Bogie, Justin. "Congress Must Stop the Abuse of Disaster and Emergency Spending." The Heritage Foundation, February 4, 2019. https://www.heritage.org/sites/default/files/2019-02/BG3380.pdf.

Boehner, John. Interview by John Dickerson. "Transcript: Boehner, Sanders, Kasich." *Face the Nation*, CBS News, September 27, 2015. https://www.cbsnews.com/news/face-the-nation-transcripts-september-27-boehner-sanders-kasich/.

Boskin, Michael J., John H. Cochrane, John F. Cogan, George P. Shultz, and John B. Taylor. "A Debt Crisis Is on the Horizon." *Washington Post*, March 27, 2018. https://www.washingtonpost.com/opinions/the-debt-crisis-is-on-our-doorstep/2018/03/27/fd28318c-27d3-11e8-bc72-077aa4dab9ef_story.html.

Bowman, Emma, and Wynne Davis. "Charlottesville Victim Heather Heyer 'Stood Up' Against What She Felt Was Wrong." NPR, August 13, 2017. https://www.npr.org/sections/thetwo-way/2017/08/13/543175919/violence-in-charlottesville-claims-3-victims.

Brandt, Eric. "Toomey Doubts Second Senate Gun-Control Vote Any Time Soon." Main Line Times, May 1, 2013. http://www.mainlinemedianews.com/mainlinetimes/news/toomey-doubts-second-senate-gun-control-vote-any-time-soon/article_0542dc39-1434-5559-822c-4c493c384c0b.html.

Brenan, Megan. "More Still Disapprove Than Approve of 2017 Tax Cuts." Gallup, October 10, 2018. https://news.gallup.com/poll/243611/disapprove-approve-2017-tax-cuts.aspx.

——. "Trump Seen Marginally as Decisive Leader, but Not Honest." Gallup, July 10, 2019. https://news.gallup.com/poll/260495/trump-seen-marginally-decisive-leader-not-honest.aspx.

——. "U.S. Voters Using Midterms to Send Trump a Message." Gallup, November 2, 2018. https://news.gallup.com/poll/244193/voters-using-midterms-send-trump-message.aspx.

"Brené Brown on 'Dare to Lead' and why vulnerability is the 'only path to courage.'" CBS *This Morning*, CBS, October 10, 2018. https://www.cbsnews.com/news/brene-brown-new-book-dare-to-lead-courage-vulnerability/.

"Brennan, Kasich, Focus Group." Interview by John Dickerson, *Face the Nation*, CBS News, February 26, 2017. https://www.cbsnews.com/news/face-the-nation-february-26-2017-transcript-brennan-kasich-focus-group/.

Broder, David S., and Ward Sinclair. "A Political Skylab Hits the Capital." *Washington Post*, July 20, 1979. https://www.washingtonpost.com/archive/politics/1979/07/20/a-political-skylab-hits-the-capital/2ed94fb9-fe0d-4a3c-872e-5a0eda93f5a1/.

Brown, Brendan. "Trump Twitter Archive." Trump Twitter Archive. http://www.trumptwitterarchive.com/.

Brown, George Rothwell. "Full Credit Accorded Aroused Nation." *San Francisco Examiner*, April 9, 1938.

Brownstein, David. "Public Service Leadership Model: Quick links resource guide." Partnership for Public Service, August 9, 2019. https://ourpublicservice.org/public-service-leadership-model-quick-links-resource-guide/.

Bryan, Bob. "Top Trump adviser says the GOP tax bill is 'death to Democrats.'" *Business Insider*, December 5, 2017. https://www.businessinsider.com/trump-gop-tax-bill-democrats-salt-deduction-text-details-2017-12.

Buckley, Jr., William F. "Our Mission Statement." *National Review*, November 19, 1955. https://www.nationalreview.com/1955/11/our-mission-statement-william-f-buckley-jr/.

"'The Buck Stops Here' Desk Sign." Harry S. Truman Library and Museum. https://www.trumanlibrary.gov/education/trivia/buck-stops-here-sign.

Budryk, Zack. "Pelosi: Progressive Dem wing represented by Ocasio-Cortez is 'like five people.'" The Hill, April 14, 2019. https://thehill.com/homenews/house/438856-pelosi-progressive-dem-wing-represented-by-ocasio-cortez-is-like-five-people.

Bump, Philip. "Donald Trump's surprisingly savvy analysis of American politics." *Washington Post*, August 16, 2015. https://www.washingtonpost.com/news/the-fix/wp/2015/08/16/donald -trumps-surprisingly-savvy-comment-about-american-politics/.

——. "The revised death toll in Puerto Rico makes Trump's comparison to Katrina look even worse." *Washington Post*, August 9, 2018. https://www.washingtonpost.com/news/politics /wp/2018/08/09/the-revised-death-toll-in-puerto-rico-makes-trumps-comparison-to-katrina -look-even-worse/.

——. "Trump's attempt to clean up the Putin event was an insult to America's intelligence." *Washington Post*, July 17, 2018. https://www.washingtonpost.com/news/politics/wp /2018/07/17/trumps-attempt-to-clean-up-the-putin-event-was-an-insult-to-americas -intelligence/.

Burns, Robert. "US intel heads list North Korea, not border, as threat to US." AP News, January 29, 2019. https://apnews.com/5bb33704147f4951a040dcb53d709586.

"Bush Asks Condi For A Bathroom Break . . ." HuffPost, March 3, 2008. https://www.huffpost .com/entry/bush-asks-condi-for-a-bat_n_7399.

Bush, George W. "Bullhorn Address to Ground Zero Rescue Workers." American Rhetoric of 9-11, September 14, 2001. https://www.americanrhetoric.com/speeches/gwbush911ground zerobullhorn.htm.

"Business Leaders Start 2020 with Lingering Concerns About Talent Shortages & Recession Risk." The Conference Board, January 2, 2020. https://www.conference-board.org/press /c-suite-survey-2020.

Campbell, David, and Geoffrey Layman. "How Trump has changed white evangelicals' views about morality." *Washington Post*, April 25, 2019. https://www.washingtonpost.com/politics /2019/04/25/how-trump-has-changed-white-evangelicals-views-about-morality/.

Cannon, Carl M. "Newt vs. Tip: Partisanship at Its Apogee?" Real Clear Politics, May 15, 2014. https://www.realclearpolitics.com/articles/2014/05/15/newt_vs_tip_partisanship_at_its _apogee_122643.html.

Cannon, Lou, and Lee Lescaze. "The Relaxed Approach." *Washington Post*, February 9, 1981. https://www.washingtonpost.com/archive/politics/1981/02/09/the-relaxed-approach /0b09571d-0f29-43b1-a813-e7395d53667b/.

Cappelli, Peter. "Your Approach to Hiring Is All Wrong." *Harvard Business Review*, June 2019. https://hbr.org/2019/05/recruiting.

Carberry, Sean D. "Clapper: Presidential transition 'will be OK.'" Federal Computer Week, September 7, 2016. https://fcw.com/articles/2016/09/07/clapper-carberry.aspx?m=1.

Caro, Robert. Interview by Steve Inskeep. "Caro's 'Passage Of Power': LBJ's Political Genius." NPR, April 30, 2012. https://www.npr.org/transcripts/151523678.

Caron, Christina. "Obama's Letter to President Trump on Inauguration Day." *New York Times*, September 3, 2017. https://www.nytimes.com/2017/09/03/us/politics/obama-trump -letter.html.

Carter, Jimmy. "Former President Jimmy Carter on Service and How the Presidency Has Changed." Interview by John Dickerson. CBS *This Morning*, CBS News, August 28, 2018. https://www.cbsnews.com/news/former-president-jimmy-carter-on-service-and-how-the -presidency-has-changed/.

——. "July 15, 1979: "Crisis of Confidence" Speech." UVA Miller Center, National Archives. https://millercenter.org/the-presidency/presidential-speeches/july-15-1979-crisis -confidence-speech.

Caruso, Justin. "'It's Devastating'—Trump Describes Writing Letters to Families of Killed Soldiers in Emotional Speech." Daily Caller, October 7, 2019. https://dailycaller.com /2019/10/07/trump-veterans-speech-devastating/.

Cassidy, John. "Can Donald Trump Learn from Ronald Reagan and Tip O'Neill?" *New Yorker*, March 28, 2017. https://www.newyorker.com/news/john-cassidy/can-donald-trump -learn-from-ronald-reagan-and-tip-oneill.

"Character Above All: An Exploration of Presidential Leadership." *PBS Newshour.* 1996. https://www.pbs.org/newshour/spc/character/.

Chaslot, Guillaume. "How Algorithms Can Learn to Discredit the Media." Medium, February 1, 2018. https://medium.com/@guillaumechaslot/how-algorithms-can-learn-to-discredit-the-media-d1360157c4fa.

———. "How YouTube's A.I. boosts alternative facts." Medium, March 31, 2017. https://medium.com/@guillaumechaslot/how-youtubes-a-i-boosts-alternative-facts-3cc276f47cf7

Chavez, Nicole, and Rafy Rivera. "Puerto Rico emergency director fired after residents discover warehouse full of Hurricane Maria supplies." CNN.com, January 19, 2020. https://www.cnn.com/2020/01/18/us/puerto-rico-emergency-director-fired/index.html.

Cheriks, Jason. "How the Obama Administration Handled The Last Crisis In The Gulf." HuffPost, August 30, 2017. https://www.huffpost.com/entry/how-the-obama-administration-handled-the-last-crisis-in-the-gulf_n_59a7080ae4b00795c2a37a81.

Chotiner, Isaac. "The Pelosi-Versus-Squad Paradigm." *New Yorker,* July 18, 2019. https://www.newyorker.com/news/q-and-a/the-pelosi-versus-squad-paradigm.

Chozick, Amy, Nicholas Confessore, and Michael Barbaro. "Leaked Speech Excerpts Show a Hillary Clinton at Ease with Wall Street." *New York Times,* October 7, 2016. https://www.nytimes.com/2016/10/08/us/politics/hillary-clinton-speeches-wikileaks.html.

Christie, Les. "Foreclosures up 75% in 2007." CNN Money, January 29, 2008. https://money.cnn.com/2008/01/29/real_estate/foreclosure_filings_2007/.

———. "Foreclosures up a record 81% in 2008." CNN Money, January 15, 2009. https://money.cnn.com/2009/01/15/real_estate/millions_in_foreclosure/.

Cillizza, Chris. "Donald Trump doesn't actually seem to think President Obama was born in the U.S." *Washington Post,* September 22, 2016. https://www.washingtonpost.com/news/the-fix/wp/2016/09/22/does-donald-trump-actually-think-president-obama-was-born-in-the-u-s-er/.

"The Civil Rights Act of 1964: A Long Struggle for Freedom." Library of Congress. https://www.loc.gov/exhibits/civil-rights-act/multimedia/randolph-challenges-fdr.html.

Clark, Robert E. "Ike Setting Up Policy of Firing Back." *Cedar Rapids Gazette,* vol. 74, no. 264, September 29, 1956.

Clements, Kendrick A. "Woodrow Wilson and Administrative Reform." *Presidential Studies Quarterly* 28, no. 2 (1998): 320–36. www.jstor.org/stable/27551862.

Clifford, George. "Can His Victory in the Fortas Case Make Sen. Robert Griffin a Power in Washington? Or Will He Be Just a One-Time Hero?" *Detroit Scope Magazine,* November 2, 1968.

Clinton, Bill. "Excerpts from Transcribed Remarks by the President and the Vice President to the People of Knoxville on Internet for Schools." Office of the Press Secretary, October 10, 1996. https://govinfo.library.unt.edu/npr/library/speeches/101096.html.

———. "Interview of the President." Interview by WWWE Radio, Cleveland, October 24, 1994. https://clintonwhitehouse6.archives.gov/1994/10/1994-10-24-interview-of-the-president-with-wwwe-radio-cleveland.html.

———. "Let's Make a Deal." C-SPAN, Presidential Leadership Scholars Program, September 12, 2014. https://www.c-span.org/video/?c4508363/user-clip-lets-make-deal.

———. "President Clinton: We Share Your Grief . . . But You Have Not Lost Everything." *New York Times,* April 24, 1995. https://www.washingtonpost.com/archive/politics/1995/04/24/president-clinton-we-share-your-grief-but-you-have-not-lost-everything/31f4ec23-7ac7-47c7-a62f-e63699eb3041/.

"Cloture Rule." United States Senate, March 8, 1917. https://www.senate.gov/artandhistory/history/minute/Cloture_Rule.htm.

Clymer, Adam. "A 'New' Hamilton Jordan Faces Challenge to President's Future." *New York Times,* July 23, 1979.

"CNBC Full Transcript: CNBC's "Your Money, Your Vote: The Republican Presidential

Debate" (Part 2)." CNBC News, October 29, 2015. https://www.cnbc.com/2015/10/29/cnbc
-full-transcript-cnbcs-your-money-your-vote-the-republican-presidential-debate-part-2
.html.

Cohen, Richard. "Mr. Cool turns cold." *Washington Post*, August 8, 2011. https://www.wash
ingtonpost.com/opinions/mr-cool-turns-cold/2011/08/08/gIQAoZlI3I_story.html.

"Colin Powell Provides An Inside Perspective on President Reagan and Trust." The Hudson
Union Society, December 25, 2012. https://www.youtube.com/watch?v=rgZ4x6D3GRs.

Collins, Jim. "Best New Year's Resolution? A 'Stop Doing' List." *USA Today*, December 30,
2003. https://www.jimcollins.com/article_topics/articles/best-new-years.html.

"Colorado Sen. Michael Bennet on Trump, McConnell and His New Book." Interview by
John Dickerson, *CBS This Morning*, CBS News, July 15, 2019. https://soundcloud.com
/cbsthismorning/colorado-sen-michael-bennet-on-trump-mcconnell-and-his-new-book.

"Communications Market Report." OfCom, August 2, 2018. https://www.ofcom.org.uk/__data
/assets/pdf_file/0022/117256/CMR-2018-narrative-report.pdf.

Condon, Jr., George E. "Howard Baker, the 'Eloquent Listener.'" *The Atlantic*, June 26, 2014.
https://www.theatlantic.com/politics/archive/2014/06/howard-baker-the-eloquent-listener
/442872/.

"Congress and the Public: Congressional Job Approval." Gallup, January 2020. https://news
.gallup.com/poll/1600/congress-public.aspx.

"Conversation with Buford Ellington and Marvin Watson, September 10, 1965." UVA Miller
Center. https://millercenter.org/the-presidency/secret-white-house-tapes/conversation
-buford-ellington-and-marvin-watson-september.

"Conversation with Robert Phillips, Marvin Watson and Russell Long, September 14, 1965."
UVA Miller Center. https://millercenter.org/the-presidency/secret-white-house-tapes
/conversation-robert-phillips-marvin-watson-and-russell-long.

Conway III, George T. "Unfit for Office." *The Atlantic*, October 3, 2019. https://www
.theatlantic.com/ideas/archive/2019/10/george-conway-trump-unfit-office/599128/.

Cook, Dave. "GOP Official Haley Barbour: Obama Not a Muslim, but He Is Mysterious."
Christian Science Monitor, September 9, 2010. https://www.csmonitor.com/USA/Politics
/monitor_breakfast/2010/0909/GOP-official-Haley-Barbour-Obama-not-a-Muslim-but-he
-is-mysterious.

"Coolidge Taken Ill, Recovers Quickly; Combination of Heat and Cantaloupe Causes a Brief
Attack of Indigestion." *New York Times*, May 24, 1925. https://timesmachine.nytimes.com
/timesmachine/1925/05/24/107059288.html?pageNumber=1.

Cooper, Michael. "Conservatives Sowed Idea of Health Care Mandate, Only to Spurn It
Later." *New York Times*, February 14, 2012. https://www.nytimes.com/2012/02/15/health
/policy/health-care-mandate-was-first-backed-by-conservatives.html.

Corwin, Edward S. "Woodrow Wilson and the Presidency." *Virginia Law Review* 42, no. 6
(1956): 761-83. doi:10.2307/1070269.

Costa, Robert, Dan Balz, and Philip Rucker. "Trump wanted to put Bill Clinton's accusers in
his family box. Debate officials said no." *Washington Post*, October 10, 2016. https://www
.washingtonpost.com/news/post-politics/wp/2016/10/10/trumps-debate-plan-to-seat-bill
-clintons-accusers-in-family-box-was-thwarted/.

Crowley, Michael. "Trump Visits Afghanistan and Says He Reopened Talks with Taliban."
New York Times, November 28, 2019. https://www.nytimes.com/2019/11/28/us/politics/trump
-afghanistan.html.

Crowley, Michael, and Carlotta Gall. "In Trump, Turkey's Erdogan Keeps Finding a Sympathetic Ear." *New York Times*, October 8, 2019. https://www.nytimes.com/2019/10/08/us
/politics/trump-erdogan-turkey-visit.html.

Cunningham, Paige Winfield. "The Health 202: Democrats have lurched leftward on health
benefits for undocumented immigrants." *Washington Post*, July 1, 2019. https://www

.washingtonpost.com/news/powerpost/paloma/the-health-202/2019/07/01/the-health-202
-democrats-have-lurched-leftward-on-health-benefits-for-undocumented-immigrants
/5d18b0a61ad2e552a21d51bf/.

Currier, Cora. "The Facts Behind Obama's Executive Privilege Claim." ProPublica, June 21,
2012. https://www.propublica.org/article/the-facts-behind-obamas-executive-privilege-claim.

Dale, Daniel. "Donald Trump has said 5276 false things as U.S. president." *Toronto Star*, May
5, 2019. https://projects.thestar.com/donald-trump-fact-check/.

Daley, Steve, and Elaine S. Povich. "House Speaker Wright Resigns." *Chicago Tribune*, June
1, 1989. https://www.chicagotribune.com/news/ct-xpm-1989-06-01-8902050821-story.html.

Dallek, Matthew. "Bipartisan Reagan-O'Neill Social Security Deal in 1983 Showed It Can Be
Done." *U.S. News & World Report*, April 2, 2009. https://www.usnews.com/opinion
/articles/2009/04/02/bipartisan-reagan-oneill-social-security-deal-in-1983-showed-it-can-be
-done.

Daugherty, Owen. "Roger Stone defends Trump's attacks on Barbara Bush: 'She's dead and
he's president.'" The Hill, April 5, 2019. https://thehill.com/blogs/blog-briefing-room/news
/437663-roger-stone-defends-trumps-attacks-on-barbara-bush-shes-dead.

Davies, Gareth. "The Historical Presidency: Lyndon Johnson and Disaster Politics." *Presidential Studies Quarterly* 47, Issue 3 (September 2017): 529–51.

———. "Pre-Modern Disaster Politics: Combating Catastrophe in the 1950s." *Journal of Federalism* 47, Issue 2 (February 2017): 271. https://doi.org/10.1093/publius/pjx016.

Dawsey, Josh. "In speech, Mulvaney says Republicans are hypocritical on deficits." *Washington Post*, February 19, 2020. https://www.washingtonpost.com/politics/in-speech-mulvaney
-admits-republicans-are-hypocritical-on-deficits/2020/02/19/28546c84-5385-11ea-9e47
-59804be1dcfb_story.html.

Dearborn, John. "The Foundations of the Modern Presidency: Presidential Representation,
the Unitary Executive Theory, and the Reorganization Act of 1939." *Presidential Studies
Quarterly* 49 (March 2018): 35. https://doi.org/10.1111/psq.12463.

DeBonis, Mike, and Seung Min Kim. "'All roads lead to Putin': Pelosi questions Trump's
loyalty in White House clash." *Washington Post*, October 17, 2019. https://www
.washingtonpost.com/powerpost/pelosi-recalls-clash-with-trump-says-she-was-probably
-telling-him-that-all-roads-lead-to-putin/2019/10/17/fdbde8d2-f0f2-11e9-8693-f487e46784aa
_story.html.

Decker, Cathleen. "Bush Brands Dukakis as Insensitive to Crime Victims." *Los Angeles Times*,
October 8, 1988. https://www.latimes.com/archives/la-xpm-1988-10-08-mn-2922-story.html.

"Defeated Quayle: 'I Will Continue to Stand Up.'" *Janesville Gazette Newspaper*, April 4,
1992.

Degan, Tom. "LBJ: The Man We Hate to Love." LBJ Presidential Library, May 14, 2012. http://
www.lbjlibrary.org/press/lbj-in-the-news/lbj-the-man-we-hate-to-love.

Delli Carpini, Michael X. "Radio's Political Past." *Media Studies Journal, Radio: the Forgotten
Medium* 7 (1993): 23–36. http://repository.upenn.edu/asc_papers/23.

Demirjian, Karoun, and Dave Weigel. "Haley calls for ignoring the 'angriest voices' this election season." *Washington Post*, January 12, 2016. https://www.washingtonpost.com/news
/powerpost/wp/2016/01/12/haley-to-call-for-ignoring-the-angriest-voices-this-election-season/.

"Democracy in Retreat." Freedom in the World, 2019. https://freedomhouse.org/sites/default
/files/Feb2019_FH_FITW_2019_Report_ForWeb-compressed.pdf.

DeSilver, Drew. "Can Presidential Speeches Change Minds? The Evidence Suggests Not."
Pew Research Center. September 10, 2013. https://www.pewresearch.org/fact-tank/2013/09
/10/can-presidential-speeches-change-minds-the-evidence-suggest-not/.

———. "Split-ticket districts, once common, are now rare." Pew Research Center, August 8,
2016. https://www.pewresearch.org/fact-tank/2016/08/08/split-ticket-districts-once-common
-are-now-rare/?utm_source=Pew+Research+Center&utm_campaign=3f5deccecc

-Weekly_August_11_20168_11_2016&utm_medium=email&utm_term=0_3e953b9b70 -3f5deccecc-400240005.

———. "Turnout in This Year's U.S. House Primaries Rose Sharply, Especially on the Democratic Side." Pew Research Center, October 3, 2018. https://www.pewresearch.org/fact -tank/2018/10/03/turnout-in-this-years-u-s-house-primaries-rose-sharply-especially-on-the -democratic-side/.

Dewar, Helen, and Ann Devroy. "Mitchell Urges Bush to Visit West Berlin." Washington Post, November 14, 1989. https://www.washingtonpost.com/archive/politics/1989/11/14/mitchell -urges-bush-to-visit-west-berlin/a61014ee-86a9-4e37-b5c1-284fa60c041e/.

De Witt, Karen. "Clinton's Prime-Time Presentation Is Shunned by 2 Networks." New York Times, April 19, 1995. https://www.nytimes.com/1995/04/19/us/clinton-s-prime-time-pre sentation-is-shunned-by-2-networks.html.

Diamond, Jeremy. "Trump: I could 'shoot somebody and I wouldn't lose voters.'" CNN.com, January 24, 2016. https://www.cnn.com/2016/01/23/politics/donald-trump-shoot-somebody -support/index.html.

Dickerson, Caitlin. "Detention of Migrant Children Has Skyrocketed to Highest Levels Ever." New York Times, September 12, 2018. https://www.nytimes.com/2018/09/12/us/migrant -children-detention.html.

Dickerson, John. "If I Were King . . ." Slate, November 30, 2011. https://slate.com/news-and -politics/2011/12/newt-gingrich-is-the-only-candidate-who-knows-how-he-would-govern -america.html.

———. "John's Notebook: Stay Generous." Face the Nation, CBS News, July 30, 2017. https:// www.cbsnews.com/news/johns-notebook-stay-generous/.

———. "Meet the Press." Slate, March 14, 2013. https://slate.com/news-and-politics/2013/03 /woodrow-wilson-held-the-first-presidential-press-conference-100-years-ago-and-they -remain-awkward-impersonal-and-no-fun-for-barack-obama-today.html.

Dickinson, Matthew. "The Real Story of Obama's Presidency." Sites Dot Middlebury: Presidential Power, August 8, 2011. http://sites.middlebury.edu/presidentialpower/tag/obamas -presidency-westen-analysis/.

"Disaster Declarations by Year: 2018." Department of Homeland Security: FEMA, Accessed October 23, 2018. https://www.fema.gov/disasters/year.

"The Disaster Relief Fund: Overview and Issues." Congressional Research Service, November 22, 2019. https://fas.org/sgp/crs/homesec/R45484.pdf.

Dittrick, Paula. "'Top hat' oil spill containment device in gulf." Oil & Gas Journal, May 12, 2010. https://www.ogj.com/general-interest/hse/article/17285188/top-hat-oil-spill-containment -device-in-gulf.

Doherty, Carroll. "Key takeaways on Americans' growing partisan divide over political values." Pew Research Center, October 5, 2017. https://www.pewresearch.org/fact-tank/2017/10/05 /takeaways-on-americans-growing-partisan-divide-over-political-values/.

"Donald Trump Presidential Campaign Announcement." C-SPAN, June 16, 2015. https://www .c-span.org/video/?326473-1/donald-trump-presidential-campaign-announcement.

"Donald Trump Really Hates Teleprompters." CNN.com, October 2015. https://www.cnn .com/videos/politics/2016/03/22/donald-trump-teleprompter-aipac-speech-election-2016-ar -origwx.cnn.

Dorning, Mike. "Trump's $28 Billion Trade War Bailout Is Overpaying Farmers." Bloomberg, December 4, 2019. https://www.bloomberg.com/news/articles/2019-12-04/trump-s-28-billion -trade-war-bailout-is-overpaying-many-farmers.

Douthat, Ross. "The Two-Emperor Problem." New York Times, November 24, 2018. https:// www.nytimes.com/2018/11/24/opinion/sunday/john-roberts-donald-trump.html.

Drew, Elizabeth. "Running." New Yorker, November 23, 1975. https://www.newyorker.com /magazine/1975/12/01/running-3.

Drezner, Daniel W. "The flight from the 'Flight 93 Election.'" Washington Post, August 10,

2018. https://www.washingtonpost.com/news/posteverything/wp/2018/04/10/the-flight-from-the-flight-93-election/.

D'Souza, Deborah. "Top 10 Donors to Trump's 2016 Campaign." Investopedia, June 25, 2019. https://www.investopedia.com/articles/investing/033116/top-10-corporate-contributors-trump-campaign.asp.

Dunlap, David W. "1966 | 'The Time Has Come for Action.'" *New York Times*, October 5, 2017. https://www.nytimes.com/2017/10/05/insider/1966-the-time-has-come-for-action.html.

Dunning, Rodney. "Charlottesville Unite the Right Rally." Flickr, August 12, 2017. https://www.flickr.com/photos/rodneydunning/36401911981/in/photostream/.

"Economy." Gallup. https://news.gallup.com/poll/1609/consumer-views-economy.aspx.

Eder, Richard. "Johnson Directs Relief." *New York Times*, September 13, 1965.

"Editorial: Candidates seeking office can't be bothered to vote." *Boston Herald*, November 17, 2018. https://www.bostonherald.com/2018/05/30/editorial-candidates-seeking-office-cant-be-bothered-to-vote/.

Edmondson, Catie, and Maggie Haberman. "Jeff Van Drew Switches Parties, Pledging 'Undying Support' for Trump." *New York Times*, December 19, 2019. https://www.nytimes.com/2019/12/19/us/politics/jeff-van-drew-trump.html.

Edsall, Thomas B. "The Trump Voters Whose 'Need for Chaos' Obliterates Everything Else." *New York Times*, September 4, 2019. https://www.nytimes.com/2019/09/04/opinion/trump-voters-chaos.html?fallback=0&recId=1QNbosgmBUOstqdIazkJuh33tGS&locked=0&geoContinent=NA&geoRegion=VA&recAlloc=top_conversion&geoCountry=US&blockId=most-popular&imp_id=73233716&action=click&module=trending&pgtype=Article&region=Footer.

———. "What Motivates Voters More Than Loyalty? Loathing." *New York Times*, March 1, 2018. https://www.nytimes.com/2018/03/01/opinion/negative-partisanship-democrats-republicans.html.

Edwards, Adrian. "Needs Soar as Number of Syrian Refugees Tops 3 Million." UN Refugee Agency, August 29, 2014. https://www.unhcr.org/53ff76c99.html.

"The Effects of the Partial Shutdown." Congressional Budget Office, January 2019. https://www.cbo.gov/system/files?file=2019-01/54937-PartialShutdownEffects.pdf.

Efron, Edith. "Can the President Think?" *Reason*, November 1994. https://reason.com/1994/11/01/can-the-president-think/.

Eisenhower, Dwight D. "Chance for Peace." UVA Miller Center, April 16, 1953. https://millercenter.org/the-presidency/presidential-speeches/april-16-1953-chance-peace.

———. "Military-Industrial Complex Speech, Dwight D. Eisenhower, 1961." The Avalon Project, https://avalon.law.yale.edu/20th_century/eisenhower001.asp.

Ekins, Emily Elisabeth. "Tea Party Fairness: How the Idea of Proportional Justice Explains the Right-Wing Populism of the Obama Era." Diss., UCLA, 2015. https://escholarship.org/uc/item/3663x343#author.

"Eleanor Roosevelt." Library of Congress. https://www.loc.gov/item/today-in-history/october-11/.

"Eleanor Roosevelt's Surprising Connection to a Dire Town." *First Ladies Revealed*, Episode 4, Smithsonian Channel, July 21, 2017. https://www.smithsonianchannel.com/videos/eleanor-roosevelts-surprising-connection-to-a-dire-town/57258.

"Election Overview." Open Secrets. https://www.opensecrets.org/overview/index.php?display=A&type=M&cycle=2008.

Ellis, Richard J., and Mark Dedrick. "The Presidential Candidate, Then and Now." *Perspectives on Political Science*, Vol. 26, no. 4 (Fall 1997): 208–216. http://www.uvm.edu/~dguber/POLS125/articles/ellis.htm.

Epstein, Jennifer. "Scaramucci Says Trump 'Intentionally' Lies to Inflame Opponents." Bloomberg, October 25, 2018. https://www.bloomberg.com/news/articles/2018-10-25/scaramucci-says-trump-intentionally-lies-to-inflame-opponents.

Erickson, Erick. "Yes the President's Behavior Is Abnormal. But the Democrats' Policies Are

Bat Crap Crazy." Resurgent, August 23, 2019. https://theresurgent.com/2019/08/23/yes-the-presidents-behavior-is-abnormal-but-the-democrats-policies-are-bat-crap-crazy/.

Eshbaugh-Soha, Matthew, and Jeffrey S. Peake. "Presidents and the Economic Agenda." *Political Research Quarterly* 58, no. 1 (2005): 127–38. doi:10.2307/3595602.

"The Ethics Charges Against Jim Wright: Excerpts: 'Wright Did Not Show Reasonable Care on Gifts.'" *Los Angeles Times*, April 18, 1989. https://www.latimes.com/archives/la-xpm-1989-04-18-mn-2024-story.html.

Everett, Burgess. "McConnell throws down the gauntlet: No Scalia replacement under Obama." Politico, February 13, 2016. https://www.politico.com/story/2016/02/mitch-mcconnell-antonin-scalia-supreme-court-nomination-219248.

Evers-Hillstrom, Karl. "Lobbying Spending Reaches $3.4 Billion in 2018, Highest in 8 Years." Open Secrets, January 25, 2010. https://www.opensecrets.org/news/2019/01/lobbying-spending-reaches-3-4-billion-in-18/.

"Exports of Goods and Services (% of GDP)." World Bank, 2019. https://data.worldbank.org/indicator/NE.EXP.GNFS.ZS.

Fahrenthold, David A. "Trump Recorded Having Extremely Lewd Conversation About Women in 2005." *Washington Post*, October 8, 2016. https://www.washingtonpost.com/politics/trump-recorded-having-extremely-lewd-conversation-about-women-in-2005/2016/10/07/3b9ce776-8cb4-11e6-bf8a-3d26847eeed4_story.html.

Fallows, James. "The Passionless Presidency." *The Atlantic*, May 1979. https://www.theatlantic.com/magazine/archive/1979/05/the-passionless-presidency/308516/.

"Feelings About Partisans and the Parties." Pew Research Center, June 22, 2016. https://www.people-press.org/2016/06/22/1-feelings-about-partisans-and-the-parties/.

Fein, Steven, George R. Goethals, and Matthew B. Kugler. "Social Influence on Political Judgments: The Case of Presidential Debates." *Political Psychology* 28, Issue 2 (March 2007): 165–92. https://onlinelibrary.wiley.com/doi/abs/10.1111/j.1467-9221.2007.00561.x.

Fesler, James W. "The Brownlow Committee Fifty Years Later." *Public Administration Review* 47, no. 4 (1987): 291–96. https://doi.org/10.2307/975308.

Feuer, Alan. "For Donald Trump, Friends in Few Places." *New York Times*, March 11, 2016. https://www.nytimes.com/2016/03/13/nyregion/for-donald-trump-friends-in-few-places.html.

"Filibuster Derails Supreme Court Appointment." United States Senate, October 1, 1968. https://www.senate.gov/artandhistory/history/minute/Filibuster_Derails_Supreme_Court_Appointment.htm.

Fiorina, Morris P. "The (Re)Nationalization of Congressional Elections." Hoover Institution, 2016. https://www.hoover.org/sites/default/files/research/docs/fiorina_renationalizationofcongressionalelections_7.pdf.

"Fire Back When Rivals Go Too Far—Ike's New Policy." *Delphos Daily Herald*, vol. 73, September 29, 1956.

"First Inaugural Address of George Washington." The Avalon Project, April 30, 1789. https://avalon.law.yale.edu/18th_century/wash1.asp.

"First-year mayors find executive training comes at the right time." Medium, July 27, 2018. https://medium.com/@BloombergCities/first-year-mayors-find-executive-training-comes-at-the-right-time-c1042448de16.

Fischer, John. "The Kennedy Era: Stage Two." *Harper's* magazine, February 14, 1962. https://archive.org/stream/harpersmagazine224janalde/harpersmagazine224janalde_djvu.txt.

Fitzgerald, Sandy. "James Baker: Trump's White House Needs Strong Chief of Staff." Newsmax, June 1, 2017. https://www.newsmax.com/politics/james-baker-trump-white-house-strong/2017/06/01/id/793612/.

Flake, Jeff and Chris Coons. Interview by Scott Pelley. "Sens. Jeff Flake and Chris Coons Explain Why They Decided to Delay Brett Kavanaugh's Confirmation." *60 Minutes*. CBS News, September 30, 2018. https://www.cbsnews.com/news/jeff-flake-lindsey-graham

-brett-kavanaugh-supreme-court-confirmation-inside-the-decision-to-delay-confirmation
-hearing/.

Flessner, Dave. "Corker: Trump's divisive talk appeals to base but weakens U.S. leadership."
Chattanooga Times Free Press, November 23, 2018. https://www.timesfreepress.com/news
/politics/local/story/2018/nov/23/rhetorical-battletrump-divisive-talk-appeals/483594/.

———. "Former U.S. Sen. Bob Corker says he doesn't recognize the Republican party today."
Chattanooga Times Free Press, October 3, 2019. https://www.timesfreepress.com/news
/local/story/2019/oct/03/former-us-sen-bob-corker-says-he-doesnt-recognize-republican
-party-today/505038/.

"Flying into the Eye of Edna." *See It Now*, CBS, September 14, 1954, Moving Image Research
Center, Library of Congress, Reel FCB8953.

Ford, Matt, and Adam Chandler. "'Hate Crime': A Mass Killing at a Historic Church." *The
Atlantic*, June 19, 2015. https://www.theatlantic.com/national/archive/2015/06/shooting
-emanuel-ame-charleston/396209/.

"Foresight—and Hindsight." Chapter 11 in *The Final 9/11 Commission Report*, National Commission on Terrorist Attacks upon the United States. https://govinfo.library.unt.edu/911
/report/911Report_Ch11.pdf.

"Foreword." *The American Political Science Review* 44, no. 3 (1950): v-ix. doi:10.2307/1950997.

Fortin, Jacey. "The Statue at the Center of Charlottesville's Storm." *New York Times*, August
13, 2017. https://www.nytimes.com/2017/08/13/us/charlottesville-rally-protest-statue.html.

Frankovic, Kathy. "America's Political Parties Remain Polarized." YouGov, May 28, 2019.
https://today.yougov.com/topics/politics/articles-reports/2019/05/28/americas-political
-parties-remain-polarized.

Frates, Chris. "Payoffs for states get Reid to 60." Politico, December 19, 2009. https://www
.politico.com/story/2009/12/payoffs-for-states-get-reid-to-60-030815.

Fredericks, Bob. "Huma on Hillary's $12M Morocco Fiasco: 'She Created This Mess and She
Knows It.'" *New York Post*, October 21, 2016. https://nypost.com/2016/10/21/huma-on
-hillarys-12m-morocco-fiasco-she-created-this-mess-and-she-knows-it/.

"FreedomWorks Blasts House Vote for $700 Billion Wall Street Bailout." Business Wire, Octo-
ber 3, 2008. https://www.businesswire.com/news/home/20081003005677/en/FreedomWorks
-Blasts-House-Vote-700-Billion-Wall.

Freeman, Joanne. "5 Challenges George Washington Faced as America's First President."
George Washington's Mount Vernon, 2020. https://www.mountvernon.org/george
-washington/the-first-president/5-challenges-of-being-americas-first-president/.

Freking, Kevin. "Trump Spotlights Confirmation of 150-Plus Federal Judges." Associated
Press, November 6, 2019. https://apnews.com/7d0c948029a54dab940e4c986cfa01a3.

French, Nancy. "What happened after my husband was attacked for critiquing Franklin Graham's Pete Buttigieg tweets." *Washington Post*, May 9, 2019. https://www.washingtonpost
.com/religion/2019/05/09/what-happened-after-my-husband-was-attacked-critiquing
-franklin-grahams-pete-buttigieg-tweets/.

"From John Adams to Thomas Jefferson, 6 December 1787," Founders Online, National Archives, https://founders.archives.gov/documents/Adams/99-02-02-0281.

Frum, David. "David Frum on Obama Lessons in Robert Caro's Lyndon Johnson." *Newsweek*,
April 15, 2012. https://www.newsweek.com/david-frum-obama-lessons-robert-caros-lyndon
-johnson-63929.

Funk, Cary, Meg Hefferon, Brian Kennedy, and Courtney Johnson. "Trust and Mistrust in
Americans' Views of Scientific Experts." Pew Research Center, August 2, 2019. https://www
.pewresearch.org/science/2019/08/02/trust-and-mistrust-in-americans-views-of-scientific
-experts/.

Galston, William. "Ethics and Character in the U.S. Presidency." *Presidential Studies Quarterly* 40, no. 1, Ethics and the Presidency (March 2010), 90–101. https://www.jstor.org
/stable/23044897.

——. "Why the 2005 Social Security Initiative Failed, and What it Means for the Future." Brookings Institution, September 21, 2007. https://www.brookings.edu/research/why-the -2005-social-security-initiative-failed-and-what-it-means-for-the-future/.

Gates, Robert. Interview by John Dickerson. "Extended Interview." *Face the Nation*, CBS News, May 14, 2017. https://www.youtube.com/watch?v=9gHDmXYNJoc.

——. "Robert Gates Recounts George H. W. Bush's 'Award' for Colleagues Who Fell Asleep in Meetings." *CBS This Morning*, CBS News, December 4, 2018. https://www.cbsnews .com/news/robert-gates-on-george-h-w-bush-legacy-humor-country-first/.

——. "Secretary Robert Gates reflects on George H. W. Bush's restraint and humor." *CBS This Morning*, CBS News, December 4, 2018. https://www.youtube.com/watch?v=COI-5wWKY7b4.

"Gen. David Petraeus: 'You can't completely get out of endless wars.'" Interview by John Dickerson, *CBS This Morning*, CBS News, October 29, 2019. https://www.cbsnews.com /news/david-petraeus-isis-abu-bakr-al-baghdadi-endless-wars-cbs-this-morning-podcast -john-dickerson/.

Geraghty, Jim. "Joe Biden Promises that If Elected, He Will Cure Cancer." *National Review*, June 12, 2019. https://www.nationalreview.com/corner/joe-biden-promises-that-if-elected -he-will-cure-cancer/.

——. "Our Political Fights Are Bad Because We Don't Agree on the Rules." *National Review*, April 12, 2019. https://www.nationalreview.com/the-morning-jolt/our-political-fights -are-bad-because-we-dont-agree-on-the-rules/.

Gibbs, Nancy, and Karen Tumulty. "Master of the House." *Time*, June 24, 2001. http://content .time.com/time/magazine/article/0,9171,133563,00.html.

Gingrich, Newt. "If Dems keep doing these five things, Trump will have a landslide victory in 2020." Fox News, July 12, 2019. https://www.foxnews.com/opinion/newt-gingrich-trump -democrats-pelosi-mcgovern.

Ginsburg, Daniel. "Ty Cobb." Society for American Baseball Research. https://sabr.org /bioproj/person/7551754a.

Gittiner, Ted, and Allen Fisher. "LBJ Champions the Civil Rights Act of 1964, Part 2." National Archives, Summer 2004. https://www.archives.gov/publications/prologue/2004/summer /civil-rights-act-2.html.

Goldberg, Jeffrey. "The Man Who Couldn't Take It Anymore." *The Atlantic*, October 2019. https://www.theatlantic.com/magazine/archive/2019/10/james-mattis-trump/596665/.

Goldberg, Jonah. "Obscuring the Issue of Trump's Character." *National Review*, January 2, 2019. https://www.nationalreview.com/corner/donald-trump-character-issue/.

Goldsmith, Marshall. "What Got You Here Won't Get You There." Talks at Google, December 10, 2007. https://talksat.withgoogle.com/talk/what-got-you-here-won-t-get-you-there.

Goodwin, Doris Kearns. "Defeat Your Opponents. Then Hire Them." *New York Times*, August 3, 2008. https://www.nytimes.com/2008/08/03/opinion/03goodwin.html.

——. "Franklin D. Roosevelt." In *Character Above All: Ten Presidents from FDR to George Bush*. New York: Simon & Schuster, 1996, PBS. https://www.pbs.org/newshour/spc /character/essays/roosevelt.html.

——. "Presidential Leadership." Interview by John Dickerson. *CBS This Morning*, CBS News, November 2, 2018. https://tunein.com/podcasts/News—Politics-Podcasts/CBS-This -Morning-p112538/?topicId=126614581.

GOPAC. "Language: A Key Mechanism of Control." Curriculum page, Wake Forest University, 1995. https://users.wfu.edu/zulick/454/gopac.html.

"GOP Tax Plan Benefits Rich, U.S. Voters Say Almost 3–1, Quinnipiac University National Poll Finds." Quinnipiac University Poll, December 5, 2017. https://poll.qu.edu/national /release-detail?ReleaseID=2504.

Gould, Joe, and Leo Shane III. "When will Trump nominate a permanent defense secretary?"

Military Times, March 28, 2019. https://www.militarytimes.com/congress/2019/03/28/when-will-trump-nominate-a-permanent-defense-secretary/.

Graham, Franklin. "Clinton's Sins Aren't Private." *Wall Street Journal*, August 27, 1998. https://www.wsj.com/articles/SB904162265981632000.

Graham, Lindsey. "Statement on Charlottesville." August 16, 2017. https://www.lgraham.senate.gov/public/index.cfm/press-releases?ID=D1258F2A-79E7-4952-9E85-FBAE64919AF4.

Graubard, Stephen R. "Presidents: The Power and the Mediocrity." *New York Times*, January 18, 1989.

"Gravely Ill, Atwater Offers Apology." *New York Times*, January 13, 1991. https://www.nytimes.com/1991/01/13/us/gravely-ill-atwater-offers-apology.html.

Green, Steve. "Report: Nearly 70 percent of LV homeowners underwater on mortgage." *Las Vegas Sun*, November 30, 2009. https://lasvegassun.com/news/2009/nov/30/report-nearly-70-percent-lv-homeowners-underwater-/.

Greenhouse, Linda. "The Nation; 'Suicide Pact.'" *New York Times*, September 22, 2002. https://www.nytimes.com/2002/09/22/weekinreview/the-nation-suicide-pact.html.

Gregorian, Dareh. "Back Pay for Federal Contractors Missing from Government Funding Bill." NBC News, February 15, 2019. https://www.nbcnews.com/politics/politics-news/back-pay-federal-contractors-missing-government-funding-bill-n971886.

Grove, Lloyd. ". . . And the Critics Sound Off." *Washington Post*, June 5, 1992. https://www.washingtonpost.com/archive/lifestyle/1992/06/05/and-the-critics-sound-off/87038381-a3d8-4a0c-a659-3998910c453d/.

"Growing Partisan Divide Over Fairness of the Nation's Tax System." Pew Research Center, April 4, 2019. https://www.people-press.org/2019/04/04/growing-partisan-divide-over-fairness-of-the-nations-tax-system/.

Grunwald, Michael. "Trump Goes Code Pink on George W. Bush." Politico, February 14, 2016. https://www.politico.com/magazine/story/2016/02/trump-code-pink-bush-iraq-9-11-213630.

Haberman, Maggie, and Michael S. Schmidt. "Trump Tied Ukraine Aid to Inquiries He Sought, Bolton Book Says." *New York Times*, January 28, 2020. https://www.nytimes.com/2020/01/26/us/politics/trump-bolton-book-ukraine.html.

Hadar, Roey. "Retired Army Gen. Stanley McChrystal: President Donald Trump immoral, doesn't tell the truth." Interview by Martha Raddatz. *This Week*, ABC News, December 30, 2018. https://abcnews.go.com/Politics/retired-army-gen-stanley-mcchrystal-president-donald-trump/story?id=60065642.

Hagan, Joe. "Beto O'Rourke: 'I'm Just Born to Be In It.'" *Vanity Fair*, March 13, 2019. https://www.vanityfair.com/news/2019/03/beto-orourke-cover-story.

"Hail to the Chief." Library of Congress, Song Collection. Washington, DC, 2002. https://www.loc.gov/item/ihas.200000009/.

Hains, Tim. "Trump's Updated ISIS Plan: 'Bomb the Shit Out Of Them,' Send In Exxon To Rebuild." Real Clear Politics, November 13, 2015. https://www.realclearpolitics.com/video/2015/11/13/trumps_updated_isis_plan_bomb_the_shit_out_of_them_send_exxon_in_to_rebuild.html.

Haley, Nikki. Interview with Norah O'Donnell. "I Was Asked by Cabinet Members to Take Sides Against the President." *CBS Sunday Morning*, CBS News, November 11, 2019. https://www.cbsnews.com/news/nikki-haley-was-asked-by-cabinet-members-john-kelly-and-rex-tillerson-to-take-sides-against-president-trump/.

Hall, Carla. "Firing One-Liners." *Washington Post*, July 21, 1979. https://www.washingtonpost.com/archive/lifestyle/1979/07/21/firing-one-liners/bde0758f-d86c-4dd5-bbbf-a5b2516f5e05/.

Halon, Yael. "Nikki Haley: Democratic leadership, candidates are the only people mourning Soleimani death." Fox News, January 6, 2020. https://www.foxnews.com/media/nikki-haley-democrats-soleimani-trump.

Hamby, Peter. "Did Twitter Kill the Boys on the Bus? Searching for a better way to cover a

campaign." Harvard University: Joan Shorenstein Center, September 2013. https://shoren
steincenter.org/wp-content/uploads/2013/08/d80_hamby.pdf.

"Harry S. Truman's Decision to Use the Atomic Bomb." National Park Service, October 25,
2017. https://www.nps.gov/articles/trumanatomicbomb.htm.

Harwood, John. "Americans Overwhelmingly Support Free Trade as Concern Grows About
Trump's Economy: NBC/WSJ poll." CNBC News, August 18, 2019. https://www.cnbc
.com/2019/08/18/americans-support-free-trade——and-are-worried-about-the-trump
-economy-poll.html.

———. "Few Americans think they're getting a Trump tax cut: NBC/WSJ poll." CNBC News,
April 8, 2019. https://www.cnbc.com/2019/04/05/few-americans-think-theyre-getting
-a-trump-tax-cut-nbcwsj-poll.html.

Hatfield, Mark O. with the Senate Historical Office. "Vice Presidents of the United States,
1789–1993." U.S. Senate: Government Printing Office, 1997. https://www.senate.gov
/artandhistory/history/resources/pdf/spiro_agnew.pdf.

Hawkings, David. "The Incredible Shrinking Split Tickets." Roll Call, February 1, 2017.
https://www.rollcall.com/2017/02/01/the-incredible-shrinking-split-tickets/.

Heilemann, John, and Mark Halperin. "The Intervention." New Yorker, November 1, 2013.
https://nymag.com/news/features/heilemann-halperin-double-down-excerpt-2013-11/.

Heim, Joe. "Jerry Falwell Jr. can't imagine Trump 'doing anything that's not good for the country.'" CBS News, January 1, 2019. https://www.washingtonpost.com/lifestyle/magazine/jerry
-falwell-jr-cant-imagine-trump-doing-anything-thats-not-good-for-the-country/2018/12/21
/6affc4c4-f19e-11e8-80d0-f7e1948d55f4_story.html?noredirect=on.

"'Helvidius' Number 4, [14 September] 1793," Founders Online, National Archives, https://
founders.archives.gov/documents/Madison/01-15-02-0070.

Henderson, Nia-Malika. "Michael Dukakis explains what happened to Michael Dukakis."
Washington Post, January 11, 2015. https://www.washingtonpost.com/news/the-fix/wp/2015
/01/11/michael-dukakis-explains-what-happened-to-michael-dukakis/.

"Here's Donald Trump's Presidential Announcement Speech." Time, June 16, 2015. https://
time.com/3923128/donald-trump-announcement-speech/.

Hesson, Ted. "Explainer: Inside the plans for Trump's expanded travel ban." Reuters, January 29, 2020. https://www.reuters.com/article/us-usa-immigration-travel-explainer/explainer
-inside-the-plans-for-trumps-expanded-travel-ban-idUSKBN1ZS2A6.

Hincks, Joseph. "ISIS Is Still Active in Iraq, Syria and Beyond. This Is What the Threat Looks
Like Now." Time, January 18, 2019. https://time.com/5506007/trump-isis-victory-islamic-state/.

"H. L. Mencken on Balder and Dash." Lapham's Quarterly, 1921, https://www.laphamsquarterly
.org/comedy/hl-mencken-balder-and-dash.

Hogue, Henry B. "Presidential Reorganization Authority: History, Recent Initiatives, and Options for Congress." Congressional Research Service, December 11, 2012. https://fas.org
/sgp/crs/misc/R42852.pdf.

Holland, Steve. "McCain suspends campaign to work on Wall Street plan." Reuters, September 24, 2008. https://www.reuters.com/article/us-usa-politicsnews1/mccain-suspends
-campaign-to-work-on-wall-street-plan-idUSTRE48N7ZP20080924?sp=true.

Holmes, Steven A. "Clinton Defines the Limits of Compromise with G.O.P.; Gingrich Urges
'Dialogue.'" New York Times, April 8, 1995. https://www.nytimes.com/1995/04/08/us/clinton
-defines-the-limits-of-compromise-with-gop-gingrich-urges-dialogue.html.

Holsendolph, Ernest. "Adams Angrily Quits Transportation Job." New York Times, July 21,
1979. https://www.nytimes.com/1979/07/21/archives/adams-angrily-quits-transportation-job
-he-says-president-ordered.html.

Hoover, Herbert. "The New Deal: Address delivered to Joint Republican Organizations." Pepperdine School of Public Policy, October 17, 1938. https://publicpolicy.pepperdine.edu
/academics/research/faculty-research/new-deal/hoover-speeches/hh101738.htm.

———. "Statement Announcing a Series of Conferences with Representatives of Business,

Industry, Agriculture, and Labor." The American Presidency Project, November 15, 1929. https://www.presidency.ucsb.edu/documents/statement-announcing-series-conferences -with-representatives-business-industry-agriculture.

Hornick, Ed. "Is oil spill 'Obama's Katrina'?." CNN.com, May 4, 2010. https://www.cnn.com /2010/POLITICS/05/04/obama.oil.fallout/index.html.

Horsley, Scott. "Obama Visits Federal Prison, A First For A Sitting President." NPR, July 16, 2015. https://www.npr.org/sections/itsallpolitics/2015/07/16/423612441/obama-visits-federal -prison-a-first-for-a-sitting-president.

Howard, Philip N., Bharath Ganesh, and Dimitra Liotsiou. "The IRA, Social Media and Political Polarization in the United States, 2012–2018." University of Oxford. https://comprop .oii.ox.ac.uk/wp-content/uploads/sites/93/2018/12/The-IRA-Social-Media-and-Political -Polarization.pdf.

Howe, Daniel Walker. "America's Century of Self-Discovery." The New York Sun, April 9, 2008. https://www.nysun.com/arts/americas-century-of-self-discovery/74392/.

Hulse, Carl. "Conservatives Viewed Bailout Plan as Last Straw." New York Times, September 26, 2008. https://www.nytimes.com/2008/09/27/business/27repubs.html.

Hurley, Lawrence. "Amid Impeachment Drama, Senate Helps Trump Move U.S. Courts to the Right." Reuters, November 20, 2019. https://www.reuters.com/article/us-usa-trump -judges/amid-impeachment-drama-senate-helps-trump-move-u-s-courts-to-the-right -idUSKBN1XU2MZ.

"Hurricane Diane—August 15–19, 1955." National Weather Service. https://www.weather.gov /mhx/HurricaneDiane1955.

"I Am Part of the Resistance Inside the Trump Administration." New York Times, September 5, 2018. https://www.nytimes.com/2018/09/05/opinion/trump-white-house-anonymous -resistance.html.

Igielnik, Ruth, and Kim Parker. "Majorities of U.S. veterans, public say the wars in Iraq and Afghanistan were not worth fighting." Pew Research Center. July 10, 2019. https://www .pewresearch.org/fact-tank/2019/07/10/majorities-of-u-s-veterans-public-say-the-wars-in -iraq-and-afghanistan-were-not-worth-fighting/.

"Ike Decides to Answer Demo 'Lies.'" Tyrone Daily Herald. September 29, 1956.

Illing, Sean. "There's a War for Your Attention. And You're Probably Losing It." Vox.com, February 11, 2018. https://www.vox.com/conversations/2016/11/17/13477142/facebook-twitter -social-media-attention-merchants.

"In Convention, Richmond, Friday, June 20, 1788." Teaching American History. https://teach- ingamericanhistory.org/resources/ratification/elliot/vol3/june20/.

"Income, Poverty, and Health Insurance: 2018." United States Census Bureau, September 2019. https://www.census.gov/content/dam/Census/newsroom/press-kits/2019/iphi/presentation -iphi-overview.pdf.

"Intermediate-Range Nuclear Forces [INF] Chronology." Federation of American Scientists. https://fas.org/nuke/control/inf/inf-chron.htm.

International Refugee Assistance Project v. Trump, No. 17-1351 (4th Cir. 2017). https://assets .documentcloud.org/documents/3524359/Doj-Brief-ca4-20170324.pdf.

"In the Interpreter's House." American Magazine, vol. 66, Phillips Publishing Co., 1908.

"In Their Own Words." New York Times, August 18, 1992. https://www.nytimes.com/1992/08/18 /news/in-their-own-words-excerpts-from-president-s-remarks-at-rally.html.

"IRS Scandal Fast Facts." CNN.com, September 26, 2019. https://www.cnn.com/2014/07/18 /politics/irs-scandal-fast-facts/index.html.

Isidore, Chris. "Bailout plan rejected—supporters scramble." CNN Money, September 29, 2008. https://money.cnn.com/2008/09/29/news/economy/bailout/.

"'I think the European Union is a foe,' Trump says ahead of Putin meeting in Helsinki." CBS News, July 15, 2018. https://www.cbsnews.com/news/donald-trump-interview-cbs-news -european-union-is-a-foe-ahead-of-putin-meeting-in-helsinki-jeff-glor/.

Jackson, David. "Donald Trump accepts GOP nomination, says 'I alone can fix' system." *USA Today*, July 21, 2016. https://www.usatoday.com/story/news/politics/elections/2016/07/21/donald-trump-republican-convention-acceptance-speech/87385658/.

Jacobson, Louis. "Donald Trump Didn't Realize His Own Website Called Marco Rubio 'Mark Zuckerberg's Personal Senator.'" Politifact, October 28, 2015. https://www.politifact.com/truth-o-meter/statements/2015/oct/28/donald-trump/donald-trump-didnt-realize-his-own-website-called-/.

James, Frank. "Nearly One In Four U.S. Homes With Mortgages 'Underwater.'" NPR, November 24, 2009. https://www.npr.org/sections/thetwo-way/2009/11/one_in_four_us_homes_underwate.html.

"John McCain's New Hampshire Primary Speech." *New York Times*, January 8, 2008. https://www.nytimes.com/2008/01/08/us/politics/08text-mccain.html.

Johnson, Lyndon B. "Telephone conversation #133, sound recording, LBJ and DAVID MCDONALD, 11/29/1963, 1:29 PM." LBJ Presidential Library, https://www.discoverlbj.org/item/tel-00133.

Johnson, Ron. Interview by Chuck Todd. "Meet the Press: February 17, 2019." *Meet the Press*, NBC News, February 17, 2019. https://www.nbcnews.com/meet-the-press/meet-press-february-17-2019-n972606.

"Joint Statement from the Department of Homeland Security and Office of the Director of National Intelligence on Election Security." U.S. Department of Homeland Security, October 7, 2016. https://www.dhs.gov/news/2016/10/07/joint-statement-department-homeland-security-and-office-director-national.

Jones, Jeffrey M. "Presidential Moral Leadership Less Important to Republicans." Gallup, May 29, 2018. https://news.gallup.com/poll/235022/presidential-moral-leadership-less-important-republicans.aspx?utm_source=alert&utm_medium=email&utm_content=morelink&utm_campaign=syndication.

———. "Support for Tax Overhaul Rising, but Law Remains Unpopular." Gallup, March 7, 2018. https://news.gallup.com/poll/228653/support-tax-overhaul-rising-law-remains-unpopular.aspx.

Kaczynski, Andrew. "Trump Isn't Into Anal, Melania Never Poops, and Other Things He Told Howard Stern." Buzzfeed, February 16, 2016. https://www.buzzfeednews.com/article/andrewkaczynski/trump-isnt-into-anal-melania-never-poops-and-other-things-he#.ldZMnyqoa.

Kaplan, Jonas T., Sarah I. Gimbel, and Sam Harris. "Neural correlates of maintaining one's political beliefs in the face of counterevidence." *Scientific Reports* 6, 39589 (December 2016). doi:10.1038/srep39589.

Kapur, Sahil, and Joshua Green. "Internal GOP Poll: 'We've Lost the Messaging Battle' on Tax Cuts." Bloomberg, September 20, 2018. https://www.bloomberg.com/news/articles/2018-09-20/internal-gop-poll-we-ve-lost-the-messaging-battle-on-tax-cuts.

Karl, Jonathan and Benjamin Siegel. "Exclusive: Rubio Won't Talk About WikiLeaks, and Neither Should Donald Trump." ABC News, October 19, 2016. https://abcnews.go.com/Politics/exclusive-rubio-talk-wikileaks-donald-trump/story?id=42895586.

Kennedy, John F. "A Force That Has Changed the Political Scene." *TV Guide*, November 14, 1959. https://museum.tv/debateweb/html/equalizer/print/tvguide_jfkforce.htm.

———. "News Conference 10, April 21, 1961." John F. Kennedy Presidential Library and Museum. https://www.jfklibrary.org/archives/other-resources/john-f-kennedy-press-conferences/news-conference-10.

———. "Remarks of Senator John F. Kennedy, at the Dalles, Oregon, May 15, 1960." John F. Kennedy Presidential Library and Museum. https://www.jfklibrary.org/archives/other-resources/john-f-kennedy-speeches/dalles-or-19600515

———. "Statement on Assassination of Martin Luther King, Jr., Indianapolis, Indiana, April 4, 1968." John F. Kennedy Presidential Library and Museum. https://www.jfklibrary.org/learn

/about-jfk/the-kennedy-family/robert-f-kennedy/robert-f-kennedy-speeches/statement-on
-assassination-of-martin-luther-king-jr-indianapolis-indiana-april-4-1968.

"Kerry discusses $87 billion comment." CNN.com, September 30, 2004. https://www.cnn
.com/2004/ALLPOLITICS/09/30/kerry.comment/.

Kessler, Glenn. "Not just misleading. Not merely false. A lie." *Washington Post*, August 22,
2018. https://www.washingtonpost.com/politics/2018/08/23/not-just-misleading-not-merely
-false-lie/.

———. "The pre-war intelligence on Iraq: Wrong or hyped by the Bush White House?" *Washington Post*, December 13, 2006. https://www.washingtonpost.com/news/fact-checker/wp
/2016/12/13/the-pre-war-intelligence-on-iraq-wrong-or-hyped-by-the-bush-white-house/.

———. "When did McConnell say he wanted to make Obama a 'one-term president'?." *Washington Post*, September 25, 2012.

Kessler, Glenn, and Scott Clement. "Trump Routinely Says Things That Aren't True. Few
Americans Believe Him." *Washington Post*, December 14, 2018. https://www.washingtonpost
.com/graphics/2018/politics/political-knowledge-poll-trump-falsehoods/.

Kessler, Glenn, Salvador Rizzo, and Meg Kelly. "President Trump has made 15,413 false or
misleading claims over 1,055 days." *Washington Post*, December 16, 2019. https://www
.washingtonpost.com/politics/2019/12/16/president-trump-has-made-false-or-misleading
-claims-over-days/.

Kheel, Rebecca. "Trump called Pelosi a 'third-rate politician' during Syria meeting, top Democrats say." The Hill, October 16, 2019. https://thehill.com/homenews/administration
/466156-trump-called-pelosi-a-third-rate-politician-during-syria-briefing-top.

Kiel, Paul, and Dan Nguyen. "Bailout Tracker: Tracking Every Dollar and Every Recipient."
ProPublica, April 15, 2009. https://projects.propublica.org/bailout/.

Kifner, John. "McVeigh's Mind: A special report.; Oklahoma Bombing Suspect: Unraveling of
a Frayed Life." *New York Times*, December 31, 1995. https://www.nytimes.com/1995/12/31
/us/mcveigh-s-mind-special-report-oklahoma-bombing-suspect-unraveling-frayed-life
.html.

Kight, Stef W. "Half of the post-millennial generation is non-white." Axios, November 16,
2018. https://www.axios.com/gen-z-post-millennials-diversity-minorities-demographics-us
-9da4ad70-cedd-4d33-b86f-4b76e9277b8f.html.

Kim, Seung Min. "Populist economic frustration threatens Trump's strongest reelection issue,
Post-ABC poll finds." *Washington Post*, April 29, 2019. https://www.washingtonpost.com
/politics/populist-economic-frustration-threatens-trumps-strongest-reelection-issue-post
-abc-poll-finds/2019/04/28/44f64cbc-6a02-11e9-9d56-1c0cf2c7ac04_story.html.

———. "Rubio says Congress can't get answers on Trump immigration order." Politico, January
30, 2017. https://www.politico.com/story/2017/01/senate-rubio-trump-immigration-234406.

Kim, Susanna, Jake Tapper, and Z. Byron Wolf. "June Jobs Report: Unemployment Rate Up
to 9.2 Percent with Only 18,000 Added Jobs." ABC News, July 7, 2011. https://abcnews.go
.com/Business/june-jobs-report-unemployment-rate-92-percent-18000/story?id=14020360.

Kirzinger, Ashley, Bianca DiJulio, Liz Hamel, Elise Sugarman, and Mollyann Brodie. "Kaiser
Health Tracking Poll—May 2017: The AHCA's Proposed Changes to Health Care."
Henry J. Kaiser Family Foundation, May 31, 2017. https://www.kff.org/health-costs/report
/kaiser-health-tracking-poll-may-2017-the-ahcas-proposed-changes-to-health-care/.

Klein, Betsy. "Trump moved by veteran's performance." CNN.com, September 30, 2019.
https://www.cnn.com/2019/09/30/politics/donald-trump-luis-avila-wounded-veteran/index
.html.

Klein, Ezra. "The Green Lantern Theory of the Presidency, explained." Vox.com, May 20,
2014. https://www.vox.com/2014/5/20/5732208/the-green-lantern-theory-of-the-presidency
-explained.

Klion, David. "The Blob." *The Nation*, October 17, 2018. https://www.thenation.com/article
/archive/ben-rhodes-and-the-crisis-of-liberal-foreign-policy/.

Knott, Stephen F. "America Was Founded on Secrets and Lies." *Foreign Policy*, February 15, 2016. https://foreignpolicy.com/2016/02/15/george-washington-spies-lies-executive-power/.

Knowledge Networks. "The Associated Press-Yahoo Poll." Associated Press, Yahoo, November 2007. http://surveys.associatedpress.com/data/KnowledgeNetworks/AP-Yahoo_2007-08_panel01.pdf.

Kolbert, Elizabeth. "Drawing the Line." *New Yorker*, June 20, 2016. https://www.newyorker.com/magazine/2016/06/27/ratfcked-the-influence-of-redistricting.

———. "The Media; Perot's 30-Minute TV Ads Defy the Experts, Again." *New York Times*, October 27, 1992. https://www.nytimes.com/1992/10/27/nyregion/the-1992-campaign-the-media-perot-s-30-minute-tv-ads-defy-the-experts-again.html.

Kosner, Edward. "'Hubert Humphrey' Review: The Man From Minnesota." *Wall Street Journal*, August 31, 2018. https://www.wsj.com/articles/hubert-humphrey-review-the-man-from-minnesota-1535751289.

Krugman, Paul. "What Happened on Election Day." *New York Times*. https://www.nytimes.com/interactive/projects/cp/opinion/election-night-2016/paul-krugman-the-economic-fallout.

Kuhn, Moritz, Moritz Schularick, and Ulrike Steins. "Research: How the Financial Crisis Drastically Increased Wealth Inequality in the U.S." *Harvard Business Review*, September 13, 2018. https://hbr.org/2018/09/research-how-the-financial-crisis-drastically-increased-wealth-inequality-in-the-u-s.

Kurtz, Howard. "Scaramucci says some ex-Trump aides back his criticism of president." Fox News, August 13, 2017. https://www.foxnews.com/media/scaramucci-says-some-ex-trump-aides-back-his-criticisms-of-president.

LaCava, Gregory, dir. *Gabriel Over the White House*. Partial Transcript via IMDb. https://www.imdb.com/title/tt0024044/characters/nm0404158.

Lafrance, Adrienne. "In 1858, People Said the Telegraph Was 'Too Fast for the Truth.'" *The Atlantic*, Jule 28, 2014. https://www.theatlantic.com/technology/archive/2014/07/in-1858-people-said-the-telegraph-was-too-fast-for-the-truth/375171/.

Lam, Bourree. "Obama's Final Jobs Report Marks 75 Consecutive Months of Growth." *The Atlantic*, January 6, 2017. https://www.theatlantic.com/business/archive/2017/01/december-jobs-report/512366/.

Landler, Mark. "The Afghan War and the Evolution of Obama." *New York Times*, January 1, 2017. https://www.nytimes.com/2017/01/01/world/asia/obama-afghanistan-war.html.

Langley, Monica, and Gerard Baker. "Donald Trump, in Exclusive Interview, Tells WSJ He Is Willing to Keep Parts of Obama Health Law." *Wall Street Journal*, November 11, 2016. https://www.wsj.com/articles/donald-trump-willing-to-keep-parts-of-health-law-1478895339.

Lawrence, Henry W. "Recalling the Strangest Inaugurations." *Santa Cruz Evening News*. March 4, 1933.

Lawrence, John. "When America Stared Into the Abyss." *The Atlantic*, January 7, 2019. https://www.theatlantic.com/ideas/archive/2019/01/john-lawrence-inside-2008-financial-crash/576574/.

"LBJ and Senator Russell Long on Hurricane Betsy." UVA Miller Center, September 9, 1965. https://millercenter.org/the-presidency/educational-resources/lbj-and-senator-russell-long-on-hurricane-betsy.

Leavitt, Michael. Interview by John Dickerson. "Face the Nation Transcript August 14, 2016: Collins, Ridge, Cohen, Hayden." *Face the Nation*, CBS News, August 14, 2016. https://www.cbsnews.com/news/face-the-nation-transcript-august-14-2016-collins-ridge-cohen-hayden/.

Lee, Jasmine C., and Kevin Quealy. "The 598 People, Places and Things Donald Trump Has Insulted on Twitter: A Complete List." *New York Times*. May 24, 2019. https://www.nytimes.com/interactive/2016/01/28/upshot/donald-trump-twitter-insults.html.

Lee, Michelle. "Fact Check: Has Trump declared bankruptcy four or six times?" *Washington Post*, September 26, 2016. https://www.washingtonpost.com/politics/2016/live-updates/general-election/real-time-fact-checking-and-analysis-of-the-first-presidential-debate/fact-check-has-trump-declared-bankruptcy-four-or-six-times/.

Lee, MJ. "How Donald Trump blasted George W. Bush in S.C.—and still won." CNN.com, February 21, 2016. https://www.cnn.com/2016/02/20/politics/donald-trump-south-carolina-military/index.html.

Leech, Margaret. "The Front Porch Campaign." *American Heritage*, vol. 1, issue 1, December 1959. https://www.americanheritage.com/front-porch-campaign.

Leibovich, Mark. "This Is the Way Paul Ryan's Speakership Ends." *New York Times Magazine*, August 7, 2018. https://www.nytimes.com/2018/08/07/magazine/paul-ryan-speakership-end-trump.html.

Leonhardt, David and Stuart A. Thompson. "Trump's Lies." *New York Times*, December 14, 2017. https://www.nytimes.com/interactive/2017/06/23/opinion/trumps-lies.html.

Lewis, Michael. "Obama's Way." *Vanity Fair*, September 11, 2012. https://www.vanityfair.com/news/2012/10/michael-lewis-profile-barack-obama.

Lewis, Paul. "The Donald Trump Show: 24 Hours with the Republican Frontrunner." *The Guardian*, August 18, 2015. https://www.theguardian.com/us-news/2015/aug/18/donald-trump-reality-tv-and-politics.

Liasson, Mara. "After Touting Negotiating Skills, Trump Struggles To Make A Deal On Health Care." *All Things Considered*, NPR, July 6, 2017. https://www.npr.org/2017/07/06/535823089/after-touting-negotiating-skills-trump-struggles-to-make-a-deal-on-health-care.

Lightman, David. "Clinton Popularity Up After Oklahoma City Bombing." *Hartford Courant*, May 9, 1995. https://www.courant.com/news/connecticut/hc-xpm-1995-05-09-9505090393-story.html.

Lincoln, Abraham. "Last Public Address." April 11, 1865. http://www.abrahamlincolnonline.org/lincoln/speeches/last.htm.

Lippmann, Walter. "Worry Is Main Burden for President." *The Tuscaloosa News*, December 28, 1955.

Liptak, Kevin. "Exclusive: Read the Inauguration Day letter Obama left for Trump." CNN.com, September 5, 2017. https://www.cnn.com/2017/09/03/politics/obama-trump-letter-inauguration-day/index.html.

———. "Trump recounts minute-by-minute details of Soleimani strike to donors at Mar-a-Lago." CNN.com, January 18, 2020. https://www.cnn.com/2020/01/18/politics/trump-soleimani-details-mar-a-lago/index.html.

Lipton, Eric. "Security Briefings for the Other Guy." *New York Times*, August 3, 2004. https://www.nytimes.com/2004/08/03/world/security-briefings-for-the-other-guy.html.

Louisville Public Advertiser, April 14, 1824.

"Lyndon B. Johnson, Clark M. Clifford, James R. 'Jim' Jones, Walt W. Rostow, and Dean Rusk on 4 November 1968." UVA Miller Center. https://prde.upress.virginia.edu/conversations/4006128.

Mackey, Robert. "Justice Department Says 2020 Census Fight Might Not Be Over, Following President's Tweet." The Intercept, July 3, 2019. https://theintercept.com/2019/07/03/justice-department-says-2020-census-fight-might-not-following-presidents-tweet/.

Madden, Richard L. "Senator Buckley 'Warns' Nixon on Support by Conservatives." *New York Times*, August 1, 1971. https://www.nytimes.com/1971/08/01/archives/senator-buckley-warns-nixon-on-support-by-conservatives.html.

Maddow, Rachel. "The limits of schmoozing." *The Rachel Maddow Show*, MSNBC News, August 7, 2013. http://www.msnbc.com/rachel-maddow-show/the-limits-schmoozing.

Madison, James. "The Federalist Papers: No. 51." The Avalon Project, February 8, 1788. https://avalon.law.yale.edu/18th_century/fed51.asp.

"Madison Debates." The Avalon Project, August 8, 1787. https://avalon.law.yale.edu/18th _century/debates_808.asp.

"Madison Debates." The Avalon Project, September 17, 1787. https://avalon.law.yale.edu/18th _century/debates_917.asp.

Manchester, Julia. "83 Percent Say the President Should Be Consoler in Chief After National Tragedies." The Hill, December 4, 2018. https://thehill.com/hilltv/what-americas-thinking /419689-83-percent-say-the-president-should-be-the-consoler-in-chief.

Maraniss, David. "Tooting His Own Horn." Washington Post, June 5, 1992. https://www .washingtonpost.com/archive/lifestyle/1992/06/05/tooting-his-own-horn/37cff9b0-07b5 -45b6-9c5b-0d9bef7fb4c9/.

Margolis, Jon. "A Hollow Ring to GOP Gripes About Bork Foes." Chicago Tribune, October 20, 1987. http://articles.chicagotribune.com/1987-10-20/news/8703190795_1_bork-foes -judge-robert-bork-conservatives.

Marrero, Tony. "Rubio: Capitalizing on Hacked WikiLeaks Material Is 'Invitation to Chaos And Havoc.'" Tampa Bay Times, October 19, 2016. https://www.tampabay.com/rubio -capitalizing-on-wikileaks-material-is-invitation-to-chaos-and-havoc/2299182/.

Marshall, Josh. "Wait . . . Wait." Talking Points Memo, September 24, 2008. https://talking-pointsmemo.com/edblog/wait-wait.

Mastrangelo, Dominick. "Trump: Nancy Pelosi Is 'Crazy as a Bedbug.'" Washington Examiner, November 22, 2019. https://www.washingtonexaminer.com/news/crazy-as-a-bedbug -trump-blasts-pelosi-and-questions-her-mental-stability.

Mattin, David. "The Future of Retail." Trend Watching, 2018. https://trendwatching.com /quarterly/2018-05/the-future-of-retail/.

Mattis, James. Interview by John Dickerson. "Transcript: Defense Secretary James Mattis on "Face the Nation." Face the Nation, CBS News, May 28, 2017. https://www.cbsnews.com /news/transcript-defense-secretary-james-mattis-on-face-the-nation-may-28-2017/.

"McCain Counters Obama 'Arab' Question." Associated Press via YouTube, October 11, 2008. https://www.youtube.com/watch?v=jrnRU30cIH4.

McCammond, Alexi, and Jonathan Swan. "Scoop: Insider leaks Trump's 'Executive Time'-filled private schedules." Axios, February 3, 2019. https://www.axios.com/donald-trump -private-schedules-leak-executive-time-34e67fbb-3af6-48df-aefb-52e02c334255.html.

McCartin, Joseph A. "The Strike That Busted Unions." New York Times, August 2, 2011. https:// www.nytimes.com/2011/08/03/opinion/reagan-vs-patco-the-strike-that-busted-unions.html.

McCartin, Joseph A., and Eliott Simons. "The Consequences of Reagan Breaking the '81 Air Traffic Controllers Strike." Real News Network, August 6, 2014. https://therealnews.com /stories/jmccartinpanelesimons0804patcopt2.

McChrystal, Stanley. "An Interview with General (Ret.) Stanley McChrystal." Prism, vol. 6, no. 3. https://cco.ndu.edu/Portals/96/Documents/prism/prism_6-3/McCrystal.pdf.

——. "Why I threw out my painting of Robert E. Lee." CBS This Morning, CBS News, October 22, 2018. https://www.cbsnews.com/news/gen-stanley-mcchrystal-why-i-threw-out -my-painting-of-robert-e-lee/.

McConnell, Robert L. "The Genesis and Ideology of 'Gabriel Over the White House.'" Cinema Journal 15, no. 2 (Spring 1976): 7–26. doi:10.2307/1224915.

McCrimmon, Ryan. "'They literally take food off their table.'" Politico, February 3, 2020. https:// www.politico.com/news/2020/02/03/trump-agriculture-department-cut-programs-109205.

McDermott, Rose, and Peter K. Hatemi. "To Go Forward, We Must Look Back: The Importance of Evolutionary Psychology for Understanding Modern Politics." Evolutionary Psychology (February 2018): 1–7. https://journals.sagepub.com/doi/pdf/10.1177/147470491876 4506.

McDowell, Scott. "The First 90 Days: Your Road Map for Success at a New Job." 99U, March 11, 2013. https://99u.adobe.com/articles/7303/the-first-90-days-your-road-map-for -success-at-a-new-job.

McKay, Brett and Kate. "Leadership Lessons from Dwight D. Eisenhower, #2: How to Not Let Anger and Criticism Get the Best of You." Art of Manliness, November 7, 2018. https://www.artofmanliness.com/articles/leadership-lessons-from-dwight-d-eisenhower-2-how-to-not-let-anger-and-criticism-get-the-best-of-you/.

Meacham, Jon. "George H.W. Bush and the Price of Politics." *New York Times*, December 1, 2018. https://www.nytimes.com/2018/12/01/opinion/george-hw-bush-death-jon-meacham.html.

Meckler, Laura, and Kristina Peterson. "Senator Says Trump Open to Comprehensive Immigration Overhaul." *Wall Street Journal*, February 9, 2017. https://www.wsj.com/articles/senator-says-trump-open-to-comprehensive-immigration-overhaul-1486675985.

Merica, Dan. "Labor's Trumka: Hillary Clinton is 'very, very qualified to be president.'" CNN Political Ticker, August 28, 2014. https://politicalticker.blogs.cnn.com/2014/08/28/labors-trumka-hillary-clinton-is-very-very-qualified-to-be-president/.

Michaels, Jon. "How Trump is dismantling a pillar of the American state." *The Guardian*, November 7, 2017. https://www.theguardian.com/commentisfree/2017/nov/07/donald-trump-dismantling-american-administrative-state.

"Militant Groups Storm Capital to 'Stop Roosevelt.'" *Pittsburgh Sun-Telegraph*, April 4, 1938.

Miller, Stephen. Interview by John Dickerson. "Transcript: Schumer, Flake, Miller." *Face the Nation*, CBS News, February 12, 2017. https://www.cbsnews.com/news/face-the-nation-transcript-february-12-2017-schumer-flake-miller/.

Mindock, Clark. "Donald Trump's Campaign Loves WikiLeaks, But Russian Hackers Could Target Republicans Next, Marco Rubio Warns." International Business Times, October 19, 2016. https://www.ibtimes.com/donald-trumps-campaign-loves-wikileaks-russian-hackers-could-target-republicans-next-2434153.

Mora, David. "Update: We Found a 'Staggering' 281 Lobbyists Who've Worked in the Trump Administration." ProPublica, October 15, 2019. https://www.propublica.org/article/we-found-a-staggering-281-lobbyists-whove-worked-in-the-trump-administration.

Moran, Lee. "Donald Trump Fires Back at the Late Barbara Bush: 'She Should Be' Nasty To Me." HuffPost, April 5, 2019. https://www.huffpost.com/entry/donald-trump-barbara-bush-interview_n_5ca70854e4b0dca032ff6b6f.

Morgan, Wesley. "Trump leaves Pentagon power vacuum." Politico, April 25, 2019. https://www.politico.com/story/2019/04/25/pentagon-acting-officials-1375772.

"Mr. Truman's Speeches." *Washington Post*, May 8, 1948.

Mueller III, Special Counsel Robert S. "Report on the Investigation into Russian Interference in the 2016 Presidential Election." U.S. Department of Justice, March 2019. https://www.justice.gov/storage/report.pdf.

Murphy, Mike. "A day later, White House says Trump meant to condemn white supremacists." Market Watch, August 13, 2017. https://www.marketwatch.com/story/a-day-later-white-house-says-trump-meant-to-condemn-white-supremacists-2017-08-13.

Nagourney, Adam, and Elisabeth Bumiller. "McCain Leaps into a Thicket." *New York Times*, September 25, 2008. https://www.nytimes.com/2008/09/26/us/politics/26campaign.html.

Nakamura, David. "In Japan, Trump calls Jimmy Carter a 'terrible president' and says Kamala Harris got 'too much credit' in debate." *Washington Post*, June 29, 2019. https://www.washingtonpost.com/politics/in-japan-trump-calls-jimmy-carter-a-terrible-president-and-says-kamala-d-harris-got-too-much-credit-in-debate/2019/06/29/27969022-9a46-11e9-830a-21b9b36b64ad_story.html.

Narayanswamy, Anu, Darla Cameron, and Matea Gold. "Money Raised as of Dec. 31." *Washington Post*, February 1, 2017. https://www.washingtonpost.com/graphics/politics/2016-election/campaign-finance/.

Natanson, Hannah, John Woodrow Cox, and Perry Stein. "Trump's words, bullied kids, scarred schools." *Washington Post*, February 13, 2020. https://www.washingtonpost.com/graphics/2020/local/school-bullying-trump-words/.

"NBC News/Wall Street Journal Survey." Hart Research, October 27–30, 2019. https://assets
.documentcloud.org/documents/6538104/19433-NBCWSJ-Late-October-Poll.pdf.

Nelson, Libby. "A heartbreaking account of Obama comforting the grieving families after
Sandy Hook." Vox.com, December 14, 2015. https://www.vox.com/2015/12/14/10106188/sandy
-hook-victims-obama.

———. "'Why we voted for Donald Trump': David Duke explains the white supremacist Charlottesville protests." Vox.com, August 12, 2017. https://www.vox.com/2017/8/12/16138358
/charlottesville-protests-david-duke-kkk.

Newbold, Stephanie P., and Larry D. Terry. "The President's Committee on Administrative
Management: The Untold Story and the Federalist Connection." *Administration & Society* 38, no. 5 (November 2006): 522–55. doi:10.1177/009539970603800503.

Newman, Caroline. "Q&A: Bush Adviser Philip Zelikow Shares Memories of the Late President." UVA Today, December 4, 2018. https://news.virginia.edu/content/qa-bush-adviser
-philip-zelikow-shares-memories-late-president.

Newport, Frank. "U.S. Public Opinion and the 2017 Tax Law." Gallup, April 29, 2019. https://
news.gallup.com/opinion/polling-matters/249161/public-opinion-2017-tax-law.aspx.

"Newt Gingrich Examines the Evolution of Conservatism." Interview by Mark Levin. *Life,
Liberty & Levin*, Fox News, October 28, 2018. https://www.foxnews.com/transcript/newt
-gingrich-examines-the-evolution-of-conservatism.

Neyfakh, Leon. "Rod Rosenstein Is a Cautionary Tale." Slate, May 11, 2017. https://slate.com
/news-and-politics/2017/05/rod-rosenstein-is-a-cautionary-tale.html.

Nixon, Richard M. "Asia After Viet Nam." *Foreign Affairs*, October 1967. https://www
.foreignaffairs.com/articles/asia/1967-10-01/asia-after-viet-nam.

Nobleman, Eli E. "The Delegation of Presidential Functions: Constitutional and Legal Aspects." *Annals of the American Academy of Political and Social Science* 307 (1956): 134–43.
www.jstor.org/stable/1031341.

"No Kick from Campaigns." *Newsweek*, November 4, 1990. https://www.newsweek.com/no
-kick-campaigns-205798.

"Nominations of Abe Fortas and Homer Thornberry." Committee on the Judiciary, United
States Senate. Washington, DC: U.S. Government Printing Office, 1965. https://www.loc
.gov/law/find/nominations/thornberry/hearing-pt1a.pdf.

Noonan, Peggy. "He Was Supposed to be Competent." *Wall Street Journal*, May 29, 2010.
https://www.wsj.com/articles/SB10001424052748704269204575270950789108846.

———. "Over Trump, We're as Divided as Ever." *Wall Street Journal*, March 8, 2018. http://
peggynoonan.com/over-trump-were-as-divided-as-ever/.

Nordlinger, Jay. "Good Ol' Tip." *National Review*, January 25, 2013. https://www.nationalreview
.com/2013/01/good-ol-tip-jay-nordlinger/.

Norman, Jim. "Solid Majority Still Opposes New Construction on Border Wall." Gallup, February 4, 2019. https://news.gallup.com/poll/246455/solid-majority-opposes-new-construction
-border-wall.aspx.

Nussbaum, Matthew. "Trump and the teleprompter: A brief history." Politico, June 7, 2016.
https://www.politico.com/story/2016/06/donald-trump-teleprompter-224039.

Obama, Barack. Interview by John Dickerson. "Transcript: President Obama." *Face the Nation*, CBS News, July 24, 2016. https://www.cbsnews.com/news/face-the-nation-transcripts
-july-24-2016-president-obama/.

———. Interview by Steve Kroft. "Transcript: Sen. Obama, Part 1." *60 Minutes*, CBS News,
September 24, 2008. https://www.cbsnews.com/news/transcript-sen-obama-part-1/.

———. "Remarks by the President in Eulogy for the Honorable Reverend Clementa Pinckney." Office of the Press Secretary, June 26, 2015. https://obamawhitehouse.archives.gov
/the-press-office/2015/06/26/remarks-president-eulogy-honorable-reverend-clementa
-pinckney.

——. "Taking the Cyberattack Threat Seriously." *Wall Street Journal*, July 19, 2012. https://www.wsj.com/articles/SB10000872396390444330904577535492693044650.

——. "Why don't YOU get a drink with Mitch McConnell?" C-SPAN, November 5, 2014. https://www.youtube.com/watch?v=HH_sXMpW4Os.

"Obama: 'If you like your health care plan, you'll be able to keep your health care plan,'" Politifact, https://www.politifact.com/obama-like-health-care-keep/.

"Obama looking for 'whose ass to kick.'" CNN.com, June 8, 2010. https://www.cnn.com/2010/POLITICS/06/07/gulf.oil.obama/index.html.

"The Oklahoma City Bombing." Oklahoma Office of Homeland Security, 2020. https://www.ok.gov/homeland/About_OKOHS/index.html.

O'Neill, Thomas P. "Frenemies: A Love Story." *New York Times*, October 5, 2012. https://campaignstops.blogs.nytimes.com/2012/10/05/frenemies-a-love-story/.

"On the Nomination (Merrick B. Garland, of Maryland, to be United States Circuit Judge for the District of Columbia Circuit.)." U.S. Congress, Senate, 105th Cong., 1st sess., March 19, 1997. https://www.senate.gov/legislative/LIS/roll_call_lists/roll_call_vote_cfm.cfm?congress=105&session=1&vote=00034.

Oreskes, Micheal. "Lee Atwater, Master of Tactics for Bush and G.O.P., Dies at 40." *New York Times*, March 30, 1991. https://www.nytimes.com/1991/03/30/obituaries/lee-atwater-master-of-tactics-for-bush-and-gop-dies-at-40.html.

O'Rourke, Beto. Interview by Chuck Todd. "Meet the Press—September 15, 2019." *Meet the Press*, NBC News, September 15, 2019. https://www.nbcnews.com/meet-the-press/meet-press-september-15-2019-n1054636.

Osborne, David. "The Swinging Days of Newt Gingrich." *Mother Jones*, November 1, 1984. https://www.motherjones.com/politics/1984/11/newt-gingrich-shining-knight-post-reagan-right/.

O'Toole, Mary. "Must Reads: John F. Kelly Says His Tenure as Trump's Chief of Staff Is Best Measured by What the President Did Not Do." *Los Angeles Times*, December 30, 2018. https://www.latimes.com/politics/la-na-pol-john-kelly-exit-interview-20181230-story.html.

O'Toole, Patricia. "The Speech That Saved Teddy Roosevelt's Life." *Smithsonian Magazine*, November 2012. https://www.smithsonianmag.com/history/the-speech-that-saved-teddy-roosevelts-life-83479091/.

"Over 7 in 10 Americans want parties in Congress to work together." The Hill TV, September 10, 2019. https://www.youtube.com/watch?v=Neyp2ApY5qA.

Page, Susan. "2016 lessons so far: Trump's takeover and an enthusiasm gap." *USA Today*, March 1, 2016. https://www.usatoday.com/story/news/politics/elections/2016/03/01/analysis-super-tuesday-trump-takeover-feelthebern-clinton-cruz-rubio-sanders/81143962/.

Paisley, Laura. "Political Polarization at Its Worst Since the Civil War." University of Southern California News, November 8, 2016. https://news.usc.edu/110124/political-polarization-at-its-worst-since-the-civil-war-2/.

Pakenham, Michael. "Johnson Views Louisiana Storm Damage with Flashlight in Hand." *Chicago Tribune*, September 11, 1965.

Palma, Bethania. "Did Trump Tweet a Picture of Himself as Rocky Balboa?" Snopes.com, November 29, 2019. https://www.snopes.com/fact-check/trump-rocky-tweet/.

Panetta, Leon. Interview by Chris Bury. "Interview: Leon Panetta." *Frontline*, PBS, June 2000. https://www.pbs.org/wgbh/pages/frontline/shows/clinton/interviews/panetta.html.

Pariser, Eli. "When the Internet Thinks It Knows You." *New York Times*, May 22, 2011. https://www.nytimes.com/2011/05/23/opinion/23pariser.html.

Parker, Ashley. "McMaster: Trump's sharing of sensitive intelligence with Russia was 'wholly appropriate.'" *Washington Post*, May 16, 2017. https://www.washingtonpost.com/news/post-politics/wp/2017/05/16/trump-acknowledges-facts-shared-with-russian-envoys-during-white-house-meeting/.

Parker, Kim. "The Growing Partisan Divide in Views of Higher Education." Pew Research Center, August 19, 2019. https://www.pewsocialtrends.org/essay/the-growing-partisan-divide -in-views-of-higher-education/.

Parscale, Brad. "Parscale: Number one reason swing voters will vote for Trump is his stance on border security." Interview by Martha MacCallum, *The Story*, Fox, January 10, 2019. https://www.foxnews.com/transcript/parscale-number-one-reason-swing-voters-will-vote -for-trump-is-his-stance-on-border-security.

"Partisanship and Political Animosity in 2016." Pew Research Center, June 22, 2016. https:// www.people-press.org/2016/06/22/partisanship-and-political-animosity-in-2016/.

"'Paul Revere Riders' Fight Dictator Bill at Capital." *Pittsburgh Sun-Telegraph*, April 8, 1938.

"'Paul Reveres' Demand Death of Dictator Bill." *San Francisco Examiner*, April 8, 1938. https://www.newspapers.com/image/457513725/?terms=paul%2Brevere.

Pence, Mike. "The Two Schools of Thought on Clinton." *The Mike Pence Show*, August 21, 1999. http://web.archive.org/web/19990821083429/http:/www.hublergroup.com:80/pence /clinton2.html.

———. "Why Clinton Must Resign Or Be Impeached." *The Mike Pence Show*. http://web .archive.org/web/20010306205858fw_/http:/www.cybertext.net/pence/pres.html.

Pennycook, Gordon, Tyrone D. Cannon, and David G. Rand. "Prior Exposure Increases Perceived Accuracy of Fake News." *Journal of Experimental Psychology: General* 147, 12 (2018): 1865–80. https://doi.org/10.1037/xge0000465.

Perle, Richard. "The Debate Over How to Deal with North Korea." *Frontline*, PBS. https:// www.pbs.org/wgbh/pages/frontline/shows/kim/themes/debate.html.

"Perot Outdraws a Playoff Game." *New York Times*, October 8, 1992. https://www.nytimes.com /1992/10/08/us/the-1992-campaign-perot-outdraws-a-playoff-game.html.

Perry, Mark. "When Presidents Get Angry." Politico Magazine, September 27, 2017. www .politico.com/magazine/story/2017/09/27/donald-trump-anger-215648.

Petersen, Michael Bang, Mathias Osmundsen, and Kevin Arceneaux. "A 'Need for Chaos' and the Sharing of Hostile Political Rumors in Advanced Democracies." PsyArXiv (2018), doi:10.31234/osf.io/6m4ts.

Pfiffner, James P. "White House Staff Versus the Cabinet: Centripetal and Centrifugal Roles." *Presidential Studies Quarterly* 16, no. 4 (1986): 666–90. www.jstor.org/stable/40574416.

Phillip, Abby, Ed O'Keefe, Nick Miroff, and Damian Paletta. "Lost Weekend: How Trump's Time at His Golf Club Hurt the Response to Maria." *Washington Post*, September 29, 2017. https://www.washingtonpost.com/politics/lost-weekend-how-trumps-time-at-his-golf-club -hurt-the-response-to-maria/2017/09/29/ce92ed0a-a522-11e7-8c37-e1d99ad6aa22_story.html.

Pollak, Joel B. "GOP Debate: Trump Did Call Rubio 'Zuckerberg's Personal Senator.'" Breitbart, October 28, 2015. https://www.breitbart.com/politics/2015/10/28/gop-debate-trump -did-call-rubio-zuckerbergs-personal-senator/.

Popken, Ben. "As Algorithms Take Over, YouTube's Recommendations Highlight a Human Problem." NBC News, April 18, 2018. https://www.nbcnews.com/tech/social-media /algorithms-take-over-youtube-s-recommendations-highlight-human-problem-n867596.

Porter, Frank C. "LBJ Sees Betsy Toll in Hundreds." *Washington Post*, September 13, 1965.

Porter, Michael E., and Nitin Nohria. "The Leader's Calendar: How CEOs Manage Time." *Harvard Business Review*, July/August 2018. https://hbr.org/2018/07/the-leaders-calendar.

Porter, Tom. "8 days after his acquittal, Trump openly admitted sending Giuliani to hunt for dirt on Joe Biden—reversing a key part of his impeachment defense." Business Insider, February 14, 2020. https://www.businessinsider.com/trump-admits-giuliani-ukraine-reversing -impeachment-defense-2020-2.

"Presidential Approval Ratings—Donald Trump." Gallup, https://news.gallup.com/poll/203198 /presidential-approval-ratings-donald-trump.aspx.

"Presidents and Labor: Harry Truman and the Strike Wave of 1946." POTUS Geeks Live Journal, September 1, 2017. https://potus-geeks.livejournal.com/882627.html.

"The President's Daily Diary for September 10, 1965." LBJ Presidential Library. http://lbjlibrary
.net/assets/documents/archives/hurricane_disaster/19650910.pdf.

"President Taft Stunned." New York Times, April 16, 1912, via Encyclopedia Titanica. https://
www.encyclopedia-titanica.org/president-taft-stunned.html.

"President Trump mocks being presidential." CNN.com. https://www.cnn.com/videos/politics
/2018/03/10/trump-pennsylvania-speech-mocking-presidential-sot.cnn.

"President Trump on Christine Blasey Ford, his relationships with Vladimir Putin and Kim
Jong Un and more." Interview by Lesley Stahl. 60 Minutes, CBS News, October 15, 2018.
https://www.cbsnews.com/news/donald-trump-full-interview-60-minutes-transcript-lesley
-stahl-2018-10-14/.

"Press Conference by President Trump." Office of the Press Secretary, September 27, 2018.
https://www.whitehouse.gov/briefings-statements/press-conference-president-trump-2/.

"PREVIEW: Trump Tells O'Reilly He 'Respects' Putin in Super Bowl Interview." Fox News,
February 4, 2017. https://insider.foxnews.com/2017/02/04/preview-bill-oreilly-donald-trump
-super-bowl-interview.

"The Primaries are More than Eyewash." Life, February 18, 1952.

"Public's Priorities for U.S. Asylum Policy: More Judges for Cases, Safe Conditions for Migrants." Pew Research Center, August 12, 2019. https://www.people-press.org/2019/08/12
/publics-priorities-for-u-s-asylum-policy-more-judges-for-cases-safe-conditions-for
-migrants/.

Qiu, Linda. "15 Claims From Trump's Speech to CPAC, Fact-Checked." New York Times,
March 2, 2019. https://www.nytimes.com/2019/03/02/us/politics/trump-cpac-fact-check.html.

Ragusa, Jordan. "If the Senate allowed a Merrick Garland vote, he might pass." Christian Science Monitor, March 18, 2016. https://www.csmonitor.com/USA/Politics/Politics-Voices
/2016/0318/If-the-Senate-allowed-a-Merrick-Garland-vote-he-might-pass.

Raju, Manu. "Cruz accuses Mitch McConnell of telling a 'flat-out lie.'" Politico, July 24, 2015.
https://www.politico.com/story/2015/07/ted-cruz-says-mitch-mcconnell-lies-export-import
-bank-120583.

Ramachandran, Vignesh. "Stanford students help bridge political divides." Stanford News.
October 16, 2019. https://news.stanford.edu/2019/10/16/bridging-political-divides/.

Rauch, Jonathan. "How American Politics Went Insane." The Atlantic, August 2016. https://www
.theatlantic.com/magazine/archive/2016/07/how-american-politics-went-insane/485570/.

Raymond, Adam K., and Matt Stieb. "Trump Hired Them, Then He Called Them Incompetent." Intelligencer, February 13, 2020. https://nymag.com/intelligencer/2020/02/dumb-as
-a-rock-9-times-trump-insulted-people-he-appointed.html.

"Read President Trump's Interview with TIME on Truth and Falsehoods." Time, March 23, 2017.
https://time.com/4710456/donald-trump-time-interview-truth-falsehood/?xid=homepage.

Reagan, Ronald. "Address to the Nation on the Explosion of the Space Shuttle Challenger."
Ronald Reagan Presidential Foundation and Institute, January 28, 1986. https://www
.reaganfoundation.org/media/128831/challenger.pdf.

———. "Remarks at a Dinner Honoring Speaker of the House of Representatives Thomas P.
O'Neill, Jr." Ronald Reagan Presidential Library and Museum, March 17, 1986. https://
www.reaganlibrary.gov/research/speeches/31786f.

Reid, Chip. "The Politics of the Oil Spill." CBS News, June 6, 2010. https://www.cbsnews.com
/news/the-politics-of-the-oil-spill/.

Reiss, Robert. "12 CEOs Describe Their Leadership Style." Forbes. October 8, 2018. https://www
.forbes.com/sites/robertreiss/2018/10/08/12-quotes-from-amazing-leaders/#ff3905a15b8e.

Relman, Eliza. "The 25 women who have accused Trump of sexual misconduct." Business
Insider, October 9, 2019. https://www.businessinsider.com/women-accused-trump-sexual
-misconduct-list-2017-12.

"Remarks by President Trump and President Putin of the Russian Federation in Joint Press
Conference." Office of the Press Secretary, July 16, 2018. https://www.whitehouse.gov

/briefings-statements/remarks-president-trump-president-putin-russian-federation-joint
-press-conference/.

Republican National Committee. "Growth & Opportunity Project." RNC Autopsy Report,
2012. https://www.documentcloud.org/documents/624581-rnc-autopsy.html.

"Republican Sen. Bob Corker says Trump's conduct 'hurts our country.'" Interview by John
Dickerson. CBS This Morning, CBS News. December 12, 2018. https://www.cbsnews.com
/news/senator-bob-corker-trump-conduct-hurts-our-country/.

Resnick, Brian. "A New Brain Study Sheds Light on Why It Can Be So Hard to Change
Someone's Political Beliefs." Vox.com, January 23, 2017. https://www.vox.com/science-and
-health/2016/12/28/14088992/brain-study-change-minds.

Reston, James. "Mr. Nixon's Finest Hour." New York Times, March 1, 1972. https://www
.nytimes.com/1972/03/01/archives/mr-nixons-finest-hour.html.

———. "Q&A; 'The President is Going Down the Wrong Road.'" New York Times, November 1, 1983. https://www.nytimes.com/1983/11/01/us/q-a-the-president-is-going-down-the
-wrong-road.html.

"Revolving Door: Former Members of the 115th Congress." Open Secrets, https://www
.opensecrets.org/revolving/departing.php?cong=115.

"Revolving Door: Former Members of the 114th Congress." Open Secrets, https://www
.opensecrets.org/revolving/departing.php?cong=114.

"Rex Tillerson reflects on firing, working for "undisciplined" Trump." CBS News, December 7, 2018. https://www.cbsnews.com/news/rex-tillerson-bob-schieffer-interview-houston
-firing-trump-tweet-tillerson-insult-2018-12-07/.

Rich, Frank. "Paar to Leno, J.F.K. to J.F.K." New York Times, February 8, 2004. https://www
.nytimes.com/2004/02/08/arts/paar-to-leno-jfk-to-jfk.html?_r=0.

Richardson, Jay. "Cherry Tree Myth." George Washington's Mount Vernon. https://www
.mountvernon.org/library/digitalhistory/digital-encyclopedia/article/cherry-tree-myth/.

Roberts, Steven V. "Bush Intensifies Debate on Pledge, Asking Why It So Upsets Dukakis."
New York Times, August 25, 1988. https://www.nytimes.com/1988/08/25/us/bush-intensifies
-debate-on-pledge-asking-why-it-so-upsets-dukakis.html.

———. "Congress; The Eclipse of the Boll Weevils." New York Times, March 26, 1983. https://
www.nytimes.com/1983/03/26/us/congress-the-eclipse-of-the-boll-weevils.html.

Robertson, Nic, Paul Cruickshank, and Tim Lister. "Document shows origins of 2006 plot for
liquid bombs on planes." CNN.com, April 30, 2012. https://www.cnn.com/2012/04/30
/world/al-qaeda-documents/index.html.

Robles, Frances, Richard Fausset, and Michael Barbaro. "Nikki Haley, South Carolina Governor, Calls for Removal of Confederate Battle Flag." New York Times, June 22, 2015.
https://www.nytimes.com/2015/06/23/us/south-carolina-confederate-flag-dylann-roof
.html.

Romero, Dennis. "John Kelly says he told Trump a 'yes man' would get him impeached."
NBC News, October 26, 2019. https://www.nbcnews.com/politics/donald-trump/john-kelly
-says-he-told-trump-yes-man-would-get-n1072491.

Romney, Mitt. "The president shapes the public character of the nation. Trump's character
falls short." Washington Post, January 1, 2019. https://www.washingtonpost.com/opinions
/mitt-romney-the-president-shapes-the-public-character-of-the-nation-trumps-character
-falls-short/2019/01/01/37a3c8c2-0d1a-11e9-8938-5898adc28fa2_story.html.

"Romney Readiness Project General Instructions: First 200 Days." Romney Readiness Project documents, Center for Presidential Transitions. https://presidentialtransition.org/wp
-content/uploads/sites/6/2016/01/0418b5bd131c3adae65bcbffea841313-1453147324.pdf.

"Romney's Harsh Trump Critique Shows Why He Lost to Obama In 2012." Investor's Business Daily, January 2, 2019. https://www.investors.com/politics/editorials/romney-trump
-criticism/.

"Romney's Strong Debate Performance Erases Obama's Lead." Pew Research Center, Octo-

ber 8, 2012. https://www.people-press.org/2012/10/08/romneys-strong-debate-performance
-erases-obamas-lead/.

Roosevelt, Franklin D. "Address at Oglethorpe University." FDR Library, May 22, 1932. https://
fdrlibrary.files.wordpress.com/2012/10/oglethorpe.pdf.

———. "Fireside Chat 13: On Purging the Democratic Party." UVA Miller Center, June 24,
1938. https://millercenter.org/the-presidency/presidential-speeches/june-24-1938-fireside
-chat-13-purging-democratic-party.

Roosevelt, Theodore. "Fellow-Feeling as a Political Factor." In *Century*, January 1900. https://
www.bartleby.com/58/4.html.

Rosenberg, Yair. "Why 'The West Wing' Is a Terrible Guide to American Democracy." *The
Atlantic*, October 1, 2012. https://www.theatlantic.com/politics/archive/2012/10/why-the
-west-wing-is-a-terrible-guide-to-american-democracy/263084/.

Rubin, Robert. Interview by Chris Bury. "Clinton Years Interview." *Frontline*, PBS, July 2000.
https://www.pbs.org/wgbh/pages/frontline/shows/clinton/interviews/rubin.html.

Rucker, Philip, and Robert Costa. "Bannon vows a daily fight for 'deconstruction of the administrative state.'" *Washington Post*, February 23, 2017. https://www.washingtonpost.com
/politics/top-wh-strategist-vows-a-daily-fight-for-deconstruction-of-the-administrative-state
/2017/02/23/03f6b8da-f9ea-11e6-bf01-d47f8cf9b643_story.html.

Rupar, Aaron. "Trump claimed ex-presidents told him they wished they built a wall. We now
know he made it up." Vox.com, January 7, 2019. https://www.vox.com/2019/1/7/18172559
/trump-ex-presidents-border-wall.

"Russian Active Measures Campaigns and Interference in the 2016 U.S. Election." Report of
the Select Committee on Intelligence, 116th Congress. https://www.intelligence.senate
.gov/sites/default/files/documents/Report_Volume2.pdf.

Russian, Ale. "Trump Boasted of Avoiding STDs While Dating: Vaginas Are 'Landmines . . .
It Is My Personal Vietnam.'" *Time*, October 15, 2016. https://people.com/politics/trump
-boasted-of-avoiding-stds-while-dating-vaginas-are-landmines-it-was-my-personal
-vietnam/.

Ryan, Paul. Interview by Michael Barbaro. "Paul Ryan's Exit Interview." *The Daily*, *New York
Times*. August 8, 2018. https://www.nytimes.com/2018/08/08/podcasts/the-daily/paul-ryan
-house-speaker-trump.html.

Ryan, Tim. "Trump Flips Another Circuit to Majority GOP Appointees." Courthouse News
Service, November 20, 2019. https://www.courthousenews.com/trump-flips-another-circuit
-to-majority-gop-appointees/.

Ryssdal, Kai, and Jana Kasperkevic. "'The enemy is forgetting': Bernanke, Geithner and Paulson on why we must remember the 2008 financial crisis." Marketplace, March 19, 2018.
https://www.marketplace.org/2018/03/19/bernanke-geithner-paulson-regulations-lesson
-crisis-warning/.

Salama, Vivian. "Trump: Mockery of Christine Blasey Ford "Doesn't Matter. We Won." *Wall
Street Journal*, October 14, 2018. https://www.wsj.com/articles/trump-mockery-of-christine
-blasey-ford-doesnt-matter-we-won-1539569094.

Salvanto, Anthony, Jennifer De Pinto, Kabir Khanna, and Fred Backus. "Americans wary of
Trump tariffs' impact, but support plan to aid farmers—CBS poll." CBS, July 29, 2018.
https://www.cbsnews.com/news/americans-wary-of-trump-tariffs-impact-but-support-plan
-to-aid-farmers-cbs-poll/?utm_source=newsletter&utm_medium=email&utm_campaign
=sendto_newslettertest&stream=top.

Samara Klar, Yanna Krupnikov, and John Barry Ryan. "Affective Polarization or Partisan Disdain? Untangling a Dislike for the Opposing Party from a Dislike of Partisanship." *Public
Opinion Quarterly* 82, 2 (Summer 2018): 379–90. https://doi.org/10.1093/poq/nfy014.

Sant, Shannon Van. "U.S. Envoy to The Coalition Against ISIS Resigns Over Trump's Syria
Policy." NPR, December 22, 2018. https://www.npr.org/2018/12/22/679535003/u-s-envoy-to
-the-coalition-against-isis-resigns-over-trumps-syria-policy.

Sasse, Ben. "We Can and We Should Do Better Than This." *U.S. Senator for Nebraska Ben Sasse*, September 4, 2018. https://www.sasse.senate.gov/public/index.cfm/press-releases?ID =9731B7D3-1CB3-4B04-AB6C-F2D91CFC5720.

Schaedel, Sydney. "Trump Didn't Ignore Disabled Child." FactCheck.org, August 3, 2017. https://www.factcheck.org/2017/08/trump-didnt-ignore-disabled-child/.

Schlender, Brent. "Exclusive: New Wisdom From Steve Jobs On Technology, Hollywood, And How 'Good Management Is Like The Beatles.'" *Fast Company*, April 17, 2012. https:// www.fastcompany.com/1829788/exclusive-new-wisdom-steve-jobs-technology-hollywood -and-how-good-management-beatles.

Schlesinger, Jr., Arthur M. "How the State Department Baffled Him." From "Part III: From J.F.K.'s Inner Circle, 'A Thousand Days.'" *Life*, vol. 59, no. 5, July 30, 1965.

Schmidt, Eric, and Maggie Haberman. "Trump Ordered Mueller Fired, but Backed Off When White House Counsel Threatened to Quit." *New York Times*, January 25, 2018. https://www.nytimes.com/2018/01/25/us/politics/trump-mueller-special-counsel-russia .html.

Schmitt, Eric, and Charlie Savage. "Bowe Bergdahl, American Soldier, Freed by Taliban in Prisoner Trade." *New York Times*, May 31, 2014. https://www.nytimes.com/2014/06/01/us /bowe-bergdahl-american-soldier-is-freed-by-taliban.html.

Schwartz, Ian. "Trump: 'I Hate to Tell You Puerto Rico But You've Thrown Our Budget A Little Out Of Whack.'" Real Clear Politics, October 3, 2017. https://www.realclearpolitics .com/video/2017/10/03/trump_i_hate_to_tell_you_puerto_rico_but_youve_thrown_our _budget_a_little_out_of_whack.html.

Scott, Eugene. "Trump denounces David Duke, KKK." CNN.com, March 3, 2016. https:// www.cnn.com/2016/03/03/politics/donald-trump-disavows-david-duke-kkk/index.html.

"The Second Presidential Debate." *New York Times*, October 7, 2008. https://www.nytimes .com/elections/2008/president/debates/transcripts/second-presidential-debate.html.

Segers, Grace. "Former top special operations commander says Trump 'needs to be held ac- countable.'" CBS News, October 4, 2019. https://www.cbsnews.com/news/former-top -special-operations-commander-says-trump-needs-to-be-held-accountable/.

"Seizure! Truman Takes the Steel Mills." Constitutional Rights Foundation, 2020. https:// www.crf-usa.org/bill-of-rights-in-action/bria-4-4-b-seizure-truman-takes-the-steel-mills .html.

Selwyn-Holmes, Alex. "The Loneliest Job." Iconic Photos, July 18, 2010. https://iconicphotos .wordpress.com/2010/07/18/the-loneliest-job/.

Semones, Evan. "Trump assails Rep. Dingell, citing her late husband, amid wave of attacks on Dems." Politico, February 8, 2020. https://www.politico.com/news/2020/02/08/trump -attacks-dingell-pelosi-112528.

"Senators compromise on aid to Poles, Hungary." *The Record*, November 14, 1989.

Sevastopulo, Demetri, and Gillian Tett. "Gary Cohn urges Trump team to do more to con- demn neo-Nazis." *Financial Times*, August 25, 2017. https://www.ft.com/content/b85beea2 -8924-11e7-bf50-e1c239b45787.

Shabad, Rebecca. "Donald Trump: I Hope Russia Finds Hillary Clinton's Emails." CBS News, July 27, 2016. https://www.cbsnews.com/news/donald-trump-i-hope-russia-finds -hillary-clintons-emails/.

———. "Speaker Ryan: GOP presidential nominee must reject bigotry." CBS News, March 1, 2016. https://www.cbsnews.com/news/speaker-ryan-gop-presidential-nominee-must-reject -bigotry/.

Shankar, Maya. "Using Behavioral Science Insights to Make Government More Effective, Simpler, and More People-Friendly." The White House Press Office, February 9, 2015. https://obamawhitehouse.archives.gov/blog/2015/02/09/behavioral-science-insights-make -government-more-effective-simpler-and-more-user-fri.

Shanker, Deena. "How to Stay Sane in a World of Crazy News." Bloomberg, February 16, 2017. https://www.bloomberg.com/news/articles/2017-02-16/how-to-stay-sane-in-a-world-of crazy news.

Shear, Michael D. and Michael S. Schmidt. "President Admits Trump Tower Meeting Was Meant to Get Dirt on Clinton." New York Times, August 5, 2018, https://www.nytimes.com /2018/08/05/us/politics/trump-tower-meeting-donald-jr.html.

Shearer, Elisa and Katerina Eva Matsa. "News Use Across Social Media Platforms 2018." Pew Research Center, September 10, 2018. https://www.journalism.org/2018/09/10/news-use -across-social-media-platforms-2018/.

Shedden, David. "The First Convention Broadcast: Radio at the 1924 Conventions." https://www .poynter.org/archive/2004/the-first-convention-broadcast-radio-at-the-1924-conventions/.

Sheffer, Bill. "From the Archive: LBJ Visits Elkhart County on Tour of Disaster Areas." Goshen News, April 10, 2015. https://www.goshennews.com/from-the-archive-lbj-visits-elkhart -county-on-tour-of/article_238e1568-dfc4-11e4-ba6a-63fcbbd4e8e9.html.

Siders, David. "Democrats preview post-Trump plan: Executive orders." Politico, May 4, 2019. https://www.politico.com/story/2019/05/04/democrats-executive-orders-2020-1301633.

Sides, John. "Script Doctor." Monkey Cage, August 7, 2011. https://themonkeycage.org/2011/08 /script-doctor/.

Silverman, Ellie. "Neo-Nazis marched past their synagogue chanting 'Sieg Heil.'" Washing- ton Post, August 26, 2017. https://www.washingtonpost.com/local/social-issues/neo-nazis -marched-past-their-synagogue-chanting-sieg-heil-two-weeks-later-the-charlottesville -jewish-community-is-still-healing/2017/08/26/d75ef1d0-8a70-11e7-a50f-e0d4e6ec070a _story.html.

Simon, Ron. "See How JFK Created a Presidency for the Television Age." Time, May 30, 2017. https://time.com/4795637/jfk-television/.

Simpson, Jeffrey. "Acting the prime minister, prepared for the role." The Globe and Mail, March 22, 2018. https://www.theglobeandmail.com/opinion/acting-the-prime-minister -prepared-for-the-role/article27256072/.

Sirak, Ron. "Founding Father." Golf Digest, November 1, 2009. https://www.golfdigest.com /story/golf_eisenhower_sirak.

Sitrin, Carly. "Read: President Trump's remarks condemning violence 'on many sides' in Char- lottesville." Vox.com, August 12, 2017. https://www.vox.com/2017/8/12/16138906/president -trump-remarks-condemning-violence-on-many-sides-charlottesville-rally.

Skelley, Geoffrey. "Just How Many Obama 2012-Trump 2016 Voters Were There?" UVA: Cen- ter for Politics, June 1, 2017. http://centerforpolitics.org/crystalball/articles/just-how-many -obama-2012-trump-2016-voters-were-there/.

Slack, Donovan. "Paul Ryan rips Trump comments as 'textbook definition of racist.'" USA Today, June 7, 2016. https://www.usatoday.com/story/news/politics/onpolitics/2016/06/07 /paul-ryan-rips-trump-comments-textbook-definition-racist/85548042/.

"Slavery in The Lowcountry." International African American Museum, 2017. https://iaamu- seum.org/history/slavery-in-charleston-and-the-lowcountry/.

Smith, Ben. "How Mitt Romney Won the First Debate." Buzzfeed, October 3, 2012. https:// www.buzzfeednews.com/article/bensmith/how-mitt-romney-won-the-first-debate.

Smith-Spark, Laura. "With more than 191,000 dead in Syria, U.N. rights chief slams global 'paralysis.'" CNN.com, August 22, 2014. https://www.cnn.com/2014/08/22/world/meast/syria -conflict/index.html.

Solomon, John, and Buck Sexton. "Trump slams Bush for 'worst single mistake' in U.S. his- tory." The Hill, September 19, 2018. https://thehill.com/hilltv/rising/407398-trump-slams -bush-for-worst-single-mistake-in-us-history.

Sorkin, Andrew Ross. "Warren Buffett, Delegator in Chief." New York Times, April 23, 2011. https://www.nytimes.com/2011/04/24/weekinreview/24buffett.html.

Sorkin, Andrew Ross, and Landon Thomas Jr. "JPMorgan Acts to Buy Ailing Bear Stearns at Huge Discount." *New York Times*, March 16, 2008. https://www.nytimes.com/2008/03/16 /business/16cnd-bear.html.

"The Speaker Steps Down; Excerpts from Phone Call About Gingrich's Future." *New York Times*, November 8, 1998. https://web.archive.org/web/20160804035421/http://www.nytimes .com/1998/11/08/us/the-speaker-steps-down-excerpts-from-phone-call-about-gingrich -s-future.html.

Spiegel, Danny. "Today in TV History: Bill Clinton and His Sax Visit Arsenio." TV Insider, June 3, 2015. https://www.tvinsider.com/2979/rerun-bill-clinton-on-arsenio-hall/.

"Spiro T. Agnew, 39th Vice President (1969–1973)." United States Senate. https://www.senate .gov/about/officers-staff/vice-president/VP_Spiro_Agnew.htm.

"Split-ticket Districts in the 2016 Presidential and U.S. House Elections." Ballotpedia, https:// ballotpedia.org/Split-ticket_districts_in_the_2016_presidential_and_U.S._House_elections #cite_note-1.

SSRS Research Refined. "General Poll." CNN.com, July 1, 2019. http://cdn.cnn.com/cnn /2019/images/07/01/rel8a.-.democrats.and.healthcare.pdf.

Stanley-Becker, Isaac. "'Horns' are growing on young people's skulls. Phone use is to blame, research suggests." *Washington Post*, June 25, 2019. https://www.washingtonpost.com/nation /2019/06/20/horns-are-growing-young-peoples-skulls-phone-use-is-blame-research-suggests/.

"State Dining Room." White House Historical Association, January 16, 2019. https://www .whitehousehistory.org/white-house-tour/state-dining-room.

"Statement from the Press Secretary." White House, October 6, 2019. https://www.whitehouse .gov/briefings-statements/statement-press-secretary-85/.

Stenholm, Charlie. "How Tip O'Neill and Ronald Reagan would make this Congress work." The Hill, March 12, 2015. https://thehill.com/blogs/pundits-blog/lawmaker-news/235409 -how-ronald-reagan-and-tip-oneill-would-make-this-congress.

Stephey, M.J. "Dukakis' Deadly Response." *Time*, October 14, 1988. http://content.time.com /time/specials/packages/article/0,28804,1844704_1844706_1844712,00.html.

Stier, Max. "My Turn: Government HR crisis is brewing." *Providence Journal*, June 16, 2018. https://www.providencejournal.com/opinion/20180616/my-turn-max-stier-government-hr -crisis-is-brewing.

———. "Op-Ed: America is rapidly approaching an HR crisis." *Los Angeles Times*, June 6, 2018. https://www.latimes.com/opinion/op-ed/la-oe-stier-federal-workers-20180606-story.html.

Stokols, Eli. "Unapologetic, Trump promises to make America rich." Politico, May 26, 2016. https://www.politico.com/story/2016/05/unapologetic-trump-promises-to-make-america -rich-223632.

Stolberg, Sheryl Gay, Maggie Haberman, and Peter Baker. "Trump Was Repeatedly Warned That Ukraine Conspiracy Theory Was 'Completely Debunked.'" *New York Times*, September 29, 2019. https://www.nytimes.com/2019/09/29/us/politics/tom-bossert-trump-ukraine .html.

Sullivan, Andrew. "Did Obama Just Throw the Entire Election Away?" The Dish, October 8, 2012. http://dish.andrewsullivan.com/2012/10/08/did-obama-just-throw-the-entire-election -away/.

———. "I Used to Be a Human Being." *New York*, September 19, 2016. http://nymag.com/intel- ligencer/2016/09/andrew-sullivan-my-distraction-sickness-and-yours.html.

Sutphen, Mona. "Rethinking the American Presidency." Moderated by Robert Bruner. UVA Miller Center, May 23, 2019. https://millercenter.org/prezfest2019/prezfest-videos/rethinking -american-presidency.

Swaine, John. "Trump inauguration crowd photos were edited after he intervened." *The Guardian*, September 6, 2018. https://www.theguardian.com/world/2018/sep/06/donald -trump-inauguration-crowd-size-photos-edited.

Swan, Jonathan, and Alayna Treene. "Scoop: Former White House counsel Don McGahn off

the record." Axios, April 7, 2019. https://www.axios.com/white-house-counsel-don-mcgahn
-trump-mueller-republican-lunch-7b687a07-4acf-4578-ac32-f0c421c74070.html.

Szep, Jason. "Cities grapple with surge in abandoned homes." Reuters, March 24, 2008. https://
www.reuters.com/article/us-usa-housing-vacant/cities-grapple-with-surge-in-abandoned
-homes-idUSN1162941020080325.

Tackett, Michael. "Some Presidents Felt Trapped in the White House Bubble. Trump Thrives
in It." New York Times, March 27, 2019. https://www.nytimes.com/2019/03/27/us/politics
/trump-white-house-travel.html.

Taft, William Howard, and Supreme Court of the United States. U.S. Reports: Myers v. United
States, 272 U.S. 52. 1926. Periodical. https://www.loc.gov/item/usrep272052/.

"Taxation of Social Security Benefits." Social Security Agency History. https://www.ssa.gov
/history/taxationofbenefits.html.

Taylor, Derrick Bryson. "Trump Mocks Greta Thunberg on Twitter, and She Jabs Back." New
York Times, December 12, 2019. https://www.nytimes.com/2019/12/12/us/politics/greta
-thunberg-trump.html.

Tenpas, Kathyn Dunn. "Tracking Turnover in the Trump administration." Brookings Institution, February 2020. https://www.brookings.edu/research/tracking-turnover-in-the-trump
-administration/.

Terkel, Amanda. "Pat Toomey: Background Checks Died Because GOP Didn't Want to Help
Obama." HuffPost, May 1, 2013. https://www.huffpost.com/entry/pat-toomey-background
-checks_n_3192690.

"Text of Truman Statement on Convention." St. Louis Post-Dispatch, July 2, 1960. https://www
.newspapers.com/image/141680791/.

"Theodore Roosevelt." History.com, May 16, 2019. https://www.history.com/topics/us-presidents
/theodore-roosevelt.

Thiessen, Marc A. "Trump could be the most honest president in modern history." Washington
Post, October 11, 2018. https://www.washingtonpost.com/opinions/trump-could-be-the-most
-honest-president-in-modern-history/2018/10/11/67aefc5a-cd76-11e8-a3e6-44daa3d35ede
_story.html.

Thompson, Dennis F. "Constitutional Character: Virtues and Vices in Presidential Leadership." Presidential Studies Quarterly 40, no. 1 (2010): 23–37. www.jstor.org/stable/23044893.

Thrush, Glenn, Manu Raju, and Josh Gerstein. "Obama under fire for spill response." Politico,
May 27, 2010. https://www.politico.com/story/2010/05/obama-under-fire-for-spill-response
-037819.

"Tillerson says Trump 'speaks for himself' on Charlottesville protests." Fox News, August
27, 2017. https://www.foxnews.com/politics/tillerson-says-trump-speaks-for-himself-on
-charlottesville-protests.

Toner, Robin. "Buchanan, Urging New Nationalism, Joins '92 Race." New York Times, December 11, 1991. https://www.nytimes.com/1991/12/11/us/buchanan-urging-new-nationalism
-joins-92-race.html.

Troy, Tevi. "Don't Worry, America: The 3 A.M. Phone Call Is a Myth." Politico Magazine. September 10, 2016. https://www.politico.com/magazine/story/2016/09/3am-phone-call-myth
-trump-214208.

———. "Presidents and Mass Shootings." National Affairs, Spring 2018. https://www.national
affairs.com/publications/detail/presidents-and-mass-shootings.

Truman, Harry S. "Mr. Truman's Memoirs: Atom Problems Arise, Installment 1, Excerpts
from 'Years of Trial and Hope.'" New York Times, January 22, 1956. https://www.nytimes
.com/1956/01/22/archives/mr-trumans-memoirs-atom-problems-arise-mr-truman-memoirs
-atom.html.

"Truman Library Discovers 1947 Truman Diary." National Archives, July 10, 2003. https://www
.archives.gov/press/press-releases/2003/nr03-54.html.

Trumbull, David. "The most important thing is sincerity. If you can fake that you've got it

made." *Post-Gazette*, December 15, 2006. http://www.trumbullofboston.org/writing/2006
-12-15.htm.

Trump, Donald. Interview by Frank Luntz. "Presidential Candidate Donald Trump at the Family Leadership Summit." C-SPAN. July 18, 2015. https://www.c-span.org/video/?327045 -5/presidential-candidate-donald-trump-family-leadership-summit.

———. "President Trump's interview in the Oval Office: Full Transcript." CBS News, May 1, 2017. https://www.cbsnews.com/news/president-trump-oval-office-interview-cbs-this-morning -full-transcript/.

———. "Remarks by President Trump and President Putin of the Russian Federation in Joint Press Conference." Office of the Press Secretary, July 16, 2018. https://www.whitehouse .gov/briefings-statements/remarks-president-trump-president-putin-russian-federation -joint-press-conference/.

———. "Remarks by President Trump at the 68th Annual National Prayer Breakfast." Office of the Press Secretary, February 6, 2020. https://www.whitehouse.gov/briefings-statements /remarks-president-trump-68th-annual-national-prayer-breakfast/.

———. "Remarks by President Trump on Infrastructure." Office of the Press Secretary, August 15, 2017. https://www.whitehouse.gov/briefings-statements/remarks-president-trump -infrastructure/.

———. "Transcript: ABC News' George Stephanopoulos' exclusive interview with President Trump." Interview by George Stephanopoulos. ABC News, June 16, 2019. https://abcnews .go.com/Politics/transcript-abc-news-george-stephanopoulos-exclusive-interview-president /story?id=63749144.

———. "Transcript: Trump, Cruz, Clinton, Priebus." Interview by John Dickerson. *Face the Nation*, CBS News, March 6, 2016. https://www.cbsnews.com/news/face-the-nation-transcripts -march-6-2016-trump-cruz-clinton-priebus/.

"Trump, Huckabee, Sullenberger." Interview by John Dickerson. *Face the Nation*, CBS News, August 2, 2015. https://www.cbsnews.com/news/face-the-nation-transcripts-august-2-2015 -trump-huckabee-sullenberger/.

"Trump Address NRA Convention on Guns." CNN Transcripts, May 20, 2016. http://transcripts .cnn.com/TRANSCRIPTS/1605/20/cnr.06.html.

"Trump disputes CIA findings that MBS ordered Khashoggi murder." Aljazeera.com, November 23, 2018. https://www.aljazeera.com/news/2018/11/trump-contradicts-cia-findings-mbs -ordered-khashoggi-murder-181123070359687.html.

"Trump: 'I Could Stand in the Middle of Fifth Avenue and Shoot Somebody and I Wouldn't Lose Any Voters.'" Real Clear Politics, January 23, 2016. https://www.realclearpolitics.com /video/2016/01/23/trump_i_could_stand_in_the_middle_of_fifth_avenue_and_shoot _somebody_and_i_wouldnt_lose_any_voters.html.

"Trust in government: 1958–2015." Pew Research Center, November 23, 2015. https://www .people-press.org/2015/11/23/1-trust-in-government-1958-2015/.

Tufekci, Zeynep. "How Social Media Took Us from Tahrir Square to Donald Trump." MIT Technology Review, August 14, 2018. https://www.technologyreview.com/s/611806/how -social-media-took-us-from-tahrir-square-to-donald-trump/.

Uhrmacher, Kevin, Kevin Schaul, and Dan Keating. "These former Obama strongholds sealed the election for Trump." *Washington Post*, November 9, 2016. https://www.washingtonpost .com/graphics/politics/2016-election/obama-trump-counties/?tid=lk_inline_manual_11.

U.S. Congress, House of Representatives. 98th Cong., 2nd sess., May 15, 1984. https://www .govinfo.gov/content/pkg/GPO-CRECB-1984-pt9/pdf/GPO-CRECB-1984-pt9-5-2.pdf.

U.S. Congress. "Operation Inherent Resolve." Lead Inspector General Report, July 1, 2019. https://www.politico.com/f/?id=0000016e-8474-d93d-ad6f-8e76571c0000&nname=play book-pm&nid=0000015a-dd3e-d536-a37b-dd7fd8af0000&nrid=0000014e-f116-dd93-ad7f -f91725480002&nlid=964328.

U.S. Congress. Senate. Homeland Security and Governmental Affairs. Presidential Transi-

tions Improvement Act of 2015. 114th Cong., 1st sess., 2015. S. Rept. 114–94. https://www
.congress.gov/congressional-report/114th-congress/senate-report/94/1.

"U.S. household income distribution from 1990 to 2018." Statistica, September 2019 https://
www.statista.com/statistics/219643/gini-coefficient-for-us-individuals-families-and
-households/.

"U.S. Senator's Daughter Says." *Evening Independent*, February 19, 1940. https://news.google
.com/newspapers?id=C8YLAAAAIBAJ&sjid=nFQDAAAAIBAJ&pg=3560,3163003&dq=
drapes.

"U.S. Voters Want to See Mueller Report," Quinnipiac University Poll, March 26, 2019. https://
poll.qu.edu/national/release-detail?ReleaseID=2609.

Van Buren, Martin. "Special Session Message." National Archives, September 4, 1937. https://
millercenter.org/the-presidency/presidential-speeches/september-4-1837-special-session
-message.

Vandermaas-Peeler, Alex, Daniel Cox, and Maxine Najle, et al. "Partisanship Trumps Gender:
Sexual Harassment, Woman Candidates, Access to Contraception, and Key Issues in 2018
Midterms." PRRI, October 3, 2018. https://www.prri.org/research/abortion-reproductive
-health-midterms-trump-kavanaugh/.

Vavreck, Lynn. "It's Not So Much the Debate. It's the Days After the Debate." *New York Times*,
June 26, 2019. https://www.nytimes.com/2019/06/26/upshot/debate-dramatic-moments
-overrated.html.

———. "A Measure of Identity: Are You Wedded to Your Party?" *New York Times*, January 31,
2017. https://www.nytimes.com/2017/01/31/upshot/are-you-married-to-your-party.html.

"Vital Statistics on Congress: Data on the U.S. Congress." Brookings Institution, April 7, 2014.
https://www.brookings.edu/wp-content/uploads/2016/06/Vital-Statistics-Chapter-2
-Congressional-Elections.pdf.

Wagner, John. "'Bing, bing, bing': Trump reveals his thinking behind firing off all those
tweets." *Washington Post*, October 20, 2017. https://www.washingtonpost.com/news/post
-politics/wp/2017/10/20/bing-bing-bing-trump-reveals-his-thinking-behind-firing-off-all
-those-tweets/.

Wagner, John, Felicia Sonmez, and Colby Itkowitz. "President celebrates Senate acquittal at
the White House, expresses no contrition and calls Democratic leaders 'vicious and
mean.'" *Washington Post*, February 6, 2020. https://www.washingtonpost.com/politics/trump
-impeachment-live-updates/2020/02/06/f45f94b4-48ce-11ea-bdbf-1dfb23249293_story.html.

Wagner, Meg, Veronica Rocha, Brian Ries, Amanda Wills, and Jessie Yeung. "The nation
honors President George H. W. Bush." CNN.com, December 13, 2018. https://www.cnn
.com/politics/live-news/george-hw-bush-funeral/h_b83e5cb050582b896b8cab9cd2c5b330.

Waidelich, Butch. "From Engineering to Peanuts to the Presidency." U.S. Department of
Transportation. https://www.transportation.gov/fastlane/engineering-peanuts-presidency.

Wallace-Wells, Benjamin. "Pete Buttigieg's Quiet Rebellion." *New Yorker*, February 9, 2019.
https://www.newyorker.com/news/the-political-scene/pete-buttigiegs-quiet-rebellion.

Walsh, Edward. "Central Role for Jordan." *Washington Post*, February 22, 1977. https://www
.washingtonpost.com/archive/politics/1977/02/22/central-role-for-jordan/d334c330-d06e
-46fb-bb29-8bb58b6384d0/.

Wang, Sam. "The Great Gerrymander of 2012." *New York Times*, February 2, 2013. https://www
.nytimes.com/2013/02/03/opinion/sunday/the-great-gerrymander-of-2012.html.

———. "Post-Debate Reaction." Princeton Election Consortium, October 3, 2012. http://elec-
tion.princeton.edu/2012/10/03/post-debate-reaction/.

Warner, Margaret Garrard. "Bush Battles The 'Wimp Factor.'" *Newsweek*, October 19, 1987.
https://www.newsweek.com/bush-battles-wimp-factor-207008.

Warren, Elizabeth. "Enough is Enough: The President's Latest Wall Street Nominee." Huff-
Post, November 19, 2014. https://www.huffpost.com/entry/presidents-wall-street-nominee
_b_6188324.

"Washington's Constitution." George Washington's Mount Vernon. https://www.mountvernon
.org/george-washington/constitutional-convention/washingtons-constitution/.

Watson, Jack. "Oral History: Interview as Transition Director." UVA Miller Center, April 17-18,
1981. https://millercenter.org/the-presidency/presidential-oral-histories/jack-h-watson-jr-oral
-history.

Waxman, Olivia B. "How Ross Perot Changed Political Campaigns." *Time*, July 9, 2019.
https://time.com/5622818/ross-perot-dead-legacy/.

Weems, Mason Locke. "The Ingenious Weems Relates Some Pleasing Anecdotes." Bartleby
.com, December 2013. https://www.bartleby.com/400/prose/602.html.

Wehner, Peter. "Christian Doomsayers Have Lost It." *New York Times*, December 6, 2019.
https://www.nytimes.com/2019/12/06/opinion/sunday/trump-christian-conservatives.html.

———. "Why the First Year Matters, Vol. 1: Dear Mr. President." First Year 2017. http://first-
year2017.org/essay/letter-to-the-new-president.html.

Weiner, Matthew. "How golf balls took on the oil spill and lost." CNN.com, May 31, 2010.
https://www.cnn.com/2010/SPORT/golf/05/31/golf.oil.spill/index.html.

Weiner, Rachel. "Chris Christie: 'Real leaders change polls.'" *Washington Post*, August 28,
2012. https://www.washingtonpost.com/news/post-politics/wp/2012/08/28/chris-christie
-real-leaders-change-polls/.

———. "Sean Hannity: I've 'evolved' on immigration." *Washington Post*, November 8, 2012.
https://www.washingtonpost.com/news/post-politics/wp/2012/11/08/sean-hannity-ive
-evolved-on-immigration/.

Weinraub, Bernard. The Political Campaign; Reagan Begins 13-State Campaign Tour. *New York
Times*, October 24, 1985. https://www.nytimes.com/1986/10/24/us/the-political-campaign
-reagan-begins-13-state-campaign-tour.html.

Wemple, Erik. "Why Tucker Carlson is (finally) blasting President Trump." *Washington Post*,
January 10, 2018. https://www.washingtonpost.com/blogs/erik-wemple/wp/2018/01/10/why
-is-tucker-carlson-blasting-president-trump/.

Westen, Drew. "What Happened to Obama?" *New York Times*, August 6, 2011. https://www
.nytimes.com/2011/08/07/opinion/sunday/what-happened-to-obamas-passion.html?_r=1&
ref=opinion&pagewanted=all.

"What psychology experiments tell you about why people deny facts." *The Economist*, December 8, 2018. https://www.economist.com/united-states/2018/12/08/what-psychology
-experiments-tell-you-about-why-people-deny-facts.

White, Richard D. "Executive Reorganization, Theodore Roosevelt and the Keep Commission." *Administrative Theory & Praxis* 24, no. 3 (2002): 507–18. www.jstor.org/stable
/25611596.

Whitlock, Craig. "The Afghanistan Papers: At War With the Truth." *Washington Post*, December 9, 2019. https://www.washingtonpost.com/graphics/2019/investigations/afghanistan
-papers/afghanistan-war-confidential-documents/.

Whitman, David. "Are Reagan's New Judges Really Closet Moderates?" *Washington Post*, August 9, 1987. https://www.washingtonpost.com/archive/opinions/1987/08/09/are-reagans
-new-judges-really-closet-moderates/60da1734-053b-4a75-a4a9-c6bcae68846f/.

"Why It Happened." Digital History ID 3432, 2019. http://www.digitalhistory.uh.edu/disp
_textbook.cfm?smtID=2&psid=3432.

Wilhelm, Colin. "Mitch McConnell blames entitlement programs for rising deficit." *Washington Examiner*, October 16, 2018. https://www.washingtonexaminer.com/policy/economy
/mitch-mcconnell-blames-entitlement-programs-for-rising-deficit.

Wilkie, Curtis. *Boston Sunday Globe*, January 1, 1978.

Will, George. "The Sound of a Lapdog." *Washington Post*, January 30, 1986. https://www
.washingtonpost.com/archive/politics/1986/01/30/george-bush-the-sound-of-a-lapdog
/9322b0c0-c006-4709-99fc-4283fcb35ea8/.

Williams, Claire. "Amid Unpopular Tax Overhaul, GOP Banking on 2019 Tax Returns." De-

cember 17, 2018. https://morningconsult.com/2018/12/17/amid-unpopular-tax-overhaul-gop
-banking-on-2019-tax-returns/.

Williams, Jack. "Hurricane Betsy hit Florida, smashed New Orleans in 1965." *USA Today*,
October 21, 2003. http://usatoday30.usatoday.com/weather/resources/askjack/2003-10-09
-hurricane-betsy_x.htm.

Williams, J. D. "The Summer of 1787: Getting a Constitution." *Brigham Young University
Quarterly* 27, Issue 3, Article 6 (July 1987). https://scholarsarchive.byu.edu/cgi/viewcontent
.cgi?article=2491&context=byusq.

Wills, Garry. "Lincoln's Greatest Speech." *The Atlantic*, September 1999. https://www.theatlantic
.com/magazine/archive/1999/09/lincolns-greatest-speech/306551/.

Wilson, Woodrow. "League of Nations." U.S. Diplomatic Mission to Germany, September 25,
1919. https://usa.usembassy.de/etexts/speeches/rhetoric/wwleague.htm.

"Winning West Virginia: JFK's Primary Campaign." John F. Kennedy Presidential Library
and Museum. *New Frontiers*, Issue 12, Spring 2010. https://www.jfklibrary.org/sites/default
/files/2018-05/Issue_12_Spring_2010_New_Frontiers.pdf.

Wolf, Zachary B. "Trump's Ukraine phone call, annotated." CNN.com, September 25, 2019.
https://www.cnn.com/interactive/2019/09/politics/trump-ukraine-transcript-annotated/.

"Women's Leaders Map Fight Against Passage." *San Francisco Examiner*, April 8, 1938.

"Woodrow Wilson's Changing Views of the Senate." United States Senate, April 12, 1907.
https://www.senate.gov/artandhistory/history/minute/Woodrow_Wilsons_Changing_Views
_of_the_Senate.htm.

"The Yes, No and Maybe on Driver's Licenses." *New York Times*, November 1, 2007. https://
www.nytimes.com/2007/11/01/us/politics/01words.html.

York, Erica. "Tracking the Economic Impact of U.S. Tariffs and Retaliatory Actions." Tax
Foundation, December 16, 2019. https://taxfoundation.org/tariffs-trump-trade-war.

Zapotosky, Matt, Greg Miller, Ellen Nakashima, and Carol D. Leoning. "Trump Pressed
Ukrainian Leader to Investigate Biden's Son, According to People Familiar with the Matter." *Washington Post*, September 20, 2019. https://www.washingtonpost.com/national
-security/trump-pressed-ukrainian-leader-to-investigate-bidens-son-according-to-people
-familiar-with-the-matter/2019/09/20/7fa39b20-dbdc-11e9-bfb1-849887369476_story.html.

Zeleny, Jeff. "Bill Clinton and Barack Obama, Together at Last." *New York Times*, October 30,
2008. https://thecaucus.blogs.nytimes.com/2008/10/30/bill-clinton-and-barack-obama/.

MANUSCRIPT COLLECTIONS

Clinton, Bill. "Weekly Compilation of Presidential Documents," April 24, 1995. Volume
31—Number 16, Pages 631-683. University of Illinois at Urbana-Champaign.

Eisenhower, Dwight David. "Dwight D. Eisenhower Letter to Dillon Anderson." *Post-
Presidential Papers, January 22, 1968*. Principal file, Box 36, Library of Congress.

"From George Washington to Edmund Pendleton, 22 January 1795." Founders Online, National Archives. https://founders.archives.gov/documents/Washington/05-17-02-0282.

"From George Washington to Henry Knox, 8 March 1787." Founders Online, National Archives. https://founders.archives.gov/documents/Washington/04-05-02-0072.

"From George Washington to Major General Stirling, 5 March 1780." Founders Online, National Archives. https://founders.archives.gov/documents/Washington/03-24-02-0525.

"From George Washington to Officers of the Army, 15 March 1783." Founders Online, National Archives. https://founders.archives.gov/documents/Washington/99-01-02-10840.

"From George Washington to the President of Congress, 17 September 1787." Founders Online, National Archives. https://founders.archives.gov/documents/Washington/04-05-02
-0306.

"From Thomas Jefferson to John Dickinson, 13 January 1807." Founders Online, National
Archives. https://founders.archives.gov/documents/Jefferson/99-01-02-4861.

"From Thomas Jefferson to William Henry Harrison, 27 February 1803." Founders Online, National Archives. https://founders.archives.gov/documents/Jefferson/01-39-02-0500.

Hamilton, Alexander. "The Federalist Papers: No. 49." The Avalon Project, February 5, 1788. https://avalon.law.yale.edu/18th_century/fed49.asp.

———. "The Federalist Papers: No. 68." The Avalon Project, March 14, 1788. https://avalon.law.yale.edu/18th_century/fed68.asp.

———. "The Federalist Papers, No. 70." The Avalon Project, March 18, 1788. https://avalon.law.yale.edu/18th_century/fed70.asp.

———. "The Federalist Papers, No. 71." The Avalon Project, March 18, 1788. https://avalon.law.yale.edu/18th_century/fed71.asp.

———. "The Federalist Papers: No. 74." The Avalon Project, March 25, 1788. https://avalon.law.yale.edu/18th_century/fed74.asp.

Hund, Gaillard, and James Brown Scott, eds. "Notes on the Debates in the Federal Convention." By James Madison. Avalon Project. https://avalon.law.yale.edu/subject_menus/debcont.asp.

Jefferson, Thomas. "Diffusion of Knowledge Bill", 1779. FE 2:221, Papers 2:526.

"Letter from Richard Wirthlin to President Reagan." Ronald Reagan Presidential Library and Museum, April 10, 1985. https://drive.google.com/file/d/1Mi6HhW1QFMSXPOF6-iThn3e6UKCjXKqg/view.

"The Madison Debates: June 1, 1787." The Avalon Project. https://avalon.law.yale.edu/18th_century/debates_601.asp.

"The Madison Debates: June 6, 1787." The Avalon Project. https://avalon.law.yale.edu/18th_century/debates_606.asp.

"The Madison Debates: June 17, 1787." The Avalon Project. https://avalon.law.yale.edu/18th_century/debates_717.asp.

"The Madison Debates: July 19, 1787." The Avalon Project. https://avalon.law.yale.edu/18th_century/debates_719.asp.

"NEVER SINCE," TJ to Pierre-Samuel du Pont de Nemours, July 14, 1807. Thomas Jefferson Papers, Library of Congress.

"Papers of Harry S. Truman Staff Member and Office Files: National Security Council File." https://www.trumanlibrary.gov/library/truman-papers/papers-harry-s-truman-staff-member-and-office-files-national-security-council.

"President Roosevelt and His Aide Lowell Mellet Talk. Side 2, 0–821 (pt. 1), 821–1640 (pt. 2). Sometime between August 22 and August 27, 1940." Franklin D. Roosevelt Presidential Library and Museum, Transcripts of White House Office Conversations, 08/22/1940–10/10/1940, http://docs.fdrlibrary.marist.edu/transcr6.html.

The Public Papers and Addresses of Franklin D. Roosevelt. Vol 1, *The Genesis of the New Deal, 1928–1932: With a Special Introduction and Explanatory Notes by President Roosevelt.* https://quod.lib.umich.edu/p/ppotpus/4925052.1928.001?rgn=main;view=fulltext.

"Thomas Jefferson to John B. Colvin, 20 September 1810." Founders Online, National Archives. https://founders.archives.gov/documents/Jefferson/03-03-02-0060.

"Thomas Jefferson to Walter Jones." Founders Online, January 2, 1814. https://founders.archives.gov/documents/Jefferson/03-07-02-0052.

TWEETS CONSULTED

Alexander, Robert. Alexander (@onuprof). "Electoral College . . ." Twitter, October 31, 2019. 6:45 P.M. https://twitter.com/onuprof/status/1190082469241839616.

Bennet, Michael. (@MichaelBennet). "If you elect . . ." Twitter, August 6, 2019, 11:27 A.M. https://twitter.com/michaelbennet/status/1158806845953323008?lang=en.

Dobbs, Lou. (@LouDobbs). "No wonder . . ." Twitter, July 4, 2019, 5:39 A.M. https://twitter.com/LouDobbs/status/1146760530033614850.

Falwell, Jerry. (@JerryFalwellJr). "Complaining . . ." Twitter, January 9, 2018, 4:50 P.M. https://twitter.com/jerryfalwelljr/status/950892514235559936?lang=en.

———. "Who are you . . ." Twitter, June 25, 2019, 1:12 P.M. https://twitter.com/JerryFalwellJr/status/1143613031450103813.

Gardner, Cory. (@SenCoryGardner). "Mr. President . . ." Twitter, August 12, 2017, 1:44 P.M. https://twitter.com/SenCoryGardner/status/896472477844385792.

Graham, Lindsey. (@LindseyGrahamSC). "By abandoning . . ." Twitter, October 7, 2019, 6:50 A.M. https://twitter.com/LindseyGrahamSC/status/1181205092554493952.

Kessler, Glenn. (@GlennKesslerWP). "Going through Trump . . ." Twitter, October 21, 2018. 10:22 A.M. https://twitter.com/GlennKesslerWP/status/1054060328928055296.

Maher, Bill. (@billmaher). "i can't believe . . ." Twitter, October 3, 2012, 7:18 P.M. https://twitter.com/billmaher/status/253680489850892289.

Mann, Merlin. (@hotdogsladies). "You eventually . . ." Twitter, April 10, 2009, 12:20 P.M. https://twitter.com/hotdogsladies/status/1492464753.

Mercieca, Jennifer. (@jenmercieca). "Never to trust . . ." Twitter, February 17, 2020. https://twitter.com/jenmercieca/status/1229487093426028544.

Moore, Russell. (@drmoore). "The reports . . ." Twitter, June 25, 2019, 12:41 A.M. https://twitter.com/drmoore/status/1143418475723055106.

Nyhan, Brendan. (@BrendanNyhan) "Apparently foreign . . ." Twitter, December 16, 2016, 10:23 A.M. https://twitter.com/BrendanNyhan/status/809826239305355264.

Parkhomenko, Adam. (@AdamParkhomeko). "Yesterday . . ." Twitter, April 4, 2019, 8:38 A.M. https://twitter.com/AdamParkhomenko/status/1113828136821645318.

Rowling, J.K. (@jk_rowling). "Trump imitated . . ." Twitter, July 28, 2017, 11:08 A.M. https://web.archive.org/web/20170731141929/https:/twitter.com/jk_rowling/status/890997400290111489.

Russian Embassy, UK. (@RussianEmbassy). "Best evidence . . ." Twitter, October 6, 2019, 8:31 A.M. https://twitter.com/RussianEmbassy/status/1180868111056195585.

Trump, Donald J. (@RealDonalTrump). "After historic . . ." Twitter, December 19, 2018, 3:10 P.M. https://twitter.com/realDonaldTrump/status/1075528854402256896.

———. ". . . . and viciously . . ." Twitter, July 14, 2019, 5:27 A.M. https://twitter.com/realDonaldTrump/status/1150381395078000643.

———. "Appreciate . . ." Twitter, June 12, 2016, 9:43 A.M. https://twitter.com/realdonaldtrump/status/742034549232766976?lang=en.

———. "As a very . . ." Twitter, May 12, 2017, 4:59 A.M. https://twitter.com/realDonaldTrump/status/863000553265270786.

———. "At least 7 dead . . ." Twitter, June 4, 2017, 4:31 A.M. https://twitter.com/realDonaldTrump/status/871328428963901440.

———. "Because Nancy's teeth . . ." Twitter, December 15, 2019, 2:11 P.M. https://twitter.com/realDonaldTrump/status/1206335971974959107.

———. "A Blue Wave . . ." Twitter, August 21, 2018, 3:38 A.M. https://twitter.com/realdonaldtrump/status/1031852996567748613?lang=en.

———. "Chuck Jones . . ." Twitter, December 7, 2016, 4:41 P.M. https://twitter.com/realDonaldTrump/status/806660011904614408.

———. ". . . the crazed and incompetent . . ." Twitter, April 1, 2019, 8:38 P.M. https://twitter.com/realDonaldTrump/status/1112922221037719552.

———. "I am going . . ." Twitter, May 21, 2015, 5:26 P.M. https://twitter.com/realDonaldTrump/status/601544572498509824.

———. "Ilhan Omar . . ." Twitter, September 18, 2019, 5:14 A.M. https://twitter.com/realDonaldTrump/status/1174295718388854784.

———. ". . . I never told then White House Counsel Don McGahn to fire Robert Mueller . . ." Twitter, April 25, 2019, 7:47 A.M. https://twitter.com/realDonaldTrump/status/1121380133137461248.

———. "The intelligence people . . ." Twitter, January 30, 2019, 5:50 A.M. https://twitter.com/realDonaldTrump/status/1090608298343190528.

———. "Mitt Romney . . ." Twitter, October 5, 2019. 7:17 A.M. https://twitter.com/realDonald Trump/status/1180487139546546182.

———. ". . . My only question . . ." Twitter, August 23, 2019, 7:57 A.M. https://twitter.com/realDonaldTrump/status/1164914610836783104.

———. "My use . . ." Twitter, July 1, 2017, 3:41 P.M. https://twitter.com/realdonaldtrump/status/881281755017355264?lang=en.

———. "Nobody . . ." Twitter, April 27, 2015, 7:33 A.M. https://twitter.com/realDonaldTrump/status/592698043629215746/.

———. "The only one . . ." Twitter, May 12, 2015, 8:12 P.M. https://twitter.com/realDonaldTrump/status/598324947140902912.

———. "PELOSI STAMMERS . . ." Twitter, May 23, 2019, 6:09 P.M. https://twitter.com/realDonaldTrump/status/1131728912835383300.

———. "Rep Tlaib . . ." Twitter, August 21, 2019, 4:52 A.M. https://twitter.com/realDonaldTrump/status/1164143118565937152.

———. "Repubs must . . ." Twitter, November 20, 2014, 6:36 A.M. https://twitter.com/realDonald Trump/status/535441553079431168.

———. ". . . a source of potential danger . . ." Twitter, January 30, 2019, 5:56 A.M. https://twitter.com/realDonaldTrump/status/1090609577006112769.

———. ". . . Such poor . . ." Twitter, September 30, 2017, 4:26 A.M. https://twitter.com/realdonald trump/status/914089003745468417.

———. "There is no . . ." Twitter, November 10, 2018, 12:08 A.M. https://twitter.com/realdonald trump/status/1061168803218948096?lang=en.

———. "This is what happens . . ." Twitter, March 4, 2020, 7:31 A.M. https://twitter.com/realDonaldTrump/status/1235181043881299969.

———. ". . . The USA should . . ." Twitter, September 11, 2019, 3:42 A.M. https://twitter.com/realDonaldTrump/status/1171735692428419072.

———. "The way . . ." Twitter, April 22, 2014, 5:23 P.M. https://twitter.com/realdonaldtrump/status/458763139866435584?lang=en.

———. "We ALL must . . ." Twitter, August 12, 2017, 10:19 A.M. https://twitter.com/realDonald Trump/status/896420822780444672.

Weigel, Dave. (@daveweigel). "A semantic battle . . ." Twitter, October 16, 2019, 10:04 A.M. https://twitter.com/daveweigel/status/1184515451780583424.

Notes

INTRODUCTION

1. James Roosevelt, *My Parents: A Differing View* (Chicago: Playboy Press, 1977).
2. Stephen E. Ambrose, *Eisenhower: Soldier and President* (New York: Simon & Schuster, 1990), 65.
3. Robert E. Clark, "Ike Setting Up Policy of Firing Back," *Cedar Rapids Gazette*, vol. 74, no. 264, September 29, 1956, 1.
4. "Fire Back When Rivals Go Too Far—Ike's New Policy," *Delphos Daily Herald*, vol. 73, September 29, 1956.
5. "Ike Decides to Answer Demo 'Lies,'" *Tyrone Daily Herald*, September 29, 1956, 1.
6. Sherman Adams, *Firsthand Report: The Story of the Eisenhower Administration* (New York: Harper & Brothers, 1961).
7. Ike could have called Stevenson an "egghead." *The New York Herald Tribune* columnist Stewart Alsop had coined the term precisely to describe the urbane, intellectual, and balding Stevenson. Ike didn't pick up that ready weapon, though. (Ike was also bald.)
8. Mark Perry, "When Presidents Get Angry," Politico Magazine, September 27, 2017, www.politico.com/magazine/story/2017/09/27/donald-trump-anger-215648.
9. Evan Thomas, *Ike's Bluff: President Eisenhower's Secret Battle to Save the World* (New York: Little, Brown and Company, 2012), 355.
10. Clarence G. Lasby, *Eisenhower's Heart Attack* (Lawrence, KS: University Press of Kansas, 1997), 19.
11. Clark, "Ike Setting Up Policy," 1.
12. Jasmine C. Lee and Kevin Quealy, "The 598 People, Places and Things Donald Trump Has Insulted on Twitter: A Complete List," *New York Times*, May 24, 2019, https://www.nytimes.com/interactive/2016/01/28/upshot/donald-trump-twitter-insults.html.
13. Jeffrey A. Engel, *When the World Seemed New: George H. W. Bush and the End of the Cold War* (Boston: Houghton Mifflin Harcourt, 2017), 8.
14. Theodore C. Sorensen, *Decision-Making in the White House: The Olive Branch or the Arrows* (New York: Columbia University Press, 2005), 701.
15. Michael Leavitt, interview by John Dickerson, "Face the Nation Transcript August 14, 2016: Collins, Ridge, Cohen, Hayden," *Face the Nation*, CBS News, August 14, 2016, https://www.cbsnews.com/news/face-the-nation-transcript-august-14-2016-collins-ridge-cohen-hayden/.
16. Peter Wehner, "Why the First Year Matters, Vol. 1: Dear Mr. President," First Year 2017, http://firstyear2017.org/essay/letter-to-the-new-president.html.

17. Richard Reeves, *President Reagan: The Triumph of Imagination* (New York: Simon & Schuster, 2005), Kindle, location 171.

18. Michael Beschloss, *Presidents of War* (New York: Crown, 2018), 103.

19. "Hail to the Chief," Library of Congress, Song Collection, Washington, DC, 2002. https://www.loc.gov/item/ihas.200000009/.

20. Clinton Rossiter, *The American Presidency* (New York: Time Inc. Book Division, 1963).

21. Interview with author.

22. Phillip G. Henderson, *Managing the Presidency* (Boulder, CO: Westview Press, 1988), 13.

23. Stef W. Kight, "Half of the post-millennial generation is non-white," Axios, November 16, 2018, https://www.axios.com/gen-z-post-millennials-diversity-minorities -demographics-us-9da4ad70-cedd-4d33-b86f-4b76e9277b8f.html.

24. Jefferson in a letter to John Vanmetre on September 4, 1800, in Stephanie P. Newbold, *All But Forgotten: Thomas Jefferson and the Development of Public Administration* (Albany: State University of New York Press, 2010).

25. Interview with author.

26. Louis Brownlow, *The President and the Presidency* (Chicago: Public Administration Service, 1953).

27. James David Barber, *The Presidential Character: Predicting Performance in the White House* (Englewood Cliffs, NJ: Prentice-Hall, 1992), Preface.

28. Stephen J. Adler, Jeff Mason, and Steve Holland, "Exclusive: Trump Says He Thought Being President Would Be Easier than His Old Life," *Reuters*, April 27, 2017, https://www.reuters.com/article/us-usa-trump-100days/exclusive-trump-says-he -thought-being-president-would-be-easier-than-his-old-life-idUSKBN17U0CA.

29. Robert Dallek, *Camelot's Court: Inside the Kennedy White House* (Sydney: HarperCollins, 2013), 3.

30. Benjamin Wallace-Wells, "Pete Buttigieg's Quiet Rebellion," *New Yorker*, February 9, 2019, https://www.newyorker.com/news/the-political-scene/pete-buttigiegs -quiet-rebellion.

31. United States Census Bureau, *Income, Poverty, and Health Insurance: 2018*, September 2019, https://www.census.gov/content/dam/Census/newsroom/press-kits/2019 /iphi/presentation-iphi-overview.pdf.

32. Interview with author.

33. Interview with author.

34. Interview with author.

35. Barack Obama, interview by John Dickerson, "Face the Nation Transcripts July 24, 2016: President Obama," *Face the Nation*, CBS News, July 24, 2016, https://www .cbsnews.com/news/face-the-nation-transcripts-july-24-2016-president-obama/.

36. Christina Caron, "Obama's Letter to President Trump on Inauguration Day," *New York Times*, September 3, 2017, https://www.nytimes.com/2017/09/03/us/politics /obama-trump-letter.html.

CHAPTER 1: EXECUTIVE IN CHIEF

1. Gregory LaCava, *Gabriel Over the White House*, partial transcript via IMDb, https://www.imdb.com/title/tt0024044/characters/nm0404158.

2. "It is not because I do less than I might do, but that I have more than I can do." "From Thomas Jefferson to William Henry Harrison, 27 February 1803," Founders Online, National Archives, https://founders.archives.gov/documents/Jefferson/01-39-02-0500.

3. Peri E. Arnold, "The Brownlow Committee, Regulation, and the Presidency: Seventy Years Later," *Public Administration Review* 67, no. 6 (2007): 1030–40, www.jstor.org/stable/4624663.

4. "Women's Leaders Map Fight Against Passage," *San Francisco Examiner*, April 8, 1938.

5. "Paul Reveres' Demand Death of Dictator Bill," *San Francisco Examiner*, April 8, 1938, 3.

6. In the newspaper photographs, the hat looked exactly like the headgear used to celebrate the cartoon mouse created ten years earlier by Walt Disney.

7. Robert Dallek, *Franklin D. Roosevelt: A Political Life* (New York: Penguin, 2018), 2.

8. Governor Landon of Kansas declared, "Even the iron hand of a national dictator is in preference to a paralytic stroke." . . . Al Smith thought the Constitution ought to be wrapped up and laid "on the shelf" until the crisis was over. *Vanity Fair*, whose associate editors included Clare Boothe Brokaw (later Luce), demanded, "Appoint a dictator!" Walter Lippmann wanted to give the President full power at the expense of Congress; "The danger," he said, "is not that we shall lose our liberties, but that we shall not be able to act with the necessary speed and comprehensiveness," and Republican Senator David A. Reed said outright, "If this country ever needed a Mussolini, it needs one now." William Manchester, *The Glory and the Dream: A Narrative History of America 1932–1972*, vols. 1 and 2 (Boston: Little, Brown, 1974), 58.

9. Robert L. McConnell, "The Genesis and Ideology of 'Gabriel Over the White House,'" *Cinema Journal* 15, no. 2 (Spring 1976): 7–26, doi:10.2307/1224915.

10. Jonathan Alter, *The Defining Moment: FDR's Hundred Days and the Triumph of Hope* (New York: Simon & Schuster, 2006), 185.

11. "Thomas Jefferson to John B. Colvin, 20 September 1810," Founders Online, National Archives, https://founders.archives.gov/documents/Jefferson/03-03-02-0060.

12. Linda Greenhouse, "The Nation; 'Suicide Pact,'" *New York Times*, September 22, 2002, https://www.nytimes.com/2002/09/22/weekinreview/the-nation-suicide-pact.html.

13. "Seizure! Truman Takes the Steel Mills," Constitutional Rights Foundation, 2020, https://www.crf-usa.org/bill-of-rights-in-action/bria-4-4-b-seizure-truman-takes-the-steel-mills.html.

14. Loretta Britten and Sarah Brash, eds., *Hard Times: The 30s (Our American Century)*, (Richmond, VA: Time-Life Books, 1998).

15. Dallek, R., *Franklin D. Roosevelt*, 5.

16. Richard Hofstadter, *The American Political Tradition and the Men Who Made It* (New York: Vintage Books, 1989), 372.

17. Barber, *Presidential Character*, 49.

18. Kimberly Amadeo, "Unemployment Rate by Year Since 1929 Compared to Inflation and GDP," The Balance, February 7, 2020, https://www.thebalance.com/unemployment-rate-by-year-3305506.

19. Franklin D. Roosevelt, "Address at Oglethorpe University," FDR Library, May 22, 1932, https://fdrlibrary.files.wordpress.com/2012/10/oglethorpe.pdf.

20. Manchester, *Glory and the Dream*, 5.

21. Benjamin Ginsberg, *Presidential Government* (New Haven: Yale University Press, 2016), 96. This sounds like Coolidge, but the quote is actually one written by his secretary, who took down his thoughts.

22. Forrest McDonald, *The American Presidency: An Intellectual History* (Lawrence, KS: University Press of Kansas, 1994), 365. Not everything came from Roosevelt's brain and brain trust. The Tennessee Valley Authority Act, the Federal Securities

Act, and the new Glass-Steagall Act were based on ideas that had long been kicked around in Congress.

23. Ginsberg, *Presidential Government*, 89.

24. Matthew J. Dickinson, *Bitter Harvest: FDR, Presidential Power and the Growth of the Presidential Branch* (Cambridge: Cambridge University Press, 1996), 47.

25. Ibid., 49.

26. United States Congress, "Looking Toward the Constitutional Bicentennial: A Proposed Amendment to Permit Members of Congress to Serve in Key Executive Branch Offices," (Washington: U.S. Government Printing Office, 1980), 80.

27. Eli E. Nobleman, "The Delegation of Presidential Functions: Constitutional and Legal Aspects," *Annals of the American Academy of Political and Social Science* 307 (1956): 134–43, www.jstor.org/stable/1031341.

28. The Committee on Department Methods was popularly known as the Keep Commission after its leader, Assistant Secretary of the Treasury Charles Keep.

29. Harold T. Pinkett, *The Keep Commission, 1905–1909: A Rooseveltian Effort for Administrative Reform* (Menasha, WI: George Banta, 1965), 310.

30. Kendrick A. Clements, "Woodrow Wilson and Administrative Reform," *Presidential Studies Quarterly* 28, no. 2 (1998): 325, www.jstor.org/stable/27551862.

31. Ibid., 327. The President's Commission on Economy and Efficiency, which had been created by President Taft in early 1911 and parsimoniously funded by Congress, recommended an expansion of the civil service, a standardization of accounting procedures throughout the government, the centralization of the executive branch under the authority of the president (as opposed to having cabinet officers report to committees of Congress), the functional grouping of administrative agencies, and the adoption of a single executive budget instead of having individual funding proposals presented to Congress by each government agency. All of these proposals were identical or similar to Wilson's own ideas about administrative reform, yet neither as president-elect nor after taking office, was he willing to ask Congress to renew the commission's funding, which ran out in June 1913.

32. James W. Fesler, "The Brownlow Committee Fifty Years Later," *Public Administration Review* 47, no. 4 (1987): 291, https://doi.org/10.2307/975308.

33. Dickinson, *Bitter Harvest*, 89.

34. Theodore J. Lowi, *The Personal President: Power Invested, Promise Unfulfilled* (Ithaca, NY: Cornell University Press, 1985), 2.

35. Louis Brownlow and United States President's Committee on Administrative Management, *Administrative Management in the Government of the United States* (Washington: U.S. Government Printing Office, 1937), 43.

36. H. R. Haldeman read this portion to his White House staff at the start of the Nixon years.

37. "Paul Revere Riders' Fight."

38. Manchester, *Glory and the Dream*, 127.

39. "Militant Groups Storm Capital to 'Stop Roosevelt,'" *Pittsburgh Sun-Telegraph*, April 4, 1938.

40. John Dearborn, "The Foundations of the Modern Presidency: Presidential Representation, the Unitary Executive Theory, and the Reorganization Act of 1939," *Presidential Studies Quarterly* 49 (March 2018): 35, https://doi.org/10.1111/psq.12463.

41. *Public Papers of the Presidents of the United States: Franklin D. Roosevelt*, vol. 9, 1940 (Washington, DC: U.S. Best Books, 1941), 302.

42. Franklin D. Roosevelt, "Fireside Chat 13: On Purging the Democratic Party," UVA Miller Center, June 24, 1938, https://millercenter.org/the-presidency/presidential -speeches/june-24-1938-fireside-chat-13-purging-democratic-party.

43. Dunn, *Roosevelt's Purge*, location 109.

44. Ibid., location 8.

45. George Rothwell Brown, "Full Credit Accorded Aroused Nation," *San Francisco Examiner*, April 9, 1938, 2.

46. Dunn, *Roosevelt's Purge*, location 17.

47. Ibid.

48. Henry B. Hogue, "Presidential Reorganization Authority: History, Recent Initiatives, and Options for Congress," Congressional Research Service (December 11, 2012), 12, https://fas.org/sgp/crs/misc/R42852.pdf.

49. Ben Sasse, "We Can And We Should Do Better Than This," *U.S. Senator for Nebraska Ben Sasse*, September 4, 2018, https://www.sasse.senate.gov/public/index .cfm/press-releases?ID=9731B7D3-1CB3-4B04-AB6C-F2D91CFC5720.

50. Ross Douthat, "The Two-Emperor Problem," *New York Times*, November 24, 2018, https://www.nytimes.com/2018/11/24/opinion/sunday/john-roberts-donald-trump .html.

51. Adam Andrzejewski, "Trump's Leaner White House 2019 Payroll Has Already Saved Taxpayers $20 Million," *Forbes*, June 28, 2019, https://www.forbes.com/sites /adamandrzejewski/2019/06/28/trumps-leaner-white-house-2019-payroll-has-already -saved-taxpayers-20-million/#1f7233b9386d.

52. Thomas E. Cronin, *The State of the Presidency* (Boston: Little, Brown, 1980), 30.

53. George W. Martin, *Madam Secretary Frances Perkins* (Lexington, MA: Plunkett Lake Press, 2019). Labor Secretary Frances Perkins usually wore a tricorn hat and pearls with a plain black dress. She noticed that when she dressed fashionably, her male colleagues were unlikely to respect her opinions. When she dressed in black with pearls, she had more success. "I tried to remind them of their mothers, and it worked," she said.

CHAPTER 2: COMMANDER IN CHIEF

1. Barack Obama, "Taking the Cyberattack Threat Seriously," *Wall Street Journal*, July 19, 2012, https://www.wsj.com/articles/SB10000872396390444330904577535492 693044650.

2. Kurt M. Campbell and James B. Steinberg, *Difficult Transitions: Foreign Policy Troubles at the Outset of Presidential Power* (Washington, DC: Brookings Institution Press, 2008).

3. Dwight D. Eisenhower Letter to Dillon Anderson, in Post-Presidential Papers, January 22, 1968, principal file, box 36, Library of Congress.

4. Chris Whipple, *The Gatekeepers: How the White House Chiefs of Staff Define Every Presidency* (New York: Crown, 2017), Kindle, location 18.

5. "In 1969 and during the first half of 1970, I was a wet-behind-the-ears, twenty-nine-year-old staff aide in the West Wing of the Nixon White House. I was working for the wisest man in that White House, Bryce Harlow, who was a friend of President Johnson, as well as the favorite staff member of President Eisenhower, and President Nixon's first appointee." "Alexander to Obama: No 'enemies list,'" Politico, October 21, 2009, https://www.politico.com/story/2009/10/alexander-to-obama-no -enemies-list-028549.

6. Interview with author.

7. Merlin Mann (@hotdogsladies), "You eventually . . ." Twitter, April 10, 2009, 12:20 P.M., https://twitter.com/hotdogsladies/status/1492464753.

8. Alexander Hamilton, "The Federalist Papers: No. 74," The Avalon Project, March 25, 1788, https://avalon.law.yale.edu/18th_century/fed74.asp.

9. Campbell and Steinberg, *Difficult Transitions*, 23–40.

10. Dallek, R., *Camelot's Court*, ii.

11. Dwight D. Eisenhower, "Military-Industrial Complex Speech, Dwight D. Eisenhower, 1961," The Avalon Project, https://avalon.law.yale.edu/20th_century /eisenhower001.asp.

12. Bill Clinton, *My Life* (New York: Alfred A. Knopf, 2004), Kindle, locations 9639–41.

13. The George Washington University National Security Archive, "The 3 A.M. Phone Call," National Security Archive Electronic Briefing Book no. 371, March 1, 2012, https://nsarchive2.gwu.edu/nukevault/ebb371/.

14. Interview with author.

15. Mark Landler, "The Afghan War and the Evolution of Obama," *New York Times*, January 1, 2017, https://www.nytimes.com/2017/01/01/world/asia/obama-afghanistan -war.html.

16. Mark Mardell, "Barack Obama defends 'just war' using drones," BBC.com, May 24, 2013, https://www.bbc.com/news/world-us-canada-22638533.

17. Michael Crowley, "Trump Visits Afghanistan and Says He Reopened Talks With Taliban," *New York Times*, November 28, 2019, https://www.nytimes.com/2019/11 /28/us/politics/trump-afghanistan.html.

18. Reeves, *President Reagan*, location 300.

19. Nixon wrote an article in *Foreign Affairs*, "Asia After Viet Nam," laying out his vision. It included a line he repeated in his inaugural address: "Taking the long view, we simply cannot afford to leave China forever outside the family of nations, there to nurture its fantasies, cherish its hates and threaten its neighbors. There is no place on this small planet for a billion of its potentially most able people to live in angry isolation." Richard M. Nixon, "Asia After Viet Nam," *Foreign Affairs*, October 1967, https://www.foreignaffairs.com/articles/asia/1967-10-01/asia-after-viet-nam.

20. Richard L. Madden, "Senator Buckley 'Warns' Nixon on Support by Conservatives," *New York Times*, August 1, 1971, https://www.nytimes.com/1971/08/01/archives /senator-buckley-warns-nixon-on-support-by-conservatives.html. The conservative thinker, writer, and publisher William F. Buckley asked conservatives to "suspend" support of Nixon because he was making the China trip.

21. Margaret MacMillan, *Nixon and Mao: The Week That Changed the World* (New York: Random House, 2008), 6.

22. James Reston, "Mr. Nixon's Finest Hour," *New York Times*, March 1, 1972, https:// www.nytimes.com/1972/03/01/archives/mr-nixons-finest-hour.html.

23. Interview with author.

24. Tevi Troy, "Don't Worry, America: The 3 A.M. Phone Call Is a Myth," Politico Magazine, September 10, 2016, https://www.politico.com/magazine/story/2016/09 /3am-phone-call-myth-trump-214208. Hillary Clinton touched on these ideas in her "3 A.M. phone call" ad, which raised the specter of a worldwide emergency. "Something is happening in the world," intoned the narrator. "Your vote will decide who answers that call." It was a great and important point, though as a political matter it did not undercut her opponent Barack Obama in the way Clinton had hoped. The senator from New York had no more experience handling 3 A.M. phone calls than did the senator from Illinois. If it was a question of judgment in a late-night emer-

gency, Obama was happy to debate that point. He was arguing that he had superior judgment because he had opposed the Iraq war and Senator Clinton had not.

25. Craig Whitlock, "The Afghanistan Papers: At War With The Truth," *Washington Post*, December 9, 2019, https://www.washingtonpost.com/graphics/2019/investigations/afghanistan-papers/afghanistan-war-confidential-documents/.

26. "The Second Presidential Debate," *New York Times*, October 7, 2008, https://www.nytimes.com/elections/2008/president/debates/transcripts/second-presidential-debate.html.

CHAPTER 3: WELCOME TO THE NFL

1. George W. Bush, "Bullhorn Address to Ground Zero Rescue Workers," American Rhetoric of 9-11, September 14, 2001, https://www.americanrhetoric.com/speeches/gwbush911groundzerobullhorn.htm.

2. Barber, *Presidential Character*, 271.

3. James Chace, *1912: Wilson, Roosevelt, Taft and Debs—The Election That Changed the Country* (New York: Simon & Schuster, 2004), 243.

4. Interview with author.

5. Interview with author.

6. "Foresight—and Hindsight," *The Final 9/11 Commission Report*, National Commission on Terrorist Attacks upon the United States, chapter 11, 341, https://govinfo.library.unt.edu/911/report/911Report_Ch11.pdf.

7. President Bush explained that he was a "war president," essentially arguing he didn't have to listen to Congress if it got in the way of doing that job. In October 2002, when he signed the Defense Appropriations Act, which included language blocking the use of torture on terrorist suspects—which President Bush had opposed—in his signing statement he said he would interpret that portion of the legislation "in a manner consistent with the constitutional authority of the president . . . and consistent with the constitutional limitations on the judicial power." Members of Congress largely acquiesced.

8. James Madison, "'Helvidius' Number 4, 14 September 1793," Founders Online, National Archives, https://founders.archives.gov/documents/Madison/01-15-02-0070.

9. Interview with author.

10. Interview with author.

11. "Democracy in Retreat."

12. Interview with author.

13. Interview with author.

14. Sean D. Carberry, "Clapper: Presidential transition 'will be OK,'" Federal Computer Week, September 7, 2016, https://fcw.com/articles/2016/09/07/clapper-carberry.aspx?m=1.

15. "Gen. David Petraeus: 'You can't completely get out of endless wars,'" interview by John Dickerson, *CBS This Morning*, CBS News, October 29, 2019, https://www.cbsnews.com/news/david-petraeus-isis-abu-bakr-al-baghdadi-endless-wars-cbs-this-morning-podcast-john-dickerson/.

16. Interview with author.

17. Interview with author.

18. Kevin Liptak, "Trump recounts minute-by-minute details of Soleimani strike to donors at Mar-a-Lago." CNN.com, January 18, 2020, https://www.cnn.com/2020/01/18/politics/trump-soleimani-details-mar-a-lago/index.html.

19. Interview with author.
20. Interview with author.
21. Interview with author.
22. Interview with author.
23. Interview with author.
24. Interview with author.
25. Interview with author.
26. Interview with author. When I talked about this with one former spy, their response was "And my basketball coach told me I should be taller as a kid." The point was that of course a better imagination was needed, but that's always the case. The flaw lies not in lacking imagination but in not having the time and attention to apply it to every threat. Your musical comedy might not be very good because you lack imagination, or it might not be very good because while you were writing it you were also writing a volume of poetry, a three-part nonfiction narrative of the American West, and an opera.
27. Interview with author.
28. Interview with author.
29. Interview with author.
30. In hunting, you set or fix traps that you later check to see if you have caught anything.
31. Interview with author.
32. John Solomon and Buck Sexton, "Trump slams Bush for 'worst single mistake' in U.S. history." The Hill, September 19, 2018, https://thehill.com/hilltv/rising/407398 -trump-slams-bush-for-worst-single-mistake-in-us-history.
33. Lou Dobbs (@LouDobbs), "No wonder . . ." Twitter, July 4, 2019, 5:39 A.M., https:// twitter.com/LouDobbs/status/1146760530033614850.
34. Ruth Igielnik and Kim Parker, "Majorities of U.S. veterans, public say the wars in Iraq and Afghanistan were not worth fighting," Pew Research Center, July 10, 2019, https://www.pewresearch.org/fact-tank/2019/07/10/majorities-of-u-s-veterans-public -say-the-wars-in-iraq-and-afghanistan-were-not-worth-fighting/.
35. Glenn Kessler, "The pre-war intelligence on Iraq: Wrong or hyped by the Bush White House?" Washington Post, December 13, 2006, https://www.washingtonpost .com/news/fact-checker/wp/2016/12/13/the-pre-war-intelligence-on-iraq-wrong-or -hyped-by-the-bush-white-house/.
36. President Trump was asked if he believed his own intelligence agencies or the Russian president when it came to the allegations of meddling in the elections. President Trump said "My people came to me—Dan Coats came to me and some others—they said they think it's Russia. I have President Putin; he just said it's not Russia. I will say this: I don't see any reason why it would be." "Remarks by President Trump and President Putin of the Russian Federation in Joint Press Conference." Office of the Press Secretary, July 16, 2018, https://www.whitehouse.gov /briefings-statements/remarks-president-trump-president-putin-russian-federation -joint-press-conference/.

    Later, he told reporters he meant to have said, "I don't see any reason why it wouldn't be Russia." Philip Bump, "Trump's attempt to clean up the Putin event was an insult to America's intelligence." Washington Post, July 17, 2018, https:// www.washingtonpost.com/news/politics/wp/2018/07/17/trumps-attempt-to-clean -up-the-putin-event-was-an-insult-to-americas-intelligence/.
37. Donald J. Trump (@realDonaldTrump), "The intelligence people . . ." Twitter,

January 30, 2019, 5:50 A.M., https://twitter.com/realDonaldTrump/status/109060 8298343190528.

38. Donald J. Trump (@realDonaldTrump), ". . . a source of potential danger . . ." Twitter, January 30, 2019, 5:56 A.M., https://twitter.com/realDonaldTrump/status /1090609577006112769.

39. Directly contradicting President Donald Trump, U.S. intelligence agencies told Congress in January 2019 that North Korea is unlikely to dismantle its nuclear arsenal, that the Islamic State group remains a threat, and that the Iran nuclear deal is working. Robert Burns, "US intel heads list North Korea, not border, as threat to US," *AP News*, January 29, 2019, https://apnews.com/5bb33704147f4951a040dcb53 d709586.

40. "Trump disputes CIA findings that MBS ordered Khashoggi murder," Aljazeera .com, November 23, 2018, https://www.aljazeera.com/news/2018/11/trump-contradicts -cia-findings-mbs-ordered-khashoggi-murder-181123070359687.html.

41. Interview with author.

42. Interview with author.

CHAPTER 4: FIRST RESPONDER

1. "President Taft Stunned," *New York Times*, April 16, 1912, Encyclopedia Titanica, https://www.encyclopedia-titanica.org/president-taft-stunned.html.

2. Gareth Davies, "The Historical Presidency: Lyndon Johnson and Disaster Politics," *Presidential Studies Quarterly* 47, Issue 3 (September 2017): 540.

3. "Foresight—and Hindsight," 349.

4. Interview with author.

5. "Overall, between 180 and 200 total fatalities were estimated to be a result of Hurricane Diane. Although it was difficult to estimate total damages stemming from Hurricane Diane, it was determined that the floods and other impacts from the hurricane caused between $832 million and $1 billion (1955 USD in damage, making it the costliest hurricane in U.S. history at the time (until it was surpassed by Hurricane Betsy in 1965)." "Hurricane Diane—August 15–19, 1955," National Weather Service, https://www.weather.gov/mhx/HurricaneDiane1955.

6. Gareth Davies, "Pre-Modern Disaster Politics: Combating Catastrophe in the 1950s," *Journal of Federalism* 47, Issue 2 (February 2017): 271, https://doi.org/10.1093 /publius/pjx016.

7. "Eisenhower Flies to Colorado For Work-Play Holiday: Mamie Waves Goodbye," *Tampa Morning Tribune*, August 15, 1955.

8. "Eisenhower Taking Grandson Trout Fishing in Colorado," *The Evening Sun*, Baltimore, August 17, 1955.
     "Eisenhower a Happy Man While Fishing and Cooking," *Reading PA Eagle*, 1955.

9. Clark, "'Mystery Woman' Appears on Eisenhower's Canvas," *Miami Daily News*, September 21, 1955.

10. Bob Considine, "Nixon Voices His Credo: 'Stick to Your Job.'" *San Francisco Examiner*, September 18, 1955, 20.

11. Davies, "The Historical Presidency," 530.

12. Ibid.

13. Davies, "Pre-Modern Disaster Politics," 270.

14. Ibid., 267.

15. William L. Painter, "The Disaster Relief Fund: Overview and Issues," Congressional Research Service, November 22, 2019, 5, https://fas.org/sgp/crs/homesec/R45484.pdf.

16. Tom Degan, "LBJ: The Man We Hate to Love," The Rant, May 14, 2012, LBJ Presidential Library, http://www.lbjlibrary.org/press/lbj-in-the-news/lbj-the-man-we-hate-to-love.

17. Jack Williams, "Hurricane Betsy hit Florida, smashed New Orleans in 1965," USA Today, October 21, 2003, http://usatoday30.usatoday.com/weather/resources/askjack/2003-10-09-hurricane-betsy_x.htm.

18. "LBJ and Senator Russell Long on Hurricane Betsy," UVA Miller Center, September 9, 1965, https://millercenter.org/the-presidency/educational-resources/lbj-and-senator-russell-long-on-hurricane-betsy.

19. "Conversation with Buford Ellington and Marvin Watson, September 10, 1965," UVA Miller Center, https://millercenter.org/the-presidency/secret-white-house-tapes/conversation-buford-ellington-and-marvin-watson-september.

20. Michael Pakenham, "Johnson Views Louisiana Storm Damage with Flashlight in Hand," Chicago Tribune, September 11, 1965.

21. Richard Eder, "Johnson Directs Relief," New York Times, September 13, 1965.

22. "The President's Daily Diary for September 10, 1965," LBJ Presidential Library, http://lbjlibrary.net/assets/documents/archives/hurricane_disaster/19650910.pdf.

23. "Conversation with Robert Phillips, Marvin Watson and Russell Long, September 14, 1965," UVA Miller Center, https://millercenter.org/the-presidency/secret-white-house-tapes/conversation-robert-phillips-marvin-watson-and-russell-long.

24. Interview with author.

25. When a president gets involved, it focuses the mind of the bureaucracy, but Fugate hastens to add that the job is simply to remind everyone to work through the existing system. It's not about reinventing the machine on the fly, which leads to messy improvisation. "The crucial part," says Fugate, "is that the president makes sure all federal agencies are working through FEMA and not freelancing. Concentration without fragmentation." Interview with author.

26. Porter, Frank C. "LBJ Sees Betsy Toll In Hundreds." Washington Post, September 13, 1965.

27. Pakenham, "Johnson Views Louisiana."

28. Eder, "Johnson Directs Relief."

29. Davies, "The Historical Presidency," 530.

30. Justin Bogie, "Congress Must Stop the Abuse of Disaster and Emergency Spending," The Heritage Foundation, February 4, 2019, https://www.heritage.org/sites/default/files/2019-02/BG3380.pdf.

31. "2017 Hurricanes and Wildfires: Initial Observations on the Federal Response and Key Recovery Challenges," United States Government Accountability Office: Report to Congressional Addresses, 14 September 2018, https://www.gao.gov/assets/700/694231.pdf.

32. "Disaster Declarations by Year: 2018," Department of Homeland Security: FEMA, https://www.fema.gov/disasters/year.

33. Manchester, Glory and the Dream, 221.

34. Ibid.

35. "Flying into the Eye of Edna," See It Now, CBS, September 14, 1954, Moving Image Research Center, Library of Congress, Reel FCB8953.

36. Davies, "Pre-Modern Disaster Politics," 270.

37. Mike Walker, *Rather Dumb: A Top Tabloid Reporter Tells CBS News How to Do News* (Nashville, TN: Nelson Current, 2005), 22.

38. Davies, "The Historical Presidency," 540.

39. Bill Sheffer, "From the Archive: LBJ Visits Elkhart County on Tour of Disaster Areas," *Goshen News,* April 10, 2015, https://www.goshennews.com/from-the-archive -lbj-visits-elkhart-county-on-tour-of/article_238e1568-dfc4-11e4-ba6a-63fcbbd4e8e9 .html.

40. Andrew Morris, *Race, Rights, and Disaster Relief: Hurricane Camille, Mississippi, and the Transformation of American Disaster Policy* (Philadelphia: University of Pennsylvania Press, forthcoming).

41. Rick Perlstein, *Nixonland: The Rise of a President and the Fracturing of America* (New York: Scribner, 2008), 422.

42. "Eleanor Roosevelt," Library of Congress, https://www.loc.gov/item/today-in-history /october-11/.

43. *First Ladies Revealed,* episode 4,"Eleanor Roosevelt's Surprising Connection to a Dire Town," Smithsonian Channel, July 21, 2017, https://www.smithsonianchannel .com/videos/eleanor-roosevelts-surprising-connection-to-a-dire-town/57258.

44. Ibid.

45. William Edward Leuchtenburg, *The FDR Years: On Roosevelt and His Legacy* (New York: Columbia University Press, 1995).

46. Fred I. Greenstein, ed., *Leadership in the Modern Presidency* (Cambridge: Harvard University Press, 1988).

47. Jon Meacham, *The Soul of America* (New York: Random House, 2018), 221.

48. Garry Wills, *Certain Trumpets* (New York: Simon & Schuster, 2013), 14.

CHAPTER 5: CONSOLER IN CHIEF

1. Ronald C. White Jr., *Lincoln's Greatest Speech: The Second Inaugural* (New York: Simon & Schuster, 2002), 182.

2. Garry Wills, "Lincoln's Greatest Speech," *The Atlantic,* September 1999, https:// www.theatlantic.com/magazine/archive/1999/09/lincolns-greatest-speech/306551/.

3. Ronald Reagan, "Address to the Nation on the Explosion of the Space Shuttle Challenger," Ronald Reagan Presidential Foundation and Institute, January 28, 1986, https://www.reaganfoundation.org/media/128831/challenger.pdf.

4. Michael Waldman, *POTUS Speaks: Finding the Words That Defined the Clinton Presidency* (New York: Simon & Schuster, 2000), 82.

5. Julia Manchester, "83 Percent Say the President Should Be Consoler in Chief After National Tragedies," The Hill, December 4, 2018.

6. Reagan, "Address to the Nation."

7. Peggy Noonan, *What I Saw at the Revolution: A Political Life in the Reagan Era* (New York: Random House, 2002), 67.

8. R. W. Apple, Jr., "The Shuttle Explosion; President as Healer," *New York Times,* January 29, 1986, https://www.nytimes.com/1986/01/29/us/the-shuttle-explosion -president-as-healer.html.

9. "Vital Statistics on Congress: Data on the U.S. Congress," Brookings Institution, April 7, 2014, https://www.brookings.edu/wp-content/uploads/2016/06/Vital-Statistics -Chapter-2-Congressional-Elections.pdf.

10. Karen De Witt, "Clinton's Prime-Time Presentation Is Shunned by 2 Networks," *New York Times,* April 19, 1995, https://www.nytimes.com/1995/04/19/us/clinton-s -prime-time-presentation-is-shunned-by-2-networks.html.

11. Steven A. Holmes, "Clinton Defines the Limits of Compromise with G.O.P.; Gingrich Urges 'Dialogue,'" *New York Times*, April 8, 1995, https://www.nytimes.com/1995/04/08/us/clinton-defines-the-limits-of-compromise-with-gop-gingrich-urges-dialogue.html.

12. Bill Clinton, "Weekly Compilation of Presidential Documents," vol. 31, no. 16, University of Illinois at Urbana-Champaign, 1995, 657.

13. "The Oklahoma City Bombing," Oklahoma Office of Homeland Security, 2020, https://www.ok.gov/homeland/About_OKOHS/index.html.

14. Bill Clinton, "President Clinton: We Share Your Grief . . . But You Have Not Lost Everything," *New York Times*, April 24, 1995, https://www.washingtonpost.com/archive/politics/1995/04/24/president-clinton-we-share-your-grief-but-you-have-not-lost-everything/31f4ec23-7ac7-47c7-a62f-e63699eb3041/.

15. David Lightman, "Clinton Popularity Up After Oklahoma City Bombing," *Hartford Courant*, May 9, 1995, https://www.courant.com/news/connecticut/hc-xpm-1995-05-09-9505090393-story.html.

16. Waldman, *POTUS Speaks*, 82.

17. Tevi Troy, "Presidents and Mass Shootings," *National Affairs*, Spring 2018, https://www.nationalaffairs.com/publications/detail/presidents-and-mass-shootings.

18. David W. Dunlap, "1966 | 'The Time Has Come for Action,'" *New York Times*, October 5, 2017, https://www.nytimes.com/2017/10/05/insider/1966-the-time-has-come-for-action.html.

19. Grant Duwe, *Mass Murder in the United States: A History* (Jefferson, NC: McFarland & Company, 2014), 27.

20. Bonnie Berkowitz, Chris Alcantara, and Denise Lu, "The Terrible Numbers That Grow with Each Mass Shooting," *Washington Post*, February 27, 2019, https://www.washingtonpost.com/graphics/2018/national/mass-shootings-in-america/.

21. Tevi Troy, "Presidents and Mass Shootings."

22. Based on data collected by Elizabeth Hinson, the researcher for this book.

23. Matt Ford and Adam Chandler, "'Hate Crime': A Mass Killing at a Historic Church," *The Atlantic*, June 19, 2015, https://www.theatlantic.com/national/archive/2015/06/shooting-emanuel-ame-charleston/396209/.

24. "Slavery in The Lowcountry," International African American Museum, 2017, https://iaamuseum.org/history/slavery-in-charleston-and-the-lowcountry/.

25. Barack Obama, "Remarks by the President in Eulogy for the Honorable Reverend Clementa Pinckney," Office of the Press Secretary, June 26, 2015, https://obamawhitehouse.archives.gov/the-press-office/2015/06/26/remarks-president-eulogy-honorable-reverend-clementa-pinckney.

26. John F. Kennedy, "Statement on Assassination of Martin Luther King, Jr., Indianapolis, Indiana, April 4, 1968," John F. Kennedy Presidential Library and Museum, https://www.jfklibrary.org/learn/about-jfk/the-kennedy-family/robert-f-kennedy/robert-f-kennedy-speeches/statement-on-assassination-of-martin-luther-king-jr-indianapolis-indiana-april-4-1968.

27. Frances Robles, Richard Fausset, and Michael Barbaro, "Nikki Haley, South Carolina Governor, Calls for Removal of Confederate Battle Flag," *New York Times*, June 22, 2015, https://www.nytimes.com/2015/06/23/us/south-carolina-confederate-flag-dylann-roof.html.

28. Jacey Fortin, "The Statue at the Center of Charlottesville's Storm," *New York Times*, August 13, 2017, https://www.nytimes.com/2017/08/13/us/charlottesville-rally-protest-statue.html.

29. Ibid.

30. Ellie Silverman, "Neo-Nazis marched past their synagogue chanting 'Sieg Heil,'" *Washington Post*, August 26, 2017, https://www.washingtonpost.com/local/social -issues/neo-nazis-marched-past-their-synagogue-chanting-sieg-heil-two-weeks-later -the-charlottesville-jewish-community-is-still-healing/2017/08/26/d75ef1do-8a70 -11e7-a50f-eod4e6eco70a_story.html.

31. Ibid.

32. Rodney Dunning, "Charlottesville Unite the Right Rally," Flickr, August 12, 2017, https://www.flickr.com/photos/rodneydunning/36401911981/in/photostream/.

33. Emma Bowman, and Wynne Davis, "Charlottesville Victim Heather Heyer 'Stood Up' Against What She Felt Was Wrong," NPR, August 13, 2017, https://www.npr .org/sections/thetwo-way/2017/08/13/543175919/violence-in-charlottesville-claims-3 -victims.

34. Libby Nelson, "'Why we voted for Donald Trump': David Duke explains the white supremacist Charlottesville protests," Vox.com, August 12, 2017, https://www .vox.com/2017/8/12/16138358/charlottesville-protests-david-duke-kkk.

35. Carly Sitrin, "Read: President Trump's remarks condemning violence 'on many sides' in Charlottesville," Vox.com, August 12, 2017, https://www.vox.com/2017/8/12 /16138906/president-trump-remarks-condemning-violence-on-many-sides -charlottesville-rally.

36. Donovan Slack, "Paul Ryan rips Trump comments as 'textbook definition of rac- ist,'" *USA Today*, June 7, 2016, https://www.usatoday.com/story/news/politics /onpolitics/2016/06/07/paul-ryan-rips-trump-comments-textbook-definition-racist /85548042/.

37. Eugene Scott, "Trump denounces David Duke, KKK," CNN.com, March 3, 2016, https://www.cnn.com/2016/03/03/politics/donald-trump-disavows-david-duke-kkk /index.html. In March 2016, CNN's Jake Tapper asked candidate Trump about David Duke and the KKK. Rather than denounce their support, Trump said he would have to see what groups Tapper was talking about. Tapper pointed out that the KKK was a well-known racist organization.

    Rebecca Shabad, "Speaker Ryan: GOP presidential nominee must reject big- otry," CBS News, March 1, 2016, https://www.cbsnews.com/news/speaker-ryan-gop -presidential-nominee-must-reject-bigotry/. House Speaker Paul Ryan told report- ers, "If a person wants to be the nominee of the Republican Party, there can be no evasion and no games. They must reject any group or cause that is built on bigotry. This party does not prey on people's prejudices."

    Susan Page, "2016 lessons so far: Trump's takeover and an enthusiasm gap," *USA Today*, March 1, 2016, https://www.usatoday.com/story/news/politics/elections /2016/03/01/analysis-super-tuesday-trump-takeover-feelthebern-clinton-cruz-rubio -sanders/81143962/. Senate Majority Leader Mitch McConnell said, "There has been a lot of talk in the last twenty-four hours about one of our presidential candi- dates and his seeming ambivalence about David Duke and the KKK, so let me make it perfectly clear, that is not the view of Republicans who have been elected to the United States Senate, and I condemn his views in the most forceful way." Members of the president's manufacturing council stepped down.

38. Cory Gardner (@SenCoryGardner), "Mr. President - we must call evil by its name. These were white supremacists and this was domestic terrorism," Twitter, August 12, 2017, 1:44 P.M., https://twitter.com/SenCoryGardner/status/896472477 844385792.

39. Demetri Sevastopulo and Gillian Tett, "Gary Cohn urges Trump team to do more to condemn neo-Nazis," *Financial Times*, August 25, 2017, https://www.ft.com /content/b85beea2-8924-11e7-bf50-e1c239b45787.

40. Rex Tillerson, "Tillerson says Trump 'speaks for himself' on Charlottesville protests," *Fox News Sunday*, August 27, 2017, https://www.foxnews.com/politics /tillerson-says-trump-speaks-for-himself-on-charlottesville-protests.

41. Donald J. Trump (@realDonaldTrump), "At least 7 dead and 48 wounded in terror attack and Mayor of London says there is "no reason to be alarmed!" Twitter, June 4, 2017, 4:31 A.M., https://twitter.com/realDonaldTrump/status/871328428963 901440.

42. Donald J. Trump (@realDonaldTrump), "There is no reason for these massive, deadly and costly forest fires in California except that forest management is so poor. Billions of dollars are given each year, with so many lives lost, all because of gross mismanagement of the forests. Remedy now, or no more Fed payments!" Twitter, November 10, 2018, 12:08 A.M., https://twitter.com/realDonaldTrump /status/1061168803218948096.

43. From September 23, 2017 to September 9, 2018, President Trump posted twenty-seven tweets and two retweets about NFL players kneeling during the national anthem. This information was tallied by Elizabeth Hinson, the researcher for this book.

44. This list, and countless others, is made possible by Brendan Brown, who created TrumpTwitterArchive.com, which sorts and catalogs Trump's tweets, even deleted tweets. This is a list of Trump's eight-four tweets about birtherism: http://www .trumptwitterarchive.com/highlights/birtherism.

45. Donald J. Trump (@realDonaldTrump), Twitter, August 12, 2017, 1:19 P.M., https://twitter.com/realDonaldTrump/status/896420822780444672. President Trump Tweeted six times following the "Unite the Right" rally on August 11, 2017 and the counterprotest the following day. This was his harshest: "We ALL must be united & condemn all that hate stands for. There is no place for this kind of violence in America. Lets come together as one!"

46. Mike Murphy, "A day later, White House says Trump meant to condemn white supremacists," Market Watch, August 13, 2017, https://www.marketwatch.com /story/a-day-later-white-house-says-trump-meant-to-condemn-white-supremacists -2017-08-13.

47. Donald J. Trump, "Remarks by President Trump on Infrastructure," Office of the Press Secretary, August 15, 2017, https://www.whitehouse.gov/briefings-statements /remarks-president-trump-infrastructure/.

48. Ibid.

49. Ibid.

50. Lindsey Graham, "Statement on Charlottesville," press release, August 16, 2017, https://www.lgraham.senate.gov/public/index.cfm/press-releases?ID=D1258F2A -79E7-4952-9E85-FBAE64919AF4.

CHAPTER 6: ACTING PRESIDENTIAL

1. Bruce Chadwick, *The General and Mrs. Washington: The Untold Story of a Marriage and a Revolution* (Naperville, IL: Sourcebooks, Inc., 2007).

2. George Washington, *The Writings of George Washington: 1785–1790* (New York: G.P. Putnam's Sons, 1891), 375.

3. Ron Chernow, *Washington: A Life* (New York: Penguin Press, 2010), 568.

4. Joseph J. Ellis, *His Excellency: George Washington* (New York: Vintage Books, 2004), Kindle, location 3227.

5. Chernow, *Washington: A Life*, 562.

6. Mike Pence, "The Two Schools of Thought on Clinton," *The Mike Pence Show*, August 21, 1999, http://web.archive.org/web/19990821083429/http:/www.hublergroup .com:80/pence/clinton2.html.

7. James Q. Wilson, *The Moral Sense* (New York: Free Press Paperbacks, 1993).

8. Evan Semones, "Trump assails Rep. Dingell, citing her late husband, amid wave of attacks on Dems," Politico, February 8, 2020, https://www.politico.com/news /2020/02/08/trump-attacks-dingell-pelosi-112528.

9. Derrick Bryson Taylor, "Trump Mocks Greta Thunberg on Twitter, and She Jabs Back." *New York Times*, December 12, 2019, https://www.nytimes.com/2019/12/12 /us/politics/greta-thunberg-trump.html.

10. William J. Bennett, *The Book of Virtues: A Treasury of Great Moral Stories* (New York: Simon & Schuster, 1993).

11. John Adams, "Quotes on Power," John Adams Heritage Historical Society, http:// www.john-adams-heritage.com/quotes/.

12. Alexander Hamilton, "The Federalist Papers, No. 70," The Avalon Project, March 18, 1788, https://avalon.law.yale.edu/18th_century/fed70.asp.

13. In the early days of his presidency, Donald Trump called the acting director of the National Park Service because he thought the official government photographs didn't reflect the accurate crowd size. John Swaine, "Trump inauguration crowd photos were edited after he intervened," *The Guardian*, September 6, 2018, https:// www.theguardian.com/world/2018/sep/06/donald-trump-inauguration-crowd-size -photos-edited.

14. Joanne Freeman, "5 Challenges George Washington Faced as America's First President," George Washington's Mount Vernon, https://www.mountvernon.org/george -washington/the-first-president/5-challenges-of-being-americas-first-president/.

15. Edward J. Larson, *The Return of George Washington* (New York: William Morrow, 2014), 101.

16. Ibid.

17. Ibid., 105.

18. Carol Sue Humphrey, *The Press of the Young Republic, 1783–1833* (Westport, CT: Greenwood Press, 1996), 8.

19. Ibid.

20. Jack Rakove, *Revolutionaries: A New History of the Invention of America* (Boston: Houghton Mifflin Harcourt, 2010), 116. The historian Jack Rakove argues in his Pulitzer Prize–winning *Revolutionaries* that Washington had a special quality for presenting himself as the leader who would inspire others. "When admirers . . . wrote to him . . . they almost seemed to understand the role they expected him to play better than he did himself," Rakove writes. "Almost—except that the knack of fostering that expectation in others was one of the traits that enabled Washington to pursue the destiny he sought to attain in himself." Washington encouraged his countrymen to fashion for him a job, like a coat that only he could wear.

21. "Thomas Jefferson to Walter Jones," Founders Online, January 2, 1814, https:// founders.archives.gov/documents/Jefferson/03-07-02-0052.

22. Edward J. Larson, *George Washington, Nationalist* (Charlottesville: University of Virginia Press, 2016).

23. Rossiter, *The American Presidency*, 167.

24. This was not entirely a compliment. Adams wrote in a letter to his friend Benja-

min Rush in 1811 that the American public's craving for entertainment was endangering principle. Larson, *The Return*, 148. Annual Historical Association for the Year 1902, (Washington: Government Printing Office, 1903), 121. How do we have records if there was secrecy? There was no TMZ correspondent listening at the keyhole. Instead, the scribing was coming from inside the house. Madison took notes. Madison did not miss a single day, "nor," as he explained, "more than a casual fraction of an hour in any day so that I could not have lost a single speech, unless a very short one." But the thirty-six-year-old future president vowed to keep his notes secret until the last delegate died. As it turns out, he was the last delegate. He died in 1836, at age eighty-five. He was the final survivor, and his heirs published his notes (edited and perhaps shined up a bit) to cover his debts.

25. J. D. Williams, "The Summer of 1787: Getting a Constitution," *Brigham Young University Quarterly* 27, issue 3, article 6 (July 1987), https://scholarsarchive.byu .edu/cgi/viewcontent.cgi?article=2491&context=byusq.

26. "The Madison Debates: June 1, 1787," The Avalon Project, https://avalon.law.yale .edu/18th_century/debates_601.asp.

27. As David O. Stewart put it, the framers of the Constitution "wrote General Washington's future job description." David O. Stewart, *The Summer of 1787: The Men Who Invented the Constitution* (New York: Simon & Schuster, 2007), 153.

28. Fragile at age eighty-one, besieged by gout and tormented by kidney stones, the former world diplomat arrived at the proceedings each day carried by local prisoners hoisting a sedan chair, a phone-booth-like box with two poles on either side. Despite his infirmity, it seemed he alone possessed the mental energy to push these matters forward. "Docr. franklin observed that it was a point of great importance," Madison records, "and wished that the gentlemen would deliver their sentiments on it before the question was put." At this point tongues were freed and debate on the presidency kicked up in earnest. How many people should serve in the executive capacity? What powers should a president have? Should Congress or the people, or both, grant power to the president? How should a person or persons be removed, and by whom and on what grounds? The date was June 1, 1787. Conversation about the presidency would continue over hill and down dale until the last moments before the final vote on ratification in mid-September. "Madison Debates."

29. Edmund Clarence Stedman, ed., *A Library of American Literature*, vol. 3, *Literature of the Revolutionary Period.* (New York: Charles L. Webster & Company, 1888), 160.

30. Chernow, *Washington: A Life*, 456.

31. "From George Washington to Major General Stirling, 5 March 1780," Founders Online, National Archives, https://founders.archives.gov/documents/Washington /03-24-02-0525.

32. "From George Washington to Henry Knox, 8 March 1787," Founders Online, National Archives, https://founders.archives.gov/documents/Washington/04-05-02 -0072.

33. Doris Kearns Goodwin, *Team of Rivals: The Political Genius of Abraham Lincoln* (New York: Simon & Schuster, 2005), 87.

34. Congressional Record: Proceedings and Debates of the United States Congress, vol. 83, part 9 (Washington: U.S. Government Printing Office, 1938).

35. Dennis F. Thompson, "Constitutional Character: Virtues and Vices in Presidential Leadership," *Presidential Studies Quarterly* 40, no. 1 (2010): 23–37, www.jstor .org/stable/23044893.

36. Jeffrey K. Tulis, *The Rhetorical Presidency* (Princeton, NJ: Princeton University Press, 1987), Kindle, location 37.

37. James Madison, "The Federalist Papers: No. 49," The Avalon Project, February 5, 1788, https://avalon.law.yale.edu/18th_century/fed49.asp.

38. Meacham, *The Soul of America*, 12.

39. On *CBS This Morning*, Brown elaborated on this idea: "You can absolutely get away—you can get masses of people behind you if you do two things: if you weaponize uncertainty, if you take people who are in uncertainty and guarantee them certainty and then give people someone to blame for their pain. You can do anything you want. The problem with that is that fear has a short shelf life and you cannot do that for very long." "Brené Brown on 'Dare To Lead' and why vulnerability is the 'only path to courage,'" *CBS This Morning*, October 10, 2018, https://www.cbsnews.com/news/brene-brown-new-book-dare-to-lead-courage-vulnerability/.

40. Karoun Demirjian and Dave Weigel, "Haley calls for ignoring the 'angriest voices' this election season," *Washington Post*, January 12, 2016, https://www.washingtonpost.com/news/powerpost/wp/2016/01/12/haley-to-call-for-ignoring-the-angriest-voices-this-election-season/.

41. Dave Flessner, "Corker: Trump's divisive talk appeals to base but weakens U.S. leadership," *Chattanooga Times Free Press*, November 23, 2018, https://www.timesfreepress.com/news/politics/local/story/2018/nov/23/rhetorical-battletrump-divisive-talk-appeals/483594/.

42. Doris Kearns Goodwin, "Franklin D. Roosevelt," in *Character Above All: Ten Presidents from FDR to George Bush* (New York: Simon & Schuster, 1996), PBS, https://www.pbs.org/newshour/spc/character/essays/roosevelt.html.

43. Meg Wagner, Veronica Rocha, Brian Ries, Amanda Wills, and Jessie Yeung, "The nation honors President George H. W. Bush," CNN.com, December 13, 2018, https://www.cnn.com/politics/live-news/george-hw-bush-funeral/h_b83e5cb05058 2b896b8cab9cd2c5b330.

44. Interview with author.

45. Fred I. Greenstein, *The Presidential Difference: Leadership Style from FDR to Barack Obama* (Princeton: Princeton University Press, 2009), 49.

46. John C. Maxwell, *The 21 Irrefutable Laws of Leadership* (Nashville: Thomas Nelson, 2007).

47. David Frum, "David Frum on Obama Lessons in Robert Caro's Lyndon Johnson," *Newsweek*, April 15, 2012, https://www.newsweek.com/david-frum-obama-lessons-robert-caros-lyndon-johnson-63929.

48. Doris Kearns Goodwin, interview by John Dickerson, "Presidential Leadership," *CBS This Morning*, CBS News, November 2, 2018, https://tunein.com/podcasts /News—Politics-Podcasts/CBS-This-Morning-p112538/?topicId=126614581. "Every man is said to have a peculiar ambition," Lincoln said. "I have no other so great as that of being truly esteemed of my fellow man, by rendering myself worthy of their esteem. How far I shall succeed in gratifying this ambition is yet to be developed. I am young and unknown to many of you." Doris Kearns Goodwin, *Leadership in Turbulent Times: Lessons from the Presidents* (New York: Simon & Schuster, 2018), 3.

CHAPTER 7: ACTION HERO PRESIDENT

1. Joseph A. McCartin, *Collision Course: Ronald Reagan, the Air Traffic Controllers, and the Strike that Changed America* (Oxford University Press, 2011), 290.

2. Joseph A. McCartin and Elliot Simons, interview by Jessica Desvarieux, "The Consequences of Reagan Breaking the '81 Air Traffic Controllers Strike," Real News Network, video, August 6, 2014, https://therealnews.com/stories/jmccartinpa nelesimonso804patcopt2.

3. Ronald Reagan, *An American Life: The Autobiography* (New York: Simon & Schuster, 1990), 283.

4. "'The Buck Stops Here' Desk Sign," Harry S. Truman Library and Museum, https://www.trumanlibrary.gov/education/trivia/buck-stops-here-sign.

5. Woodrow Wilson, *A Crossroads of Freedom: The 1912 Speeches of Woodrow Wilson* (Yale University Press, 1956), 302.

6. Scott Horsley, "Obama Visits Federal Prison, a First for a Sitting President," NPR, July 16, 2015, https://www.npr.org/sections/itsallpolitics/2015/07/16/423612441/obama -visits-federal-prison-a-first-for-a-sitting-president. The only federal prison to be visited by a sitting president: Barack Obama in 2015.

7. Ibid.

8. David McCullough, *Truman* (New York: Simon & Schuster, 2003), Kindle, locations 16161–17614.

9. White, Jr., *Lincoln's Greatest Speech*, 189.

10. "'The Buck Stops Here' Desk Sign," Harry S. Truman Library and Museum, https://www.trumanlibrary.gov/education/trivia/buck-stops-here-sign.

11. David Herbert Donald, *Lincoln* (New York: Simon & Schuster, 1995), Kindle, location 113.

12. Glenn Thrush, Manu Raju, and Josh Gerstein, "Obama under fire for spill response," Politico, May 27, 2010, https://www.politico.com/story/2010/05/obama -under-fire-for-spill-response-037819.

13. Peggy Noonan, "He Was Supposed to be Competent," *Wall Street Journal*, May 29, 2010, https://www.wsj.com/articles/SB100014240527487042692045752709 50789108846.

14. Interview with author.

15. Tevi Troy, "Don't Worry."

16. H. R. Haldeman, *The Haldeman Diaries: Inside the Nixon White House* (New York: G. P. Putnam's Sons, 1994), Kindle, location 3726.

17. Interview with author.

18. Associated Press, "Rapper Blasts Bush Over Katrina," CBS News, September 3, 2005, https://www.cbsnews.com/news/rapper-blasts-bush-over-katrina/.

19. Associated Press, "Katrina disaster prompts Bush to cut his vacation," NBC News, August 31, 2005, http://www.nbcnews.com/id/9134533/ns/us_news-katrina_the_long _road_back/t/katrina-disaster-prompts-bush-cut-vacation/#.XlhXRWhKhPY.

20. Peter Baker, *Days of Fire: Bush and Cheney in the White House* (New York: Anchor Books, 2013), Kindle, location 8438.

21. Ibid., location 8581.

22. Ed Hornick, "Is oil spill 'Obama's Katrina'?" CNN.com, May 4, 2010, https://www .cnn.com/2010/POLITICS/05/04/obama.oil.fallout/index.html.

23. Jason Cheriks, "How The Obama Administration Handled The Last Crisis In The Gulf," HuffPost, August 30, 2017, https://www.huffpost.com/entry/how-the -obama-administration-handled-the-last-crisis-in-the-gulf_n_59a7080ae4b00795 c2a37a81.

24. Paula Dittrick, "'Top hat' oil spill containment device in gulf," *Oil & Gas Journal*, May 12, 2010, https://www.ogj.com/general-interest/hse/article/17285188/top-hat-oil -spill-containment-device-in-gulf.

25. Matthew Weiner, "How golf balls took on the oil spill and lost," CNN.com, May 31, 2010, https://www.cnn.com/2010/SPORT/golf/05/31/golf.oil.spill/index.html.

26. "Obama looking for 'whose ass to kick,'" CNN.com, June 8, 2010, https.//www.cnn .com/2010/POLITICS/06/07/gulf.oil.obama/index.html.

27. Chip Reid, "The Politics of the Oil Spill," CBS News, June 6, 2010, https://www .cbsnews.com/news/the-politics-of-the-oil-spill/.

28. Ezra Klein, "The Green Lantern Theory of the Presidency, explained," Vox, May 20, 2014, https://www.vox.com/2014/5/20/5732208/the-green-lantern-theory-of -the-presidency-explained.

29. Interview with author.

30. Edgar F. Puryear, *Nineteen Stars: A Study in Military Character and Leadership* (Novato, CA: Presidio Press, 1981), 289.

31. Michael Bloomberg, interview by Margaret Brennan, "Transcript: Cotton, Feinstein, Bloomberg," *Face the Nation*, CBS News, April 22, 2018, https://www.cbsnews .com/news/full-transcript-face-the-nation-on-april-22-2018/.

32. Interview with author.

33. Interview with author.

34. Cora Currier, "The Facts Behind Obama's Executive Privilege Claim," ProPublica, June 21, 2012, https://www.propublica.org/article/the-facts-behind-obamas -executive-privilege-claim.

35. "IRS Scandal Fast Facts," CNN.com, September 26, 2019, https://www.cnn.com /2014/07/18/politics/irs-scandal-fast-facts/index.html.

36. Woodrow Wilson, *Congressional Government: A Study in American Politics* (Boston: Houghton, Mifflin and Company), 1885.

37. Brian Balogh and Bruce J. Schulman, eds., *Recapturing the Oval Office: New Historical Approaches to the American Presidency* (Ithaca, NY: Cornell University Press, 2015), Kindle, location 16.

38. Ibid., location 19.

39. Interview with author.

40. Abby Phillip, Ed O'Keefe, Nick Miroff, and Damian Paletta, "Lost Weekend: How Trump's Time at His Golf Club Hurt the Response to Maria," *Washington Post*, September 29, 2017, https://www.washingtonpost.com/politics/lost-weekend-how -trumps-time-at-his-golf-club-hurt-the-response-to-maria/2017/09/29/ce92ed0a-a522 -11e7-8c37-e1d99ad6aa22_story.html.

41. Donald J. Trump (@realDonaldTrump), ". . . Such poor leadership ability by the Mayor of San Juan, and others in Puerto Rico, who are not able to get their workers to help. They . . . want everything to be done for them when it should be a community effort. 10,000 Federal workers now on Island doing a fantastic job," Twitter, September 30, 2017, 6:26 A.M., https://twitter.com/realdonaldtrump/status /914089003745468417.

42. Interview with author.

43. Nicole Chavez and Rafy Rivera, "Puerto Rico emergency director fired after residents discover warehouse full of Hurricane Maria supplies," CNN.com, January 19, 2020, https://www.cnn.com/2020/01/18/us/puerto-rico-emergency-director -fired/index.html.

44. Interview with author.

45. Ian Schwartz, "Trump: 'I Hate To Tell You Puerto Rico But You've Thrown Our Budget A Little Out Of Whack,'" Real Clear Politics, October 3, 2017, https://www .realclearpolitics.com/video/2017/10/03/trump_i_hate_to_tell_you_puerto_rico _but_youve_thrown_our_budget_a_little_out_of_whack.html.

46. Philip Bump, "The revised death toll in Puerto Rico makes Trump's comparison to Katrina look even worse," *Washington Post*, August 9, 2018, https://www.washingtonpost.com/news/politics/wp/2018/08/09/the-revised-death-toll-in-puerto-rico-makes-trumps-comparison-to-katrina-look-even-worse/.

47. Donald J. Trump (@realDonaldTrump) ". . . the crazed and incompetent . . ." Twitter, April 1, 2019, 8:38 P.M., http://twitter.com/realDonaldTrump/status/111292222/037719552.

CHAPTER 8: CONFIDENCE MAN: THE ECONOMY

1. Gerard Helferich, *An Unlikely Trust: Theodore Roosevelt, J. P. Morgan, and the Improbable Partnership That Remade American Business* (Guilford, CT: Lyons Press / Globe Pequot, 2018), Kindle, location 1214.

2. Ibid., locations 1201–4.

3. Ibid., location 1229.

4. Daniel Gross, *Forbes Business Stories of All Time* (New York: John Wiley & Sons, Inc., 1996), 71.

5. Herbert Hoover, "Statement Announcing a Series of Conferences With Representatives of Business, Industry, Agriculture, and Labor," The American Presidency Project, November 15, 1929, https://www.presidency.ucsb.edu/documents/statement-announcing-series-conferences-with-representatives-business-industry-agriculture."

6. Steve Holland, "McCain suspends campaign to work on Wall Street plan," Reuters, September 24, 2008, https://www.reuters.com/article/us-usa-politicsnews1/mccain-suspends-campaign-to-work-on-wall-street-plan-idUSTRE48N7ZP20080924?sp=true.

7. Josh Marshall, "Wait . . . Wait," Talking Points Memo, September 24, 2008, https://talkingpointsmemo.com/edblog/wait-wait.

8. Ben S. Bernanke, Henry M. Paulson, Jr., and Timothy F. Geithner, *Firefighting: The Financial Crisis and Its Lessons* (New York: Penguin Books, 2019), Kindle, location 1172.

9. Emily Elisabeth Ekins, "Tea Party Fairness: How the Idea of Proportional Justice Explains the Right-Wing Populism of the Obama Era," (diss., UCLA, 2015), https://escholarship.org/uc/item/3663x343#author.

10. "FreedomWorks Blasts House Vote for $700 Billion Wall Street Bailout," Business Wire, October 3, 2008, https://www.businesswire.com/news/home/20081003005677/en/FreedomWorks-Blasts-House-Vote-700-Billion-Wall.

11. Bernanke, Paulson, and Geithner, *Firefighting*, location 1183.

12. Ibid.

13. John Lawrence, "When America Stared Into the Abyss," *The Atlantic*, January 7, 2019, https://www.theatlantic.com/ideas/archive/2019/01/john-lawrence-inside-2008-financial-crash/576574/.

14. Interview with author.

15. Lynn Adler, "Foreclosures jump 57 percent in last 12 months." Reuters, April 15, 2008, https://www.reuters.com/article/us-usa-mortgages-foreclosures/foreclosures-jump-57-percent-in-last-12-months-idUSN1435957820080415. In January 2008, there were 57 percent more foreclosures than twelve months earlier.

    Steve Green, "Report: Nearly 70 percent of LV homeowners underwater on mortgage," *Las Vegas Sun*, November 30, 2009, https://lasvegassun.com/news/2009

/nov/30/report-nearly-70-percent-lv-homeowners-underwater-/. In Nevada, once an American boom town, 65 percent of the homes were "underwater." This led to more foreclosures than those investment bankers were expecting.

Les Christie, "Foreclosures up a record 81% in 2008," CNN Money, January 15, 2009, https://money.cnn.com/2009/01/15/real_estate/millions_in_foreclosure/. U.S. foreclosure filings spiked by more than 81 percent in 2008, a record, and up 225 percent compared with 2006.

Ibid. One out of every fifty-four households received a foreclosure notice. In Las Vegas, a real estate group hired buses to give tours of foreclosed homes to prospective buyers in order to clear inventory.

16. Frank James, "Nearly One In Four U.S. Homes With Mortgages 'Underwater,'" NPR, November 24, 2009, https://www.npr.org/sections/thetwo-way/2009/11/one_in_four_us_homes_underwate.html.

17. Christie, "Foreclosures up 81%."

18. Jason Szep, "Cities grapple with surge in abandoned homes," Reuters, March 24, 2008, https://www.reuters.com/article/us-usa-housing-vacant/cities-grapple-with-surge-in-abandoned-homes-idUSN1162941020080325.

19. Bernanke, Paulson, and Geithner, *Firefighting*, location 259.

20. Ibid.

21. Robert E. Rubin and Jacob Weisberg, *In an Uncertain World: Tough Choices from Wall Street to Washington* (New York: Random House, 2003), 355.

22. Blake Abbot, "'A Widespread Loss of Confidence.' TARP, Presidential Rhetoric, and the Crisis of Neoliberalism," *Communication Quarterly*, 66:5, 463–480, doi.org10.1080/01463373.2018.1446034.

23. Goodwin, *Leadership in Turbulent Times*, 180.

24. "Why It Happened," Digital History ID 3432, 2019, http://www.digitalhistory.uh.edu/disp_textbook.cfm?smtID=2&psid=3432.

25. Martin Van Buren, "Special Session Message," National Archives, September 4, 1937, https://millercenter.org/the-presidency/presidential-speeches/september-4-1837-special-session-message.

26. Henry M. Paulson, *On the Brink: Inside the Race to Stop the Collapse of the Global Financial System* (New York: Business Plus, 2010), Kindle, location 92.

27. Andrew Ross Sorkin and Landon Thomas, Jr., "JPMorgan Acts to Buy Ailing Bear Stearns at Huge Discount," *New York Times*, March 16, 2008, https://www.nytimes.com/2008/03/16/business/16cnd-bear.html. JPMorgan Chase purchased the company at the bargain basement rate of $2 per share—down from $30 per share just days before the sale.

28. The government went further. It rescued insurance giant AIG with $85 billion. The 158-year-old investment bank Lehman Brothers collapsed, the largest bankruptcy in U.S. history; Merrill Lynch collapsed and had to be resuscitated by Bank of America. Two banks, Washington Mutual and Wachovia, failed. They were the two largest failures of federally insured banks in U.S. history.

29. Lawrence, "When America Stared."

30. Interview with author.

31. "Exports of Goods and Services (% of GDP)," World Bank, 2019, https://data.worldbank.org/indicator/NE.EXP.GNFS.ZS.

32. Clinton, *My Life*, location 13128.

33. Ibid., location 13157.

34. Rubin and Weisberg, *Uncertain World*, 365.

35. Derek Chollet and James Goldgeier, *America Between the Wars: From 11/9 to 9/11; The Misunderstood Years Between the Fall of the Berlin Wall and the Start of the War on Terror* (New York: PublicAffairs Books, 2008), 166.

36. Clinton, *My Life*, location 13157.

37. Ibid.

38. Lawrence, "When America Stared."

39. Ibid.

40. Ibid.

41. Ibid.

42. Carl Hulse, "Conservatives Viewed Bailout Plan as Last Straw," *New York Times*, September 26, 2008, https://www.nytimes.com/2008/09/27/business/27repubs.html.

43. Lawrence, "When America Stared."

44. Interview with author.

45. Interview with author.

46. When John Maynard Keynes met with FDR, the president, unimpressed by his "rigamarole of figures," told his secretary of labor, "He must be a mathematician rather than a political economist." Hofstadter, *American Political Tradition*, 432.

47. Interview with author.

48. Interview with author.

49. Paul Kiel and Dan Nguyen, "Bailout Tracker: Tracking Every Dollar and Every Recipient," ProPublica, April 15, 2009, https://projects.propublica.org/bailout/.

50. Elizabeth Warren, "Enough is Enough: The President's Latest Wall Street Nominee," HuffPost, November 19, 2014, https://www.huffpost.com/entry/presidents-wall-street-nominee_b_6188324.

51. Dan Merica, "Labor's Trumka: Hillary Clinton is 'very, very qualified to be president,'" CNN Political Ticker, August 28, 2014, https://politicalticker.blogs.cnn.com/2014/08/28/labors-trumka-hillary-clinton-is-very-very-qualified-to-be-president/.

52. Interview with author.

53. Michael J. Boskin, John H. Cochrane, John F. Cogan, George P. Shultz, and John B. Taylor, "A Debt Crisis Is on the Horizon," *Washington Post*, March 27, 2018, https://www.washingtonpost.com/opinions/the-debt-crisis-is-on-our-doorstep/2018/03/27/fd28318c-27d3-11e8-bc72-077aa4dab9ef_story.html.

54. Interview with author.

55. Chris Isidore, "Bailout plan rejected—supporters scramble," CNN Money, September 29, 2008, https://money.cnn.com/2008/09/29/news/economy/bailout/.

56. Kai Ryssdal and Jana Kasperkevic, "'The enemy is forgetting': Bernanke, Geithner and Paulson on why we must remember the 2008 financial crisis," Marketplace, March 19, 2018, https://www.marketplace.org/2018/03/19/bernanke-geithner-paulson-regulations-lesson-crisis-warning/.

57. Kenneth J. Arrow, "I Know a Hawk from a Handsaw," in *Eminent Economists: Their Life and Philosophies*, edited by Michael Szenberg (New York: Cambridge University Press, 1993), 42–50.

58. Ibid.

59. "U.S. household income distribution from 1990 to 2018," Statistica, September 2019, https://www.statista.com/statistics/219643/gini-coefficient-for-us-individuals-families-and-households/. The Gini coefficient, which measures income distribution in the United States, stood at 0.46 in 2007 and has increased to 0.49. (A Gini coefficient of zero represents perfect equality where all values are the same, for example, where everyone has equal income.)

60. Moritz Kuhn, Moritz Schularick, and Ulrike Steins, "Research: How the Financial

Crisis Drastically Increased Wealth Inequality in the U.S," *Harvard Business Review*, September 13, 2018, https://hbr.org/2018/09/research-how-the-financial-crisis -drastically-increased-wealth-inequality in the u 0.

61. Seung Min Kim, "Populist economic frustration threatens Trump's strongest re-election issue, Post-ABC poll finds," *Washington Post*, April 29, 2019, https://www .washingtonpost.com/politics/populist-economic-frustration-threatens-trumps -strongest-reelection-issue-post-abc-poll-finds/2019/04/28/44f64cbc-6a02-11e9-9d56 -1c0cf2c7ac04_story.html.

62. Frank Newport, "U.S. Public Opinion and the 2017 Tax Law," Gallup, April 29, 2019, https://news.gallup.com/opinion/polling-matters/249161/public-opinion-2017 -tax-law.aspx. In reality, eight in ten Americans stood to receive tax cuts in 2018 under the law, according to an analysis by the nonpartisan Tax Policy Center.

    John Harwood, "Few Americans think they're getting a Trump tax cut: NBC/ WSJ poll," CNBC News, April 8, 2019, https://www.cnbc.com/2019/04/05/few -americans-think-theyre-getting-a-trump-tax-cut-nbcwsj-poll.html. Yet the cuts for most taxpayers are so small that many didn't notice.

63. Sahil Kapur and Joshua Green, "Internal GOP Poll: 'We've Lost the Messaging Battle' on Tax Cuts," Bloomberg, September 20, 2018, https://www.bloomberg.com /news/articles/2018-09-20/internal-gop-poll-we-ve-lost-the-messaging-battle-on-tax -cuts.

64. Kim Parker, "The Growing Partisan Divide in Views of Higher Education," Pew Research Center, August 19, 2019, https://www.pewsocialtrends.org/essay/the -growing-partisan-divide-in-views-of-higher-education/.

65. Bourree Lam, "Obama's Final Jobs Report Marks 75 Consecutive Months of Growth," *The Atlantic*, January 6, 2017, https://www.theatlantic.com/business /archive/2017/01/december-jobs-report/512366/.

CHAPTER 9: A HISTORIC PARTISAN GAP

1. Chris Matthews, *Tip and the Gipper: When Politics Worked* (New York: Simon & Schuster, 2013), 73.
2. Interview with the author.
3. George W. Bush, *Decision Points* (New York: Crown, 2010), Kindle, location 5863.
4. Bob Corker, interview by John Dickerson, "Republican Sen. Bob Corker says Trump's conduct 'hurts our country,'" *CBS This Morning*, CBS News, December 12, 2018, https://www.cbsnews.com/news/senator-bob-corker-trump-conduct -hurts-our-country/.
5. O'Neill's leadership aide Burt Hoffman wrote the Speaker a note about his new role: "Until such time as we nominate a new presidential candidate, you are the leader of the Democratic Party as well as the highest public official of that party. You are also, more than ever, the only person in a position to continue representing the ideals of justice and compassion." John A. Farrell, *Tip O'Neill and the Democratic Century: A Biography* (New York: Little, Brown, 2001), Kindle, location 540.
6. Matthews, *Tip and the Gipper*, 233.
7. Jay Nordlinger, "Good Ol' Tip," *National Review*, January 25, 2013, https://www .nationalreview.com/2013/01/good-ol-tip-jay-nordlinger/.
8. Thomas P. O'Neill, "Frenemies: A Love Story," *New York Times*, October 5, 2012, https://campaignstops.blogs.nytimes.com/2012/10/05/frenemies-a-love-story/.
9. Farrell, *Tip O'Neill*, location 540.
10. James Reston, "Q&A; 'The President is Going Down the Wrong Road,'" *New York*

Times, November 1, 1983, https://www.nytimes.com/1983/11/01/us/q-a-the-president-is-going-down-the-wrong-road.html.

11. Farrell, *Tip O'Neill,* location 574.

12. Ibid.

13. Douglas Brinkley, ed., *The Reagan Diaries* (New York: HarperCollins, 2007), 4.

14. Ibid., 3.

15. Nordlinger, "Good Ol' Tip."

16. "Taxation of Social Security Benefits," Social Security Agency History, https://www.ssa.gov/history/taxationofbenefits.html. Under the 1983 amendments to the Social Security Act, a previously enacted increase in the payroll tax rate was accelerated, additional employees were added to the system, the full-benefit retirement age was slowly increased, and up to one-half of the value of the Social Security benefit was made potentially taxable income.

17. John Cassidy, "Can Donald Trump Learn from Ronald Reagan and Tip O'Neill?" *New Yorker,* March 28, 2017, https://www.newyorker.com/news/john-cassidy/can-donald-trump-learn-from-ronald-reagan-and-tip-oneill.

18. Charlie Stenholm, "How Tip O'Neill and Ronald Reagan would make this Congress work," The Hill, March 12, 2015, https://thehill.com/blogs/pundits-blog/lawmaker-news/235409-how-ronald-reagan-and-tip-oneill-would-make-this-congress.

19. Paul Bedard, "Tip O'Neill and Reagan and Model for Breaking Partisan Gridlock," *U.S. News & World Report,* February 17, 2010, https://www.usnews.com/news/blogs/washington-whispers/2010/02/17/tip-oneill-and-reagan-and-model-for-breaking-partisan-gridlock.

20. Matthew Dallek, "Bipartisan Reagan-O'Neill Social Security Deal in 1983 Showed It Can Be Done," *U.S. News & World Report,* April 2, 2009, https://www.usnews.com/opinion/articles/2009/04/02/bipartisan-reagan-oneill-social-security-deal-in-1983-showed-it-can-be-done.

21. Colin Wilhelm, "Mitch McConnell blames entitlement programs for rising deficit," *Washington Examiner,* October 16, 2018, https://www.washingtonexaminer.com/policy/economy/mitch-mcconnell-blames-entitlement-programs-for-rising-deficit.

22. Mike DeBonis and Seung Min Kim, "'All roads lead to Putin': Pelosi questions Trump's loyalty in White House clash," *Washington Post,* October 17, 2019, https://www.washingtonpost.com/powerpost/pelosi-recalls-clash-with-trump-says-she-was-probably-telling-him-that-all-roads-lead-to-putin/2019/10/17/fdbde8d2-f0f2-11e9-8693-f487e46784aa_story.html.

23. Rebecca Kheel, "Trump called Pelosi a 'third-rate politician' during Syria meeting, top Democrats say," The Hill, October 16, 2019, https://thehill.com/homenews/administration/466156-trump-called-pelosi-a-third-rate-politician-during-syria-briefing-top.

24. Dominick Mastrangelo, "Trump: Nancy Pelosi Is 'Crazy as a Bedbug,'" *Washington Examiner,* November 22, 2019, https://www.washingtonexaminer.com/news/crazy-as-a-bedbug-trump-blasts-pelosi-and-questions-her-mental-stability.

25. Donald J. Trump (@realDonaldTrump), "Because Nancy's teeth were falling out of her mouth, and she didn't have time to think!" Twitter, December 15, 2019, 2:11 P.M., https://twitter.com/realDonaldTrump/status/1206335971974959107.

26. Mitch McConnell, *The Long Game* (New York: Penguin Publishing Group, 2019), 3.

27. Robert G. Kaiser, *Act of Congress* (New York: Alfred A. Knopf, 2013), 135.

28. "1980 Presidential Election, Results by Congressional District," Dave Leip's Atlas of U.S. Presidential Elections, https://upload.wikimedia.org/wikipedia/commons /2/29/1980_Presidential_Election%2C_Results_by_Congressional_District.png, United States. Bureau of the Census. *Congressional District Atlas*, 95th Congress 1977. HathiTrust, https://hdl.handle.net/2027/pur1.32754073474441.

In 1980, Reagan won districts in the following states: Arizona (2), California (16), Colorado (3), Connecticut (3), Florida (8), Hawaii (1), Illinois (3), Indiana (5), Iowa (3), Kansas (1), Kentucky (1), Louisiana (4), Maryland (4), Massachusetts (4), Michigan (6), Mississippi (1), Missouri (4), Montana (1), Nevada (1), New Hampshire (1), New Jersey (6), New York (20), North Carolina (3), North Dakota (1), Ohio (6), Oklahoma (5), Oregon (2), Pennsylvania (6), South Dakota (1), Tennessee (2), Texas (13), Virginia (1), Washington (5), Wisconsin (1)

29. Steven V. Roberts, "Congress; The Eclipse of the Boll Weevils," *New York Times*, March 26, 1983, https://www.nytimes.com/1983/03/26/us/congress-the-eclipse-of -the-boll-weevils.html.

30. David Hawkings, "The Incredible Shrinking Split Tickets," Roll Call, February 1, 2017, https://www.rollcall.com/2017/02/01/the-incredible-shrinking-split-tickets/.

31. Ibid.

32. "2008 Electoral College by Congressional District," FrontloadingHQ, March 10, 2009, http://frontloading.blogspot.com/2009/03/2008-electoral-college-by-congres sional.html.

33. Drew DeSilver, "Split-ticket districts, once common, are now rare," Pew Research Center, August 8, 2016, https://www.pewresearch.org/fact-tank/2016/08/08/split -ticket-districts-once-common-are-now-rare/?utm_source=Pew+Research+Center &utm_campaign=3f5deccecc-Weekly_August_11_20168_11_2016&utm_medium= email&utm_term=0_3e953b9b70-3f5deccecc-400240005.

34. "Split-ticket Districts in the 2016 Presidential and U.S. House Elections," Ballot-pedia, https://ballotpedia.org/Split-ticket_districts_in_the_2016_presidential_and _U.S._House_elections#cite_note-1.

35. Refer to endnote 6, p. 529.

36. Hawkings, "Incredible Shrinking."

37. Ibid.

38. Ibid.

39. Elizabeth Kolbert, "Drawing the Line," *The New Yorker*, June 20, 2016.

40. Sam Wang, "The Great Gerrymander of 2012," *New York Times*, February 2, 2013, https://www.nytimes.com/2013/02/03/opinion/sunday/the-great-gerrymander-of -2012.html.

41. Bill Bishop, *The Big Sort* (Boston: Houghton Mifflin Harcourt, 2008), 5–6.

42. Ibid.

43. Morris P. Fiorina, "The (RE) Nationalization of Congressional Elections," Hoover Institution, 2016, 11, https://www.hoover.org/sites/default/files/research/docs/fiorina _renationalizationofcongressionalelections_7.pdf.

44. "Election Overview," Open Secrets, https://www.opensecrets.org/overview/index .php?display=A&type=M&cycle=2008. The average amount raised for members in House races increased by about 51% from $1,441,545 in 2008 to $2,182,068 in 2018. During that same period, the average raised for members in Senate races went from $3,128,436 to $5,795,174. That's an 85.2% increase. In the 2016 presidential election, Democratic candidates on average raised $133,343,288 while Republican candidates raised $38,096,042.

45. Megan Brenan, "U.S. Voters Using Midterms to Send Trump a Message," Gallup,

November 2, 2018, https://news.gallup.com/poll/244193/voters-using-midterms-send-trump-message.aspx.

46. Ibid.

47. Kantar/CMAG.

48. Laura Paisley, "Political Polarization at Its Worst Since the Civil War," University of Southern California News, November 8, 2016, https://news.usc.edu/110124/political-polarization-at-its-worst-since-the-civil-war-2/.

49. Mark Gitenstein, *Matters of Principle: An Insider's Account of America's Rejection of Robert Bork's Nomination to the Supreme Court* (New York: Simon & Schuster, 1992).

50. Jon Margolis, "A Hollow Ring to GOP Gripes About Bork Foes," *Chicago Tribune*, October 20, 1987, http://articles.chicagotribune.com/1987-10-20/news/8703190795_1_bork-foes-judge-robert-bork-conservatives.

51. Interview with author.

52. Gitenstein, *Matters of Principle*, 44.

53. David Whitman, "Are Reagan's New Judges Really Closet Moderates?" *Washington Post*, August 9, 1987, https://www.washingtonpost.com/archive/opinions/1987/08/09/are-reagans-new-judges-really-closet-moderates/60da1734-053b-4a75-a4a9-c6bcae68846f/.

54. Kathy Frankovic, "America's Political Parties Remain Polarized," YouGov, May 28, 2019, https://today.yougov.com/topics/politics/articles-reports/2019/05/28/americas-political-parties-remain-polarized.

55. "Feelings About Partisans and the Parties," Pew Research Center, June 22, 2016, https://www.people-press.org/2016/06/22/1-feelings-about-partisans-and-the-parties/.

56. Lynn Vavreck, "A Measure of Identity: Are You Wedded to Your Party?" *New York Times*, January 31, 2017, https://www.nytimes.com/2017/01/31/upshot/are-you-married-to-your-party.html.

57. Carroll Doherty, "Key takeaways on Americans' growing partisan divide over political values," Pew Research Center, October 5, 2017, https://www.pewresearch.org/fact-tank/2017/10/05/takeaways-on-americans-growing-partisan-divide-over-political-values/.

58. "Presidential Approval Ratings—Donald Trump," Gallup, https://news.gallup.com/poll/203198/presidential-approval-ratings-donald-trump.aspx. Gallup poll October 14–31, 2019: Trump's lowest approval rating among Dems was 3 percent in the period from August 15 to 30, 2019. The highest his approval rating has ever been among Dems is 13 percent, the first week after his inauguration and again in the period from April 30 to May 6, 2018.

59. Drew DeSilver, "Turnout in This Year's U.S. House Primaries Rose Sharply, Especially on the Democratic Side," Pew Research Center, October 3, 2018, https://www.pewresearch.org/fact-tank/2018/10/03/turnout-in-this-years-u-s-house-primaries-rose-sharply-especially-on-the-democratic-side/. Nearly a fifth (19.6 percent) of registered voters—about 37 million—cast ballots in House primary elections, according to the analysis of state election results. That may not sound like a lot, but it was a 56 percent increase over the 23.7 million who voted in 2014's House primaries; turnout that year was 13.7 percent of registered voters. While the battle for control of the House has gotten a lot of public and media attention, turnout rates were also substantially higher in 2018's Senate (22.2 percent) and gubernatorial (26.5 percent) primaries than in 2014 (16.6 and 18.6 percent, respectively), though the increases were relatively similar for both parties.

60. Jeff Flake and Chris Coons, interview by Scott Pelley, "Sens. Jeff Flake and Chris

Coons Explain Why They Decided to Delay Brett Kavanaugh's Confirmation," *60 Minutes*, CBS News, September 30, 2018, https://www.cbsnews.com/news/jeff -flake-lindsey-graham-brett-kavanaugh-supreme-court-confirmation-inside-the -decision-to-delay-confirmation-hearing/.

61. Interview with author. (This rule is not absolute. Republicans have been able to break a little bit with Donald Trump on national security issues—punishing Russia when Trump was reluctant to and bucking his decision to withdraw troops from Syria—because those issues do not touch the bond Donald Trump shares with his voters.)

62. Mitch McConnell wrote about South Carolina Republican Senator Jim DeMint who blasted GOP leaders negotiating to reduce the deficit with no appreciation for the fact that a Democrat was in the White House and had a say in negotiations too. "This exchange perfectly illustrated the hypocrisy of DeMint and his whole enterprise. People like him were depending on me to pick up the pieces by brokering deals. He'd say it was the best we could do, privately, and then fund-raise by blasting me for the same deals. I found the fact that DeMint would shake my hand after railing against this deal both jaw-dropping and revealing, and I didn't remain quiet about my frustration." McConnell, *Long Game*, 211.

63. Associated Press, "President Trump picks Ratcliffe to be top intelligence official again," Fox10 Phoenix, February 28, 2020, https://www.fox10phoenix.com/news /president-trump-picks-ratcliffe-to-be-top-intelligence-official-again.

64. Isaac Chotiner, "The Pelosi-Versus-Squad Paradigm," *New Yorker*, July 18, 2019, https://www.newyorker.com/news/q-and-a/the-pelosi-versus-squad-paradigm.

65. Zack Budryk, "Pelosi: Progressive Dem wing represented by Ocasio-Cortez is 'like five people,'" The Hill, April 14, 2019, https://thehill.com/homenews/house/438856 -pelosi-progressive-dem-wing-represented-by-ocasio-cortez-is-like-five-people.

66. John Boehner, interview by John Dickerson, "Transcript: Boehner, Sanders, Kasich," *Face the Nation*, CBS News, September 27, 2015, https://www.cbsnews.com /news/face-the-nation-transcripts-september-27-boehner-sanders-kasich/.

67. Interview with author.

CHAPTER 10: A NEW ERA OF PARTISAN WARFARE

1. GOPAC, "Language: A Key Mechanism of Control," (Curriculum page, Wake Forest University, Winston-Salem, NC, 1995), https://users.wfu.edu/zulick/454/gopac .html.

2. Jon Meacham, *Destiny and Power: The American Odyssey of George Herbert Walker Bush* (New York: Random House, 2015), 445.

3. Carl M. Cannon, "Newt vs. Tip: Partisanship at Its Apogee?" Real Clear Politics, May 15, 2014, https://www.realclearpolitics.com/articles/2014/05/15/newt_vs_tip _partisanship_at_its_apogee_122643.html. Even though they were stricken from the record, C-SPAN has a home for every noteworthy and unworthy floor speech. O'Neill's from May 15, 1984 can be seen here: https://www.c-span.org/video /?c4456736/speaker-oneils-words-taken.

4. U.S. Congress, House of Representatives, 98th Cong., 2nd sess., May 15, 1984, 12211, https://www.govinfo.gov/content/pkg/GPO-CRECB-1984-pt9/pdf/GPO-CRECB -1984-pt9-5-2.pdf.

5. "The Ethics Charges Against Jim Wright: Excerpts: 'Wright Did Not Show Reasonable Care on Gifts,'" *Los Angeles Times*, April 18, 1989, https://www.latimes .com/archives/la-xpm-1989-04-18-mn-2024-story.html.

6. Steven M. Gillon, *The Pact: Bill Clinton, Newt Gingrich, and the Rivalry That Defined a Generation* (New York: Oxford University Press, 2008), 61.

7. Dan Balz, "The Whip Who Would Be Speaker," *Washington Post*, October 20, 1994, https://www.washingtonpost.com/archive/politics/1994/10/20/the-whip-who-would-be-speaker/9e5dfbdd-808a-4ca6-aff1-70d6980c2ff6/.

8. Gingrich explained to a group of conservative activists, he had been giving "organized, systematic, researched, one-hour lectures. Did CBS rush in and ask if they could tape one of my one-hour lectures? No. But the minute Tip O'Neill attacked me, he and I got 90 seconds at the close of all three network news shows. You have to give them confrontations. When you give them confrontations, you get attention; when you get attention, you can educate." David Osborne, "The Swinging Days of Newt Gingrich," *Mother Jones*, November 1, 1984, https://www.motherjones.com/politics/1984/11/newt-gingrich-shining-knight-post-reagan-right/.

9. Steve Daley and Elaine S. Povich, "House Speaker Wright Resigns," *Chicago Tribune*, June 1, 1989, https://www.chicagotribune.com/news/ct-xpm-1989-06-01-8902050821-story.html.

10. Meacham, *Destiny and Power*, xxi.

11. Ibid., 415.

12. Ibid., 413.

13. Robin Toner, "Buchanan, Urging New Nationalism, Joins '92 Race," *New York Times*, December 11, 1991, https://www.nytimes.com/1991/12/11/us/buchanan-urging-new-nationalism-joins-92-race.html.

14. Meacham, *Destiny and Power*, 365.

15. "The Speaker Steps Down; Excerpts from Phone Call About Gingrich's Future," *New York Times*, November 8, 1998, https://web.archive.org/web/20160804035421/http://www.nytimes.com/1998/11/08/us/the-speaker-steps-down-excerpts-from-phone-call-about-gingrich-s-future.html.

16. Frances E. Lee, *Insecure Majorities: Congress and the Perpetual Campaign* (Chicago: University of Chicago Press, 2016), 1.

17. Meacham, *Destiny and Power*, 362.

18. Robert Draper, *Do Not Ask What Good We Do: Inside the U.S. House of Representatives* (New York: Simon & Schuster, 2012), xviii.

19. This is a portion of the interview McConnell did with the *National Journal* on October 23, 2010 when he made that statement:

McConnell: We need to be honest with the public. This election is about them, not us. And we need to treat this election as the first step in retaking the government. We need to say to everyone on Election Day, "Those of you who helped make this a good day, you need to go out and help us finish the job."

NJ: What's the job?

McConnell: The single most important thing we want to achieve is for President Obama to be a one-term president.

NJ: Does that mean endless, or at least frequent, confrontation with the president?

McConnell: If President Obama does a Clintonian backflip, if he's willing to meet us halfway on some of the biggest issues, it's not inappropriate for us to do business with him.

NJ: What are the big issues?

McConnell: It is possible the president's advisers will tell him he has to do something to get right with the public on his levels of spending and on lowering the national debt. If he were to heed that advice, he would, I imagine, find more support among our conference than he would among some in the Senate in his own party. I don't want the president to fail; I want him to change. Glenn Kessler, "When did McConnell say he wanted to make Obama a 'one-term president'?" *Washington Post*, September 25, 2012, https://www.washingtonpost.com/blogs/fact -checker/post/when-did-mcconnell-say-he-wanted-to-make-obama-a-one-term -president/2012/09/24/79fd5cd8-0696-11e2-afff-d6c7f20a83bf_blog.html.

20. Interview with author.

CHAPTER 11: ON THE SEPARATION OF POWERS

1. George F. Hoar, *Autobiography of Seventy Years*, vol. 2 (New York: Charles Scribner's Sons, 1903), 46.

2. James Madison, "The Federalist Papers: No. 51," February 8, 1788, https://avalon .law.yale.edu/18th_century/fed51.asp.

3. John Adams, "John Adams, Clarendon, no. 3," in *Papers of John Adams*, edited by Robert J. Taylor et al. (Cambridge, MA: Belknap Press of Harvard University Press, 1977), http://press-pubs.uchicago.edu/founders/documents/v1ch17s12.html.

4. This also made it easier for the candidate of the log cabin and hard cider to be all things to all people, of course, but still, that he could hide behind this norm of congressional supremacy meant it existed.

5. "Woodrow Wilson's Changing Views of the Senate," United States Senate, April 12, 1907, https://www.senate.gov/artandhistory/history/minute/Woodrow_Wilsons _Changing_Views_of_the_Senate.htm.

6. "Spiro T. Agnew, 39th Vice President (1969–1973)," United States Senate, https:// www.senate.gov/about/officers-staff/vice-president/VP_Spiro_Agnew.htm.

7. Eric Schmitt and Charlie Savage, "Bowe Bergdahl, American Soldier, Freed by Taliban in Prisoner Trade," *New York Times*, May 31, 2014, https://www.nytimes .com/2014/06/01/us/bowe-bergdahl-american-soldier-is-freed-by-taliban.html. Barack Obama released five Taliban detainees from Guantanamo Bay in a prisoner swap for Army Sergeant Bowe Bergdahl, ignoring a federal law that required him to notify Congress thirty days before releasing detainees.

8. Interview with author.

9. Ron Johnson, interview by Chuck Todd, "Meet the Press: February 17, 2019," *Meet the Press*, NBC News, February 17, 2019, https://www.nbcnews.com/meet-the -press/meet-press-february-17-2019-n972606.

10. Brakkton Booker, "Trump Administration Diverts $3.8 Billion in Pentagon Funding to Border Wall," NPR, February 13, 2020, https://www.npr.org/2020/02/13 /805796618/trump-administration-diverts-3-8-billion-in-pentagon-funding-to -border-wall.

11. Jonathan Chait, "Trump Lawyers Argue No President Can Be Impeached for Any Abuse of Power," *New York*, January 19, 2020, https://nymag.com/intelligencer /2020/01/trump-brief-impeachment-trial-abuse-power-crime-dershowitz.html.

12. "McConnell says he's waiting on Trump to chart path on guns," *Los Angeles Times*, September 4, 2019, https://www.latimes.com/politics/story/2019-09-04/mcconnell -trump-gun-violence-legislation.

13. Yael Halon, "Nikki Haley: Democratic leadership, candidates are the only people mourning Soleimani death," Fox News, January 6, 2020, https://www.foxnews.com /media/nikki-haley-democrats-soleimani-trump.

14. Mitt Romney, "The president shapes the public character of the nation. Trump's

character falls short," *Washington Post*, January 1, 2019, https://www.washingtonpost
.com/opinions/mitt-romney-the-president-shapes-the-public-character-of-the-nation
-trumps-character-falls-short/2019/01/01/37a3c8c2-0d1a-11e9-8938-5898adc28fa2
_story.html.

15. "Romney's Harsh Trump Critique Shows Why He Lost to Obama In 2012," Investor's Business Daily, January 2, 2019, https://www.investors.com/politics/editorials
/romney-trump-criticism/.

16. "I don't like people who use their faith as justification for doing what they know is
wrong," said President Trump in February 2020 at the National Prayer Breakfast.
"Nor do I like people who say 'I pray for you' when they know that that's not so. So
many people have been hurt and we can't let that go on." Donald J. Trump, "Remarks by President Trump at the 68th Annual National Prayer Breakfast," Office
of the Press Secretary, February 6, 2020, https://www.whitehouse.gov/briefings
-statements/remarks-president-trump-68th-annual-national-prayer-breakfast/.

   Later that day in a press conference he also targeted Romney: "And then you
had some that used religion as a crutch. They never used it before. But you know,
it's a failed presidential candidate, so things can happen when you fail so badly
running for president." John Wagner, Felicia Sonmez, and Colby Itkowitz, "President celebrates Senate acquittal at the White House, expresses no contrition and
calls Democratic leaders 'vicious and mean,'" *Washington Post*, February 6, 2020,
https://www.washingtonpost.com/politics/trump-impeachment-live-updates/2020
/02/06/f45f94b4-48ce-11ea-bdbf-1dfb23249293_story.html.

17. Herbert Hoover, "The New Deal: Address delivered to Joint Republican Organizations," Pepperdine School of Public Policy, October 17, 1938, https://publicpolicy
.pepperdine.edu/academics/research/faculty-research/new-deal/hoover-speeches
/hh101738.htm.

18. Ibid.

19. Ibid.

20. William Galston, "Ethics and Character in the U.S. Presidency," *Presidential
Studies Quarterly*, 40, no. 1, Ethics and the Presidency (March 2010), 90–101,
https://www.jstor.org/stable/23044897.

21. Jonathan Elliot, ed., *The Debates in the Several States on the Adoption of the Federal Constitution, as Recommended by the General Convention at Philadelphia in
1787*, vol. 5, 2nd ed. (Buffalo, NY: William S. Hein & Co., 1996), 136. In this case
"want" means "lack" (that is, the people are not in want of virtue).

22. Madison, "The Federalist Papers: No. 51."

23. Bertrand Russell would also speak to the primacy of power: "The fundamental
concept in social science is Power, in the same sense in which Energy is the fundamental concept in physics." Bernard Bailyn, *The Ideological Origins of the
American Revolution* (Cambridge, MA: Belknap Press of Harvard University Press,
1967), 56.

24. "What turned power into a malignant force," writes Bailyn, "was . . . the nature of
man—a susceptibility to corruption and his lust for self-aggrandizement." Ibid., 59.

25. Congressional Record: Proceedings and Debates of the United States Congress,
vol. 107, part 15, (Washington: U.S. Government Printing Office, 1961), 19956. I
know some of you are expecting it, so here's the quote that came to mind as you
were reading this: "Power tends to corrupt and absolute power corrupts absolutely"
(Lord Acton). It has become so overused I couldn't bring myself to repeat it in the
text.

26. Bailyn, *Ideological Origins*, 60.

27. Hofstadter, *American Political Tradition*, 5.

28. John Adams referred to this mechanism that would balance society's conflicting interests as "A frame, a scheme, a system, a combination of powers for a certain end, namely—the good of the whole community."

29. William Howard Taft and Supreme Court of the United States, *U.S. Reports: Myers v. United States*, 272 *U.S.* 52, 1926, periodical, https://www.loc.gov/item /usrep272052/.

30. Stewart, *Summer of 1787*, 154.

31. Edward J. Larson and Michael P. Winship, *The Constitutional Convention: A Narrative History from the Notes of James Madison* (New York: Modern Library, 2005), 26.

32. Richard Beeman, *Plain, Honest Men: The Making of the American Constitution* (New York: Random House, 2009), 304.

33. Delegate James McHenry of Maryland, who started to keep brief notes on the proceedings, wrote about "desultory conversation on that part of the report respecting the mode of chusing the President." Ibid., 304.

34. Ray Raphael, *Mr. President* (New York: Vintage Books, 2013), 121. Delegate Hugh Williamson of North Carolina asked to lower the threshold of votes in Congress required to override a presidential veto. Requiring too many votes to override, he argued, "puts too much in the power of the President." Four weeks before, he had stood to argue for the opposite position. He wanted to raise the threshold for the number of votes needed to thwart a president. He worried at that time that Congress had too much power. He changed his mind because he believed that other choices made in the interim had put the balance of powers out of whack.

35. Even on the day of adoption, delegates adjusted the balance, lowering the population requirements for representation in the House. More members representing fewer people would mean the body was likely to more accurately reflect the public will. It was a matter on which George Washington had made one of his only contributions, saying the "smallness of the proportion of representatives was an insufficient security for the rights and interests of the people." "From George Washington to the President of Congress, 17 September 1787," Founders Online, National Archives, https://founders.archives.gov/documents/Washington/04-05-02-0306.

36. James Madison also explained in his Convention notes that Governor Morris had a rare quality of mind that explained why he was chosen to write the final draft of the Constitution: "It is but due to Mr. M to remark that to the brilliancy and fertility of his genius, he added what is too rare, a candid surrender of his opinions when the lights of discussion satisfied him that they had been too hastily formed, and a readiness to aid in making the best of measures in which he had been overruled." Gaillard Hunt, ed., *The Writings of James Madison*, vol. 11, *1819–1836* (New York: G. P. Putnam's Sons, 1910), 450.

37. Richard J. Ellis, *The Development of the American Presidency* (New York: Taylor & Francis, 2012).

38. "Madison Debates."

CHAPTER 12: JUST BE LIKE LBJ!

1. Lyndon B. Johnson, "Telephone conversation #133, sound recording, LBJ and DAVID MCDONALD, 11/29/1963, 1:29 PM," LBJ Presidential Library, https://www .discoverlbj.org/item/tel-00133.

2. Ted Gittiner and Allen Fisher, "LBJ Champions the Civil Rights Act of 1964, Part 2,"

National Archives, Summer 2004, https://www.archives.gov/publications/prologue/2004/summer/civil-rights-act-2.html.

3. Barack Obama, "Why don't YOU get a drink with Mitch McConnell?" C-SPAN, November 5, 2014, https://www.youtube.com/watch?v=HH_sXMpW4Os.

4. Edward S. Corwin, "Woodrow Wilson and the Presidency," *Virginia Law Review* 42, no. 6 (1956): 766, doi:10.2307/1070269.

5. The country didn't blame the Senate as an institution for this condition. Warren Harding succeeded Wilson. He was the first sitting senator ever to be elected to the presidency. Ibid.

6. Barack Obama, interview by Steve Kroft, "Transcript: Sen. Obama, Part 1," *60 Minutes*, CBS News, September 24, 2008, https://www.cbsnews.com/news/transcript-sen-obama-part-1/.

7. Russell Berman, "Hillary Clinton, Uniter?" *The Atlantic*, February 27, 2015, https://www.theatlantic.com/politics/archive/2015/02/hillary-clintons-warm-purple-space/386288/.

8. Mara Liasson, "After Touting Negotiating Skills, Trump Struggles To Make A Deal On Health Care," *All Things Considered*, NPR, July 6, 2017, https://www.npr.org/2017/07/06/535823089/after-touting-negotiating-skills-trump-struggles-to-make-a-deal-on-health-care.

9. Biden made this statement at a stump speech during the 2020 presidential campaign.

10. Rachel Maddow, "The limits of schmoozing," *The Rachel Maddow Show*, MSNBC News, August 7, 2013, http://www.msnbc.com/rachel-maddow-show/the-limits-schmoozing.

11. McConnell, *Long Game*, 209.

12. Interview with author.

13. Bailey also quotes Kennedy reflecting, "I used to wonder when I was a member of the House how President Truman got in so much trouble. Now I am beginning to get the idea. It is not difficult." Thomas A. Bailey, *Presidential Greatness: The Image and the Man from George Washington to the Present* (New York: Appleton-Century-Crofts), 1966, 239.

14. George E. Condon, Jr., "Howard Baker, the 'Eloquent Listener,'" *The Atlantic*, June 26, 2014, https://www.theatlantic.com/politics/archive/2014/06/howard-baker-the-eloquent-listener/442872/. This tradition continued after Johnson was out of office. As late as 1978, Republican Senate minority leader Howard Baker was willing to risk his own aspirations as a presidential candidate in 1980 to help Democratic president Jimmy Carter secure the 67 votes needed to give Panama control of the Panama Canal. At the time, conservative Republicans argued that keeping control of the canal was a crucial national security priority.

15. Gittiner and Fisher, "LBJ Champions."

16. Burgess Everett, "McConnell throws down the gauntlet: No Scalia replacement under Obama," Politico, February 13, 2016, https://www.politico.com/story/2016/02/mitch-mcconnell-antonin-scalia-supreme-court-nomination-219248.

17. "Nominations of Abe Fortas and Homer Thornberry," Committee on the Judiciary, United States Senate (Washington: U.S. Government Printing Office, 1965), 46, https://www.loc.gov/law/find/nominations/thornberry/hearing-pt1a.pdf.

18. George Clifford, "Can His Victory in the Fortas Case Make Sen. Robert Griffin a Power in Washington? Or Will He Be Just a One-Time Hero?" *Detroit Scope Magazine*, November 2, 1968.

19. Michael Bennet, interview by John Dickerson, "Colorado Sen. Michael Bennet on

Trump, McConnell and His New Book," *CBS This Morning*, CBS News, July 15, 2019, https://soundcloud.com/cbsthismorning/colorado-sen-michael-bennet-on trump-mcconnell-and-his-new-book.

20. Ibid.

21. Robert A. Caro, *The Passage of Power: The Years of Lyndon Johnson* (New York: Knopf Doubleday Publishing Group, 2012), 600.

22. Ibid.

23. Todd S. Purdum, *An Idea Whose Time Has Come: Two Presidents, Two Parties, and the Battle for the Civil Rights Act of 1964* (New York: Henry, Holt and Company, 2014), 277.

24. Robert Caro, interview by Steve Inskeep, "Caro's 'Passage Of Power': LBJ's Political Genius," NPR, April 30, 2012, https://www.npr.org/transcripts/151523678.

25. Caro, *Passage of Power*, 552.

26. Frum, "David Frum on Obama Lessons."

27. Chris Frates, "Payoffs for states get Reid to 60," Politico, December 19, 2009, https://www.politico.com/story/2009/12/payoffs-for-states-get-reid-to-60-030815.

28. Interview with author.

29. James Mattis, interview by John Dickerson, "Transcript: Defense Secretary James Mattis on 'Face the Nation,' May 28, 2017," *Face the Nation*, CBS News, https://www.cbsnews.com/news/transcript-defense-secretary-james-mattis-on-face-the-nation-may-28-2017/.

30. Doris Kearns Goodwin, *The Bully Pulpit: Theodore Roosevelt, William Howard Taft, and the Golden Age of Journalism* (New York: Simon & Schuster, 2013), 85.

31. Reagan, *American Life*, location 171.

32. Ronald Reagan, "Remarks at a Dinner Honoring Speaker of the House of Representatives Thomas P. O'Neill, Jr.," Ronald Reagan Presidential Library and Museum, March 17, 1986, https://www.reaganlibrary.gov/research/speeches/31786f.

CHAPTER 13: THE END DEPENDS ON THE BEGINNING

1. Goodwin, *Team of Rivals*, 175.

2. Ibid.

3. Donald T. Phillips, *Lincoln on Leadership* (New York: Business Plus, 1992), 31.

4. "First-year mayors find executive training comes at the right time," Medium, July 27, 2018, https://medium.com/@BloombergCities/first-year-mayors-find-executive-training-comes-at-the-right-time-c1042448de16.

5. This quote has been widely attributed to Roosevelt, but no known source for it exists.

6. Anu Narayanswamy, Darla Cameron, and Matea Gold, "Money Raised as of Dec. 31," *Washington Post*, February 1, 2017, https://www.washingtonpost.com/graphics/politics/2016-election/campaign-finance/.

7. Jim Collins, *Good to Great: Why Some Companies Make the Leap . . . And Others Don't* (New York: Harper Business, 2011).

8. Robert J. Chapman, *The Rules of Project Risk Management: Implementation Guidelines for Major Projects* (New York: Routledge, Taylor & Francis Group, 2016), 109.

9. Brent Schlender, "Exclusive: New Wisdom From Steve Jobs On Technology, Hollywood, And How 'Good Management Is Like The Beatles,'" *Fast Company*, April 17, 2012, https://www.fastcompany.com/1829788/exclusive-new-wisdom-steve-jobs-technology-hollywood-and-how-good-management-beatles.

10. Peter Drucker, *Managing the Non-Profit Organization: Principles and Practices* (New York: Harper Collins, 2010), 18.

11. Stanley McChrystal, "Why I threw out my painting of Robert E. Lee," *CBS This Morning*, CBS News, October 22, 2018, https://www.cbsnews.com/news/gen-stanley -mcchrystal-why-i-threw-out-my-painting-of-robert-e-lee/.

12. Interview with author.

13. Interview with author.

14. John Dickerson, "If I Were King . . ." Slate, November 30, 2011, https://slate.com /news-and-politics/2011/12/newt-gingrich-is-the-only-candidate-who-knows-how-he -would-govern-america.html.

15. Interview with author.

16. Bloomberg, "Transcript: Cotton, Feinstein, Bloomberg."

17. James A. Baker III, *Work Hard, Study . . . And Keep Out of Politics!* (New York: G. P. Putnam's Sons, 2006), 121.

18. Ibid.

19. Lou Cannon, *President Reagan: The Role of a Lifetime* (New York: PublicAffairs, 2000), 78.

20. Barack Obama, interview by John Dickerson, "Transcript: President Obama."

21. Ibid.

22. Interview with author.

23. Clinton, *My Life*, location 9513.

24. Interview with author.

25. Goodwin, *Team of Rivals*, 320.

26. Donald, *Lincoln*, location 5467.

27. Goodwin, *Team of Rivals*, 320.

28. Ibid., 318.

29. Ibid.

CHAPTER 14: LOST IN TRANSITION

1. Harry S. Truman, *Memoirs by Harry S. Truman, 1945: Year of Decisions* (New York: Smithmark, 1995), 10–11.

2. Haldeman, *Haldeman Diaries*, location 6985.

3. Adler, Mason, and Holland, "Being President Would Be Easier."

4. Kimberly Amadeo, "US Federal Budget Breakdown," The Balance, December 31, 2019, https://www.thebalance.com/u-s-federal-budget-breakdown-3305789.

5. "Romney Readiness Project General Instructions: First 200 Days," Romney Readiness Project documents, Center for Presidential Transitions, https://presidential transition.org/wp-content/uploads/sites/6/2016/01/0418b5bd131c3adae65bcbffea841 313-1453147324.pdf.

6. That expression appears to have come from a whimsical article in the *Evening Independent*. This bit of light fare concerned the activities of the wives of the possible presidential nominees. Referring to the wife of Ohio Republican senator Bob Taft, the son of the twenty-seventh president, the reporter writes, " 'Martha Taft is sure that 'Bob is going to get it.' She is ready to answer questions in regular stump style, though she refuses to say whether she will change the drawing room drapes in the White House." "U.S. Senator's Daughter Says," *Evening Independent*, February 19, 1940 https://news.google.com/newspapers?id=C8YLAAAAIBAJ&sjid= nFQDAAAAIBAJ&pg=3560,3163003&dq=drapes.

7. "In Their Own Words," *New York Times*, August 18, 1992, https://www.nytimes

.com/1992/08/18/news/in-their-own-words-excerpts-from-president-s-remarks-at -rally.html. Let's not be too hard on George H. W. Bush. Even Lincoln mangled his metaphors. Speaking of Stephen Douglas's policy on slavery: It "is as thin as the homeopathic soup that was made by boiling the shadow of a pigeon that had been starved to death." Donald, *Lincoln*, location 4681.

8. Interview with author.

9. Interview with author. Christie and his team met regularly with top Obama officials, as did Hillary Clinton's staff. Working for seven months out of a Washington, D.C., office, they devised a hundred-day plan detailing how to turn Donald Trump's greatest stadium rally hits into action items. They even consulted Justice Department lawyers to make sure executive orders Trump might want to issue in his first days in office could survive any legal challenges. They built teams to parachute into federal agencies quickly so that the Trump brand could be infused into the existing government workforce. Ten former U.S. attorneys worked in a special secure room, investigating lists of candidates for top posts in the cabinet and the White House. For each vital position, these lawyers with the special key cards identified prospects capable of clearing the vetting hurdles.

10. Interview with author.

11. Interview with author.

12. Jack Watson, "Oral History: Interview as Transition Director," UVA Miller Center, April 17–18, 1981, https://millercenter.org/the-presidency/presidential-oral-histories /jack-h-watson-jr-oral-history.

13. Whipple, *Gatekeepers*, location 1529.

14. Carl M. Brauer, *Presidential Transitions: Eisenhower Through Reagan* (New York: Oxford University Press, 1986), 64.

15. Theodore C. Sorensen, *Kennedy* (New York: Harper & Row, 1965), 229.

16. Interview with author.

17. Campbell, K., and Steinberg, *Difficult Transitions*, ix.

18. Interview with author.

19. Adam K. Raymond and Matt Stieb, "Trump Hired Them, Then He Called Them Incompetent," Intelligencer, February 13, 2020, https://nymag.com/intelligencer /2020/02/dumb-as-a-rock-9-times-trump-insulted-people-he-appointed.html.

20. Kathryn Dunn Tenpas, "Tracking Turnover in the Trump administration," Brookings Institution, February 2020, https://www.brookings.edu/research/tracking-turnover -in-the-trump-administration/.

21. Interview with author. Furthermore, White argues, by viewing the existing workforce as a liability, the administration misses the entrepreneurial opportunity to transform it for long after Trump is out of office. Ronald Reagan, by contrast, rebuilt the regulatory process in a fashion that every subsequent president carried forward.

22. Wesley Morgan, "Trump leaves Pentagon power vacuum," Politico, April 25, 2019, https://www.politico.com/story/2019/04/25/pentagon-acting-officials-1375772.

23. Joe Gould and Leo Shane III, "When will Trump nominate a permanent defense secretary?" Military Times, March 28, 2019, https://www.militarytimes.com/congress /2019/03/28/when-will-trump-nominate-a-permanent-defense-secretary/.

24. Ibid.

25. Interview with author. The problems mounted as the calendar pages turned. At one point in July 2019, the administration had an acting secretary of labor, an acting secretary of Homeland Security and no deputy secretary, an acting secretary of defense and no deputy secretary, an acting White House chief of staff, an acting

commissioner of Customs and Border Protection, an acting director of Immigration and Customs Enforcement, an acting director of the Citizenship and Immigration Services, an acting ambassador to the United Nations, an acting commissioner of the Food and Drug Administration, an acting director of the Office of Management and Budget, an acting secretary of the Army, an acting secretary of the Air Force, an acting undersecretary of Homeland Security for management, no undersecretary of Homeland Security for science and technology, no undersecretary of Homeland Security for strategy, policy, and plans, and an acting administrator of the Federal Emergency Management Agency.

CHAPTER 15: HARD AT THE START

1. John Fischer, "The Kennedy Era: Stage Two," *Harper's* magazine, February 14, 1962, https://archive.org/stream/harpersmagazine224janalde/harpersmagazine224janalde_djvu.txt.
2. Dallek, R., *Camelot's Court*, 3.
3. James P. Pfiffner, "White House Staff Versus the Cabinet: Centripetal and Centrifugal Roles," *Presidential Studies Quarterly* 16, no. 4 (1986): 666–90, www.jstor.org/stable/40574416.
4. Interview with author.
5. Interview with author.
6. Interview with author.
7. Stephen Miller, interview by John Dickerson, "Transcript: Schumer, Flake, Miller," *Face the Nation*, CBS News, February 12, 2017, https://www.cbsnews.com/news/face-the-nation-transcript-february-12-2017-schumer-flake-miller/. This was in the answer to a question about what they'd learned from this experience.
8. Interview with author.
9. Interview with author.
10. "I Am Part of the Resistance Inside the Trump Administration," *New York Times*, September 5, 2018, https://www.nytimes.com/2018/09/05/opinion/trump-white-house-anonymous-resistance.html.
11. Interview with author.
12. Interview with author.
13. David E. Sanger, *Confront and Conceal: Obama's Secret Wars and Surprising Use of American Power* (New York: Crown, 2012), Kindle, location 58.
14. Michael Lewis, *The Fifth Risk* (New York: W. W. Norton, 2018), 60.
15. Mona Sutphen, "Rethinking the American Presidency," moderated by Robert Bruner, UVA Miller Center, May 23, 2019, https://millercenter.org/prezfest2019/prezfest-videos/rethinking-american-presidency.
16. Interview with author.
17. Interview with author.
18. Haldeman, *Haldeman Diaries*, location 393.
19. Richard Tanner Johnson, *Managing the White House: An Intimate Study of the Presidency* (New York: Harper & Row, Publishers, 1974), xiii.
20. Philip Rucker and Robert Costa, "Bannon vows a daily fight for 'deconstruction of the administrative state,'" *Washington Post*, February 23, 2017, https://www.washingtonpost.com/politics/top-wh-strategist-vows-a-daily-fight-for-deconstruction-of-the-administrative-state/2017/02/23/03f6b8da-f9ea-11e6-bf01-d47f8cf9b643_story.html.

21. Stephen Hess, *Organizing the Presidency* (Washington, DC: Brookings Institution Press, 2002), 5.

22. Lewis, *Fifth Risk*, 47, 73.

23. Ryan McCrimmon, "'They literally take food off their table,'" Politico, February 3, 2020, https://www.politico.com/news/2020/02/03/trump-agriculture-department-cut-programs-109205.

24. Interview with author.

25. Interview with author.

26. Dave Weigel (@daveweigel), "A semantic battle . . ." Twitter, October 16, 2019, 10:04 A.M., https://twitter.com/daveweigel/status/1184515451780583424. I have put this term in quotation marks because, as *The Washington Post*'s David Weigel has pointed out, this expression is inaccurate. A person who changes position flips, or flops. If they "flip-flop," they change a position and then change back to the original one.

27. Tim Harford, *Adapt: Why Success Always Starts with Failure* (New York: Farrar, Strauss and Giroux, 2011), 20.

28. David Brownstein, "Public Service Leadership Model: Quick links resource guide," Partnership for Public Service, August 9, 2019, https://ourpublicservice.org/public-service-leadership-model-quick-links-resource-guide/.

29. Max Stier, "My Turn: Government HR crisis is brewing," *Providence Journal*, June 16, 2018, https://www.providencejournal.com/opinion/20180616/my-turn-max-stier-government-hr-crisis-is-brewing.

30. Interview with author. This is based on a calculation taken from the first page of James Q. Wilson's *Bureaucracy: What Government Agencies Do and Why They Do It*, and adding the Bush effort and the Obama effort. It does not include Trump, but it could.

31. Scott McDowell, "The First 90 Days: Your Road Map For Success at a New Job," 99U, March 11, 2013, https://99u.adobe.com/articles/7303/the-first-90-days-your-road-map-for-success-at-a-new-job.

32. Congress had started the ball rolling in the previous century. In 1887 the Cockrell Committee was called to investigate the executive, and in 1893 the Dockery-Cockrell Commission did the same thing. There has never been a Senator Hickory, which has spared us the Hickory-Dockery-Cockrell Inquiry.

33. Roosevelt had seized the day. After years of thwarting presidents, in February 1903, Congress cracked open the door to executive reorganization when it created the Department of Commerce and Labor and gave the president authority to "transfer any unit engaged in statistical or scientific work, together with their duties and authority" (Stat. 827).

    Richard D. White, "Executive Reorganization, Theodore Roosevelt and the Keep Commission," *Administrative Theory & Praxis* 24, no. 3 (2002): 507–18, www.jstor.org/stable/25611596. For the first time, Congress delegated to the president the authority to reorganize (at least in this new department) as he saw fit. For Roosevelt, this small delegation of authority was all he needed to embark upon a much more ambitious reorganization effort.

34. Charles Rappleye, *Herbert Hoover in the White House: The Ordeal of the Presidency* (New York: Simon & Schuster, 2016), 11.

35. James Q. Wilson, *Bureaucracy: What Government Agencies Do and Why They Do It* (New York: Basic Books, 1989).

36. Jonathan D. Breul, "Three Bush Administration Management Reform Initiatives:

The President's Management Agenda, Freedom to Manage Legislative Proposals, and the Program Assessment Rating Tool," *Public Administration Review* 67, no. 1 (2007): 21–26, www.jstor.org/stable/4624536.

37. Maya Shankar, "Using Behavioral Science Insights to Make Government More Effective, Simpler, and More People-Friendly," The White House Press Office, February 9, 2015, https://obamawhitehouse.archives.gov/blog/2015/02/09/behavioral -science-insights-make-government-more-effective-simpler-and-more-user-fri.

38. Jon Michaels, "How Trump is dismantling a pillar of the American state," *The Guardian*, November 7, 2017, https://www.theguardian.com/commentisfree/2017 /nov/07/donald-trump-dismantling-american-administrative-state.

39. Neil MacNeil and Harold William Metz, *The Hoover Report, 1953–1955: What It Means to You as a Citizen and Taxpayer* (New York: MacMillan, 1956), 9.

40. Interview with author.

41. Theodore Roosevelt, *An Autobiography* (New York: Charles Scribner's Sons, 1921), 368.

CHAPTER 16: HOW A PRESIDENT DECIDES

1. "Colin Powell Provides An Inside Perspective on President Reagan and Trust." The Hudson Union Society, December 25, 2012, https://www.youtube.com/watch ?v=rgZ4x6D3GRs.

2. Walter R. Borneman, *Polk: The Man Who Transformed the Presidency and America* (New York: Random House, 2009), 319.

3. Calvin Coolidge, *The Autobiography of Calvin Coolidge* (Walking Through The Word Publishers, 2014), Kindle, location 1646.

4. Daniel Ginsburg, "Ty Cobb," Society for American Baseball Research, https://sabr .org/bioproj/person/7551754a. Ty Cobb's lifetime batting average was .366.

5. Actual baseball games are so languidly paced that there is a built-in pause for the seventh inning stretch. Baseball is the only professional sport in which spectators must engage in calisthenics to keep their blood moving.

6. Yair Rosenberg, "Why 'The West Wing' Is a Terrible Guide to American Democracy," *The Atlantic*, October 1, 2012, https://www.theatlantic.com/politics/archive /2012/10/why-the-west-wing-is-a-terrible-guide-to-american-democracy/263084/.

7. Coolidge, *Autobiography*, location 1645.

8. Sorensen, *Decision-Making*, xxix.

9. Michael Lewis, "Obama's Way," *Vanity Fair*, September 11, 2012, https://www .vanityfair.com/news/2012/10/michael-lewis-profile-barack-obama.

10. Jon Meacham, *Thomas Jefferson: The Art of Power* (New York: Random House, 2012), Kindle, locations 8641–2.

11. Laura Smith-Spark, "With more than 191,000 dead in Syria, U.N. rights chief slams global 'paralysis,'" CNN.com, August 22, 2014, https://www.cnn.com/2014 /08/22/world/meast/syria-conflict/index.html. 191,369 men, women and children were reported killed in Syria between March 2011 and the end of April 2014.

12. Adrian Edwards, "Needs Soar as Number of Syrian Refugees Tops 3 Million," UN Refugee Agency, August 29, 2014, https://www.unhcr.org/53ff76c99.html. As of August 2014, the UN refugee agency reported that Syria's intensifying refugee crisis had passed a record three million people, amid reports of horrifying conditions inside the country. These included cities where populations were surrounded, people were going hungry, and civilians were being indiscriminately killed.

Shane Bauer, "Part One of Two: Behind the Lines," *Mother Jones*, May/June

2019, https://www.motherjones.com/politics/2019/06/behind-the-lines-syria-part-one/. As of June 2019, at least half a million people had been killed in the Syrian war. The exact number is unknown. Twelve million Syrians — more than half the country's prewar population — have been displaced, including 5.6 million refugees.

13. Interview with author.

14. Robert Rubin, interview by Chris Bury, "Clinton Years Interview," *Frontline*, PBS, July 2000, https://www.pbs.org/wgbh/pages/frontline/shows/clinton/interviews/rubin .html.

15. Leon Panetta, interview by Chris Bury, "Interview: Leon Panetta," *Frontline*, PBS, June 2000, https://www.pbs.org/wgbh/pages/frontline/shows/clinton/interviews /panetta.html.

16. Edith Efron, "Can the President Think?" *Reason*, November 1994, https://reason .com/1994/11/01/can-the-president-think/.

17. Interview with author.

18. Richard Neustadt, *Presidential Power and the Modern Presidents* (New York: Free Press, 1990), 209.

19. Whipple, *Gatekeepers*.

20. Ernest Holsendolph, "Adams Angrily Quits Transportation Job," *New York Times*, July 21, 1979, https://www.nytimes.com/1979/07/21/archives/adams-angrily-quits -transportation-job-he-says-president-ordered.html.

21. Nikki Haley, *With All Due Respect: Defending America with Grit and Grace* (New York: St. Martin's Publishing Group, 2019), 184. In this story the U.N. ambassador explains she was anxious to tell the president his joint press conference with Vladimir Putin had not gone well.

22. Alexi McCammond and Jonathan Swan, "Scoop: Insider leaks Trump's 'Executive Time'-filled private schedules," Axios, February 3, 2019, https://www.axios.com /donald-trump-private-schedules-leak-executive-time-34e67fbb-3af6-48df-aefb -52e02c334255.html.

23. Michael E. Porter and Nitin Nohria, "The Leader's Calendar: How CEOs Manage Time," *Harvard Business Review*, July/August 2018, https://hbr.org/2018/07/the -leaders-calendar.

24. Interview with author.

25. Robert J. Donovan, "The Nixon Team: Decision-Making Will Be Different," *Los Angeles Times*, November 8, 1968.

26. Haldeman, *Haldeman Diaries*, location 422.

27. Whipple, *Gatekeepers*, location 23.

28. Interview with author.

29. Whipple, *Gatekeepers*, location 23.

30. Interview with author.

31. William Safire, *Before the Fall: An Inside View of the Pre-Watergate White House* (New Brunswick, NJ: Transaction Publishers), 2005, 17.

32. Interview with author.

33. Anthony J. Bennett, *The American President's Cabinet: From Kennedy to Bush* (London: Macmillan Publishers, 1996), 219.

34. George Stephanopoulos, *All Too Human* (New York: Little, Brown, 1999), 285.

35. Sandy Fitzgerald, "James Baker: Trump's White House Needs Strong Chief of Staff," Newsmax, June 1, 2017, https://www.newsmax.com/politics/james-baker -trump-white-house-strong/2017/06/01/id/793612/.

36. Robert Gates, interview by John Dickerson, "Extended Interview," *Face the Nation*, CBS News, May 14, 2017, https://www.youtube.com/watch?v=9gHDmXYNJoc.

37. Donald J. Trump, interview by John Dickerson, "President Trump's interview in the Oval Office: Full Transcript," *CBS This Morning*, CBS News, May 1, 2017, https://www.cbsnews.com/news/president-trump-oval-office-interview-cbs-this-morning-full-transcript/.

38. Andrew Ross Sorkin, "Warren Buffett, Delegator in Chief," *New York Times*, April 23, 2011, https://www.nytimes.com/2011/04/24/weekinreview/24buffett.html.

39. Whipple, *Gatekeepers*, location 106.

40. Bloomberg, "Transcript: Cotton, Feinstein, Bloomberg."

41. Interview with author.

42. James Fallows, "The Passionless Presidency," *The Atlantic*, May 1979, https://www.theatlantic.com/magazine/archive/1979/05/the-passionless-presidency/308516/.

43. David S. Broder and Ward Sinclair, "A Political Skylab Hits the Capital," *Washington Post*, July 20, 1979, https://www.washingtonpost.com/archive/politics/1979/07/20/a-political-skylab-hits-the-capital/2ed94fb9-fe0d-4a3c-872e-5a0eda93f5a1/.

44. Ibid.

45. Carla Hall, "Firing One-Liners," *Washington Post*, July 21, 1979, https://www.washingtonpost.com/archive/lifestyle/1979/07/21/firing-one-liners/bde0758f-d86c-4dd5-bbbf-a5b2516f5e05/.

46. "Proclamations about 'cabinet government' are a reaction by recent presidents to make it seem as if they are running a participatory form of government," said Jack Knebel, Ford's Agriculture Secretary. "But you've got to remember that you just can't have that in our system. We elect one man to make the decisions." A. Bennett, *American President's Cabinet*, 218.

47. Interview with author.

CHAPTER 17: IMPULSE PRESIDENCY

1. "Papers of Harry S. Truman Staff Member and Office Files: National Security Council File," Harry S. Truman Library and Museum, https://www.trumanlibrary.gov/library/truman-papers/papers-harry-s-truman-staff-member-and-office-files-national-security-council.

2. McCullough, *Truman*, location 17612.

3. The Youngstown Sheet and Tube Company, et al., Republic Steel Corporation, Armco Steel Corporation, et al., Bethlehem Steel Company, et al., Jones & Laughlin Steel Corporation, United States Steel Company, and E.J. Lavino & Company v. Sawyer, 744, 579–768 (1951).

4. Donald J. Trump (@realDonaldTrump), "As a very active President with lots of things happening, it is not possible for my surrogates to stand at podium with perfect accuracy!. . . ." Twitter, May 12, 2017, 4:59 A.M., https://twitter.com/realDonaldTrump/status/863000553265270786.

5. Dennis Romero, "John Kelly says he told Trump a 'yes man' would get him impeached," NBC News, October 26, 2019, https://www.nbcnews.com/politics/donald-trump/john-kelly-says-he-told-trump-yes-man-would-get-n1072491.

6. McCullough, *Truman*, location 9689. A special thanks to Tammy Williams at the Truman Presidential Library and Museum for providing us with copies of Truman's handwritten draft of the speech he didn't give.

7. David McCullough, *Kissinger: A Biography* (New York: Simon & Schuster, 2005), 492.

8. Interview with author.

9. Mary O'Toole, "Must Reads: John F. Kelly Says His Tenure as Trump's Chief of

Staff Is Best Measured by What the President Did Not Do," *Los Angeles Times*, December 30, 2018, https://www.latimes.com/politics/la-na-pol-john-kelly-exit interview 20181230 story.html.

10. Paul Ryan, interview by Michael Barbaro, "Paul Ryan's Exit Interview," *The Daily*, *New York Times*, August 8, 2018, https://www.nytimes.com/2018/08/08/podcasts/the -daily/paul-ryan-house-speaker-trump.html.

11. Nikki Haley, interview by Norah O'Donnell, "I Was Asked by Cabinet Members to Take Sides Against the President," *CBS Sunday Morning*, CBS News, November 11, 2019, https://www.cbsnews.com/news/nikki-haley-was-asked-by-cabinet -members-john-kelly-and-rex-tillerson-to-take-sides-against-president-trump/.

12. Manchester, *Glory and the Dream*, 562.

13. Geoffrey Skelley, "Just How Many Obama 2012-Trump 2016 Voters Were There?" UVA: Center for Politics, June 1, 2017, http://centerforpolitics.org/crystalball /articles/just-how-many-obama-2012-trump-2016-voters-were-there/.

14. Kevin Uhrmacher, Kevin Schaul, and Dan Keating, "These former Obama strongholds sealed the election for Trump," *Washington Post*, November 9, 2016, https://www.washingtonpost.com/graphics/politics/2016-election/obama-trump -counties/?tid=lk_inline_manual_11.

15. David Klion, "The Blob," *The Nation*, October 17, 2018, https://www.thenation .com/article/archive/ben-rhodes-and-the-crisis-of-liberal-foreign-policy/.

16. Gates, "Extended Interview."

17. Tom Porter, "8 days after his acquittal, Trump openly admitted sending Giuliani to hunt for dirt on Joe Biden — reversing a key part of his impeachment defense," Business Insider, February 14, 2020, https://www.businessinsider.com/trump-admits -giuliani-ukraine-reversing-impeachment-defense-2020-2.

18. Eric Schmidt and Maggie Haberman, "Trump Ordered Mueller Fired, but Backed Off When White House Counsel Threatened to Quit," *New York Times*, January 25, 2018, https://www.nytimes.com/2018/01/25/us/politics/trump-mueller-special -counsel-russia.html.

19. "Rex Tillerson reflects on firing, working for 'undisciplined' Trump," *CBS News*, December 7, 2018, https://www.cbsnews.com/news/rex-tillerson-bob-schieffer-inter view-houston-firing-trump-tweet-tillerson-insult-2018-12-07/.

20. Interview with author.

21. Interview with author.

22. Whitlock, "The Afghanistan Papers."

23. David Halberstam, *The Best and the Brightest* (New York: Fawcett Books, 1992).

24. Arthur M. Schlesinger, Jr., "How the State Department Baffled Him," from "Part III: From J.F.K.'s Inner Circle, 'A Thousand Days,'" *Life*, vol. 59, no. 5, July 30, 1965.

25. Interview with author.

26. Carol D. and Philip Rucker, *A Very Stable Genius: Donald J. Trump's Testing of America* (New York, Penguin Press, 2020).

27. Alan Feuer, "For Donald Trump, Friends in Few Places," *New York Times*, March 11, 2016, https://www.nytimes.com/2016/03/13/nyregion/for-donald-trump -friends-in-few-places.html. LeFrak first told this to *New York Times* then explained it to me in an interview I did with him in January 2017.

28. Interview with author.

29. Interview with author.

30. Interview with author.

31. Seung Min Kim, "Rubio says Congress can't get answers on Trump immigration

order," Politico, January 30, 2017, https://www.politico.com/story/2017/01/senate
-rubio-trump-immigration-234406.

32. Interview with author.

33. Donald J. Trump (@realDonaldTrump), "After historic victories against ISIS, it's
time to bring our great young people home!" Twitter, December 19, 2018, 3:10 P.M.,
https://twitter.com/realDonaldTrump/status/1075528854402256896.

34. Shannon Van Sant, "U.S. Envoy To The Coalition Against ISIS Resigns Over
Trump's Syria Policy," NPR, December 22, 2018, https://www.npr.org/2018/12/22
/679535003/u-s-envoy-to-the-coalition-against-isis-resigns-over-trumps-syria-policy.

35. Joseph Hincks, "ISIS Is Still Active in Iraq, Syria and Beyond. This Is What the
Threat Looks Like Now," Time, January 18, 2019, https://time.com/5506007/trump
-isis-victory-islamic-state/.

36. Jeffrey Goldberg, "The Man Who Couldn't Take It Anymore." The Atlantic, October 2019, https://www.theatlantic.com/magazine/archive/2019/10/james-mattis
-trump/596665/.

37. Interview with author.

38. Michael Crowley and Carlotta Gall, "In Trump, Turkey's Erdogan Keeps Finding
a Sympathetic Ear," New York Times, October 8, 2019, https://www.nytimes.com
/2019/10/08/us/politics/trump-erdogan-turkey-visit.html.

39. "Press Conference by President Trump," Office of the Press Secretary, September 27, 2018, https://www.whitehouse.gov/briefings-statements/press-conference
-president-trump-2/.

40. "Turkey will soon be moving forward with its long-planned operation into Northern Syria," the White House said in a statement released just before 11 P.M. in
Washington. "The United States Armed Forces will not support or be involved
in the operation, and United States forces, having defeated the ISIS territorial
'Caliphate,' will no longer be in the immediate area." "Statement from the Press
Secretary," White House, October 6, 2019, https://www.whitehouse.gov/briefings
-statements/statement-press-secretary-85/.

41. Lindsey Graham (@LindseyGrahamSC., "By abandoning . . ." Twitter, October 7,
2019, 6:50 A.M., https://twitter.com/LindseyGrahamSC/status/1181205092554493952.

42. U.S. Congress, "Operation Inherent Resolve," Lead Inspector General Report,
July 1, 2019, https://www.politico.com/f/?id=0000016e-8474-d93d-ad6f-8e76571c0000
&nname=playbook-pm&nid=0000015a-dd3e-d536-a37b-dd7fd8af0000&nrid=
0000014e-f116-dd93-ad7f-f91725480002&nlid=964328.

43. The president has bristled over alliances. He is skeptical of their long-term benefit; obligations to alliances either irritate him because they block what he wants
to do quickly, or they require maintenance duties he thinks aren't worth the
payoff. Trump has repeatedly disparaged and minimized American allies for no
discernible reason. Asked to identify America's greatest foe, he named the European Union, easily America's greatest ally. (Donald J. Trump, interviewed by Jeff
Glor, "'I think the European Union is a foe,' Trump says ahead of Putin meeting
in Helsinki," CBS News, July 15, 2018, https://www.cbsnews.com/news/donald
-trump-interview-cbs-news-european-union-is-a-foe-ahead-of-putin-meeting-in
-helsinki-jeff-glor/.) His obsession over NATO member countries paying their
dues overshadowed the security agenda for the alliance. It was the source of regular tension with former Defense Secretary James Mattis, who consistently made
the case that alliances are necessary to bolster the United States in the event of
unforeseen threats in the future. President Trump's positions have often aligned

with Russian goals, which, according to his own security officials, included undermining the very alliances in Europe that Trump was helping to weaken. The president's improvisations in the moment also put U.S. adversary Russia on the same moral plane, a significant shift in U.S. policy seemingly made for momentary reasons. In February 2017, when Fox News host Bill O'Reilly said Vladimir Putin was a killer, Trump retorted, "You think our country is so innocent?" "PREVIEW: Trump Tells O'Reilly He 'Respects' Putin in Super Bowl Interview," Fox News, February 4, 2017, https://insider.foxnews.com/2017/02/04/preview-bill -oreilly-donald-trump-super-bowl-interview.

At a press conference in Helsinki, Finland, in July 2018, when asked whether he held Russia accountable for the state of relations between the two countries after Russia disrupted the 2016 election, the president said, "I hold both countries responsible. I think that the United States has been foolish." Donald J. Trump, "Remarks by President Trump and President Putin of the Russian Federation in Joint Press Conference," Office of the Press Secretary, July 16, 2018, https://www .whitehouse.gov/briefings-statements/remarks-president-trump-president-putin -russian-federation-joint-press-conference/.

A year later, *The Washington Post* reported that Trump had told Theresa May he didn't think the Russians poisoned a UK citizen, Sergei Skripal, as UK intelligence agencies had claimed. The Russian government used President Trump's statement against the United Kingdom: "Best evidence that no evidence of Russian involvement exists," wrote the Russian embassy on its Twitter feed. Russian Embassy, UK (@RussianEmbassy), "Best evidence that no evidence of Russian involvement exists," Twitter, October 6, 2019, 8:31 A.M., https://twitter.com/RussianEmbassy /status/1180868111056195585.

44. Michael Crowley, "Trump Visits Afghanistan and Says He Reopened Talks With Taliban," *New York Times*, November 28, 2019, https://www.nytimes.com/2019/11 /28/us/politics/trump-afghanistan.html.

45. Donald J. Trump (@realDonaldTrump), ". . . . My only question is, who is our bigger enemy, Jay Powell or Chairman Xi?" Twitter, August 23, 2019, 7:57 A.M., https://twitter.com/realDonaldTrump/status/1164914610836783104.

46. Donald J. Trump (@realDonaldTrump), ". . . . The USA should always be paying the the lowest rate . . ." Twitter, September 11, 2019, 3:42 A.M., https://twitter.com /realDonaldTrump/status/1171735692428419072.

47. Francesco Bianchi, Howard Kung, and Thilo Kind, "Threats to Central Bank Independence: High-Frequency Identification with Twitter," National Bureau of Economic Research, Working Paper No. 26308 (September 2019), https://www .nber.org/papers/w26308.

48. Aaron Blake, "Trump's extraordinary Oval Office squabble with Chuck Schumer and Nancy Pelosi, annotated," *Washington Post*, December 11, 2018, https://www .washingtonpost.com/politics/2018/12/11/trumps-extraordinary-oval-office-squabble -with-chuck-schumer-nancy-pelosi-annotated/.

49. "The Effects of the Partial Shutdown," Congressional Budget Office, January 2019, https://www.cbo.gov/system/files?file=2019-01/54937-PartialShutdownEffects.pdf.

50. Dareh Gregorian, "Back Pay for Federal Contractors Missing from Government Funding Bill," NBC News, February 15, 2019, https://www.nbcnews.com/politics /politics-news/back-pay-federal-contractors-missing-government-funding-bill -n971886. The exact number of contract workers affected is unclear. It's been estimated that 1.2 million people—from highly paid engineers working with NASA to

low-paid cafeteria workers—were affected, though some were able to work at other jobs. Among those who weren't paid during the longest shutdown in U.S. history and now aren't getting back pay are two thousand workers for SourceAmerica, which places employees with a wide range of disabilities through a nationwide nonprofit network.

51. Leon Neyfakh, "Rod Rosenstein Is a Cautionary Tale," Slate, May 11, 2017, https:// slate.com/news-and-politics/2017/05/rod-rosenstein-is-a-cautionary-tale.html.

52. Ashley Parker, "McMaster: Trump's sharing of sensitive intelligence with Russia was 'wholly appropriate,'" Washington Post, May 16, 2017, https://www.washingtonpost .com/news/post-politics/wp/2017/05/16/trump-acknowledges-facts-shared-with -russian-envoys-during-white-house-meeting/.

53. Robert Mackey, "Justice Department Says 2020 Census Fight Might Not Be Over, Following President's Tweet," The Intercept, July 3, 2019, https://theintercept.com /2019/07/03/justice-department-says-2020-census-fight-might-not-following -presidents-tweet/.

54. Maggie Haberman and Michael S. Schmidt, "Trump Tied Ukraine Aid to Inqui-ries He Sought, Bolton Book Says," New York Times, January 28, 2020, https://www .nytimes.com/2020/01/26/us/politics/trump-bolton-book-ukraine.html.

55. Bennett, A., American President's Cabinet, 215.

56. Whipple, Gatekeepers.

57. Stuart E. Eizenstat, President Carter: The White House Years (New York: St. Mar-tin's Press, 2018), Kindle, locations 1518–23.

58. "The Carter presidency fell outside the Democratic mold," writes the political scientist James Sterling. Erwin C. Hargrove, Jimmy Carter as President (Baton Rouge: Louisiana State University Press, 1988), xvi.

59. Curtis Wilkie, Boston Sunday Globe, January 1, 1978, A4.

60. "All right, Peter, just listen. Everything is going to be fine. You're very high right now. You will probably be that way for five more hours. Try taking some Vita-min B complex, Vitamin C complex . . . if you have beer, go ahead and drink it. . . . Just remember you're a living organism on this planet, and you're very safe. You've just taken a heavy drug. Relax, stay inside, and listen to some music. Do you have any Allman Brothers?" Doug Hill and Jeff Weingrad, Saturday Night: A Backstage History of "Saturday Night Live" (San Francisco: Untreed Reads, 1986).

61. Eizenstat, President Carter, location 13790.

62. Whipple, Gatekeepers.

63. Jimmy Carter, White House Diary: Jimmy Carter (New York: Farrar, Straus and Giroux, 2010), 118.

64. Adam Clymer, "A 'New' Hamilton Jordan Faces Challenge to President's Future," New York Times, July 23, 1979.

65. Jonathan Swan and Alayna Treene, "Scoop: Former White House counsel Don McGahn off the record," Axios, April 7, 2019, https://www.axios.com/white-house -counsel-don-mcgahn-trump-mueller-republican-lunch-7b687a07-4acf-4578-ac32 -f0c421c74070.html.

66. David Nakamura, "In Japan, Trump calls Jimmy Carter a 'terrible president' and says Kamala Harris got 'too much credit' in debate," Washington Post, June 29, 2019, https://www.washingtonpost.com/politics/in-japan-trump-calls-jimmy-carter -a-terrible-president-and-says-kamala-d-harris-got-too-much-credit-in-debate/2019 /06/29/27969022-9a46-11e9-830a-21b9b36b64ad_story.html.

67. Interview with author.

68. Interview with author.

CHAPTER 18: THE EXPECTATION

1. Inauguration Day moved to January 20 beginning in 1937, following ratification of the Twentieth Amendment to the Constitution, where it has remained since.
2. "Wilson, In Friendly Chat, Says He Likes Reporters," *Washington Post*, March 16, 1913.
3. "Wilson Wins Newspaper Men; Amazed to Have 125 Call, He Makes a Hit by His Frank Talk," *New York Times*, March 16, 1913.
4. Barber, *Presidential Character*, 49.
5. Brinkley, ed., *Reagan Diaries*, 2.
6. Bill Clinton, "Excerpts from Transcribed Remarks by the President and the Vice President to the People of Knoxville on Internet for Schools," Office of the Press Secretary, October 10, 1996, https://govinfo.library.unt.edu/npr/library/speeches /101096.html.
7. Interview with author.
8. This photo was taken by White House photographer George Tames on February 10, 1961. Tames remembers: "President Kennedy's back was broken during the war, when that torpedo boat of his was hit by the Japanese destroyer. As a result of that injury he wore a brace on his back most of his life. Quite a few people didn't realize that. Also he could never sit for any length of time, more than thirty or forty minutes in a chair without having to get up and walk around. Particularly when it felt bad he had a habit, in the House, and the Senate, and into the Presidency, of carrying his weight on his shoulders, literally, by leaning over a desk, putting down his palms out flat, and leaning over and carrying the weight of his upper body by his shoulder muscles, and sort of stretching or easing his back. He would read and work that way, which was something I had seen him do many times. When I saw him doing that, I walked in, stood by his rocking chair, and then I looked down and framed him between the two windows, and I shot that picture." Alex Selwyn-Holmes, "The Loneliest Job," Iconic Photos, July 18, 2010, https://iconicphotos .wordpress.com/2010/07/18/the-loneliest-job/.
9. "Truman Library Discovers 1947 Truman Diary," National Archives, July 10, 2003, https://www.archives.gov/press/press-releases/2003/nr03-54.html.
10. Ibid.
11. Michael Tackett, "Some Presidents Felt Trapped in the White House Bubble. Trump Thrives in It," *New York Times*, March 27, 2019, https://www.nytimes.com /2019/03/27/us/politics/trump-white-house-travel.html.
12. Interview with author.
13. Interview with author.
14. Bailey, *Presidential Greatness*, 130.
15. "In the Interpreter's House," *American Magazine*, vol. 66, Phillips Publishing Co., 1908, 519.
16. Interview with author.
17. Reeves, *President Reagan*, xiv.
18. Troy, T., "Don't Worry."
19. Interview with author.
20. Barber, *Presidential Character*, 5.
21. Lou Cannon and Lee Lescaze, "The Relaxed Approach," *Washington Post*, February 9, 1981, https://www.washingtonpost.com/archive/politics/1981/02/09/the-relaxed -approach/0b09571d-0f29-43b1-a813-e7395d53667b/.
22. Interview with author.

23. Martha Washington: Although she maintained her calm, cheerful, and dignified demeanor, she felt she was (as she told her niece) "more like a state prisoner than anything else." J. Ellis, *His Excellency: George Washington*, location 191.

24. "From Thomas Jefferson to John Dickinson, 13 January 1807," Founders Online, National Archives, https://founders.archives.gov/documents/Jefferson/99-01-02-4861.

25. Edward Connery Lanthem, *Your Son, Calvin Coolidge: A Selection of Letters from Calvin Coolidge to His Father* (Montpelier: Vermont Historical Society, 1968), 219.

26. My mother told me that he called her in such a condition when she covered his White House for NBC.

27. Matthew Algeo, *The President Is a Sick Man* (Chicago Review Press, 2011).

28. Robert Dallek explains: "Given the closeness of the final tally and the problems Kennedy had convincing voters that his Catholicism and youth or inexperience should not be a bar to his election, adding a discussion of his medical history would probably have put his victory out of reach." Dallek, R., *Camelot's Court*, 79.

29. "Trust in government: 1958–2015," Pew Research Center, November 23, 2015, https://www.people-press.org/2015/11/23/1-trust-in-government-1958-2015/.

30. "Coolidge Taken Ill, Recovers Quickly; Combination of Heat and Cantaloupe Causes a Brief Attack of Indigestion," *New York Times*, May 24, 1925, https://timesmachine.nytimes.com/timesmachine/1925/05/24/107059288.html?pageNumber=1.

31. "Bush Asks Condi For A Bathroom Break . . ." HuffPost, March 3, 2008, https://www.huffpost.com/entry/bush-asks-condi-for-a-bat_n_7399.

32. Interview with author.

33. Interview with author.

34. John Dickerson, "John's Notebook: Stay Generous," *Face the Nation*, CBS News, July 30, 2017, https://www.cbsnews.com/news/johns-notebook-stay-generous/.

35. J. K. Rowling (@jk_rowling), "Trump imitated . . ." Twitter, July 28, 2017, 11:08 A.M., https://web.archive.org/web/20170731141929/https:/twitter.com/jk_rowling/status/890997400290111489.

36. Interview with author.

37. Anthony Salvanto, Jennifer De Pinto, Kabir Khanna, and Fred Backus, "Americans wary of Trump tariffs' impact, but support plan to aid farmers — CBS poll," CBS, July 29, 2018, https://www.cbsnews.com/news/americans-wary-of-trump-tariffs-impact-but-support-plan-to-aid-farmers-cbs-poll/?utm_source=newsletter&utm_medium=email&utm_campaign=sendto_newslettertest&stream=top.

38. Bandy X. Lee, ed., *The Dangerous Case of Donald Trump* (New York: St. Martin's Press, 2017).

39. George T. Conway III, "Unfit for Office," *The Atlantic*, October 3, 2019, https://www.theatlantic.com/ideas/archive/2019/10/george-conway-trump-unfit-office/599128/.

40. Bethania Palma, "Did Trump Tweet a Picture of Himself as Rocky Balboa?" Snopes.com, November 29, 2019, https://www.snopes.com/fact-check/trump-rocky-tweet/.

41. Barber, *Presidential Character*.

42. Ibid., 48.

43. Wilson stroke; Harding heart attack; FDR heart attack; Eisenhower heart attack.

44. Walter Lippmann, "Worry Is Main Burden For President," *The Tuscaloosa News*, December 28, 1955.

45. McCullough, *Truman*, location 21898.

46. Interview with author.

47. Justin Caruso, " 'It's Devastating' — Trump Describes Writing Letters To Families

Of Killed Soldiers In Emotional Speech," *Daily Caller*, October 7, 2019. https://dailycaller.com/2019/10/07/trump-veterans-speech-devastating/.

48. Interview with author.

49. Interview with author.

50. Lady Bird Johnson, diary entry of September 11, 1965, *A White House Diary* (Austin: University of Texas Press, 1970), 320.

51. Libby Nelson, "A heartbreaking account of Obama comforting the grieving families after Sandy Hook," Vox.com, December 14, 2015, https://www.vox.com/2015/12/14/10106188/sandy-hook-victims-obama.

52. Alter, *Defining Moment*, 157.

53. Leuchtenburg, *FDR Years*, 2.

54. Dallek, R., *Franklin D. Roosevelt*, 15.

55. Blanche Wiesen Cook, *Eleanor Roosevelt*, vol. 3, *The War Years and After* (New York: Penguin Random House, 2016), 421.

56. Geoffrey C. Ward, *A First-Class Temperament: The Emergence of Franklin Roosevelt* (New York: Vintage Books, 1989), xvi.

57. Donald, *Lincoln*, location 159.

58. Hofstadter, *American Political Tradition*, 392.

59. Hamilton, "The Federalist Papers, No. 70."

60. Henry Raymont, "Johnson's Memoirs Due in November," *New York Times*, May 14, 1971.

61. Nic Robertson, Paul Cruickshank, and Tim Lister, "Document shows origins of 2006 plot for liquid bombs on planes," CNN.com, April 30, 2012, https://www.cnn.com/2012/04/30/world/al-qaeda-documents/index.html.

62. Interview with author.

63. Ronald Reagan, *Book 1: January 1 to June 28, 1985* (United States Government Printing Office, 1988), 179.

64. Dallek, R., *Franklin D. Roosevelt*, 221.

65. Ibid.

66. Lasby, *Eisenhower's Heart Attack*, 53.

67. Ron Sirak, "Founding Father," *Golf Digest*, November 1, 2009, https://www.golfdigest.com/story/golf_eisenhower_sirak.

68. Brett and Kate McKay, "Leadership Lessons from Dwight D. Eisenhower, #2: How to Not Let Anger and Criticism Get the Best of You," Art of Manliness, November 7, 2018, https://www.artofmanliness.com/articles/leadership-lessons-from-dwight-d-eisenhower-2-how-to-not-let-anger-and-criticism-get-the-best-of-you/.

69. Ibid.

70. Lewis, "Obama's Way."

CHAPTER 19: THE IMPOSSIBLE PRESIDENCY

1. Lowi, *Personal President*, 10.

2. Harold Bloom, *Genius: A Mosaic of One Hundred Exemplary Creative Minds* (Burbank, CA: Warner, 2002). This expression I am borrowing from Derek Thompson who was quoting Harold Bloom quoting what Charles Lamb once said of Coleridge.

3. Jeremi Suri, *The Impossible Presidency: The Rise and Fall of America's Highest Office* (New York: Basic Books, 2017), 290.

4. Harold M. Barger, *The Impossible Presidency: Illusions and Realities of Executive Power* (Glenview, IL: Scott, Foresman, 1984).

CHAPTER 20: CANDIDATE OF THE PEOPLE

1. Gore Vidal, *The Best Man*, Dramatists Play Service, 2001.
2. "From John Adams to Thomas Jefferson, 6 December 1787," Founders Online, National Archives, https://founders.archives.gov/documents/Adams/99-02-02-0281.
3. Wilson Woodrow, *The Papers of Woodrow Wilson*, edited by Arthur S. Link, 69 volumes (Princeton: Princeton University Press, 1966–1994), 475.
4. John F. Kennedy, "A Force That Has Changed The Political Scene," *TV Guide*, November 14, 1959, https://museum.tv/debateweb/html/equalizer/print/tvguide_jfkforce.htm.
5. Ibid.
6. John F. Kennedy, "Remarks of Senator John F. Kennedy, at the Dalles, Oregon, May 15, 1960," John F. Kennedy Presidential Library and Museum, https://www.jfklibrary.org/archives/other-resources/john-f-kennedy-speeches/dalles-or-19600515.
7. Donald J. Davidson, ed., *The Wisdom of Theodore Roosevelt* (New York: Citadel Press Books, 2003), 170.
8. John M. Hilpert, *American Cyclone: Theodore Roosevelt and His 1900 Whistle-Stop Campaign* (Jackson: University Press of Mississippi, 2015), 34. Letter to Henry Clay Payne, August 18, 1900.
9. Patricia O'Toole, "The Speech That Saved Teddy Roosevelt's Life," *Smithsonian Magazine*, November 2012, https://www.smithsonianmag.com/history/the-speech-that-saved-teddy-roosevelts-life-83479091/.
10. "Scott Lucas: The 'Paper Majority' Leader," United States Senate. https://www.senate.gov/artandhistory/history/common/generic/People_Leaders_Lucas.htm.
11. "1952 Eisenhower vs. Stevenson," The Living Room Candidate: Presidential Campaign Commercials 1952–2016, http://www.livingroomcandidate.org/commercials/1952.
12. "Winning West Virginia: JFK's Primary Campaign," John F. Kennedy Presidential Library and Museum, *New Frontiers*, issue 12, Spring 2010, https://www.jfklibrary.org/sites/default/files/2018-05/Issue_12_Spring_2010_New_Frontiers.pdf.
13. Ron Simon, "See How JFK Created a Presidency for the Television Age," *Time*, May 30, 2017, https://time.com/4795637/jfk-television/.
14. "The Primaries are More than Eyewash," *Life*, February 18, 1952.
15. McCullough, *Truman*, location 21898.
16. Gary A. Donaldson, *Truman Defeats Dewey* (Lexington: University Press of Kentucky, 1999), 180.
17. Balogh and Schulman, *Recapturing the Oval Office*, 164.
18. Ibid., 163.

CHAPTER 21: NO HIRING MANUAL FOR THE PRESIDENCY

1. Kevin Liptak, "Exclusive: Read the Inauguration Day letter Obama left for Trump," CNN.com, September 5, 2017, https://www.cnn.com/2017/09/03/politics/obama-trump-letter-inauguration-day/index.html.
2. "The Debates and Proceedings in the Congress of the United States. Fifteenth Congress—First Session" (Washington: Gales and Seaton, 1854), 180.
3. Stephen R. Graubard, "Presidents: The Power and the Mediocrity," *New York Times*, January 18, 1989; also "Debates and Proceedings," 180.
4. James Bryce, *The American Commonwealth*, vol. 1 (London: MacMillian and Co., 1891), 75.

5. Delegates who wanted the president determined by popular election ran into problems with the Southern slave states, which would not have as much say in an election determined that way. "The right of suffrage was much more diffusive i e , extensive. In the Northern than the Southern States," explained James Madison, "and the latter could have no influence in the election on the score of Negroes." "Madison Debates."

Southern states would not let the one million slaves vote, and as a result would have fewer voters to influence the choice of a president. On the other hand, presidents couldn't be picked by the legislature because that would make them beholden to that branch. The Electoral College was created to balance both desires. "The substitution of electors obviated this difficulty and seemed on the whole to be liable to fewest objections," said Madison. Ibid.

A solution with the "fewest objections" doesn't exactly recommend itself as exemplary, and that aspect of its origin certainly gives ammunition to those who want to abolish it today. "The Electoral College really was a Frankenstein's mashup of the different ideas they considered to select the president, and the one they designed was largely obsolete within ten years," says Robert M. Alexander, author of *Representation and the Electoral College*. Robert Alexander (@onuprof), "Electoral College scholar here . . ." Twitter, October 31, 2019, 6:45 P.M., https://twitter.com/onuprof/status/1190082469241839616.

6. Raphael, *Mr. President*, 146.

7. Alexander Hamilton, "The Federalist Papers: No. 68," The Avalon Project, March 14, 1788, https://avalon.law.yale.edu/18th_century/fed68.asp.

8. Ellis, J., *His Excellency: George Washington*, location 189.

9. James W. Ceaser, *Presidential Selection: Theory and Development. Princeton* (NJ: Princeton University Press, 1979), ix.

10. Miscellaneous Documents of the House of Representatives, Second Session of the Forty-Fourth Congress, Volume 292; Volume 294 (Washington, Government Printing Office, 1877), 703.

11. Gil Troy, *See How They Ran: The Changing Role of the Presidential Candidate* (Cambridge, MA: Harvard University Press, 1996), Kindle, location 171.

12. Jennifer Mercieca (@jenmercieca), "Never to trust political power to anyone who seeks political power," Twitter, February 17, 2020, 2:25 P.M., https://twitter.com/jenmercieca/status/1229487093426028544.

13. Ellis, R., *Development of the American Presidency*, 49.

14. Phillip G. Henderson, ed., *The Presidency Then and Now* (Lanham, MD: Rowman & Littlefield, 2000), 186.

15. Hamilton, "The Federalist Papers, No. 70."

16. Ceaser, *Presidential Selection*, 43.

17. "Madison Debates."

18. Alexander Hamilton, "The Federalist Papers, No. 71," The Avalon Project, March 18, 1788, https://avalon.law.yale.edu/18th_century/fed71.asp.

19. *Louisville Public Advertiser*, April 14, 1824.

20. Troy, G., *See How They Ran*, location 639.

21. Donald John Ratcliffe, *The One-Party Presidential Contest: Adams, Jackson, and 1824's Five-Horse Race* (Lawrence: University Press of Kansas, 2015), Kindle, location 4797.

22. Michaels, "How Trump is Dismantling."

23. Henry W. Lawrence, "Recalling the Strangest Inaugurations," *Santa Cruz Evening News*, March 4, 1933.

24. Troy, G., *See How They Ran*, location 1765.
25. Michael E. McGerr, *The Decline of Popular Politics* (New York: Oxford University Press, 1986), 14.
26. Troy, G., *See How They Ran*, location 1093.
27. Ibid., location 1356.
28. Ibid., location 1882.
29. Ibid., location 1731.
30. Gary Hart, *Right from the Start: A Chronicle of the McGovern Campaign* (Princeton: Quadrangle, 1973).
31. Interview with author.
32. Interview with author.
33. Henry S. Randall, *The Life of Thomas Jefferson*, vol. 1 (Philadelphia: J. B. Lippincott & Co., 1871), 609.
34. Interview with author.
35. A concept you've affirmed by reading this far.
36. Gene Healy, *The Cult of the Presidency* (Washington, DC: Cato Institute, 2008), 1.
37. "Editorial: Candidates seeking office can't be bothered to vote," *Boston Herald*, November 17, 2018, https://www.bostonherald.com/2018/05/30/editorial-candidates-seeking-office-cant-be-bothered-to-vote/.
38. Richard Norton Smith, *An Uncommon Man: The Triumph of Herbert Hoover* (Worland, WY: High Plains Publishing Company, Inc., 1984), 103.
39. Jonathan Rauch, "How American Politics Went Insane," *The Atlantic*, August 2016, https://www.theatlantic.com/magazine/archive/2016/07/how-american-politics-went-insane/485570/.
40. Manu Raju, "Cruz accuses Mitch McConnell of telling a 'flat-out lie,'" Politico, July 24, 2015, https://www.politico.com/story/2015/07/ted-cruz-says-mitch-mcconnell-lies-export-import-bank-120583.
41. Ceaser, *Presidential Selection*, 5.
42. Jody Avirgan and Clare Malone, "Why The Dean Screams Sounded So Different on TV," FiveThirtyEight, February 4, 2016, https://fivethirtyeight.com/features/why-the-dean-scream-sounded-so-different-on-tv/.
43. Interview with author.
44. Troy, G., *See How They Ran*, location 491.
45. Jim Geraghty, "Joe Biden Promises that If Elected, He Will Cure Cancer," *National Review*, June 12, 2019, https://www.nationalreview.com/corner/joe-biden-promises-that-if-elected-he-will-cure-cancer/.
46. "Barack Obama's Remarks in St. Paul." *New York Times*, June 3, 2008. https://www.nytimes.com/2008/06/03/us/politics/03text-obama.html.
    https://docs.google.com/document/d/1MKPvp-Yi7vlPTMy5e7okl7T9uCvNavoUYvuYY7Rblec/edit
47. David Jackson, "Donald Trump accepts GOP nomination, says 'I alone can fix' system," *USA Today*, July 21, 2016, https://www.usatoday.com/story/news/politics/elections/2016/07/21/donald-trump-republican-convention-acceptance-speech/87385658/.
48. Eli Stokols, "Unapologetic, Trump promises to make America rich," Politico, May 26, 2016, https://www.politico.com/story/2016/05/unapologetic-trump-promises-to-make-america-rich-223632.
49. Donald J. Trump (@realDonaldTrump), "The only one . . ." Twitter, May 12, 2015, 8:12 P.M., https://twitter.com/realDonaldTrump/status/598324947140902912.

50. Donald J. Trump (@realDonaldTrump), "I am going . . ." Twitter, May 21, 2015, 5:26 P.M., https://twitter.com/realDonaldTrump/status/601544572498509824.

51. Donald J. Trump (@realDonaldTrump), "Nobody . . ." Twitter, April 27, 2015, 7:33 A.M., https://twitter.com/realDonaldTrump/status/592698043629215746/.

52. "Foreword," *The American Political Science Review* 44, no. 3 (1950): v–ix, doi:10 .2307/1950997.

CHAPTER 22: WHAT GOT YOU HERE WON'T GET YOU THERE

1. "Mr. Truman's Speeches," *Washington Post*, May 8, 1948.

2. Baker, P., *Days of Fire*, location 12557.

3. Ginsberg, *Presidential Government*.

4. Marshall Goldsmith, "What Got You Here Won't Get You There," Talks at Google, December 10, 2007, https://talksat.withgoogle.com/talk/what-got-you-here-won't -get-you-there.

5. Interview with author.

6. Neustadt, *Presidential Power*, 9.

7. General David Petraeus has described a view of adaptive leadership very similar to Eisenhower's: "I have always sought to adjust my leadership style to be one that will, individually, bring out the best in each of those who report directly to me and also bring out the best in the organization I am privileged to lead. The style, e.g., that achieves that objective as the Commander of the Multinational Force with multiple senior officer direct reports is very different from that which is employed to do the same as a young Airborne Infantry Platoon Leader. In short, leaders need to work hard to understand what leadership style will enable each of the individuals who report to them to be all that they can be—and to do the same with respect to the organization overall, as well." Robert Reiss, "12 CEOs Describe Their Leadership Style," *Forbes*, October 8, 2018, https://www.forbes.com/sites/robertreiss /2018/10/08/12-quotes-from-amazing-leaders/#ff3905a15b8e.

8. Greenstein, *Leadership*. "We shall attack and attack until we are exhausted, and then we shall attack again" was Patton's motto. In Sicily he invaded with the U.S. 7th Army, and the mission was a historic success, though it is the location of a serious blow to Patton's reputation: In an Italian field hospital he slapped a soldier suffering from shell shock and accused him of cowardice. He was forced to issue a public apology and earned a sharp reprimand from General Dwight D. Eisenhower.

9. Eisenhower added a postscript to his letter to Marshall that demonstrated his understanding of the way presidential behavior affects troops in the field: "If you can conveniently do so I should like very much for you to pay my respects to the Secretary and the President. I appreciate the obviously solid support they have given to decisions that possibly looked, at the time, risky." Joseph P. Hobbs, *Dear General: Eisenhower's Wartime Letters to Marshall* (Baltimore: Johns Hopkins University Press, 1999), 131.

10. Bill Clinton, "Let's Make a Deal," C-SPAN, Presidential Leadership Scholars Program, September 12, 2014, https://www.c-span.org/video/?c4508363/user-clip-lets -make-deal.

11. "Defeated Quayle: 'I Will Continue to Stand Up,'" *Janesville Gazette Newspaper*, April 4, 1992.

12. Barack Obama, interview by Steve Kroft, "Transcript: Sen. Obama, Part 1," 60

Minutes, CBS News, September 24, 2008, https://www.cbsnews.com/news/transcript-sen-obama-part-1/.

13. Jeff Zeleny, "Bill Clinton and Barack Obama, Together at Last," *New York Times*, October 30, 2008, https://thecaucus.blogs.nytimes.com/2008/10/30/bill-clinton-and-barack-obama/.

14. "Read President Trump's Interview with TIME on Truth and Falsehoods," *Time*, March 23, 2017, https://time.com/4710456/donald-trump-time-interview-truth-falsehood/?xid=homepage.

15. Donald J. Trump, interview by Lesley Stahl, "President Trump on Christine Blasey Ford, his relationships with Vladimir Putin and Kim Jong Un and more," *60 Minutes*, CBS News, October 15, 2018, https://www.cbsnews.com/news/donald-trump-full-interview-60-minutes-transcript-lesley-stahl-2018-10-14/.

16. Tulis, *Rhetorical Presidency*, location 183.

17. Jeffrey Simpson, "Acting the prime minister, prepared for the role," *The Globe and Mail*, March 22, 2018, https://www.theglobeandmail.com/opinion/acting-the-prime-minister-prepared-for-the-role/article27256072/.

18. Interview with author.

19. Bill Clinton, interview by WWWE Radio, Cleveland, "Interview of the President," October 24, 1994, https://clintonwhitehouse6.archives.gov/1994/10/1994-10-24-interview-of-the-president-with-wwwe-radio-cleveland.html.

20. Ron Suskind, *Confidence Men: Wall Street, Washington, and the Education of a President* (New York: Harper, 2012).

21. Lindsey Boerma, "Obama reflects on his biggest mistake as president," CBS News, July 12, 2012, https://www.cbsnews.com/news/obama-reflects-on-his-biggest-mistake-as-president/.

22. Jimmy Carter, "July 15, 1979: 'Crisis of Confidence' Speech," UVA Miller Center, National Archives, https://millercenter.org/the-presidency/presidential-speeches/july-15-1979-crisis-confidence-speech. Yes, this is the "malaise" speech, but Carter never used that word. It was used by White House aides in the run-up to the speech, and the news media used that word to describe the speech, but the word never emerged from President Carter's mouth during that address.

23. Drew Westen, "What Happened to Obama?" *New York Times*, August 6, 2011, https://www.nytimes.com/2011/08/07/opinion/sunday/what-happened-to-obamas-passion.html?_r=1&ref=opinion&pagewanted=all.

24. Richard Cohen, "Mr. Cool turns cold," *Washington Post*, August 8, 2011, https://www.washingtonpost.com/opinions/mr-cool-turns-cold/2011/08/08/gIQAoZlI3I_story.html.

25. Matthew Dickinson, "The Real Story of Obama's Presidency," Sites Dot Middlebury: Presidential Power, August 8, 2011, http://sites.middlebury.edu/presidentialpower/tag/obamas-presidency-westen-analysis/.

26. John Sides, "Script Doctor," Monkey Cage, August 7, 2011, https://themonkeycage.org/2011/08/script-doctor/.

27. Susanna Kim, Jake Tapper, and Z. Byron Wolf, "June Jobs Report: Unemployment Rate Up to 9.2 Percent With Only 18,000 Added Jobs," ABC News, July 7, 2011, https://abcnews.go.com/Business/june-jobs-report-unemployment-rate-92-percent-18000/story?id=14020360.

28. Matthew Eshbaugh-Soha and Jeffrey S. Peake, "Presidents and the Economic Agenda," *Political Research Quarterly* 58, no. 1 (2005): 128. www.jstor.org/stable/3595602, doi:10.2307/3595602.

29. Ibid., 134.

30. Michael J. Hogan, *Woodrow Wilson's Western Tour: Rhetoric, Public Opinion, and the League of Nations* (College Station: Texas A&M University Press, 2006), 28.

31. Woodrow Wilson, "League of Nations," U.S. Diplomatic Mission to Germany, September 25, 1919, https://usa.usembassy.de/etexts/speeches/rhetoric/wwleague.htm.

32. Scott A. Berg, *Wilson* (New York: Simon & Schuster, 2013), 612.

33. Monica Langley and Gerard Baker, "Donald Trump, in Exclusive Interview, Tells WSJ He Is Willing to Keep Parts of Obama Health Law," *Wall Street Journal*, November 11, 2016, https://www.wsj.com/articles/donald-trump-willing-to-keep-parts-of-health-law-1478895339.

34. Vivian Salama, "Trump: Mockery of Christine Blasey Ford 'Doesn't Matter. We Won,'" *Wall Street Journal*, October 14, 2018, https://www.wsj.com/articles/trump-mockery-of-christine-blasey-ford-doesnt-matter-we-won-1539569094.

35. Interview with author.

36. Drew DeSilver, "Can Presidential Speeches Change Minds? The Evidence Suggests Not," Pew Research Center, September 10, 2013, https://www.pewresearch.org/fact-tank/2013/09/10/can-presidential-speeches-change-minds-the-evidence-suggest-not/.

37. Reagan, *American Life*, locations 7051–2.

38. Memo, Richard Wirthlin to Ronald Reagan, April 10, 1985, ID #312590, PR015, WHORM: Subject File, Ronald Reagan Library.

39. Ibid.

40. DeSilver, "Presidential Speeches."

41. Clinton, "Interview of the President."

42. Bush, *Decision Points*, location 5782.

43. Ibid., location 5815.

44. After announcing his sixty cities in sixty days tour, Bush ended up only giving twenty-five speeches in that time period and traveling to even less cities, information cataloged and tallied by Elizabeth Hinson, the researcher for this book.

45. Bush, *Decision Points*, location 5862.

46. "April 2009 Health Tracking Poll," Henry J. Kaiser Family Foundation, April 1, 2019, https://www.kff.org/health-reform/poll-finding/april-2009-health-tracking-poll/.

47. Michael Cooper, "Conservatives Sowed Idea of Health Care Mandate, Only to Spurn It Later," *New York Times*, February 14, 2012, https://www.nytimes.com/2012/02/15/health/policy/health-care-mandate-was-first-backed-by-conservatives.html.

48. Amanda Terkel, "Pat Toomey: Background Checks Died Because GOP Didn't Want To Help Obama," HuffPost, May 1, 2013, https://www.huffpost.com/entry/pat-toomey-background-checks_n_3192690.

49. "GOP Tax Plan Benefits Rich, U.S. Voters Say Almost 3-1, Quinnipiac University National Poll Finds," Quinnipiac University Poll, December 5, 2017. https://poll.qu.edu/images/polling/us/us12052017_ufrt567.pdf/.

    Claire Williams, "Amid Unpopular Tax Overhaul, GOP Banking on 2019 Tax Returns," December 17, 2018, https://morningconsult.com/2018/12/17/amid-unpopular-tax-overhaul-gop-banking-on-2019-tax-returns/.

50. Ashley Kirzinger, Bianca DiJulio, Liz Hamel, Elise Sugarman, and Mollyann Brodie, "Kaiser Health Tracking Poll—May 2017: The AHCA's Proposed Changes to Health Care," Henry J. Kaiser Family Foundation, May 31, 2017, https://www.kff.org/health-costs/report/kaiser-health-tracking-poll-may-2017-the-ahcas-proposed-changes-to-health-care/.

51. Jim Norman, "Solid Majority Still Opposes New Construction on Border Wall,"

Gallup, February 4, 2019, https://news.gallup.com/poll/246455/solid-majority-opposes-new-construction-border-wall.aspx.

52. "Revolving Door: Former Members of the 115th Congress," Open Secrets, https://www.opensecrets.org/revolving/departing.php?cong=115.

53. "Revolving Door: Former Members of the 114th Congress," Open Secrets, https://www.opensecrets.org/revolving/departing.php?cong=114.

54. The process of crafting a speech focuses an administration, and it's good for people to hear what a president professes to care about, but if you really want to understand a president's true intent, the State of the Union address is less significant than the Federal Register and the budget, which don't get a tenth of the coverage.

55. Goodwin, *Team of Rivals*, 206.

56. Interview with author.

57. "The Civil Rights Act of 1964: A Long Struggle for Freedom," Library of Congress, https://www.loc.gov/exhibits/civil-rights-act/multimedia/randolph-challenges-fdr.html.

58. "I call these receptions my public-opinion baths . . . and, though they may not be pleasant in all particulars, the effect as a whole is renovating and invigorating to my perceptions of responsibility and duty. It would never do for a President to have guards with drawn sabres at his door, as if he fancied he were, or were trying to be, or were assuming to be, an emperor." Arthur M. Schlesinger, Jr., *The Imperial Presidency* (New York: Houghton Mifflin Harcourt, 2004), 494.

59. The reporters were baffled when Wilson made this request. "Our function, at least as we saw it, leaving aside our duty, was to inform the country what Washington was doing," wrote *The New York Times* Washington bureau chief Richard Oulahan later. The president, he said, "had come to Washington with a distinct prejudice against the place and what he conceived to be its mental atmosphere." John Dickerson, "Meet the Press," Slate, March 14, 2013, https://slate.com/news-and-politics/2013/03/woodrow-wilson-held-the-first-presidential-press-conference-100-years-ago-and-they-remain-awkward-impersonal-and-no-fun-for-barack-obama-today.html.

60. Rachel Weiner, "Chris Christie: 'Real leaders change polls,'" *Washington Post*, August 28, 2012, https://www.washingtonpost.com/news/post-politics/wp/2012/08/28/chris-christie-real-leaders-change-polls/.

61. Elaine C. Kamarck, *Why Presidents Fail And How They Can Succeed Again* (Washington: Brookings Institution Press, 2016), Kindle, location 4.

62. Michael Bennet (@MichaelBennet), "If you elect . . ." Twitter, August 6, 2019, 11:27 A.M., https://twitter.com/michaelbennet/status/1158806845953323008?lang=en.

CHAPTER 23: RESTRAINT

1. Jack W. Germond and Jules Witcover, *Whose Broad Stripes and Bright Stars: The Trivial Pursuit of the Presidency* (New York: Warner Books, 1989).

2. Wystan Hugh Auden and Louis Kronenberger, *The Viking Book of Aphorisms* (New York: Dorset Press, 1981).

3. "No Kick from Campaigns," *Newsweek*, November 4, 1990, https://www.newsweek.com/no-kick-campaigns-205798.

4. "Berlin Wall," History.com, November 9, 2019, https://www.history.com/topics/cold-war/berlin-wall.

5. Meacham, *Destiny and Power*, 381.

6. Greenstein, *Leadership*, 80.

7. Barber, *Presidential Character*.

8. Abraham Lincoln, "Last Public Address," April 11, 1865, http://www.abrahamlincoln online.org/lincoln/speeches/last.htm.

9. Campaign indifference to restraint is repealed when wars don't go well—then, candidates boast about it. Donald Trump supported military action in Iraq and Libya, but by the 2016 campaign, when those actions were no longer popular, he bragged that he'd been against both. That was a lie, but candidate Trump was willing to get caught lying rather than be associated with unpopular wars. That inclination to restraint goes only so far, though. Asked about ISIS, Trump promised to "bomb the shit out of them," (Tim Hains, "Trump's Updated ISIS Plan: 'Bomb The Shit Out Of Them,' Send In Exxon To Rebuild," Real Clear Politics, November 13, 2015, https://www.realclearpolitics.com/video/2015/11/13/trumps _updated_isis_plan_bomb_the_shit_out_of_them_send_exxon_in_to_rebuild .html.) a promise he kept once in office. During the 2004 campaign, John Kerry got mangled in the intersection of changing public opinion about warfare. Voters wanted a strong commander in chief, which is why John Kerry nodded to his Vietnam War duty when he accepted the Democratic nomination. Arriving at the podium, he saluted and said, "John Kerry reporting for duty." But Democratic voters had soured on the war, which is why he had voted against continuing to fund it. Trying to hit both targets, Kerry responded to a question during the campaign about war funding by saying "I actually did vote for the $87 billion before I voted against it." ("Kerry discusses $87 billion comment," CNN.com, September 30, 2004, https://www.cnn.com/2004/ALLPOLITICS/09/30/kerry.comment/.) Barack Obama, running for office in 2008, was the only recent candidate to win office using a legitimate antiwar claim as proof of his restraint.

10. Peggy Noonan, "Over Trump, We're as Divided as Ever," *Wall Street Journal*, March 8, 2018, http://peggynoonan.com/over-trump-were-as-divided-as-ever/.

11. "President Trump mocks being presidential," CNN.com, https://www.cnn.com /videos/politics/2018/03/10/trump-pennsylvania-speech-mocking-presidential-sot .cnn.

12. Fred I. Greenstein, *The Hidden-Hand Presidency: Eisenhower as Leader* (Baltimore: Johns Hopkins University Press, 1994).

13. Ibid.

14. Beschloss, *Presidents of War*, 20.

15. "NEVER SINCE," TJ to Pierre-Samuel du Pont de Nemours, July 14, 1807, Thomas Jefferson Papers, LOC.

16. Strengthened the New York bankers. (This is the fight he had with Hamilton— one of them, anyway—when Hamilton wanted to consolidate the Revolutionary War debts from the states.)

17. Beschloss, *Presidents of War*, 35.

18. Helen Dewar and Ann Devroy, "Mitchell Urges Bush to Visit West Berlin," *Washington Post*, November 14, 1989, https://www.washingtonpost.com/archive/politics /1989/11/14/mitchell-urges-bush-to-visit-west-berlin/a61014ee-86a9-4e37-b5c1 -284fa60c041e/.

19. "Senators compromise on aid to Poles, Hungary," *The Record*, November 14, 1989, 31.

20. "American Experience: George H. W. Bush," PBS, Part 1, 2008, http://www .shoppbs.pbs.org/wgbh/amex/bush41/program/pt.html#part1.

21. Engel, *When the World*.

22. Goldsmith, "What Got You Here."

23. Meacham, *Destiny and Power*, 382.

24. William Taubman, *Gorbachev: His Life and Times* (New York: W.W. Norton & Company, 2017).

25. George Bush, *All the Best, George Bush: My Life in Letters and Other Writings* (New York: Simon & Schuster, 2014), 441.

26. Robert Gates, "Robert Gates Recounts George H. W. Bush's 'Award' for Colleagues Who Fell Asleep in Meetings," *CBS This Morning*, CBS News, December 4, 2018, https://www.cbsnews.com/news/robert-gates-on-george-h-w-bush-legacy-humor-country-first/.

27. Bush, *All the Best*, 442.

28. Neustadt, *Presidential Power*, xv.

29. Stanley McChrystal, "An Interview with General (Ret.) Stanley McChrystal," *Prism*, vol. 6, no. 3, https://cco.ndu.edu/Portals/96/Documents/prism/prism_6-3/McCrystal.pdf.

30. The January 26, 1987, issue of *Time* magazine included an article titled "Where Is the Real George Bush?" One of the anecdotes in that story made "the vision thing" a famous example of Bush's locution. A friend suggested that Bush go alone to Camp David for a few days to figure out where he wanted to take the country: "'Oh,' Bush said, exasperated, 'the vision thing.'" Robert Ajemian, "Where Is the Real George Bush?" *Time*, January 26, 1987, http://content.time.com/time/subscriber/article/0,33009,963342-1,00.html.

31. Garry Wills, *Certain Trumpets* (New York: Simon & Schuster, 2013), 50.

32. Though Bush claimed to have been "out of the loop" about the arms for hostages crisis, his biographer, Jon Meacham, who delivered the eulogy at Bush's funeral, notes, "The record is clear that Bush was aware that the United States, in contravention of its own stated policy, was trading arms for hostages as part of an initiative to reach out to moderate elements in Iran." Meacham, *Destiny and Power*, 299.

33. Germond and Witcover, *Broad Stripes*.

34. Elizabeth Drew, "Running," *New Yorker*, November 23, 1975, https://www.newyorker.com/magazine/1975/12/01/running-3.

35. Jon Meacham, "George H.W. Bush and the Price of Politics," *New York Times*, December 1, 2018, https://www.nytimes.com/2018/12/01/opinion/george-hw-bush-death-jon-meacham.html.

36. Ibid.

37. Richard P. McCormick, *The Presidential Game: The Origins of American Presidential Politics* (New York: Oxford University Press, 1982).

38. Meacham, *Destiny and Power*, 232. Only the man's name was not Green. It was John Breen, editor of the Nashua *Telegraph*, who had agreed to moderate the debate.

39. "Dear Reader, to read a more full account of this moment in campaign history I recommend Whistlestop."

40. George Will, "The Sound Of a Lapdog," *Washington Post*, January 30, 1986, https://www.washingtonpost.com/archive/politics/1986/01/30/george-bush-the-sound-of-a-lapdog/9322b0c0-c006-4709-99fc-4283fcb35ea8/.

41. Meacham, *Destiny and Power*, 319.

42. Steven V. Roberts, "Bush Intensifies Debate on Pledge, Asking Why It So Upsets Dukakis," *New York Times*, August 25, 1988, https://www.nytimes.com/1988/08/25/us/bush-intensifies-debate-on-pledge-asking-why-it-so-upsets-dukakis.html.

43. Cathleen Decker, "Bush Brands Dukakis as Insensitive to Crime Victims," *Los*

Angeles Times, October 8, 1988, https://www.latimes.com/archives/la-xpm-1988-10
-08-mn-2922-story.html.

44. "Gravely Ill, Atwater Offers Apology," *New York Times*, January 13, 1991, https://
www.nytimes.com/1991/01/13/us/gravely-ill-atwater-offers-apology.html.

45. Micheal Oreskes, "Lee Atwater, Master of Tactics For Bush and G.O.P., Dies at 40,"
New York Times, March 30, 1991, https://www.nytimes.com/1991/03/30/obituaries
/lee-atwater-master-of-tactics-for-bush-and-gop-dies-at-40.html.

46. Nia-Malika Henderson, "Michael Dukakis explains what happened to Michael
Dukakis," *Washington Post*, January 11, 2015, https://www.washingtonpost.com
/news/the-fix/wp/2015/01/11/michael-dukakis-explains-what-happened-to-michael
-dukakis/.

47. M. J. Stephey, "Dukakis' Deadly Response," *Time*, October 14, 1988, http://content
.time.com/time/specials/packages/article/0,28804,1844704_1844706_1844712,00
.html.

48. Meacham, *Destiny and Power*, 413.

49. Ibid.

50. Michael Grunwald, "Trump Goes Code Pink on George W. Bush," Politico, February 14, 2016, https://www.politico.com/magazine/story/2016/02/trump-code-pink
-bush-iraq-9-11-213630.

51. Alex Vandermaas-Peeler, Daniel Cox, and Maxine Najle, et al, "Partisanship
Trumps Gender: Sexual Harassment, Woman Candidates, Access to Contraception, and Key Issues in 2018 Midterms," PRRI, October 3, 2018, https://www.prri
.org/research/abortion-reproductive-health-midterms-trump-kavanaugh/.

52. MJ Lee, "How Donald Trump blasted George W. Bush in S.C.—and still won,"
CNN.com, February 21, 2016, https://www.cnn.com/2016/02/20/politics/donald
-trump-south-carolina-military/index.html.

53. Lee Moran, "Donald Trump Fires Back At The Late Barbara Bush: 'She Should
Be' Nasty To Me," HuffPost, April 5, 2019, https://www.huffpost.com/entry/donald
-trump-barbara-bush-interview_n_5ca70854e4b0dca032ff6b6f.

54. Owen Daugherty, "Roger Stone defends Trump's attacks on Barbara Bush: 'She's
dead and he's president,'" The Hill, April 5, 2019, https://thehill.com/blogs/blog
-briefing-room/news/437663-roger-stone-defends-trumps-attacks-on-barbara-bush
-shes-dead.

CHAPTER 24: THE CHURCH OF PERPETUAL DISAPPOINTMENT

1. David Shedden, "The First Convention Broadcast: Radio at the 1924 Conventions," Poynter, September 1, 2004, https://www.poynter.org/archive/2004/the-first
-convention-broadcast-radio-at-the-1924-conventions/.

2. Edward J. Larson, *A Magnificent Catastrophe: The Tumultuous Election of 1800,
America's First Presidential Campaign* (New York: Free Press, 2007), 111.

3. Troy, G., *See How They Ran*, location 4.

4. Robert A. Slayton, *Empire Statesman: The Rise and Redemption of Al Smith* (New
York: Free Press, 2001), 317.

5. Drew, "Running."

6. Ben Smith, "How Mitt Romney Won the First Debate," Buzzfeed, October 3,
2012, https://www.buzzfeednews.com/article/bensmith/how-mitt-romney-won-the
-first-debate.

7. Bill Maher (@billmaher), "I can't believe I'm saying this, but Obama looks like he

DOES need a teleprompter," Twitter, October 3, 2012, 7:18 P.M., https://twitter
.com/billmaher/status/253680489850892289.

8. Peter Hamby, "Did Twitter Kill the Boys on the Bus? Searching for a better way to
cover a campaign," Harvard University: Joan Shorenstein Center, September 2013,
https://shorensteincenter.org/wp-content/uploads/2013/08/d80_hamby.pdf.

9. Lynn Vavreck, "It's Not So Much the Debate. It's the Days After the Debate," *New
York Times*, June 26, 2019, https://www.nytimes.com/2019/06/26/upshot/debate
-dramatic-moments-overrated.html.

10. Andrew Sullivan, "Did Obama Just Throw the Entire Election Away?" dish
.andrewsullivan.com, October 8, 2012, https://dish.andrewsullivan.com/2012/10/08
/did-obama-just-throw-the-entire-election-away/.

11. "Romney's Strong Debate Performance Erases Obama's Lead," Pew Research
Center, October 8, 2012, https://www.people-press.org/2012/10/08/romneys-strong
-debate-performance-erases-obamas-lead/.

12. Sam Wang, "Post-Debate Reaction," Princeton Election Consortium, October 3,
2012, https://election.princeton.edu/2012/10/03/post-debate-reaction/.

13. John Heilemann and Mark Halperin, "The Intervention," *New Yorker*, November 1,
2013, https://nymag.com/news/features/heilemann-halperin-double-down-excerpt
-2013-11/.

14. Newt Gingrich, *Understanding Trump* (New York: Center Street, 2017), xii.

15. David A. Fahrenthold, "Trump Recorded Having Extremely Lewd Conversation About Women in 2005," *Washington Post*, October 8, 2016, https://www
.washingtonpost.com/politics/trump-recorded-having-extremely-lewd-conversation
-about-women-in-2005/2016/10/07/3b9ce776-8cb4-11e6-bf8a-3d26847eeed4_story
.html.

16. Robert Costa, Dan Balz, and Philip Rucker, "Trump wanted to put Bill Clinton's
accusers in his family box. Debate officials said no," October 10, 2016, https://www
.washingtonpost.com/news/post-politics/wp/2016/10/10/trumps-debate-plan-to-seat
-bill-clintons-accusers-in-family-box-was-thwarted/.

17. Charles Francis Adams, ed., *Memoirs of John Quincy Adams: Comprising Portions of His Diary from 1795 to 1848* (Philadelphia: J. B. Lippincott & Co., 1876),
468.

18. Joseph Cummins, *Anything for a Vote: Dirty Tricks, Cheap Shots, and October
Surprises in U.S. Presidential Campaigns* (Philadelphia: Quirk Books, 2007),
26–28.

19. Ibid., 30.

20. Interview with author.

21. Congressional Record: Proceedings and Debates of the United States Congress,
vol. 113, part 6 (Washington: U.S. Government Printing Office, 1967), 7527.

22. Thomas Jefferson, "Diffusion of Knowledge Bill," 1779. FE 2:221, Papers 2:526.

23. *The Voter's Non-Partisan Handbook and Campaign Guide: Great Issues and National Leaders of 1908* (Philadelphia: W. E. Scull, 1908).

24. David Greenberg, *Republic of Spin: An Inside History of the American Presidency*
(New York: W. W. Norton, 2016), 26.

25. The Democratic politician William McAdoo described a Harding speech as "an
army of pompous phrases moving over the landscape in search of an idea." One of
Harding's expressions was "Let's be done with wiggle and wobble." Ibid., 133.

26. "H. L. Mencken on Balder and Dash," *Lapham's Quarterly*, 1921, https://www
.laphamsquarterly.org/comedy/hl-mencken-balder-and-dash.

27. "1952 Eisenhower vs. Stevenson," The Living Room Candidate: Presidential Cam-

paign Commercials 1952–2016, http://www.livingroomcandidate.org/commercials /1952.

28. Balogh and Schulman, *Recapturing the Oval Office*, 163.

29. Frank Rich, "Paar to Leno, J.F.K. to J.F.K.," *New York Times*, February 8, 2004, https://www.nytimes.com/2004/02/08/arts/paar-to-leno-jfk-to-jfk.html?_r=0.

30. Greenberg, *Republic of Spin*, 389.

31. David Trumbull, "The most important thing is sincerity. If you can fake that you've got it made," *Post-Gazette*, December 15, 2006, http://www.trumbullofboston .org/writing/2006-12-15.htm.

32. Lloyd Grove, ". . . And the Critics Sound Off," *Washington Post*, June 5, 1992, https://www.washingtonpost.com/archive/lifestyle/1992/06/05/and-the-critics-sound -off/87038381-a3d8-4a0c-a659-3998910c453d/.

33. Danny Spiegel, "Today in TV History: Bill Clinton and His Sax Visit Arsenio," TV Insider, June 3, 2015, https://www.tvinsider.com/2979/rerun-bill-clinton-on-arsenio -hall/.

34. David Maraniss, "Tooting His Own Horn," *Washington Post*, June 5, 1992, https:// www.washingtonpost.com/archive/lifestyle/1992/06/05/tooting-his-own-horn /37cff9b0-07b5-45b6-9c5b-0d9bef7fb4c9/.

35. Spiegel, "Today in TV History."

36. Adrienne Lafrance, "In 1858, People Said the Telegraph Was 'Too Fast for the Truth,'" *The Atlantic*, Jule 28, 2014, https://www.theatlantic.com/technology/archive /2014/07/in-1858-people-said-the-telegraph-was-too-fast-for-the-truth/375171/.

37. Daniel Walker Howe, "America's Century of Self-Discovery," *The Sun*, April 9, 2008, https://www.nysun.com/arts/americas-century-of-self-discovery/74392/.

38. Michael X Delli Carpini, "Radio's Political Past," *Media Studies Journal, Radio: the Forgotten Medium* 7 (1993): 23–36, http://repository.upenn.edu/asc_papers/23.

39. David B. Valley, *A History and Analysis of Democratic Presidential Nomination Acceptance Speeches to 1968* (Lanham, MD: University Press of America, 1988).

40. Merle Miller, *Plain Speaking: An Oral Biography of Harry S. Truman* (New York: Berkley Books, 1981).

41. According to Merriam Webster, a "wonk" is someone preoccupied with arcane details or procedures in a specialized field.

42. "Perot Outdraws a Playoff Game," *New York Times*, October 8, 1992, https://www .nytimes.com/1992/10/08/us/the-1992-campaign-perot-outdraws-a-playoff-game .html.

43. Olivia B. Waxman, "How Ross Perot Changed Political Campaigns," *Time*, July 9, 2019, https://time.com/5622818/ross-perot-dead-legacy/.

44. Philip Bump, "Donald Trump's surprisingly savvy analysis of American politics," *Washington Post*, August 16, 2015, https://www.washingtonpost.com/news/the-fix /wp/2015/08/16/donald-trumps-surprisingly-savvy-comment-about-american -politics/.

45. Karl Evers-Hillstrom, "Lobbying Spending Reaches $3.4 Billion in 2018, Highest in 8 Years," Open Secrets, January 25, 2010, https://www.opensecrets.org/news/2019 /01/lobbying-spending-reaches-3-4-billion-in-18/.

46. David Mora, "Update: We Found a 'Staggering' 281 Lobbyists Who've Worked in the Trump Administration," ProPublica, October 15, 2019, https://www.propublica .org/article/we-found-a-staggering-281-lobbyists-whove-worked-in-the-trump -administration.

47. Randy Alfred, "Aug. 9, 1854: Thoreau Warns, 'The Railroad Rides on Us,'" *Wired*, August 9, 2010, https://www.wired.com/2010/08/0809thoreau-walden-published/.

48. "1928," *New York Times*, January 1, 1928, 38.

49. "Communications Market Report," OfCom, August 2, 2018, https://www.ofcom.org.uk/__data/assets/pdf_file/0022/117256/CMR-2018-narrative-report.pdf.

50. Isaac Stanley-Becker, "'Horns' are growing on young people's skulls. Phone use is to blame, research suggests," *Washington Post*, June 25, 2019, https://www.washingtonpost.com/nation/2019/06/20/horns-are-growing-young-peoples-skulls-phone-use-is-blame-research-suggests/. Younger users check their phones even more frequently, causing some to develop hornlike spikes at the back of their skulls as a result of the forward tilt of the head required to peer into their handheld screens. For most of us, it takes thirty minutes to refocus on a task after a self-interruption. (The math is yours to do: If we're interrupting ourselves every twelve minutes, how does that allow for the thirty-minute reset?)

51. Andrew Sullivan, "I Used to Be a Human Being," *New York*, September 19, 2016, http://nymag.com/intelligencer/2016/09/andrew-sullivan-my-distraction-sickness-and-yours.html.

52. Ben Popken, "As Algorithms Take Over, YouTube's Recommendations Highlight a Human Problem," NBC News, April 18, 2018, https://www.nbcnews.com/tech/social-media/algorithms-take-over-youtube-s-recommendations-highlight-human-problem-n867596.

53. Eli Pariser, "When the Internet Thinks It Knows You," *New York Times*, May 22, 2011, https://www.nytimes.com/2011/05/23/opinion/23pariser.html.

54. Jasmin Barmore, "Bethany Gaskin Is the Queen of Eating Shellfish Online." *New York Times*, June 11, 2019, https://www.nytimes.com/2019/06/11/style/youtube-mukbang-bloveslife-bethany-gaskin.html.

55. Paul Roberts, *The Impulse Society: America in the Age of Instant Gratification*, (London: Bloomsbury, 2014), 73.

56. "Alibaba CEO: On-Demand Delivery Is Infrastructure for Future of Retail," CNBC News, November 12, 2018, https://www.cnbc.com/video/2018/11/12/alibaba-ceo-on-demand-delivery-is-infrastructure-for-future-of-retail.html.

57. David Mattin, "The Future of Retail," Trend Watching, 2018, https://trendwatching.com/quarterly/2018-05/the-future-of-retail/.

58. Sean Illing, "There's a War for Your Attention. And You're Probably Losing It," Vox.com, February 11, 2018, https://www.vox.com/conversations/2016/11/17/13477142/facebook-twitter-social-media-attention-merchants.

59. Mike Allen, "Sean Parker Unloads on Facebook: 'God Only Knows What It's Doing to Our Children's Brains,'" Axios, November 9, 2017, https://www.axios.com/sean-parker-unloads-on-facebook-god-only-knows-what-its-doing-to-our-childrens-brains-1513306792-f855e7b4-4e99-4d60-8d51-2775559c2671.html.

60. Joe Hagan, "Beto O'Rourke: 'I'm Just Born to Be In It,'" *Vanity Fair*, March 13, 2019, https://www.vanityfair.com/news/2019/03/beto-orourke-cover-story.

61. "John McCain's New Hampshire Primary Speech," *New York Times*, January 8, 2008, https://www.nytimes.com/2008/01/08/us/politics/08text-mccain.html.

62. "Here's Donald Trump's Presidential Announcement Speech," *Time*, June 16, 2015, https://time.com/3923128/donald-trump-announcement-speech/.

63. Ale Russian, "Trump Boasted of Avoiding STDs While Dating: Vaginas Are 'Landmines . . . It Is My Personal Vietnam,'" *Time*, October 15, 2016, https://people.com/politics/trump-boasted-of-avoiding-stds-while-dating-vaginas-are-landmines-it-was-my-personal-vietnam/.

64. "Mr. Truman's Speeches," *Washington Post*, May 8, 1948.

65. Matthew Nussbaum, "Trump and the teleprompter: A brief history," Politico,

June 7, 2016, https://www.politico.com/story/2016/06/donald-trump-teleprompter-224039.

66. Marjorie R. Hershey, *Guide to U.S. Political Parties* (Washington: CQ Press, 2014), 150.

67. Elisa Shearer and Katerina Eva Matsa, "News Use Across Social Media Platforms 2018," Pew Research Center, September 10, 2018, https://www.journalism.org/2018/09/10/news-use-across-social-media-platforms-2018/.

68. Zeynep Tufekci, "How Social Media Took Us from Tahrir Square to Donald Trump," MIT *Technology Review*, August 14, 2018, https://www.technologyreview.com/s/611806/how-social-media-took-us-from-tahrir-square-to-donald-trump/.

69. Rose McDermott and Peter K. Hatemi, "To Go Forward, We Must Look Back: The Importance of Evolutionary Psychology for Understanding Modern Politics," *Evolutionary Psychology* (February 2018): 1–7. https://journals.sagepub.com/doi/pdf/10.1177/1474704918764506.

70. Steven Fein, George R. Goethals, and Matthew B. Kugler, "Social Influence on Political Judgments: The Case of Presidential Debates," *Political Psychology* 28, Issue 2 (March 2007): 165–92. https://onlinelibrary.wiley.com/doi/abs/10.1111/j.1467-9221.2007.00561.x.

71. "Partisanship and Political Animosity in 2016," Pew Research Center, June 22, 2016, https://www.people-press.org/2016/06/22/partisanship-and-political-animosity-in-2016/.

72. Edsall, "What Motivates?"

73. "Partisanship and Political Animosity."

74. Adam Parkhomenko, "Yesterday . . ." Twitter, April 4, 2019, 8:38 A.M., https://twitter.com/AdamParkhomenko/status/1113828136821645318.

75. Riley Beggin, "Trump again boosts a baseless conspiracy theory, this one about Jeffrey Epstein," Vox, August 11, 2019, https://www.vox.com/policy-and-politics/2019/8/11/20800787/jeffrey-epstein-donald-trump-conspiracy-theory-clinton-body-count-retweet-killed-death-by-suicide.

76. "Newt Gingrich Examines the Evolution of Conservatism," interview by Mark Levin, *Life, Liberty & Levin*, FOX News, October 28, 2018, https://www.foxnews.com/transcript/newt-gingrich-examines-the-evolution-of-conservatism.

77. Erick Erickson, "Yes the President's Behavior Is Abnormal. But the Democrats' Policies Are Bat Crap Crazy," Resurgent, August 23, 2019, https://theresurgent.com/2019/08/23/yes-the-presidents-behavior-is-abnormal-but-the-democrats-policies-are-bat-crap-crazy/.

78. Brian Resnick, "A New Brain Study Sheds Light on Why It Can Be So Hard to Change Someone's Political Beliefs," Vox, January 23, 2017, https://www.vox.com/science-and-health/2016/12/28/14088992/brain-study-change-minds.

79. "What psychology experiments tell you about why people deny facts." *The Economist*, December 8, 2018, https://www.economist.com/united-states/2018/12/08/what-psychology-experiments-tell-you-about-why-people-deny-facts.

80. Brendan Nyhan (@BrendanNyhan), "Apparently foreign espionage in US elections is ok if what comes out is true. Partisanship is a hell of a drug," Twitter, December 16, 2016, 10:23 A.M., https://twitter.com/BrendanNyhan/status/809826239305355264.

81. Jim Geraghty, "Our Political Fights Are Bad Because We Don't Agree on the Rules," *National Review*, April 12, 2019, https://www.nationalreview.com/the-morning-jolt/our-political-fights-are-bad-because-we-dont-agree-on-the-rules/.

82. Illing, "There's a War."

CHAPTER 25: AMPING UP THE AWFUL

1. "McCain Counters Obama 'Arab' Question," Associated Press via YouTube, October 11, 2008, https://www.youtube.com/watch?v=jrnRU3ocIH4.

2. "From George Washington to Edmund Pendleton, 22 January 1795," Founders Online, National Archives, https://founders.archives.gov/documents/Washington /05-17-02-0282. Original source: *The Papers of George Washington*, Presidential Series, vol. 17, 1 October 1794–31 March 1795, edited by David R. Hoth and Carol S. Ebel (Charlottesville: University of Virginia Press, 2013), 424–28.

3. Guillaume Chaslot, "How YouTube's A.I. boosts alternative facts," Medium, March 31, 2017, https://medium.com/@guillaumechaslot/how-youtubes-a-i-boosts -alternative-facts-3cc276f47cf7. The former YouTube programmer Guillaume Chaslot studied how algorithms designed to keep users on the site amped up the content. The site's artificial intelligence is designed to maximize clicks and time spent online. If a video causes users to spend more time online, it is offered to other users. He found that searching "Is the earth flat or round?" and following recommendations five times discovered that more than 90 percent of recommended videos state that the earth is flat. A *Wall Street Journal* reporter helping his son search for information about Saturn quickly found himself routed to pro-Putin propaganda videos.

4. In the 2020 election, Beto O'Rourke relied on this relationship between political correctness and authenticity by swearing. NBC's Chuck Todd asked him about his language, which he was amping up when talking about gun control: "Do you find it a bit frustrating that it takes, sometimes, theatrics to get the attention of the press corps, to get the attention of the American public?" O'Rourke replied: "I think what people want us to do, and what I'm trying to do in this campaign, is just to see things as clearly as I possibly can and speak as honestly as I possibly can without triangulating or polling, or, you know, focus group testing what the message is." Beto O'Rourke, interview by Chuck Todd, "Meet the Press—September 15, 2019," *Meet the Press*, NBC News, September 15, 2019, https://www.nbcnews.com /meet-the-press/meet-press-september-15-2019-n1054636.

   Breaking the norms of polite speech became a signal that he was maximally committed to the cause, which was deeply popular in Democratic circles and also sent a signal of how vigorously he would work for the issue when in office.

5. Thomas B. Edsall, "The Trump Voters Whose 'Need for Chaos' Obliterates Everything Else," *New York Times*, September 4, 2019, https://www.nytimes.com/2019/09 /04/opinion/trump-voters-chaos.html?fallback=0&recId=1QNbosgmBUOstqdI azkJuh33tGS&locked=0&geoContinent=NA&geoRegion=VA&recAlloc=top _conversion&geoCountry=US&blockId=most-popular&imp_id=73233716& action=click&module=trending&pgtype=Article&region=Footer.

6. Ibid.

7. Hugo Mercier and Dan Sperber, *The Enigma of Reason* (Cambridge, MA: Harvard University Press, 2017), 8.

8. Gordon Pennycook, Tyrone D. Cannon, and David G. Rand, "Prior Exposure Increases Perceived Accuracy of Fake News," *Journal of Experimental Psychology: General* 147, 12 (2018): 1865–80, https://doi.org/10.1037/xge0000465.

9. "From George Washington to Edmund Pendleton, 22 January 1795," Founders Online, National Archives, https://founders.archives.gov/documents/Washington /05-17-02-0282.

10. Pennycook, Cannon, and Rand, "Prior Exposure."

11. Jeremy Diamond, "Trump: I could 'shoot somebody and I wouldn't lose voters,'" CNN.com, January 24, 2016, https://www.cnn.com/2016/01/23/politics/donald-trump -shoot-somebody-support/index.html.

12. "Russian Active Measures Campaigns and Interference in the 2016 U.S. Election," Report of the Select Committee on Intelligence, 116th Congress, https://www .intelligence.senate.gov/sites/default/files/documents/Report_Volume2.pdf.

13. Philip N. Howard, Bharath Ganesh, and Dimitra Liotsiou, "The IRA, Social Media and Political Polarization in the United States, 2012–2018," University of Oxford, https://comprop.oii.ox.ac.uk/wp-content/uploads/sites/93/2018/12/The-IRA -Social-Media-and-Political-Polarization.pdf.

CHAPTER 26: WINNING ABOVE ALL

1. "Joint Statement from the Department of Homeland Security and Office of the Director of National Intelligence on Election Security," U.S. Department of Homeland Security, October 7, 2016, https://www.dhs.gov/news/2016/10/07/joint -statement-department-homeland-security-and-office-director-national.

2. Jonathan Karl and Benjamin Siegel, "Exclusive: Rubio Won't Talk About Wiki-Leaks, and Neither Should Donald Trump," ABC News, October 19, 2016, https:// abcnews.go.com/Politics/exclusive-rubio-talk-wikileaks-donald-trump/story?id= 42895586.

3. Amy Chozick, Nicholas Confessore, and Michael Barbaro, "Leaked Speech Excerpts Show a Hillary Clinton at Ease with Wall Street," New York Times, October 7, 2016, https://www.nytimes.com/2016/10/08/us/politics/hillary-clinton-speeches -wikileaks.html.

4. Clark Mindock, "Donald Trump's Campaign Loves WikiLeaks, But Russian Hackers Could Target Republicans Next, Marco Rubio Warns," International Business Times, October 19, 2016, https://www.ibtimes.com/donald-trumps-campaign -loves-wikileaks-russian-hackers-could-target-republicans-next-2434153.

5. Ben Popken, "As Algorithms Take Over, YouTube's Recommendations Highlight a Human Problem," NBC News, April 18, 2018, https://www.nbcnews.com/tech /social-media/algorithms-take-over-youtube-s-recommendations-highlight-human -problem-n867596.

6. Eric Lipton, "Security Briefings for the Other Guy," New York Times, August 3, 2004, https://www.nytimes.com/2004/08/03/world/security-briefings-for-the-other -guy.html.

7. Berg, Wilson. This was before the Presidential Succession Act of 1947 restored the speaker of the house and president pro tempore of the Senate to the line of succession and placed them ahead of the members of the cabinet.

8. "Keep Anna Chennault working on SVN," Nixon ordered Haldeman. John A. Farrell, Richard Nixon: The Life (New York: Doubleday, 2017).

9. "Lyndon B. Johnson, Clark M. Clifford, James R. 'Jim' Jones, Walt W. Rostow, and Dean Rusk on 4 November 1968," UVA Miller Center, https://prde.upress .virginia.edu/conversations/4006128.

10. Rebecca Shabad, "Donald Trump: I Hope Russia Finds Hillary Clinton's Emails," CBS News, July 27, 2016, https://www.cbsnews.com/news/donald-trump-i-hope -russia-finds-hillary-clintons-emails/.

11. Donald J. Trump, interview by George Stephanopoulos, "Transcript: ABC News'

George Stephanopoulos' exclusive interview with President Trump," ABC News, June 16, 2019, https://abcnews.go.com/Politics/transcript-abc-news-george -stephanopoulos-exclusive-interview-president/story?id=63749144.

12. Benjamin Wittes and Susan Hennessey, *Unmaking the Presidency: Donald Trump's War on the World's Most Powerful Office* (New York: Farrar, Straus and Giroux, 2020), 18.

13. Haberman and Schmidt, "Trump Tied Ukraine Aid."

14. Sheryl Gay Stolberg, Maggie Haberman, and Peter Baker, "Trump Was Repeatedly Warned That Ukraine Conspiracy Theory Was 'Completely Debunked,'" *New York Times*, September 29, 2019, https://www.nytimes.com/2019/09/29/us /politics/tom-bossert-trump-ukraine.html.

15. Tom Porter, "8 days after his acquittal."

16. Peter Baker, "'We Absolutely Could Not Do That': When Seeking Foreign Help Was Out of the Question," *New York Times*, October 6, 2019, https://www.nytimes .com/2019/10/06/us/politics/trump-foreign-influence.html.

17. "President Roosevelt and His Aide Lowell Mellet Talk. Side 2, 0–821 (pt. 1), 821–1640 (pt. 2). Sometime between August 22 and August 27, 1940," Franklin D. Roosevelt Presidential Library and Museum, transcripts of White House Office Conversations, 08/22/1940–10/10/1940, http://docs.fdrlibrary.marist.edu/transcr6.html.

18. Donald J. Trump (@realDonaldTrump), "PELOSI STAMMERS THROUGH NEWS CONFERENCE," Twitter, May 23, 2019, 6:09 P.M., https://twitter.com /realDonaldTrump/status/1131728912835383300.

19. Donald J. Trump (@realDonaldTrump), "Ilhan Omar . . ." Twitter, September 18, 2019, 5:14 A.M., https://twitter.com/realDonaldTrump/status/1174295718388854784.

20. Interview with author.

21. Donald J. Trump (@realDonaldTrump), "Mitt Romney . . ." Twitter, October 5, 2019, 7:17 A.M., https://twitter.com/realDonaldTrump/status/1180487139546546182.

CHAPTER 27: RESOLVE TO BE HONEST

1. Donald, *Lincoln*, 149.

2. George Bush, *Public Papers of the Presidents of the United States: George Bush, 1992–1993* (New York: Best Books, 1993), 1825.

3. Pence, "The Two Schools of Thought."

4. Bennett, *Book of Virtues*, 11.

5. Louis Jacobson, "Donald Trump Didn't Realize His Own Website Called Marco Rubio 'Mark Zuckerberg's Personal Senator,'" Politifact, October 28, 2015, https:// www.politifact.com/truth-o-meter/statements/2015/oct/28/donald-trump/donald -trump-didnt-realize-his-own-website-called-/.

6. Joel B. Pollak, "GOP Debate: Trump Did Call Rubio 'Zuckerberg's Personal Senator,'" Breitbart, October 28, 2015, https://www.breitbart.com/politics/2015/10/28 /gop-debate-trump-did-call-rubio-zuckerbergs-personal-senator/.

7. Glenn Kessler, Salvador Rizzo, and Meg Kelly, "President Trump has made 15,413 false or misleading claims over 1,055 days," *Washington Post*, December 16, 2019, https://www.washingtonpost.com/politics/2019/12/16/president-trump-has-made -false-or-misleading-claims-over-days/; David Leonhardt and Stuart A. Thompson, "Trump's Lies," *New York Times*, December 14, 2017, https://www.nytimes.com /interactive/2017/06/23/opinion/trumps-lies.html.

The most recent tally as of this writing was done by *The Washington Post* in

December 2019. Its database is the only publication that has continued to tally his false or misleading claims. By Trump's 1,055th day in office, he had made 15,413 false or misleading claims, according to the Fact Checker database that analyzes, categorizes, and tracks every suspect statement he has uttered. That's an average of more than thirty-two new false claims a day.

The New York Times stopped recording the president's "demonstrably false statements" on November 11, 2017. Based on a broad standard—one that includes Trump's misleading statements (like exaggerating military spending in the Middle East)—Trump said something untrue, in public, every day for the first forty days of his presidency. The streak didn't end until March 1.

Daniel Dale, "Donald Trump has said 5276 false things as U.S. president," Toronto Star, May 5, 2019, https://projects.thestar.com/donald-trump-fact-check/. Daniel Dale, Washington bureau chief for the Toronto Star, reports that Trump had said 5,276 false things as president as of May 5, 2019. For comparison: As of May 5, 2019, according to The Washington Post's fact checking database, Trump had made 10,216 false or misleading claims.

8. Marc Thiessen, "Trump could be the most honest president in modern history," Washington Post, October 11, 2018, https://www.washingtonpost.com/opinions /trump-could-be-the-most-honest-president-in-modern-history/2018/10/11/67aefc5a -cd76-11e8-a3e6-44daa3d35ede_story.html.

9. Megan Brenan, "Trump Seen Marginally as Decisive Leader, but Not Honest," Gallup, July 10, 2019, https://news.gallup.com/poll/260495/trump-seen-marginally -decisive-leader-not-honest.aspx.

10. "NBC News/Wall Street Journal Survey," Hart Research, October 27–30, 2019, https://assets.documentcloud.org/documents/6538104/19433-NBCWSJ-Late -October-Poll.pdf.

11. According to Washington's estate at Mount Vernon, "this iconic story about the value of honesty was invented." Jay Richardson, "Cherry Tree Myth," George Washington's Mount Vernon, https://www.mountvernon.org/library/digitalhistory /digital-encyclopedia/article/cherry-tree-myth/.

12. Phillips, Lincoln on Leadership, 52.

13. Dave Cook, "GOP Official Haley Barbour: Obama Not a Muslim, but He Is Mysterious," Christian Science Monitor, September 9, 2010, https://www.csmonitor .com/USA/Politics/monitor_breakfast/2010/0909/GOP-official-Haley-Barbour -Obama-not-a-Muslim-but-he-is-mysterious.

14. Troy, G., See How They Ran, location 10.

15. According to David Herbert Donald's Lincoln, when Lincoln was on his way to Washington and his first inaugural, he told the New Jersey Senate that Weems's account of Washington's heroic struggles at Trenton—"the crossing of the river; the contest with the Hessians; the great hardships endured at that time"—had made an indelible mark on his mind. "I recollect thinking then, boy even though I was," he said, "that there must have been something more than common that those men struggled for." Donald, Lincoln, location 483.

16. Ibid., location 11467.

17. "State Dining Room," White House Historical Association, January 16, 2019, https://www.whitehousehistory.org/white-house-tour/state-dining-room.

18. H. R. McMaster, Dereliction of Duty (New York: HarperCollins, 2011), location 6821.

19. Interview with author.

20. Washington, *The Writings of George Washington*, 200.
21. "Obama: 'If you like your health care plan, you'll be able to keep your health care plan,'" Politifact, https://www.politifact.com/obama-like-health-care-keep/.
22. Donald Trump said Senate Majority Leader Mitch McConnell said his phone call with Ukraine was perfect. McConnell said the two never discussed the matter. Ted Barrett, Phil Mattingly, Ali Zaslav, et al., "McConnell denies he told Trump his call with the Ukrainian President was perfect," CNN.com, October 22, 2019.

   Trump said he talked to previous presidents who told him they wished they'd built the wall. Every living president said they had no such conversation. Aaron Rupar, "Trump claimed ex-presidents told him they wished they built a wall. We now know he made it up," Vox, January 7, 2019. (Statement from President Carter: "I have not discussed the border wall with President Trump, and do not support him on the issue." Politico: Clinton and Obama haven't had conversations with Trump since his inauguration. A spokesperson for George W. Bush said Bush never discussed a border wall with Trump.)

   Trump said he had nothing to do with a statement about his son's meeting with an official from the Russian government. He helped dictate portions of it. (Michael D. Shear and Michael S. Schmidt, "President Admits Trump Tower Meeting Was Meant to Get Dirt on Clinton," *New York Times*, August 5, 2018, https://www.nytimes.com/2018/08/05/us/politics/trump-tower-meeting-donald-jr.html.)

   He said he did not try to fire Special Counsel Robert Mueller. He tried at least twice. (Donald J. Trump (@realDonaldTrump), ". . . I never told then White House Counsel Don McGahn to fire Robert Mueller . . ." Twitter, April 25, 2019, 7:47 A.M., https://twitter.com/realDonaldTrump/status/1121380133137461248.)

   He said he didn't send Rudy Giuliani to Ukraine. He did. (*Roadkill with Geraldo* podcast: Journalist Geraldo Rivera asked, "Was it strange to send Rudy Giuliani to Ukraine, your personal lawyer? Are you sorry you did that?" Trump responded, "No, not at all," and praised Giuliani's role as a "crime fighter.")
23. "In Convention, Richmond, Friday, June 20, 1788," Teaching American History, https://teachingamericanhistory.org/resources/ratification/elliot/vol3/june20/.

CHAPTER 28: CHARACTER COUNTS

1. Ellis, J., *His Excellency: George Washington*, location 2561.
2. *The Writings of George Washington, Being His Correspondence, Addresses, Messages and Other Papers, Official and Private, Selected and Published from the Original Manuscripts; with a Life of the Author, Notes, and Illustrations*, edited by Jared Sparks, vol. 8 (Boston: Ferdinand Andrews, Publisher, 1839), 72.
3. Ellis, J., *His Excellency: George Washington*, location 2561.
4. John Trumbull to Johnathan Trumbull Jr., May 10, 1784, quoted in Garry Wills, *Cincinnatus: George Washington and the Enlightenment* (New York: Doubleday, 1984), 13.
5. Ellis, J., *His Excellency: George Washington*, location 139.
6. Timothy P. Roth, *Morality, Political Economy and American Constitutionalism* (Cheltenham, UK: Edward Elgar Publishing, 2007), 23.
7. "From George Washington to Officers of the Army, 15 March 1783," Founders Online, National Archives, https://founders.archives.gov/documents/Washington/99-01-02-10840.

8. Edward G. Lengel, *General George Washington: A Military Life* (New York: Random House, 2007), 348.

9. Beeman, *Plain, Honest Men*, 6.

10. Ibid., 7.

11. Ibid., 5.

12. Ibid., 4.

13. Ellis, J., *His Excellency: George Washington*, location 141.

14. David Cobb, who served on Washington's staff during the Newburgh Conspiracy, as it came to be known, reflected on Washington's commitment to the early form of American government and its effect on the nation: "I have ever considered that the United States are indebted for their republican form of government solely to the firm and determined republicanism of George Washington at this time." Paul F. Boller, Jr., *Presidential Campaigns* (New York: Oxford University Press, 1984), 15.

15. James Q. Wilson, *On Character: Essays* (Washington, DC: American Enterprise Institute, 1995), 5.

16. Bob Woodward, *Fear: Trump in the White House* (New York: Simon & Schuster, 2018), 234.

17. Betsy Klein, "Trump moved by veteran's performance," CNN.com, September 30, 2019, https://www.cnn.com/2019/09/30/politics/donald-trump-luis-avila-wounded-veteran/index.html.

18. Donald J. Trump, "Appreciate . . ." Twitter, June 12, 2016, 9:43 A.M., https://twitter.com/realdonaldtrump/status/742034549232766976?lang=en.

19. Interview with author.

20. This idea comes from reading Garry Wills on FDR in *Certain Trumpets*. Garry Wills, *Certain Trumpets* (New York: Simon & Schuster, 2013).

21. Theodore Roosevelt, "Fellow-Feeling As a Political Factor," in *Century*, January, 1900, https://www.bartleby.com/58/4.html.

22. Peter Singer, *The Expanding Circle: Ethics and Sociobiology* (Princeton, NJ: Princeton University Press, 2011).

23. Francis Fukuyama, *Identity: The Demand for Dignity and the Politics of Resentment* (New York: Farrar, Straus and Giroux, 2018), Kindle, location 173.

24. Ted Allbeury, *Show Me a Hero* (Mineola, NY: Courier Dover Publications, 1992), 150.

25. Clark M. Clifford, *Counsel to the President* (New York: Knopf Doubleday, 1992), 89.

26. When Donald Trump wanted to attack a labor leader, he could do so quickly and without interruption. When Chuck Jones, president of Steelworkers 1999, scoffed at Trump's promise that he would save eleven hundred jobs at the Indiana Carrier plant, the then president-elect gave him the bing, bing, bing: "Chuck Jones, who is President of United Steelworkers 1999, has done a terrible job representing workers. No wonder companies flee country!" Donald J. Trump (@realDonaldTrump), "Chuck Jones . . ." Twitter, December 7, 2016, 4:41 P.M., https://twitter.com/realDonaldTrump/status/806660011904614408.

27. Interview with author.

28. Neustadt, *Presidential Power*, 87.

29. George F. Will, *The Conservative Sensibility* (New York: Hachette Books, 2019).

30. "Transcript: Brennan, Kasich, Focus Group," interview by John Dickerson, *Face the Nation*, CBS News, February 26, 2017, https://www.cbsnews.com/news/face-the-nation-february-26-2017-transcript-brennan-kasich-focus-group/.

31. The reason this praise for honesty is morally wobbly was explained by Max Beer-

bohm at the turn of the twentieth century, "I hold that Candor is good only when it reveals good actions or good sentiments, and that when it reveals evil, itself is evil, even also." Max Beerbohm, "The Happy Hypocrite," in *The Yellow Book*, vol. 11 (London: Ballantyne Press, 1896), 11.

32. Brinkley, ed., *Reagan Diaries*, 520. It's hard to think of a smaller job to be concerned about. Nevertheless, it was a matter brought before the president and one he felt was important enough to make a record of: "Took up matter of George Allen. He's heading up our physical fitness program & the Foundation for the same. We have to ask him to resign from Foundation—he's not allowed to do both in addition to maintaining his interests in the private sector."

33. Dan Balz, "Nos. 44 and 45 Broke The Mold. What Does That Mean for the Future of the Presidency?" *Washington Post*, May 18, 2019, https://www.washingtonpost .com/politics/nos-44-and-45-broke-the-mold-what-does-that-mean-for-the-future -of-the-presidency/2019/05/18/97d64320-77e9-11e9-bd25-c989555e7766_story.html.

34. Jerry Falwell (@JerryFalwellJr), "Complaining . . ." Twitter, January 9, 2018, 4:50 P.M., https://twitter.com/jerryfalwelljr/status/950892514235559936?lang=en.

35. John Wagner, " 'Bing, bing, bing': Trump reveals his thinking behind firing off all those tweets," *Washington Post*, October 20, 2017, https://www.washingtonpost .com/news/post-politics/wp/2017/10/20/bing-bing-bing-trump-reveals-his-thinking -behind-firing-off-all-those-tweets/.

36. From 9:02 to 9:23 A.M. on September 29, 2019, Trump shared more than twenty tweets mentioning Ed Henry, tallied by Elizabeth Hinson, the researcher for this book.

CHAPTER 29: IT'S MY PARTY

1. Diamond, "Trump: I could 'shoot somebody.' "

2. "On the Nomination (Merrick B. Garland, of Maryland, to be United States Circuit Judge for the District of Columbia Circuit.)," U.S. Congress, Senate, 105th Cong., 1st sess., March 19, 1997, https://www.senate.gov/legislative/LIS/roll_call _lists/roll_call_vote_cfm.cfm?congress=105&session=1&vote=00034.

3. Jordan Ragusa, "If the Senate allowed a Merrick Garland vote, he might pass," *Christian Science Monitor*, March 18, 2016, https://www.csmonitor.com/USA /Politics/Politics-Voices/2016/0318/If-the-Senate-allowed-a-Merrick-Garland-vote -he-might-pass.

4. Everett, "McConnell throws down the gauntlet."

5. Tim Ryan, "Trump Flips Another Circuit to Majority GOP Appointees," Courthouse News Service, November 20, 2019, https://www.courthousenews.com/trump -flips-another-circuit-to-majority-gop-appointees/.

6. Kevin Freking, "Trump Spotlights Confirmation of 150-Plus Federal Judges," Associated Press, November 6, 2019, https://apnews.com/7d0c948029a54dab940e4c9 86cfao1a3.

7. Lawrence Hurley, "Amid Impeachment Drama, Senate Helps Trump Move U.S. Courts to the Right," Reuters, November 20, 2019, https://www.reuters.com/article /us-usa-trump-judges/amid-impeachment-drama-senate-helps-trump-move-u-s -courts-to-the-right-idUSKBN1XU2MZ. It's a benchmark that means he'll have filled one-quarter of such judgeships in under three years in office. By comparison, President Barack Obama nominated fifty-five circuit judges who were confirmed over eight years. Freking, "Trump Spotlights."

8. "Fox contributor Ken Starr says Trump's Supreme Court appointments cover 'a

multitude of sins,'" Media Matters, December 18, 2019, https://www.mediamatters
.org/fox-news/ken-starr-says-trumps-supreme-court-appointments-cover-multitude
-sins.

9. Interview with author.

10. Interview with author.

11. Interview with author.

12. Flessner, "Corker," https://www.timesfreepress.com/news/politics/local/story/2018
/nov/23/rhetorical-battletrump-divisive-talk-appeals/483594/.

13. Republican National Committee, "Growth & Opportunity Project," RNC Autopsy
Report, 2012, https://www.documentcloud.org/documents/624581-rnc-autopsy.html.

14. Rachel Weiner, "Sean Hannity: I've 'evolved' on immigration," *Washington Post*,
November 8, 2012, https://www.washingtonpost.com/news/post-politics/wp/2012/11
/08/sean-hannity-ive-evolved-on-immigration/.

15. The rejected commercial features footage of an undocumented immigrant from
Mexico, Luis Bracamontes, bragging about his murder of two California police
officers in 2014. Ominous music plays, followed by images of the migrant caravan
that originated in Central America.

16. Erica York, "Tracking the Economic Impact of U.S. Tariffs and Retaliatory Actions," Tax Foundation, December 16, 2019, https://taxfoundation.org/tariffs-trump
-trade-war.

17. Mike Dorning, "Trump's $28 Billion Trade War Bailout Is Overpaying Farmers,"
Bloomberg, December 4, 2019, https://www.bloomberg.com/news/articles/2019-12
-04/trump-s-28-billion-trade-war-bailout-is-overpaying-many-farmers.

    Liberals will say Republicans never really believed in deficit reduction and
used it only to constrain Democratic presidents. David Stockman certainly discovered that the commitment to budget deficits was not what it seemed during the
Reagan years, but George H. W. Bush likely lost an election because he chose tax
cuts to balance the budget, and John Kasich worked very hard to balance the
budget with Bill Clinton in 1997.

18. The historical dig that a candidate for office "couldn't be elected dogcatcher"
dates back to 1889 when Louisville's *Weekly Courier Journal* wrote that President
Grover Cleveland was so unpopular in Washington, D.C., that the district's residents wouldn't even elect him as the man in charge of rounding up stray dogs.
The political epithet is also sometimes used to denote the lowest-possible office.
Of course, dogcatchers are not in fact popularly elected nor are they phoning it
in—the National Animal Control Association requires eighty hours of training for
its new officers.

19. Josh Dawsey, "In speech, Mulvaney says Republicans are hypocritical on deficits,"
Washington Post, February 19, 2020, https://www.washingtonpost.com/politics/in
-speech-mulvaney-admits-republicans-are-hypocritical-on-deficits/2020/02/19
/28546c84-5385-11ea-9e47-59804be1dcfb_story.html.

20. David Campbell and Geoffrey Layman, "How Trump has changed white evangelicals' views about morality," *Washington Post*, April 25, 2019, https://www
.washingtonpost.com/politics/2019/04/25/how-trump-has-changed-white
-evangelicals-views-about-morality/.

21. Jeffrey M. Jones, "Presidential Moral Leadership Less Important to Republicans,"
Gallup, May 29, 2018, https://news.gallup.com/poll/235022/presidential-moral
-leadership-less-important-republicans.aspx?utm_source=alert&utm_medium=
email&utm_content=morelink&utm_campaign=syndication.

22. Knowledge Networks, "The Associated Press-Yahoo Poll," Associated Press, Yahoo,

November 2007, http://surveys.associatedpress.com/data/KnowledgeNetworks/AP
-Yahoo_2007-08_panel01.pdf.

23. Glenn Kessler and Scott Clement, "Trump Routinely Says Things That Aren't
True. Few Americans Believe Him," *Washington Post*, December 14, 2018, https://
www.washingtonpost.com/graphics/2018/politics/political-knowledge-poll-trump
-falsehoods/.

24. Caitlin Dickerson, "Detention of Migrant Children Has Skyrocketed to Highest
Levels Ever," *New York Times*, September 12, 2018, https://www.nytimes.com/2018
/09/12/us/migrant-children-detention.html.

25. Russell Moore (@drmoore), "The reports . . ." Twitter, June 25, 2019, 12:41 A.M.,
https://twitter.com/drmoore/status/1143418475723055106.

26. Jerry Falwell (@JerryFalwellJr), "Who are you . . ." Twitter, June 25, 2019, 1:12 P.M.,
https://twitter.com/JerryFalwellJr/status/1143613031450103813.

27. Nancy French, "What happened after my husband was attacked for critiquing
Franklin Graham's Pete Buttigieg tweets," *Washington Post*, May 9, 2019, https://
www.washingtonpost.com/religion/2019/05/09/what-happened-after-my-husband
-was-attacked-critiquing-franklin-grahams-pete-buttigieg-tweets/.

28. Donald J. Trump (@realDonaldTrump), "The way . . ." Twitter, April 22, 2014,
5:23 P.M., https://twitter.com/realdonaldtrump/status/458763139866435584?lang=en.

29. Donald J. Trump (@realDonaldTrump), "AGAIN, TO OUR VERY FOOLISH
LEADER, DO NOT ATTACK SYRIA—IF YOU DO MANY VERY BAD
THINGS WILL HAPPEN & FROM THAT FIGHT THE U.S. GETS NOTH-
ING!" Twitter, September 5, 2013, 9:20 A.M., https://twitter.com/realDonaldTrump
/status/375609403376144384; "Only the Obama WH can get away with attacking
Bob Woodward," Twitter, March 1, 2013, 3:04 P.M., https://twitter.com/realDonald
Trump/status/307582196196188160; "Yesterday Obama campaigned with JayZ &
Springsteen while Hurricane Sandy victims across NY & NJ are still decimated
by Sandy. Wrong!" Twitter, November 6, 2012, 3:01 P.M., https://twitter.com
/realdonaldtrump/status/265906714518384640?lang=en; "3 Chief of Staffs in less
than 3 years of being President: Part of the reason why @BarackObama can't manage to pass his agenda," Twitter, January 10, 2010, 3:07 P.M., https://twitter.com
/realDonaldTrump/status/1568295912673280000?s=20.

30. Donald J. Trump (@realDonaldTrump), "Repubs must . . ." Twitter, November 20,
2014, 6:36 A.M., https://twitter.com/realDonaldTrump/status/535441553079431168.

31. He belittled, mocked, and forced out Attorney General Jeff Sessions. When Sessions ran for his old Senate seat, his first commercial proclaimed how well Trump
was doing and showed him donning a "Make America Great Again" hat. After Sessions fared poorly in his party primary, Trump tweeted: "This is what happens to
someone who loyally gets appointed Attorney General of the United States & then
doesn't have the wisdom or courage to stare down & end the phony Russia Witch
Hunt," and included a link to a story about Sessions's runoff against former Auburn
football coach Tommy Tuberville. He added: "Recuses himself on FIRST DAY in
office, and the Mueller Scam begins!" Donald J. Trump (@realDonaldTrump),
"This is what happens . . ." Twitter, March 4, 2020, 7:31 A.M., https://twitter.com
/realDonaldTrump/status/1235181043881299969.

CHAPTER 30: THE UNCERTAIN NEVER TRUMPER

1. Victor Davis Hanson, *The Case for Trump* (New York: Basic Books, 2019), 5.

2. Linda Qiu, "15 Claims from Trump's Speech to CPAC, Fact-Checked," *New York*

Times, March 2, 2019, https://www.nytimes.com/2019/03/02/us/politics/trump-cpac
-fact-check.html.

3. Bennett, *Book of Virtues*.
4. Jennifer Epstein, "Scaramucci Says Trump 'Intentionally' Lies to Inflame Opponents," Bloomberg, October 25, 2018, https://www.bloomberg.com/news/articles
/2018-10-25/scaramucci-says-trump-intentionally-lies-to-inflame-opponents.
5. Politics is not the only venue in which those who called for enforcement standards bristle when they are applied to the home team. The National Basketball Association learned this when they worked to improve the quality of their refereeing. As Michael Lewis chronicles in his podcast *Against the Rules*, after complaints about referees, the league spent millions training court officials. The games became objectively more fair, but fans didn't like it—particularly the season ticket holders. Referees had been subtly bending the rules toward the home team. Fans asking for better whistleblowing weren't asking for more objectivity. They were asking for less.
6. Hanson, *Case for Trump*, 116.
7. Ibid., 380.
8. Richard Perle, "The Debate Over How to Deal with North Korea," *Frontline*, https://www.pbs.org/wgbh/pages/frontline/shows/kim/themes/debate.html.
9. Daniel W. Drezner, "The flight from the 'Flight 93 Election,'" *Washington Post*, August 10, 2018, https://www.washingtonpost.com/news/posteverything/wp/2018/04
/10/the-flight-from-the-flight-93-election/.
10. "Washington's Constitution," George Washington's Mount Vernon, https://www
.mountvernon.org/george-washington/constitutional-convention/washingtons
-constitution/.
11. William F. Buckley, Jr., "Our Mission Statement," *National Review*, November 19, 1955. https://www.nationalreview.com/1955/11/our-mission-statement-william-f
-buckley-jr/.
12. "Rep. DeLay's Remarks on Impeachment," Associated Press, December 19, 1998, https://www.washingtonpost.com/wp-srv/politics/special/clinton/stories/delaytext
121998.htm.
13. Jonah Goldberg, "Obscuring the Issue of Trump's Character," *National Review*, January 2, 2019, https://www.nationalreview.com/corner/donald-trump-character
-issue/.
14. William J. Bennett, *The Death of Outrage: Bill Clinton and the Assault on American Ideals* (New York: Simon & Schuster, 1998), 34–36.
15. "U.S. Voters Want To See Mueller Report," Quinnipiac University Poll, March 26, 2019, https://poll.qu.edu/national/release-detail?ReleaseID=2609.
16. Hannah Natanson, John Woodrow Cox, and Perry Stein, "Trump's words, bullied kids, scarred schools," *Washington Post*, February 13, 2020, https://www
.washingtonpost.com/graphics/2020/local/school-bullying-trump-words/.
17. French, "What happened after."
18. Peter Wehner, *The Death of Politics: How to Heal Our Frayed Republic After Trump* (New York: HarperCollins, 2019).
19. Eliza Relman, "The 25 women who have accused Trump of sexual misconduct," Business Insider, October 9, 2019, https://www.businessinsider.com/women-accused
-trump-sexual-misconduct-list-2017-12.
20. Glenn Kessler, "Not just misleading. Not merely false. A lie," *Washington Post*, August 22, 2018, https://www.washingtonpost.com/politics/2018/08/23/not-just-mis
leading-not-merely-false-lie/.

21. Mike Pence, "Why Clinton Must Resign Or Be Impeached," *The Mike Pence Show*, http://web.archive.org/web/20010306205858fw_/http:/www.cybertext.net/pence/pres .html.

22. "First Inaugural Address of George Washington," The Avalon Project, April 30, 1789, https://avalon.law.yale.edu/18th_century/wash1.asp.

23. Roey Hadar, "Retired Army Gen. Stanley McChrystal: President Donald Trump immoral, doesn't tell the truth," interview by Martha Raddatz, *This Week*, ABC News, December 30, 2018, https://abcnews.go.com/Politics/retired-army-gen -stanley-mcchrystal-president-donald-trump/story?id=60065642.

24. Grace Segers, "Former top special operations commander says Trump 'needs to be held accountable,'" CBS News, October 4, 2019, https://www.cbsnews.com /news/former-top-special-operations-commander-says-trump-needs-to-be-held -accountable/.

CHAPTER 31: DONALD TRUMP'S AMERICA

1. Bob Bryan, "Top Trump adviser says the GOP tax bill is 'death to Democrats,'" Business Insider, December 5, 2017, https://www.businessinsider.com/trump-gop -tax-bill-democrats-salt-deduction-text-details-2017-12. The legislation goes "after state and local taxes, which weakens public employee unions. They go after university endowments, and universities have become play pens of the left. And getting rid of the individual mandate is to eventually dismantle Obamacare." The modification of the state and local tax deduction caused turmoil in high-tax states like New York and California that traditionally vote for Democratic presidential candidates. By increasing the tax bite on those who own property in those states, the tax code discouraged home ownership and put federal pressure on states to lower their taxes, which might or might not be in a state's interests.

2. Donald J. Trump (@realDonaldTrump), ". . . . and viciously . . ." Twitter, July 14, 2019, 5:27 A.M., https://twitter.com/realDonaldTrump/status/1150381395078000643.

3. Donald J. Trump (@realDonaldTrump), "A Blue Wave . . ." Twitter, August 21, 2018, 3:38 A.M., https://twitter.com/realdonaldtrump/status/1031852996567748613 ?lang=en.

4. "Parscale: Number one reason swing voters will vote for Trump is his stance on border security," interview by Martha MacCallum, *The Story*, Fox, January 10, 2019, https://www.foxnews.com/transcript/parscale-number-one-reason-swing-voters -will-vote-for-trump-is-his-stance-on-border-security.

5. Todd Beamon, "Steve Bannon, Unrepentant, Dismisses Far Right as 'Clowns,'" Newsmax, August 16, 2017, https://www.newsmax.com/Politics/bannon-dismisses -far-right-clowns/2017/08/16/id/808082/.

6. SSRS, "General Poll," CNN.com, July 1, 2019, http://cdn.cnn.com/cnn/2019 /images/07/01/rel8a.-.democrats.and.healthcare.pdf.

7. Paige Winfield Cunningham, "The Health 202: Democrats have lurched leftward on health benefits for undocumented immigrants," *Washington Post*, July 1, 2019, https://www.washingtonpost.com/news/powerpost/paloma/the-health-202/2019/07 /01/the-health-202-democrats-have-lurched-leftward-on-health-benefits-for -undocumented-immigrants/5d18b0a61ad2e552a21d51bf/.

8. "The Yes, No and Maybe on Driver's Licenses," *New York Times*, November 1, 2007, https://www.nytimes.com/2007/11/01/us/politics/01words.html.

9. "Public's Priorities for U.S. Asylum Policy: More Judges for Cases, Safe Conditions for Migrants," Pew Research Center, August 12, 2019, https://www.people

-press.org/2019/08/12/publics-priorities-for-u-s-asylum-policy-more-judges-for-cases
-safe-conditions-for-migrants/.

10. Newt Gingrich, "If Dems keep doing these five things, Trump will have a landslide victory in 2020," Fox News, July 12, 2019, https://www.foxnews.com/opinion
/newt-gingrich-trump-democrats-pelosi-mcgovern.

11. Paul Krugman, "What Happened on Election Day," *New York Times*, https://www
.nytimes.com/interactive/projects/cp/opinion/election-night-2016/paul-krugman
-the-economic-fallout.

12. Megan Brenan, "More Still Disapprove Than Approve of 2017 Tax Cuts," Gallup,
October 10, 2018, https://news.gallup.com/poll/243611/disapprove-approve-2017-tax
-cuts.aspx.
    One year after Obama signed it into law in March 2011, 46 percent of Ameri-
cans said his signature domestic legislation, the Affordable Care Act, was a "good
thing" and 44 percent said it was a "bad thing."

13. "Economy," Gallup, https://news.gallup.com/poll/1609/consumer-views-economy
.aspx.

14. Catie Edmondson and Maggie Haberman, "Jeff Van Drew Switches Parties,
Pledging 'Undying Support' for Trump," *New York Times*, December 19, 2019,
https://www.nytimes.com/2019/12/19/us/politics/jeff-van-drew-trump.html.

15. "Over 7 in 10 Americans want parties in Congress to work together," The Hill TV,
September 10, 2019, https://www.youtube.com/watch?v=Neyp2ApY5qA.

16. "Transcript: Trump, Huckabee, Sullenberger," interview by John Dickerson, *Face
the Nation*, CBS News, August 2, 2015, https://www.cbsnews.com/news/face-the
-nation-transcripts-august-2-2015-trump-huckabee-sullenberger/.

17. Interview with author.

18. Interview with author.

19. Interview with author.

20. Glenn Kessler (@GlennKesslerWP), "Going through Trump speeches to update
our database. He tells audiences the opioid bill passed 'very little Democrat support.' The vote was 98 to 1, with only Utah Sen. Mike Lee (R) opposing it. The
House passed it 393 to 8. Even a rare bipartisan achievement can't be celebrated?"
Twitter, October 21, 2018, 10:22 A.M., https://twitter.com/GlennKesslerWP/status
/1054060328928055296.

21. "President Trump mocks being presidential," CNN.com, https://www.cnn.com
/videos/politics/2018/03/10/trump-pennsylvania-speech-mocking-presidential-sot
.cnn.

22. Wilson, *On Character*, 2.

23. "Donald Trump Presidential Campaign Announcement," C-SPAN, June 16, 2015,
https://www.c-span.org/video/?326473-1/donald-trump-presidential-campaign
-announcement.

24. Fukuyama, *Identity*, location 109.

25. Laura Meckler and Kristina Peterson, "Senator Says Trump Open to Comprehensive Immigration Overhaul," *Wall Street Journal*, February 9, 2017, https://www.wsj
.com/articles/senator-says-trump-open-to-comprehensive-immigration-overhaul
-1486675985.

26. Erik Wemple, "Why Tucker Carlson is (finally) blasting President Trump," *Washington Post*, January 10, 2018, https://www.washingtonpost.com/blogs/erik-wemple
/wp/2018/01/10/why-is-tucker-carlson-blasting-president-trump/.

27. During negotiations with the White House over how to win Democratic votes for
the tax bill, President Trump called into a meeting between White House staff

and Senate Democrats. According to several senators in the room, he essentially just yelled at the Democrats. "Halfway through this rant," says North Dakota Senator Heidi Heitkamp, "we pretended that the link was breaking apart so we could get him off the phone."

CONCLUSION

1. "Madison Debates."
2. John Stauffer and Henry Louis Gates, Jr., eds., *The Portable Frederick Douglass*. (New York: Penguin Books, 2016), 257
3. Interview with author.
4. Harvard Business Review, *The Peter Drucker Reader* (Boston: Harvard Business Review Press, 2017).
5. "Business Leaders Start 2020 with Lingering Concerns About Talent Shortages & Recession Risk," The Conference Board, January 2, 2020, https://www.conference-board.org/press/c-suite-survey-2020. Only 28 percent of talent acquisition leaders today report that internal candidates are an important source of people to fill vacancies—presumably because of less internal development and fewer clear career ladders.
6. Peter Cappelli, "Your Approach to Hiring Is All Wrong," *Harvard Business Review*, June 2019, https://hbr.org/2019/05/recruiting.
7. "Assessment & Selection: Realistic Job Previews," OPM, https://www.opm.gov/policy-data-oversight/assessment-and-selection/other-assessment-methods/realistic-job-previews/.
8. What do I mean? Well, I have spent much of my career identifying hypocrisy. There's no more core function of what journalists do. But not all hypocrisies are of equal value. Sometimes we choose to point out a hypocrisy and spend a lot of time on it when it's not the most vital issue in the public square. Or, when committed to a duty like fact-checking, and I was slow to learn—as we discussed in a previous chapter—that politicians often invite the fact-checking process in order to spread disinformation.
9. Interview with author.
10. Eric Schmidt, Jonathan Rosenberg, and Alan Eagle, *Trillion Dollar Coach* (New York: Harper Business, 2019), 26.
11. Interview with author.
12. Thomas E. Cronin and Michael A. Genovese, *The Paradoxes of the American Presidency* (New York: Oxford University Press, 2010), 19.
13. David Siders, "Democrats preview post-Trump plan: Executive orders," Politico, May 4, 2019, https://www.politico.com/story/2019/05/04/democrats-executive-orders-2020-1301633.
14. Interview with author.
15. Schlesinger, *Imperial Presidency*, 494.
16. Bailey, *Presidential Greatness*, 36.
17. "Bush urged Obama to preserve two classified programs, the cyberattacks on Iran and the drone program in Pakistan. The Iranians, Obama was told, were still clueless about why their centrifuges were blowing up. Obama took Bush's advice." Sanger, *Confront and Conceal*, location 52.
18. Dwight D. Eisenhower, "Chance for Peace," UVA Miller Center, April 16, 1953, https://millercenter.org/the-presidency/presidential-speeches/april-16-1953-chance-peace.

19. Donald J. Trump, interview by John Dickerson, "Transcript: Trump, Cruz, Clinton, Priebus," *Face the Nation*, CBS News, March 6, 2016, https://www.cbsnews .com/news/face-the-nation-transcripts-march-6-2016-trump-cruz-clinton-priebus/.

20. Caroline Newman, "Q&A: Bush Adviser Philip Zelikow Shares Memories of the Late President," UVA Today, December 4, 2018, https://news.virginia.edu/content /qa-bush-adviser-philip-zelikow-shares-memories-late-president.

21. Lindsey Boerma, "Cain: No need to name my economic, foreign policy advisers," CBS News, October 14, 2011, https://www.cbsnews.com/news/cain-no-need -to-name-my-economic-foreign-policy-advisers/.

22. Joe Heim, "Jerry Falwell Jr. can't imagine Trump 'doing anything that's not good for the country,'" CBS News, January 1, 2019, https://www.washingtonpost.com /lifestyle/magazine/jerry-falwell-jr-cant-imagine-trump-doing-anything-thats-not -good-for-the-country/2018/12/21/6affc4c4-f19e-11e8-80d0-f7e1948d55f4_story.html ?noredirect=on.

23. Michelle Lee, "Fact Check: Has Trump declared bankruptcy four or six times?" *Washington Post*, September 26, 2016, https://www.washingtonpost.com/politics /2016/live-updates/general-election/real-time-fact-checking-and-analysis-of-the -first-presidential-debate/fact-check-has-trump-declared-bankruptcy-four-or-six -times/.

24. "I was the first & only potential GOP candidate to state there will be no cuts to Social Security, Medicare, and & Medicaid," Trump boasted on Twitter in May of 2015. Medicare spending grew 6.4 percent to $750.2 billion in 2018, or 21 percent of total National Health Expenditure (NHE). Medicaid spending grew 3.0 percent to $597.4 billion in 2018, or 16 percent of total NHE. Health spending is projected to grow 0.8 percentage point faster than Gross Domestic Product (GDP) per year over the 2018–27 period; as a result, the health share of GDP is expected to rise from 17.9 percent in 2017 to 19.4 percent by 2027.

25. It's not Congress's fault that they're spending. GOP leaders tried to engage Trump in budget-cutting discussions, but he has been largely disinterested.

26. Interview with author.

27. Interview with author

28. Jim Collins, "Best New Year's Resolution? A 'Stop Doing' List," USA *Today*, December 30, 2003, https://www.jimcollins.com/article_topics/articles/best-new-years .html.

29. Interview with author.

30. Interview with author.

31. Interview with author

32. In 1965, the ratio of full-time federal civil servants (1.9 million) to the total U.S. population (193 million) was about 1 to 100. In 2013, with a civilian workforce of 2.1 million and a U.S. population of 316 million, that ratio was about 1 to 150. The Census Bureau estimates that the nation's population by 2035 will be about 370 million.

33. That Morris was chosen because he showed the greatest intellectual flexibility is amusing, since Morris's word choices in drafting the final document, particularly on the question of executive powers, have built the foundation of unwavering modern opinions of total certainty. Hamilton, for example, maintained that the textual difference between the two vesting clauses Morris wrote for Congress and the Executive indicated that the president had all executive powers—except where the Constitution explicitly provided otherwise—whereas Congress only had the powers Morris specified in the Constitution. Whether these were Morris's

choices or merely his faithful effort to convey the conclusion of the Convention has also been a subject of intense debate.

34. "The admission of slaves into the representation, when fairly explained, comes to this,—that the inhabitant of Georgia and South Carolina who goes to the coast of Africa, and, in defiance of the most sacred laws of humanity, tears away his fellow creatures from their dearest connexions, and damns them to the most cruel bondage, shall have more votes in a government instituted for protection of the rights of mankind, than the citizen of Pennsylvania or New Jersey, who views with a laudable horror so nefarious a practice." "Madison Debates."

35. Emily Badger and Quoctrung Bui, "Americans Say Their Politics Don't Define Them. But It's Complicated," *New York Times*, October 12, 2018, https://www.nytimes.com/interactive/2018/10/12/upshot/us-politics-identity.html.

36. Samara Klar, Yanna Krupnikov, and John Barry Ryan, "Affective Polarization or Partisan Disdain? Untangling a Dislike for the Opposing Party from a Dislike of Partisanship," *Public Opinion Quarterly*, 82, 2 (Summer 2018): 379–90, https://doi.org/10.1093/poq/nfy014.

Illustration List and Credits

Nixons' arrival in Peking, China, February 21, 1972. Courtesy The Richard Nixon Presidential Library and Museum/ National Archives and Records Administration

26 President George W. Bush with retired firefighter Bob Beckwith at the scene of the World Trade Center disaster, September 14, 2001. Win McNamee/Reuters

30 Henry Stimson, Secretary of War, letter to President Harry S. Truman, April 24, 1945. Harry S. Truman Papers, Confidential File, Harry S. Truman Presidential Library, Independence, Missouri

44 President Lyndon Johnson surveying damage in Elkhart County, Indiana, after the Palm Sunday Tornadoes, 1965. Mel Troyer/The Goshen News/ From the collections of the Elkhart County Historical Museum, Bristol, Indiana

47 Wearing a miner's cap and accompanied by mine officials and representatives of the United Mine Workers, Mrs. Franklin D. Roosevelt starts her two-and-a-half mile trip into the heart of a drift coal mine at Neffs, Ohio, May 21, 1935. Bettmann/Getty Images

52 President Ronald Reagan in the Oval Office addressing the nation on the space shuttle *Challenger* disaster, after postponing his scheduled State of the Union Address, January 28, 1986. Bettmann/Getty Images

55 President Bill Clinton and First Lady Hillary Clinton talk to children at the White House after delivering a joint radio address about the tragedy of the bombing in Oklahoma; President and Mrs. Clinton sought to reassure children made fearful by the bombing, April 22, 1995. Michael Geissinger/AFP via Getty Images

60 Demonstrators hold Confederate and Nazi flags during the Unite the Right rally in Charlottesville, Virginia, August 12, 2017. Andy Campbell/ HuffPost/© 2017 Oath Inc. All rights reserved. Used under license.

68 Signing of the United States Constitution on September 17, 1787, in Independence Hall, Philadelphia, by Howard Chandler Christy, 1940. WDC Photos/Alamy Stock Photo

72 President Franklin D. Roosevelt signs the Social Security Act, August 14, 1935. FPG/Archive Photos/Getty Images

77 Senator Barack Obama poses in front of the Superman statue in Metropolis, Illinois, August 14, 2006. Clyde Wills/Courtesy of the Metropolis Planet

79 Cartoon by Nick Anderson of President Barack Obama and the Deepwater Horizon oil spill, June 17, 2010. Nick Anderson Editorial Cartoon used with the permission of Nick Anderson, The Washington Post Writers Group and The Cartoonist Group. All rights reserved. CG Image Number 48609.

79 (inset) First Lady Michelle Obama highlights Gulf Coast vacation destinations, Panama City Beach, Florida, July 12, 2010. US Coast Guard Photograph/ Alamy Stock Photograph

80 (top) President Lyndon Johnson aboard Air Force One surveys damage to Louisiana following Hurricane Betsy, September 10, 1965. LBJ Library photograph by Yoichi Okamoto

80 (bottom) President George W. Bush looks out over devastation from Hurricane Katrina as he heads back to Washington D.C., aboard Air Force One, August 31, 2005. Paul Morse/White House via Getty Images

84 President Jimmy Carter, Roslyn Carter, Harold Denton and Governor

Dick Thornburgh in the control room of the Three Mile Island nuclear power plant, Middletown, Pennsylvania, April 1, 1979. Associated Press

96 President George W. Bush flanked by Federal Reserve Chairman Ben Bernanke, U.S. Treasury Secretary Henry Paulson, and SEC Chairman Christopher Cox, speaks about a plan by the federal government to try and shore up failing financial markets, September 19, 2008. Win McNamee/Getty Images

99 Specie Claws, political cartoon about the Specie Circular or "Specie Clause" associated with the Jackson and Van Buren administrations, published by H. R. Robinson, circa 1838. Library of Congress Prints and Photographs Division, Washington, D.C., Reproduction Number LC-USZ62-36585

105 Demonstrators from the D.C. Jobs for Justice rally, against the $700 billion bailout, outside the U.S. Capitol Building in Washington, D.C., October 2, 2008. Jim Watson /AFP via Getty Images

115 President Ronald Reagan, Speaker of the House Tip O'Neill, and Nancy Reagan during the President's seventieth birthday party in the Oval Office, February 6, 1981. Courtesy Ronald Reagan Library

126 Speaker of the House Nancy Pelosi confronts President Donald Trump in the Cabinet Room of the White House, October, 16, 2019. Shealah Craighead/White House Photo/Alamy Stock Photo

132 Congressman Newt Gingrich, 1984. Associated Press

134 President George H. W. Bush stands with members of the Congressional leadership in the Rose Garden of the White House to announce a budget agreement, September 30, 1990. Mark Reinstein/Alamy Stock Photo

140 President Woodrow Wilson addressing the public on the League of Nations Peace Tour, Tacoma, Washington, September 18, 1919. Bettmann/Getty Images

144 Oliver Twist political cartoon by Joseph L. Parrish, published in the *Chicago Tribune*, January 16, 1937. © 1937 Chicago Tribune. All rights reserved. Distributed by Tribune Content Agency, LLC. Cartoon courtesy of the Franklin D. Roosevelt Presidential Library and Museum, Hyde Park, New York.

152 Martin Luther King, Jr. (center), with Roy Wilkins, James Farmer, and Whitney Young, meet with President Lyndon Johnson in the Oval Office, January 18, 1964. LBJ Library photograph by Yoichi Okamoto

158 President Barack Obama talks with Senate Minority Leader Mitch McConnell on the Colonnade of the White House, November 7, 2014, following the Republican victories during the elections. White House Photo/Alamy Stock Photo

165 Illustration of Abraham Lincoln reading the Emancipation Proclamation before his cabinet members, from an engraving by Alexander Hay Ritchie, after a painting by Francis Carpenter. Bettmann/Getty Images

169 President Ronald Reagan and James Baker during a Regional Forum on the National Commission on Excellence in Education Report at Farragut High School in Knoxville, Tennessee, June 14, 1983. Courtesy of the Ronald Reagan Library

178 President Richard Nixon and his family on Inauguration Day with Lyndon Johnson and Lady Bird Johnson, January 20, 1969. Corbis via Getty Images

192 Presidents Dwight Eisenhower and John Kennedy meet after the failed Bay of Pigs invasion, Camp David, Maryland, April 22, 1961. Everett Collection Historical/Alamy Stock Photo

202 President Ronald Reagan feeds acorns to some White House squirrels outside the Oval Office adjacent to the Rose Garden, November 16, 1983. Bettmann/Getty Images

208 President Richard Nixon and H. R. Haldeman aboard Air Force One, February 20, 1972. Courtesy of The Richard Nixon Presidential Library and Museum/National Archives and Records Administration

211 President Bill Clinton with White House Chief of Staff Leon Panetta walking on the South Lawn at the White House, April 7, 1995. Joshua Roberts/AFP via Getty Images

219 Outgoing U.S. Ambassador to the United Nations Nikki Haley talks with President Donald Trump in the Oval Office, October 9, 2018. Jonathan Ernst/Reuters

231 The heads of the Ford and Carter transition teams meet at the White House: Richard Cheney, White House chief of staff; Jack Watson, head of the Carter transition team; and John Marsh, head of the Ford transition team, November 05, 1976. Bettmann/Getty Images

234 All eyes are on you, Mr. President; political cartoon of President Woodrow Wilson by Udo J. Keppler, 1913. Library of Congress Prints and Photographs Division, Washington, D.C., Reproduction Number LC-DIG-ppmsca-27925

238 President John F. Kennedy in the Oval Office, February 10, 1961. George Tames/The New York Times/Redux

240 President George W. Bush writes a note to Secretary of State Condoleezza Rice during a Security Council meeting at the United Nations in New York, September 14, 2005. Rick Wilking/Reuters

246 President Donald Trump greets Montgomery Weer, a three-year-old boy with spina bifida, at the White House, July 24, 2017. Tom Brenner/The New York Times/Redux

252 (top) President Barack Obama speaks at the annual White House Correspondents' Association dinner in Washington, D.C., April 30, 2011. Martin H. Simon/Pool via Bloomberg/Getty Images

252 (bottom) President Barack Obama, along with members of the national security team, receive an update on the mission against Osama bin Laden in the Situation Room of the White House, May 1, 2011. Pete Souza/Courtesy of the Barack Obama Presidential Library

254 President Ronald Reagan and Nancy Reagan with horses at Camp David, July 21, 1984. Courtesy Ronald Reagan Library

256 Weight of the World cartoon showing President Ulysses S. Grant struggling beneath the burdens of corruption that beset his government, and pursued by the hounds of the press, circa 1876. MPI/Getty Images

259 Democratic presidential nominee John F. Kennedy and his wife, Jacqueline, ride up Broadway in a ticker-tape parade, October 19, 1960. Frank Hurley/New York Daily News Archive via Getty Images

265 Theodore Rooosevelt giving a campaign speech, 1912. Bettmann/Getty Images

267 Sen. John F. Kennedy campaigning at a coal mine, 1960. Hank Walker/The Life Picture Collection via Getty Images

282　"A Chicken in Every Pot" political ad for Herbert Hoover during the campaign of 1928. Alpha Stock Alamy Stock Photo

284　Presidential candidate Vermont governor Howard Dean yells during caucus night party, West Des Moines, Iowa, January 19, 2004. Paul Sancya/Associated Press

293　President Jimmy Carter speaking to the nation from the Oval Office, July 15, 1979. Associated Press

303　The president of the Brotherhood of Sleeping Car Porters, A. Philip Randolph, making his report to the Porters, 1937. Rex Hardy Jr./The Life Picture Collection via Getty Images

312　President George H. W. Bush and Soviet president Mikhail Gorbachev chatting at the Malta Summit press conference, December 03, 1989. Dirck Halstead/The Life Images Collection via Getty Images

317　Cover of *Newsweek* magazine, October 19, 1987, featuring George H. W. Bush. Used with the permission of Newsweek/copyright © 2020. All rights reserved. Photograph by David Valdez/George H. W. Bush Presidential Library and Museum.

322　RCA Radiola advertisement promoting the radio for listening to upcoming political conventions, from the June 1924 issue of *Radio*. Courtesy of The Linda Hall Library of Science, Engineering, and Technology, Kansas City, Missouri

331　Bill Clinton plays the saxophone during a campaign stop on *The Arsenio Hall Show*, June 3, 1992. Reed Saxon/Associated Press

334 (top)　President Donald Trump addresses a crowd during a campaign rally, Columbia, Missouri, November 1, 2018. Charlie Riedel/Associated Press

334 (bottom)　President Barack Obama greets the crowd at a rally at the University of Wisconsin, Madison, Wisconsin, September 28, 2010. Charles Dharapak/Associated Press

353　Supporters take photographs of President Donald Trump during a Make American Great Again rally, Mesa, Arizona, October 19, 2018. Doug Mills/The New York Times/Redux

354　President-elect Donald Trump and Vice President-elect Mike Pence at their election night rally in Manhattan, New York, November 9, 2016. Mike Segar/Reuters

364　Abraham Lincoln "Honest Old Abe Lincoln & Hamlin" campaign ribbon, 1860. Heritage Auctions, HA.com

370　John Adams' blessing engraved in the mantel of the State Dining Room in the White House. White House Collection/White House Historical Association

377　*General George Washington Resigning His Commission* by John Trumbull, 1824. Architect of the Capitol

383　President and Mrs. Ford read a petition, signed by all one hundred members of the United States Senate, following the First Lady's breast cancer surgery at Bethesda Naval Hospital, Bethesda, Maryland, October 2, 1974. David Hume Kennerly/Courtesy of the Gerald R. Ford Library

391　President Donald Trump and Senate Majority Leader Mitch McConnell speak to supporters during the Make America Great Again rally in Lexington, Kentucky, November 4, 2019. Preston Ehrler/SOPA Images/LightRocket via Getty Images

399　Republican presidential candidate Donald Trump greets supporters after his rally at Ladd-Peebles Stadium, Mobile, Alabama, August 21, 2015. Mark Wallheiser/Getty Images

429　"We are against his politics, but we like his grit," political cartoon of President Teddy Roosevelt delivering speech with a bullet in his chest by W. A. Rogers, October 16, 1912. Cabinet of American Illustration, Library of Congress Prints and Photographs Division, Washington, D.C., Reproduction Number LC-DIG-cai-2a14471

433　Frederick Douglass, circa 1855. Everett Collection

446　Benjamin Franklin by David Martin, 1767. White House Collection/White House Historical Association

Index

Page numbers of photographs and their captions appear in italics.

ABOUT THE AUTHOR

JOHN DICKERSON is a *60 Minutes* correspondent and senior political analyst for CBS News. Prior to that, he was a co-host of *CBS This Morning*, the anchor of *Face the Nation*, and CBS News's chief Washington correspondent. Dickerson is also a contributing writer to *The Atlantic*, co-host of *Slate's* Political Gabfest podcast, and host of the *Whistlestop* podcast. Dickerson won the Ford Prize for Distinguished Reporting on the Presidency as *Slate's* chief political correspondent. Dickerson covered the White House for *Time* during his twelve years at the magazine. The 2020 presidential campaign will be the seventh he has covered.

ABOUT THE TYPE

This book was set in Electra, a typeface designed for Linotype by renowned type designer W. A. Dwiggins (1880–1956). Electra is a fluid typeface, avoiding the contrasts of thick and thin strokes that are prevalent in most modern typefaces.